**W9-AZF-874**

| | | |
|---|---|---|
| Customer service analysis | Database design, querying, and reporting | Chapter 8, p. 285 |
| Sales lead and customer analysis | Database design, querying, and reporting | Chapter 11, p. 396 |
| Web page design | Word processing Web page creation or Web page development tool | Chapter 12, p. 428 |

## Internet Skills

| | |
|---|---|
| Using online software tools to calculate shipping costs | Chapter 1, p. 33 |
| Using online interactive mapping software to plan efficient transportation routes | Chapter 2, p. 71 |
| Researching product information Evaluating Web sites for auto sales | Chapter 3, p. 102 |
| Researching travel costs using online travel sites | Chapter 4, p. 144 |
| Searching online databases for products and services | Chapter 5, p. 175 |
| Using Web search engines for business research | Chapter 6, p. 220 |
| Researching and evaluating business outsourcing services | Chapter 7, p. 255 |
| Researching and evaluating supply chain management services | Chapter 8, p. 286 |
| Evaluating e-commerce hosting services | Chapter 9, p. 322 |
| Using shopping bots to compare product price, features, and availability | Chapter 10, p. 361 |
| Analyzing Web site design | Chapter 11, p. 397 |
| Using Internet newsgroups for marketing | Chapter 12, p. 429 |

## Analytical, Writing and Presentation Skills

| Business Problem | Chapter and page |
|---|---|
| Management analysis of a business | Chapter 1, p. 33 |
| Value chain and competitive forces analysis Business strategy formulation | Chapter 3, p. 102 |
| Employee productivity analysis | Chapter 6, p. 219 |
| Disaster recovery planning | Chapter 7, p. 255 |
| Locating and evaluating suppliers | Chapter 8, p. 286 |
| Developing an e-commerce strategy | Chapter 9, p. 321 |
| Formulating a corporate privacy policy | Chapter 12, p. 428 |

# Essentials of Business Information Systems

*Seventh Edition*

**Kenneth C. Laudon**

*New York University*

**Jane P. Laudon**

*Azimuth Information Systems*

PEARSON

Prentice
Hall

*Upper Saddle River, New Jersey 07458*

**Library of Congress Cataloging-in-Publication Data**

Laudon, Kenneth C.
  Essentials of business information systems / Kenneth C. Laudon, Jane P. Laudon, — 7th ed.
    p. cm.
  Rev. ed. of: Essentials of management information systems : managing the digital firm /
Kenneth C. Laudon, Jane P. Laudon. c2005
  Includes bibliographical references and index.
  ISBN 0-13-227781-6
  1.   Management information systems.   I. Laudon, Jane Price.   II. Title.
  T58.6.L3753 2006
  658.4'038011—dc22

                     2006005781

AVP/Executive Editor: Bob Horan
VP/Editorial Director: Jeff Shelstad
Manager, Product Development: Pamela Hersperger
Editorial Assistant/Project Manager: Ana Cordero
Media Project Manager: Peter Snell
AVP/Executive Marketing Manager: Deb Clare
Marketing Assistant: Joanna Sabella
Associate Director, Production Editorial: Judy Leale
Senior Managing Editor: Cynthia Regan
Senior Production Editor: Anne Graydon
Permissions Coordinator: Charles Morris
Associate Director, Manufacturing: Vinnie Scelta
Manufacturing Buyer: Diane Peirano
Design/Composition Manager: Christy Mahon
Composition Liaison: Nancy Thompson
Designer: Janet Slowik
Cover Design: Kiwi Design
Cover Photo: Picto's/Stock Image/Getty Images, Inc.
Illustration (Interior): Carlisle Publishing Services
Manager, Multimedia Production: Richard Bretan
Director, Image Resource Center: Melinda Reo
Manager, Rights and Permissions: Zina Arabia
Manager, Visual Research: Beth Brenzel
Manager, Cover Visual Research & Permissions: Karen Sanatar
Image Permission Coordinator: Angelique Sharps
Photo Researcher: Melinda Alexander
Composition: Carlisle Publishing Services
Full-Service Project Management: Ann Imhof, Carlisle Editorial Services
Printer/Binder: Courier Kendallville
Typeface: 10/12 Times

Credits and acknowledgments borrowed from other sources and reproduced, with permission, in this textbook appear on appropriate page within text or on page P-1.

Microsoft® and Windows® are registered trademarks of the Microsoft Corporation in the U.S.A. and other countries. Screen shots and icons reprinted with permission from the Microsoft Corporation. This book is not sponsored or endorsed by or affiliated with the Microsoft Corporation.

**Pearson Prentice Hall™** is a trademark of Pearson Education, Inc.
**Pearson®** is a registered trademark of Pearson plc
**Prentice Hall®** is a registered trademark of Pearson Education, Inc.

Pearson Education LTD.
Pearson Education Singapore, Pte. Ltd
Pearson Education, Canada, Ltd
Pearson Education–Japan

Pearson Education Australia PTY, Limited
Pearson Education North Asia Ltd
Pearson Educación de Mexico, S.A. de C.V.
Pearson Education Malaysia, Pte. Ltd.

10 9 8 7 6 5 4 3 2 1
ISBN: 0-13-227820-0

*For Erica and Elisabeth*

**Kenneth C. Laudon**  is a Professor of Information Systems at New York University's Stern School of Business. He holds a B.A. in Economics from Stanford and a Ph.D. from Columbia University. He has authored 12 books dealing with electronic commerce, information systems, organizations, and society. Professor Laudon has also written over 40 articles concerned with the social, organizational, and management impacts of information systems, privacy, ethics, and multimedia technology.

Professor Laudon's current research is on the planning and management of large-scale information systems and multimedia information technology. He has received grants from the National Science Foundation to study the evolution of national information systems at the Social Security Administration, the IRS, and the FBI. Ken's research focuses on enterprise system implementation, computer-related organizational and occupational changes in large organizations, changes in management ideology, changes in public policy, and understanding productivity change in the knowledge sector.

Ken Laudon has testified as an expert before the United States Congress. He has been a researcher and consultant to the Office of Technology Assessment (United States Congress) and to the Office of the President, several executive branch agencies, and Congressional Committees. Professor Laudon also acts as an in-house educator for several consulting firms and as a consultant on systems planning and strategy to several Fortune 500 firms. At NYU's Stern School of Business, Ken Laudon teaches courses on Managing the Digital Firm, Information Technology and Corporate Strategy, Professional Responsibility (Ethics), and Electronic Commerce and Digital Markets. Ken Laudon's hobby is sailing and he is a veteran Newport to Bermuda Race captain.

**Jane Price Laudon**  is a management consultant in the information systems area and the author of seven books. Her special interests include systems analysis, data management, MIS auditing, software evaluation, and teaching business professionals how to design and use information systems.

Jane received her Ph.D. from Columbia University, her M.A. from Harvard University, and her B.A. from Barnard College. She has taught at Columbia University and the New York University Graduate School of Business. She maintains a lifelong interest in Oriental languages and civilizations.

The Laudons have two daughters, Erica and Elisabeth.

# BRIEF CONTENTS

# CONTENTS

**3**  Achieving Competitive Advantage with Information Systems   74

## II  Information Technology Infrastructure    107

### 4  IT Infrastructure: Hardware and Software    108

**Chapter-Opening Case:** DreamWorks Animation Turns to Technology for Production Support    109

## III Key System Applications for the Digital Age  259

## IV  Building and Managing Systems   365

## 11  Building Information Systems   366

**Chapter-Opening Case: A New Ordering System for Girl Scout Cookies   367**

We wrote this book for business school students who wanted a brief but in-depth look at how business firms in the United States use information technologies and systems to achieve corporate objectives. The premise of this book is that all business school students—regardless of their majors—require some basic understanding and knowledge of how to use information systems and technologies on their jobs. The reason for this is quite simple: Information systems are one of the major tools available to business managers for achieving corporate goals, such as operational excellence, developing new products and services, improving decision making, and achieving competitive advantage.

When interviewing potential employees, business firms often look for new hires who know how to use information systems and technologies for achieving bottom-line business results. Regardless of whether you are an accounting, finance, management, operations management, marketing, or information systems major, the knowledge and information you find in this book will be valuable throughout your business career.

## It's a New World of Business

A continuing stream of information technology innovations, combined with new business practices and superb management decisions, is transforming the way we do business, the way revenues are generated, and the way customers receive products and services. New avenues of telecommunication, such as high-speed wireless Wi-Fi networks, cellular phone networks and high-speed telecommunications service to the home and small business, coupled with entirely new hardware platforms, such as smart phones, personal digital assistants, and very powerful wireless laptop computers, are changing how people work, where they work, and what they do when they work. In the process, some old businesses, even industries, are being destroyed while new businesses are springing up.

For instance, the emergence of online music stores—driven by millions of consumers who prefer iPods and MP3 players to CDs—has forever changed the older business model of distributing music on physical devices, such as records and CDs. The emergence of online DVD rentals has transformed the old model of distributing films through theaters and then through DVD rentals at physical stores. New high-speed broadband connections to the home have supported these two business changes, and in addition, permanently altered the marketing and advertising worlds as newspaper advertising declines and Internet advertising explodes.

Likewise, the management of business firms has changed: The emergence of powerful mobile phones based on high-speed digital networks means even remote salespeople on the road are only seconds away from their managers' questions and oversight. The growth of enterprise-wide information systems that provide extraordinarily rich data to managers on customers, suppliers, and employees, means that managers no longer operate in a fog of confusion but instead have online, nearly instant, access to the really important information they need to make accurate and timely decisions.

## What Do You Really Need to Know About Information Systems and Technologies?

One of the challenges in writing this book was discovering exactly what a business student needs to know about information systems and technologies. We decided early on that knowing how the technology works in detail might be important for information systems (IS) majors, or for the curious, but less important for accounting, finance, management, marketing, operations research, and other business majors. What was important for all groups of business students—including IS majors—was a solid knowledge of *how businesses today use the technology* to achieve business objectives.

But what are the most important business objectives through which to examine IS? We decided the most important objectives that drive the use of information systems and technologies are the following:

- Operational excellence
- New products and services
- Customer and supplier intimacy
- Improved decision making by all employees
- Competitive advantage
- Survival

## A Problem-Solving Perspective

Achieving these objectives is usually not easy, and it presents many challenges to real-world businesses. Companies turn to information systems to meet these challenges, along with changes in organizational culture and structure, and employee behavior. We came to realize that a *problem-solving perspective* is very useful for explaining how businesses go about achieving their business objectives by using information systems. We want students to understand this business problem-solving and critical-thinking perspective because it will be an important asset for them to demonstrate when seeking employment opportunities. Businesses seek out problem solvers. Throughout the book, beginning in Chapter 1, we use the problem-solving perspective by showing how real-world companies identified and ultimately solved key business challenges using information systems and technologies.

## New to the Seventh Edition

This edition has been totally rewritten as a concise, student-friendly introduction to information systems for business students. It shows how information systems help businesses achieve their core objectives and integrates a career orientation that demonstrates the relevance of information systems to all business students regardless of their majors. This edition also puts more emphasis on showing students how to use information systems in business problem solving. The following features and content reflect this new direction.

### Streamlined Student-Friendly Content

We've streamlined the text into 12 chapters to make it more accessible for students. The revision focuses on the essential information systems concepts students need, making the text suitable for quarter courses or courses where the instructor wishes to supplement the text with additional projects.

## Career Resources Integrated Throughout

This edition contains several new features showing how the text and the course are directly useful in future business careers.

### New Heads Up Section

A new **Heads Up** section at the beginning of each chapter shows why students need to know about the chapter contents and how this knowledge will help them in their future careers in finance and accounting; human resources; manufacturing, production, and operations management; and sales and marketing.

### New Career Guidelines

Chapter 1 includes a detailed discussion of information systems skills required of accounting, finance, management, marketing, operations management, and information systems majors.

### New Structured Digital Portfolio

Concluding the text is a new Building Your Digital Portfolio section to help students with career building. It shows how to use the text with a template on the Laudon student Web site for building a structured digital portfolio demonstrating the business knowledge, application software proficiency, and Internet skills they have acquired from using this text. This portfolio can be included in a resume or job application or used as a learning assessment tool for instructors.

### New Career Opportunities Slide Presentation

A slide presentation prepared by Kenneth Laudon examines the future occupational and employment outlook for information systems majors until 2012. This presentation is available to adopters on the Laudon Web site.

## Modularization: New Learning Tracks Feature

A new **Learning Tracks** feature gives instructors the flexibility to provide in-depth coverage of the topics they choose. A Learning Tracks section at the end of each chapter directs students to supplementary material on the Laudon student Web site. This optional content provides additional details on chapter topics that instructors can select for more in-depth coverage. For example, the Learning Tracks provide additional coverage of topics such as developments in computer processing, storage, and networking that have transformed IT infrastructure for the hardware/software chapter; entity-relationship diagramming and normalization for the database chapter; general and application controls for information systems in the security chapter; or capital budgeting methods for new information systems in the building information systems chapter.

---

**LEARNING TRACKS**

1. If you want to learn more about entity-relationship diagramming and normalization, you will find a Learning Track on Database Design, Normalization, and Entity-Relationship Diagramming at the Laudon Web site for this chapter.
2. If you want to learn more about using SQL to query a database, you will find a Learning Track on SQL at the Laudon Web site for this chapter.

## Problem-Solving and Skills Emphasis

This edition puts more emphasis on showing students how to use information systems to solve business problems than did earlier editions.

- Chapter 1 introduces a **four-step problem-solving method** that students can use throughout the course. They will learn how to identify a business problem, design alternative solutions, choose the correct solution, and implement the solution.

*This four-step method helps students analyze information systems problems and develop solutions.*

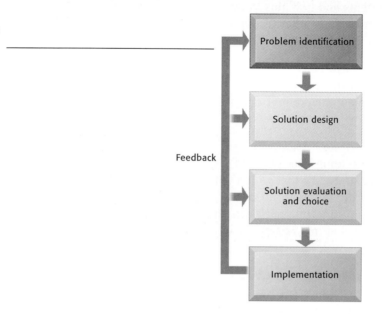

- Case studies in the text require students to use this problem-solving method to analyze the case and answer the case study questions.
- The end of each chapter provides an array of hands-on projects that promote higher-order thinking and encourage students to apply information from the course to real-world business problems. These projects include hands-on application software exercises, running case projects, and exercises for building Internet skills. Each end-of-chapter project identifies both the business skills and the software skills required for the solution.

## New Leading-Edge Topics

This edition includes up-to-date treatment of the following topics:

- Offshore and domestic outsourcing (Chapters 1, 4, 11)
- Wi-Fi, WiMax, and broadband cellular networks (Chapter 6)
- Radio frequency identification (RFID) systems (Chapter 6)
- Internet telephony (VoIP) (Chapter 6)
- RSS (Chapter 6)
- Wireless sensor networks (Chapter 6)
- Digital convergence (convergence of communications and computing; Chapters 4 and 6)
- Software mashups (Chapter 4)
- Grid computing, edge computing, and autonomic computing (Chapter 4)
- Web services and service-oriented architecture (Chapter 4)

- Wi-Fi security issues (Chapter 7)
- Information system implications of Sarbanes–Oxley, HIPAA, and other government regulations (Chapter 7)
- Blogging and social networking (Chapter 9)

## Video Cases

A video segment for each chapter in the text is available on the Laudon Web site and interactive CD-ROM. These videos cases include companies such as Lands' End, Acxiom, Cisco Systems, UPS, Oracle-PeopleSoft, and Verisign. Each video illustrates chapter concepts and includes questions for students to answer to help them apply what they have learned.

# Hallmark Features of This Text

As in all Laudon texts, *Essentials of Business Information Systems,* seventh edition, has many unique features designed to create an active, dynamic learning environment.

## Integrated Framework for Describing and Analyzing Information Systems

An integrated framework portrays information systems as being composed of people, organization, and technology elements. This framework is used throughout the text to describe and analyze information systems and information systems problems, and is reinforced in the student projects and case studies.

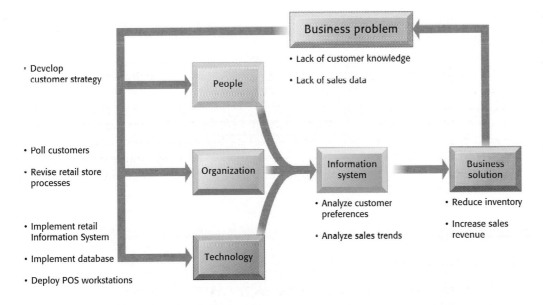

*A special diagram accompanying each chapter-opening case graphically illustrates how people, organization, and technology elements work together to create an information system solution to the business challenges discussed in the case.*

## Extensive Real-World Examples

Real-world examples drawn from business and public organizations are used throughout the text to illustrate text concepts. All opening and ending cases, as well as in-chapter cases, describe companies or organizations that are familiar to students, such as Google, eBay, Kazaa, Amazon, iTunes, Procter & Gamble, Marriott, Seven-Eleven, and the Girl Scouts. Recognizing the global nature of business today, the cases and in-text discussions include numerous companies in Canada, Europe, Australia, Asia, Latin America, and the Middle East.

## Variety of Hands-On Projects

### Hands-On Application Software Exercises

Each chapter features a hands-on Application Software Exercise where students can solve problems using spreadsheet, database, Web-page development tool, or electronic presentation software. Some of these exercises require students to use these application software tools in conjuction with Web activities. The Application Software Exercises include business problems dealing with supply chain management (Chapter 2), inventory management (Chapter 5), customer relationship management (Chapters 8 and 11), and break-even analysis (Chapter 10).

The application exercises are included in each chapter, and their data files are available on the Laudon Web site and in the Laudon interactive CD-ROM along with complete instructions.

### Running Case Study

A running case study at the end of each chapter provides students with opportunities for problem solving in an ongoing real-world business scenario. Students learn about a simulated company, Dirt Bikes U.S.A., where they can apply their information systems knowledge to problems facing this growing firm. Examples of running case projects include the following:

- Performing a competitive analysis for Dirt Bikes (Chapter 3)
- Redesigning Dirt Bikes's database for customer relationship management (Chapter 5)
- Identifying supply chain management solutions for Dirt Bikes (Chapter 8)
- Analyzing the impact of price changes in product components (Chapter 10)

The running case and any required files are on the Laudon Web site and the Laudon interactive CD-ROM.

*Students can use their application software skills to solve real-world business problems based on chapter concepts.*

*Each chapter contains a project requiring students to use application software, Web tools, or analytical skills to solve a problem that Dirt Bikes U.S.A. has encountered.*

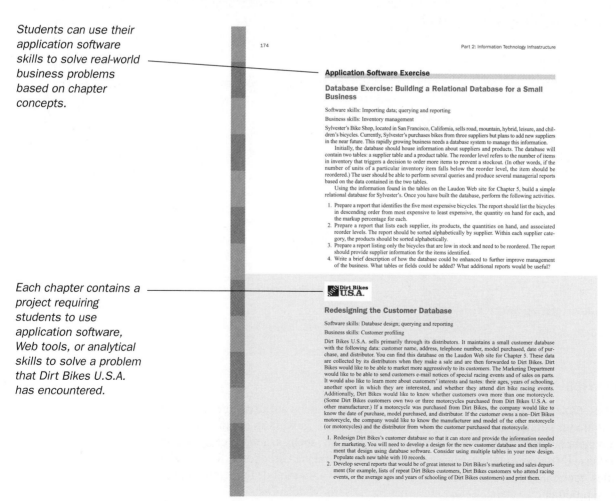

174                                                                              Part 2: Information Technology Infrastructure

**Application Software Exercise**

**Database Exercise: Building a Relational Database for a Small Business**

Software skills: Importing data; querying and reporting

Business skills: Inventory management

Sylvester's Bike Shop, located in San Francisco, California, sells road, mountain, hybrid, leisure, and children's bicycles. Currently, Sylvester's purchases bikes from three suppliers but plans to add new suppliers in the near future. This rapidly growing business needs a database system to manage this information.

Initially, the database should house information about suppliers and products. The database will contain two tables: a supplier table and a product table. The reorder level refers to the number of items in inventory that triggers a decision to order more items to prevent a stockout. (In other words, if the number of units of a particular inventory item falls below the reorder level, the item should be reordered.) The user should be able to perform several queries and produce several managerial reports based on the data contained in the two tables.

Using the information found in the tables on the Laudon Web site for Chapter 5, build a simple relational database for Sylvester's. Once you have built the database, perform the following activities.

1. Prepare a report that identifies the five most expensive bicycles. The report should list the bicycles in descending order from most expensive to least expensive, the quantity on hand for each, and the markup percentage for each.
2. Prepare a report that lists each supplier, its products, the quantities on hand, and associated reorder levels. The report should be sorted alphabetically by supplier. Within each supplier category, the products should be sorted alphabetically.
3. Prepare a report listing only the bicycles that are low in stock and need to be reordered. The report should provide supplier information for the items identified.
4. Write a brief description of how the database could be enhanced to further improve management of the business. What tables or fields could be added? What additional reports would be useful?

**Dirt Bikes U.S.A.**

**Redesigning the Customer Database**

Software skills: Database design; querying and reporting

Business skills: Customer profiling

Dirt Bikes U.S.A. sells primarily through its distributors. It maintains a small customer database with the following data: customer name, address, telephone number, model purchased, date of purchase, and distributor. You can find this database on the Laudon Web site for Chapter 5. These data are collected by its distributors when they make a sale and are then forwarded to Dirt Bikes. Dirt Bikes would like to be able to market more aggressively to its customers. The Marketing Department would like to be able to send customers e-mail notices of special racing events and of sales on parts. It would also like to learn more about customers' interests and tastes: their ages, years of schooling, another sport in which they are interested, and whether they attend dirt bike racing events. Additionally, Dirt Bikes would like to know whether customers own more than one motorcycle. (Some Dirt Bikes customers own two or three motorcycles purchased from Dirt Bikes U.S.A. or other manufacturer.) If a motorcycle was purchased from Dirt Bikes, the company would like to know the date of purchase, model purchased, and distributor. If the customer owns a non–Dirt Bikes motorcycle, the company would like to know the manufacturer and model of the other motorcycle (or motorcycles) and the distributor from whom the customer purchased that motorcycle.

1. Redesign Dirt Bikes's customer database so that it can store and provide the information needed for marketing. You will need to develop a design for the new customer database and then implement that design using database software. Consider using multiple tables in your new design. Populate each new table with 10 records.
2. Develop several reports that would be of great interest to Dirt Bikes's marketing and sales department (for example, lists of repeat Dirt Bikes customers, Dirt Bikes customers who attend racing events, or the average ages and years of schooling of Dirt Bikes customers) and print them.

Each Application Software Exercise and Dirt Bikes project lists both business and software skills required for the solution.

### Building Internet Skills Projects

A Building Internet Skills project concludes each chapter. These projects require students to use Web research tools and explore business resources on the Internet, and include assignments such as configuring and pricing an automobile (Chapter 3), searching online databases (Chapter 5), using Web search engines for business research (Chapter 6), or evaluating supply chain management services (Chapter 8).

## Variety of Case Studies

This text provides a variety of case studies to help students synthesize chapter concepts and apply their new knowledge to real-world problems and scenarios. Every chapter contains a short chapter-opening case, two short **Focus On** cases, and a long chapter-ending case.

Electronic case studies on both U.S. and non-U.S. companies at the Laudon Web site provide additional opportunities for problem solving.

**FOCUS ON ORGANIZATIONS** | Southwest Airlines: New Strategy, New Systems

In a tumultuous time for the airline industry, when some of the major players are taking the hardest hits, Southwest Airlines stands alone in the profit column. It has posted a profit for an unparalleled 32 straight years.

What began as a small Texas airline is now one of the largest airlines in the United States, transporting more than 70 million people each year to 60 cities in the continental United States and Hawaii. Southwest "took off" with a "keep it simple" philosophy that focused on the leisure traveler who was willing to sacrifice luxury for lower airfares and casual service. It used a single style of aircraft (the Boeing 737), alternative airports, reusable boarding passes, and unassigned seating, rapidly turning around its planes when they landed to keep them in the air as much as possible. No domestic airline in the United States has such a low cost structure.

Southwest's approach to information technology was equally no-frills. Unlike other airlines, it did not automate aircraft maintenance, for example, or use systems that analyzed an extensive pool of customer data to improve marketing and customer loyalty. Management did not think Southwest's size justified automation in these areas. Although the airline had digital systems for ticketing and reservations, until recently, getting the boarding pass was a manual operation.

These no-frill days appear to be ending. Southwest is no longer a regional airline and is expanding into markets where the larger carriers, such as Delta, American, and United, operate. It must also compete with JetBlue, which combines low fares with extras, such as more legroom, leather seats, and personal satellite TV screens. In these markets, Southwest has to manage passengers more efficiently, know customers better, and shorten the amount of time that aircraft spend out of service.

Southwest is upgrading its information systems so that, as CEO Gary Kelly puts it, "we can continue to be tops in all categories" and "be the low-fare airline." To provide high-touch customer service, Southwest will have to automate processes that it previously accomplished without technology.

Southwest.com is the company's main sales channel, accounting for more than $3 billion in annual sales, or 65 percent of total revenue. Swabiz.com is a business travel portal the company started in 2000. Southwest moved to e-tickets in the mid-1990s, and today it uses paper tickets for only 5 percent of transactions. Direct e-ticketing saves the airline travel agency commissions, which cost about $10 per booking. Electronic bookings cost at most $1. Customers now have the convenience of obtaining board-

ing passes at multiple airport locations or online instead of waiting on a line at the gate.

Southwest's information systems team is also addressing the issue of maintenance modernization. The system has reduced the time that planes are out of service for regular maintenance by 10 to 15 percent. Inspectors detail problems on Panasonic tablets, which wirelessly transmit the problems to a centralized content library that publishes information in real time to kiosks used by maintenance crews. The kiosks reduce the amount of time technicians spend searching for information, which used to take up to 30 to 40 percent of their working days. An improved optimization capability to integrate and analyze scheduling and maintenance systems will ensure that costs are kept low and that maintenance remains a high priority.

Passengers will see a greater presence of self-service kiosks. By replacing the legacy check-in systems, agents will be able to access check-in, ticketing, baggage, and security modules through the kiosk interface, thereby shortening wait time for passengers and reducing data entry keystroking. One way that Kelly measures the level of efficiency at Southwest is by a ratio of employees to aircraft. In 2000, the airline employed about 95 people per aircraft. Today, the number is down to about 70.

Southwest is enhancing its customer systems, which, until recently, held only the transactional records of customers who paid by credit cards, gift cards, or airline vouchers, and obtained e-tickets. An old legacy reservations system contains data on each passenger's specific booking, including those who pay by check or cash. These data will be added to the basic customer data, along with frequent-flier data stored in another system. The combined data will give the airline a broader view of all passengers to alert airport workers to particular passenger requirements, predict market trends and buying habits, and conduct targeted marketing.

*Sources: Tony Kontzer, "Wings of Change," InformationWeek, March 28, 2005, and "Customer Connections," InformationWeek, March 14, 2005; Tom Steinert-Threlkeld, "Southwest Airlines: Flying Low," Baseline, April 10, 2005; and Susan Carey, "Amid JetBlue's Rapid Ascent, CEO Adopts Big Rivals' Traits," The Wall Street Journal, August 25, 2005.*

**To Think About:**
What is Southwest Airline's business strategy? How is Southwest dealing with the current problems plaguing the airline industry? What role do information systems play in Southwest's strategy and business model? How much will information systems help Southwest deal with its problems and compete in the industry?

*Each chapter contains two Focus On boxes (Focus on People, Focus on Organizations, or Focus on Technology) that present real-world examples illustrating the people, organization, and technology issues in the chapter.*

## Interactive CD-ROM

An interactive CD-ROM version of the text is available with the text. In addition to the full text and bullet text summaries by chapter, the CD-ROM features audio/video overviews explaining key concepts, online quizzes, hyperlinks to the exercises on the Laudon Web site, video cases, the complete running case and application software exercises with required files, technology updates, and more. Students can use the CD-ROM edition as an interactive supplement or as an alternative to the traditional text.

*Bulleted text highlights the key points of each chapter to help students review material before quizzes and exams. Students can reinforce and extend their knowledge of chapter concepts using the glossaries and other interactive resources in the CD-ROM edition.*

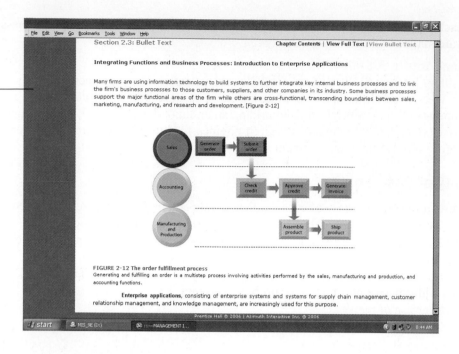

## Overview of the Text

### Table of Contents

Part I introduces the major themes and the problem-solving approach that are used throughout the book. While surveying the role of information systems in today's businesses, this part addresses several major questions: What is an information system? Why are information systems so essential in businesses today? How can information systems help businesses become more competitive? What do I need to know about information systems to succeed in my business career?

Part II provides the technical foundation for understanding information systems by examining hardware, software, databases, networking technologies, and tools and techniques for security and control. This part answers questions such as these: What technologies and tools do businesses today need to accomplish their work? What do I need to know about these technologies to make sure they enhance the performance of my firm? How are these technologies likely to change in the future?

Part III examines the core information systems applications businesses are using today to improve operational excellence and decision making. These applications include enterprise systems; systems for supply chain management, customer relationship management, and knowledge management; e-commerce applications; decision-support systems; and executive support systems. This part answers questions such as these: How can enterprise applications improve business performance? How do firms use e-commerce to extend the reach of their business? How can systems improve decision making and help companies make better use of their knowledge assets?

Part IV shows how to use the knowledge acquired in earlier chapters to analyze and design information systems solutions to business problems. This part answers questions such as these: How can I develop a solution to an information system problem that provides genuine business benefits? How can the firm adjust to the changes introduced by the new system solution? What alternative approaches are available for building system solutions? What broader ethical and social issues should be addressed when building and using information systems?

## Chapter Outline

Each chapter contains the following elements:

- A chapter-opening case describing a real-world organization to establish the theme and importance of the chapter
- A diagram analyzing the opening case in terms of the people, organization, and technology model used throughout the text
- A series of Student Objectives to identify learning outcomes
- Two short case studies
- A Learning Tracks section identifying supplementary material on the Laudon Web site
- A chapter Summary keyed to the Student Objectives
- A list of Key Terms that students can use to review concepts
- Review Questions for students to test their comprehension of chapter material
- Discussion Questions raised by the broader themes of the chapter
- An Application Software Exercise requiring students to use application software tools to develop solutions to real-world business problems based on chapter concepts
- A Dirt Bikes U.S.A. running case project
- A Building Internet Skills exercise
- A Video Case
- A Teamwork project to develop teamwork and presentation skills
- A chapter-ending case study illustrating important themes

## Instructional Support Materials

### Instructor's Resource CD-ROM

Most of the support materials described in the following sections are conveniently available for adopters on the Instructor's Resource CD-ROM. The CD includes the Instructor's

Resource Manual, Test Item File, TestGen, PowerPoint slides, and the helpful lecture tool "Image Library."

### Image Library (on Instructor's Resource CD-ROM)

The Image Library is an impressive resource to help instructors create vibrant lecture presentations. Almost every figure and photo in the text is provided and organized by chapter for convenience. These images and lecture notes can be imported easily into Microsoft PowerPoint to create new presentations or to add to existing ones.

### Instructor's Manual (on Web and Instructor's Resource CD-ROM)

The Instructor's Manual features not only answers to review, discussion, case study, and teamwork questions but also an in-depth lecture outline, teaching objectives, key terms, teaching suggestions, and Internet resources. This supplement can be downloaded from the secure faculty section of the Laudon Web site and is also available on the Instructor's Resource CD-ROM.

### Test Item File (on Instructor's Resource CD-ROM)

The Test Item File is a comprehensive collection of true–false, multiple-choice, fill-in-the-blank, and essay questions, including questions on the case study material. The questions are rated by difficulty level and the answers are referenced by section. An electronic version of the Test Item File is available in TestGen on the Instructor's Resource CD-ROM.

### PowerPoint Slides (on Web and Instructor's Resource CD-ROM)

Electronic color slides created by Azimuth Interactive Corporation, Inc., are available in Microsoft PowerPoint. The slides illuminate and build on key concepts in the text. Both students and faculty can download the PowerPoint slides from the Web site, and they are also provided on the Instructor's Resource CD-ROM.

### Web Site

The Laudon/Laudon text is supported by an excellent Web site at http://www.prenhall.com/laudon that truly reinforces and enhances text material with the Dirt Bikes U.S.A. running case, Video Cases, data files for the hands-on Application Software Exercises, an Interactive Study Guide, International Resources, additional case studies, PowerPoint slides for the course, and a special PowerPoint slide show on IT careers custom-prepared by Kenneth Laudon. The Web site also features a secure password-protected faculty area from which instructors can download the Instructor's Manual and suggested answers to the running case, Application Software Exercise, and Building Internet Skills projects. The site has an improved online syllabus tool to help professors add their own personal syllabi to the site in minutes.

### Videos

**Prentice Hall MIS Video, Volume 1.** The first video in the Prentice Hall MIS Video Library includes custom clips created exclusively for Prentice Hall featuring real companies, such as Andersen Consulting, Lands' End, Lotus Development Corporation, Oracle Corporation, and Pillsbury Company.

**Prentice Hall MIS Video, Volume 2.** Video clips are provided to adopters to enhance class discussion and projects. These clips highlight real-world corporations and organizations and illustrate key concepts found in the text.

### Online Courses

**OneKey** http://www.prenhall.com/onekey. OneKey is a dynamic, interactive, online course management tool powered exclusively for Pearson Education by Blackboard. This exciting product allows you to teach market-leading Pearson Education content in an easy-to-use customizable format.

**WebCT** http://www.prenhall.com/webct. Gold Level customer support, available exclusively to adopters of Prentice Hall courses, is provided free of charge on adoption and provides priority assistance, training discounts, and dedicated technical support.

**BlackBoard** http://www.prenhall.com/blackboard. Prentice Hall's abundant online content, combined with Blackboard's popular tools and interface, result in robust, Web-based courses that are easy to implement, manage, and use—taking your courses to new heights in student interaction and learning.

### Tutorial Software

For instructors seeking application software support to use with this text, Prentice Hall is pleased to offer the PH Train IT CD-ROM and the Web-delivered PH Train and Assess IT. These exciting tutorial and assessment products are fully certified up to the expert level of the Microsoft Office User Specialist (MOUS) Certification Program. These items can be packaged with the Laudon/Laudon text at an additional charge. Please go to http://www.prenhall.com/phit for an online demonstration of these products or contact your local Prentice Hall representative for more details.

### Software Cases

A series of optional management software cases, *Solve It! Management Problem Solving with PC Software,* has been developed to support the text. *Solve It!* consists of 12 spreadsheet cases, 12 database cases, and 6 Internet projects drawn from real-world businesses, plus the data files associated with the cases. The cases are graduated in difficulty. The case book contains complete tutorial documentation showing how to use spreadsheet, database, and Web browser software to solve the problems. A new version of *Solve It!* with all new cases is published every year. *Solve It!* must be adopted for an entire class. It can be purchased directly from the supplier, Azimuth Interactive Corporation, Inc., 23 North Division Street, Peekskill, New York, 10566 (telephone: 800-416-6786; Web site: www.mysolveit.com).

Also available for supplementing the text is *MIS Cases: Decision Making with Application Software,* 2nd ed., by M. Lisa Miller. This casebook features 24 cases using spreadsheet, database, Web-page development, or presentation graphics software.

## Acknowledgments

The production of any book involves valued contributions from a number of persons. We would like to thank all of our editors for encouragement, insight, and strong support for many years. Bob Horan did a wonderful job guiding the development of this edition. We remain grateful to Jeff Shelstad for his support of this project. We thank Debbie Clare, AVP/Executive Marketing Manager, for her superb and vigorous marketing work.

We praise Anne Graydon for her outstanding role in managing the production work for this project and thank Ann Imhof for supervising production of this text. We thank Melinda Alexander for her fine photo research work. Our special thanks go to our supplement authors for their work. We are indebted to Kenneth Rosenblatt for his assistance in the preparation of the text and to Diana R. Craig for her help with the database chapter.

Special thanks to colleagues at the Stern School of Business at New York University; to Professor Edward Stohr of Stevens Institute of Technology; to Professors Al Croker and Michael Palley of Baruch College and New York University; to Professor Lawrence Andrew of Western Illinois University; to Professor Lutz Kolbe of the University of St. Gallen; and to Professor Donald Marchand of the International Institute for Management Development, who provided additional suggestions for improvement.

We like to especially thank all our reviewers whose suggestions helped improve our texts. Reviewers for this edition include the following:

Ron Morgan, Franklin University

David Reavis, Texas A&M University, Texarkana

Stan Lewis, University of Southern Mississippi

Ray Tsai, St. Cloud State University

Leonard Presby, William Paterson University

Kevin McCormack, North Carolina State University

Jon Erickson, University of Nebraska, Omaha

Doris Duncan, California State University, Hayward

Clint King, University of Southern Alabama

Tom Harris, Ball State University

Connie Wells, Roosevelt University

*K.C.L.*
*J.P.L.*

# Information Systems in the Digital Age

**PART I**

Part I introduces the major themes and the problem-solving approaches that are used throughout the book. While surveying the role of information systems in today's businesses, this part raises several major questions: What is an information system? Why are information systems so essential in businesses today? How can information systems help businesses become more competitive? What do I need to know about information systems to succeed in my business career?

# Business Information Systems in Your Career

**CHAPTER 1**

## STUDENT OBJECTIVES

**After completing this chapter, you will be able to:**

1. Explain why information systems are so essential in business today.

2. Define an information system from both a technical and a business perspective, and distinguish between computer literacy and information systems literacy.

3. Apply a four-step method for business problem solving to solve information system–related problems.

4. Assess how information systems will affect business careers in accounting, finance, management, marketing, operations management, and information systems and identify the information systems skills and knowledge essential for all business careers.

## MAJOR LEAGUE BASEBALL HITS A HOME RUN WITH INFORMATION SYSTEMS

**Technology is helping** Major League Baseball (MLB) raise its batting average. MLB is responsible for operating the two top baseball leagues in North America—the National League and the American League. Although baseball is a sport, Major League Baseball is also a big business, requiring revenue from tickets to games, television broadcasts, and other sources to pay for its stadiums and teams. One of the functions of MLB is to help promote and grow that business.

Major League Baseball has its own set of business challenges. As salaries for top players ballooned, so have ticket prices. Many fans now watch games on television rather than attending them in person. Although some teams fill the stadiums, others, such as the Pittsburgh Pirates, have seen their fan base dwindle. Shea Stadium, the home field of the New York Mets, was half empty most of the 2004 baseball season.

MLB still uses traditional print and broadcast media—newspapers, television, and radio—to publicize games, and retail outlets and stadiums to sell baseball tickets and souvenirs. But MLB's new emphasis is on using the Internet and information technology. It now runs a high-tech production/Internet spin-off based in New York called MLB Advanced Media (MLBAM), which oversees MLB video productions, the Web sites for each of MLB's 30 teams, and its own Web site, www.MLB.com.

Bib Bowman, CEO and president of MLBAM, wants to find more customers and turn them into devoted fans who will go to more games and buy more baseball-related merchandise. "A lot of people just go to one game per year, and we need to encourage that fan to be more active with his or her favorite team," he says. Teams such as the Mets, which had ranked seventeenth in attendance among MLB's 30 teams in 2004, have benefited. The MLB Web sites have helped publicize information about the Mets and increased season ticket sales.

It's easy to see why. At MLB.com, for example, fans can check game scores; purchase game tickets; shop for caps, jerseys, baseball cards, and memorabilia; post opinions on electronic message boards; use e-mail; and find out more about their favorite teams and players. The site also features fantasy baseball games, where fans compete with each other by managing "fantasy teams" based on real players' statistics.

In 2004, all of the MLB Web sites sold 11.2 million game tickets online and expected to sell 30 to 40 percent more in 2005. MLBAM is trying to boost ticket sales further by broadcasting offers to fans' cell phones. For instance, Mets fans who have shown interest in ticket offers may receive a text message that there are still seats available for a Mets game at Shea Stadium and they can purchase tickets using their cell phones. If the fan purchases, a bar code is transmitted to his or her cell phone to use as a ticket that will be accepted at the gate. MLBAM also sold more than one million cell phone wallpapers, ring tones, and other content during that baseball season. It has started to offer live audio broadcast feeds of games and fantasy games to owners of color-screen phones at all the major cellular services.

To learn more about who its customers were and what they wanted, MLBAM worked with SAS Inc. on software to collect and analyze its customer data. These data come from subscriptions; e-commerce transactions on MLB Web sites; and e-mail addresses collected from sweepstakes, online newsletters, and other offers. Special Web site tracking tools provide information on the most popular parts of MLB Web sites, which ball games participants watch or download, which online games they play, and which team merchandise or tickets they buy. ■

*Sources:* Jon Surmacz, "In a League of Its Own," *CIO Magazine,* April 15, 2005; W. David Gardner, "Fans Say 'Take Me Out to the Web Site,'" *InformationWeek,* August 22, 2005; Peter J. Howe, "Major League Baseball Pitches Cell Phone Content," *Boston Globe,* March 14, 2005; Tony Kontzer, "Finding the Customer," *InformationWeek,* August 1, 2005; and Jonathan Eig, "The New Face of Baseball," *The Wall Street Journal,* October 22–23, 2005.

The challenges facing Major League Baseball show why information systems are so essential today. MLB is a business as well as a sport, and it needs to help its member teams stay in business and increase their revenues. Ticket prices have risen, stadium attendance is down for some teams, and many fans prefer to watch baseball games on television. The sport must also compete with other forms of entertainment, including electronic games.

To increase game attendance, MLB could have increased its advertising budget with traditional media, such as newspapers, television, or radio. But these media are very expensive, and the amount of information they provide about MLB teams is very limited. MLB chose instead a solution that takes advantage of new marketing and selling opportunities on the Internet.

MLB set up a series of Web sites, one for each member team and a Web site for all of Major League Baseball called www.MLB.com. These Web sites provide fans with easy access to extensive information about teams, games, and players; the ability to purchase tickets via computer or cell phone; and the ability to purchase souvenirs and memorabilia over the Web. The Web sites include community-building features, such as e-mail and electronic messaging, and new products for sale, such as cell phone content and fantasy games, that are not available through traditional channels. Use of the Internet and the Web makes it possible for MLB to use new tools for analyzing customers. Thanks to all of these new information system initiatives, MLB ticket sales are up.

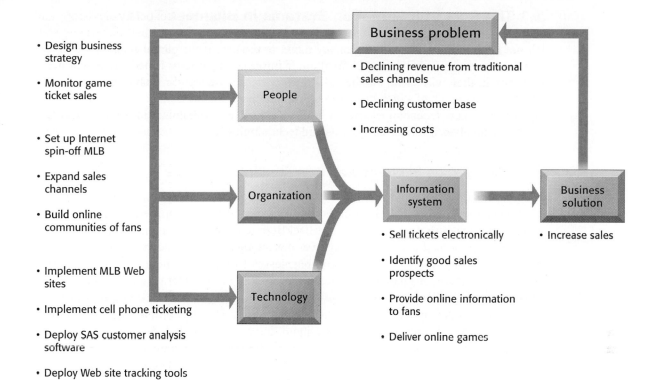

- Design business strategy
- Monitor game ticket sales
- Set up Internet spin-off MLB
- Expand sales channels
- Build online communities of fans
- Implement MLB Web sites
- Implement cell phone ticketing
- Deploy SAS customer analysis software
- Deploy Web site tracking tools

**Business problem**

- Declining revenue from traditional sales channels
- Declining customer base
- Increasing costs

People

Organization

Technology

**Information system**

- Sell tickets electronically
- Identify good sales prospects
- Provide online information to fans
- Deliver online games

**Business solution**

- Increase sales

---

**HEADS UP**

This chapter introduces you to the roles that information systems and technologies play in business firms. All firms today, large and small, local, national and global, use information systems to achieve important business objectives, such as operational efficiency, customer and supplier intimacy, better decision making, and new products and services. Information systems and technologies will also play large roles in your career. You will need to know how to use information systems and technologies to help your firm solve problems and overcome challenges.

•   If your career is in finance or accounting, you will find a detailed discussion of the impact of information systems on accounting and finance careers in Section 1.5 of the chapter.

•   If your career is in human resources or management, you will find a detailed discussion of the impact of information systems on management careers in Section 1.5 of the chapter.

•   If your career is in manufacturing, production, or operations management, you will find a detailed discussion of the impact of information systems on operations management in service and manufacturing in Section 1.5 of the chapter.

•   If your career is in sales and marketing, you will find a detailed discussion of the impact of information systems on marketing and sales careers in Section 1.5 of the chapter.

---

This chapter begins our investigation of information systems. First we explain why information systems are so essential in business today. Then we define information systems, showing that they are composed of people, organization, and technology elements. We introduce a four-step method for analyzing information systems problems in business. We conclude with a detailed discussion of how you will be using information systems in your future business career.

## 1.1 The Role of Information Systems in Business Today

It's not business as usual in America any more, or the rest of the global economy. In 2006, American businesses will invest $1.8 trillion in information systems hardware and software. In addition, they will spend another $1.7 trillion on business and management consulting and services—much of which involves redesigning firms' business operations to take advantage of these new technologies. About half of all business investment in the United States each year involves information systems and technologies.

### How Information Systems Are Transforming Business

You can see the results of this massive spending around you every day by observing how people conduct business. More wireless cell phone accounts were opened in 2005 than telephone land lines installed. Cell phones, BlackBerrys, handhelds, e-mail, online conferencing, and international teleconferencing over the Internet have all become essential tools of business. In 2005, more than 40 million businesses had dot-com Internet sites registered. Five million Americans purchase something every day on the Internet and another 19 million research a product.

In 2005, FedEx moved in the United States nearly 100 million packages and United Parcel Service (UPS) moved more than 380 million packages to help businesses respond to rapidly changing customer demand, minimize inventories, and operate more efficiently. The responsiveness of this new "FedEx" economy has led many experts to believe the era of massive recessions and booms of the typical business cycle is over, replaced by much smaller contractions and expansions, and strong long-term growth.

As newspaper readership continues to decline, more than 35 million people receive their news online. Thirty-two million Americans now read blogs, and eight million write blogs, creating an explosion of new writers and new forms of customer feedback that did not exist in 2000 (Pew, 2005).

E-commerce and Internet advertising are booming: Google's online ad revenues surpassed $6 billion in 2005, and Internet advertising continues to grow at more than 30 percent a year, reaching more than $11 billion in revenues in 2005.

New federal security and accounting laws, requiring many businesses to keep e-mail messages for five years, coupled with existing occupational and health laws requiring firms to store employee chemical exposure data for up to 60 years, are spurring the growth of digital information now estimated to be 5 exabytes, equivalent to 37,000 Libraries of Congress.

Briefly, it's a new world of doing business, one that will greatly affect your future business career. Along with the changes in business come changes in jobs and careers. No matter whether you are a finance, accounting, management, marketing, operations management, or information systems major, how you work, where you work, and how well you are compensated will all be affected by business information systems. The purpose of this book is to help you understand and benefit from these new business realities.

### Business Objectives of Information Systems

What makes information systems so essential today? Why are businesses investing so much in information systems and technologies? They do so to achieve six important business objectives: operational excellence; new products, services, and business models; customer and supplier intimacy; improved decision making; competitive advantage; and survival.

#### Operational Excellence
Businesses continuously seek to improve the efficiency of their operations in order to achieve higher profitability. Information systems and technologies are some of the most important tools available to managers for achieving higher levels of efficiency and productivity in business operations, especially when coupled with changes in business practices and management behavior.

Wal-Mart, the largest retailer on Earth, exemplifies the power of information systems coupled with brilliant business practices and supportive management to achieve world-class operational efficiency. In 2005, Wal-Mart achieved more than $285 billion in sales—nearly one-tenth of retail sales in the United States—in large part because of its RetailLink system, which digitally links its suppliers to every one of Wal-Mart's 5,289 stores worldwide. As soon as a customer purchases an item, the supplier monitoring the item knows to ship a replacement to the shelf. Wal-Mart is the most efficient retail store in the industry, achieving sales of more than $28 per square foot, compared to its closest competitor, Target, at $23 per square foot, and other retail firms producing less than $12 per square foot.

### New Products, Services, and Business Models

Information systems and technologies are a major enabling tool for firms to create new products and services, as well as entirely new business models. A **business model** describes how a company produces, delivers, and sells a product or service to create wealth. Today's music industry is vastly different from the industry in 2000. Apple Inc. transformed an old business model of music distribution based on vinyl records, tapes, and CDs into an online, legal distribution model based on its own iPod technology platform (see the case study concluding this chapter). Apple has prospered from a continuing stream of iPod innovations, including the original iPod, the iPod nano, the iTunes music service, and the iPod video player.

### Customer and Supplier Intimacy

When a business really knows its customers, and serves them well, the way they want to be served, the customers generally respond by returning and purchasing more. This raises revenues and profits. Likewise with suppliers: the more a business engages its suppliers, the better the suppliers can provide vital inputs. This lowers costs. How to really know your customers, or suppliers, is a central problem for businesses with millions of off-line and online customers.

The Mandarin Oriental in Manhattan and other high-end hotels exemplify the use of information systems and technologies to achieve customer intimacy. These hotels use computers to keep track of guests' preferences, such as their preferred room temperature, check-in time, frequently dialed telephone numbers, and television programs, and store these data in a giant data repository. Individual rooms in the hotels are networked to a central server computer so that they can be remotely monitored or controlled. When a customer arrives at one of these hotels, the system automatically changes the room conditions, such as dimming the

*Apple's iPod, iPod nano, and iPod video player are popular new products based on information technology that are transforming the music and entertainment industries.*

*TAL Apparel Ltd. uses networked information systems to manage production and inventory for clients such as JC Penney.*

lights, setting the room temperature, or selecting appropriate music, based on the customer's digital profile. The hotels also analyze their customer data to identify their best customers and to develop individualized marketing campaigns based on customers' preferences.

JC Penney exemplifies the benefits of information systems–enabled supplier intimacy. Every time a dress shirt is bought at a Penney store in the United States, the record of the sale appears immediately on computers in Hong Kong at the TAL Apparel Ltd. supplier, a giant contract manufacturer that produces one in eight dress shirts sold in the United States. TAL runs the numbers through a computer model it developed and then decides how many replacement shirts to make, and in what styles, colors, and sizes. TAL then sends the shirts to each Penney store, completely bypassing the retailer's warehouses. In other words, Penney's shirt inventory is near zero, as is the cost of storing it.

### Improved Decision Making

Many business managers operate in an information fog bank, never really having the right information at the right time to make an informed decision. Instead, managers rely on forecasts, best guesses, and luck. The result is over- or underproduction of goods and services, misallocation of resources, and poor response times. These poor outcomes raise costs and lose customers. In the past 10 years, information systems and technologies have made it possible for managers to use real-time data from the marketplace when making decisions.

For instance, Verizon Corporation, one of the largest telecommunications service companies in the United States, uses a Web-based digital dashboard to provide managers with precise real-time information on customer complaints, network performance for each locality served, and line outages or storm-damaged lines. Using this information, managers can immediately allocate repair resources to affected areas, inform consumers of repair efforts, and restore service fast.

### Competitive Advantage

When firms achieve one or more of these business objectives—operational excellence; new products, services, and business models; customer/supplier intimacy; and improved decision making—chances are they have already achieved a competitive advantage. Doing things better than your competitors, charging less for superior products, and responding to customers and suppliers in real time all add up to higher sales and higher profits that your competitors cannot match.

Perhaps no other U.S. company exemplifies all of these attributes leading to competitive advantage more than Dell Computer. In a period when PC prices have been falling at 25 percent a year, forcing most manufacturers into losses, Dell Computer has shown consistent profitability during its life span of 25 years. It has achieved such a high level of operational efficiency at its PC assembly plants that competitors struggle to keep up. A large part of its operational efficiency results from "mass customization," staying close to the customer by

Business Objects' digital dashboard delivers comprehensive and accurate information for decision making. The graphical overview of key performance indicators helps managers quickly spot areas that need attention.

using a Web-based order entry model that can build and ship a customized PC to any of its millions of consumers in only a few days, even overnight if the customer is really in a hurry. Dell has used its commanding position to introduce many new products and services, especially to corporate customers, such as a custom Dell Web page for corporate accounts.

## Survival

Business firms also invest in information systems and technologies because they are necessities of doing business. Sometimes these "necessities" are driven by industry-level changes. For instance, after Citibank introduced the first automatic teller machines (ATMs) in the New York region in 1977 to attract customers through higher service levels, its competitors rushed to provide ATMs to their customers to keep up with Citibank. Today, virtually all banks in the United States have regional ATMs and link to national and international ATM networks, such as CIRRUS. Providing ATM services to retail banking customers is simply a requirement of being in and surviving in the retail banking business.

There are many federal and state statutes and regulations that create a legal duty for companies and their employees to retain records, including digital records. For instance, the Toxic Substances Control Act (1976), which regulates the exposure of U.S. workers to more than 75,000 toxic chemicals, requires firms to retain records on employee exposure for

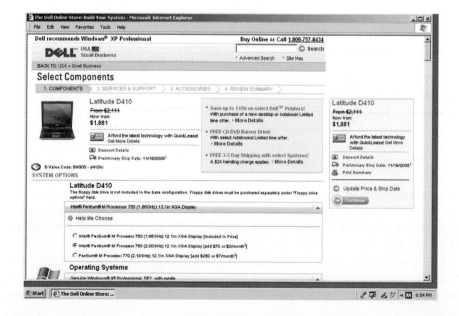

On the Dell Computer Web site, customers can select the options they want and order their computer custom built to these specifications. Dell's assemble-to-order system is a major source of competitive advantage.

*Retail banks today need to provide ATM services to their customers in order to stay in business.*

30 years. The Sarbanes-Oxley Act (2002), which was intended to improve the accountability of public firms and their auditors, requires public companies to retain audit working papers and records, including all e-mails, for five years. There are many other pieces of federal and state legislation in healthcare, financial services, education, and privacy protection that impose significant information retention and reporting requirements on U.S. businesses. Firms turn to information systems and technologies to provide the capability to respond to these requirements.

## 1.2 Perspectives on Information Systems and Information Technology

So far we've used *information systems* and *technologies* informally without defining the terms. **Information technology (IT)** consists of all the hardware and software that a firm needs to use in order to achieve its business objectives. This includes not only computer machines, disk drives, handheld personal digital assistants, and, yes, even iPods (where they are used for a business purpose) but also software, such as the Windows or Linux operating systems, the Microsoft Office desktop productivity suite, and the many thousands of computer programs that can be found in a typical large firm. "Information systems" are more complex and can best be understood by looking at them from both a technology and a business perspective.

### What Is an Information System?

An **information system** can be defined technically as a set of interrelated components that collect (or retrieve), process, store, and distribute information to support decision making and control in an organization. In addition to supporting decision making, coordination, and control, information systems also help managers and workers analyze problems, visualize complex subjects, and create new products.

Information systems contain information about significant people, places, and things within the organization or in the environment surrounding it. By **information** we mean data that have been shaped into a form that is meaningful and useful to human beings. **Data**, in contrast, are streams of raw facts representing events occurring in organizations or the physical environment before they have been organized and arranged into a form that people can understand and use.

A brief example contrasting information and data may prove useful. Supermarket checkout counters scan millions of pieces of data, such as bar codes, that describe each product. Such pieces of data can be totaled and analyzed to provide meaningful information, such as

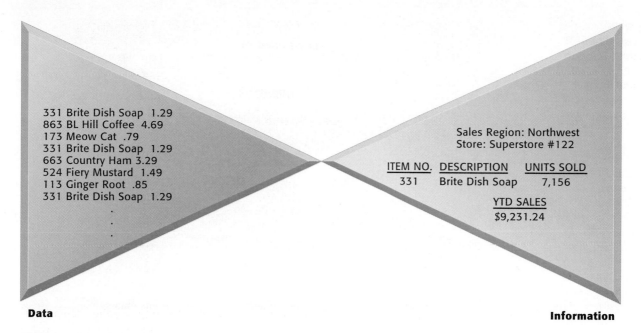

**Figure 1-1**
Data and Information
*Raw data from a supermarket checkout counter can be processed and organized to produce meaningful information, such as the total unit sales of dish detergent or the total sales revenue from dish detergent for a specific store or sales territory.*

the total number of bottles of dish detergent sold at a particular store, which brands of dish detergent were selling the most rapidly at that store or sales territory, or the total amount spent on that brand of dish detergent at that store or sales region (see Figure 1-1).

Three activities in an information system produce the information that organizations need to make decisions, control operations, analyze problems, and create new products or services. These activities are input, processing, and output (see Figure 1-2). **Input** captures or collects raw data from within the organization or from its external environment. **Processing** converts this raw input into a meaningful form. **Output** transfers the processed information to the people who will use it or to the activities for which it will be used. Information systems also require **feedback**, which is output that is returned to appropriate members of the organization to help them evaluate or correct the input stage.

In Major League Baseball's system for selling tickets through its Web site, the raw input consists of order data for tickets, such as the purchaser's name, address, credit card number, number of tickets ordered, and date and location of the game for which the ticket is being purchased. MLB's computers store these data and process them to calculate order totals, to track ticket purchases, and to send requests for payment to credit card companies. MLB's computers also analyze the data collected to determine fans' interests and to identify receptive individuals for targeting messages about upcoming game tickets and other products. The output consists of tickets to print out online, receipts for orders, and reports on online ticket orders. The system provides meaningful information, such as the number of tickets sold online for a particular game, the total number of online tickets sold each year, and the customers most interested in receiving information about tickets for upcoming games.

Although computer-based information systems use computer technology to process raw data into meaningful information, there is a sharp distinction between a computer and a computer program on the one hand, and an information system on the other. Electronic computers and related software programs are the technical foundation, the tools and materials, of modern information systems. Computers provide the equipment for storing and processing information. Computer programs, or software, are sets of operating instructions that direct and control computer processing. Knowing how computers and computer programs work is

**Figure 1-2**
Functions of an
Information System
*An information system
contains information
about an organization
and its surrounding envi-
ronment. Three basic
activities—input, pro-
cessing, and output—
produce the information
organizations need.
Feedback is output
returned to appropriate
people or activities in
the organization to eval-
uate and refine the
input. Environmental
actors, such as cus-
tomers, suppliers, com-
petitors, stockholders,
and regulatory agen-
cies, interact with the
organization and its
information systems.*

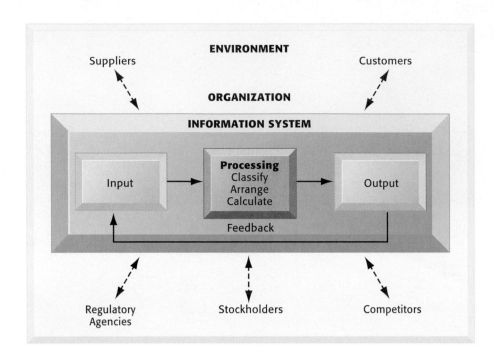

important in designing solutions to organizational problems, but computers are only part of
an information system.

A house is an appropriate analogy. Houses are built with hammers, nails, and wood, but
these do not make a house. The architecture, design, setting, landscaping, and all of the decisions that lead to the creation of these features are part of the house and are crucial for solving the problem of putting a roof over one's head. Computers and programs are the hammer,
nails, and lumber of computer-based information systems, but alone they cannot produce the
information a particular organization needs. To understand information systems, you must
understand the problems they are designed to solve, their architectural and design elements,
and the organizational processes that lead to these solutions.

## 1.3 It Isn't Simply Technology: The Role of People and Organizations

To fully understand information systems, you will need to be aware of the broader organization, people, and information technology dimensions of systems (see Figure 1-3) and their
power to provide solutions to challenges and problems in the business environment. We
refer to this broader understanding of information systems, which encompasses an understanding of the people and organizational dimensions of systems as well as the technical
dimensions of systems, as **information systems literacy**. Information systems literacy
includes a behavioral as well as a technical approach to studying information systems.
**Computer literacy**, in contrast, focuses primarily on knowledge of information technology.

The field of **management information systems (MIS)** tries to achieve this broader
information systems literacy. MIS deals with behavioral issues as well as technical issues
surrounding the development, use, and impact of information systems used by managers and
employees in the firm.

### Dimensions of Information Systems

Let's examine each of the dimensions of information systems—organizations, people, and
information technology.

**Figure 1-3**
Information Systems
Are More Than
Computers
*Using information sys-
tems effectively
requires an understand-
ing of the organization,
people, and information
technology shaping the
systems. An information
system provides a solu-
tion to important busi-
ness problems or chal-
lenges facing the firm.*

## Organizations

Information systems are an integral part of organizations. And although we tend to think about information technology changing organizations and business firms, it is, in fact, a two-way street: The history and culture of business firms also affects how the technology is used and how it should be used. In order to understand how a specific business firm uses information systems, you need to know something about the structure, history, and culture of the company.

Organizations have a structure that is composed of different levels and specialties. Their structures reveal a clear-cut division of labor. Authority and responsibility in a business firm is organized as a hierarchy, or a pyramid structure, of rising authority and responsibility. The upper levels of the hierarchy consist of managerial, professional, and technical employees, whereas the lower levels consist of operational personnel. Experts are employed and trained for different business functions, such as sales and marketing, manufacturing and production, finance and accounting, and human resources. Information systems are built by the firm in order to serve these different specialties and different levels of the firm. Chapter 2 provides more detail on these business functions and organizational levels and the ways in which they are supported by information systems.

An organization accomplishes and coordinates work through this structured hierarchy and through its **business processes**, which are logically related tasks and behaviors for accomplishing work. Developing a new product, fulfilling an order, or hiring a new employee are examples of business processes.

Most organizations' business processes include formal rules that have been developed over a long time for accomplishing tasks. These rules guide employees in a variety of procedures, from writing an invoice to responding to customer complaints. Some of these business processes have been written down, but others are informal work practices, such as a requirement to return telephone calls from co-workers or customers, that are not formally documented. Information systems automate many business processes. For instance, how a customer receives credit or how a customer is billed is often determined by an information system that incorporates a set of formal business processes.

Each organization has a unique **culture**, or fundamental set of assumptions, values, and ways of doing things, that has been accepted by most of its members. Parts of an organization's culture can always be found embedded in its information systems. For instance, the United Parcel Service's concern with placing service to the customer first is an aspect of its organizational culture that can be found in the company's package tracking systems, which we describe in the Focus on Organizations.

Different levels and specialties in an organization create different interests and points of view. These views often conflict. Conflict is the basis for organizational politics. Information systems come out of this cauldron of differing perspectives, conflicts, compromises, and agreements that are a natural part of all organizations.

### People

A business is only as good as the people who work there and run it. Likewise with information systems—they are useless without skilled people to build and maintain them, and without people who can understand how to use the information in a system to achieve business objectives.

For instance, a call center that provides help to customers using an advanced customer relationship management system (described in later chapters) is useless if employees are not adequately trained to deal with customers, find solutions to their problems, and leave the customer feeling that the company cares for them. Likewise, employee attitudes about their jobs, employers, or technology can have a powerful effect on their abilities to use information systems productively.

Business firms require many different kinds of skills and people, including managers as well as rank-and-file employees. The job of managers is to make sense out of the many situations faced by organizations, make decisions, and formulate action plans to solve organizational problems. Managers perceive business challenges in the environment; they set the organizational strategy for responding to those challenges; and they allocate the human and financial resources to coordinate the work and achieve success. Throughout, they must exercise responsible leadership.

But managers must do more than manage what already exists. They must also create new products and services and even re-create the organization from time to time. A substantial part of management responsibility is creative work driven by new knowledge and information. Information technology can play a powerful role in helping managers develop novel solutions to a broad range of problems.

As you will learn throughout this text, technology is today relatively inexpensive, but people are very expensive. Because people are the only ones capable of business problem solving and converting information technology into useful business solutions, we spend considerable effort in this text looking at the people dimension of information systems.

### Technology

Information technology is one of many tools managers use to cope with change. **Computer hardware** is the physical equipment used for input, processing, and output activities in an information system. It consists of the following: computers of various sizes and shapes; various input, output, and storage devices; and physical media to link these devices together.

**Computer software** consists of the detailed, preprogrammed instructions that control and coordinate the computer hardware components in an information system. Chapter 4 describes the contemporary software and hardware platforms used by firms today in greater detail.

**Data management technology** consists of the software governing the organization of data on physical storage media. More detail on data organization and access methods can be found in Chapter 5.

**Networking and telecommunications technology**, consisting of both physical devices and software, links the various pieces of hardware and transfers data from one physical location to another. Computers and communications equipment can be connected in networks for sharing voice, data, images, sound, and video. A **network** links two or more computers to share data or resources, such as a printer.

The world's largest and most widely used network is the **Internet**, Inc. The Internet is a global "network of networks" that uses universal standards (described in Chapter 6) to connect millions of different networks with more than 350 million host computers in over 200 countries around the world (Internet Systems Consortium, 2005).

The Internet has created a new "universal" technology platform on which to build new products, services, strategies, and business models. This same technology platform has internal uses, providing the connectivity to link different systems and networks within the firm. Internal corporate networks based on Internet technology are called **intranets**. Private intranets extended to authorized users outside the organization are called **extranets**, and firms use such networks to coordinate their activities with other firms for making purchases, collaborating on design, and other interorganizational work. For most business firms today, using Internet technology is both a business necessity and a competitive advantage.

The **World Wide Web** is a service provided by the Internet that uses universally accepted standards for storing, retrieving, formatting, and displaying information in a page format on the Internet. Web pages contain text, graphics, animations, sound, and video and are linked to other Web pages. By clicking on highlighted words or buttons on a Web page, you can link to related pages to find additional information and links to other locations on the Web. The Web can serve as the foundation for new kinds of information systems such as UPS's Web-based package tracking system or MLB's online systems for ordering tickets and playing "fantasy" baseball described earlier in this chapter.

All of these technologies, along with the people required to run and manage them, represent resources that can be shared throughout the organization and constitute the firm's **information technology (IT) infrastructure**. The IT infrastructure provides the foundation, or *platform,* on which the firm can build its specific information systems. Each organization must carefully design and manage its information technology infrastructure so that it has the set of technology services it needs for the work it wants to accomplish with information systems. Chapters 4 through 7 of this text examine each major technology component of information technology infrastructure and show how they all work together to create the technology platform for the organization.

The Focus on Technology describes some of the typical technologies used in computer-based information systems today. United Parcel Service (UPS) invests heavily in information systems technology to make its business more efficient and customer oriented. It uses an array of information technologies including bar code scanning systems, wireless networks, large mainframe computers, handheld computers, the Internet, and many different pieces of software for tracking packages, calculating fees, maintaining customer accounts, and managing logistics. As you read this case, try to identify the problem this company was facing, what alternative solutions were available to management, and how well the chosen solution worked.

Let's identify the organization, people, and technology elements in the UPS package tracking system. The organization element anchors the package tracking system in UPS's sales and production functions (the main product of UPS is a service–package delivery). It

Using a handheld computer called a Delivery Information Acquisition Device (DIAD), UPS drivers automatically capture customers' signatures along with pickup, delivery, and time-card information. UPS information systems use these data to track packages while they are being transported.

# FOCUS ON TECHNOLOGY   UPS Competes Globally with Information Technology

United Parcel Service (UPS) is the world's largest air and ground package-distribution company. It started out in 1907 in a closet-sized basement office. Jim Casey and Claude Ryan—two teenagers from Seattle with two bicycles and one phone—promised the "best service and lowest rates." UPS has used this formula successfully for more than 90 years and is now the world's largest ground and air package-distribution company.

Today UPS delivers more than 14.1 million parcels and documents each day in the United States and more than 200 other countries and territories. The firm has been able to maintain leadership in small-package delivery services despite stiff competition from FedEx and Airborne Express by investing heavily in advanced information technology. During the past decade, UPS has poured billions of dollars into technology and systems to boost customer service while keeping costs low and streamlining its overall operations.

Using a handheld computer called a Delivery Information Acquisition Device (DIAD), a UPS driver can automatically capture customers' signatures along with pickup, delivery, and time-card information. The driver then places the DIAD into the UPS truck's vehicle adapter, an information-transmitting device that is connected to the cellular telephone network. Package tracking information is then transmitted to UPS's computer network for storage and processing in UPS's main computers in Mahwah, New Jersey, and Alpharetta, Georgia. From there, the information can be accessed worldwide to provide proof of delivery to customers or to respond to customer queries.

Through its automated package tracking system, UPS can monitor packages throughout the delivery process. At various points along the route from sender to receiver, bar code devices scan shipping information on the package label; the information is then fed into the central computer. Customer service representatives can check the status of any package from desktop computers linked to the central computers and are able to respond immediately to inquiries from customers. UPS customers can also access this information from the company's Web site using their own computers or wireless devices, such as pagers and cell phones.

Anyone with a package to ship can access the UPS Web site to track packages, check delivery routes, calculate shipping rates, determine time in transit, and schedule a pickup. Businesses anywhere can use the Web site to arrange UPS shipments and bill the shipments to the company's UPS account number or to a credit card. The data collected at the UPS Web site are transmitted to the UPS central computer and then back to the customer after processing. UPS also provides tools that enable customers, such as Cisco Systems, to embed UPS functions, such as tracking and cost calculations, into their own Web sites so that they can track shipments without visiting the UPS site.

Information technology helps UPS reinvent itself and keep growing. UPS implemented a suite of custom-built software that uses operations research and mapping technology to optimize the way packages are loaded and delivered. Because UPS delivers 14 million small packages each day, the resulting information is cutting the distance that delivery trucks travel by more than 100 million miles each year.

UPS is now leveraging its decades of expertise managing its own global delivery network to manage logistics and supply-chain management for other companies. It created a UPS Supply Chain Solutions division that provides a complete bundle of standardized services to subscribing companies at a fraction of what it would cost to build their own systems and infrastructure. These services include supply-chain design and management, freight forwarding, customs brokerage, mail services, multimodal transportation, and financial services, in addition to logistics services.

Birkenstock Footprint Sandals is one of many companies benefiting from these services. Birkenstock's German plants pack shoes in crates that are bar coded with their U.S. destination. UPS contracts with ocean carriers in Rotterdam to transport the shoe crates across the Atlantic to New Jersey ports instead of routing them through the Panama Canal to Birkenstock's California warehouses. UPS trucks whisk each incoming shipment to a UPS distribution hub and, within hours, to 3,000 different retailers. By handing this work over to UPS, Birkenstock has cut the time to get its shoes to stores by half. Along the way, UPS uses bar code scanning to keep track of every shipment until the merchant signs off on it.

*Sources:* Elena Malykhina, "UPS Seeks Reliability, End-to-End Visibility," *InformationWeek,* March 7, 2005; Dave Barnes, "Delivering Corporate Citizenship," *Optimize,* September 2005; Tom Steinert-Threlkeld, "UPS Delivers Real Presence for Virtual Bank," *CIO Insight,* September 7, 2005; Dean Foust, "Big Brown's New Bag," and "Online Extra: UPS's Eskew on 'the Next Logical Step,'" *BusinessWeek,* July 19, 2004; and Galen Gruman, "UPS vs. FedEx: Head-to-Head on Wireless" and "New Technologies Hit Mainstream," *CIO Magazine,* June 1, 2004.

## To Think About:

What are the inputs, processing, and outputs of UPS's package tracking system? What technologies are used? How are these technologies related to UPS's business strategy? What problems do these technologies solve? What would happen if these technologies were not available?

specifies the required procedures for identifying packages with both sender and recipient information, taking inventory, tracking the packages en route, and providing package status reports for UPS customers and customer service representatives.

The system must also provide information to satisfy the needs of managers and workers. UPS drivers need to be trained in both package pickup and delivery procedures and in how to use the package tracking system so that they can work efficiently and effectively. UPS customers may need some training to use UPS in-house package tracking software or the UPS Web site.

UPS's management is responsible for monitoring service levels and costs and for promoting the company's strategy of combining low cost and superior service. Management decided to use automation to increase the ease of sending a package using UPS and of checking its delivery status, thereby reducing delivery costs and increasing sales revenues.

The technology supporting this system consists of handheld computers, bar code scanners, wired and wireless communications networks, desktop computers, UPS's central computer, storage technology for the package delivery data, UPS in-house package tracking software, and software to access the World Wide Web. The result is an information system solution to the business challenge of providing a high level of service with low prices in the face of mounting competition.

## 1.4 Understanding Information Systems: A Business Problem-Solving Approach

Our approach to understanding information systems is to consider information systems and technologies as solutions to a variety of business challenges and problems. We refer to this as a "problem solving approach." Businesses face many challenges and problems, and information systems are one major way of solving these problems. All of the cases in this book illustrate how a company used information systems to solve a specific problem.

The problem-solving approach has direct relevance to your future career. Your future employers will hire you because you are able to solve business problems and achieve business objectives. Your knowledge of how information systems contribute to problem solving will be very helpful to both you and your employers. Let's take a closer look at the problem-solving approach that is used throughout the book.

### The Problem-Solving Approach

At first glance, problem solving in daily life seems to be perfectly straightforward: A machine breaks down, parts and oil spill all over the floor, and, obviously, somebody has to do something about it. So, of course, you find a tool around the shop and start repairing the machine. After cleanup and a proper inspection of other parts, you start the machine, and production resumes.

No doubt some problems in business are this straightforward. But few problems are this simple in the real world of business. In real-world business firms, a number of major factors are simultaneously involved in problems. These major factors can usefully be grouped into three categories: *organization, technology,* and *people.* In other words, a whole set of problems is usually involved.

### A Model of the Problem-Solving Process

There is a simple model of problem solving that you can use to help you understand and solve business problems using information systems. You can think of business problem solving as a four-step process (see Figure 1-4). Most problem solvers work through this model on their way to finding a solution. Let's take a brief look at each step.

#### Problem Identification

The first step in the problem-solving process is to understand what kind of problem exists. Contrary to popular beliefs, problems are not like basketballs on a court simply waiting to be

**Figure 1-4**
Problem Solving Is a
Continuous Four-Step
Process
*During implementation
and thereafter, the out-
come must be continu-
ally measured and the
information about how
well the solution is
working is fed back to
the problem solvers. In
this way, the identifica-
tion of the problem can
change over time, solu-
tions can be changed,
and new choices
made, all based on
experience.*

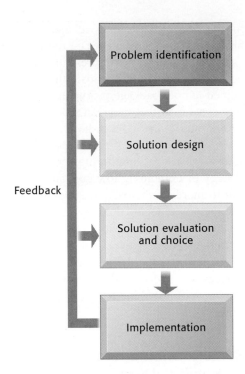

picked up by some "objective" problem solver. Before problems can be solved, there must be agreement in a business that a problem exists, about what the problem is, about what its causes are, and about what can be done about the problem given the limited resources of the organization. Problems have to be properly defined by people in an organization before they can be solved.

For instance, what at first glance might seem like a problem with employees not ade-quately responding to customers in a timely and accurate manner might in reality be a result of an older, out-of-date information system for keeping track of customers. Or it might be a combination of both poor employee incentives for treating customers well and an outdated system. Once you understand this critical fact, you can start to solve problems creatively. Finding answers to these questions will require fact gathering, interviews with people involved in the problem, and analysis of documents.

In this text we emphasize three different and typical dimensions of business problems: organizations, technology, and people (see Table 1.1). Typical organizational problems include poor business processes (usually inherited from the past), unsupportive culture, political in-fighting, and changes in the organization's surrounding environment. Typical technology problems include insufficient or aging hardware, outdated software, inadequate data management, insufficient telecommunications capacity, and the incompatibility of old systems with new technology. Typical people problems include employee training, difficul-ties of evaluating performance, legal and regulatory compliance, ergonomics, poor or inde-cisive management, and employee support and participation. When you begin to analyze a business problem, you will find these dimensions are helpful guides to understanding the kind of problem with which you are working.

### Solution Design

The second step is to design solutions to the problem(s) you have identified. As it turns out, there are usually a great many "solutions" to any given problem, and the choice of solution often reflects the differing perspectives of people in an organization. You should try to con-sider as many different solutions as possible so that you can understand the range of possi-ble solutions. Some solutions emphasize technology; others, change in the organization and people aspects of the problem. As you will find throughout the text, most successful solu-tions result from an integrated approach in which new technologies are accompanied by changes in organization and people.

| Dimension | Description |
|---|---|
| Organizational dimensions | Outdated business processes |
| | Unsupportive culture and attitudes |
| | Political conflict |
| | Turbulent business environment, change |
| | Complexity of task |
| | Inadequate resources |
| Technology dimensions | Insufficient or aging hardware |
| | Outdated software |
| | Inadequate data management |
| | Insufficient telecommunications capacity |
| | Incompatibility of old systems with new technology |
| | Rapid technological change |
| People dimensions | Lack of employee training |
| | Difficulties of evaluating performance |
| | Legal and regulatory compliance |
| | Work environment |
| | Lack of employee support and participation |
| | Indecisive management |
| | Poor management |

**TABLE 1.1**

**Dimensions of Business Problems**

## Choice

Choosing the "best" solution for your business firm is the next step in the process. Some of the factors to consider when trying to find the "best" single solution are the cost of the solution, the feasibility of the solution for your business given existing resources and skills, and the length of time required to build and implement the solution. Also very important at this point are the attitudes and support of your employees and managers. A solution that does not have the support of all the major interests in the business can quickly turn into a disaster.

## Implementation

The best solution is one that can be implemented. Implementation of an information system solution involves building the solution and introducing it into the organization. This includes purchasing or building the software and hardware—the technology part of the equation. The software must be tested in a realistic business setting; then employees need to be trained, and documentation about how to use the new system needs to be written.

You will definitely need to think about change management. **Change management** refers to the many techniques used to bring about successful change in a business. Nearly all information systems require changes in the firm's business processes and, therefore, changes in what hundreds or even thousands of employees do every day. You will have to design new, more efficient business processes, and then figure out how to encourage employees to adapt to these new ways of doing business. This may require meeting sessions to introduce the change to groups of employees, new training modules to bring employees quickly up to speed on the new information systems and processes, and finally some kind of rewards or incentives to encourage people to enthusiastically support the changes.

Implementation also includes the measurement of outcomes. After a solution has been implemented, it must be evaluated to determine how well it is working and whether any additional changes are required to meet the original objectives. This information is fed back to the problem solvers. In this way, the identification of the problem can change over time, solutions can be changed, and new choices made, all based on experience.

## Problem Solving: A Process, Not an Event

It is often assumed that once a problem is "solved," it goes away and can be forgotten about. And it is easy to fall into the trap of thinking about problem solving as an event that is "over" at some point, like a relay race or a baseball game. Often in the real world this does not happen. Sometimes the solution chosen does not work, and new solutions are required.

For instance, the U.S. National Aeronautics and Space Administration (NASA) spent more than $1 billion to fix a problem with shedding foam on the space shuttle. Experience proved the initial solution did not work. More often, the solution chosen partially works but needs a lot of continuous changes to truly "fit" the situation. Initial solutions are often rough approximations at first of what ultimately "works." Sometimes, the nature of the problem changes in a way that makes the initial solution ineffective. For instance, hackers create new variations on computer viruses that require continually evolving antivirus programs to hold them in check. For all these reasons, problem solving is a continuous process rather than a single event.

## The Role of Critical Thinking in Problem Solving

It is amazingly easy to accept someone else's definition of a problem or to adopt the opinions of some authoritative group that has "objectively" analyzed the problem and offers quick solutions. You should try to resist this tendency to accept existing definitions of any problem. Through the natural flow of decision making, it is essential that you try to maintain some distance from any specific solution until you are sure you have properly identified the problem, developed understanding, and analyzed alternatives. Otherwise, you may leap off in the wrong direction, solve the wrong problem, and waste resources. You will have to engage in some critical-thinking exercises.

**Critical thinking** can be briefly defined as the sustained suspension of judgment with an awareness of multiple perspectives and alternatives. It involves at least four elements:

- Maintaining doubt and suspending judgment
- Being aware of different perspectives
- Testing alternatives and letting experience guide
- Being aware of organizational and personal limitations

Simply following a rote pattern of decision making, or a model, does not guarantee a correct solution. The best protection against incorrect results is to engage in critical thinking throughout the problem-solving process.

First, maintain doubt and suspend judgment. Perhaps the most frequent error in problem solving is to arrive prematurely at a judgment about the nature of the problem. By doubting all solutions at first and refusing to rush to a judgment, you create the necessary mental conditions to take a fresh, creative look at problems, and you keep open the chance to make a creative contribution.

Second, recognize that all interesting business problems have many dimensions and that the same problem can be viewed from different perspectives. In this text we have emphasized the usefulness of three perspectives on business problems: technology, organizations, and people. Within each of these very broad perspectives are many subperspectives, or views. The *technology perspective,* for instance, includes a consideration of all the components in the firm's IT infrastructure and the way they work together. The *organization perspective* includes a consideration of a firm's business processes, structure, culture, and politics. The *people perspective* includes consideration of the firm's management, as well as employees as individuals and their interrelationships in workgroups.

You will have to decide for yourself which major perspectives are useful for viewing a given problem. The ultimate criterion here is usefulness: Does adopting a certain perspective tell you something more about the problem that is useful for solving the problem? If not, reject that perspective as being not meaningful in this situation and look for other perspectives.

The third element of critical thinking involves testing alternatives, or modeling solutions to problems, letting experience be the guide. Not all contingencies can be known in advance, and much can be learned through experience. Therefore, experiment, gather data, and reassess the problem periodically.

## The Connection Between Business Objectives, Problems, and Solutions

Now let's make the connection between business information systems and the problem-solving approach. At the beginning of this chapter we talked about the six reasons business firms invest in information systems and technologies. We identified six business objectives of information systems: operational excellence; new products, services, and business models; customer/supplier intimacy; improved decision making; strategic advantage; and survival. When firms cannot achieve these objectives, they become "challenges" or "problems" that receive attention. Managers and employees who are aware of these challenges often turn to information systems as one of the solutions, or the entire solution.

Review the diagram at the beginning of this chapter. The diagram shows how MLB's Web-based systems solved the business problem presented by declining interest in baseball games and competition from television and other media. These systems provided a solution that takes advantage of new opportunities created by the Internet. They opened new sales channels and gathered information to help the organization make better decisions about how to promote its teams and sell tickets and related products. The diagram also illustrates how people, technology, and organizational elements work together to create the systems.

Each chapter of this text begins with a diagram similar to this one to help you analyze the chapter-opening case. You can use this diagram as a starting point for analyzing any information system or information system problem you encounter.

Table 1.2 further highlights the connection between business objectives, problem solving, and information system solutions by describing other cases in this text that illustrate how businesses use information systems to solve business problems and, thereby, achieve business objectives.

**TABLE 1.2**

**Business Objectives, Problems, and Information System Solutions**

| Business Objective: Case | Problem/Challenge | Information System Solution |
|---|---|---|
| Operational excellence: TransAlta | Became a deregulated power provider that had to focus on service level and costs | Uses systems based on wireless radio frequency identification (RFID) technology to maintain equipment more efficiently |
| New products and services: MLB | Revenue and customer base were waning | Created Web site for online tickets sales and delivery of new online "fantasy" baseball games |
| Customer/supplier intimacy: Seven-Eleven Stores | Retail stores were unable to stock inventory efficiently and respond to changes in customer demand | Implemented Retail Information System that collects and analyzes point-of-sale data to determine customer demand at each store location |
| Improved decision making: Whirlpool | Managers could not get information in a timely fashion to make decisions about stocking inventory | Implemented new supply-chain management systems |
| Competitive advantage: Blockbuster | New competitors taking away market share | Created an online system for movie rentals to compete with NetFlix |
| Survival: China Telecom | Existing systems could not respond to government reporting regulations | Implemented an enterprise system to comply with international reporting regulations of publicly traded companies |

## 1.5 Information Systems and Your Career

It's not business as usual, and it's not the same old labor market either. Work and careers are changing, and for you to succeed in this new labor market you will need a broad skill set if you are to help business firms achieve their objectives. Looking out to 2012, the U.S. economy will create 21.6 million new jobs, expanding the labor force to 165 million. In this same period about 28.5 million existing jobs will open up as their occupants retire. More than 95 percent of the new jobs will be created in the service sector. Many of these new jobs and replacement jobs will require a college degree to perform (Statistical Abstract, 2004–2005; U.S. Bureau of Labor Statistics, 2005).

What this means is that U.S. business firms are looking for candidates who have a broad range of problem-solving skills—the ability to read, write, and present ideas—as well as the technical skills required for specific tasks. Regardless of your business school major, or your future occupation, information systems and technologies will play a major and expanding role in your day-to-day work and your career. Your career opportunities, and your compensation, will in part depend on your ability to help business firms use information systems to achieve their objectives.

The Focus on People provides an example of an outstanding manager who knows how to use information technology wisely. Mitchell Gregory, who is in charge of information systems at Sonic Corporation, combines a strong business background with an appreciation for how information technology can benefit the business. As you read this case, try to identify the problem Sonic Corporation was facing, what alternative solutions were available to management, and how well the chosen solution worked. Also look at the kinds of skills that helped Mitchell Gregory become such a successful business problem solver.

### How Information Systems Will Affect Business Careers

In the following sections we describe how specific occupations will be affected by information systems and what skills you should be building in order to function effectively in this new, emerging labor market. Let's look at the career opportunities for business school majors.

#### Accounting

There are about 1.1 million accountants in the U.S. labor force today, and the field is expected to expand by 20 percent to the year 2012, adding 200,000 new jobs, and a similar number of jobs to replace retirees. This above-average growth in accounting is in part driven by new accounting laws for public companies, greater scrutiny of public and private firms by government tax auditors, and a growing demand for management and operational advice.

*Accountants depend heavily on information systems for organizing data, summarizing transations, and preparing financial statements.*

# FOCUS ON PEOPLE    A Top Information Manager Puts Business Before Technology

Oklahoma City–based Sonic Corporation is only one-fifth the size of McDonald's domestic hamburger business. However, it occupies a special place of its own as the largest chain of drive-in restaurants in the United States. As of August 31, 2004, the company had 2,885 Sonic Drive-Ins in operation, primarily in the southern two-thirds of the country.

At a typical Sonic Drive-In, a customer drives into one of 24 to 36 covered drive-in spaces, orders through an intercom speaker system, and has the food delivered by a carhop within an average of four minutes. The carhop carries a wireless credit card reader to accept credit card payments as well as cash. Many Sonic Drive-Ins include patio seating.

Sonic is known for signature items, such as made-to-order sandwiches and hamburgers, extra-long cheese coney hot dogs, hand-battered onion rings, tater tots, specialty soft drinks including cherry limeades and slushes, and frozen desserts. Sonic Drive-Ins also offer a breakfast menu. Sonic tries to stand out from competitors by offering a wide variety of made-to-order items, quality, value, and quick, personalized service from its carhops.

Sonic lives and dies by how its food is accepted by consumers, so Sonic devotes a great deal of energy to finding out what its customers want using traditional marketing techniques as well as new technology. The company continues to use traditional market research and focus groups, including polls, testing, and customer interviews, to determine how customers will react to a potential product. Sonic also uses data from point-of-sales terminals in each of its drive-ins to track customer trends. After analyzing point-of-sale data, the company learned that ice cream sundaes accounted for as much as 30 percent of one Texas franchisee's sales and encouraged other restaurants in the chain to promote desserts. At other chains, desserts typically account for 2 percent of sales, but at Sonic they account for 17 percent of the total.

Helping Sonic sell food and keep its customers returning to its drive-ins is Mitchell Gregory, the company's chief information officer (CIO). Gregory's job description includes monitoring taste tests for items such as the SuperSonic Jalapeño Cheeseburger and other market research as well as overseeing Sonic's information systems. Sonic's main mission is to sell food and keep customers coming back to its drive-ins, whereas the role of information systems is to support the business, he says. Having one executive responsible for both technology and market research helps ensure that the company will use information to support its goals.

Although Gregory oversees all of Sonic's information systems, he did not start out as a technology specialist. Before assuming the CIO position, he was Sonic's vice president of brand development and before that, director of market research. Prior to joining Sonic, Gregory worked in sales, financial analysis, business planning, and accounting at PepsiCo. "I'm not a technology person and my background is in general business, so I come at things from the other side of the fence," he notes.

This background makes it easy for Gregory to identify business issues where technology can help the company, but he doesn't always know how to identify the right technology to solve the problem. Gregory's solution is to encourage his information systems staff to learn about the business as much as they can so that they can make good recommendations and communicate more easily with him. For example, he will encourage a programmer who is a specialist in Java software to become involved in a market research project.

Gregory and his team developed an intranet that allows stores connected via the Web to compare their performance to that of their peers, report sales, and track responses to promotions company-wide. The company analyzes its high-level data, such as regional sales for a new burger, but leaves the detailed analysis, such as soda sales in July, to each drive-in manager.

Thanks to Gregory's leadership, *Baseline Magazine* ranked Sonic Corp. among the top 500 publicly traded U.S. companies that manage information the best. The actual systems these companies use don't all have to be highly automated or leading-edge, but the companies need to use information wisely to add value to their financial performance. Managing information includes far more than technology. It also includes brainpower, insight, good work processes, and the ability to manage teams well. Sonic earned its *Baseline* ranking not by relying heavily on technology but by relegating it to a secondary role.

*Sources:* Larry Dignan, "Here's the Beef," *Baseline,* October 15, 2005; Jennifer A. Kingson, "Wireless Moves the Cash Register Where You Are," *New York Times,* November 25, 2005; Sonic Corp. 10-K Report, November 15, 2004; and Lea Goldman, "Greased Lightning," *Forbes,* October 28, 2002.

**To Think About:**

What problems and challenges does Sonic face? How is it trying to solve these problems? What alternative solutions are available? Is CIO Mitchell Gregory a good problem solver for this company? Why or why not?

There are many different types of accountants. They can be broadly classified as public accountants, management accountants, government accountants, and internal auditors. Accountants provide a broad range of services to business firms including preparing, analyzing, and verifying financial documents; budget analysis; financial planning; information technology consulting; and limited legal services.

In addition, a new, rapidly growing specialty called "forensic accounting" has emerged as a result of the financial scandals in public firms. Forensic accountants investigate white-collar crimes, such as securities fraud and embezzlement, bankruptcies and contract disputes, and other possibly criminal financial transactions.

Accounting was one of the very first applications to use computers, beginning in the 1950s when the first commercial computers were used to develop accounting information systems such as general ledger and payroll. Accountants increasingly rely on information systems to summarize transactions, create financial records, organize data, and perform financial analysis. In fact, there is no way that firms today can perform even basic accounting functions without extensive investment in systems. As a result of new public laws, accountants are beginning to perform more technical duties, such as implementing, controlling, and auditing systems and networks, and developing technology plans and budgets.

What kinds of information system skills are really important for accounting majors given these changes in the accounting profession? Here is a short list:

- Knowledge of current and likely future changes in information technology, including hardware, software, and telecommunications, which will be used by public and private firms, government agencies, and financial advisors as they perform auditing and accounting functions. Also essential is an understanding of accounting and financial applications and design factors to ensure firms are able to maintain accounting records and perform auditing functions, and an understanding of system and network security issues, which are vital to protect the integrity of accounting systems.
- Understanding of enterprise systems capabilities for corporate-wide financial reporting on a global and national scale. Because so many transactions are occurring over the Internet, accountants need to understand online transaction and reporting systems, and how systems are used to achieve accounting functions in an online, wireless, and mobile business environment.

### Finance

Finance majors perform a wide variety of jobs in the U.S. economy. Financial managers develop financial reports, direct investment activities, and implement cash management strategies. There are about 600,000 financial managers in the U.S. labor force and this occupation is expected to grow by about 20 percent by 2012, adding about 120,000 new jobs, and requiring the replacement of about 100,000 additional jobs.

In addition, a huge financial services industry (which includes the banking, brokerage, insurance, and real estate industries) employs many more college graduates who are finance majors. The financial services industry alone employs more than 7 percent of the U.S. labor force, or about 10 million people. This includes job titles such as broker, trader, sales representative, insurance agent, and bank officer. Employment growth in the financial services industry is expected to be above average as more Americans retire and need extensive financial advice and services. In the next six years financial services sector employment is expected to add an additional one million new jobs, and replace another 800,000.

Financial managers require strong system skills and play important roles in planning, organizing, and implementing information system strategies for their firms. Financial managers work directly with a firm's board of directors and senior management to ensure investments in information systems help achieve corporate goals and achieve high returns. The relationship between information systems and the practice of modern financial management and services is so strong that many advise finance majors to also co-major in information systems (and vice versa).

What kinds of information system skills should finance majors develop? Following is brief list:

- An understanding of likely future changes in information technology, including hardware, software, and telecommunications, that will be used by financial managers and financial service firms. This includes an understanding of financial applications and design factors to ensure firms are able to manage their investments, cash, and risks; new kinds of mobile and wireless applications to manage financial reporting; and development of online systems for financial transactions. As new trading systems emerge, financial service firms and managers will need to understand how these systems work and how they will change their firm's business.
- Knowledge of the new role played by enterprise-wide financial reporting systems for achieving corporate-wide financial reporting on a global and national scale. As more and more transactions move online, finance majors need to understand online transaction reporting systems and management of online system investments.

## Marketing

Thanks to the Internet, no field has undergone more technology-driven change in the past five years than marketing and advertising. The explosion in e-commerce activity described earlier in this chapter means that eyeballs are moving rapidly to the Internet. As a result, Internet advertising is the fastest-growing form of advertising, expanding at more than 30 percent annually and reaching $13 billion in 2006. (Other forms of marketing communications are growing at a much slower 5 percent rate.) All this means that branding products and communicating with customers are moving online at a fast pace.

Marketing majors perform a wide variety of jobs in U.S. industry. There are three major categories of jobs: marketing, sales, and public relations. In each of these categories college degrees are essential, and marketing requires strong creative writing and analytical skills. Marketing managers develop the firm's detailed marketing and branding strategy and work with product development managers, market research managers, creative and media managers, and promotion managers. Sales managers are responsible for making sales, which includes managing a sales force, developing sales campaigns, and ensuring sales meet business targets. Public relations managers develop publicity programs that support the firm's overall marketing and sales objectives, and communicate with key groups, such as shareholders, consumers, and government regulators.

There are about 900,000 marketing, public relations, sales, and advertising managers in the 2005 U.S. labor force. This field is growing faster than average and is expected to add more than 200,000 jobs by 2012 and replace an additional 150,000 employees who are retiring. There is a much larger group of 2.6 million nonmanagerial employees in marketing-related occupations (art, design, entertainment, sports, and media) and more than 15.9 million employees in sales. These occupations together are expected to create an additional 1.8 million jobs by 2012.

For each of the major occupational groups within marketing, information systems skills are crucial because marketing activities, branding, promotion, and public relations increasingly involve an understanding of the Internet as well as internal corporate marketing and sales information systems. The field of marketing—including sales and public relations— has also been affected by major changes in legislation, as has accounting and finance, witnessing major lawsuits involving product liability claims, misrepresentation, and fraud. Marketing and sales managers are increasingly held partially responsible for product claims and product promotion strategies. This new legal and ethical environment forces marketing and sales managers to become involved in corporate record retention policies for e-mail and other records. Following are the general information systems skills on which marketing majors should focus:

- An ability to understand emerging new hardware and software platforms, and how they impact traditional marketing activities, such as brand development, production promotion, and sales. This would include an understanding of Internet and marketing database systems and design factors to ensure firms are able to market their products, develop reports on product performance, retrieve feedback from customers, and manage product development.

- An understanding of how enterprise-wide systems for product management, sales force management, and customer relationship management are used to develop products that consumers want, to manage the customer relationship, and to manage an increasingly mobile sales force.

## Operations Management in Services and Manufacturing

The growing size and complexity of modern industrial production and the emergence of huge global service companies have created a growing demand for employees who can coordinate and optimize the resources required to produce goods and services. Operations management as a discipline is directly relevant to three occupational categories: industrial production managers, administrative service managers, and operations analysts.

Industrial production managers work in goods production and are responsible for production planning, staffing, procurement, quality control, inventory control, and coordination with other departments, such as marketing and finance. Today's production managers work in highly computerized environments where flows of raw, intermediate, and final products are very precisely coordinated to reduce inventory costs to a minimum, speed time to market, and achieve exceptionally high quality. There are about 180,000 industrial production managers in the U.S. labor force.

Administrative service managers work in service organizations, such as banks, insurance companies, food services, hotel and lodging services, and government services, which together employ more than 60 percent of the U.S. labor force. Administrative service managers—like industrial production managers—are responsible for allocating and coordinating the resources and human resources needed to produce services. There are about 320,000 administrative service managers in the U.S. labor force.

Operations analysts (also known as operations research analysts) use analytical methods from mathematics and engineering to solve business problems. They work on diverse problems, such as planning and forecasting, performance management, scheduling, facilities design, supply chain management, and transportation and distribution, often relying on the analysis of data stored in large databases. There are around 60,000 operations analysts in the U.S. labor force.

*MineMAX Planner uses optimization and 3-D interactive visualization technologies to provide a mining engineer with a user-friendly, fast tool for determining optimal pits and performing strategic analysis. Information systems help solve production problems in mining and other industries.*

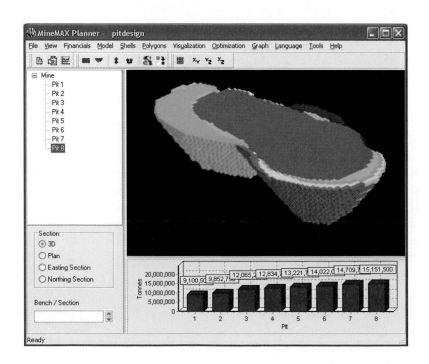

Although industrial production will continue to rise, the number of people employed in goods production at all levels will remain static or decline slightly. However, the services sector will be expanding rapidly, creating strong job opportunities for operations management majors as business firms in diverse service sector industries, from finance, to real estate, restaurants, lodging and travel, seek to improve their efficiency and competitiveness.

Production managers, administrative service managers, and operations analysts will be employing information systems and technologies every day to accomplish their jobs, with extensive use of database and analytical software. Here are the general information systems skills on which operations management majors should focus:

- Knowledge of the changing hardware and software platforms that will be used in operations management. This would include an understanding of the role that databases, modeling tools, and business analytical software play in production and services management.
- An in-depth understanding of how enterprise-wide information systems for production management, supplier management, sales force management, and customer relationship management are used to achieve efficient operations and meet other firm objectives.

## Management

Management is the largest single group in the U.S. business labor force with more than 14 million members, not including an additional 547,000 management consultants. Overall, the management corps in the United States is expected to expand faster than other occupational groups, adding about 3.8 million new jobs by 2012, with about two million replacement openings in this period as a result of retirements. There are more than 20 different types of managers tracked by the Bureau of Labor Statistics, all the way from chief executive officer, to human resource managers, production managers, project managers, lodging managers, medical managers, and community service managers.

Managers perform a wide range of activities in all industries throughout the economy, including planning, leading, organizing, coordinating, and communicating. Managers are responsible for the efficient operation of business firms and for supervision of employees. Most management jobs today require college degrees; strong leadership; and analytical, presentation, and writing skills.

Information systems skills are crucial as the job of management increasingly is enabled by digital technologies, such as the Internet, e-mail, cell phones, and BlackBerry handhelds, that permit managers to observe and monitor employees, customers, and suppliers more precisely and improve decision making. As with other business fields, management is under increasing social, ethical, and legal scrutiny of both government regulators and the public. It is management, for instance, that is responsible for meeting equal employment opportunity guidelines, occupational health and safety requirements, public health requirements, information retention policies, and a host of requirements mandated by law.

The job of management has been transformed by information systems, and, arguably, it would be impossible to manage business firms today without the extensive use of information systems, even very small firms. Nearly all of the 14 million managers in the United States use information systems and technologies every day to accomplish their jobs, from desktop productivity tools to applications coordinating the entire enterprise. Here are the general information systems skills on which management majors should focus:

- Knowledge of new hardware and software that can make management more efficient and effective, enhance leadership and coordination capabilities, and improve the achievement of corporate business objectives in the broadest sense. This would include an understanding of the role that databases play in managing information resources of the firm.
- An in-depth understanding of how enterprise-wide information systems for production management, supplier management, sales force management, and customer relationship

management are used to achieve efficient operations and help managers make better decisions for improving firm performance.

## Information Systems

The information systems field is arguably one of the most fast changing and dynamic of all the business professions because it is directly tied to the rapid evolution of information technologies, which are among the most important tools for achieving business firms' key objectives. The explosive growth of business information systems has generated a growing demand for information systems employees and managers who, working with other business professionals in accounting, finance, marketing, production and operations management, and general management, design and develop new hardware and software systems to serve the needs of business. Of the top 20 fastest-growing occupations through 2012, five are information system occupations.

Information systems occupations can broadly be separated into two groups: technical and managerial, although the distinction can be fluid. Technical information systems specialists focus primarily on building new systems and maintenance and operation of existing systems. Managerial information systems specialists focus on the management of existing systems, planning and implementing new systems, and coordinating the overall systems effort with larger business objectives and other business managers.

In the technical areas, there are about one million computer systems analysts, programmers, programmer analysts, database administrators, Webmasters, Web developers, and computer scientists in the U.S. labor force, and these jobs are expected to grow at above-average rates to produce nearly 400,000 new jobs by 2012 and fill another 200,000 replacement jobs. This is more than a 36 percent growth rate to 2012, making information systems one of the fastest-growing occupational groups.

There are about 284,000 information system managers in the United States, with an estimated growth rate of 36 percent through 2012, expanding the number of new jobs by more than 100,000 new positions, with an additional 50,000 new hires required for replacements. As businesses and government agencies increasingly rely on the Internet for communication and computing resources, system and network security management positions are growing very rapidly.

**Outsourcing** The Internet has created new opportunities for outsourcing many information systems jobs, along with many other service sector and manufacturing jobs. Offshore outsourcing to low-wage countries has been controversial because U.S. workers fear it will reduce demand for U.S. information systems employment. However, this fear is overblown given the huge demand for new information system hires in the United States through 2012. In fact, reducing the cost of providing information technology services to U.S. corporations by offshoring labor-intensive and lower-level jobs may increase the demand for U.S.-based information system workers as firms find the price of investing in IT falls relative to other capital investments while its power to increase revenues and profits grows.

There are two kinds of outsourcing: outsourcing to domestic U.S. firms and offshore outsourcing to low-wage countries, such as India and eastern European countries. Even this distinction becomes problematic as domestic service providers, such as IBM, develop global outsourcing centers in India.

The impact of *domestic* outsourcing on the overall demand for information technology employment through 2012 is most likely quite small. Service provider firms, such as IBM, Hewlett Packard, and Accenture, add domestic IT employees as they expand their domestic IT services, while domestic information systems departments lose some employees or do not hire new employees.

The impact of *offshore* outsourcing on U.S. domestic IT jobs is more problematic because, ostensibly, jobs that move offshore decrease demand for workers in the United States. The most common and successful offshore outsourcing projects involve production programming and system maintenance programming work, along with call center work related to customer relationship management systems (Gurbaxani and Jorion, 2005). Hence, the largest impact of offshore outsourcing will mostly likely be on technical positions in information systems and less on managerial positions. Even so, offshore outsourcing is unlikely to fulfill the demand for technical information systems specialists in the United States through 2012, and may only replace 100,000 to 150,000 U.S. workers.

Given all these factors in the IT labor market, on what kinds of skills should information system majors focus? Following is a list of general skills we believe will optimize employment opportunities:

- An in-depth knowledge of how new and emerging hardware and software can be used by business firms to make them more efficient and effective, enhance customer and supplier intimacy, improve decision making, achieve competitive advantage, and ensure firm survival. This includes an in-depth understanding of databases, database design, implementation, and management.
- An in-depth understanding of how enterprise-wide information systems for production management, supplier management, sales force management, and customer relationship management are used to achieve efficient operations and meet other firm objectives.
- An ability to lead in the design and implementation of new information systems, work with other business professionals to ensure systems meet business objectives, and work with software packages providing new system solutions.

## Information Systems and Your Career Wrap-Up

Looking back at the information system skills required for specific majors, there are some common themes that affect all business majors. Following is a list of these common requirements for information system skills and knowledge:

- All business students, regardless of major, need an understanding of how information systems are used by firms to achieve business objectives such as achieving operational efficiency, developing new products and services, and maintaining customer intimacy.
- Perhaps the most dominant theme that pervades this review of necessary job skills is the central role of databases in a modern firm. Each of the careers we have just described relies heavily in practice on databases. Chapter 5 features a detailed discussion of databases and data management.
- With the pervasive growth in databases comes inevitably an exponential growth in digital information and a resulting challenge to managers trying to understand all this information. Regardless of major, business students need to develop skills in analysis of information and helping firms understand and make sense out of their environments.
- All business majors need to be able to work with specialists and system designers who build and implement information systems. This is necessary to ensure that the systems that are built actually service business purposes and provide the information and understanding required by managers and employees.
- Each of the business majors will be impacted by changes in the ethical, social, and legal environment of business. Business school students need to understand how information systems can be used to meet business requirements for reporting to government regulators and the public and how information systems impact the ethical issues in their fields.

## How This Book Prepares You for the Future

This book is explicitly designed to prepare you for your future business career. It provides you with the necessary knowledge and foundation concepts for understanding the role of information systems in business organizations. You will be able to use this knowledge to identify opportunities for increasing the effectiveness of your business. You will learn how to use information systems to improve operations, create new products and services, improve decision making, increase customer intimacy, and promote competitive advantage.

Equally important, this book develops your ability to use information systems to solve problems that you will encounter on the job. You will learn how to analyze and define a business problem and how to design an appropriate information system solution. You will deepen your critical-thinking and problem-solving skills. The following features of the text and the accompanying learning package reinforce this problem-solving and career orientation.

### A Framework for Describing and Analyzing Information Systems

The text provides you with a framework for analyzing and solving problems by examining the people, organizational, and technology components of information systems. This framework is used repeatedly throughout the text to help you understand information systems in business and analyze information systems problems.

### A Four-Step Model for Problem Solving

The text provides you with a four-step method for solving business problems, which we introduced in this chapter. You will learn how to identify a business problem, design alternative solutions, choose the correct solution, and implement the solution. You will be asked to use this problem-solving method to solve the case studies in each chapter. Chapter 11 will show you how to use this approach to design and build new information systems.

### Hands-on Projects for Stimulating Critical Thinking and Problem Solving

Each chapter concludes with a series of hands-on projects to sharpen your critical-thinking and problem-solving skills. These projects include hands-on Application Software Exercises, projects tied to the Dirt Bikes running case, and projects for building Internet skills. For each of these projects, we identify both the business skills and the software skills required for the solution.

### Career Resources Integrated Throughout

To make sure you can see exactly how the text is directly useful in your future business career, we've added the following career resources: the Heads Up feature and the digital portfolio.

**Heads Up**  At the beginning of each chapter is a Heads Up section showing exactly why you need to know about the contents of the chapter and how this knowledge will help you in future careers in finance and accounting, management and human resources, manufacturing and production, and sales and marketing.

**Digital Portfolio**  We have provided you with a template for preparing a structured digital portfolio to demonstrate the business knowledge, application software skills, Internet skills, and analytical skills you have acquired in this course. You can include this portfolio in your resume or job applications. Your professors can also use the portfolio to assess the skills you have learned.

---

**LEARNING TRACKS**

1. If you would like to learn more about the debate about How Much Does IT Matter? you will find a Learning Track on this topic at the Laudon Web site for this chapter.
2. If you would like to learn more about the changing business environment for information technology, you will find a Learning Track on this topic at the Laudon Web site for this chapter.
3. If you want to learn more about the business information value chain, you will find a Learning Track on this topic at the Laudon Web site for this chapter.

# Summary

**1** **Explain why information systems are so essential in business today.** Information systems are a foundation for conducting business today. In many industries, survival and even existence is difficult without extensive use of information technology. Businesses today use information systems to achieve six major objectives: operational excellence; new products, services, and business models; customer/supplier intimacy; improved decision making; competitive advantage; and day-to-day survival.

**2** **Define an information system from both a technical and a business perspective, and distinguish between computer literacy and information systems literacy.** From a technical perspective, an information system collects, stores, and disseminates information from an organization's environment and internal operations to support organizational functions and decision making, communication, coordination, control, analysis, and visualization. Information systems transform raw data into useful information through three basic activities: input, processing, and output. From a business perspective, an information system provides a solution to a problem or challenge facing a firm and represents a combination of people, organization, and technology elements. The people dimension of information systems involves issues such as training, job attitudes, and management behavior. The technology dimension consists of computer hardware, software, data management technology, and networking/telecommunications technology. The organization dimension of information systems involves issues such as the organization's hierarchy, functional specialties, business processes, culture, and political interest groups.

Information systems literacy requires an understanding of the organizational and people dimensions of information systems as well as the technical dimensions addressed by computer literacy. Information systems literacy draws on both technical and behavioral approaches to studying information systems.

**3** **Apply a four-step method for problem solving to solve information system–related problems.** Business problem solving involves four steps: problem identification, solution design, choice, and implementation. Problem identification involves understanding what kind of problem is being presented—whether it stems from people, organizational, or technology factors or a combination of these. Solution design involves designing several alternative solutions to the problem that has been identified. Choice entails selecting the best solution, taking into account its cost and the available resources and skills in the business. Implementation of an information system solution entails purchasing or building hardware and software, testing the software, providing employees with training and documentation, managing change as the system is introduced into the organization, and measuring the outcome. Problem solving requires critical thinking in which one suspends judgment to consider multiple perspectives and alternatives.

**4** **Assess how information systems will affect business careers in accounting, finance, management, marketing, operations management, and information systems and identify the information systems skills and knowledge essential for all business careers.** Each of the major business fields requires an understanding of information systems. Accountants need to understand future changes in hardware, software, and network security essential for protecting the integrity of accounting systems along with new technologies for reporting in online and wireless business environments. Finance majors need to understand future IT changes, financial database systems, and online trading systems for managing investments and cash. Marketing majors require an understanding of marketing database systems and systems for customer relationship management as well as Web-based systems for online sales. Operations management careers need knowledge of changing hardware, software, and database technologies used in production and services management and an in-depth understanding of how enterprise-wide information systems for production management, supplier management, sales force management, and customer relationship management achieve efficient operations. Careers in management and human resources need knowledge of how hardware and software can make management more efficient, enhance coordination, and achieve major business objectives.

Information systems majors clearly need to understand the central role databases play in managing information resources of the firm and how new hardware and software technologies can enhance business performance. They also need skills for leading the design and implementation of new management systems, working with other business professionals to ensure systems meet business objectives, and working with software packages providing new system solutions.

Common information systems skills and knowledge for all business careers include an understanding of how information systems help firms achieve major business objectives; an appreciation of the central role of databases; skills in information analysis and business intelligence; sensitivity to the ethical, social, and legal issues raised by systems; and the ability to work with technology specialists and other business professionals in designing and building systems.

## Key Terms

Business model, 7
Business processes, 13
Change management, 19
Computer hardware, 14
Computer literacy, 12
Computer software, 14
Critical thinking, 20
Culture, 13
Data, 10
Data management technology, 14

Extranets, 15
Feedback, 11
Information, 10
Information system, 10
Information systems literacy, 12
Information technology (IT), 10
Information technology (IT) infrastructure, 15
Input, 11

Internet, 14
Intranets, 15
Management information systems (MIS), 12
Network, 14
Networking and telecommunications technology, 14
Output, 11
Processing, 11
World Wide Web, 15

## Review Questions

**1.1** List and describe six reasons why information systems are so important for business today.

**1.2** What is an information system? What activities does it perform?

**1.3** What is the difference between data and information?

**1.4** What is information systems literacy? How does it differ from computer literacy?

**1.5** List and describe the organizational, people, and technology dimensions of information systems.

**1.6** What are the Internet and the World Wide Web? How have they changed the roles played by information systems in organizations?

**1.7** List and describe each of the four steps for solving business problems.

**1.8** Give some examples of people, organizational, and technology problems found in businesses.

**1.9** What role does critical thinking play in problem solving?

**1.10** What role do information systems play in business problem solving?

**1.11** What role do information systems play in careers in accounting, finance, marketing, management, and operations management? How have careers in information systems been affected by new technologies and outsourcing?

**1.12** What information system skills and knowledge are essential for all business careers?

## Discussion Questions

**1.1** Information systems are too important to be left to computer specialists. Do you agree? Why or why not?

**1.2** If you were setting up the Web sites for Major League Baseball, what people, organization, and technology issues might you encounter?

## Application Software Exercise

## Database Exercise: Converting Data into Useful Information

Software skills: Database querying and reporting

Business skills: Sales trend analysis

Effective information systems transform data into meaningful information for decisions that improve business performance. At the Laudon Web site for Chapter 1, you can find a Store and Regional Sales Database with raw data on weekly store sales of computer equipment in various sales regions. The database includes fields for store identification number, sales region number, item number, item description, unit price, units sold, and the weekly sales period when the sales were made. Develop some reports and queries to make this information more useful for running the business. Modify the database table, if necessary, to provide all of the information you require. Here are some questions you might consider:

1. Which are the best-performing stores and sales regions?
2. What are the best-selling products?
3. Which stores and sales regions sell the most of which products?
4. When are the strongest and weakest selling periods? For which stores? Which sales regions? Which products?
5. How can your company improve sales in the weakest store and sales region? (Answers will vary.)

## Preparing a Management Overview of the Company

Business skills: Management analysis of a business

Dirt Bikes's management has asked you to prepare a management analysis of the company to help it assess the firm's current situation and future plans. Review Dirt Bikes's company history, organization chart, products and services, and sales and marketing in the Introduction to Dirt Bikes, which can be found at the Laudon Web site. Then prepare a report that addresses these questions:

1. What are the company's goals and culture?
2. What products and services does Dirt Bikes U.S.A. provide? How many types of products and services are available to customers? How does Dirt Bikes sell its products?
3. How many employees are managers, production workers, or knowledge or information workers? Are there levels of management?
4. What kinds of information systems and technologies would be the most important for a company such as Dirt Bikes?
5. (Optional) Use electronic presentation software to summarize your analysis for management.

## Building Internet Skills

## Analyzing Shipping Costs

This project will help develop your Internet skills in using online software tools to calculate shipping costs and in analyzing package-delivery services.

You are the shipping clerk of a small firm that prints, binds, and ships popular books for a mid-level publisher. Your production facilities are located in Albany, New York (ZIP code 12250). Your customers' warehouses are located in Rye, New York (10580); Irving, Texas (75015); Charlotte, North Carolina (28201); Sioux Falls, South Dakota (57117); and Tustin, California

(92680). The production facility operates 250 days per year. Your books are usually shipped in one of two sized packages:

(A) Height: 9 inches, Length: 13 inches, Width: 17 inches, Weight: 45 pounds
(B) Height: 10 inches, Length: 6 inches, Width: 12 inches, Weight: 16 pounds

The company ships about four of the A boxes to each of the warehouses on an average day and about eight B boxes daily.

Your task is to select the best shipper for your company. Compare three shippers, such as Federal Express (www.fedex.com), UPS (www.ups.com), and the U.S. Post Office (www.usps.gov). Consider not only costs but also such issues as delivery speed, pickup schedules, drop-off locations, tracking ability, and ease of use of the Web site. Which service did you select? Explain why.

## Video Case

You will find a video case illustrating some of the concepts in this chapter on the Laudon Web site at **www.prenhall.com/laudon** along with questions to help you analyze the case.

## Teamwork

### Analyzing a Business System

In a group with three or four classmates, find a description in a computer or business magazine of an information system used by an organization. Look for information about the company on the Web to gain further insight into the company, and prepare a brief description of the business. Describe the system you have selected in terms of its inputs, processes, and outputs and in terms of its organization, people, and technology features and the importance of the system to the company. If possible, use electronic presentation software to present your analysis to the class.

# BUSINESS PROBLEM-SOLVING CASE

## Can the Music Industry Change Its Tune?

Would you pay $15.99 for a CD of your favorite recording artist if you could get it for free on the Web? This question has shaken the music industry to its foundations. A tremendous number of Internet users have taken advantage of online file-sharing services from which they can download digitized music files from other users free of charge.

The first such service to achieve widespread popularity was Napster. Its Web site provided software and services that enabled users to locate any of the one billion digitized MP3 music files on the computers of other online Napster members and copy the files onto their own computers for free. Napster's own computers did not store any music files. Instead, they acted as an intermediary between a user and a supplier. To obtain a specific music file, you would sign on to the Napster Web site and type in the name of the desired song. Napster's central title index would display a list of the connected computers with that specific song. You would select a computer and Napster would establish a direct connection between

your computer and the one storing the requested music file. Your Napster software then downloaded the file to your computer. You could play the song on your computer or copy it onto a CD. Once stored on your computer, others could copy it from you. The lure of free music caused the size of the Napster community to swell to 80 million users worldwide by 2001.

Napster users could legally copy uncopyrighted material, but reproducing and distributing copyrighted files without permission is illegal because the recipient does not compensate the owner for the use of the intellectual property. In December 1999, the Recording Industry Association of America (RIAA), representing the five major music recording companies at that time (Universal Music, Sony Music, Warner Music, BMG, and EMI), which together accounted for 80 percent of recorded music, sued Napster for violating copyright laws. U.S. courts ordered Napster to stop allowing users to share copyrighted music files and the site closed down in July 2002, declaring bankruptcy. It has since been transformed into a legal fee-based online digital music subscription service.

Napster was held liable for the illegal copying of copyrighted songs because it maintained a central index of members' music on its own central computer. Its closure did not stop widespread illegal music file sharing, however. Alternative peer-to-peer approaches to free downloading were developed. These networks did not require a centralized computer to manage the file swapping. Services using this approach included Kazaa, Morpheus, Grokster, and WinMX.

Kazaa established its headquarters in Vanuatu, a tiny independent island near Australia that is considered a tax haven and enables corporations to operate with little regulation. Kazaa software is stored on individual computers, enabling anyone to locate computers where individuals have stored music files available to be copied. Once the user located the desired song, the software established a direct peer-to-peer link between the two computers and downloaded the song without the user paying a fee. Distributors of the software claimed that it had valuable legal uses and they were not responsible if millions of people used it illegally.

To profit from its software, Kazaa allowed pop-up advertisements and unsolicited e-mail from vendors who paid for the service. Because the free trading of digitized materials did not pass through a centralized computer, no one knew who was downloading or how many songs were being downloaded. In June 2003, Kazaa claimed that its Media Desktop software for computer-to-computer file sharing had been downloaded 270 million times.

On October 2, 2001, through the RIAA, the major record labels filed suit against Kazaa, Morpheus, and other peer-to-peer services, alleging copyright infringement. However, because the exchange of music files was strictly between individuals, these companies claimed they were not breaking any laws and could not be forced to shut down. Individual users, however, could be punished.

The recording companies suffered a major blow on April 25, 2003, when a suit brought by the record labels, movie studios, and music publishers against Grokster Ltd. and StreamCast Networks Inc. (creators of Morpheus) was decided in favor of the file-sharing services. The U.S. District Court in Los Angeles ruled that the companies could not be held responsible for illegal music swapping with their software because they could not monitor or control how users of their software exchanged files. The companies were not breaking laws by making their software available.

In the fall of 2002 the RIAA began to prosecute individuals, starting with students, for using the Internet to download music illegally. Shortly thereafter, many universities began to block file-sharing services on their campus networks. In the spring of 2003, the RIAA also started sending instant messages to users of Kazaa and Grokster warning them that they were risking legal penalties by stealing music. Within the next year and a half, the RIAA sued more than 1,500 members of the general population, with the majority of cases settled in favor of the record companies.

Legal ramifications did not by themselves win the battle against illegal file sharing. The industry strongly pronounced that file sharing was still causing the sales of CDs to plummet and illegal downloading was costing them billions of dollars. Many users of Kazaa, Grokster, and WinMX remained undeterred by the threat of legal action.

The music industry presented sales data to back up its claims. In 2000, CD sales brought the industry about $35.5 billion. In 2001, sales fell to $33.7 billion, a decrease of 5 percent. Nielsen SoundScan measured another 8.8 percent drop in 2002. The following year, U.S. sales only fell 0.8 percent, but worldwide sales tumbled 10 percent. Critics of the recording industry's position pointed to a weaker economy as the main culprit for poorer sales. The critics also noted that record companies were releasing fewer titles than they had in the past and that the average price of a CD rose more than a dollar between 1999 and 2001. Adding to the criticism, researchers declared that users of file-sharing services were more likely to increase their spending on music than nonusers because the users' greater exposure to music fed their enthusiasm for it. Increased competition for the entertainment dollar from DVDs, video games, and the Internet itself also received credit for cutting into CD sales.

The music industry was slow to change the way it did business. Record companies resisted licensing their songs for legal sale online. When they did make their catalogs available, they attached restrictive technical safeguards to prevent abuse, such as prohibiting files from being copied to CDs or portable music players. The restrictions, as well as the prices, did not appeal to music enthusiasts. However, as far back as 2002, the major record labels were experimenting with pricing structures that would be appealing. Some executives believed that the industry should not offer individual songs for download because people would pay for a whole CD to get one or two songs. When tests showed that above $1 per song sales decreased significantly, John Rose, executive vice president of EMI, proposed, "If all consumers who pirate tracks today bought them for a buck, that would be a $5 billion a month business."

The entire perception of legal music downloading changed on April 29, 2003, when Apple Computer announced a new Web site named the iTunes Music Store. The venture succeeded immediately, selling 1.4 million songs in its first week and 100 million by August 2004. Consumer enthusiasm for iTunes stunned the industry and awakened it to new possibilities. iTunes charged 99 cents per song and offered most complete CDs for about $10. At its launch, the store offered 200,000 songs. Apple subsequently reached licensing agreements with all five major record labels to boost its catalog to more than two million songs.

To date, iTunes Music Store shoppers have purchased more than 900 million songs. With cooperation from the labels, iTunes even relaxed some of the restrictions it originally imposed on downloaded songs. Users can now burn songs to an unlimited number of CDs, sync their music to an unlimited number of iPods, and play songs purchased from iTunes on as many as five computers. Apple's iPod portable digital music player became a pop culture phenomenon, helping Apple hold 75 percent of the online, legal, music download marketplace.

Following the success of iTunes, Apple had no shortage of rivals. RealNetworks, MSN, Yahoo!, Napster, and MusicMatch all developed models for the purchase of music online. Unlike iTunes, some of them offered subscription models or streaming access to songs rather than downloads. But most of them dispelled the one doubt that the record labels held onto for so long: Money could be made by selling music over the Internet and digital cellular networks. Third-generation (3G) cell phone services with high-speed transmission capacities brought streaming music and video to users on demand wherever they were. In November 2005, Sprint opened an online store for downloading songs to cell phones, initially offering 250,000 titles.

The music industry still faced a decline in sales of music on a physical format, such as CDs. At the end of the first half of 2005, the International Federation of the Phonographic Industry (IFPI) calculated that worldwide digital music sales had tripled to $790 million from the preceding year. Digital music sales accounted for 6 percent of total industry sales. According to the IFPI, total industry sales dropped 1.9 percent over the same time from $13.4 billion to $13.2 billion. Physical format sales were down 6.3 percent; CD sales, specifically, fell 6.7 percent.

In June, the U.S. Supreme Court delivered a positive ruling for the industry in the *MGM* vs. *Grokster* case. The Court ruled that the developers of technology used by others to infringe on copyrights may be liable for the infringements if the developer promotes or encourages the use of the tool for such undertakings. The RIAA interpreted the decision as a strong victory.

Sam Yagan, the president of MetaMachine, which produces eDonkey peer-to-peer file-sharing software, stated before a Senate Judiciary Committee that companies such as his would have little choice but to change their business models. He surmised that if his company did not become more like iTunes or the new Napster, the costs of fighting off legal action from the RIAA would be too high to overcome. On November 7, 2005, Grokster shut down as part of a legal settlement with the music industry.

BitTorrent, an organization that operates a network with technology for downloading very large files, hired a capital management firm to help it raise $8.75 million in funding to create a legal commercial download service. This was also good news for the film industry, which in recent years had discovered that movie piracy had been dramatically boosted by file sharing.

FrontCode Technologies, the company that released the WinMX file-sharing client on October 8, 2000, received a cease and desist order from the RIAA on September 13, 2005. A little more than a week later, the WinMX community was shocked to discover that the www.WinMX.com domain had been taken down. They soon learned that www.WinMX.com had been reregistered in Vanuatu, where it might be able escape legal threats. Yagan of MetaMachine believed that this might be the strategy of file-sharing companies that lacked the resources to establish legal downloading services.

The music industry received more good news in September 2005 when a federal judge in Australia ruled that Kazaa violated Australian copyright laws by enabling users to infringe on copyrighted recordings. The judge ordered Kazaa to alter its software so that search results would not display files with names that appear on a roster of copyrighted works compiled by record companies. While the music industry celebrated the decision, some experts believed that the defeat of a major file-trading network, such as Kazaa, simply opened the door for others to create new technologies that would escape the reach of the ruling. The original Napster case had a similar effect.

Although the conversion of some peer-to-peer companies to legitimate online retailers, the shutting down of others, and new legal support suggest that the tide is turning for the music industry, reality reveals waters that are still murky. The music-tracking research firm Big Champagne Online Media Measurement conservatively estimated that individuals were still illegally downloading 10 billion songs per year, or 20 times as many as had been downloaded legally from iTunes in its history. The major record labels have cut back on staff, and two of them even consolidated to reduce the Big Five to the Big Four. The RIAA has sued more than 15,000 individuals to date. According to Big Champagne, in April 2005, the number of Americans trading copyrighted music illegally was double the number measured when the RIAA first took legal action in September 2003.

*Sources:* Sarah McBride, "For Grokster, It's the Day the Music Died," *The Wall Street Journal,* November 8, 2005; David Pogue, "At Last, Phone Some Tunes to Yourself," *The New York Times,* November 10, 2005; Nancy Gohring, "File-Sharing Doomed, Warns Exec," *IDG News Service,* September 30, 2005; "Sales of Digital Music Triple," Associated Press, October 3, 2005; Thomas C. Green, "Congress Mulls 'Post-Grokster' Legislation," *The Register,* September 29, 2005; "RIAA Statement on *MGM* vs. *Grokster* Supreme Court Ruling," www.riaa.com, accessed June 27, 2005; "Napster Announces College Deals," *Los Angeles Business Journal,* September 15, 2005; "MPAA Files New Piracy Lawsuits," www.newsfactor.com, accessed October 14, 2005; Stephen Williams, "3G Does It All-Fast," *Newsday,* October 11, 2005; Anne Broache, "Congress to Legislate File Swapping?" *CNET News,* September 28, 2005; David Canton, "Music Industry Hails Decision Against Kazaa," *London Free Press,* October 8, 2005; Thomas Mennecke, "WinMX—The Beginning, The Middle, The End," *Slyck News,* October 4, 2005; John Borland, "The Supreme Court's Ruling Against P2P," *CNET News,* June 27, 2005; Nick Wingfield and Sarah McBride, "Green Light for Grokster," *The Wall Street Journal,* August 20, 2004; Nick Wingfield, "Price War in Online Music," *The Wall Street Journal,* August 17, 2004, and "Online Music's Latest Tune," *The Wall Street Journal,* August 27, 2004; Sarah McBride, "Stop the Music!" *The Wall Street Journal,* August 23, 2004; Alex Veiga, "Recording Industry Sues 532 over Swapping," Associated Press, March 23, 2004; David McGuire, "Study: File-Sharing No Threat to Music Sales," *The Washington Post,* March 30, 2004; Nick Wingfield and Ethan Smith, "With the Web Shaking Up Music, a Free-for-All in Online Songs," *The Wall Street Journal,* November 19, 2003, and "New Ways to Pay 99 Cents for Music," *The Wall Street Journal,* October 9, 2003; Amy Harmon, "Despite Suits, Music File Sharers Shrug Off Guilt and Keep Sharing," *The New York Times,* September 19, 2003; Amy Harmon, "Industry Offers a Carrot in Online Music Fight," *The New York Times,* June 8, 2003; "Kazaa Stays on Track to Be Most Downloaded Program," news.yahoo.com, accessed May 25, 2003; Amy Harmon, "Music Swappers Get a Message on PC Screens: Stop It Now," *The New York Times,* May 19, 2003; Jane Black, "Big Music: Win Some, Lose a Lot More?" *BusinessWeek Online,* May 5, 2003;

Amy Harmon, "Suit Settled for Students Downloading Music Online," *The New York Times,* May 2, 2003; Pui-Wing Tam, "Apple Launches Online Store Offering Downloadable Music," *The Wall Street Journal,* April 29, 2003; Anna Wilde Mathews and Nick Wingfield, "Entertainment Industry Loses Important File-Sharing Battle," *The Wall Street Journal,* April 28, 2003; Jane Black, "Web Music Gets Its Act Together," *BusinessWeek Online,* April 22, 2003; Saul Hansell, "E-Music Settles on Prices. It's a Start," *The New York Times,* March 3, 2003; Anne Wilde Mathews and Charles Goldsmith, "Music Industry Faces New Threats on Web," *The Wall Street Journal,* February 21, 2003; Jane Black, "Big Music's Broken Record," *BusinessWeek Online,* February 13, 2003; and Laura M. Holson and Geraldine Fabrikant, "Music Industry Braces for a Shift," *The New York Times,* January 13, 2003.

**Case Study Questions**

1. Describe the problem raised by this case. What caused this problem? What was its impact?
2. Did the recording industry correctly identify the problem and its people, organizational, and technology issues?
3. What solutions to illegal music downloading were available? Which solution is the most effective? Was the correct solution chosen?
4. Do you think the current solution is viable? Why or why not? Explain your answer.

# E-Business: How Businesses Use Information Systems

## CHAPTER 2

## STUDENT OBJECTIVES

After completing this chapter, you will be able to:

1. Identify and describe the major features of a business that are important for understanding the role of information systems.

2. Describe the information systems supporting the major business functions: sales and marketing, manufacturing and production, finance and accounting, and human resources.

3. Evaluate the role played by systems serving the various levels of management in a business and their relationship to each other.

4. Explain how enterprise applications and intranets promote business process integration and improve organizational performance.

5. Assess the role of the information systems function in a business.

## CHAPTER OUTLINE

### INFORMATION SYSTEMS HELP KIA SOLVE ITS QUALITY PROBLEMS

**Information systems are helping Kia's** cars stay in the race. Korean car manufacturer Kia Motors started selling in the North American market, promising high-quality vehicles at prices well below the competition. In 1995, Kia sold 12,000 cars, and by 2004, Kia had sold 270,000 cars. From a marketing and sales standpoint, Kia has been a phenomenal success. But until 2002 Kia ranked at the bottom of J. D. Power and Associates' annual initial-quality survey of new vehicle owners. In 1997, when the average North American car had 1.1 defects per vehicle, Kia had 2.75. In 2002 Kia had improved to 2.12 defects per vehicle, but the industry average was 1.33. Kia had a long way to go, and it was affecting its ability to sell cars, retain customers, and keep operational costs down.

Like all manufacturers of vehicles sold in North America, Kia had to create a system by December 1, 2003 to report any defects, accidents, or injuries involving its vehicles to the U.S. National Highway Traffic Safety Administration (NHTSA).

This was a major challenge for the company. The information Kia had to report was stored in at least seven different systems run by Kia's warranty, parts, consumer, and legal affairs departments.

Fragmentation of this information in different systems prevented Kia from getting a complete picture of defects. Parts sales are the first indicator of a defect, warranty claims the second, and consumer complaints the third. Looking at parts sales alone won't provide an answer. A sudden increase in brake pad orders from Kia dealers making repairs indicates there might be a problem with a particular pad. By examining warranty claims, Kia might discover that brake pads were only being ordered for four-wheel drive models of one of its vehicles and not for two-wheel drive models. This additional information might show that the problem was actually a result of excess vibration caused by the vehicle's design rather than the brake pads.

Kia could have created a series of stopgap software programs to extract the required information out of these various computer systems and collate it manually. But this would have been time-consuming and would not provide any other benefits to the company. So Kia's management decided instead to create a defect early warning system that could identify potential problems, such as faulty brake parts, by combining warranty claims, parts orders, field reports, and consumer complaints.

Kia enlisted Infogain, a Los Gatos, California, software consulting firm to help it design a new system solution. Infogain created a software "engine" that examines six Kia systems for warranty claims, parts sales, vehicle identification number master storage files, and vehicle inventories and stores the essential information in a single common data repository. The system automatically breaks down and categorizes reports based on individual components, such as steering assemblies or headlights, and links to Kia's Clarify customer relationship management system, tracking consumer complaints received by phone, e-mail, or postal mail.

Once the data have been stored in a single place, Kia can use Crystal Analysis software to analyze them, highlighting events, such as spikes in warranty claims related to a particular vehicle model, unusual increases in parts orders, or high numbers of accidents resulting in serious injury or death, on an early warning dashboard. Managers are able to analyze the data by daily, weekly, or monthly reporting periods and by specific car models, model years, and components. They also can break down the data in detail to see how many complaints or warranty claims are associated with a specific item, such as a steering assembly.

Information from this system is helping Kia determine what percentage of its vehicles is likely to have problems. The company can now determine the most cost-effective strategy for dealing with defect problems. For example, should Kia recall all batteries if battery defects occur in extreme heat or limit recalls to states in the southern United States? In quality rankings released on May 18, 2005, J. D. Power reported that Kia had 1.40 problems per vehicle, finishing second for quality in the compact-car category behind the Toyota Prius. ■

*Sources*: Mel Duvall, "Kia Motors America: Lemon Aid," *Baseline Magazine*, June 2005; and www.kia.com, accessed August 23, 2005.

**K**ia Motors' experience illustrates how much companies today rely on information systems for running their businesses. Without a system for tracking and identifying defects, Kia did not know how serious its quality control problem was until customer complaints piled up. The high incidence of defects in Kia products affected marketplace perceptions of the Kia brand, customer retention rates, and Kia's ability to continue ramping up sales. Kia's quality problems obviously affected its profitability and long-term survival.

The information required to track defects was scattered among multiple systems. Kia could have created some software on the fly that merely pushed the required information out of these systems, but then the information would have to be collated manually. This solution would have been very time-consuming and also limit Kia's flexibility in what it could do with the information. The solution that worked best for Kia was to develop a system that extracted the required data from all of the systems, integrated the data, and then analyzed them, with capabilities for displaying overall trends and for drilling down into details.

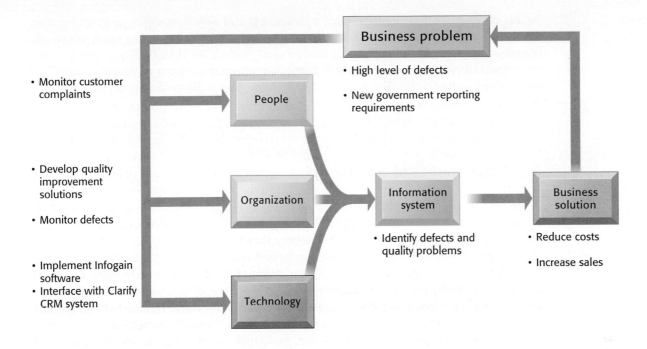

Kia's defect reporting system helps it increase profitability and even strategic advantage. Kia has tried to keep customers happy despite its quality problems by offering a 10 Year/100,000 Mile Warranty Program, which provides coverage until either the yearly or total mileage figure is reached, whichever occurs first. That means that Kia must pay for repairs on all warrantied items in its vehicles for many more years than its competitors are willing to do for their products, which raises operating costs and eats into profits. Better information from the new system helps Kia pinpoint the sources of defects so it can improve its production processes before defects become too widespread, thus lowering its costs for warranty repairs. Higher levels of quality and a lower incidence of repairs also increase customer satisfaction and make it more likely that both new and existing customers will purchase from Kia.

---

**HEADS UP**

This chapter provides you with an overview of how business firms use and organize information systems, and provides you with the basic vocabulary and concepts of business information systems that are used throughout the book. Many of the topics we cover here are covered in greater detail in later chapters, but this brief introduction to the entire field will help prepare you for later chapters and will quickly give you a better idea of the significant role that information systems play in a business.

•  If your career is in finance and accounting, you will be working with systems that keep track of your company's assets, fund flows, and overall financial performance.

•  If your career is in human resources, information systems will help you develop staffing requirements; identify potential new employees; maintain employee records; track employee training, skills, and job performance; and design appropriate plans for employee compensation and career development.

•  If your career is in manufacturing, production, or operations managmement, information systems will help you solve problems related to the planning, development, and delivery of products and services and control the flow of production.

•  If your career is in sales and marketing, information systems will help you promote products, contact customers, track sales, identify profitable customers, provide ongoing service and support, and analyze the performance of the firm's sales staff.

In this chapter, we first describe what a business is and why businesses need information systems. We show how businesses use information systems to achieve the goals of specific business functions and of different organizational groups. We then briefly examine enterprise applications and Internet tools that integrate information from disparate systems and parts of the business. Finally, we describe the role of the information systems function in business.

## 2.1 Components of a Business

A **business** is a formal organization whose aim is to produce products or provide services for a profit—that is, to sell products at a price greater than the costs of production. Customers are willing to pay this price because they believe they receive a value greater than or equal to the sale price. Business firms purchase inputs and resources from the larger environment (suppliers who are often other firms). Employees of the firm transform these inputs by adding value to them in the production process. There are, of course, nonprofit firms and organizations, and government agencies that are complex formal organizations that produce services and products but do not operate in order to produce a profit. Nevertheless, even these kinds of organizations consume resources from their environments, add value to these inputs, and deliver their outputs to constituents and customers. In general, the information systems found in nonprofit organizations are remarkably similar to those found in private industry.

### Organizing a Business: Basic Business Functions

Imagine that you wanted to set up your own business. Simply deciding to go into business would be the most important decision, but next would come the question of what product or what service you wanted to produce. The decision of what to produce is called a strategic choice because it determines who are your likely customers, the kinds of employees you will need, the production methods and facilities needed, the marketing themes, and many other choices.

Once you decide what to produce, what kind of organization would you need? First, you would have to design some sort of production division—an arrangement of people, machines, and business processes (procedures) that could produce the product. Second, you would need a sales and marketing group who could attract customers, sell the product, and keep track of after-sales issues, such as warranties and maintenance. Third, once you generate sales you will need a finance and accounting group to keep track of current financial transactions, such as orders, invoices, disbursements, and payroll. In addition, this group would seek out sources of credit and finance. Finally, you would want a group of people to focus on recruiting, hiring, training, and retaining employees. Figure 2-1 summarizes the four basic functions found in every business.

Of course, if you were an entrepreneur or your business was very small with only a few employees, you would not need, and probably could not afford, all these separate groups of people. Instead, in small firms, you would be performing all these functions yourself or with a few others. No wonder small firms have a high mortality rate! In any event, even in small firms the four basic functions of a firm are required. Larger firms often will have separate departments for each function: manufacturing and production, sales and marketing, finance and accounting, and human resources.

Figure 2-1 is also useful for thinking about the basic entities that make up a business. The five basic entities in a business with which it must deal are: suppliers, customers, employees, invoices/payments, and, of course, products and services. There are many other entities that a business must manage and monitor, but these are the basic ones at the foundation of any business.

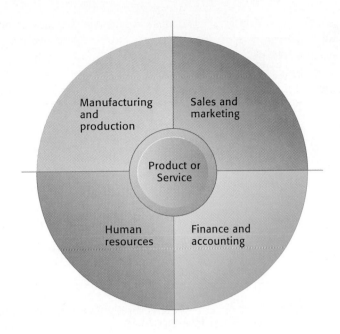

**Figure 2-1**
The Four Major Functions of a Business
*Every business, regardless of its size, must perform four functions to succeed. It must produce the product or service; market and sell the product; keep track of accounting and financial transactions; and perform basic human resources tasks, such as hiring and retaining employees.*

## Business Processes

Once you identify the basic business functions and entities for your business, your next job will be to describe exactly how you want your employees to perform these functions. What specific tasks do you want your sales personnel to perform, in what order, and on what schedule? What steps do you want production employees to follow as they transform raw resources into finished products? How will customer orders be fulfilled? How will vendor bills be paid? The actual steps and tasks that describe how work is organized in a business are called *business processes*, which we introduced in Chapter 1. A business process is a logically related set of activities that define how specific business tasks are performed.

Every business in fact can be seen as a collection of business processes. Large businesses have thousands of business processes, some more important than others. To a large extent, the efficiency of a business firm depends on how well its business processes are designed and coordinated.

Many business processes are tied to a specific functional area. For example, the sales and marketing function would be responsible for identifying customers, and the human resources function would be responsible for hiring employees. Other business processes cross many different functional areas and require coordination across departments. For instance, consider the seemingly simple business process of fulfilling a customer order (see Figure 2-2). Initially, the sales department receives a sales order. The order passes first to accounting to ensure the customer can pay for the order either by a credit verification or request for immediate payment prior to shipping. Once the customer credit is established, the production department has to pull the product from inventory or produce the product. Then the product will need to be shipped (and this may require working with a logistics firm, such as UPS or FedEx). A bill or invoice will then have to be generated by the accounting department, and a notice will be sent to the customer indicating that the product has shipped. Sales will have to be notified of the shipment and prepare to support the customer by answering calls or fulfilling warranty claims.

What at first appears to be a simple process, fulfilling an order, turns out to be a very complicated series of steps that require the close coordination of major functional groups in a firm. Second, to efficiently perform all these steps in the order fulfillment process requires a great deal of information and, in order to be efficient, the rapid flow of information both within the firm; with business partners, such as delivery firms; and with the customer.

**Figure 2-2**
The Order Fulfillment
Process
*Fulfilling a customer
order involves a com-
plex set of steps that
requires the close coor-
dination of the sales,
accounting, and manu-
facturing functions.*

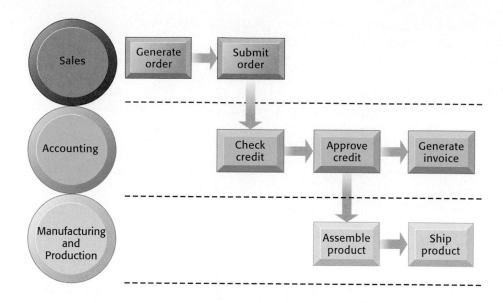

## Managing a Business and Firm Hierarchies

What is missing from Figures 2-1 and 2-2 is any notion of how to coordinate and control the four major functions, their departments, and their business processes. Each of these functional departments has its own goals and processes, and they obviously need to cooperate in order for the whole business to succeed. Business firms, like all organizations, achieve coordination by hiring managers whose responsibility is to ensure all the various parts of an organization work together. Firms coordinate the work of employees in various divisions by developing a hierarchy in which authority (responsibility and accountability) is concentrated at the top.

The hierarchy of management is composed of **senior management**, which makes long-range strategic decisions about products and services as well as ensures financial performance of the firm; **middle management**, which carries out the programs and plans of senior management; and **operational management**, which is responsible for monitoring the daily activities of the business. **Knowledge workers**, such as engineers, scientists, or architects, design products or services and create new knowledge for the firm, whereas **data workers**, such as secretaries or clerks, assist with paperwork at all levels of the firm. **Production or service workers** actually produce the product and deliver the service (see Figure 2-3).

**Figure 2-3**
Levels in a Firm
*Business organizations
are hierarchies consist-
ing of three principal
levels: senior manage-
ment, middle manage-
ment, and operational
management.
Information systems
serve each of these lev-
els. Scientists and
knowledge workers
often work with middle
management.*

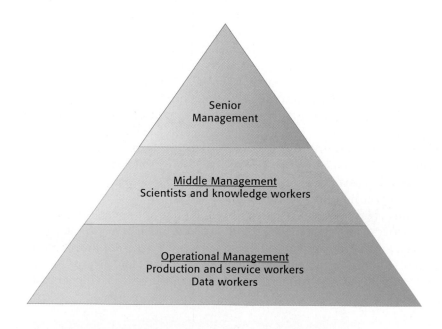

Each of these groups has different needs for information given their different responsibilities, and each can be seen as major information constituents. Senior managers need summary information that can quickly inform them about the overall performance of the firm, such as gross sales revenues, sales by product group and region, and overall profitability. Middle managers need more specific information on the results of specific functional areas and departments of the firm, such as sales contacts by the sales force, production statistics for specific factories or product lines, employment levels and costs, and sales revenues for each month or even each day. Operational managers need transaction-level information, such as the number of parts in inventory each day or the number of hours logged on Tuesday by each employee. Knowledge workers may need access to external scientific databases or internal databases with organizational knowledge. Finally, production or service workers need access to information from production machines, and service workers need access to customer records in order to take orders and answer questions from customers.

## The Business Environment

So far we have talked about business as if it operated in a vacuum. Nothing could be further from the truth. In fact, business firms depend heavily on their environments to supply capital, labor, customers, new technology, services and products, stable markets and legal systems, and general educational resources. Even a pizza parlor cannot survive long without a supportive environment that delivers the cheese, tomato sauce, and flour!

Figure 2-4 summarizes the key actors in the environment of every business. To stay in business, a firm must monitor changes in its environment and share information with the key entities in that environment. For instance, a firm must respond to political shifts, respond to changes in the overall economy (such as changes in labor rates and price inflation), keep track of new technologies, and respond to changes in the global business environment (such as foreign exchange rates). In its immediate environment, firms need to track and share information with suppliers, customers, stockholders, regulators, and logistic partners (such as shipping firms).

Business environments are constantly changing; new developments in technology, politics, customer preferences, and regulations happen all the time. In general, when businesses fail, it is often because they failed to respond adequately to changes in their environments.

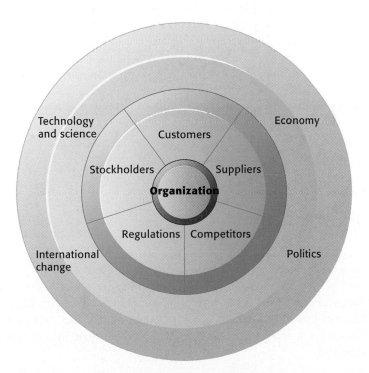

**Figure 2-4**
The Business Environment
*To be successful, an organization must constantly monitor and respond to—or even anticipate—developments in its environment. A firm's environment includes specific groups with which the business must deal directly, such as customers, suppliers, and competitors, as well as the broader general environment, including socioeconomic trends, political conditions, technological innovations, and global events.*

For instance, changes in technology, such as the Internet, are forcing entire industries and leading firms to change their business models or suffer failure. The case study concluding Chapter 1 describes how new technology—the Internet—is making the music industry's traditional business model based on distributing music on CDs obsolete. Another example is the photography business. Digital photography has forced Eastman Kodak to downsize and move into digital cameras and Internet photography services because most of the consumer marketplace no longer wants to use traditional cameras with film.

## The Role of Information Systems in a Business

Until now we have not mentioned information systems. But from the brief review of business functions, entities, and environments, you can see the critical role that information plays in the life of a business. Up until the mid-1950s, firms managed all this information and information flow with paper records. During the past 50 years more and more business information and the flow of information among key business actors in the environment has been computerized.

Businesses invest in information systems as a way to cope with and manage their internal production functions and to cope with the demands of key actors in their environments. Specifically, as we noted in Chapter 1, firms invest in information systems for the following business objectives:

- To achieve operational excellence (productivity, efficiency, agility)
- To develop new products and services
- To attain customer intimacy and service
- To improve decision making (accuracy and speed)
- To promote competitive advantage
- To ensure survival

## 2.2 Types of Business Information Systems

Now it is time to look more closely at how businesses use information systems to achieve these goals. Because there are different interests, specialties, and levels in an organization, there are different kinds of systems. No single system can provide all the information an organization needs. In fact large- and medium-size firms have thousands of computer programs and hundreds of different systems. Even small firms have a collection of different systems: a system for conducting e-mail campaigns to customers, a system for monitoring advertisements placed on Google, a system for keeping track of basic sales transactions, a system for keeping track of vendors, and so forth. At first glance it can be difficult to comprehend all the different systems in a business, and even more difficult to understand how they relate to one another.

We attempt to describe this complex situation by looking at all these different systems from two different perspectives: a functional perspective identifying systems by their major business function, and a constituency perspective that identifies systems in terms of the major organizational groups that they serve.

### Systems from a Functional Perspective

We will start by describing systems using a functional perspective because this is the most straightforward approach, and, in fact, because this is how you will likely first encounter systems in a business. For instance, if you are a marketing major and take a job in marketing, you will be working on the job first with marketing information systems. If you are an accounting major, you will be working with accounting and financial systems first. From a historical perspective, functional systems were the first kinds of systems developed by business firms. These systems were located in specific departments, such as accounting, marketing and sales, production, and human resources. Let's take a close look at systems from this functional perspective.

| System | Description | Groups Served |
|---|---|---|
| Order processing | Enter, process, and track orders | Operational management<br>Employees |
| Pricing analysis | Determine prices for products and services | Middle management |
| Sales trend forecasting | Prepare five-year sales forecasts | Senior management |

**TABLE 2.1**

**Examples of Sales and Marketing Information Systems**

## Sales and Marketing Systems

The sales and marketing function is responsible for selling the organization's products or services. Marketing is concerned with identifying the customers for the firm's products or services, determining what customers need or want, planning and developing products and services to meet their needs, and advertising and promoting these products and services. Sales is concerned with contacting customers, selling the products and services, taking orders, and following up on sales. **Sales and marketing information systems** support these activities.

Table 2.1 shows that information systems are used in sales and marketing in a number of ways. Sales and marketing systems help senior management monitor trends affecting new products and sales opportunities, support planning for new products and services, and monitor the performance of competitors. Sales and marketing systems aid middle management by supporting market research and by analyzing advertising and promotional campaigns, pricing decisions, and sales performance. Sales and marketing systems assist operational management and employees in locating and contacting prospective customers, tracking sales, processing orders, and providing customer service support.

Figure 2-5 illustrates a sales information system used by retailers, such as The Gap or Target. Point-of-sale devices (usually handheld scanners at the checkout counter) capture data about each item sold, which update the sales system's figures about sales and send data

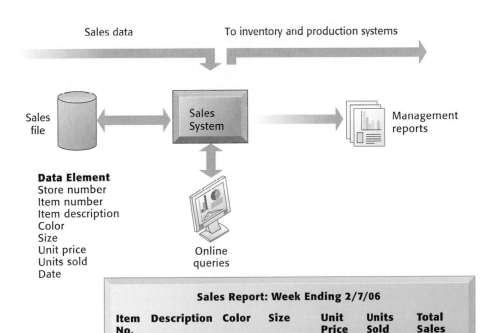

**Figure 2-5**
Example of a Sales Information System
*This system captures sales data at the moment the sale takes place to help the business monitor sales transactions and to provide information to help management analyze sales trends and the effectiveness of marketing campaigns.*

**Sales Report: Week Ending 2/7/06**

| Item No. | Description | Color | Size | Unit Price | Units Sold | Total Sales |
|---|---|---|---|---|---|---|
| 294 | Sports bag | Black | Small | 10.00 | 10,451 | $104,510 |
| 295 | Sports bag | Black | Medium | 20.00 | 21,800 | $436,000 |
| 394 | Sports bag | Red | Small | 10.00 | 5,331 | $53,310 |

*Information systems can guide the actions of machines and equipment to help pharmaceutical and other types of firms monitor and control the manufacturing process.*

about items sold to related systems dealing with items remaining in inventory and with production. These businesses use this information to track which items have been sold, to determine sales revenue, and to identify hot-selling items and other sales trends.

## Manufacturing and Production Systems

The manufacturing and production function is responsible for actually producing the firm's goods and services. Manufacturing and production systems deal with the planning, development, and maintenance of production facilities; the establishment of production goals; the acquisition, storage, and availability of production materials; and the scheduling of equipment, facilities, materials, and labor required to fashion finished products. **Manufacturing and production information systems** support these activities.

Table 2.2 shows some typical manufacturing and production information systems for each major organizational group. Senior management uses manufacturing and production systems that deal with the firm's long-term manufacturing goals, such as where to locate new plants or whether to invest in new manufacturing technology. Manufacturing and production systems for middle management analyze and monitor manufacturing and production costs and resources. Operational management uses manufacturing and production systems that deal with the status of production tasks.

Most manufacturing and production systems use some sort of inventory system, as illustrated in Figure 2-6. Data about each item in inventory, such as the number of units depleted because of a shipment or purchase or the number of units replenished by reordering or returns, are either scanned or keyed into the system. The inventory master file contains basic data about

| TABLE 2.2 | System | Description | Groups Served |
|---|---|---|---|
| **Examples of Manufacturing and Production Information Systems** | Machine control | Controls the actions of machines and equipment | Operational management |
| | Production planning | Decides when and how many products should be produced | Middle management |
| | Facilities location | Decides where to locate new production facilities | Senior management |

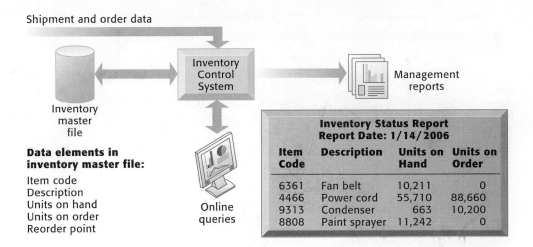

**Figure 2-6**
Overview of an Inventory System
*This system provides information about the number of items available in inventory to support manufacturing and production activities.*

each item, including the unique identification code for each item, a description of the item, the number of units on hand, the number of units on order, and the reorder point (the number of units in inventory that triggers a decision to reorder to prevent a stockout). Companies can estimate the number of items to reorder, or they can use a formula for calculating the least expensive quantity to reorder called the *economic order quantity*. The system produces reports that give information about such things as the number of each item available in inventory, the number of units of each item to reorder, or items in inventory that must be replenished.

## Finance and Accounting Systems

The finance function is responsible for managing the firm's financial assets, such as cash, stocks, bonds, and other investments, to maximize the return on these financial assets. The finance function is also in charge of managing the capitalization of the firm (finding new financial assets in stocks, bonds, or other forms of debt). To determine whether the firm is getting the best return on its investments, the finance function must obtain a considerable amount of information from sources external to the firm.

The accounting function is responsible for maintaining and managing the firm's financial records—receipts, disbursements, depreciation, payroll—to account for the flow of funds in a firm. Finance and accounting share related problems—how to keep track of a firm's financial assets and fund flows. They provide answers to questions such as these: What is the current inventory of financial assets? What records exist for disbursements, receipts, payroll, and other fund flows?

Table 2.3 shows some of the typical **finance and accounting information systems** found in large organizations. Senior management uses finance and accounting systems to establish long-term investment goals for the firm and to provide long-range forecasts of the firm's financial performance. Middle management uses systems to oversee and control the firm's financial resources. Operational management uses finance and accounting systems to track the flow of funds in the firm through transactions, such as paychecks, payments to vendors, securities reports, and receipts.

Figure 2-7 illustrates an accounts receivable system, which keeps track of what customers who have made purchases on credit owe to a company. Every invoice generates an "account

| System | Description | Groups Served |
|---|---|---|
| Accounts receivable | Tracks money owed the firm | Operational management |
| Budgeting | Prepares short-term budgets | Middle management |
| Profit planning | Plans long-term profits | Senior management |

**TABLE 2.3**

**Examples of Finance and Accounting Information Systems**

**Figure 2-7**
An Accounts
Receivable System

*An accounts receivable system tracks and stores important customer data, such as payment history, credit rating, and billing history.*

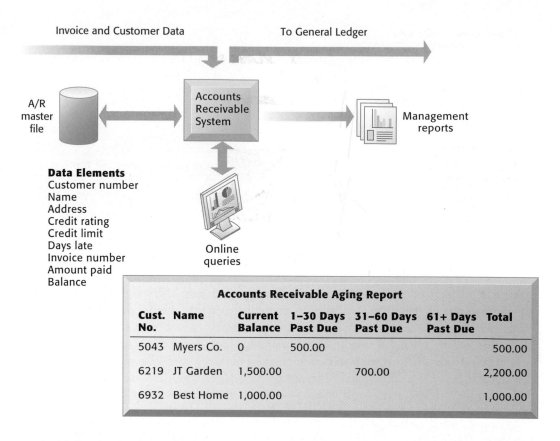

Invoice and Customer Data                    To General Ledger

**Data Elements**
Customer number
Name
Address
Credit rating
Credit limit
Days late
Invoice number
Amount paid
Balance

Online queries

**Accounts Receivable Aging Report**

| Cust. No. | Name | Current Balance | 1–30 Days Past Due | 31–60 Days Past Due | 61+ Days Past Due | Total |
|-----------|------|-----------------|--------------------|--------------------|-------------------|-------|
| 5043 | Myers Co. | 0 | 500.00 | | | 500.00 |
| 6219 | JT Garden | 1,500.00 | | 700.00 | | 2,200.00 |
| 6932 | Best Home | 1,000.00 | | | | 1,000.00 |

receivable"—that is, the customer owes the firm money. Some customers pay immediately in cash, but others are granted credit. The accounts receivable system records each invoice in a master file that also contains information on each customer, including that person's credit rating. The system keeps track of all the bills outstanding and can produce a variety of output reports, both on paper and on the computer screen, to help the business collect bills. The system also answers queries about a customer's credit rating and payment history.

### Human Resources Systems

The human resources function is responsible for attracting, developing, and maintaining the firm's workforce. **Human resources information systems** support activities such as identifying potential employees, maintaining complete records on existing employees, and creating programs to develop employees' talents and skills.

Human resources systems help senior management identify the manpower requirements (skills, educational level, types of positions, number of positions, and cost) for meeting the firm's long-term business plans. Middle management uses human resources systems to monitor and analyze the recruitment, allocation, and compensation of employees. Operational management uses human resources systems to track the recruitment and placement of the firm's employees (see Table 2.4).

**TABLE 2.4**

**Examples of Human Resources Information Systems**

| System | Description | Groups Served |
|--------|-------------|---------------|
| Training and development | Tracks employee training, skills, and performance appraisals | Operational management |
| Compensation analysis | Monitors the range and distribution of employee wages, salaries, and benefits | Middle management |
| Human resources planning | Plans the long-term labor force needs of the organization | Senior management |

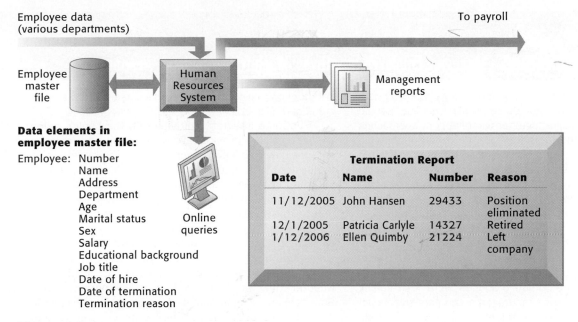

**Figure 2-8**
An Employee Record Keeping System
*This system maintains data on the firm's employees to support the human resources function.*

Figure 2-8 illustrates a typical human resources system for employee record keeping. It maintains basic employee data, such as the employee's name, age, sex, marital status, address, educational background, salary, job title, date of hire, and date of termination. The system can produce a variety of reports, such as lists of newly hired employees, employees who are terminated or on leaves of absence, employees classified by job type or educational level, or employee job performance evaluations. Such systems are typically designed to provide data that can satisfy federal and state record keeping requirements for Equal Employment Opportunity (EEO) and other purposes.

The Focus on Organizations describes a human resources system with more of a strategic orientation. Wachovia Bank, the result of the merged Wachovia and First Union Banks, needed to find a way of optimizing employee performance in both sales and customer service. The bank implemented an incentive and compensation management system that lets it model the business impact of different combinations of employee rewards and incentives. As you read this case, try to identify the problem this company was facing; what alternative solutions were available to management; how well the chosen solution worked; and the people, organization, and technology issues that had to be addressed when developing the solution.

## Systems from a Constituency Perspective

Although a functional perspective is very useful for understanding how business systems serve specific functions, this perspective does not tell us how systems help managers manage the firm. Here we need a perspective that examines systems in terms of the various levels of management and types of decisions that they support. Each of three main management constituencies we described earlier uses a different type of system to deliver the information required to manage the company.

### Transaction Processing Systems

Operational managers need systems that keep track of the elementary activities and transactions of the organization, such as sales, receipts, cash deposits, payroll, credit decisions, and the flow of materials in a factory. **Transaction processing systems (TPS)** provide this kind of information. A transaction processing system is a computerized system that performs and records the daily routine transactions necessary to conduct business, such as sales order entry, hotel reservations, payroll, employee record keeping, and shipping.

# FOCUS ON ORGANIZATIONS  Managing Employee Incentives: Wachovia's Strategic Weapon

When First Union Corp. of Charlotte, North Carolina, and Wachovia Corp. of Winston-Salem, North Carolina, merged in 2001, they brought together two divergent approaches to banking. Wachovia had a first-rate reputation in customer service. At Wachovia branches, customers interacted with bank staff for most transactions. Wachovia monitored the quality of its customer service by sending "mystery shoppers" to evaluate the service skills of its employees. The bank rewarded employees that rated well and their branch managers. In a 1999 survey of the 20 largest banks in the United States by *Consumer Reports*, Wachovia finished fourth in customer service.

In the same survey, First Union ranked last in customer service. First Union branches were lean selling machines. Employees encouraged customers to conduct their business at ATMs or telephone kiosks rather than visiting tellers. First Union rewarded its employees with commissions and incentives for bringing in new business, such as credit card accounts or loans. This approach brought each of First Union's 2,200 branches an average of $2 million in loans per quarter. Each of Wachovia's 700 branches produced average loan sales of less than half a million dollars per quarter.

For all of its selling success, First Union was struggling. Customer satisfaction was so low that the bank experienced a customer attrition rate of 20 percent in the first quarter of 1999. At the same time, employees were dissatisfied, with bank tellers turning over at a rate of 49 percent.

The merger presented the new company with the opportunity to combine the winning sales tactics of First Union with the superior customer service of Wachovia. The merged bank shrewdly opted to use the Wachovia name and started restructuring its employee rewards and incentives programs to optimize both product sales and customer service.

Prior to the merger, First Union ran its very successful incentive and compensation programs on a two-decade-old financial spreadsheet application named Nomad. The program could log transactions and calculate commissions and bonuses, but the staff could not reprogram the software to create new incentive programs or model alternative scenarios. Furthermore, the system required manual reporting and was, therefore, vulnerable to frequent data entry errors, usually overpayments of rewards, which cost the bank about $7.5 million a year.

In 2003, Wachovia selected Callidus Software's TrueComp system as the bank's new enterprise incentive management (EIM) solution and went live with the new system in June 2004. With TrueComp, Wachovia was able to automate its compensation programs. The software keeps track of 31 different incentive plans for more than 25,000 employees, considering factors such as customer satisfaction, investment referrals, loan referrals, and credit card sign-ups.

TrueComp integrates directly with the bank's sales application, known as SOLD. As soon as an employee enters a new sale (new account, loan, mortgage, etc.) into the system, SOLD sends the relevant employee reward information directly to TrueComp. The investment in TrueComp will pay for itself in only one year if the system reduces the number of reward overpayments by 5 percent.

Even more valuable to Wachovia are TrueComp's modeling capabilities. By modeling different compensation scenarios before enacting them, Wachovia can see how certain incentive programs will affect the bottom line and whether new strategies will fulfill corporate goals. Suppose, for example, that senior management wants the bank to sign up one million new checking and savings accounts in 2006. The system will let management see if increasing teller incentives from, say, $25 per new account signing to $35 per new account is the best strategy for reaching that goal or whether increasing incentives for customer satisfaction ratings will have a bigger impact.

The system shows the bank whether it is more profitable to award bonuses for referrals, opening new accounts, or customer service ratings. If the bank wants to take away incentives for referrals to investment advisers but raise incentive amounts based on customer service ratings for bank branches or individual employees, the software simulates whether the likely increase in new customers and a lower customer turnover rate will produce more revenue than if those incentives were directed toward investments.

Average per-branch quarterly loan sales at Wachovia now stand at $2.3 million, which is more than First Union was doing on its own before the merger and 450 percent more than Wachovia premerger branches produced. Wachovia has enjoyed a simultaneous increase in customer satisfaction, according to a 2004 Gallup survey. On a scale of 1 to 7, Wachovia rated 6.57, up from 5.59 in 1999.

*Sources*: Mel Duval, "Wachovia: Best Incentives," *Baseline Magazine*, January 13, 2005; Christopher Caggiano, "Front-end Alignment," *Computerworld*, April 8, 2005; Press release, "Callidus Software Helps Wachovia to Optimize Its Incentive Compensation," www.callidussoftware.com, November 16, 2004, accessed August 16, 2005; and Glen Fest, "Incentive Pay: Compensating for Good Relationships," *Bank Technology News*, www.banktechnews.com, accessed June 2005.

**To Think About:**

What problems did First Union and Wachovia face when they merged? What solutions were available to Wachovia to solve its problems and meet its goals? What did the TrueComp EIM system do for Wachovia? How did the system benefit the business?

The principal purpose of systems at this level is to answer routine questions and to track the flow of transactions through the organization. How many parts are in inventory? What happened to Mr. Williams's payment? To answer these kinds of questions, information generally must be easily available, current, and accurate.

At the operational level, tasks, resources, and goals are predefined and highly structured. The decision to grant credit to a customer, for instance, is made by a lower-level supervisor according to predefined criteria. All that must be determined is whether the customer meets the criteria. The systems illustrated in Figures 2-7 and 2-8 are transaction processing systems.

Managers need TPS to monitor the status of internal operations and the firm's relations with the external environment. TPS are also major producers of information for the other types of systems. (For example, the accounts receivable system illustrated in Figure 2-7, along with other accounting TPS, supplies data to the company's general ledger system, which is responsible for maintaining records of the firm's income and expenses and for producing reports such as income statements and balance sheets.)

Transaction processing systems are often so central to a business that TPS failure for a few hours can lead to a firm's demise and perhaps that of other firms linked to it. Imagine what would happen to UPS if its package tracking system were not working! What would the airlines do without their computerized reservation systems?

## Management Information Systems and Decision-Support Systems

Middle management needs systems to help with monitoring, controlling, decision-making, and administrative activities. The principal question addressed by such systems is this: Are things working well?

In Chapter 1, we define management information systems as the study of information systems in business and management. The term **management information systems (MIS)** also designates a specific category of information systems serving middle management. MIS provide middle managers with reports on the organization's current performance. This information is used to monitor and control the business and predict future performance.

MIS summarize and report on the company's basic operations using data supplied by transaction processing systems. The basic transaction data from TPS are compressed and usually presented in reports that are produced on a regular schedule. Today, many of these reports are delivered online. Figure 2-9 shows how a typical MIS transforms transaction-level data from inventory, production, and accounting into MIS files that are used to provide managers with reports. Figure 2-10 shows a sample report from this system.

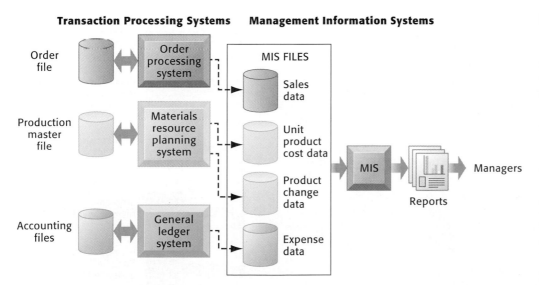

**Figure 2-9**

How Management Information Systems Obtain Their Data from the Organization's TPS
*In the system illustrated by this diagram, three TPS supply summarized transaction data to the MIS reporting system at the end of the time period. Managers gain access to the organizational data through the MIS, which provides them with the appropriate reports.*

**Figure 2-10**
Sample MIS Report
*This report, showing
summarized annual
sales data, was pro-
duced by the MIS in
Figure 2-9.*

Consolidated Consumer Products Corporation Sales by Product and Sales Region: 2006

| PRODUCT CODE | PRODUCT DESCRIPTION | SALES REGION | ACTUAL SALES | PLANNED | ACTUAL versus PLANNED |
|---|---|---|---|---|---|
| 4469 | Carpet Cleaner | Northeast | 4,066,700 | 4,800,000 | 0.85 |
| | | South | 3,778,112 | 3,750,000 | 1.01 |
| | | Midwest | 4,867,001 | 4,600,000 | 1.06 |
| | | West | 4,003,440 | 4,400,000 | 0.91 |
| | TOTAL | | 16,715,253 | 17,550,000 | 0.95 |
| 5674 | Room Freshener | Northeast | 3,676,700 | 3,900,000 | 0.94 |
| | | South | 5,608,112 | 4,700,000 | 1.19 |
| | | Midwest | 4,711,001 | 4,200,000 | 1.12 |
| | | West | 4,563,440 | 4,900,000 | 0.93 |
| | TOTAL | | 18,559,253 | 17,700,000 | 1.05 |

MIS serve managers primarily interested in weekly, monthly, and yearly results, although some MIS enable managers to drill down to see daily or hourly data if required. MIS generally provide answers to routine questions that have been specified in advance and have a predefined procedure for answering them. For instance, MIS reports might list the total pounds of lettuce used this quarter by a fast-food chain or, as illustrated in Figure 2-10, compare total annual sales figures for specific products to planned targets. These systems generally are not flexible and have little analytical capability. Most MIS use simple routines, such as summaries and comparisons, as opposed to sophisticated mathematical models or statistical techniques.

**Decision-support systems (DSS)** support nonroutine decision making for middle management. They focus on problems that are unique and rapidly changing, for which the procedure for arriving at a solution may not be fully predefined in advance. They try to answer questions such as these: What would be the impact on production schedules if we were to double sales in the month of December? What would happen to our return on investment if a factory schedule were delayed for six months?

Although DSS use internal information from TPS and MIS, they often bring in information from external sources, such as current stock prices or product prices of competitors. These systems use a variety of models to analyze data, or they condense large amounts of data into a form in which decision makers can analyze them. DSS are

**Figure 2-11**
Voyage-Estimating
Decision-Support
System
*This DSS operates on a
powerful PC. It is used
daily by managers who
must develop bids on
shipping contracts.*

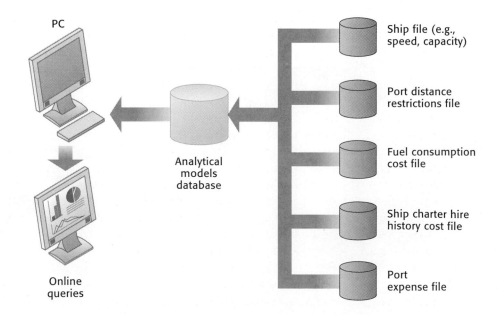

designed so that users can work with them directly; these systems explicitly include user-friendly software.

An interesting, small, but powerful, DSS is the voyage-estimating system of a subsidiary of a large American metals company that exists primarily to carry bulk cargoes of coal, oil, ores, and finished products for its parent company. The firm owns some vessels, charters others, and bids for shipping contracts in the open market to carry general cargo. A voyage-estimating system calculates financial and technical voyage details. Financial calculations include ship/time costs (fuel, labor, capital), freight rates for various types of cargo, and port expenses. Technical details include a myriad of factors, such as ship cargo capacity, speed, port distances, fuel and water consumption, and loading patterns (location of cargo for different ports).

The system can answer questions such as the following: Given a customer delivery schedule and an offered freight rate, which vessel should be assigned at what rate to maximize profits? What is the optimal speed at which a particular vessel can optimize its profit and still meet its delivery schedule? What is the optimal loading pattern for a ship bound for the U.S. West Coast from Malaysia? Figure 2-11 illustrates the DSS built for this company. The system operates on a powerful desktop personal computer, providing a system of menus that makes it easy for users to enter data or obtain information.

This voyage-estimating DSS draws heavily on analytical models. Other types of DSS are less model driven, focusing instead on extracting useful information to support decision making from massive quantities of data. For example, Intrawest—the largest ski operator in North America—collects and stores vast amounts of customer data from its Web site, call center, lodging reservations, ski schools, and ski equipment rental stores. It uses special software to analyze these data to determine the value, revenue potential, and loyalty of each customer so managers can make better decisions on how to target their marketing programs. The system segments customers into seven categories based on needs, attitudes, and behaviors, ranging from "passionate experts" to "value-minded family vacationers." The company then e-mails video clips that would appeal to each segment to encourage more visits to its resorts.

Sometimes you'll hear DSS referred to as *business intelligence systems* because they focus on helping users make better business decisions. You'll learn more about them in Chapters 5 and 10.

## Executive Support Systems

Senior managers need systems that address strategic issues and long-term trends, both in the firm and in the external environment. They are concerned with questions such as these: What will employment levels be in five years? What are the long-term industry cost trends, and where does our firm fit in? What products should we be making in five years? What new acquisitions would protect us from cyclical business swings?

**Executive support systems (ESS)** help senior management make these decisions. ESS address nonroutine decisions requiring judgment, evaluation, and insight because there is no agreed-on procedure for arriving at a solution. ESS provide a generalized computing and communications capacity that can be applied to a changing array of problems.

ESS are designed to incorporate data about external events, such as new tax laws or competitors, but they also draw summarized information from internal MIS and DSS. They filter, compress, and track critical data, displaying the data of greatest importance to senior managers. For example, the CEO of Leiner Health Products, the largest manufacturer of private-label vitamins and supplements in the United States, has an ESS that provides on his desktop a minute-to-minute view of the firm's financial performance as measured by working capital, accounts receivable, accounts payable, cash flow, and inventory.

ESS present graphs and data from many sources through an interface that is easy for senior managers to use. Often the information is delivered to senior executives through a **portal**, which uses a Web interface to present integrated personalized business content. You will learn more about other applications of portals in Chapters 9 and 10.

Figure 2-12 illustrates a model of an ESS. It consists of workstations with menus, interactive graphics, and communications capabilities that can be used to access historical and competitive data from internal corporate systems and external databases such as Dow Jones

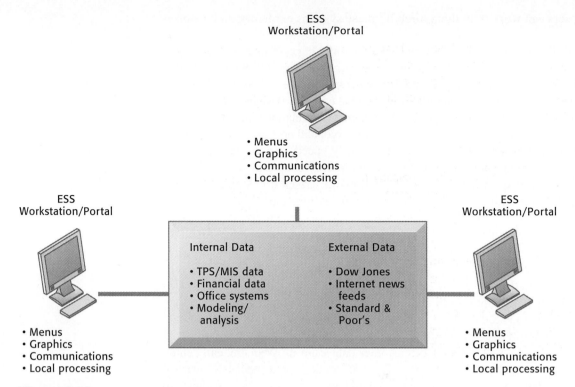

**Figure 2-12**
Model of an Executive Support System
*This system pools data from diverse internal and external sources and makes them available to executives in an easy-to-use form.*

News/Retrieval or the Gallup Poll. More details on leading-edge applications of DSS and ESS can be found in Chapter 10.

## Relationship of Systems to One Another

The systems we have just described are interrelated, as illustrated in Figure 2-13. TPS are typically a major source of data for other systems, whereas ESS are primarily a recipient of data from lower-level systems. The other types of systems may exchange data with each other as well. Data also may be exchanged among systems serving different functional areas. For example, an order captured by a sales system may be transmitted to a manufacturing system as a transaction for producing or delivering the product specified in the order or to an MIS for financial reporting. In most organizations, these systems have been loosely integrated.

**Figure 2-13**
Interrelationships Among Systems
*The various types of systems in the organization have interdependencies. TPS are major producers of information that is required by many other systems in the firm, which, in turn, produce information for other systems. These different types of systems have been loosely coupled in most organizations.*

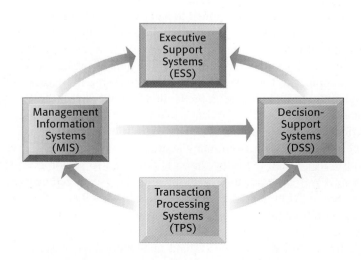

## 2.3 Systems That Span the Enterprise

Reviewing all the different types of systems we have just described, you might wonder how a business can manage all the information in these different systems. You might also wonder how costly it is to maintain so many different systems. And you might wonder how these different systems can share information. In fact, these are all excellent questions and challenges for businesses today.

### Enterprise Applications

Getting all the different kinds of systems in a company to work together is a major challenge. Typically, corporations are put together both through normal "organic" growth and through acquisition of smaller firms. Over a period of time, corporations end up with a collection of systems, most of them older, and face the challenge of getting them all to "talk" with one another and work together as one corporate system. There are several solutions to this problem.

One solution is to implement **enterprise applications**, which are systems that span functional areas, focus on executing business processes across the business firm, and include all levels of management. Enterprise applications help businesses become more flexible and productive by coordinating their business processes more closely and integrating groups of processes so they focus on efficient management of resources and customer service.

There are four major enterprise applications: enterprise systems, supply chain management systems, customer relationship management systems, and knowledge management systems. Each of these enterprise applications integrates a related set of functions and business processes to enhance the performance of the organization as a whole. Figure 2-14 shows that the architecture for these enterprise applications encompasses processes spanning the entire

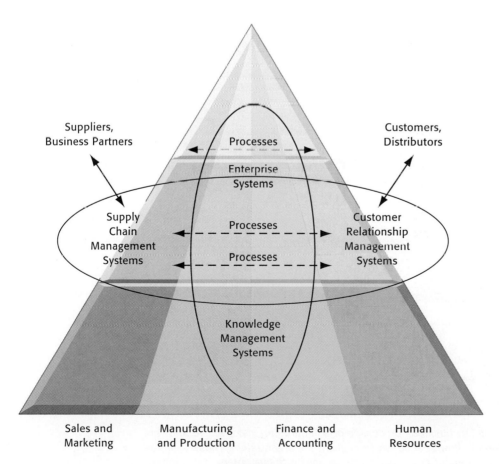

**Figure 2-14**
Enterprise Application Architecture
*Enterprise applications automate processes that span multiple business functions and organizational levels and may extend outside the organization.*

organization and, in some cases, extending beyond the organization to customers, suppliers, and other key business partners.

### Enterprise Systems

A large organization typically has many different kinds of information systems built around different functions, organizational levels, and business processes that cannot automatically exchange information. Managers might have a hard time assembling the data they need for a comprehensive, overall picture of the organization's operations. For instance, sales personnel might not be able to tell at the time they place an order whether the items that were ordered are in inventory, customers cannot track their orders, and manufacturing cannot communicate easily with finance to plan for new production. This fragmentation of data in hundreds of separate systems degrades organizational efficiency and business performance.

For example, Alcoa, the world's leading producer of aluminum and aluminum products with operations spanning 41 countries and 500 locations, had initially been organized around lines of business, each of which had its own set of information systems. Many of these systems were redundant and inefficient. Alcoa's costs for executing requisition-to-pay and financial processes were much higher and its cycle times were longer than those of other companies in its industry. (Cycle time refers to the total elapsed time from the beginning to the end of a process.) The company could not operate as a single worldwide entity (Oracle, 2005; Sullivan, 2005).

**Enterprise systems,** also known as *enterprise resource planning (ERP) systems,* solve this problem by collecting data from various key business processes in manufacturing and production, finance and accounting, sales and marketing, and human resources and storing the data in a single central data repository. This makes it possible for information that was previously fragmented in different systems to be shared across the firm and for different parts of the business to work more closely together (see Figure 2-15).

Enterprise systems speed communication of information throughout the company, making it easier for businesses to coordinate their daily operations. When a customer places an

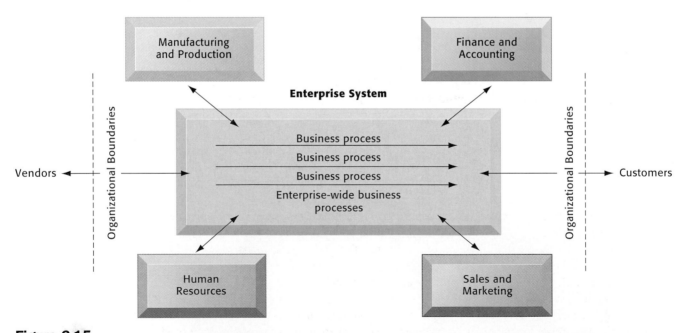

### Figure 2-15
Enterprise Systems
*Enterprise systems integrate the key business processes of an entire firm into a single software system that enables information to flow seamlessly throughout the organization. These systems focus primarily on internal processes but may include transactions with customers and vendors.*

order, the data flow automatically to other parts of the company that are affected by them. The order transaction triggers the warehouse to pick the ordered products and schedule shipment. The warehouse informs the factory to replenish whatever has depleted. The accounting department is notified to send the customer an invoice. Customer service representatives track the progress of the order through every step to inform customers about the status of their orders.

Enterprise systems give companies the flexibility to respond rapidly to customer requests while producing and stocking inventory only with what is needed to fulfill existing orders. Their ability to increase accurate and on-time shipments, minimize costs, and increase customer satisfaction adds to the firms profitability.

After implementing enterprise software from Oracle, Alcoa eliminated many redundant processes and systems. The enterprise system helped Alcoa reduce requisition-to-pay cycle time (the total elapsed time from the time a purchase requisition is generated to the time the payment for the purchase is made) by verifying receipt of goods and automatically generating receipts for payment. Alcoa's accounts payable transaction processing dropped 89 percent. Alcoa was able to centralize financial and procurement activities, which helped the company reduce nearly 20 percent of its worldwide costs. The company expects continued use of the enterprise system to reduce inventory by 25 percent, increase productivity by 15 percent, reduce materials costs by 5 percent, and improve customer service by 20 percent.

Enterprise systems provide much valuable information for improving management decision making. Corporate headquarters has access to up-to-the-minute data on sales, inventory, and production and uses this information to create more accurate sales and production forecasts. Enterprise systems provide company-wide information to help managers analyze overall product profitability or cost structures. For example, Alcoa's new enterprise system includes functionality for global human resources management that shows correlations between investment in employee training and quality; measures the company-wide costs of delivering services to employees; and measures the effectiveness of employee recruitment, compensation, and training.

### Supply Chain Management Systems

**Supply chain management (SCM) systems** help businesses manage relationships with their suppliers. These systems provide information to help suppliers, purchasing firms, distributors, and logistics companies share information about orders, production, inventory levels, and delivery of products and services so that they can source, produce, and deliver goods and services efficiently. The ultimate objective is to get the right amount of products from their source to their point of consumption with the least amount of time and with the lowest cost.

If a company and its supply network do not have accurate information, they will most likely be saddled by excessive inventories, inaccurate manufacturing plans, and missed production schedules. Inability to move products efficiently through the supply chain raises costs while degrading customer service.

For example, until it implemented a supply chain management system from SAP, Alcan Packaging had trouble fulfilling customer orders for its packaging materials for food, pharmaceuticals, and cosmetics. It did not have the information to make good decisions about how much to produce, how to allocate personnel, or how to meet the delivery dates requested by customers. It would go from working employees overtime one month to cutting back staff the next. It could not accurately project when it would meet shipment requirements (SAP, 2005).

Table 2.5 describes how firms can benefit from supply chain management systems. These systems increase firm profitability by lowering the costs of moving and making products and by enabling managers to make better decisions about how to organize and schedule sourcing, production, and distribution. Alcan expects its supply chain management system to reduce overtime by 25 percent, reduce setup costs by up to 7.5 percent, and reduce inventory carrying costs by up to 10 percent.

**TABLE 2.5**

**How Information Systems Facilitate Supply Chain Management**

| Information from supply chain management systems helps firms |
| --- |
| Decide when and what to produce, store, and move |
| Rapidly communicate orders |
| Track the status of orders |
| Check inventory availability and monitor inventory levels |
| Reduce inventory, transportation, and warehousing costs |
| Track shipments |
| Plan production based on actual customer demand |
| Rapidly communicate changes in product design |

Supply chain management systems are one type of **interorganizational system** because they automate the flow of information across organizational boundaries. You will find examples of other types of interorganizational information systems throughout this text because such systems make it possible for firms to link electronically to customers and to outsource their work to other companies.

Figure 2-16 illustrates the supply chain management systems used by Haworth Incorporated, a world-leading manufacturer and designer of office furniture. The Focus on Technology describes how Haworth implemented new systems for transportation management and warehouse management to improve coordination between its manufacturing and distribution activities. As you read this case, try to identify the problem this company was facing; what alternative solutions were available to management; how well the chosen solution worked; and the people, organization, and technology issues that had to be addressed when developing the solution.

### Customer Relationship Management Systems

**Customer relationship management (CRM) systems** help firms manage their relationships with their customers. CRM systems provide information to coordinate all of the business processes that deal with customers in sales, marketing, and service to optimize revenue, customer satisfaction, and customer retention. This information helps firms identify, attract, and retain the most profitable customers; provide better service to existing customers; and increase sales.

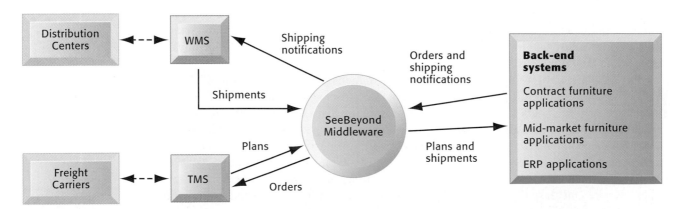

### Figure 2-16

Haworth's Supply Chain Management Systems

*Customer orders, shipping notifications, optimized shipping plans, and other supply chain information flow among Haworth's Warehouse Management System (WMS), Transportation Management System (TMS), and its back-end enterprise systems and other corporate applications.*

# FOCUS ON TECHNOLOGY | Haworth Overhauls Supply Chain Management

Haworth Incorporated, headquartered in Holland, Michigan, is the world's second-largest designer and manufacturer of office furniture and workspaces. The company offers a full range of furniture known for its innovative design, including desks, chairs, tables, partitions, and storage products. Haworth operates in more than 120 countries, with 9,000 employees, 40 manufacturing locations, 60 showrooms, and more than 600 independent dealers around the world.

Haworth was particularly successful during the booming economy of the late 1990s, which stimulated demand for new offices and office space. But the company was hit hard when many dot-coms went under because these companies glutted the market with their slightly used Haworth products.

To bring costs back in line with declining revenue, Haworth started an ambitious overhaul of its supply chain management systems in 2002. Haworth's 15 North American manufacturing facilities are located in North Carolina, Arkansas, Michigan, Mississippi, Texas, Ontario, Alberta, and Quebec. These facilities supply inventory to distribution centers in Michigan, Pennsylvania, Georgia, and Arkansas. Haworth needed to coordinate order fulfillment from multiple distribution centers with products received from all of its manufacturing facilities. The distribution centers needed to communicate effectively with the manufacturing facilities to better plan the processing of customer orders.

Haworth's existing distribution system was an old-style mainframe locator application that could only handle inventory data for a single building and could not differentiate between facilities. Each distribution center used a different version of the system based on the computer system with which it interfaced. The system did not provide a way to preplan shipments, so Haworth could not cross-dock material directly to an outbound shipment as efficiently as it desired, raising labor and freight costs. Cross-docking enables goods earmarked for a specific customer to move directly from the receiving dock to the shipping dock without being checked into the system and picked from inventory.

To solve these problems, Haworth implemented a new Warehouse Management System (WMS) based on IristaWarehouse software from Irista in Milwaukee. WMS tracks and controls the flow of finished goods from the receiving dock at any of Haworth's distribution centers to the customer site. The system has cross-docking capabilities to reduce labor costs in the warehouse. WMS interfaces with the various ERP applications running in the four distribution centers and with Haworth's Transportation Management System (TMS). Acting on shipping plans from TMS, WMS directs the movement of goods based on immediate conditions for space, equipment, inventory, and personnel.

The TMS uses optimization and carrier communication software from Manugistics Group in Rockville, Maryland. The system examines customer orders, factory schedules, carrier rates and availability, and shipping costs to produce optimal lowest-cost delivery plans. These plans are generated daily and updated every 15 minutes. TMS has an automated interface that enables Haworth to negotiate deliveries with its carriers. To find the minimal freight cost for deliveries, TMS maps out efficient routes that minimize "less-than-truckload" shipments and damage to goods.

TMS also electronically sends carriers "tenders," which are requests to bid on a shipment. These tenders are transmitted over a private network or the Web, and carriers transmit bids back automatically. In the past, that process required two phone calls. If a carrier does not reply within a specified time, the system automatically contacts another carrier.

Both TMS and WMS run on server computers from Hewlett-Packard using the Unix operating system. They interface with two sets of order entry, manufacturing planning, and shipping systems that service two different furniture markets. To tie these applications, Haworth uses special "middleware" software from SeeBeyond Technology in Monrovia, California. The middleware passes customer orders, shipping plans, and shipping notifications among the applications.

According to Jim Rohrer, a business applications process manager and key liaison between Haworth's information systems and supply chain operations, the new systems have not merely optimized business processes—they've transformed them. Haworth used to have a "signpost" system where distribution centers received information on labels or on screens and then decided what to do with it. Now the system is more directed. TMS sets up a plan, feeds it to WMS, and WMS specifies the tasks that need to be accomplished.

The payoff from these systems was considerable: Warehouse worker productivity increased 35 percent, freight costs were reduced 16 percent, and "less-than-truckload" shipments and damaged goods in transit declined 50 percent. Haworth's investment in these supply chain management systems paid for itself in only nine months.

*Sources:* Irista Inc., "Haworth: Synchronizing the Supply Chain," www.irista.com, accessed August 18, 2005; Gary H. Anthes, "Refurnishing the Supply Chain" and "Haworth's Supply Chain Project," *Computerworld*, June 7, 2004; and www.haworth.com, accessed August 18, 2005.

**To Think About:**

What problems did Haworth face? How did they affect the way the company ran its business? How did the company solve these problems? What people, organization, and technology issues did the solution have to address? How successful was the solution?

*Illustrated here are some of the capabilities of salesforce.com, a market-leading provider of on-demand customer relationship management (CRM) software. CRM systems integrate information from sales, marketing, and customer service.*

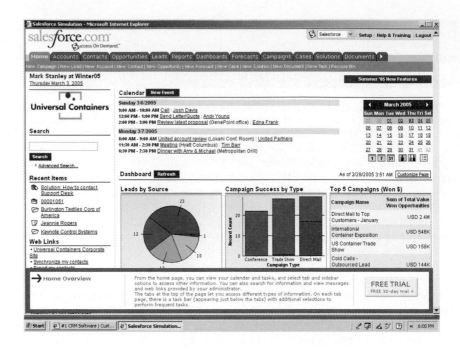

In the past, a firm's processes for sales, service, and marketing were highly compartmentalized, and these departments did not share much essential customer information. Some information on a specific customer might be stored and organized in terms of that person's account with the company. Other pieces of information about the same customer might be organized by products that were purchased. There was no way to consolidate all of this information to provide a unified view of a customer across the company.

For example, until recently, Saab U.S.A., which imports and distributes Saab vehicles to U.S. dealerships, had a splintered view of its customers. It had been engaging customers through three channels: its dealer network, a customer assistance center dealing with service inquiries, and a lead management center handling marketing and information requests from prospective customers. Each of these channels maintained customer data in its own systems. Fragmented customer data meant that a prospective customer might receive a direct mail offer from Saab one week and e-mail with an unrelated offer from a third-party marketing company the next week. The local dealer might not know about either of these offers, which prevented the dealer from delivering an effective pitch when the prospect visited the showroom. Lead quality was highly variable so many dealers ignored the leads and the company had no way of tracking leads faxed to dealers.

CRM systems try to solve this problem by integrating the firm's customer-related processes and consolidating customer information from multiple communication channels—telephone, e-mail, wireless devices, retail outlets, or the Web. Detailed and accurate knowledge of customers and their preferences helps firms increase the effectiveness of their marketing campaigns and provide higher-quality customer service and support.

After Saab U.S.A. implemented three CRM applications for automotive dealers from Siebel Systems, it was able to have a 360-degree view of each customer, including prior service-related questions and all the marketing communication the customer had ever received. Saab can track the status of referred leads by monitoring events, such as the salesperson's initial call to the customer and the scheduling and completion of a test drive. The systems provide detailed information to measure the sales results of specific leads, and target leads are directed more precisely to the right salespeople at the right dealerships. Since the CRM applications were implemented, Saab's follow-up rate on sales leads has increased from 38 to 50 percent and customer satisfaction rose from 69 to 75 percent (Picarille, 2004; Siebel, 2005).

### Knowledge Management Systems

The value of a firm's products and services is based not only on its physical resources but also on intangible knowledge assets. Some firms perform better than others because they have better knowledge about how to create, produce, and deliver products and services. This firm knowledge is difficult to imitate, unique, and can be leveraged into long-term strategic benefits. **Knowledge management systems (KMS)** enable organizations to better manage processes for capturing and applying knowledge and expertise. These systems collect all relevant knowledge and experience in the firm, and make it available wherever and whenever it is needed to improve business processes and management decisions. They also link the firm to external sources of knowledge.

KMS support processes for acquiring, storing, distributing, and applying knowledge, as well as processes for creating new knowledge and integrating it into the organization. They include enterprise-wide systems for managing and distributing documents, graphics, and other digital knowledge objects; systems for creating corporate knowledge directories of employees with special areas of expertise; office systems for distributing knowledge and information; and knowledge work systems to facilitate knowledge creation. Other knowledge management applications use intelligent techniques that codify knowledge for use by other members of the organization and tools for knowledge discovery that recognize patterns and important relationships in large pools of data.

We examine enterprise systems and systems for supply chain management and customer relationship management in greater detail in Chapter 8 and cover knowledge management applications in Chapter 10.

## Intranets and Extranets

Enterprise applications create deep-seated changes in the way the firm conducts its business, and they are often costly to implement. Companies that do not have the resources to invest in enterprise applications can still achieve some measure of information integration by using intranets and extranets, which we introduced in Chapter 1.

Intranets and extranets are really more technology platforms than specific applications, but they deserve mention here as one of the tools firms use to increase integration and expedite the flow of information within the firm, and with customers and suppliers. Intranets are internal networks built with the same tools and communication standards as the Internet and are used for the internal distribution of information to employees, and as repositories of corporate policies, programs, and data. Extranets are intranets extended to authorized users outside the company. We describe the technology for intranets and extranets in more detail in Chapter 6.

An intranet typically centers on a portal that provides a single point of access to information from several different systems and to documents using a Web interface. Such portals can be customized to suit the information needs of specific business groups and individual users if required. They may also feature e-mail, collaboration tools, and tools for searching internal corporate systems and documents.

For example, SwissAir's corporate intranet for sales provides its salespeople with sales leads, fares, statistics, libraries of best practices, access to incentive programs, discussion groups, and collaborative workspaces. The intranet includes a Sales Ticket capability that displays bulletins about unfilled airplane seats around the world to help the sales staff work with colleagues and with travel agents who can help them fill those seats.

Companies can connect their intranets to internal company transaction systems, enabling employees to take actions central to a company's operations, such as checking the status of an order or granting a customer credit. SwissAir's intranet connects to its reservation system. GUESS Jeans has an intranet called ApparelBuy.com that links to its core order processing systems.

Extranets expedite the flow of information between the firm and its suppliers and customers. SwissAir uses an extranet to provide travel agents with fare data from its intranet electronically. GUESS Jeans allows store buyers to order merchandise electronically from ApparelBuy.com. The buyers can use this extranet to track their orders through fulfillment or delivery.

Extranets allow different firms to work collaboratively on product design, marketing, and production. Engineers at Johnson Controls and DaimlerChrysler used an extranet design and collaboration system to design part of the Jeep Liberty interior together. Hewlett-Packard (HP) Laserjet Imaging Systems uses an extranet workgroup collaboration system to share information with its contract manufacturers, distribution centers, and resellers. The application makes parts plans from HP's internal production system available on a shared electronic workspace that can be accessed by suppliers. Suppliers then adjust their plans to coordinate their inventory with that of HP.

### E-Business, E-Commerce, and E-Government

The systems and technologies we have just described are transforming firms' relationships with customers, employees, suppliers, and logistic partners into digital relationships using networks and the Internet. So much business is now enabled by or based upon digital networks that we use the terms *electronic business* and *electronic commerce* frequently throughout this text. **Electronic business**, or **e-business**, refers to the use of digital technology and the Internet to execute the major business processes in the enterprise. E-business includes activities for the internal management of the firm and for coordination with suppliers and other business partners. It also includes **electronic commerce**, or **e-commerce**. E-commerce is the part of e-business that deals with the buying and selling of goods and services over the Internet. It also encompasses activities supporting those market transactions, such as advertising, marketing, customer support, security, delivery, and payment.

The technologies associated with e-business have also brought about similar changes in the public sector. Governments on all levels are using Internet technology to deliver information and services to citizens, employees, and businesses with which they work. **E-government** refers to the application of the Internet and networking technologies to digitally enable government and public sector agencies' relationships with citizens, businesses, and other arms of government. In addition to improving delivery of government services, e-government can make government operations more efficient and also empower citizens by giving them easier access to information and the ability to network electronically with other citizens. For example, citizens in some states can renew their driver's licenses or apply for unemployment benefits online, and the Internet has become a powerful tool for instantly mobilizing interest groups for political action and fund-raising.

## 2.4 The Information Systems Function in Business

We've seen that businesses need information systems to operate today and that they use many different kinds of systems. But who is responsible for running these systems? Who is responsible for making sure the hardware, software, and other technologies used by these systems are running properly and are up to date? End users manage their systems from a business standpoint, but managing the technology requires a special information systems function.

In all but the smallest of firms, the **information systems department** is the formal organizational unit responsible for information technology services. The information systems department is responsible for maintaining the hardware, software, data management technology, and networks that comprise the firm's IT infrastructure. We describe IT infrastructure in detail in Chapter 4.

### The Information Systems Department

The information systems department consists of specialists, such as programmers, systems analysts, project leaders, and information systems managers. **Programmers** are highly trained technical specialists who write the software instructions for computers. **Systems analysts** constitute the principal liaisons between the information systems groups and the rest of the organization. It is the systems analyst's job to translate business problems and requirements into information requirements and systems. **Information systems managers** are leaders of teams of programmers and analysts, project managers, physical facility managers, telecommunications managers, or database specialists. They are also managers of computer operations and data entry staff. Also, external specialists, such as hardware vendors and manufacturers, software firms, and consultants, frequently participate in the day-to-day operations and long-term planning of information systems.

In many companies, the information systems department is headed by a **chief information officer (CIO)**. The CIO is a senior manager who oversees the use of information technology in the firm.

**End users** are representatives of departments outside of the information systems group for whom applications are developed. These users are playing an increasingly large role in the design and development of information systems.

In the early years of computing, the information systems group was composed mostly of programmers who performed very highly specialized but limited technical functions. Today, a growing proportion of staff members are systems analysts and network specialists, with the information systems department acting as a powerful change agent in the organization. The information systems department suggests new business strategies and new information-based products and services, and coordinates both the development of the technology and the planned changes in the organization.

Services provided by the information systems department include the following:

- Computing platforms provide computing services that connect employees, customers, and suppliers into a coherent digital environment, including large mainframes, desktop and laptop computers, personal digital assistants (PDAs), and Internet appliances.
- Telecommunications services provide data, voice, and video connectivity to employees, customers, and suppliers.
- Data management services store and manage corporate data, and provide capabilities for analyzing the data.
- Application software services provide development and support services for the firm's business systems, including enterprise-wide capabilities, such as enterprise resource planning, customer relationship management, supply chain management, and knowledge management systems, that are shared by all business units.
- Physical facilities management services develop and manage the physical installations required for computing, telecommunications, and data management services.
- IT management services plan and develop the infrastructure, coordinate with the business units for IT services, manage accounting for the IT expenditure, and provide project management services.
- IT standards services provide the firm and its business units with policies that determine which information technology will be used, when, and how.
- IT educational services provide training in system use to employees and offer managers training in how to plan for and manage IT investments.
- IT research and development services provide the firm with research on potential future information systems projects and investments that could help the firm differentiate itself in the marketplace.

In the past, firms generally built their own software and managed their own computing facilities. Today, many firms are turning to external vendors to provide these services (see Chapters 4 and 11) and are using their information systems departments to manage these service providers.

## Organizing the Information Systems Function

There are many types of business firms, and there are many ways in which the IT function is organized within the firm (see Figure 2-17). A very small company will not have a formal information systems group. It might have one employee who is responsible for keeping its networks and applications running, or it might use consultants for these services. Larger companies will have a separate information systems department, which may be organized along several different lines, depending on the nature and interests of the firm.

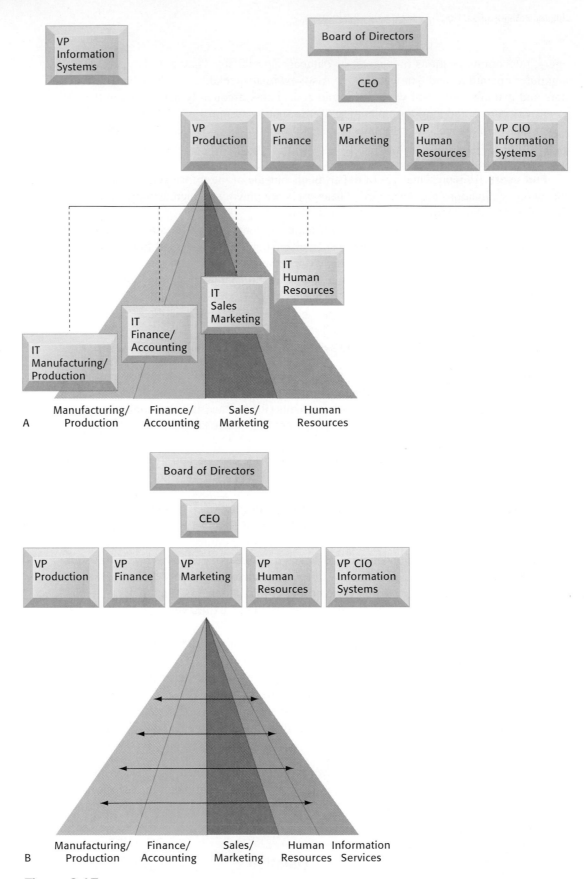

**Figure 2-17**

Organization of the Information Systems Function

*There are alternative ways of organizing the information systems function within the business: within each functional area (A), as a separate department under central control (B), or represented in each division of a large multidivisional company but under centralized control (C).*

**Figure 2-17**
(*continued*)

Sometimes you'll see a decentralized arrangement where each functional area of the business has its own information systems department and management that typically reports to a senior manager or chief information officer. In other words, the marketing department would have its own information systems group as would manufacturing and each of the other business functions. The job of the CIO is to review information technology invest ments and decisions in the functional areas. The advantage of this approach is that systems are built that directly address the business needs of the functional areas. However, central guidance is weak and the danger is high that many incompatible systems will be built, increasing costs as each group makes its own technology purchases.

In another arrangement, the information systems function operates as a separate depart ment similar to the other functional departments with a large staff, a group of middle man agers, and a senior management group that fights for its share of the company's resources. You'll see this approach in many large firms. This central information systems department makes technology decisions for the entire company, which is more likely to produce more compatible systems and more coherent long-term systems development plans.

Very large "Fortune 1,000"-size firms with multiple divisions and product lines might allow each division (such as the Consumer Products Division or the Chemicals and Additives Division) to have its own information systems group. All of these divisional infor mation systems groups report to a high-level central information systems group and CIO. The central IS group establishes corporate-wide standards, centralizes purchasing, and develops long-term plans for evolving the corporate computing platform. This model com bines some divisional independence with some centralization.

---

**LEARNING TRACKS**

1. If you want to learn more about the challenges of using all the different types of information systems in a business, you will find a Learning Track on this topic at the Laudon Web site for this chapter.

# Summary

1 **Identify and describe the major features of a business that are important for understanding the role of information systems.** A business is a formal complex organization that seeks to produce products or services for a profit. Businesses have specialized functions, such as finance and accounting, human resources, manufacturing and production, and sales and marketing. Business organizations are arranged hierarchically in levels composed of senior management, middle management, and operational management. A business process is a logically related set of activities that define how specific business tasks are performed, and a business can be viewed as a collection of business processes. Business firms must deal with their environments. A firm must respond to political shifts, respond to changes in the overall economy, keep track of new technologies, and respond to changes in the global business environment. In its immediate task environment, a firm needs to track and share information with suppliers, customers, stockholders, regulators, and logistic partners.

2 **Describe the information systems supporting the major business functions: sales and marketing, manufacturing and production, finance and accounting, and human resources.** At each level of the organization, information systems support the major functional areas of the business. Sales and marketing systems help the firm identify customers for the firm's products or services, develop products and services to meet customers' needs, promote the products and services, sell the products and services, and provide ongoing customer support. Manufacturing and production systems deal with the planning, development, and production of products and services, and control the flow of production. Finance and accounting systems keep track of the firm's financial assets and fund flows. Human resources systems maintain employee records; track employee skills, job performance, and training; and support planning for employee compensation and career development.

3 **Evaluate the role played by systems serving the various levels of management in a business and their relationship to each other.** There are four major types of information systems in contemporary organizations serving operational, middle, and senior management. Systems serving operational management are transaction processing systems (TPS), such as payroll or order processing, that track the flow of the daily routine transactions necessary to conduct business. MIS and DSS provide middle management with reports and access to the organization's current performance and historical records. Most MIS reports condense information from TPS and are not highly analytical. DSS support management decisions when these decisions are unique, rapidly changing, and not specified easily in advance. They have more advanced analytical models and data analysis capabilities than MIS and often draw on information from external as well as internal sources. ESS support senior management by providing data of greatest importance to senior management decision makers, often in the form of graphs and charts delivered via portals. They have limited analytical capabilities but can draw on sophisticated graphics software and many sources of internal and external information.

4 **Explain how enterprise applications and intranets promote business process integration and improve organizational performance.** Enterprise applications, such as enterprise systems, supply chain management systems, customer relationship management systems, and knowledge management systems, are designed to support organization-wide process coordination and integration so that the organization can operate efficiently. They span multiple functions and business processes and may be tied to the business processes of other organizations. Enterprise systems integrate the key internal business processes of a firm into a single software system so that information can flow throughout the organization, improving coordination, efficiency, and decision making. Supply chain management systems help the firm manage its relationship with suppliers to optimize the planning, sourcing, manufacturing, and delivery of products and services. Customer relationship management uses information systems to coordinate all of the business processes surrounding the firm's interactions with its customers to optimize firm revenue and customer satisfaction. Knowledge management systems enable firms to optimize the creation, sharing, and distribution of knowledge to improve business processes and management decisions.

Intranets and extranets use Internet technology and standards to assemble information from various systems and present it to the user in a Web page format. Extranets make portions of private corporate intranets available to outsiders.

5 **Assess the role of the information systems function in a business.** The information systems department is the formal organizational unit responsible for information technology services. The information systems department is responsible for maintaining the hardware, software, data management technology, and networks that comprise the firm's IT infrastructure. The information

systems department consists of specialists, such as programmers, systems analysts, project leaders, and information systems managers, and is often headed by a CIO.

There are alternative ways of organizing the IT function within the firm. A very small company will not have a formal information systems group. Larger companies will have a separate information systems department, which may be organized along several different lines, depending on the nature and interests of the firm. Each functional area of the business may have its own information systems department, overseen by a corporate CIO. The information systems function may be run as a separate department similar to the other functional departments. A third arrangement found in very large firms with multiple divisions and product lines is to have an information systems department for each division reporting to a high-level central information systems group and CIO.

## Key Terms

| | | |
|---|---|---|
| Business, 42 | Executive support systems (ESS), 55 | Manufacturing and production information systems, 48 |
| Chief information officer (CIO), 65 | Finance and accounting information systems, 49 | Middle management, 44 |
| Customer relationship management (CRM) systems, 60 | Human resources information systems, 50 | Operational management, 44 |
| Data workers, 44 | Information systems department, 64 | Portal, 55 |
| Decision-support systems (DSS), 54 | Information systems managers, 64 | Production or service workers, 44 |
| Electronic business (e-business), 64 | Interorganizational system, 60 | Programmers, 64 |
| Electronic commerce (e-commerce), 64 | Knowledge management systems (KMS), 63 | Sales and marketing information systems, 47 |
| E-government, 64 | Knowledge workers, 44 | Senior management, 44 |
| End users, 65 | Management information systems (MIS), 53 | Supply chain management (SCM) systems, 59 |
| Enterprise applications, 57 | | Systems analysts, 64 |
| Enterprise systems, 58 | | Transaction processing systems (TPS), 51 |

## Review Questions

**2.1** What is a business? What are the major business functions?

**2.2** What are business processes? What role do they play in organizations?

**2.3** Identify and describe the different levels in a business firm and their information needs.

**2.4** Why are environments important for understanding a business?

**2.5** List and describe the information systems serving each of the major functional areas of a business.

**2.6** What are the characteristics of transaction processing systems? What role do they play in a business?

**2.7** What are the characteristics of MIS? How do MIS differ from TPS? From DSS?

**2.8** What are the characteristics of DSS? How do they differ from those of ESS?

**2.9** Describe the relationship between TPS, MIS, DSS, and ESS.

**2.10** Why are organizations trying to integrate their business processes? What are the four key enterprise applications?

**2.11** What are enterprise systems? How do they change the way an organization works?

**2.12** What are supply chain management systems? How do they benefit businesses?

**2.13** What are customer relationship management systems? How do they benefit businesses?

**2.14** What is the role of knowledge management systems in the enterprise?

**2.15** Describe how the information systems function supports a business. What roles are played by programmers, systems analysts, information systems managers, and the chief information officer (CIO)?

**2.16** Describe alternative ways of organizing the information systems function in a business.

## Discussion Questions

**2.1** How could information systems be used to support the order fulfillment process illustrated in Figure 2-2? What are the most important pieces of information these systems should capture? Explain your answer.

**2.2** Adopting an enterprise application is a key business decision as well as a technology decision. Do you agree? Why or why not? Who should make this decision?

## Application Software Exercise

### Spreadsheet Exercise: Improving Supply Chain Management

Software skills: Spreadsheet date functions, data filtering, database functions

Business skills: Analyzing supplier performance and pricing

You run a company that manufactures aircraft components. You have many competitors who are trying to offer lower prices and better service to customers, and you are trying to determine whether you can benefit from better supply chain management. At the Laudon Web site for Chapter 2, you can find a spreadsheet file that contains a list of all of the items that your firm has ordered from its suppliers during the past three months. The fields in the spreadsheet file include vendor name, vendor identification number, purchaser's order number, item identification number and item description (for each item ordered from the vendor), cost per item, number of units of the item ordered, total cost of each order, vendor's accounts payable terms, promised shipping date, promised transit time, and actual arrival date for each order.

Prepare a recommendation of how you can use the data in this spreadsheet database to improve your supply chain management. You may wish to consider ways to identify preferred suppliers or other ways of improving the movement and production of your products. Some criteria you might consider include the supplier's track record for on-time deliveries, suppliers offering the best accounts payable terms, and suppliers offering lower pricing when the same item can be provided by multiple suppliers. Use your spreadsheet software to prepare reports and, if appropriate, graphs to support your recommendations.

### Analyzing Financial Performance

Software skills: Spreadsheet charts and formulas

Business skills: Financial statement analysis

As part of your analysis of the company for management, you have been asked to analyze data on Dirt Bikes's financial performance. Review Dirt Bikes's selected financial data in the Introduction to Dirt Bikes, which can be found at the Laudon Web site. There you will find Dirt Bikes's income statement and summary balance sheet data from 2003 to 2005, annual sales of Dirt Bikes models between 2001 and 2005, and total domestic versus international sales between 2001 and 2005.

Use your spreadsheet software to create graphs of Dirt Bikes's sales history from 2001 to 2005 and its domestic versus international sales from 2001 to 2005. Select the type of graph that is most appropriate for presenting the data you are analyzing.

Use the instructions at the Laudon Web site and your spreadsheet software to calculate the gross and net margins in Dirt Bikes's income statements from 2003 to 2005. You can also create graphs showing trends in selected pieces of Dirt Bikes's income statement and balance sheet data if you wish. (You may want to rearrange the historical ordering of the data if you decide to do this.)

Prepare an addition to your management report that answers these questions:

1. What are Dirt Bikes's best- and worst-performing products? What is the proportion of domestic to international sales? Have international sales grown relative to domestic sales?

2. Are sales (revenues) growing steadily, and, if so, at what rate? What is the cost of goods sold compared to revenues? Is it increasing or decreasing? Are the firm's gross and net margins increasing or decreasing? Are the firm's operating expenses increasing or decreasing? Is the firm heavily in debt? Does it have assets to pay for expenses and to finance the development of new products and information systems?

3. (Optional) Use electronic presentation software to summarize your analysis of Dirt Bikes's performance for management.

## Building Internet Skills

## Planning Transportation Logistics

This project will help develop your Internet skills in using online interactive mapping software to plan efficient transportation routes.

The MapQuest (www.mapquest.com) and Rand McNally (www.randmcnally.com) Web sites include interactive capabilities for planning a trip, as well as a service offering maps of numerous cities around the world, down to the street level. The software on the sites can calculate the distance between two points and provide itemized driving directions to any location. You can also click maps of your starting and ending locations to see detailed street maps and places of interest.

You have just started working as a dispatcher for Cross-Country Transport, a new trucking and delivery service based in Cleveland, Ohio. Your first assignment is to plan a delivery of office equipment and furniture from Omaha, Nebraska (at the corner of North 17th and Howard Streets), to Easton, Pennsylvania (corner of Ferry and South 12th Streets). To guide your trucker, you need to know the distance between the two cities and the most efficient route between them. The distance is too long to drive in one day, given the driver will drive for only 10 hours a day. Therefore, you also need to plan one or more stopovers. Use both sites to plan this trip, and select the one you would use in the future, considering ease of use, cost (if any), clarity of the maps, and driving instructions.

Which service did you decide to use, and why? What changes would you suggest to the developers of that site? Consider all aspects of the site, including ease of viewing the route, help planning stopovers, time of route segments, and so forth.

## Video Case

You will find a video case illustrating some of the concepts in this chapter on the Laudon Web site at **www.prenhall.com/laudon** along with questions to help you analyze the case.

## Teamwork

## Describing Management Decisions and Systems

With a group of three or four other students, find a description of a manager in a corporation in *Business Week, Forbes, Fortune,* or another business magazine. Write a description of the kinds of decisions this manager has to make and the kind of information that manager would need for those decisions. Suggest how information systems could supply this information. If possible, use presentation software to present your findings to the class.

# BUSINESS PROBLEM-SOLVING CASE

## Can Information Systems Help Danaher Work Leaner?

Danaher Corporation designs, manufactures, and markets industrial instruments for measurement, display, and control. Danaher divides its $6 billion business into three segments: Professional Instrumentation, Industrial Technologies, and Tools & Components. One of the three focused niche businesses in the Industrial Technologies segment is Danaher Sensors and Controls, a leading manufacturer of process/environmental controls and tools and components.

Danaher is a believer in lean manufacturing, which focuses on continuous improvement of the manufacturing process and elimination of nonproductive time. Lean manufacturers use waste reduction and improved processes to keep inventory levels low, reduce working capital, and fulfill orders faster. Tom Mathis, vice president of supply chain management for Danaher Sensors and Controls, is in charge of keeping his division lean.

Danaher employs the Japanese kanban method of supply chain management instead of relying on a manufacturing resource planning (MRP) system. An MRP reorders parts based on projections of need from the factory floor. The kanban method uses actual need, as observed on the factory floor, to replenish parts just before they run out. Kanban is the Japanese word for "sign" or "signboard."

Manufacturers who use a kanban system for material or parts replenishment affix kanban cards to the fronts of the their storage bins. When a storage bin is low in supply, a worker transports the card to the appropriate storage area to signal the need for more parts. At Danaher, the worker who collects kanban cards from bins is called a pacer. The pacer hand delivers stacks of cards to the factory's buyers, who in turn initiate orders based on the supplier, part number, and quantity information printed on the cards. Each factory in Danaher's Sensors and Controls division requires between 30,000 and 40,000 parts, so the process is taxing. Still, this traditional execution of the kanban system is suitable for operations that are confined to a factory.

However, cards often disappear, by accident or through carelessness. One study of major auto suppliers found that 1 percent of kanban cards was lost every day. As a result, 1 percent of inventory replenishment orders do not go through and the inventory for those supplies runs dry. Production suffers, and both the buyers and the purchasers have to make up for the lost transactions.

Before Mathis joined Danaher in 2002, the company's kanban system was heavily manual. The controls division did maintain a Mapics MRP system solely to track inventory and orders. Other than that use, Danaher purposely avoided any significant applications of information technology to its lean efforts. Over the years, the corporation had acquired a number of smaller companies and succeeded at reducing their inventory levels and increasing their production rates using a relatively pure form of kanban. Danaher effectively scrutinized and improved the flow of materials and parts through its factories without committing large expenditures to technology.

Despite the efficacy of the systems in place, Mathis had to find a way to make his division's operations even leaner. One of his goals was to lower costs by purchasing more supplies from overseas vendors. Mathis knew that this strategy would increase shipping and lead times for parts and that his buyers would have to devote time to researching and procuring new vendors overseas. Therefore, the purchasing process would have to become even more efficient.

Mathis saw this as an opportunity to switch from a card-based kanban system into an electronic kanban system. His main argument was that the flaws of the manual system diverted the attention of key employees away from tasks that were of greater value to the operation. For example, rather than chasing down transaction errors that had been caused by lost cards, materials buyers could be developing supplier relationships and discovering new sources for parts overseas.

An e-kanban system strengthens communications between the manufacturer and its suppliers by eliminating manual processes that are prone to errors. Some manufacturers that do not use e-kanban rely on faxes or e-mailing spreadsheets to signal their suppliers that inventory needs to be refilled. Under the electronic system, the kanban cards on storage containers have bar codes, which factory workers can scan to send an electronic signal to a supplier. There are no faxes to lose, no data entry keying mistakes, and no e-mail attachments to handle. E-kanban orders are usually placed with a blanket purchase order, further diminishing the possibility of errors. The e-kanban system also eliminates problems related to physical distance. Because the manufacturer does not have to deliver physical kanban cards upstream to its supplier, it is much easier to use suppliers that are located far away, especially overseas. Suppliers can log into an e-kanban system to retrieve order notifications, as well as send immediate alerts if they are unable to fulfill an order.

Mathis had a difficult time selling the idea of an e-kanban system at Danaher. His colleagues at the Gurnee, Illinois, plant, which was to be the first launch site, believed that they were too busy keeping the plant running to make such a significant change. Mathis directed a series of planning sessions with the intention of establishing a leaner procurement process. He realized that Danaher did not have the internal resources to support the type of system he wanted to implement.

In late 2002, Mathis began to evaluate products from supply chain management vendors. In early 2003, he settled on SupplyWorks, a vendor based in Bedford, Massachusetts. The SupplyWorks system, SupplyWorks MAX, operates over the Web, with SupplyWorks providing the servers and their administration. This arrangement left Danaher's staff free to pursue supplier procurement goals that Mathis had laid out. However, the implementation of the SupplyWorks suite at the Gurnee plant would be a mix of steps forward and backward.

The first challenge for Danaher was to integrate the plant's Mapics inventory database with the SupplyWorks system. Danaher would reap added value from never having to reprint the cards with new supplier or part quantity information—someone could simply enter the new information in the database and the bar codes would never have to change. Mathis pointed out that employees would save 28 minutes a day that was spent previously updating kanban cards. Other automations made possible by SupplyWorks would increase the staff's availability for strategic initiatives, rather than routine tasks.

The implementation of SupplyWorks began as a pilot program at Gurnee using only a segment of the plant's parts inventory. The results included a 75.6 percent reduction in buyer activities that Mathis had marked as wasteful, which had totaled 105 hours per week. The full deployment at Gurnee, which began in June 2004, did not achieve such a high rate of success. The new system reduced nonproductive time by 57 percent. Although this number seems more than respectable, some Danaher employees viewed the transition with tepid optimism.

A number of technical problems prevented the SupplyWorks system from operating to its potential. With the e-kanban implementation, Gurnee installed a new wireless inventory system to accommodate the scanning of kanban card bar codes. Unfortunately, the physical layout of the Gurnee plant provided a poor environment for radio signals. Radio interference was a common problem.

The problem was exacerbated by untested software in the handheld devices that Danaher's pacers used for scanning. If the pacers lost their connection while uploading data to the inventory database, they didn't know what to do. They often returned to rescan storage bins, which negated the time-saving features of the whole system. SupplyWorks updated the software so that it included connection failure warnings and prompts. The vendor stated that the software was not losing data but that the workers did need assistance to guide them through connection failures. Mathis hoped to solve the wireless connection problem at Gurnee fully by replacing the original Hewlett-Packard handheld units with units from Symbol Technologies, which have stronger radio reception. The three other factories now using the e-kanban system have had far fewer radio reception problems and will keep using their HP handhelds.

Danaher also found fault with the SupplyWorks mechanism for sending e-mail alerts to suppliers. The system sometimes inundated suppliers with unnecessary alerts. In some cases, the system would prompt a supplier to send advance notification of a shipment when the shipment had already arrived at Danaher. SupplyWorks adjusted its software in this case, enabling Danaher to control the alerts. However, in other areas, SupplyWorks was not so keen on customization, preferring updates that could be rolled out for multiple customers. To some Danaher employees, SupplyWorks's size and approach were a little unnerving. The employees described the vendor as energetic but often not prepared to deal with the problems that Danaher presented along the way.

In mid-2005, Mathis remained positive about the experience, both in dealing with SupplyWorks and in making his division leaner. He selected a small vendor because he believed that Danaher would receive better service.

He calculated that a product from a large ERP vendor would have cost twice as much as SupplyWorks MAX. Mathis knew that he set high expectations for the project in order to get approval for it, but he believed that the results would continue to improve and approach those expectations. The percentage of parts that Danaher bought through SupplyWorks was on the rise, whereas material costs and nonproductive time were declining. For its part, in July 2005, SupplyWorks was named a "Supply & Demand Chain Executive 100" solution vendor by *Supply & Demand Chain Executive* magazine for its work with Danaher.

*Sources*: David Carr, "Danaher Corp.: Leaner Machine," *Baseline Magazine*, June 10, 2005; Nancy Bartels, "Lean, in the Most General Sense," *Manufacturing Business Technology*, April 2005; David Drickhamer, "The Kanban E-volution," *Material Handling Management*, March 2005; Sarah Murray and Andrew K. Reese, "The 2005 Supply & Demand Chain Executive 100," *Supply & Demand Chain Executive*, www.sdcexec.com, accessed August 11, 2005; News release, "SupplyWorks Named to *Supply & Demand Chain Executive* 100 List for Productivity Results at Danaher," www.supplyworks.com, July 13, 2005, accessed August 11, 2005; and Danaher Corporation report on Form 10-K.

## Case Study Questions

1. What was the problem that Tom Mathis and Danaher Sensors and Controls needed to solve in this case? What were the surrounding issues of the problem?

2. What solutions were available to solve the problem? Were there any solutions of which Danaher did not think? What are they?

3. How much did Danaher have to change the way it conducted business to take advantage of the SupplyWorks software? What were the changes? What were the obstacles to change?

4. What did the new system do? How did it benefit the business? Were there any negative issues concerning the new system? What were they?

5. What were the results of implementing the new system? Was it a successful solution? Why or why not?

# Achieving Competitive Advantage with Information Systems

**CHAPTER 3**

## STUDENT OBJECTIVES

After completing this chapter, you will be able to:

1. Demonstrate how Porter's competitive forces model helps companies develop competitive strategies using information systems.

2. Demonstrate how the value chain and value web models help businesses identify opportunities for strategic information systems applications.

3. Assess how information systems help businesses use synergies, core competencies, and network-based strategies to achieve competitive advantage.

4. Assess how competing on a global scale and promoting quality enhance competitive advantage.

5. Evaluate the role of business process reengineering (BPR) in enhancing competitiveness.

## CHAPTER OUTLINE

## AMAZON.COM: AN INTERNET GIANT FINE-TUNES ITS STRATEGY

**Amazon.com made Internet history as** one of the first successful enterprises to sell over the Web. It has grown to become one of the largest Internet retailers on earth. In 1995, former investment banker Jeff Bezos took advantage of new business opportunities created by the Internet by setting up a Web site to sell books directly to customers online. There were three million titles in print, and any one physical bookstore could only stock a fraction of them. A "virtual" bookstore could offer a much larger selection of titles. Bezos believed consumers did not need to actually "touch and feel" a book before buying it, and Amazon.com provided online synopses, tables of contents, and reviews to help with selection. Amazon.com was able to charge lower prices than physical bookstores because it maintained very little of its own inventory (relying instead on distributors) and did not have to pay for maintaining physical storefronts or a large retail sales staff.

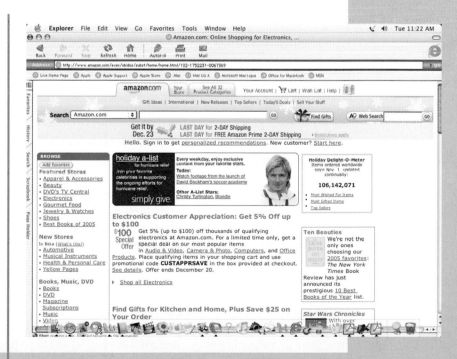

Amazon tried to provide superior customer service through e-mail and telephone customer support, automated order confirmation, online tracking and shipping information, and the ability to pay for purchases with a single click of the mouse using credit card and personal information a customer had provided during a previous purchase. This was called "1-Click" express shopping, and it made the shopping experience even more convenient.

In 1998, Amazon started selling music, CDs, videos, and DVDs, revising its business strategy "to become the best place to buy, find, and discover any product or service available online"—the online Wal-Mart. Its offerings grew to include electronics, toys, home improvement products, video games, apparel, gourmet food, and jewelry. It also introduced Amazon.com Auctions (similar to those offered by eBay), and zShops (online storefronts for small retailers). To service these new product lines, Amazon significantly expanded its warehouse and distribution capabilities and hired large numbers of employees. These moves strained its ability to adhere to its original vision of being a "virtual" retailer with lean inventories, low head count, and significant cost savings over traditional bookstores.

In 2001 and 2002, Amazon tried to increase revenue by cutting prices, offering free shipping, and leveraging its technology infrastructure to provide e-commerce services to other businesses. Amazon's Merchants@ and Amazon Marketplace allow other businesses to fully integrate their Web sites into Amazon's site to sell their branded goods using Amazon's fulfillment and payment systems. Nordstrom, Toys 'R' Us, The Gap, and Target stores use Amazon to sell their goods and then pay Amazon commissions and fees. In the Amazon Marketplace program, individuals are encouraged to sell their used or new goods on Amazon's Web site even when they compete directly with Amazon's sales of the same goods. Sales by third parties now represent 25 percent of Amazon's revenues.

Amazon refined its business model to focus more on efficient operations while maintaining a steady commitment to keeping its 49 million customers satisfied. In early 2001, Amazon closed two of its eight warehouses, laid off 15 percent of its workforce, and consolidated orders from around the country prior to shipping to reduce shipping costs. Amazon used six sigma quality measures to reduce errors in fulfillment. These measures reduced fulfillment costs from 15 percent of revenue in 2000 to 10 percent by 2003.

Amazon has finally become profitable and remains an online retailing powerhouse. But it faces powerful online retail competitors such as eBay and Yahoo! who keep innovating. Amazon is countering with new offerings, such as a digital mapping service with street-level photographs and selling short stories online for 49 cents apiece, along with additional expenditures to improve customer convenience and the shopping experience. The question is this: Can Amazon keep adapting its strategy to remain profitable and powerful? ■

*Sources*: Gary Rivlin, "A Retail Revolution Turns 10," *The New York Times*, July 10, 2005; Shaheen Pasha, "Amazon Has New Stories to Tell," *CNN Money*, August 22, 2005; Chris Gaither, "Amazon.Com Maps Show Street Photos," *Los Angeles Times*, accessed August 16, 2005; Amazon.com, Inc. Form 10-K for the fiscal year ended December 31, 2004, filed with the Securities and Exchange Commission on March 24, 2005; "Tabs on Tech: The Internet," Laurie Kawakami, *The Wall Street Journal*, June 1, 2005; and Mylene Mangalindan, "Amazon Net Falls As Rivals Take Toll," *"The Wall Street Journal*, April 27, 2005.

The story of Amazon.com illustrates some of the ways that information systems help businesses compete—and also the challenges of sustaining a competitive advantage today. When Jeff Bezos and his partners started the company, the Internet was in its infancy. They were among the first to sell over the Web. The question they had to answer was "How can we make money selling over the Web?"

Amazon's initial response was to sell books at lower prices than physical bookstores while providing additional value and customer service. This strategy catapulted Amazon to become one of the first— and largest—Internet retailers. Today, its name is still synonymous with Internet retailing. However, this strategy was not enough to provide adequate revenue growth for profitability. Amazon changed its strategy from being an online bookstore to being an online superstore, selling the same range of goods as Wal-Mart. The move increased its presence on the Internet but raised costs.

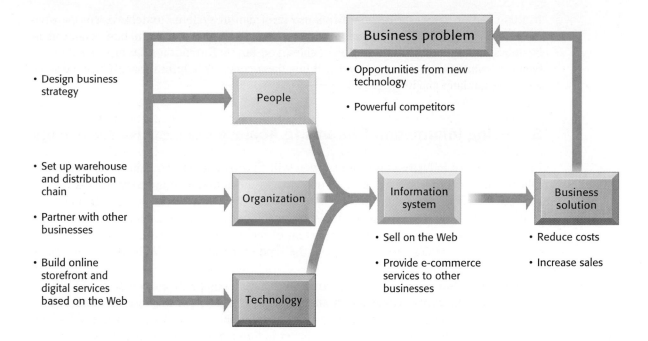

Amazon tried to solve this new set of problems by finding ways to reorganize its business to reduce operational costs and by charging other businesses to use its online storefront to reach new customers. And it has tried to keep innovating with new products while maintaining its brand image of reliability, quality, and high customer service. But the Internet makes it easier for other companies to compete on the same playing field, and Amazon will probably have to continue fine-tuning its strategy to remain competitive.

---

**HEADS UP**

In the past decade, firms using the Internet and the Web, and other kinds of information systems, have created entirely new products and services, and entire new industries and businesses. Other firms have achieved operational excellence and much closer relationships with customers and suppliers. In so doing, these firms often have achieved competitive advantages over others. Every business student and future manager should know about the strategic uses of information technology.

•   If your career is in finance and accounting, you will be working with financial products and services based on information systems, such as ATMs, online financial services, and credit cards.

•   If your career is in human resources, you will be working with systems that help the firm compete by providing information and communication capabilities that lower the cost of managing employees or by organizing jobs and work assignments to reduce operational costs.

•   If your career is in manufacturing, production, or operations management, you will use information systems that help your firm compete by lowering supply chain costs, increasing quality, and enabling the firm to design and bring new products to market more rapidly.

•   If your career is in sales and marketing, you will be working with information systems that analyze vast pools of data for highly targeted marketing campaigns or that generate unique new products and services that the business can sell.

In this chapter, we describe how firms use information systems to achieve competitive advantages over other firms in their industries. We will begin with several basic concepts in business strategy and design, and then show you how information systems contribute to business competitive advantage. You will find these concepts helpful for analyzing the business cases in later chapters.

## 3.1 Using Information Systems to Achieve Competitive Advantage

In almost every industry you examine, you will find that some firms do better than most others. There's almost always a stand-out firm. In the automotive industry, Toyota is considered a superior performer. In pure online retail, Amazon is the leader; in off-line retail Wal-Mart, the largest retailer on Earth, is the leader. In online music, Apple's iTunes is considered the leader with more than 75 percent of the downloaded music market, and in the related industry of digital music players, the iPod is the leader. In Web search, Google is considered the leader.

Firms that "do better" than others are said to have a competitive advantage over others: They either have access to special resources that others do not, or they are able to use commonly available resources more efficiently—usually because of superior knowledge and information assets. In any event, they do better in terms of revenue growth, profitability, or productivity growth (efficiency), all of which ultimately translate into higher stock market valuations than their competitors.

But why do some firms do better than others and how do they achieve competitive advantage? How can you analyze a business and identify its strategic advantages? How can you develop a strategic advantage for your own business? And how do information systems contribute to strategic advantages? Business scholars have come up with several answers to these questions.

### Types of Competitive Advantage

First, let's look at the various ways firms achieve an advantage over other firms. There are four major types of competitive advantage (Greenwald and Kahn, 2005).

#### Barriers to Entry That Restrict Supply

If you have an exclusive contract to a Hollywood movie star, or if you have a patent on a valuable new medicine, then no one else can enter your market space and you can charge high prices. You have a monopoly or a near monopoly on supply.

#### Demand Control

If you have a powerful brand name and customers use your product because of its superior qualities (perceived or real), or if the cost of switching to another competitor's product is high, then you can control customer demand. For instance, switching from the Microsoft Office suite to the competing StarOffice suite, which sells for a much lower price, imposes a very high switching cost on customers who are used to Word and Excel, and their familiar file formats. **Switching cost** refers to the cost of switching from one product to a competing product. About 95 percent of the world's one billion computers use Microsoft's operating system and Office personal productivity products. It is nice to be able to share files with all these other users. Brand names and switching costs allow you to keep prices high and increase profits.

#### Economies of Scale

If you can run your fixed cost plant and equipment at a more efficient scale of operations, say 24 hours a day, versus a competitor running the same plant and equipment only 8 hours a day, you can keep operating costs lower while expanding sales, thereby increasing your profit margins. Firms with national and global markets try to achieve such economies of scale without introducing radically new production processes. Financial service firms heavily dependent on information technology can greatly reduce their cost of operations by merging with other firms, combining back-office operations.

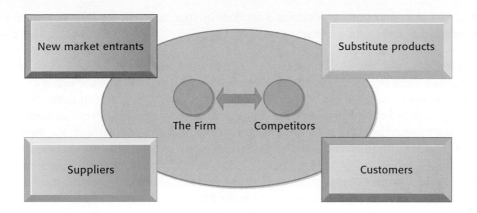

**Figure 3-1**
Porter's Competitive
Forces Model
*In Porter's competitive
forces model, the
strategic position of the
firm and its strategies
are determined not only
by competition with its
traditional direct com-
petitors but also by four
forces in the industry's
environment: new mar-
ket entrants, substitute
products, customers,
and suppliers.*

### Process Efficiency

If you can create new, more efficient production and service processes, either based on special expertise or simply on your superior ability to implement new technologies, then you
will gain a cost advantage over competitors.

But how can you tell whether your business can attain any of these advantages? One
answer to that question is Michael Porter's competitive forces model.

## Porter's Competitive Forces Model

Arguably, the most widely used model for understanding competitive advantage is Michael
Porter's **competitive forces model** (see Figure 3-1). This model provides a general view of
the firm, its competitors, and the firm's environment. Recall in Chapter 2 we described the
importance of a firm's environment and the dependence of firms on environments. Porter's
model is all about the firm's general business environment. In this model, five competitive
forces shape the fate of the firm.

### Traditional Competitors

All firms share market space with other competitors who are continuously devising new, more
efficient ways to produce, introducing new products and services, and attempting to attract
customers by developing their brands and imposing switching costs on their customers.

### New Market Entrants

In a free economy with mobile labor and financial resources, new companies are always
entering the marketplace. In some industries, there are very low barriers to entry, whereas in
other industries, entry is very difficult. For instance, it is fairly easy to start a pizza business
or just about any small retail business, but it is much more expensive and difficult to enter
the computer chip business, which has very high capital costs and requires significant expertise and knowledge that is hard to obtain. New companies have several possible advantages:
They are not locked into old plants and equipment, they often hire younger workers who are
less expensive and perhaps more innovative, they are not encumbered by old worn out brand
names, and they are "more hungry" (more highly motivated) than traditional occupants of an
industry. These advantages are also their weakness: They depend on outside financing for
new plants and equipment, which can be expensive; they have a less experienced workforce;
and they have little brand recognition.

### Substitute Products and Services

In just about every industry, there are substitutes that your customers might use if your prices
become too high. New technologies create new substitutes all the time. Even oil has substitutes: Ethanol can substitute for gasoline in cars; vegetable oil for diesel fuel in trucks; and
wind, solar, coal, and hydro power for industrial electricity generation. Likewise, Internet
telephone service can substitute for traditional telephone service, and fiber-optic telephone
lines to the home can substitute for cable TV lines. And, of course, an Internet music service
that allows you to download music tracks to an iPod is a substitute for CD-based music

stores. The more substitute products and services in your industry, the less you can control pricing and the lower your profit margins.

### Customers

A profitable company depends in large measure on its ability to attract and retain customers (while denying them to competitors), and charge high prices. The power of customers grows if they can easily switch to a competitor's products and services, or if they can force a business and its competitors to compete on price alone in a transparent marketplace where there is little **product differentiation**, and all prices are known instantly (such as on the Internet). For instance, in the used college textbook market on the Internet, students (customers) can find multiple suppliers of just about any current college textbook. In this case, online customers have extraordinary power over used-book firms.

### Suppliers

The market power of suppliers can have a significant impact on firm profits, especially when the firm cannot raise prices as fast as can suppliers. The more different suppliers a firm has, the greater control it can exercise over suppliers in terms of price, quality, and delivery schedules. For instance, manufacturers of laptop PCs almost always have multiple competing suppliers of key components, such as keyboards, hard drives, and display screens.

## Information System Strategies for Dealing with Competitive Forces

So what is a firm to do when it is faced with all these competitive forces? And how can the firm use information systems to counteract some of these forces? How do you prevent substitutes and inhibit new market entrants? There are four generic strategies, each of which often is enabled by using information technology and systems: low-cost leadership, product differentiation, focus on market niche, and strengthening customer and supplier intimacy.

### Low-Cost Leadership

Use information systems to achieve the lowest operational costs and the lowest prices. The classic example is Wal-Mart. By keeping prices low and shelves well stocked using a legendary inventory replenishment system, Wal-Mart became the leading retail business in the United States. Wal-Mart's continuous replenishment system sends orders for new merchandise directly to suppliers as soon as consumers pay for their purchases at the cash register. Point-of-sale terminals record the bar code of each item passing the checkout counter and send a purchase transaction directly to a central computer at Wal-Mart headquarters. The computer collects the orders from all Wal-Mart stores and transmits them to suppliers. Suppliers can also access Wal-Mart's sales and inventory data using Web technology.

*Wal-Mart's continuous inventory replenishment system uses sales data captured at the checkout counter to transmit orders to restock merchandise directly to its suppliers. The system enables Wal-Mart to keep costs low while fine-tuning its merchandise to meet customer demands.*

Because the system replenishes inventory with lightning speed, Wal-Mart does not need to spend much money on maintaining large inventories of goods in its own warehouses. The system also enables Wal-Mart to adjust purchases of store items to meet customer demands. Competitors, such as Sears, have been spending 24.9 percent of sales on overhead. But by using systems to keep operating costs low, Wal-Mart pays only 16.6 percent of sales revenue for overhead. (Operating costs average 20.7 percent of sales in the retail industry.)

Wal-Mart's continuous replenishment system is also an example of an **efficient customer response system**. An efficient customer response system directly links consumer behavior to distribution and production and supply chains. Wal-Mart's continuous replenishment system provides such an efficient customer response. Dell Computer Corporation's assemble-to-order system, described in the following discussion, is another example of an efficient customer response system.

## Product Differentiation

Use information systems to enable new products and services, or greatly change the customer convenience in using your existing products and services. For instance, Google continuously introduces new and unique search services on its Web site, such as Google Maps. By purchasing PayPal, an electronic payment system, in 2003, eBay made it much easier for customers to pay sellers and expanded use of its auction marketplace. Apple created iPod, a unique portable digital music player, plus a unique online Web music service where songs can be purchased for 99 cents. Continuing to innovate, Apple recently introduced a portable iPod video player.

Manufacturers and retailers are starting to use information systems to create products and services that are customized and personalized to fit the precise specifications of individual customers. Dell Computer Corporation sells directly to customers using assemble-to-order manufacturing. Individuals, businesses, and government agencies can buy computers directly from Dell, customized with the exact features and components they need. They can place their orders directly using a toll-free telephone number or by accessing Dell's Web site. Once Dell's production control receives an order, it directs an assembly plant to assemble the computer using components from an on-site warehouse based on the configuration specified by the customer.

Lands' End customers can use its Web site to order jeans, dress pants, chino pants, and shirts custom-tailored to their own specifications. Customers enter their measurements into a form on the Web site, which then transmits each customer's specifications over a network to a computer that develops an electronic made-to-measure pattern for that customer. The individual patterns are then transmitted electronically to a manufacturing plant, where they are used to drive fabric-cutting equipment. There are almost no extra production costs because the process does not require additional warehousing, production overruns, and

*The Internet makes it possible for Spacestore. com to provide a new service selling NASA space theme products online. International sales make up fifteen percent of its business.*

| TABLE 3.1 | | |
|---|---|---|

**TABLE 3.1**

**IS-Enabled New Products and Services Providing Competitive Advantage**

| | |
|---|---|
| Amazon: One-click shopping | Amazon holds a patent on one-click shopping that it licenses to other online retailers |
| Online music: Apple iPod and iTunes | An integrated handheld player backed up with an online library of 1.5 million songs; 900 million songs downloaded so far |
| Golf club customization: Ping | Customers can select from more than one million different golf club options; a build-to-order system ships their customized clubs within 48 hours |
| Online bill payment: CheckFree.com | Forty million households pay their bills online, as of 2005 |
| Online person-to-person payment: PayPal.com | Enables online transfer of money between individual bank accounts and between bank accounts and credit card accounts |

inventories, and the cost to the customer is only slightly higher than that of a mass-produced garment. Fourteen percent of Lands' End shirt and pants sales are now customized. This ability to offer individually tailored products or services using the same production resources as mass production is called **mass customization**.

Table 3.1 lists a number of companies that have developed IS-based products and services that other firms have found difficult to copy, or at least needed a long time to copy.

### Focus on Market Niche

Use information systems to enable a specific market focus, and serve this narrow target market better than competitors. Information systems support this strategy by producing and analyzing data for finely tuned sales and marketing techniques. Information systems enable companies to analyze customer buying patterns, tastes, and preferences closely so that they efficiently pitch advertising and marketing campaigns to smaller and smaller target markets.

The data come from a range of sources—credit card transactions, demographic data, purchase data from checkout counter scanners at supermarkets and retail stores, and data collected when people access and interact with Web sites. Sophisticated software tools find patterns in these large pools of data and infer rules from them that can be used to guide decision making. Analysis of such data drives one-to-one marketing where personal messages can be created based on individualized preferences. Contemporary customer relationship management (CRM) systems feature analytical capabilities for this type of intensive data analysis (see Chapters 2 and 8).

*Information systems make it possible for Ping Inc. to offer customers more than one million custom golf club options with different combinations of club heads, grips, shafts, and lie angles. Ping is able to fulfill many orders within 48 hours.*

Hilton Hotels uses a customer information system called OnQ, which contains detailed data about active guests in every property across the eight hotel brands owned by Hilton. Employees at the front desk tapping into the system instantly search through 180 million records to find out the preferences of customers checking in and their past experiences with Hilton so they can give these guests exactly what they want. OnQ establishes the value of each customer to Hilton, based on personal history and on predictions about the value of that person's future business with Hilton. OnQ can also identify customers who are clearly not profitable. Profitable customers receive extra privileges and attention, such as the ability to check out late without paying additional fees. After Hilton started using the system, the rate of staying at Hilton Hotels rather than at competing hotels soared from 41 percent to 61 percent (Kontzer, 2004).

### Strengthen Customer and Supplier Intimacy

Use information systems to tighten linkages with suppliers and develop intimacy with customers. Chrysler Corporation uses information systems to facilitate direct access from suppliers to its production schedules, and even permits suppliers to decide how and when to ship supplies to Chrysler factories. This allows suppliers more lead time in producing goods. On the customer side, Amazon.com keeps track of user preferences for book and CD purchases, and can recommend titles purchased by others to its customers. Strong linkages to customers and suppliers increase switching costs, and loyalty to your firm.

The Focus on Technology provides another example of a company that has found a way to bind customers. Even though the concrete business is considered to be very inefficient, low-tech, and something of a commodity, Cemex is able to charge customers a premium price because it can deliver just-in-time products. The company used a series of information systems to become a lean, agile machine that can respond immediately to changing customer orders and schedules. As you read this case, try to identify the problem this company

Cemex uses a sophisticated scheduling system to expedite cement delivery. Cemex manages deliveries and all of its manufacturing and production processes from a highly computerized control room.

## FOCUS ON TECHNOLOGY    Cemex Turns a Commodity into a Global Brand

Cemex, based in Monterrey, Mexico, is a century-old company that sells cement and ready-mix concrete products. It has 53 plants around the globe in more than 30 countries. Through acquisitions and organic growth it has been transformed from a local Mexican cement producer into the world's third-largest cement and concrete manufacturer. It is also an industry leader in innovating with information systems.

The concrete business is an asset-intensive, low-efficiency business with unpredictable demand. Cemex dispatchers used to take orders for 8,000 grades of mixed concrete and forward them to six regional mixing plants, each with its own fleet of trucks. Customers routinely changed half of their orders, sometimes only hours before delivery, and these orders might have to be rerouted because of weather changes, traffic jams, or problems with building permits. Cemex's phone lines were often jammed as customers, truckers, and dispatchers tried to get orders straight. Many orders were lost.

Lorenzo Zambrano, a grandson of the founder of the company, took over the business in 1985. Zambrano believed he could overcome the traditional view that cement was a commodity and did not need a special branding. He decided to apply information technology to these problems. He and Cemex chief information officer Gelacio Iniguez developed a series of systems that would enable Cemex to manage unforecastable demand better than its competitors.

Zambrano and Iniguez used ideas gleaned from visits to U.S. companies, such as Federal Express, Exxon, and Houston's 911 emergency dispatch system, to see how other organizations anticipated demand for their services. They built a system linking Cemex delivery trucks to a global positioning system satellite to help dispatchers monitor the location, direction, and speed of every vehicle. This information helps Cemex send the right truck to deliver a specific grade of cement or redirect deliveries when prompted by last-minute changes.

The company has reduced average delivery time from three hours to 20 minutes, realizing huge savings in fuel, maintenance, and personnel costs. Cemex now uses 35 percent fewer trucks to deliver the same amount of cement. Customers are willing to pay premium prices to Cemex because they do not have to keep work crews idle waiting for cement deliveries to show up.

Cemex's production facilities previously operated independently, without precise knowledge of customer demand. A satellite communications system called CemexNet now electronically links all the firm's production facilities and coordinates them from a central clearing-house. Dispatchers know the exact location, speed, and direction of all vehicles at all times and can quickly select the most optimal arrangement of trucks and mixing plant locations to fill an order.

Customers, distributors, and suppliers use the Internet to place orders directly, check shipment delivery times, and review payment records without having to telephone a customer service representative. Zambrano and his managers now have access to almost every detail about Cemex operations within 24 hours, whereas competitors are working with month-old data.

Zambrano built a sophisticated executive information system that enables him to monitor closely from his laptop computer operations in the 35 countries where Cemex operates. If a region is colored green, it is doing well. Yellow signals a potential problem, and red indicates a real problem. Zambrano can then systematically determine the details of any area of interest. At that level of detail, he can even read the e-mail exchanges about a production problem at an individual plant. Sometimes, Zambrano will send an e-mail about production issues to plant workers to let them know he is watching.

Cemex also designed software to make it easier for company executives and plant managers to keep tabs on power use. Managers use the software to plan each month's energy consumption, ensuring that conveyors, electric grinders, and other equipment run mainly during hours of off-peak electricity rates. As a result, Cemex cut its energy bills by 17 percent in the past four years.

Cemex's productivity has outpaced all of its major rivals in Mexico, and production output has grown sixfold since 1985. Its profit margins are higher than its bigger rivals, Zurich-based Holcim Limited and Paris-based Lafarge SA. In an industry known for tough price competition and thin profit margins, Cemex revenue has grown at a rate of 9 percent during the past decade.

*Sources:* Donald A. Marchand, William J. Kettinger, and Rebecca Chung, "The Cemex Way: The Right Balance Between Local Business Flexibility and Global Standardization," International Institute for Management Development, 2005; Mohan Sawhney, "Technology Is the Secret," *Financial Times*, August 23, 2005; www.cemex.com, accessed September 5, 2005; and Andrew Rowsell-Jones, "The Best of Both Worlds," *CIO Australia*, July 12, 2004.

**To Think About:**

What is Cemex's business strategy? What challenges and problems does the company face? What role do information systems play in Cemex's strategy and business model? How much do information systems help Cemex deal with its problems and compete in the industry?

| Strategy | Description | Example |
|---|---|---|
| Low-cost leadership | Use information systems to produce products and services at a lower price than competitors while enhancing quality and level of service | Wal-Mart |
| Product differentiation | Use information systems to differentiate products, and enable new services and products | Google, eBay, Apple, Lands' End |
| Focus on market niche | Use information systems to enable a focused strategy on a single market niche; specialize | Hilton Hotels, Harrah's |
| Customer and supplier intimacy | Use information systems to develop strong ties and loyalty with customers and suppliers | Chrysler Corporation, Amazon.com |

**TABLE 3.2**

**Four Basic Competitive Strategies**

was facing; what alternative solutions were available to management; how well the chosen solution worked; and the people, organization, and technology issues that had to be addressed when developing the solution.

Table 3.2 summarizes the competitive strategies we have just described. Some companies focus on one of these strategies, but you will often see companies pursuing several of them simultaneously. For example, Dell Computer tries to emphasize low cost as well as the ability to customize its personal computers. The Focus on Organizations describes how Southwest Airlines, which formerly competed on the basis of cost, is pursuing a multipronged strategy to stay competitive as it expands into large national markets. As you read this case, try to identify the problem this company was facing; what alternative solutions were available to management; how well the chosen solution worked; and the people, organization, and technology issues that had to be addressed when developing the solution.

Implementing any of these strategies is no simple matter. But it is possible, as evidenced by the many firms that obviously dominate their markets and that have used information systems to enable their strategies. As you will see later in the book, successfully using information systems to achieve a competitive advantage requires a precise coordination of technology, organizations, and people. Indeed, as many have noted with regard to Wal-Mart, Dell, and Amazon, the ability to successfully implement information systems is not equally distributed, and some firms are much better at it than others. It is not simply a matter of purchasing computers and plugging them into the wall socket. We discuss these topics throughout the book.

## The Internet's Impact on Competitive Advantage

The Internet has nearly destroyed some industries and has severely threatened more. The Internet has also created entirely new markets and formed the basis for thousands of new businesses. The first wave of e-commerce transformed the business world of books, music, and air travel. In the second wave, eight new industries are facing a similar transformation scenario: telephone services, movies, television, jewelry, real estate, hotels, bill payments, and software. The breadth of e-commerce offerings grows, especially in travel, information clearinghouses, entertainment, retail apparel, appliances, and home furnishings.

For instance, the printed encyclopedia industry and the travel agency industry have been nearly decimated by the availability of substitutes over the Internet. Likewise, the Internet has had a significant impact on the retail, music, book, brokerage, and newspaper

# FOCUS ON ORGANIZATIONS   Southwest Airlines: New Strategy, New Systems

In a tumultuous time for the airline industry, when some of the major players are taking the hardest hits, Southwest Airlines stands alone in the profit column. It has posted a profit for an unparalleled 32 straight years.

What began as a small Texas airline is now one of the largest airlines in the United States, transporting more than 70 million people each year to 60 cities in the continental United States and Hawaii. Southwest "took off" with a "keep it simple" philosophy that focused on the leisure traveler who was willing to sacrifice luxury for lower airfares and casual service. It used a single style of aircraft (the Boeing 737), alternative airports, reusable boarding passes, and unassigned seating, rapidly turning around its planes when they landed to keep them in the air as much as possible. No domestic airline in the United States has such a low cost structure.

Southwest's approach to information technology was equally no-frills. Unlike other airlines, it did not automate aircraft maintenance, for example, or use systems that analyzed an extensive pool of customer data to improve marketing and customer loyalty. Management did not think Southwest's size justified automation in these areas. Although the airline had digital systems for ticketing and reservations, until recently, getting the boarding pass was a manual operation.

These no-frill days appear to be ending. Southwest is no longer a regional airline and is expanding into markets where the larger carriers, such as Delta, American, and United, operate. It must also compete with JetBlue, which combines low fares with extras, such as more legroom, leather seats, and personal satellite TV screens. In these markets, Southwest has to manage passengers more efficiently, know customers better, and shorten the amount of time that aircraft spend out of service.

Southwest is upgrading its information systems so that, as CEO Gary Kelly puts it, "we can continue to be tops in all categories" and "be the low-fare airline." To provide high-touch customer service, Southwest will have to automate processes that it previously accomplished without technology.

Southwest.com is the company's main sales channel, accounting for more than $3 billion in annual sales, or 65 percent of total revenue. Swabiz.com is a business travel portal the company started in 2000. Southwest moved to e-tickets in the mid-1990s, and today it uses paper tickets for only 5 percent of transactions. Direct e-ticketing saves the airline travel agency commissions, which cost about $10 per booking. Electronic bookings cost at most $1. Customers now have the convenience of obtaining board-ing passes at multiple airport locations or online instead of waiting in a line at the gate.

Southwest's information systems team is also addressing the issue of maintenance modernization. The system has reduced the time that planes are out of service for regular maintenance by 10 to 15 percent. Inspectors detail problems on Panasonic tablets, which wirelessly transmit the problems to a centralized content library that publishes information in real time to kiosks used by maintenance crews. The kiosks reduce the amount of time technicians spend searching for information, which used to take up to 30 to 40 percent of their working days. An improved optimization capability to integrate and analyze scheduling and maintenance systems will ensure that costs are kept low and that maintenance remains a high priority.

Passengers will see a greater presence of self-service kiosks. By replacing the legacy check-in systems, agents will be able to access check-in, ticketing, baggage, and security modules through the kiosk interface, thereby shortening wait time for passengers and reducing data entry keystroking. One way that Kelly measures the level of efficiency at Southwest is by a ratio of employees to aircraft. In 2000, the airline employed about 95 people per aircraft. Today, the number is down to about 70.

Southwest is enhancing its customer systems, which, until recently, held only the transactional records of customers who paid by credit cards, gift cards, or airline vouchers, and obtained e-tickets. An old legacy reservations system contains data on each passenger's specific booking, including those who pay by check or cash. These data will be added to the basic customer data, along with frequent-flier data stored in another system. The combined data will give the airline a broader view of all passengers to alert airport workers to particular passenger requirements, predict market trends and buying habits, and conduct targeted marketing.

*Sources*: Tony Kontzer, "Wings of Change," *InformationWeek*, March 28, 2005, and "Customer Connections," *InformationWeek*, March 14, 2005; Tom Steinert-Threlkeld, "Southwest Airlines: Flying Low," *Baseline*, April 10, 2005; and Susan Carey, "Amid JetBlue's Rapid Ascent, CEO Adopts Big Rivals' Traits," *The Wall Street Journal*, August 25, 2005.

**To Think About:**

What is Southwest Airlines' business strategy? How is Southwest dealing with the current problems plaguing the airline industry? What role do information systems play in Southwest's strategy and business model? How much will information systems help Southwest deal with its problems and compete in the industry?

| Competitive Force | Impact of the Internet |
|---|---|
| Substitute products or services | Enables new substitutes to emerge with new approaches to meeting needs and performing functions |
| Customers' bargaining power | Availability of global price and product information shifts bargaining power to customers |
| Suppliers' bargaining power | Procurement over the Internet tends to raise bargaining power over suppliers; suppliers can also benefit from reduced barriers to entry and from the elimination of distributors and other intermediaries standing between them and their users |
| Threat of new entrants | The Internet reduces barriers to entry, such as the need for a sales force, access to channels, and physical assets; it provides a technology for driving business processes that makes other things easier to do |
| Positioning and rivalry among existing competitors | Widens the geographic market, increasing the number of competitors, and reducing differences among competitors; makes it more difficult to sustain operational advantages; puts pressure to compete on price |

**TABLE 3.3**

**Impact of the Internet on Competitive Forces and Industry Structure**

industries. At the same time, the Internet has enabled new products and services, new business models, and new industries to spring up every day from eBay and Amazon, to iTunes and Google. In this sense, the Internet is "transforming" entire industries, forcing firms to change how they do business.

Because of the Internet, the traditional competitive forces are still at work, but competitive rivalry has become much more intense (Porter, 2001). Internet technology is based on universal standards that any company can use, making it easy for rivals to compete on price alone and for new competitors to enter the market. Because information is available to everyone, the Internet raises the bargaining power of customers, who can quickly find the lowest-cost provider on the Web. Profits have been dampened. Some industries, such as the travel industry and the financial services industry, have been more impacted than others. Table 3.3 summarizes some of the potentially negative impacts of the Internet on business firms identified by Porter.

However, contrary to Porter's somewhat negative assessment, the Internet also creates new opportunities for building brands and building very large and loyal customer bases that are willing to pay a premium for the brand, for example, Yahoo!, eBay, BlueNile, RedEnvelope, Overstock.com, Amazon, Google, and many others. In addition, as with all IT-enabled business initiatives, some firms are far better at using the Internet than other firms are, which creates new strategic opportunities for the successful firms.

## The Business Value Chain Model

Although the Porter model is very helpful for identifying competitive forces and suggesting generic strategies, it is not very specific about what exactly to do, and it does not provide a methodology to follow for achieving competitive advantages. If your goal is to achieve operational excellence, where do you start? Here's where the business value chain model is helpful.

The **value chain model** highlights specific activities in the business where competitive strategies can best be applied (Porter, 1985) and where information systems are most likely to have a strategic impact. This model identifies specific, critical-leverage points where a firm can use information technology most effectively to enhance its competitive position.

**Figure 3-2**
The Value Chain
Model
*This figure provides
examples of systems for
both primary and sup-
port activities of a firm
and of its value partners
that would add a margin
of value to a firm's products or services.*

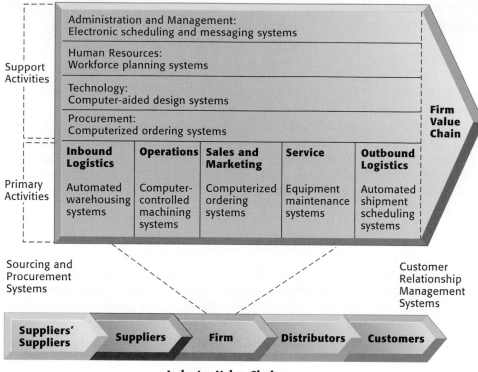

**Industry Value Chain**

The value chain model views the firm as a series or chain of basic activities that add a margin of value to a firm's products or services. These activities can be categorized as either primary activities or support activities (see Figure 3-2).

**Primary activities** are most directly related to the production and distribution of the firm's products and services, which create value for the customer. Primary activities include inbound logistics, operations, outbound logistics, sales and marketing, and service. Inbound logistics includes receiving and storing materials for distribution to production. Operations transforms inputs into finished products. Outbound logistics entails storing and distributing finished products. Sales and marketing includes promoting and selling the firm's products. The service activity includes maintenance and repair of the firm's goods and services.

**Support activities** make the delivery of the primary activities possible and consist of organization infrastructure (administration and management), human resources (employee recruiting, hiring, and training), technology (improving products and the production process), and procurement (purchasing input).

Now you can ask at each stage of the value chain, "How can we use information systems to improve operational efficiency, and improve customer and supplier intimacy?" This will force you to critically examine how you perform value-adding activities at each stage and how the business processes might be improved. You can also begin to ask how information systems can be used to improve the relationship with customers and with suppliers who lie outside the firm value chain but belong to the firm's extended value chain where they are absolutely critical to your success. Here, supply chain management systems that coordinate the flow of resources into your firm, and customer relationship management systems that coordinate your sales and support employees with customers are two of the most common system applications that result from a business value chain analysis. We discuss these enterprise applications in detail later in Chapter 8.

Using the business value chain model will also cause you to consider benchmarking your business processes against your competitors or others in related industries, and identifying industry best practices. **Benchmarking** involves comparing the efficiency and effectiveness of your business processes against strict standards and then measuring performance against those standards. Industry **best practices** are usually identified by consulting companies, research organizations, government agencies, and industry associations as the most successful solutions or problem-solving methods for consistently and effectively achieving a business objective.

Once you have analyzed the various stages in the value chain at your business, you can come up with candidate applications of information systems. Then, once you have a list of candidate applications, you can decide which to develop first. By making improvements in your own business value chain that your competitors might miss, you can achieve competitive advantage by attaining operational excellence, lowering costs, improving profit margins, and forging a closer relationship with customers and suppliers. If your competitors are making similar improvements, then at least you will not be at a competitive disadvantage—the worst of all cases!

### Extending the Value Chain: The Value Web

Figure 3-2 shows that a firm's value chain is linked to the value chains of its suppliers, distributors, and customers. After all, the performance of most firms depends not only on what goes inside a firm but also on how well the firm coordinates with direct and indirect suppliers, delivery firms (logistics partners, such as FedEx or UPS), and, of course, customers.

How can information systems be used to achieve strategic advantage at the industry level? By working with other firms, industry participants can use information technology to develop industry-wide standards for exchanging information or business transactions electronically, which force all market participants to subscribe to similar standards. Such efforts increase efficiency, making product substitution less likely and perhaps raising entry costs—thus discouraging new entrants. Also, industry members can build industry-wide, IT-supported consortia, symposia, and communications networks to coordinate activities concerning government agencies, foreign competition, and competing industries.

Looking at the industry value chain encourages you to think about how to use information systems to link up more efficiently with your suppliers, strategic partners, and customers. Strategic advantage derives from your ability to relate your value chain to the value chains of other partners in the process. For instance, if you are Amazon.com, you would want to build systems that

- Make it easy for suppliers to display goods and open stores on the Amazon site
- Make it easy for customers to pay for goods
- Coordinate the shipment of goods to customers
- Track shipments for customers

In fact, this is exactly what Amazon has done to make it one of the Web's most satisfying online retail shopping sites.

Internet technology has made it possible to create highly synchronized industry value chains called value webs. A **value web** is a collection of independent firms that use information technology to coordinate their value chains to produce a product or service for a market collectively. It is more customer driven and operates in a less linear fashion than the traditional value chain.

Figure 3-3 shows that this value web synchronizes the business processes of customers, suppliers, and trading partners among different companies in an industry or in related industries. These value webs are flexible and adaptive to changes in supply and demand. Relationships can be bundled or unbundled in response to changing market conditions. Firms will accelerate time to market and to customers by optimizing their value web relationships to make quick decisions on who can deliver the required products or services at the right price and location.

**Figure 3-3**
The Value Web
*The value web is a networked system that can synchronize the value chains of business partners within an industry to respond rapidly to changes in supply and demand.*

## Synergies, Core Competencies, and Network-Based Strategies

A large corporation is typically a collection of businesses. Often, the firm is organized financially as a collection of strategic business units and the returns to the firm are directly tied to the performance of all the strategic business units. Information systems can improve the overall performance of these business units by promoting synergies and core competencies.

### Synergies

The idea of synergies is that when the output of some units can be used as inputs to other units, or two organizations can pool markets and expertise, these relationships lower costs and generate profits. Recent bank and financial firm mergers, such as the merger of JP Morgan Chase and Bank One Corporation, Bank of America and FleetBoston Financial Corporation, and Deutsche Bank and Bankers Trust, occurred precisely for this purpose.

One use of information technology in these synergy situations is to tie together the operations of disparate business units so that they can act as a whole. For example, merging with Bank One provided JP Morgan Chase with a massive network of retail branches in the Midwest and Southwest. Information systems would help the merged banks lower retailing costs and increase cross-marketing of financial products.

### Enhancing Core Competencies

Yet another way to use information systems for competitive advantage is to think about ways that systems can enhance core competencies. The argument is that the performance of all business units can increase insofar as these business units develop, or create, a central core of competencies. A **core competency** is an activity for which a firm is a world-class leader. Core competencies may involve being the world's best miniature parts designer, the best package-delivery service, or the best thin-film manufacturer. In general, a core competency relies on knowledge that is gained over many years of experience and a first-class research organization or simply key people who follow the literature and stay abreast of new external knowledge.

Any information system that encourages the sharing of knowledge across business units enhances competency. Such systems might encourage or enhance existing competencies and help employees become aware of new external knowledge; such systems might also help a business leverage existing competencies to related markets.

For example, Procter & Gamble (P&G), a world leader in brand management and consumer product innovation, uses a series of systems to enhance its core competencies. P&G uses an intranet called InnovationNet to help people working on similar problems share ideas and expertise. The system connects those working in research and development (R&D), engineering, purchasing, marketing, legal affairs, and business information systems around the world, using a portal to provide browser-based access to documents, reports, charts, videos, and other data from various sources. In 2001, InnovationNet added a directory of subject matter experts who can be tapped to give advice or collaborate on problem solving and product development, and created links to outside research scientists and 150 entrepreneurs who are searching for new, innovative products worldwide.

P&G sells more than 300 different branded products, with separate lines of business for Fabric and Home Care, Baby and Family Care, Beauty Care, Health Care, and Snacks and Beverages. It now uses custom-developed marketing management software to help all these groups share marketing ideas and data for marketing campaigns. This system supports strategic planning, research, advertising, direct mail, and events, and can analyze the impact of marketing projects on the business.

## Network-Based Strategies

The availability of Internet and networking technology have inspired strategies that take advantage of firms' abilities to create networks or network with each other. Network-based strategies include the use of network economics and a virtual company model.

Business models based on a network may help firms strategically by taking advantage of **network economics**. In traditional economics—the economics of factories and agriculture—production experiences diminishing returns. The more any given resource is applied to production, the lower the marginal gain in output, until a point is reached where the additional inputs produce no additional outputs. This is the law of diminishing returns, and it is the foundation for most of modern economics.

In some situations, the law of diminishing returns does not work. For instance, in a network, the marginal costs of adding another participant are about zero, whereas the marginal gain is much larger. The larger the number of subscribers in a telephone system or the Internet, the greater the value to all participants because each user can interact with more people. It is no more expensive to operate a television station with 1,000 subscribers than with 10 million subscribers. The value of a community of people grows with size, whereas the cost of adding new members is inconsequential.

From this network economics perspective, information technology can be strategically useful. Internet sites can be used by firms to build *communities of users*—like-minded customers who want to share their experiences. This can build customer loyalty and enjoyment, and build unique ties to customers. eBay, the giant online auction site, and iVillage, an online community for women, are examples. Both businesses are based on networks of millions of users, and both companies have used the Web and Internet communication tools to build communities. The more people offering products on eBay, the more valuable the eBay site is to everyone because more products are listed, and more competition among suppliers lowers prices. Network economics can also provide strategic benefits to commercial software vendors. The value of their software and complementary software products increases as more people use them, and there is a larger installed base to justify continued use of the product and vendor support.

Another network-based strategy uses the model of a virtual company to create a competitive business. A **virtual company**, also known as a *virtual organization,* uses networks to link people, assets, and ideas, enabling it to ally with other companies to create and distribute products and services without being limited by traditional organizational boundaries or physical locations. One company can use the capabilities of another company without being physically tied to that company. The virtual company model is useful when a company finds it cheaper to acquire products, services, or capabilities from an external vendor or when it needs to move quickly to exploit new market opportunities and lacks the time and resources to respond on its own.

For example, Calyx and Corolla is a networked virtual organization selling fresh flowers directly to customers, bypassing traditional florists. The firm takes orders over the telephone or from its Web site and transmits them to grower farms. Farmers pick and ship the flowers directly to customers using refrigerated vans supplied by Federal Express. The flowers are delivered a day or two after being picked, weeks fresher than flowers provided by traditional florists.

Fashion companies, such as GUESS, Ann Taylor, Levi Strauss, and Reebok, enlist Hong Kong–based Li & Fung to manage production and shipment of their garments. Li & Fung handles product development, raw material sourcing, production planning, quality assurance, and shipping. Li & Fung does not own any fabric, factories, or machines, outsourcing all of its work to a network of more than 7,500 suppliers in 37 countries all over the world. Customers place orders to Li & Fung over its private extranet. Li & Fung then sends instructions to appropriate raw material suppliers and factories where the clothing is produced. The Li & Fung extranet tracks the entire production process for each order. Working as a virtual company keeps Li & Fung flexible and adaptable so that it can design and produce the products ordered by its clients in short order to keep pace with rapidly changing fashion trends.

## 3.2 Competing on a Global Scale

On the iPod box you will find an interesting statement: "Designed in California." But the iPods are assembled in Asia from parts virtually all made in Asia, except for one important part that is manufactured in the United States and shipped to Asian assembly lines: the central processor. Look closely at your jeans or sneakers. Even if they have a U.S. label, they were probably designed in California and stitched together in Hong Kong or Guatemala using materials from China or India. Call up Microsoft Help, or Verizon Help, and chances are good you will be speaking to a customer service representative located in India.

Consider the path to market for the Hewlett-Packard (HP) ProLiant ML150 server for small businesses, which is illustrated in Figure 3-4. The idea for the product was hatched by HP engineers in Singapore, who did the initial design work. HP headquarters in Houston approved the concept. Contractors in Taiwan did the machine's engineering design and initial manufacture. Final assembly of the server takes place in Singapore, China, India, and Australia (Buckman, 2004).

Foreign trade now accounts for more than 25 percent of the goods and services produced in the United States and even more in Germany and Japan. Today, and even more in the future, the success of your firm will depend on your ability to take advantage of the strategic opportunities in international markets.

### Globalization Opportunities

Globalization has created new opportunities for using information systems to coordinate the work of different parts of the company and to communicate with customers and suppliers. Competing on a global scale has many attractions. In the United States, 250 million consumers above the age of 15 account for $3.7 trillion in retail sales. Impressive numbers. But in the world economy, with a population of 6.4 billion people, there are an estimated 4.6 billion consumers above the age of 15, accounting for an estimated global gross domestic product of $55 trillion, a worldwide retail goods market of about $13.75 trillion, and a worldwide retail services market of about $18 trillion (CIA, 2005; *Statistical Abstract,* 2004; World Bank, 2005).

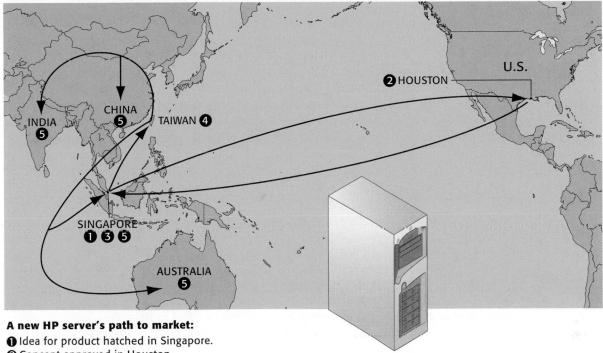

**A new HP server's path to market:**

❶ Idea for product hatched in Singapore.
❷ Concept approved in Houston.
❸ Concept design done in Singapore.
❹ Engineering design in Taiwan, where many computer components are made; initial manufacture by a Taiwanese contractor.
❺ Final assembly in Singapore, Australia, China, and India. Products made in Australia, China, and India are primarily for those markets; machines made in Singapore go to all of Southeast Asia.

## Figure 3-4
A New HP Server's Path to Market
*Hewlett-Packard and other electronics companies assign distribution and production of high-end products to a number of different countries.*

The U.S. labor force has about 140 million workers of all kinds (part time, full time, self-employed, and wage or salary earners), with an average hourly wage of a little more than $17. But the global labor force has about 3.8 billion workers with nonfarm average wages in countries such as India and the People's Republic of China of about 85 cents an hour (International Labor Organization, 2005). In Africa, Bangladesh, Pakistan, and parts of Latin America, wages are even lower. Obviously, firms that can sell their products on a global scale can reach a much larger marketplace; firms that can produce goods and services on a global scale can also achieve extraordinary cost reductions, permitting them to reduce costs or at least keep the costs down. Firms that cannot compete on this global scale are disadvantaged.

### The Internet and Globalization
Up until the mid-1990s, competing on a global scale was dominated by huge multinational firms such as General Electric, General Motors, Toyota, and IBM. These large firms could afford huge investments in factories, warehouses, and distribution centers in foreign countries and proprietary networks and systems that could operate on a global scale. The emergence of the Internet into a full-blown international communications system has drastically reduced the costs of operating on a global scale, deepening the possibilities for large companies but simultaneously creating many opportunities for small and medium-sized firms.

The global Internet, along with internal information systems, puts manufacturing firms in nearly instant contact with their suppliers; Internet telephony permits millions of service calls to U.S. companies to be answered in India and Jamaica, just as easily and cheaply as if the help desk were in New Jersey or California. Likewise, the Internet makes it possible to move very large computer files with hundreds of graphics, or complex industrial designs, across the globe in seconds.

Small firms and medium-sized firms have created an entirely new class of "micromulti-national firms." For instance, Rashima Sinha, a Silicon Valley entrepreneur, has six employ-ees in her software firm: two in the United States and four in India. She manages this global operation using e-mail, Internet telephones, and conference calls. Cosima Spera, another entrepreneur, operates a global mobile phone software and service company with five employees in the United States, eight in Spain, and two in Italy using e-mail, FTP file trans-fers for large-file Web pages, and Internet telephones (Varian, 2005).

BlueTie.com is a small-business e-mail and software service company in Rochester, New York, that, without advertising, has attracted foreign business users that account for 10 per-cent of its revenues. Www.spacestore.com started out wanting to sell NASA memorabilia and souvenirs to the U.S. market and ended up with 15 percent of its business coming from over-seas (Www.bluetie.com, 2005; www.spacestore.com, 2005).

## Global Business and System Strategies

Firms pursuing a global strategy benefit from scale economies and resource cost reduction (usually wage cost reduction). HP spread design and production for the ProLiant ML150 server and other products over multiple countries overseas to reduce logistics, tariffs, and labor costs. Firms with extensive global operations are generally able to operate their facto-ries at higher utilization rates, thereby economizing on fixed capital costs and achieving a lower cost per unit of production. Digital content firms that produce Hollywood movies are able to sell millions more copies of DVDs of popular films by using foreign markets. Internet service firms, such as Google and eBay, are able to replicate their business models and services in multiple countries without having to redesign their expensive fixed-cost information systems infrastructure.

Global operations also unleash other competitive advantages, such as speeding products to market. Hewlett-Packard had its ProLiant ML 150 server assembled in Singapore, China, India, and Australia so that it could be quickly shipped to targeted customers in Asian coun-tries. HP products made in Australia, China, and India are primarily for those markets. Machines made in Singapore go to all of Southeast Asia.

Dräger Safety, a producer of safety products, such as protective suits, breathing equip-ment, and gas detection systems, organized sales, production, shipping, and warehousing along transnational lines. In a **transnational** business organization, sales and production activities are managed from a global perspective without reference to national borders. Dräger is based in Luebeck, Germany, and has more than 40 subsidiaries in Europe, Asia, and North America. The company might take an order in Canada, generate a purchase order in Germany, source the product in the United States, and then ship it to Canada. Dräger uses middleware software that links the enterprise systems from all its subsidiaries to coordinate these operations from so many different locations. Its entire order process is fully automated and can track orders worldwide. Dräger can centralize inventory in each region and ship products directly to customers from the closest regional warehouse. About 93 percent of all orders are delivered to customers within 48 hours. By moving to transnational business processes and information systems, Dräger has been able to reduce its global inventory by 40 percent, slash inventory at sales locations by 95 percent, and lower process costs by 30 percent (Caudron, 2004).

## 3.3 Competing on Quality and Design

Quality has developed from a business buzzword into a very serious goal for many compa-nies. Quality is a form of differentiation. Companies with reputations for high quality, such as Lexus or Nordstrom, are able to charge premium prices for their products and services. Information systems have a major contribution to make in this drive for quality. In the ser-vices industries in particular, quality strategies are generally enabled by superior informa-tion systems and services.

## What Is Quality?

**Quality** can be defined from both producer and customer perspectives. From the perspective of the producer, quality signifies conformance to specifications or the absence of variation from those specifications. The specifications for a telephone might include one that states the strength of the phone should be such that it will not be dented or otherwise damaged by a drop from a four-foot height onto a wooden floor. A simple test will allow this specification to be measured. In order for this producer perspective on quality to pay off, the organization must be willing to take the actions needed to bring its products up to specifications when they fall short.

A customer definition of quality is much broader. First, customers are concerned with the quality of the physical product—its durability, safety, ease of use, and installation. Second, customers are concerned with the quality of service, by which they mean the accuracy and truthfulness of advertising, responsiveness to warranties and ongoing product support. Finally, customer concepts of quality include psychological aspects: the company's knowledge of its products, the courtesy and sensitivity of sales and support staff, and the reputation of the product.

Today, as the quality movement in business progresses, the definition of quality is increasingly from the perspective of the customer. Customers are concerned with getting value for their dollar and product fitness, performance, durability, and support.

Many companies have embraced the concept of **total quality management (TQM)**. Total quality management makes quality the responsibility of all people and functions within an organization. TQM holds that the achievement of quality control is an end in itself. Everyone is expected to contribute to the overall improvement of quality—the engineer who avoids design errors, the production worker who spots defects, the sales representative who presents the product properly to potential customers, and even the secretary who avoids typing mistakes. TQM derives from quality management concepts developed by American quality experts, such as W. Edwards Deming and Joseph Juran, but the Japanese popularized it.

Another quality concept that is being widely implemented today is six sigma, which Amazon.com used to reduce errors in order fulfillment (see the chapter-opening case). **Six sigma** is a specific measure of quality, representing 3.4 defects per million opportunities. Most companies cannot achieve this level of quality but use six sigma as a goal to implement a set of methodologies and techniques for improving quality and reducing costs. Studies have repeatedly shown that the earlier in the business cycle a problem is eliminated, the less it costs the company. Thus, quality improvements not only raise the level of product and service quality but they can also lower costs.

## How Information Systems Improve Quality

Let's examine some of the ways companies face the challenge of improving quality to see how information systems can be part of the process.

### Simplify the Product and the Production Process

The fewer steps in a process, the less time and opportunity for an error to occur. 800-Flowers, a multimillion-dollar company selling flowers by telephone or over the Web, used to be a much smaller company that spent too much money on advertising because it could not retain its customers. It had poor service, inconsistent quality, and a cumbersome manual order-taking process. Telephone representatives had to write each order, obtain credit card approval, determine which participating florist was closest to the delivery location, select a floral arrangement, and forward the order to the florist. Each step in the manual process increased the chance of human error, and the whole process took at least a half hour. Owners Jim and Chris McCann installed a new information system that downloads orders taken in telecenters or over the Web to a central computer and electronically transmits them to local florists. Orders are more accurate and arrive at the florist within two minutes.

### Benchmark

Companies achieve quality by using benchmarking to set strict standards for products, services, and other activities, and then measuring performance against those standards. Companies may use external industry standards; standards set by other companies; internally developed high standards; or some combination of the three. L. L. Bean, the Freeport, Maine, outdoor clothing company, used benchmarking to achieve an order-shipping accuracy of 99.9 percent. Its old batch order fulfillment system could not handle the surging volume and variety of items to be shipped. After studying German and Scandinavian companies with leading-edge order fulfillment operations, L. L. Bean carefully redesigned its order fulfillment process and information systems so that orders could be processed as soon as they were received and shipped within 24 hours.

### Use Customer Demands to Improve Products and Services

Improving customer service, making customer service the number one priority, will improve the quality of the product itself. Delta Airlines decided to focus on its customers, installing a customer care system at its airport gates. For each flight, the airplane seating chart, reservations, check-in information, and boarding data are linked in a central database. Airline personnel can track which passengers are on board regardless of where they checked in and use this information to help passengers reach their destination quickly, even if delays cause them to miss connecting flights.

### Reduce Cycle Time

Studies have shown that probably the best single way to reduce quality problems is to reduce **cycle time**, which refers to the total elapsed time from the beginning of a process to its end. Shorter cycle times mean that problems are caught earlier in the process, often before the production of a defective product is completed, saving some of the hidden costs of producing it. Moreover, because a shorter cycle time is easier to grasp and understand than a longer cycle time, employees are less likely to make mistakes. Finally, finding ways to reduce cycle time often means finding ways to simplify production steps.

Information systems contribute by eliminating critical time delays, as Rockwell International discovered. The Downey, California, defense contractor found that slow communication between its manufacturing plant in Palmdale, California, other Rockwell design facilities, and the Kennedy Space Center in Florida was causing errors to be made or to go undetected as the Space Center staff was preparing for a space shuttle launching. To correct the problem, the Rockwell information systems department installed an automated imaging system and networked it to all relevant sites. Now engineers can transmit design changes instantaneously to wherever they are needed or review problems at the Space Center immediately.

### Improve Design Quality and Precision

Computer-aided design (CAD) software has made a major contribution to quality improvements in many companies, from producers of automobiles to producers of razor blades. A **computer-aided design (CAD) system** automates the creation and revision of designs, using computers and sophisticated graphics software. The software enables users to create a digital model of a part, a product, or a structure and make changes to the design on the computer without having to build physical prototypes.

Clarion Malaysia, a manufacturer of sound and car audio electronics, used a CAD system to reduce the amount of time to design its products while creating new designs and improving their quality. Clarion implemented Catia V5 CAD software from Dassault Systems and IBM. Before implementing this software, Clarion Malaysia's designers needed 14 months to complete a new design model for a product. The software enables the company's design teams to complete a model in less than nine months. The time savings allow the company to be more competitive and to make more design revisions, which has improved product quality. Catia V5 has three-dimensional modeling capabilities that helped Clarion users grasp the nuances of design and see errors that would have been expensive if not detected until production (IBM, 2005).

*Computer-aided design (CAD) systems improve the quality and precision of product design by performing much of the design and testing work on the computer.*

### Improve Production Precision and Tighten Production Tolerances

For many products, quality can be enhanced by making the production process more precise, thereby decreasing the amount of variation from one part to another. CAD software often produces design specifications for tooling and manufacturing processes, saving additional time and money while producing a manufacturing process with far fewer problems. The user of this software is able to design a more precise production system, a system with tighter tolerances, than could ever be done manually. Clarion Malaysia's Catia software provided product data to tooling suppliers, which enabled them to cut tooling preparation time by 60 percent.

## 3.4 Competing on Business Processes

Technology alone is often not enough to make organizations more competitive, efficient, or quality oriented. The organization itself may need to be changed to take advantage of the power of information technology. Sometimes these changes require minor adjustments in work activities, but, often, entire business processes may need to be redesigned. This radical rethinking and redesign of business processes to take advantage of information systems is called **business process reengineering (BPR)**.

American firms have been going through a period of extreme business process reengineering over the past decade, largely driven by information systems and the Internet. In 2004, the business consulting market totaled about $400 billion, and a significant portion of this amount was spent on reengineering companies' business processes.

### Business Process Reengineering

In business process reengineering, the steps required to accomplish a particular task are combined and streamlined to eliminate repetitive and redundant work. To reengineer successfully, the business must ask some basic questions: Why do we do what we do? Why do we do it the way we do? If we could start from scratch, what would we do now and how would we do it? Then the business needs to reinvent these processes anew, without regard to traditional responsibilities of workgroups, departments, or divisions.

Here's how reengineering worked for banks engaged in mortgage processing: The application process for a home mortgage used to take about six to eight weeks and cost about $3,000. The goal of mortgage banks, such as Wells Fargo, Washington Mutual, and JP Morgan Chase, has been to reduce that cost to $1,000 and the time to obtain a mortgage to about one week (see Figure 3-5).

In the past, a mortgage applicant filled out a paper loan application. The bank entered the application into its computer system. Specialists, such as credit analysts and underwriters from

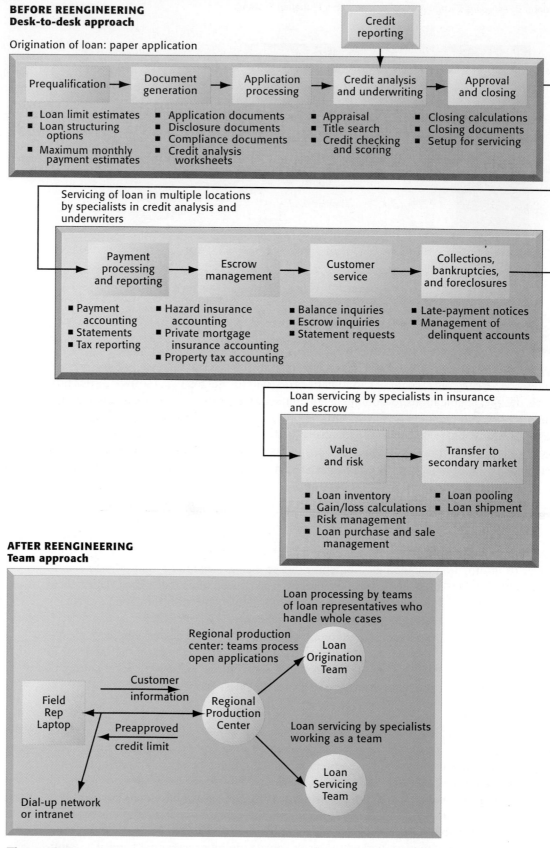

**Figure 3-5**
Redesigning Mortgage Processing in the United States
*By redesigning their mortgage processing systems and the mortgage application process, mortgage banks are able to reduce the costs of processing the average mortgage from $3,000 to $1,000 and reduce the time of approval from six weeks to one week or less. Some banks are even preapproving mortgages and locking interest rates on the same day the customer applies.*

perhaps eight different departments, accessed and evaluated the application individually. If the loan application was approved, the closing was scheduled. After the closing, bank specialists dealing with insurance or funds in escrow serviced the loan. This "desk-to-desk" assembly-line approach might take up to 17 days.

The banks replaced the sequential desk-to-desk approach with a speedier "work cell" or team approach. Now, loan originators in the field enter the mortgage application directly into laptop computers. Software checks the application transaction to make sure that all of the information is correct and complete. The loan originators transmit the loan applications over a network to regional production centers. Instead of working on the application individually, the credit analysts, loan underwriters, and other specialists convene electronically, working as a team to approve the mortgage.

After closing, another team of specialists sets up the loan for servicing. The entire loan application process can take as little as two days. Loan information is easier to access than before, when the loan application could be in eight or nine different departments. Loan originators also can dial into the bank's network to obtain information on mortgage loan costs or to check the status of a loan for the customer.

By radically rethinking their approaches to mortgage processing, mortgage banks have achieved remarkable efficiencies. They have not focused on redesigning a single business process but instead they have reexamined the entire set of logically connected processes required to obtain a mortgage.

To support the new mortgage application process, the banks have implemented work-flow and document management software. **Workflow management** is the process of stream-lining business procedures so that documents can be moved easily and efficiently. Workflow and document management software automates processes, such as routing documents to different locations, securing approvals, scheduling, and generating reports. Two or more people can work simultaneously on the same document, allowing much quicker completion time. Work need not be delayed because a file is out or a document is in transit. And with a properly designed indexing system, users will be able to retrieve files in many different ways, based on the content of the document.

## Steps In Effective Reengineering

One of the most important strategic decisions that a firm can make is not deciding how to use computers to improve business processes but rather understanding what business processes need improvement. When systems are used to strengthen the wrong business model or business processes, the business can become more efficient at doing what it should not do. As a result, the firm becomes vulnerable to competitors who may have discovered the right business model. Considerable time and cost may also be spent improving business processes that have little impact on overall firm performance and revenue. Managers need to determine what business processes are the most important to focus on when applying new information technology and how improving these processes will help the firm execute its strategy.

Management must also understand and measure the performance of existing processes as baselines. If, for example, the objective of reengineering is to reduce time and cost in developing a new product or filling an order, the business needs to measure the time and cost consumed by the unchanged process.

Following these steps does not automatically guarantee that reengineering will always be successful. Many reengineering projects do not achieve breakthrough gains in business performance because the organizational changes are often very difficult to manage. Managing change is neither simple nor intuitive, and companies committed to reengineering need a good change-management strategy (see Chapter 11).

Today's e-business environment involves much closer coordination of a firm's business processes with those of customers, suppliers, and other business partners than in the past. Organizations are required to make business process changes that span organizational boundaries. These interorganizational processes, such as those for supply chain management, not only need to be streamlined but also coordinated and integrated with those of other business partners. In such cases, reengineering will involve many companies working together to jointly redesign their shared processes.

---

**LEARNING TRACKS**

1. If you want to learn more about the challenges of building and using information systems for competitive advantage, you will find a Learning Track on this topic at the Laudon Web site for this chapter.

2. If you want to learn more about international information systems, you will find a Learning Track on this topic at the Laudon Web site for this chapter.

---

## Summary

**1** **Demonstrate how Porter's competitive forces model helps companies develop competitive strategies using information systems.** In Porter's competitive forces model, the strategic position of the firm, and its strategies, are determined by competition with its traditional direct competitors but also they are greatly affected by new market entrants, substitute products and services, suppliers, and customers. Information systems help companies compete by maintaining low costs, differentiating products or services, focusing on market niche, strengthening ties with customers and suppliers, and increasing barriers to market entry with high levels of operational excellence.

**2** **Demonstrate how the value chain and value web models help businesses identify opportunities for strategic information system applications.** The value chain model highlights specific activities in the business where competitive strategies and information systems will have the greatest impact. The model views the firm as a series of primary and support activities that add value to a firm's products or services. Primary activities are directly related to production and distribution, whereas support activities make the delivery of primary activities possible. A firm's value chain can be linked to the value chains of its suppliers, distributors, and customers. Information systems enhance competitiveness at the industry level by promoting the use of standards and industry-wide consortia, and by enabling businesses to work more efficiently with their value partners.

**3** **Assess how information systems help businesses use synergies, core competencies, and network-based strategies to achieve competitive advantage.** Because firms consist of multiple business units, information systems achieve additional efficiencies or enhanced services by tying together the operations of disparate business units. Information systems help businesses leverage their core competencies by promoting the sharing of knowledge across business units. Information systems facilitate business models based on large networks of users or subscribers that take advantage of network economics. A virtual company strategy uses networks to link to other firms so that a company can use the capabilities of other companies to build, market, and distribute products and services.

**4** **Assess how competing on a global scale and promoting quality enhance competitive advantage.** Information systems and the Internet can help companies operate internationally by facilitating coordination of geographically dispersed units of the company and communication with faraway customers and suppliers. Information systems can enhance quality by simplifying a product or service, facilitating benchmarking, reducing product development cycle time, and improving quality and precision in design and production.

**5** **Evaluate the role of business process reengineering (BPR) in enhancing competitiveness.** Organizations often have to change their business processes in order to execute their business strategies successfully. If these business processes use technology, they can be redesigned to make the technology more effective. BPR combines and streamlines the steps in a business process to eliminate repetitive and redundant work and to achieve dramatic improvements in quality, service, and speed. BPR is most effective when it is used to strengthen a good business model and when it strengthens processes that have a major impact on firm performance.

## Key Terms

| | | |
|---|---|---|
| Benchmarking, 89 | Efficient customer response | Switching cost, 78 |
| Best practices, 89 | system, 81 | Total quality management |
| Business process | Mass customization, 82 | (TQM), 95 |
| reengineering (BPR), 97 | Network economics, 91 | Transnational, 94 |
| Competitive forces model, 79 | Primary activities, 88 | Value chain model, 87 |
| Computer-aided design | Product differentiation, 80 | Value web, 89 |
| (CAD) system, 96 | Quality, 95 | Virtual company, 91 |
| Core competency, 90 | Six sigma, 95 | Workflow management, 99 |
| Cycle time, 96 | Support activities, 88 | |

## Review Questions

**3.1** Describe the four different kinds of competitive advantage for businesses.

**3.2** What is Porter's competitive forces model? How does it work? What does it explain about competitive advantage?

**3.3** What are four competitive strategies enabled by information systems that firms can pursue? How can information systems support each of these competitive strategies? Give examples.

**3.4** What is the value chain model? How can it be used to identify opportunities for information systems?

**3.5** What is the value web? How is it related to the value chain? How does it help identify opportunities for strategic information systems?

**3.6** How has the Internet changed competitive forces and competitive advantage?

**3.7** How do information systems promote synergies and core competencies? How does this enhance competitive advantage?

**3.8** How can businesses benefit by using network economics?

**3.9** What is a virtual company? What are the benefits of pursuing a virtual company strategy?

**3.10** How has globalization increased opportunities for businesses? Why do firms pursue a global strategy?

**3.11** What is quality? Compare the producer and consumer definitions of quality.

**3.12** Describe the various ways in which information systems can improve quality.

**3.13** What is business process reengineering (BPR)? How does it help firms become more competitive?

**3.14** What is workflow management? How is it related to BPR?

**3.15** What steps should companies take to make sure BPR is successful?

## Discussion Questions

**3.1** It has been said that there is no such thing as a sustainable competitive advantage. Do you agree? Why or why not?

**3.2** What are some of the issues to consider in determining whether the Internet would provide your business with a competitive advantage?

## Application Software Exercise

### Database Exercise: Using a Database for Strategic Business Development

Software skills: Database querying and reporting; database design

Business skills: Reservation systems; customer analysis

The Presidents' Inn is a small three-story hotel on the Atlantic Ocean in Cape May, New Jersey, a popular northeastern U.S. resort. Ten rooms overlook side streets, 10 rooms have bay windows that offer limited views of the ocean, and the remaining 10 rooms in the front of the hotel face the ocean. Room rates are based on room choice, length of stay, and number of guests per room. Room rates are the same for one to four guests. Fifth and sixth guests must pay an additional $20 charge each per day. Guests staying for seven days or more receive a 10 percent discount on their daily room rates.

Business has grown steadily during the past 10 years. Now totally renovated, the inn uses a romantic weekend package to attract couples, a vacation package to attract young families, and a weekday discount package to attract business travelers. The owners currently use a manual reservation and bookkeeping system, which has caused many problems. Sometimes two families have been booked in the same room at the same time. Management does not have immediate data about the hotel's daily operations and income.

Use the information provided in this description and in the database tables on the Laudon Web site for Chapter 3 to develop reports that would provide information to help management make the business more competitive and profitable. The database and related queries should be designed to make it easy to identify information, such as the average length of stay per room type, the average number of visitors per room type, and the base income per room (i.e., length of visit multiplied by the daily rate) during a specified period of time.

After identifying the preceding information, write a brief report describing what the database information reveals about the current business situation. For example, what is the strongest customer base? Which specific business strategies might be pursued to increase room occupancy and revenue? How could the database be improved to provide better information for strategic decisions?

## Performing a Competitive Analysis for Dirt Bikes

Business skills: Value chain and competitive forces analysis; business strategy formulation

Dirt Bikes's management would like to be sure it is pursuing the right competitive strategy. You have been asked to perform a competitive analysis of the company using the Web to find the information you need. Prepare a report that analyzes Dirt Bikes using the value chain and competitive forces models. Your report should include the following:

1. Which activities at Dirt Bikes create the most value?
2. How does Dirt Bikes provide value to its customers?
3. Who are Dirt Bikes's major competitors? How do their products compare in price to those of Dirt Bikes's products? What are some of the product features they emphasize?
4. What are the competitive forces that can affect the industry?
5. What competitive strategy should Dirt Bikes pursue?
6. (Optional) Use electronic presentation software to summarize your findings for management.

## Building Internet Skills

### Configuring and Pricing an Automobile

This project will help develop your Internet skills in researching product information and evaluating Web sites for auto sales.

Your current seven-year-old car has tried your patience one too many times and you decide to purchase a new automobile. You have been interested in a Ford family car and want to investigate the Ford Taurus (if you are personally interested in another car, domestic or foreign, investigate that one instead). Go to the Web site of CarsDirect (www.carsdirect.com) and begin your investigation. Locate the Ford Taurus. Research the various specific automobiles available in that model and determine which you prefer. Explore the full details about the specific car, including pricing, standard features, and options. Locate and read at least two reviews if possible. Investigate the safety of that model based on the U.S. government crash tests performed by the National Highway Traffic Safety Administration if those test results are available. Explore the features for locating a vehicle in inventory and purchasing directly. Finally, explore the other capabilities of the CarsDirect site for financing.

Having recorded or printed the information you need from CarsDirect for your purchase decision, surf the Web site of the manufacturer, in this case, Ford (www.ford.com). Compare the information available on Ford's Web site with that of CarsDirect for the Ford Taurus. Be sure to check the price and any incentives being offered (which may not agree with what you found at CarsDirect). Next, find a dealer on the Ford site so that you can view the car before making your purchase decision. Explore the other features of Ford's Web site.

Try to locate the lowest price for the car you want in a local dealer's inventory. Which site would you use to purchase your car? Why? Suggest improvements for the sites of CarsDirect and Ford.

## Video Case

You will find a video case illustrating some of the concepts in this chapter on the Laudon Web site at **www.prenhall.com/laudon** along with questions to help you analyze the case.

## Teamwork

### Identifying Opportunities for Strategic Information Systems

With a group of three or four students, select a company described in *The Wall Street Journal*, *Fortune*, *Forbes*, or another business publication. Visit the company's Web site to find additional information about that company and to see how the firm is using the Web. On the basis of this information, identify important business processes and its business strategy. Suggest information systems that might give that particular business a competitive advantage, including those based on Internet technology, if appropriate. If possible, use electronic presentation software to present your findings to the class.

## BUSINESS PROBLEM-SOLVING CASE

### Can Blockbuster Stand Up to Netflix?

Dominating the video rental business used to be a relatively simple task for Blockbuster Inc. When Blockbuster entered the scene in 1985, the industry consisted mostly of independent, mom-and-pop-style stores whose entire reach may have been two towns or a few city blocks. In its first 20 years of business, the rental giant opened 9,100 stores in 25 countries, gaining a market share that has been enjoyed by few companies in any industry.

Blockbuster equipped each of its video rental stores with custom software it had designed to simplify rental and sale transactions. An automated point-of-sale system uses a laser bar code scanner to read data from items being rented or sold and from a Blockbuster customer's identification card. These data are transmitted to Blockbuster's corporate computer center. Management uses these data to monitor sales and to analyze the demographics, and rental and sales patterns for each store to improve its marketing decisions.

Blockbuster's early success was based on video tape rentals. The company transitioned from VHS tapes to DVDs with little difficulty. Traditionally, the movie studios' wholesale price for video tapes of movies available for rental was $80 to $90. The price often deterred consumers from purchasing movies and directed them toward rental stores. DVDs were much cheaper to produce, with a wholesale price around $20. The price break motivated far more consumers to buy their own copies of movies rather than renting them for a few days. By 2004, estimates of the U.S. video rental market varied from nearly $7 billion of business per year to $9 billion; Blockbuster possessed a 40 percent share of that market. Video sales, however, had increased to around $16 billion.

The greatest threat to Blockbuster's viability came from the emergence of a new business model in the video rental market. Launched in 1998, Netflix Inc. intended to cater to those video rental customers who valued convenience above all else. First, the upstart eliminated the need for a physical store. All interactions between Netflix and its customers took place on the Internet and through the postal service. Users could go online and create a wish list of movies they wanted to rent. For a monthly service fee, Netflix mailed up to three movies at a time, which the customer could keep for as long as he or she wanted without incurring late charges. When finished with a movie, the customer mailed it back to Netflix in pre-stamped packaging provided by the company. Returning a movie prompted Netflix to send the next title on the customer's wish list. For $19.95 a month, Netflix customers had access to thousands of movie titles without leaving their homes.

According to Kagan Research LLC, revenues from online movie rentals, which were basically nonexistent in 1998, rose to $522 million in 2004. Kagan projected that the total revenue would approach $1 billion in 2005 and $3 billion by 2009. As Netflix caught on and its subscription model became popular, Blockbuster faced a new type of competitor. Unlike the performances of traditional competitors, Hollywood Entertainment and Movie Gallery, Netflix's gains in market share, from 2 to 7 percent between 2003 and 2004, gave Blockbuster true cause for concern.

To compete in the changing marketplace, Blockbuster made some dramatic changes in its business beginning in 2003. They include an online rental service; Movie Pass, a monthly subscription service for in-store customers; Game Pass, a subscription service for video games; a trading service for movies and games; and the infamous "No More Late Fees" program. The entire question of how to address a new source of competition was a complicated matter. Blockbuster could have chosen to launch an online rental store similar to Netflix and leave it at that. Or, the company could have focused only on its traditional business in an attempt to lure customers back from the rising online tide. Instead, with the initiatives previously mentioned, Blockbuster tried to do both.

Blockbuster's $100 million increase in capital expenditures from 2003 to 2004 hints at the scale of the restructuring of the business. Many of those millions found their way to the information technology department, which took Netflix on directly by establishing Blockbuster's own online subscription service. This venture required Blockbuster to construct a new business model within its existing operations. Rather than meld the two channels, Blockbuster created a new online division with its own offices near corporate headquarters in Dallas.

Part of Blockbuster's initial strategy for defeating the competition was to undercut Netflix in both pricing and distribution. Blockbuster set the price for its three-movies-at-a-time monthly subscription at $19.99, which was, at the time, two dollars less than Netflix's competing plan. Blockbuster had a strategic advantage in distribution as well. Netflix was serving its customers from 35 distribution centers around the country. Blockbuster had 30 such facilities but also had 4,500 stores in the United States to deliver DVDs to most of its customers in only a day or two at lower shipping costs. Blockbuster also enticed online customers to maintain a relationship with the physical stores by offering coupons for free in-store rentals. Blockbuster's original intent was to integrate the online and in-store services so that customers could float back and forth between the two channels with no restrictions. However, the disparate requirements for revenue recognition and inventory management have so far been too complex to make the plan a reality.

After a year in existence, the report card on Blockbuster's online store was mixed. The service had acquired one million subscribers and the company hoped to double that number within seven months or so. At the same time, Netflix had surpassed three million sub-scribers and was on its way to four million by the end of the year. Blockbuster continued to pursue gains through pricing, at one point lowering its three-movie plan to $14.99 per month versus $17.99 at Netflix. Both companies offer plan variations such as unlimited rentals of one DVD at a time for $9.99 per month and two at a time with a limit of four per month for $11.99.

In September 2005, research firm SG Cowen declared that Blockbuster's online DVD rental service "remains inferior" to Netflix. The researcher stated that Blockbuster had improved on movie availability but actually fell further behind in ratings of its user interface. The evaluation by SG Cowen came on the heels of rocky financial reports for Blockbuster. For the second quarter of 2005, Blockbuster posted a loss of $57.2 million, which was double the loss predicted on Wall Street. In comparison, the same quarter in 2004 brought a profit of $48.6 million. The news prompted an 11 percent drop in Blockbuster's stock price, which had peaked in 2002.

The reasons behind Blockbuster's losses are numerous, and include expenditures and loss of business as a result of competition. Blockbuster also endured an expensive split with Viacom in 2004 in which the communications and entertainment giant demanded a special $5-per-share payout. However, Blockbuster's most costly change was likely the "No More Late Fees" campaign it launched in January 2005. The goal of the program was to lure more customers and position Blockbuster better in the market alongside Netflix, which never charged late fees. However, the program may have created more problems than it solved. Blockbuster did measure an increase in in-store rentals after eliminating late fees, but early returns did not suggest that the increase offset the $250 million to $300 million in annual late fee revenue that was no longer being collected.

The "No More Late Fees" program also turned into a public relations problem for Blockbuster. Customers assumed that no late fees meant no due dates and no extra charges. They were outraged that Blockbuster was not more forthcoming about the fine print of the policy. In truth, customers had seven days to return a rental without incurring a charge. After seven days, Blockbuster automatically charged the customer's credit card with the full sale price of the movie. At that point, the customer had an additional 30 days to return the movie for a credit of the sale price minus a small restocking fee. More confusion was created when some Blockbuster stores declined to participate in the program. In the end, Blockbuster was forced to embark on a new multimedia advertising campaign to make the details of the program more transparent and to fend off false advertising claims filed by the attorneys general of several states.

"No More Late Fees" presented a fresh set of challenges for Blockbuster's information systems department. The 10-year-old on-site Digital Equipment Corp. Alpha servers in some stores had difficulty recognizing the new late fee rules. Additionally, programmers had to code the rules in such a way that nonparticipating stores could enforce late fees. Many of these stores adjusted their fee schedules so that late returns were charged only by the day rather than by a full rental period. On top of these adjustments, the information systems department had to closely watch how all of these changes and new programs affected inventory, rental volume, and sales. CIO John Polizzi summed up the IT challenge by saying, "When you go through 50 states, and 25 countries and 9,100 stores globally, understanding all those variables, and making it effective for the people who have to account for the supply chain, is a key part of what we have to do through IT."

Well-known corporate raider Carl Icahn took advantage of Blockbuster's low share price and acquired 9 percent of the company, entitling him to a position on the board of directors. Icahn harshly criticized CEO John Antico's business strategy. Icahn believed that Blockbuster's new initiatives, such as online rentals, were too expensive and too risky. He believed that the company should take advantage of its prevailing position in the bricks-and-mortar rental industry, even if that industry were slowly dying. Icahn brought a sense of financial stability to Blockbuster.

Despite the presence of Icahn, Antico maintained that online rentals were the only segment of the industry open to growth. He stated that the company would be profitable in the fourth quarter of 2005 and in the fiscal year 2006. He also expected the company to recover from the loss of late fee revenue by the first part of 2006. Stacy Widlitz, an analyst with Fulcrum Global Partners, disputed this view, saying, "I don't think they will ever make up for the late fee loss."

Blockbuster watched as Wal-Mart, the largest retailer in the world, failed at both in-store and online video rentals. Wal-Mart retreated from the rental market to focus on selling DVDs at low prices. Developments such as this reinforced Antico's desire to be aggressive with innovations. Blockbuster plans to expand its in-store DVD trading program as well as its focus on new markets, such as video game rentals. Still, other threats loom. Fifteen million cable subscribers use video-on-demand (VOD) technology to watch movies and programs that are not yet available on DVD. TiVo and similar digital video recorders combined with VOD could make the rental of movies obsolete. Some analysts still insist that the economics do not make sense for movie studios to abandon

DVD sales, which account for 50 percent of their profits, in favor of VOD. And technology does not currently permit the bandwidth for VOD suppliers to provide nearly the number of titles that Blockbuster can. Down the road, however, Blockbuster likely will have to address VOD, especially if the studios can eliminate companies like Blockbuster as an intermediary.

In the meantime, Antico wants Blockbuster to stay very close to the cutting edge of technology in his industry. Doing so, he believes, will enable the company to replace directly any rental revenues lost to new technology. Meanwhile, add Amazon to the list of competitive threats on which Blockbuster must also keep a careful eye. Amazon.com already operates an online movie rental service in the United Kingdom. Could there be another player to compete with Blockbuster and Netflix? Or could a new partnership shake up the industry again?

*Sources:* Janet Rae-Dupree, "Blockbuster: Movie Business Remains a Moving Target," *CIO Insight,* August 10, 2005; Rick Aristotle Munarriz, "Blockbuster Keeps the Change," Fool.com, accessed September 2, 2005; Gina Keating and Brad Dorfman, "Blockbuster Posts Loss, Drops Forecast, Stock Hit," Reuters, August 9, 2005; Greg Levine, "Blockbuster's Antico Faces Netflix—And Icahn," Forbes.com, accessed August 9, 2005; Teresa F. Linderman, "Nine Area Blockbuster Stores Say Yes to Late Fees," *Pittsburgh Post-Gazette,* August 26, 2005; Seth Sutel, "Viacom to Shed Blockbuster Stake," The Associated Press, February 10, 2004; Peter Kang, "Blockbuster 'Remains Inferior' to Netflix," Forbes.com, accessed September 7, 2005; Dinesh C. Sharma, "Blockbuster Enters Online DVD Rental Business," cnetNews.com, accessed August 11, 2004; Michael Kanellos, "Blockbuster's Brick-and-Mortar Netflix Defense," cnetNews.com, accessed October 27, 2004; Whitney Matheson, "Pop Candy–On the Tube, Demands Are in Season," *Yahoo News,* August 24, 2005; and Blockbuster 10-K Report, March 29, 2005.

### Case Study Questions

1. What is Blockbuster's business model? How successful has it been?
2. What industry and technology forces have challenged that business model? What problems have they created?
3. Is Blockbuster developing successful solutions to its problems? Are there other solutions it should have considered?
4. Do you think Blockbuster will succeed in the future? Explain your answer.

# Information Technology Infrastructure

## PART II

**P**art II provides the technical foundation for understanding information systems by examining hardware, software, databases, networking technologies, and tools and techniques for security and control. This part answers questions such as these: What technologies and tools do businesses today need to accomplish their work? What do I need to know about these technologies to make sure they enhance the performance of my firm? How are these technologies likely to change in the future?

# IT Infrastructure: Hardware and Software

CHAPTER 4

## STUDENT OBJECTIVES

After completing this chapter, you will be able to:

1. Identify and describe the components of IT infrastructure.

2. Identify and describe the major types of computer hardware, data storage, and input and output technology.

3. Identify and describe the major types of computer software used in business.

4. Assess contemporary hardware and software trends.

5. Evaluate the principal issues in managing hardware and software technology.

## CHAPTER OUTLINE

## DREAMWORKS ANIMATION TURNS TO TECHNOLOGY FOR PRODUCTION SUPPORT

**Can technology help DreamWorks Animation** do better? Its management certainly sees it as a key factor in their success. It uses world-class creative talent and advanced computer technology to produce such successful computer-generated (CG) animated films as *Shrek, Shrek 2, Shark Tale,* and *Madagascar.* To date, *Shrek 2* is the third-highest-grossing movie ever, and the number one animated film of all time.

Nevertheless, DreamWorks has plenty of competition. Pixar Studios, DreamWorks' archrival in computer animation, has prospered from a string of six blockbuster hits, including *The Incredibles, Finding Nemo* and *Monsters Inc.* Computer animation house

Blue Sky Studios is another competitor, as is Disney. Sony Pictures Entertainment and Lucasfilm have also begun producing computer-animated films.

To gain an edge in this fiercely competitive market, DreamWorks Animation has set out to make entertaining films that appeal to all audiences, while leveraging the latest technology and finest talent available. With this strategy in mind, the company established a very ambitious production schedule that no other studio has ever tried before—the release of two animated movies per year. In order to meet this schedule, DreamWorks' staff often find themselves working on more than one movie at the same time, sharing technology among the various projects, and scaling up to work on multiple features.

How is DreamWorks able to make this happen? One of the solutions is to use the finest technology available. DreamWorks has implemented a high-speed network to link the powerful computers required for animation for three key animation pipelines, two in Los Angeles and one in Redwood City, California. A sophisticated video-teleconferencing system that projects nearly life-size images on the wall enables all three groups to collaborate as never before.

Additionally, DreamWorks animators use proprietary software developed in-house called EMO for nearly every stage of their work. In DreamWorks' *Madagascar,* this software enabled animators to adopt traditional "squash & stretch" techniques and place their characters in a digital environment. The software made each frame in *Madagascar* exquisitely detailed, right down to the animals' fur. According to the company's CEO Jeffrey Katzenberg, "Technically, we couldn't have made this movie a year ago."

DreamWorks Animation's management believes that its exclusive software and other technology investments will pay off. DreamWorks Animation's investments in technology are leveraged across all pipelines and all future films as well. To render a CG film, DreamWorks technicians use a network of 2,700 Hewlett-Packard (HP) processors running the Linux operating system, which are organized to act as a single computer system that is distributed among the company's studios and an HP research lab facility in Palo Alto, California.

At the end of the day, it takes approximately 400 artists, animators, and technicians, over 200 characters modeled and surfaced, 15 terabytes of disk, 2700 processors, and over 10 million CPU rendering hours and 18 months of core production to complete any one film. DreamWorks Animation has orchestrated its people, processes, and physical assets into an effective balance that produces world class CG content effectively and efficiently. ▪

*Sources:* Aaron Ricadela, "High-Tech Reveries," *InformationWeek*, May 23, 2005; www.dreamworksanimation.com, accessed September 29, 2005; and DreamWorks Animation, December 2, 2005.

**D**reamWorks Animation has an enviable track record in producing successful high-quality, computer-generated animated films. But it also has a series of formidable competitors and a finicky mass audience to please. It was not as profitable as it could be.

DreamWorks could have chosen a solution that focused on assembling better creative talent than its competitors. But even with superior "people" resources, DreamWorks would have been hampered by the limitations of commercially available rendering software. Management believed that solution would not be sufficient to produce better animations than its competitors or to produce films more rapidly. Instead, DreamWorks decided to outclass its competitors by investing heavily in computer hardware and software to increase animation quality and to produce animated films more rapidly.

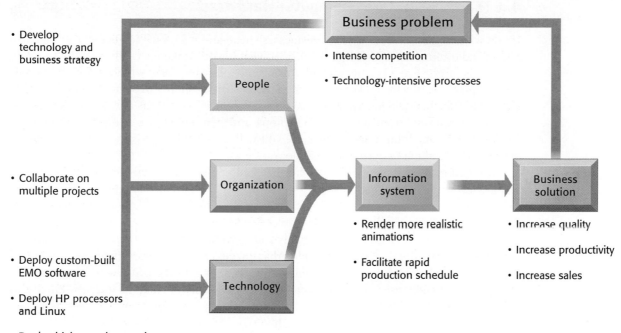

• Develop technology and business strategy

• Collaborate on multiple projects

• Deploy custom-built EMO software

• Deploy HP processors and Linux

• Deploy high-speed network

**People**

**Organization**

**Technology**

**Business problem**

• Intense competition

• Technology-intensive processes

**Information system**

• Render more realistic animations

• Facilitate rapid production schedule

**Business solution**

• Increase quality

• Increase productivity

• Increase sales

---

**HEADS UP**

This chapter describes the kind of software and hardware you will need to operate a business. In your business career, you will inevitably be making decisions about what information technology to buy, from whom to buy it, and how much to spend for it. You'll need to know how to select technology that enhances the performance of your business, is cost-effective, and is appropriate for the kind of work you will be doing.

•    If your career is in accounting and finance, you will be working with application software packages for corporate accounting, tax calculations, payroll processing, or investment planning.

•    If your career is in human resources, you will be evaluating software productivity tools for employees and arranging for training so that employees can use hardware and software effectively.

•    If your career is in manufacturing, production, or operations management, you will be using applications based on client/server computing to control the flow of work on the factory floor and workstations for product design.

•    If your career is in sales and marketing, you will be using hardware and software technologies that provide customers and sales staff with rapid access to data collected by digital scanners and other input technologies.

---

This chapter provides an overview of the computer hardware and software technology and services that are typically used in business. We first introduce the concept of information technology (IT) infrastructure and briefly describe infrastructure components. Next we discuss computer hardware and software components of IT infrastructure and the role they play in business. Finally, we examine the most important issues in managing hardware and software technologies.

## 4.1 IT Infrastructure: Computer Hardware

If you want to know why American businesses spend about $1.8 trillion every year on computing and information systems, just consider what it would take for you personally to set up a business or manage a business today. Businesses today require a wide variety of computing equipment, software, and communications capabilities simply to operate and solve basic business problems. Obviously, you need computers, and, as it turns out, a wide variety of computers ranging from desktops to laptops and handhelds, are available. If you are employed by a medium to large business, you will also need larger server computers, perhaps a minicomputer or even a mainframe.

You will also need plenty of software. Each computer will require an operating system and a wide range of application software capable of dealing with spreadsheets, documents, and data files. Unless you're a single-person business, you'll most likely want to have a network to link all the people in your business together and perhaps your customers and suppliers. As a matter of fact, you will probably want several networks: a local-area network for employees physically in your office and perhaps access to a wireless network so employees can share e-mail and computer files while they are out of the office. You will also, no doubt, want all your employees to have access to the telephone network and the Internet. Finally, to make all this equipment and software work harmoniously, you'll need the services of trained people to help you run and manage this technology.

All of these elements we have just described combine to make up the firm's information technology (IT) infrastructure, which we first defined in Chapter 1. A firm's IT infrastructure provides the foundation, or platform, for supporting all the information systems in the business.

### Infrastructure Components

IT infrastructure today is composed of five major components: computer hardware, computer software, data management technology, networking and telecommunications technology, and technology services (see Figure 4-1). These components must be coordinated with each other.

#### Computer Hardware

Computer hardware consists of technology for computer processing, data storage, input, and output. This component includes large mainframes, servers, midrange computers, desktop and laptop computers, handheld personal digital assistants (PDAs), and mobile devices for

**Figure 4-1**

IT Infrastructure Components

*A firm's IT infrastructure is composed of hardware, software, data management technology, networking technology, and technology services.*

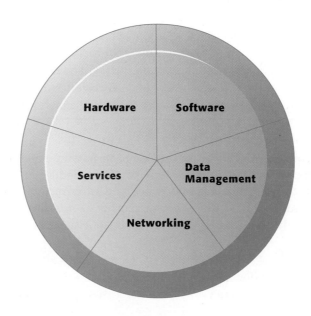

accessing corporate data and the Internet. It also includes equipment for gathering and inputting data, physical media for storing the data, and devices for delivering the processed information as output.

### Computer Software

Computer software includes both system software and application software. **System software** manages the resources and activities of the computer. **Application software** applies the computer to a specific task for an end user, such as processing an order or generating a mailing list. Today, most system and application software is no longer custom programmed but rather is purchased from outside vendors.

In addition to software for applications used by specific groups or business units, many firms are making large investments in software for enterprise integration to tie together disparate business functions and business processes and make information flow freely throughout the business. We describe all these types of software in detail in Section 4.2 and in Chapter 8.

### Data Management Technology

In addition to physical media for storing the firm's data, businesses need specialized software to organize the data and make it available to business users. **Data management software** organizes, manages, and processes business data concerned with inventory, customers, and vendors. Chapter 5 describes data management software in detail.

### Networking and Telecommunications Technology

Networking and telecommunications technology provides data, voice, and video connectivity to employees, customers, and suppliers. It includes technology for running a company's internal networks, services from telecommunications/telephone companies, and technology for running Web sites and linking to other computer systems through the Internet. Chapter 6 provides an in-depth description of these technologies.

### Technology Services

Businesses need people to run and manage the other infrastructure components we have just described and to train employees in how to use these technologies for their work. Chapter 2 described the role of the information systems department, which is the firm's internal business unit set up for this purpose. Today, many businesses supplement their in-house information systems staff with external technology consultants. Even large firms do not have the staff, the skills, the budget, or the necessary experience to implement and run the wide array of technologies that would be required. When businesses need to make major system changes or implement an entirely new IT infrastructure, they typically turn to external consultants to help them with systems integration.

**Systems integration** means ensuring that the new infrastructure works with the firm's older, so-called legacy systems and that the new elements of the infrastructure work with one another. **Legacy systems** are generally older transaction processing systems created for mainframe computers that continue to be used to avoid the high cost of replacing or redesigning them.

There are many thousands of technology vendors supplying IT infrastructure components and services and an equally large number of ways of putting them together. This chapter is about the hardware and software components of infrastructure you'll need to run a business. Chapter 5 describes the data management component, and Chapter 6 is devoted to the networking and telecommunications technology component. Chapter 7 deals with hardware and software for ensuring that information systems are reliable and secure, and Chapter 8 discusses software for enterprise applications.

## Types of Computers

Business firms face many different challenges and problems that can be solved by computers and information systems. In order to be efficient, firms need to match the right computer

**TABLE 4.1**

**Computer Performance**

| Computer ES | Processor/Speed | Performance | Comment |
|---|---|---|---|
| Personal digital assistant (PDA) Palm handheld | Intel™ PXA270/312 MHz | 500 FLOPS | PDAs are generally asked to perform one task at a time by the operator. Most of the processing power is used to draw the screen and handle voice messages. |
| Personal computer Dell XPS | Pentium® D Dual Core Processor/3.20 GHz | 4 Giga FLOPS | High-end game machine. Most PCs used in business are 1–2 GHz, with 2 GFLOPS performance, plenty for word processing, Web surfing, and spreadsheets. |
| Server computer (midrange computer) Sun Fire E4900 Server | UltraSPARC IV+/1.5 GHz | 32 Giga FLOPS | Up to 16 processors can be used with this powerful server. |
| Mainframe computer IBM Z990 Enterprise Server | Z990/1.2 GHz | 1 Tera FLOPS | Up to 54 processors can be used in this enterprise mainframe. |
| SuperComputer IBM Blue Gene/L | PowerPC 440 700 MHz | ˜136–183 Tera FLOPS | About 64,000 PowerPC processors wired into a single machine. |
| Distributed Computing Grid Folding@home | Various PC processors, whatever is available on the Internet | ˜160 Tera FLOPS | A volunteer program with 180,000 CPUs online; the largest and fastest online distributed computing project devoted to studying protein folding. |

hardware to the nature of the business challenge, neither overspending nor underspending for the technology.

Computers come in an array of sizes with differing capabilities for processing information, from the smallest handheld devices to the largest mainframes and supercomputers. Table 4.1 illustrates the different broad categories of computers and their relative performance.

Although there are many factors that enter into a computer system's performance, one way to think about the performance of computers is to measure how long it takes them to perform a FLOPS (FLoating point Operations Per Second). A floating point operation is essentially long division. The faster a computer system can calculate long division problems, the higher its overall performance. Computers range in power from about 500 FLOPS (a handheld) to a trillion or more FLOPS for supercomputers.

If you're working alone or with a few other people in a small business, you'll probably be using a desktop or laptop **personal computer (PC)**, which is sometimes referred to as a microcomputer. You might carry around a mobile device with some computing capability—either a personal digital assistant, such as a BlackBerry or Palm handheld, or a cell phone with some computing capability. If you're doing advanced design or engineering work requiring powerful graphics or computational capabilities, you might use a **workstation**, which fits on a desktop but has more powerful mathematical and graphics-processing capabilities than a PC.

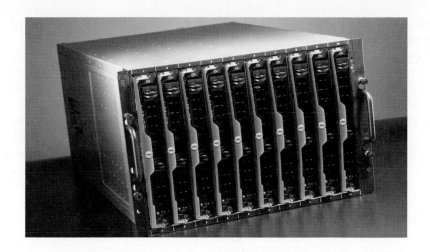

*Blade servers are ultra-thin computers consisting of a circuit board with processors, memory, and network connections that are stored in racks. They take up less space than traditional box-based servers. Illustrated here is the Dell PowerEdge™ 1855 blade server.*

If your business has a number of computers networked together or maintains a Web site, it will need a **server**. Server computers are specifically optimized to support a computer network, enabling users to share files, software, peripheral devices (such as printers), or other network resources. Servers are classified as **midrange computers** as are **minicomputers**, which are used in systems for universities, factories, or research laboratories.

Servers have become important components of firms' IT infrastructures because they provide the hardware platform for electronic commerce. By adding special software, they can be customized to deliver Web pages, process purchase and sale transactions, or exchange data with systems inside the company. You'll sometimes find many servers linked together to provide all the processing needs for large companies. If your company has to process millions of financial transactions or customer records, you'll need one of these midrange computers (32 giga FLOPS) or mainframes (up to one Tera FLOPS or a trillion FLOPS) to solve these challenges.

Mainframe computers first appeared in the mid-1960s, and ever since they have been used by large banks, insurance companies, stock brokerages, airline reservation systems, government agencies, and many other types of firms to keep track of hundreds of thousands, even millions, of records and transactions. A **mainframe** is a large-capacity, high-performance computer that can process vast amounts of data very rapidly. Airlines, for instance, use mainframes to process upwards of 3,000 reservation transactions per second. Contrary to expectations, the mainframe market has grown steadily over the past decade. IBM, the leading mainframe vendor, has repurposed its mainframe systems so they can be used as giant servers for large-scale enterprise networks and corporate Web sites. A single IBM mainframe can run enough instances of Linux or Windows server software to replace thousands of smaller Windows-based servers.

A **supercomputer** is a specially designed and more sophisticated computer that is used for tasks requiring extremely rapid and complex calculations with thousands of variables, millions of measurements, and thousands of equations. Supercomputers traditionally have been used in engineering analysis of structures, scientific exploration and simulations, and military work, such as classified weapons research and weather forecasting. A few private business firms use supercomputers. For instance, Volvo and most other automobile manufacturers use supercomputers to simulate vehicle crash tests; NuTex Sciences purchased a supercomputer to conduct genetic simulations.

If you're a long-term weather forecaster, such as the National Oceanic and Atmospheric Administration (NOAA), or the National Hurricane Center, and your challenge is to predict the movement of weather systems based on hundreds of thousands of measurements, and thousands of equations, you would want access to a supercomputer or a distributed network of computers called a grid (130 to 180 Tera FLOPS).

**Grid computing** involves connecting geographically remote computers into a single network to create a "virtual supercomputer" by combining the computational power of all computers on the grid. Grid computing takes advantage of the fact that most computers in the United States use their central processing units on average only 25 percent of the time for the work they have been assigned, leaving these idle resources available for other processing tasks. By using the combined power of thousands of PCs and other computers networked together, the grid is able to solve complicated problems at supercomputer speeds at a far lower cost.

Private firms are beginning to use computing grids because of their greater reliability than supercomputers or even standard mainframes, higher capacity, and lower cost. For example, Johnson & Johnson's pharmaceuticals research and development unit is harnessing the spare power of 400 PCs and 64 Linux servers for a "virtual" drug-screening pilot program in Belgium. In the United States, the company is using more than 100 PCs and workstations for modeling clinical drug trials (Ricadela, 2005).

### Computer Networks and Client/Server Computing

Unless you're in a small business with a stand-alone computer, you'll be using networked computers for most processing tasks. The use of multiple computers linked by a communications network for processing is called **distributed processing**. (**Centralized processing**, in which all processing is accomplished by one large central computer is much less common.)

One widely used form of distributed processing is **client/server computing**. Client/server computing splits processing between "clients" and "servers." Both are on the network, but each machine is assigned functions it is best suited to perform. The **client** is the user point of entry for the required function and is normally a desktop computer, workstation, or laptop computer. The user generally interacts directly only with the client portion of the application, often to input data or retrieve data for further analysis. The server provides the client with services. Servers store and process shared data and also perform back-end functions not visible to users, such as managing network activities. Figure 4-2 illustrates the client/server computing concept. Computing on the Internet uses the client/server model (see Chapter 6).

Figure 4-2 illustrates the simplest client/server network, consisting of a client computer networked to a server computer, with processing split between the two types of machines. This is called a two-tiered client/server architecture. Whereas simple client/server networks can be found in small businesses, most corporations have more complex, **multitiered** (often called **N-tier**) **client/server architectures**, in which the work of the entire network is balanced over several different levels of servers, depending on the kind of service being requested (see Figure 4-3).

For instance, at the first level a **Web server** will serve a Web page to a client in response to a request for service. Web server software is responsible for locating and managing stored Web pages. If the client requests access to a corporate system (a product list or price information, for instance), the request is passed along to an **application server**. Application

**Figure 4-2**
Client/Server
Computing
*In client/server computing, computer processing is split between client machines and server machines linked by a network. Users interface with the client machines.*

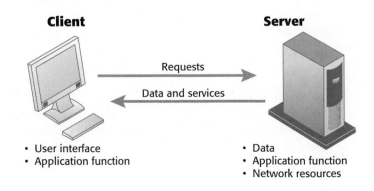

Client

Server

Requests

Data and services

• User interface
• Application function

• Data
• Application function
• Network resources

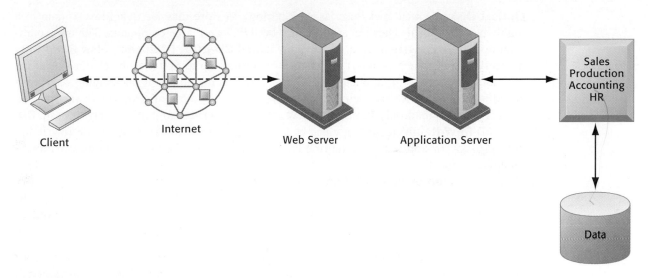

**Figure 4-3**
A Multitiered Client/Server Network (N-Tier)
*In a multitiered client/server network, client requests for service are handled by different levels of servers.*

server software handles all application operations between a user and an organization's back-end business systems. The application server may reside on the same computer as the Web server or on its own dedicated computer. Chapters 5 and 6 provide more detail on other pieces of software that are used in multitiered client/server architectures for e-commerce and e-business.

Client/server computing enables businesses to distribute computing work across a series of smaller, inexpensive machines that cost much less than minicomputers or centralized mainframe systems. The result is an explosion in computing power and applications throughout the firm. The process of transferring applications from large computers to smaller ones is called **downsizing**.

## Storage, Input, and Output Technology

In addition to hardware for processing data, you'll need technologies for data storage, and input and output. Storage and input and output devices are called peripheral devices because they are outside the main computer system unit.

### Secondary Storage Technology

Electronic commerce and electronic business, and regulations, such as Sarbanes-Oxley, have made storage a strategic technology. The amount of data that companies now need to store is doubling every 12 to 18 months. The primary storage technologies are magnetic disk, optical disk, magnetic tape, and storage networks.

**Magnetic Disk** The most widely used secondary storage medium today is the **magnetic disk**. PCs have **hard drives**, and large mainframe or midrange computer systems have multiple hard disk drives because they require immense disk storage capacity in the gigabyte and terabyte range. Some PCs use floppy disks, but they have been largely supplanted by **USB flash drives**, also known as USB drives. A USB flash drive provides portable flash memory storage by plugging into a computer's USB port. It can provide up to 6 gigabytes of portable storage capacity and is small enough to fit into a pocket.

Large computers with massive storage requirements use a disk technology called **RAID (Redundant Array of Inexpensive Disks)**. RAID devices package more than 100 disk drives, a controller chip, and specialized software into a single, large unit delivering data over multiple paths simultaneously.

**Optical Disks** Optical disks use laser technology to store massive quantities of data in a highly compact form. They are available for both PCs and large computers. The most common optical disk system used with PCs is called **CD-ROM (Compact Disk Read-Only Memory)**. A 4.75-inch compact disk for PCs can store up to 660 megabytes. Optical disks are most appropriate for applications where enormous quantities of unchanging data must be stored compactly for easy retrieval or for applications combining text, sound, and images.

CD-ROM is read-only storage. No new data can be written to it; it can only be read. **CD-RW (CD-ReWritable)** technology has been developed to allow users to create rewritable optical disks for applications requiring large volumes of storage where the information is only occasionally updated.

**Digital video disks (DVDs)** are optical disks the same size as CD-ROMs but of even higher capacity. They can hold a minimum of 4.7 gigabytes of data, enough to store a full-length, high-quality motion picture. DVDs are being used to store video and digitized text, graphics, and audio data. Rewritable DVD drives and media are now available.

**Magnetic Tape  Magnetic tape** is an older storage technology that still is employed for secondary storage of large quantities of data that are needed rapidly but not instantly. It stores data sequentially and is relatively slow compared to the speed of other secondary storage media. In order to find an individual record stored on magnetic tape, such as an employment record, the tape must be read from the beginning up to the location of the desired record.

**Storage Networking** Large firms are turning to network-based storage technologies to deal with the complexity and cost of mushrooming storage requirements. **Storage area networks (SANs)** connect multiple storage devices on a separate high-speed network dedicated to storage. The SAN creates a large central pool of storage that can be rapidly accessed and shared by multiple servers (see Figure 4-4).

### Input and Output Devices

Human beings interact with computer systems largely through input and output devices. **Input devices** gather data and convert them into electronic form for use by the computer, whereas **output devices** display data after they have been processed. Table 4.2 describes the principal input and output devices.

**Figure 4-4**
A Storage Area Network (SAN)
*A typical SAN consists of a server, storage devices, and networking devices and is used strictly for storage. The SAN stores data on many different types of storage devices, providing data to the enterprise. The SAN supports communication between any server and the storage unit as well as between different storage devices in the network.*

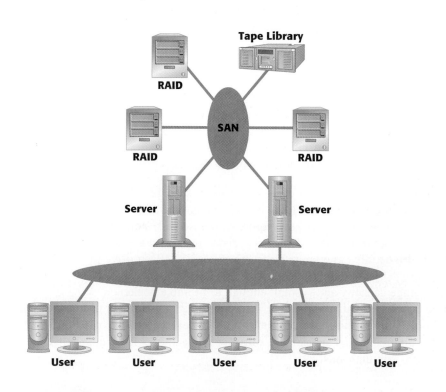

## TABLE 4.2

**Input and Output Devices**

| Input Device | Description |
|---|---|
| Keyboard | Principal method of data entry for text and numerical data. |
| Computer mouse | Handheld device with point-and-click capabilities that is usually connected to the computer by a cable. The computer user can move the mouse around on a desktop to control the cursor's position on a computer display screen, pushing a button to select a command. Trackballs and touch pads often are used in place of the mouse as pointing devices on laptop PCs. |
| Touch screen | Device that allows users to enter limited amounts of data by touching the surface of a sensitized video display monitor with a finger or a pointer. Often found in information kiosks in retail stores, restaurants, and shopping malls. |
| Optical character recognition | Device that can translate specially designed marks, characters, and codes into digital form. The most widely used optical code is the bar code, which is used in point-of-sale systems in supermarkets and retail stores. The codes can include time, date, and location data in addition to identification data. |
| Magnetic ink character recognition (MICR) | Technology used primarily in check processing for the banking industry. Characters on the bottom of a check identify the bank, checking account, and check number and are preprinted using special magnetic ink. A MICR reader translates these characters into digital form for the computer. |
| Pen-based input | Handwriting-recognition devices, such as pen-based tablets, notebooks, and notepads, that convert the motion made by an electronic stylus pressing on a touch-sensitive tablet screen into digital form. |
| Digital scanner | Device that translates images, such as pictures or documents, into digital form; essential component of image processing systems. |
| Audio input | Voice input devices that convert spoken words into digital form for processing by the computer. Microphones and tape cassette players can serve as input devices for music and other sounds. |
| Sensors | Devices that collect data directly from the environment for input into a computer system. For instance, today's farmers can use sensors to monitor the moisture of the soil in their fields to help them with irrigation. |
| **Output Device** | **Description** |
| Cathode ray tube (CRT) | Electronic gun that shoots a beam of electrons illuminating pixels on a display screen. Laptop computers use flat-panel displays, which are less bulky than CRT monitors. |
| Printers | Devices that produce a printed hard copy of information output. They include impact printers (such as dot matrix printers) and nonimpact printers (such as laser, inkjet, and thermal transfer printers). |
| Audio output | Voice output devices that convert digital output data back into intelligible speech. Other audio output, such as music, can be delivered by speakers connected to the computer. |

## Batch and Online Input and Processing

Information systems collect and process information in one of two ways: through batch or through online processing. In **batch processing**, transactions, such as orders or payroll time cards, are accumulated and stored in a group or batch until the time when, because of some reporting cycle, it is efficient or necessary to process them. Batch processing is found primarily in older systems where users need only occasional reports. In **online processing**, the user enters transactions into a device (such as a data entry keyboard or bar code reader) that is directly connected to the computer system. The transactions usually are processed immediately. Most processing today is online processing. Batch systems often use tape as a storage medium, whereas online processing systems use disk storage, which permits immediate access to specific items.

## Contemporary Hardware Trends

The exploding power of computer hardware and networking technology has dramatically changed how businesses organize their computing power, putting more of this power on networks. We look at three trends: technology convergence, edge computing, and autonomic computing.

### The Integration of Computing and Telecommunications Platforms

Arguably the most dominant theme in hardware platforms today is the convergence of telecommunications and computing platforms to the point where, increasingly, computing takes place over the network. You can see this convergence at several levels.

*The Palm Treo 650 combines a mobile phone, e-mail, messaging, personal organizer, Web access, digital music player, and digital camera that captures video in a single compact device. Convergence of computing and communications technologies has turned cell phones into mobile computing platforms.*

Communication devices, such as cell phones, are taking on functions of handheld computers, whereas handheld PDAs are taking on cell phone functions. For instance, the Palm Treo 650 digital handheld integrates phone, camera, digital music player, and handheld computer in one device. Short films and audio clips are now available over cell phones. Television, radio, and video are moving toward all-digital production and distribution.

The growing success of Internet telephone systems (now the fastest-growing type of telephone service) demonstrates how historically separate telecommunications and computing platforms are converging toward a single network—the Internet. Chapter 6 describes the convergence of computing and telecommunications in greater depth.

### Edge Computing

**Edge computing** is a multitier, load-balancing scheme for Web-based applications in which significant parts of Web site content, logic, and processing are performed by smaller, less expensive servers located nearby the user in order to increase response time and resilience while lowering technology costs. In this sense, edge computing is another technique like grid computing for using the Internet to share the workload experienced by a firm across many computers located remotely on the network.

Figure 4-5 illustrates the components of edge computing. There are three tiers in edge computing: the local client; the nearby edge computing platform, which consists of servers positioned at any of the 5,000-plus Internet service providers in the United States; and enterprise computers located at the firm's main data center. The edge computing platform is owned by a service firm, such as Akamai, which employs about 15,000 edge servers around the United States.

In an edge platform application, the edge servers initially process requests from the user client computer. Presentation components, such as static Web page content, reusable code fragments, and interactive elements gathered on forms, are delivered by the edge server to the client. Database and business logic elements are delivered by the enterprise computing platform.

### Autonomic Computing

With large systems encompassing many thousands of networked devices, computer systems have become so complex today that some experts believe they may not be manageable in the future. One approach to dealing with this problem from a computer hardware perspective is to employ autonomic computing. **Autonomic computing** is an industry-wide effort to develop systems that can configure themselves, optimize and tune themselves, heal themselves when broken, and protect themselves from outside intruders and self-destruction.

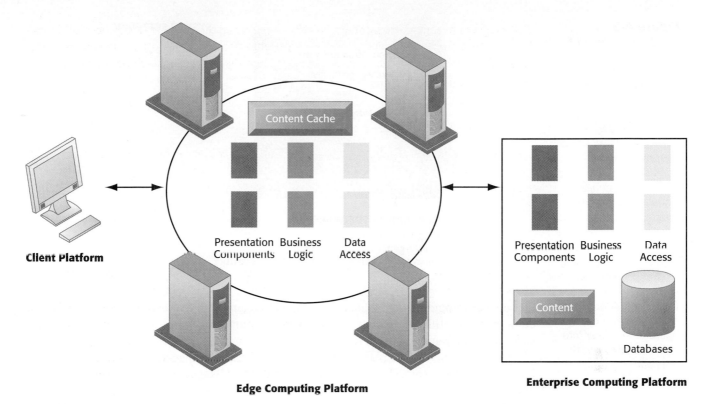

**Figure 4-5**
Edge Computing Platform
*Edge computing involves the use of the Internet to balance the processing load of enterprise platforms across the client and edge computing platform.*

Imagine, for instance, a desktop PC that could know it was invaded by a computer virus. Instead of blindly allowing the virus to invade, the PC would identify and eradicate the virus or, alternatively, turn its workload over to another processor and shut itself down before the virus destroyed any files.

You can glimpse some of these capabilities in your desktop system. For instance, virus and firewall protection software can detect viruses on PCs, automatically defeat the viruses, and alert operators. These programs can be updated automatically as the need arises by connecting to an online virus protection service such as McAfee. Other key elements of autonomic computing are still missing but are sure to be on the agenda of research centers in the next decade.

## 4.2 IT Infrastructure: Computer Software

In order to use computer hardware, you'll need software, which provides the detailed instructions that direct the computer's work. Computer software includes both system software and application software, which we defined earlier in this chapter. Both types of software are interrelated and can be thought of as a set of nested boxes, each of which must interact closely with the other boxes surrounding it. Figure 4-6 illustrates this relationship. The system software surrounds and controls access to the hardware. Application software must work through the system software in order to operate. End users work primarily with application software. Each type of software must be specially designed for a specific machine to ensure its compatibility.

### Operating System Software

The system software that manages and controls the computer's activities is called the **operating system**. Other system software consists of computer language translation programs

**Figure 4-6**
The Major Types of
Software
*The relationship
between the system
software, application
software, and users can
be illustrated by a
series of nested boxes.
System software—
consisting of operating
systems, language
translators, and utility
programs—controls
access to the hardware.
Application software,
including programming
languages and "fourth-
generation" languages,
must work through the
system software to
operate. The user inter-
acts primarily with the
application software.*

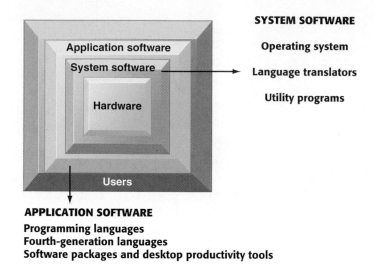

that convert programming languages into machine language that can be understood by the computer and utility programs that perform common processing tasks, such as copying, sorting, or computing a square root.

The operating system is the computer system's chief manager, enabling the system to handle many different tasks and users at the same time. The operating system allocates and assigns system resources, schedules the use of computer resources and computer jobs, and monitors computer system activities. The operating system provides locations in primary memory for data and programs, and controls the input and output devices, such as printers, terminals, and telecommunication links. The operating system also coordinates the scheduling of work in various areas of the computer so that different parts of different jobs can be worked on at the same time. Finally, the operating system keeps track of each computer job and may also keep track of who is using the system, of what programs have been run, and of any unauthorized attempts to access the system.

### PC Operating Systems and Graphical User Interfaces

Like any other software, the PC software you use is based on specific operating systems and computer hardware. Software written for one PC operating system generally cannot run on another. Table 4.3 compares the leading PC operating systems. These include the Windows family of operating systems (Windows Vista, Windows XP, Windows Server 2003, and Windows CE), UNIX, Linux, and the Macintosh operating system.

When a user interacts with a computer, including a PC, the interaction is controlled by an operating system. A user communicates with an operating system through the user interface of that operating system. Contemporary PC operating systems use a **graphical user interface**, often called a **GUI**, which makes extensive use of icons, buttons, bars, and boxes to perform tasks. It has become the dominant model for the user interface of PC operating systems and for many types of application software.

Microsoft's Windows family of operating systems has both client and server versions and a streamlined graphical user interface that arranges icons to provide instant access to common tasks. Windows systems can perform multiple programming tasks simultaneously and have powerful networking capabilities, including the capability to integrate fax, e-mail, and scheduling programs and to access information from the Internet. **Windows XP** (for eXPerience) is reliable, robust, and relatively easy to use, with both Home and Professional versions. **Windows Vista**, formerly code-named Longhorn, features improved security; diagnostics; parental controls; usability; desktop searching; synchronization with mobile devices, cameras, and Internet services; and better support for video and TV.

Windows operating systems for network servers provide network management functions, including tools for creating and operating Web sites and other Internet services. They include the server version of Windows Vista and **Windows Server 2003**, which has multi-

**TABLE 4.3**

**Leading PC Operating Systems**

| Operating System | Features |
|---|---|
| Windows Vista | Most recent Windows operating system, with improved security; desktop searching; and synchronization with mobile devices, cameras, and Internet services, as well as better support for video and TV. |
| Windows XP | Reliable, robust operating system for powerful PCs with versions for both home and corporate users. Features support of Internet access; multimedia; and group collaboration; along with powerful networking, security, and corporate management capabilities. |
| Windows Server 2003 | Most recent Windows operating system for servers. |
| Windows CE | Windows platform for devices with minimal storage, such as small handheld computers, personal digital assistants, wireless communication devices, and other information appliances. |
| UNIX | Used for powerful PCs, workstations, and network servers. Supports multitasking, multiuser processing, and networking. Is portable to different models of computer hardware. |
| Linux | Free, reliable alternative to UNIX and Windows operating systems that runs on many different types of computer hardware and can be modified by software developers. |
| Mac OS X Tiger | Most recent version of the operating system for the Macintosh computer, featuring a very fast Web browser, multiway video- and audioconferencing, powerful search capabilities, support for video and image processing, and an elegant user interface. |

ple versions for small, medium, and large businesses, and for businesses that have massive computer centers and processing requirements. Windows Server 2003 has functions to facilitate wireless connections to corporate networks, tools for Web services, and tighter links to Microsoft data management and desktop software products. Windows 2000 and Windows NT were earlier versions of this software.

**UNIX** is an interactive, multiuser, multitasking operating system developed by Bell Laboratories in 1969 to help scientific researchers share data. UNIX was designed to connect various machines together and is highly supportive of communications and networking. UNIX is often used on workstations and servers, and provides the reliability and scalability for running large systems on high-end servers. UNIX can run on many different kinds of computers and can be easily customized. Application programs that run under UNIX can be ported from one computer to run on a different computer with little modification. Graphical user interfaces have been developed for UNIX. UNIX poses some security problems because multiple jobs and users can access the same files simultaneously. Vendors have developed different versions of UNIX that are incompatible, thereby limiting software portability.

**Linux** is a UNIX-like operating system that can be downloaded from the Internet free of charge or purchased for a small fee from companies that provide additional tools for the software. It is free, reliable, compactly designed, and capable of running on many different hardware platforms, including servers, handheld computers, and consumer electronics. Linux has become popular during the past few years as a robust low-cost alternative to UNIX and the Windows operating systems.

Applications for the Linux operating system are rapidly growing. Many of these applications are embedded in cell phones, PDAs, and other handheld devices. Linux plays a major role in the back office, running Web servers and local-area networks. Linux now has a 23 percent share of the $50.9 billion U.S. server market. Its use in desktop computers is growing steadily. According to IBM, 10 million desktops ran Linux in 2004, a 40 percent increase from the previous year (*Business Week*, 2005). IBM, HP, Intel, Dell, and Sun have made

Linux a central part of their offerings to corporations, and major software vendors are starting to provide versions of their products that can run on Linux.

Linux is an example of **open-source software**, which provides all computer users with free access to its program code, so they can modify the code to fix errors or to make improvements. Open-source software, such as Linux, is not owned by any company or individual. A global network of programmers and users manages and modifies the software, usually without being paid to do so. Open-source software is by definition not restricted to any specific operating system or hardware technology, although most open-source software is currently based on Linux or UNIX.

Thousands of open-source programs are available from hundreds of Web sites. The range of open-source software extends from operating systems to office suites, Web browsers, and games. The open-source Web browser Mozilla Firefox now has 8 percent of the Web browser market and is a direct competitor to Microsoft's Internet Explorer. Several large software companies are converting some of their commercial programs to open source. More than two dozen countries in Asia, Europe, and Latin America have adopted open-source software and Linux.

The Focus on Technology describes why business use of open-source software and Linux is growing. As you read this case, try to identify the problem these companies were facing; what alternative solutions were available to management; how well the chosen solution worked; and the people, organization, and technology issues that had to be addressed when developing the solution.

## Application Software and Desktop Productivity Tools

Today, businesses have access to an array of tools for developing their application software. These include traditional programming languages, fourth-generation languages, application software packages and desktop productivity tools, software for developing Internet applications, and software for enterprise integration. It's important to know which software tools and programming languages are appropriate for the work your business wants to accomplish.

### Application Programming Languages for Business

For business applications, the most important programming languages have been COBOL, C, C++, and Visual Basic. **COBOL (COmmon Business Oriented Language)** was developed in the early 1960s for processing large data files with alphanumeric characters (mixed alphabetic and numeric data) and for business reporting. **C** is a powerful and efficient language developed in the early 1970s that combines machine portability with tight control and efficient use of computer resources. C is used primarily by professional programmers to create operating systems and application software, especially for PCs. **C++** is a newer version of C that has all the capabilities of C plus additional features for working with software objects. Unlike traditional programs, which separate data from the actions to be taken on the data, a software **object** combines data and procedures. Chapter 11 describes object-oriented software development in detail. **Visual Basic** is a widely used visual programming tool and environment for creating applications that run on Microsoft Windows operating systems. A **visual programming language** allows users to manipulate graphic or iconic elements to create programs.

### Fourth-Generation Languages

**Fourth-generation languages** consist of a variety of software tools that enable end users to develop software applications with minimal or no technical assistance or that enhance professional programmers' productivity. Fourth-generation languages tend to be nonprocedural, or less procedural, than conventional programming languages. Procedural languages require specification of the sequence of steps, or procedures, that tell the computer what to do and how to do it. Nonprocedural languages need only specify what has to be accomplished rather than provide details about how to carry out the task. Some of these nonprocedural

# FOCUS ON TECHNOLOGY   The Corporate World Migrates to Open-Source

Without the benefit of multimillion-dollar advertising campaigns, the open-source operating system Linux has gained a foothold in the corporate world. Open-source is appealing on the enterprise level because it offers more flexibility and lower costs than most commercial products. The movement is new and the territory is uncharted, so open-source converts are proceeding deliberately rather than making sweeping changes.

The most obvious benefit of open-source is access to source code that companies can use to integrate Linux with their existing business applications and improve it for their purposes. Robert Lefkowitz is vice president of research and executive education at Optaros, a company that assists other organizations that are switching to open-source applications. Lefkowitz stresses the amount of user control that open-source offers to his clients. He explains that it is easier to troubleshoot problems and maintain the availability and reliability of systems when you can "look under the hood yourself."

Siegenia-Aubi KG, a German maker of windows, doors, and ventilating equipment, replaced the Windows operating system on its Compaq servers with Linux to run mySAP customer relationship management software, and the open-source Apache Web server and MySQL database. Being able to manipulate Linux source code makes it easier to integrate with business applications the company uses. Linux is also more reliable than Windows. The company had to reboot its Compaq servers every two weeks when they were running Windows because the operating system malfunctioned. Siegenia-Aubi is now trying to move more of its business systems to Linux.

Adopters of open-source have seen other benefits as well. Movie studio DreamWorks Animation SKG realized savings when it switched to Linux desktops from Silicon Graphics proprietary RISC workstations. The studio had been paying between $30,000 and $40,000 per designer for the workstations. According to Jim Mainard, head of research and development, the move to Linux has saved the studio 20 percent per year on licensing and operating expenses. Mainard also believes that Linux has made the studio more secure against virus attacks.

Against these benefits, executives and managers must weigh the issues and challenges that accompany the incorporation of open-source into an IT infrastructure. For example, a successful open-source deployment requires proper support and maintenance. If companies do not have access to resources that can provide such support, they may negate the advantages they gained by adopting open-source. Larry Kinder, CIO of Cendant, reflects, "You're always weighing the value of having a company like Microsoft behind you or relying on an open-source community you have no control over."

Kamal Nasser, vice president of IT strategy for Nielsen Media Research notes that adoption of Linux at his company has not progressed freely because the knowledge base of the IT staff is Sun Solaris. Florian Kainz, computer graphics principal engineer at Industrial Light & Magic, asserts that companies migrating from UNIX to Linux are more likely to have better results than companies starting from Windows because the technical support skills for UNIX and Linux are similar. Vendors of open-source applications can provide support but may be stymied if customers have altered code and created problems whose origins cannot be easily uncovered.

Another obstacle for companies using open-source is the decentralized and unregulated communities that develop applications. When an upgrade is released, mission-critical features may have disappeared without warning because the developers determined they lacked value.

The undefined structure of the development community also exposes companies to legal issues that they do not confront when using commercial applications. Large businesses fear that intellectual property lawsuits could result from using a product built by, in some cases, thousands of people across the globe who may claim ownership. License agreements for open-source do not always grant complete freedom for distributing and modifying code. Yahoo! and United Parcel Service (UPS), major adopters of Linux servers, both scrutinize and manage the usage rights and licenses of the open-source software they deploy.

In addition to evaluating open-source software for legality issues, companies such as UPS and E*TRADE employ rigorous evaluations to determine the value of the software to a particular project or initiative. They also ensure that the open-source offerings will fit into their operating environments. Most companies are not ripping out the commercial software in which they have invested quite heavily. For example, Yahoo! uses open-source to create and support the services that its users are most drawn to, such as e-mail and Web page templates. However, Yahoo! has no plans to abandon the commercial applications that run its search technology, customer billing, and online ads. UPS, however, expects to run all of the traffic on UPS.com through Linux servers by 2007.

*Sources:* Larry Greenmeier, "Open Source Goes Corporate," *InformationWeek,* September 26, 2005; Laurie Sullivan, "Apps Migrate to Open Source," *InformationWeek,* September 5, 2005; and Michael Hardy, "Open Wide: Linux's Appeal Grows as Applications Flourish," *Federal Computer Week,* April 4, 2005.

**To Think About:**
What problems do Linux and other open-source software help companies address? How does open-source software help? What issues and challenges does deploying open-source software raise? What can be done to address these issues? Describe what you think is a sound strategy for deploying Linux and other open-source components at this stage of their evolution.

### Table 4.4

**Categories of Fourth-Generation Languages**

| Fourth-Generation Tool | Description | Example | |
|---|---|---|---|
| PC software tools | General-purpose application software packages for PCs. | WordPerfect<br>Microsoft Access | **Oriented toward end users** |
| Query language | Languages for retrieving data stored in databases or files. Capable of supporting requests for information that are not predefined. | SQL | |
| Report generator | Extract data from files or databases to create customized reports in a wide range of formats not routinely produced by an information system. Generally provide more control over the way data are formatted, organized, and displayed than query languages. | Crystal Reports | |
| Graphics language | Retrieve data from files or databases and display them in graphic format. Some graphics software can perform arithmetic or logical operations on data as well. | SAS Graph<br>Systat | |
| Application generator | Contain preprogrammed modules that can generate entire applications, including Web sites, greatly speeding development. A user can specify what needs to be done, and the application generator will create the appropriate program code for input, validation, update, processing, and reporting. | FOCUS<br>Microsoft FrontPage | |
| Application software package | Software programs sold or leased by commercial vendors that eliminate the need for custom-written, in-house software. | Oracle PeopleSoft HCM<br>mySAP ERP | |
| Very high-level programming language | Generate program code with fewer instructions than conventional languages, such as COBOL or FORTRAN. Designed primarily as productivity tools for professional programmers. | APL<br>Nomad2 | **Oriented toward IS professionals** |

languages are **natural languages** that enable users to communicate with the computer using conversational commands resembling human speech.

Table 4.4 shows that there are seven categories of fourth-generation languages: PC software tools, query languages, report generators, graphics languages, application generators, application software packages, and very high-level programming languages. The table lists the tools in order of ease of use by nonprogramming end users. End users are most likely to work with PC software tools and query languages. **Query languages** are software tools that provide immediate online answers to requests for information that are not predefined, such as "Who are the highest-performing sales representatives?" Query languages are often tied to data management software (described later in this section) and to database management systems (see Chapter 5).

### Software Packages and Desktop Productivity Tools

Much of the software used in businesses today is not custom programmed but consists of application software packages and desktop productivity tools. A **software package** is a prewritten, precoded, commercially available set of programs that eliminates the need for individuals or organizations to write their own software programs for certain functions. There are software packages for system software, but most package software is application software.

Software packages that run on mainframes and larger computers usually require professional programmers for their installation and support. Desktop productivity software packages for word processing, spreadsheets, data management, presentation graphics, e-mail,

Web browsers, and groupware are the most widely used software tools among business and consumer users.

**Word Processing Software** If you work in an office or attend school, you probably use word processing software every day. **Word processing software** stores text data electronically as a computer file rather than on paper. The word processing software allows the user to make changes in the document electronically in memory. This eliminates the need to retype an entire page to incorporate corrections. The software has formatting options to make changes in line spacing, margins, character size, and column width. Microsoft Word and WordPerfect are popular word processing packages.

Most word processing software has advanced features that automate other writing tasks: spelling checkers; style checkers (to analyze grammar and punctuation); thesaurus programs; and mail merge programs, which link letters or other text documents with names and addresses in a mailing list. The software now includes capabilities for creating and accessing Web pages.

Businesses that need to create highly professional looking brochures, manuals, or books will likely use desktop publishing software for this purpose. **Desktop publishing** software provides more control over the placement of text, graphics, and photos in the layout of a page than does word processing software. Adobe PageMaker and QuarkXpress are two popular desktop publishing packages.

**Spreadsheets** **Spreadsheet** software is valuable for applications in which numerous calculations with pieces of data must be related to each other. It organizes data into a grid of columns and rows. When you change a value or values, all other related values on the spreadsheet will be automatically recomputed.

You'll often see spreadsheets in applications that require modeling and "what-if" analysis. After the user has constructed a set of mathematical relationships, the spreadsheet can be recalculated instantaneously using a different set of assumptions. A number of alternatives easily can be evaluated by changing one or two pieces of data without having to rekey in the rest of the worksheet. Spreadsheet packages include graphics functions to present data in the form of line graphs, bar graphs, or pie charts. The most popular spreadsheet package is Microsoft Excel. The newest versions of this software can read and write Web files. Figure 4-7 illustrates the output from a spreadsheet for a break-even analysis and its accompanying graph.

**Data Management Software** Although spreadsheet programs are powerful tools for manipulating quantitative data, data management software, which we defined earlier in this chapter, is more suitable for creating and manipulating lists and for combining information from different files. PC database management packages have programming features and easy-to-learn menus that enable nonspecialists to build small information systems.

Data management software typically has facilities for creating files and databases and for storing, modifying, and manipulating data for reports and queries. Popular database management software for the personal computer includes Microsoft Access, which has been enhanced to publish data on the Web. Figure 4-8 shows a screen from Microsoft Access illustrating some of its capabilities. We discuss data management software in greater detail in Chapter 5.

**Presentation Graphics** **Presentation graphics** software allows users to create professional-quality graphics presentations. This software can convert numeric data into charts and other types of graphics and can include multimedia displays of sound, animation, photos, and video clips. The leading presentation graphics packages include capabilities for computer-generated slide shows and translating content for the Web. Microsoft PowerPoint and Lotus Freelance Graphics are popular presentation graphics packages.

**Integrated Software Packages and Software Suites** **Integrated software packages** combine the functions of the most important PC software packages, such as word processing, spreadsheets, presentation graphics, and data management. This integration provides a more general-purpose software tool and eliminates redundant data entry and data maintenance. For example, the break-even analysis spreadsheet illustrated in Figure 4-7 could be reformatted into a polished report with word processing software without separately keying

**Figure 4-7**
Spreadsheet
Software
*Spreadsheet software organizes data into columns and rows for analysis and manipulation. Contemporary spreadsheet software provides graphing abilities for a clear, visual representation of the data in the spreadsheets. This sample break-even analysis is represented as numbers in a spreadsheet as well as a line graph for easy interpretation.*

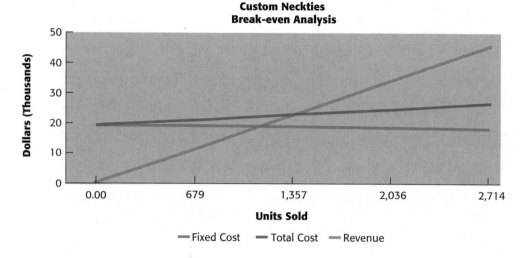

| Total fixed cost | 19,000.00 |
| Variable cost per unit | 3.00 |
| Average sales price | 17.00 |
| Contribution margin | 14.00 |
| Break-even point | 1,357 |

**Custom Neckties Pro Forma Income Statement**

| | | | | | |
|---|---|---|---|---|---|
| Units sold | 0.00 | 679 | 1,357 | 2,036 | 2,714 |
| Revenue | 0 | 11,536 | 23,071 | 34,607 | 46,143 |
| Fixed cost | 19,000 | 19,000 | 19,000 | 19,000 | 19,000 |
| Variable cost | 0 | 2,036 | 4,071 | 6,107 | 8,143 |
| Total cost | 19,000 | 21,036 | 23,071 | 25,107 | 27,143 |
| Profit/Loss | (19,000) | (9,500) | 0 | 9,500 | 19,000 |

the data into both programs. Although integrated packages can do many things well, they generally do not have the same power and depth as single-purpose packages.

Integrated software packages should be distinguished from **software suites**, which are full-featured versions of application software sold as a unit. Microsoft Office is an example. There are different versions of Office for home and business users, but the core desktop tools include Word word processing software; Excel spreadsheet software; Access database software; PowerPoint presentation graphics software; and Outlook, a set of tools for e-mail, scheduling, and contact management.

**Figure 4-8**
Data Management
Software
*This screen from Microsoft Access illustrates some of its powerful capabilities for managing and organizing information.*

**Office XP** and **Office 2003** contain capabilities to support collaborative work on the Web, publish Web documents, and update documents with information from the Web. Some Office 2003 capabilities are not on the desktop but must be accessed as services from the Microsoft server. OpenOffice (which can be downloaded over the Internet) and Sun Microsystems's StarOffice are low-cost alternatives to Microsoft Office tools that can run on Linux.

**E-Mail Software Electronic mail (e-mail)** is used for the computer-to-computer exchange of messages over a network and is an important tool for communication and collaborative work. In addition to providing electronic messaging, e-mail software has capabilities for routing messages to multiple recipients, message forwarding, and attaching text and multimedia files to messages. Large companies operate their own internal e-mail systems but small businesses and individual users typically use the e-mail software provided by commercial online information services, such as America Online, or Internet services.

**Web Browsers Web browsers** are easy-to-use software tools for displaying Web pages and for accessing the Web and other Internet resources. Web browser software features a point-and-click graphical user interface that can be employed throughout the Internet to access and display information stored on computers at other Internet sites. Browsers can display or present graphics, audio, and video information, as well as traditional text, and they allow you to click on-screen buttons or highlighted words to link to related Web sites. Web browsers have become the primary interface for accessing the Internet or for using networked systems based on Internet technology. The leading Web browsers today are Microsoft's Internet Explorer, Mozilla Firefox, and Netscape Navigator.

**Groupware Groupware** provides functions and services to support the collaborative activities of workgroups. Groupware includes software for group writing and commenting, information-sharing, electronic meetings, scheduling, and e-mail and a network to connect the members of the group as they work on their own desktop computers, often in widely scattered locations. Any group member can review the ideas of others at any time and add to them, or individuals can post a document for others to comment on or edit. Leading commercial groupware products include Lotus Notes and OpenText's LiveLink, and they have been enhanced so that they can be integrated with the Internet or private intranets. Groove is a groupware tool based on peer-to-peer technology, which enables people to work directly with other people over the Internet without going through a central server. Business versions of Microsoft's Office software suite feature Web-based groupware services.

## Software for the Web: Java and HTML

Special software tools help businesses build Web sites and applications that run on the Web. Java is used for building applications that run on the Web and HTML is used for creating Web pages.

### Java

**Java** is an operating system–independent, processor-independent, object-oriented programming language that has become the leading interactive programming environment for the Web. If an object moves on the Web or takes input from the user, a Java applet is likely behind it. Java enables users to manipulate data on networked systems using Web browsers, reducing the need to write specialized software. At the enterprise level, Java is being used for more complex e-commerce and e-business applications that require communication with an organization's back-end transaction processing systems.

Java was created by James Gosling and the Green Team at Sun Microsystems in 1992, but it did not become popular until large numbers of people started using the World Wide

Web and Internet. Nearly all Web browser software has a Java platform built in. More recently, the Java platform has migrated into cell phones, automobiles, music players, game machines, and, finally, into set-top cable television systems serving interactive content and pay-per-view services.

Java software is designed to run on any computer or computing device, regardless of the specific microprocessor or operating system the device uses. A Macintosh PC, an IBM PC running Windows, a Sun server running UNIX, and even a smart cell phone or personal digital assistant can share the same Java application. For each of the computing environments in which Java is used, Sun has created a Java Virtual Machine that interprets Java programming code for that machine. In this manner, the code is written once and can be used on any machine for which there exists a Java Virtual Machine.

Java is particularly useful in network environments, such as the Internet. Here, Java is used to create miniature programs called applets that are designed to reside on centralized network servers. The network delivers to client computers only the applets required for a specific function. With Java applets residing on a network, a user can download only the software functions and data that he or she needs to perform a particular task, such as analyzing the revenue from one sales territory. The user does not need to maintain large software programs or data files on his or her desktop machine.

### Hypertext Markup Language (HTML)

**Hypertext markup language (HTML)** is a page description language for specifying how text, graphics, video, and sound are placed on a Web page and for creating dynamic links to other Web pages and objects. Using these links, a user need only point at a highlighted keyword or graphic, click on it, and immediately be transported to another document. Table 4.5 illustrates some sample HTML statements.

HTML programs can be custom written, but they also can be created using the HTML authoring capabilities of Web browsers or of popular word processing, spreadsheet, data management, and presentation graphics software packages. HTML editors, such as Microsoft FrontPage and Adobe GoLive, are more powerful HTML authoring tool programs for creating Web pages.

### Software for Enterprise Integration

In the past, business firms typically built their own custom software and made their own choices about their software platforms (all of the various pieces of software that need to work together). This strategy produced hundreds of thousands of computer programs that frequently could not communicate with other software programs, were difficult and expensive to maintain, and were nearly impossible to change quickly as business models changed.

One solution is to replace isolated systems that cannot communicate with enterprise applications for customer relationship management, supply chain management, knowledge management, and enterprise systems, which integrate multiple business processes. Chapter 8 provides a detailed description of these enterprise applications and their roles in digitally integrating the enterprise.

| TABLE 4.5 | | |
|---|---|---|
| **Examples of HTML** | **Plain English** | **HTML** |
| | Subcompact | <TITLE>Automobile</TITLE> |
| | 4 passenger | <LI>4 passenger |
| | $16,800 | <LI>$16,800 |

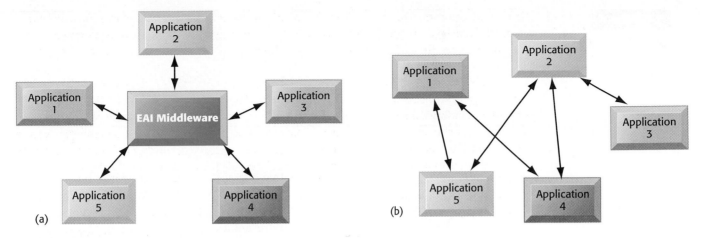

**Figure 4-9**

Enterprise Application Integration (EAI) Software Versus Traditional Integration

*EAI software (a) uses special middleware that creates a common platform with which all applications can freely communicate with each other. EAI requires much less programming than traditional point-to-point integration (b).*

Not all firms can jettison all of their legacy systems to convert to enterprise-wide platforms, however. These existing legacy mainframe applications are essential to daily operations and are very risky to change, but they can become more useful if their information and business logic can be integrated with other applications.

Some integration of legacy applications can be achieved by using special software called **middleware** to create an interface or bridge between two different systems. Middleware is software that connects two otherwise separate applications, enabling them to communicate with each other and to exchange data.

Firms may choose to write their own software to connect one application to another, but, increasingly, they are purchasing **enterprise application integration (EAI) software** packages to connect disparate applications or application clusters. This software enables multiple systems to exchange data through a single software hub rather than building countless custom software interfaces to link each system (see Figure 4-9). WebMethods, Tibco, CrossWorlds, SeeBeyond, BEA, and Vitria are leading enterprise application integration software vendors.

## Web Services and Service-Oriented Architecture

EAI software tools are product specific, meaning that they can work only with certain pieces of application software and operating systems. For example, one EAI tool to connect a specific piece of sales order entry software to manufacturing, shipping, and billing applications might not work with another vendor's order entry software. Web services provide a standardized alternative for dealing with integration.

**Web services** refer to a set of loosely coupled software components that exchange information with each other using universal Web communication standards and languages. They can exchange information between two different systems regardless of the operating systems or programming languages on which the systems are based. They can be used to build open-standard, Web-based applications linking systems of two different organizations, and they can also be used to create applications that link disparate systems within a single company. Web services are not tied to any one operating system or programming language, and different applications can use them to communicate with each other in a standard way without time-consuming custom coding.

The foundation technology for Web services is **XML**, which stands for **eXtensible Markup Language**. This language was developed in 1996 by the World Wide Web

**TABLE 4.6**

**Examples of XML**

| Plain English | XML |
|---|---|
| Subcompact | <AUTOMOBILETYPE="Subcompact"> |
| 4 passenger | <PASSENGERUNIT="PASS">4</PASSENGER> |
| $16,800 | <PRICE CURRENCY="USD">$16,800</PRICE> |

Consortium (W3C, the international body that oversees the development of the Web) as a more powerful and flexible markup language than hypertext markup language (HTML) for Web pages. Whereas HTML is limited to describing how data should be presented in the form of Web pages, XML can perform presentation, communication, and storage of data. In XML, a number is not simply a number; the XML tag specifies whether the number represents a price, a date, or a ZIP code. Table 4.6 illustrates some sample XML statements.

By tagging selected elements of the content of documents for their meanings, XML makes it possible for computers to manipulate and interpret their data automatically and perform operations on the data without human intervention. Web browsers and computer programs, such as order processing or enterprise resource planning (ERP) software, can follow programmed rules for applying and displaying the data. XML provides a standard format for data exchange, enabling Web services to pass data from one process to another.

Web services communicate through XML messages over standard Web protocols. **SOAP**, which stands for **Simple Object Access Protocol**, is a set of rules for structuring messages that enables applications to pass data and instructions to one another. **WSDL** stands for **Web services description language**; it is a common framework for describing the tasks performed by a Web service and the commands and data it will accept so that it can be used by other applications. **UDDI**, which stands for **Universal Description**, **Discovery**, and **Integration**, enables a Web service to be listed in a directory of Web services so that it can be easily located. Companies discover and locate Web services through this directory much as they would locate services in the Yellow Pages of a telephone book. Using these protocols, a software application can connect freely to other applications without custom programming for each different application with which it wants to communicate. Everyone shares the same standards.

The collection of Web services that are used to build a firm's software systems constitutes what is known as a service-oriented architecture. A **service-oriented architecture (SOA)** is a set of self-contained services that communicate with each other to create a working software application. Business tasks are accomplished by executing a series of these services. Software developers reuse these services in other combinations to assemble other applications as needed.

Virtually all major software vendors, such as IBM, Microsoft, Sun, and HP, provide tools and entire platforms for building and integrating software applications using Web services. IBM includes Web services tools in its WebSphere e-business software platform, and Microsoft has incorporated Web services tools in its Microsoft .NET platform.

Dollar Rent-A-Car's systems use Web services to link its online booking system with Southwest Airlines' Web site. Although both companies' systems are based on different technology platforms, a person booking a flight on Southwest.com can reserve a car from Dollar without leaving the airline's Web site. Instead of struggling to get Dollar's reservation system to share data with Southwest's information systems, Dollar used Microsoft .NET Web services technology as an intermediary. Reservations from Southwest are translated into Web services protocols, which are then translated into formats that can be understood by Dollar's computers.

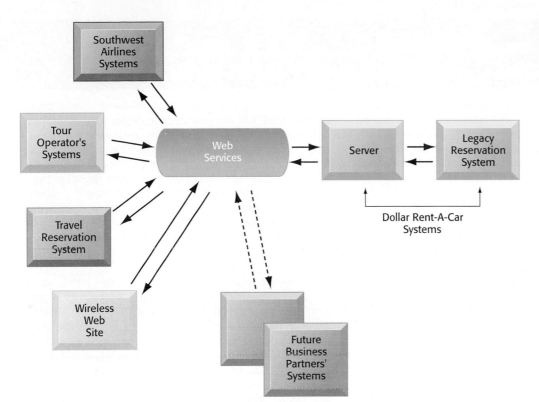

**Figure 4-10**
How Dollar Rent-A-Car Uses Web Services
*Dollar Rent-A-Car uses Web services to provide a standard intermediate layer of software to "talk" to other companies' information systems. Dollar Rent-A-Car can use this set of Web services to link to other companies' information systems without having to build a separate link to each firm's systems.*

Other car rental companies have linked their information systems to airline companies' Web sites before. But without Web services, these connections had to be built one at a time. Web services provide a standard way for Dollar's computers to "talk" to other companies' information systems without having to build special links to each one. Dollar is expanding its use of Web services to link directly to the systems of a small tour operator and a large travel reservation system as well as a Wireless Web site for mobile phones and PDAs. It does not have to write new software code for each new partner's information systems or each new wireless device (see Figure 4-10).

The Focus on Organizations describes how other businesses have benefited from a service-oriented architecture. As you read this case, try to identify the problem these companies were facing; what alternative solutions were available to management; how well the chosen solution worked; and the people, organization, and technology issues that had to be addressed when developing the solution.

## Software Trends: Mashups, Web 2.0, and Distributed Software Applications

With the development of highly distributed computing platforms comes the possibility of developing highly distributed software applications. In the past, software such as Microsoft Word or Adobe Illustrator came in a box and was designed to operate on a single machine. Increasingly, software is downloadable from the Internet and designed to combine the processing power of multiple machines and to integrate freely with other applications on the Internet. An extreme example of distributed computing is Google, which uses more than 100,000 processors spread across the world in 12 computer centers.

On a smaller scale, entrepreneurs are creating new software applications and services based on combining different online software applications. Called **mashups**, these new combined applications depend on high-speed data networks, universal communication standards, and open-source code. The idea is to take different sources and produce a new work that is "greater than" the sum of its parts.

# FOCUS ON ORGANIZATIONS  The Benefits and Challenges of a Service-Oriented Architecture

To increase flexibility to develop new business capabilities, create new products and services, boost customer loyalty, and lower operating costs, businesses are increasingly adopting service-oriented architectures (SOAs). For example, First Command Financial Planning Inc., which provides banking, insurance, and investment services to the families of more than 500,000 U.S. armed services personnel, used SOA to develop a capability to present customers with all their financial information plus tools for viewing the data. After developing software to integrate all the customer data into formats required by various applications, First Command's information systems staff used XML to create a "calculator" as a common service for multiple applications. Instead of embedding the "calculator" in each application, First Command can deliver the "calculator" service to all of its applications.

Next, First Command created a service that lets customers see all of their financial assets, regardless of where these assets are located. The service pulls data from other Web sites to an online portal if the user supplies the correct log-in and password. First Command's CIO John Quinones foresees a future in which all of the company's applications are based on services rather than being custom coded. First Command's existing applications are difficult and expensive to change because a change in any one of them requires changing the way many applications interface with each other.

TSYS Prepaid Inc., a provider of prepaid debit-card services for businesses and banks, initially offered its services to card issuers as part of a large Java application. The system evolved into an SOA when the company used Systinet Corp.'s Java server to divide the single application into individual applications that communicate through an SOA. The SOA enables TSYS to meet customer needs much faster than before, meanwhile enabling its clients to issue cards more rapidly and to have more flexibility in how they manage support for cardholders. Card issuers now access the features they want to use and have the option of integrating those services with their own customer service systems, use TSYS-supplied Web interfaces, or use TSYS as an outsourced customer service unit.

ProCard, a provider of credit card services, used SOA to fend off its competition in an innovative way. ProCard was already a leader in its industry with customer service capabilities that surpassed most of its competitors. For example, ProCard could increase a credit card customer's credit limit or change a billing address in real time as opposed to waiting for an overnight batch process to put

the change into effect. However, powerful competitors, such as Visa, had the resources to deploy similar technology. ProCard decided to convert its credit card processing tools into a service-based product that the company could offer to multiple partners, including competitors such as Visa. The SOA approach would be more lucrative than building a custom product for one partner and it would also serve as the foundation for future service products. Banks that were not willing to buy new suites of credit card processing tools were eager to acquire individual service components to enhance their own customer service capabilities.

Experts advise that an SOA should start with a small or lucrative segment of the business serving as a test case. The organization should have a staff with the technical expertise for designing and building an SOA. The organization must be able to train the staff properly as well.

Even some of those who believe strongly in the potential of an SOA recognize that that is not always the answer. Enzo Micali, CIO of 1–800-Flowers.com, knows that his decision making must reflect a balance between the desire to optimize his company's operations and the necessity to satisfy users. Sometimes, this means that developing a specific application on time or to exact specifications takes precedence over the company's greater plans. Executives, such as Micali, must also take into account that building an SOA is not a finite task. Service maintenance and repackaging can result in additional costs that make building a single-use custom application the better solution. Moreover, although some organizations already possess the tools necessary to construct an SOA, others may need to invest in technologies such as Web-services application programming interfaces (APIs) and XML compatibility before they can begin. All involved seem to agree that an SOA project is not likely to succeed without establishing limits, managing risk, and satisfying the needs of business users.

*Sources:* Tony Kontzer, "The Customer Comes First," *InformationWeek*, February 7, 2005; Christopher Lindquist, "A New Blueprint for IT," *CIO Magazine*, August 15, 2005; and Michael Meehan, "Covad: SOA Scary, Slow and Worth It," SearchWebServices.com, accessed October 3, 2005.

## To Think About:

What problems do Web services and service-oriented architectures help companies solve? How did companies described in this case benefit from SOA? How can the benefits of an SOA trickle down to consumers and the clients of companies that employ the architecture? What challenges and issues were raised by those who have experience with SOAs? Is an SOA the best solution in all cases?

Part of a movement called Web 2.0, and in the spirit of musical mashups, Web mashups combine the capabilities of two or more online applications to create a kind of hybrid that provides more customer value than the original sources alone. One area of great innovation is the mashup of mapping and satellite image software with local content. For instance, Paul Rademacher, a Silicon Valley programmer, opened a Web site called housingmaps.com that makes it possible to display real estate listings in local areas from Craigslist.com overlaid on Google Maps, with pushpins showing the location of each listing. The site has attracted more than half a million visitors and receives about 10,000 visits a day.

Although building communication links among software applications using Web services is not new, online mapping applications are driving a whole new set of recombinant applications. Other map- and satellite-image-based mashups are in the works, encouraged by Google and Yahoo!, both of which in 2005 released for programmers the application programming interfaces (APIs) that allow other applications to pull in information from Google's and Yahoo!'s map and satellite images. Microsoft will release a competing map and satellite service called Virtual Earth, which programmers will be able to use.

What's different about Google's service, however, is that it has simplified the process of using its mapping data down to the level of inserting four lines of Java script into a program. This simplification has made the process of integrating maps into other applications extremely easy for thousands of Web site designers. Publicly available APIs provide programmers with the tools for pulling data from many different Web sites and combining them with other information to make an entirely new Web service. The result is that instead of the Web being a collection of pages, it becomes a collection of capabilities, a platform where thousands of programmers can create new services quickly and inexpensively.

Some other recent mashup applications include chcapgas.com, which provides maps showing where gas can be purchased for less; chicagocrime.org, which uses Google Maps to display where crimes occur in Chicago; and bookburro.com, which allows users to compare book prices based on Amazon's API and other screen-scraping tools that scour the Web for other book sites' prices. One hot new mashup application is a new job listing site, indeed.com, which pulls job listings from many different Web job sites and organizes them by city. Even the Web browser developers are getting into the action. A new add-on to the Firefox browser, called Greasemonkey, allows users to install scripts on their computers that customize the way a Web site works on a specific PC.

## 4.3 Managing Hardware and Software Technology

Selection and use of computer hardware and software technology has a profound impact on business performance. We now describe the most important issues you'll face when managing hardware and software technology: capacity planning and scalability; determining the total cost of technology assets; and determining whether to own and maintain your own hardware, software, and other infrastructure components or lease them from an external technology service provider.

### Capacity Planning and Scalability

E-commerce and e-business are placing heavy new demands on hardware technology. Much larger processing and storage resources are required to process and store the surging digital transactions flowing between different parts of the firm, and between the firm and its customers and suppliers. Many people using a Web site simultaneously place great strains on a computer system, as does hosting large numbers of interactive Web pages with data-intensive graphics or video.

Managers and information systems specialists now need to pay more attention to hardware capacity planning and scalability than before. **Capacity planning** is the process of predicting when a computer hardware system becomes saturated. It considers factors such as the maximum number of users that the system can accommodate at one time; the impact of existing and future software applications; and performance measures, such as minimum response time for processing business transactions. Capacity planning ensures that the firm has enough computing power for its current and future needs. For example, the Nasdaq Stock Market performs ongoing capacity planning to identify peaks in the volume of stock trading transactions and to ensure it has enough computing capacity to handle large surges in volume when trading is very heavy.

Although information systems specialists perform capacity planning, input from business managers is essential. Business managers need to determine acceptable levels of computer response time and availability for the firm's mission-critical systems to maintain the level of business performance they expect. New applications, mergers and acquisitions, and changes in business volume all impact computer workload and must be considered when planning hardware capacity.

**Scalability** refers to the ability of a computer, product, or system to expand to serve a large number of users without breaking down. Electronic commerce and electronic business both call for scalable IT infrastructures that have the capacity to grow with the business as the size of a Web site and number of visitors increase. Organizations must make sure they have sufficient computer processing, storage, and network resources to handle surging volumes of digital transactions and to make such data immediately available online.

## Total Cost of Ownership (TCO) of Technology Assets

When you calculate how much your hardware and software cost, their purchase price is only the beginning. You must also consider ongoing administration costs for hardware and software upgrades, maintenance, technical support, training, and even utility and real estate costs for running and housing the technology. The **total cost of ownership (TCO)** model can be used to analyze these direct and indirect costs to help determine the actual cost of owning a specific technology. Table 4.7 describes the most important TCO components to consider in a TCO analysis.

**TABLE 4.7**

**Total Cost of Ownership (TCO) Cost Components**

| | |
|---|---|
| Hardware acquisition | Purchase price of computer hardware equipment, including computers, terminals, storage, and printers |
| Software acquisition | Purchase or license of software for each user |
| Installation | Cost to install computers and software |
| Training | Cost to provide training to information systems specialists and end users |
| Support | Cost to provide ongoing technical support, help desks, and so forth |
| Maintenance | Cost to upgrade the hardware and software |
| Infrastructure | Cost to acquire, maintain, and support related infrastructure, such as networks and specialized equipment (including storage backup units) |
| Downtime | Lost productivity if hardware or software failures cause the system to be unavailable for processing and user tasks |
| Space and energy | Real estate and utility costs for housing and providing power for the technology |

When all these cost components are considered, the TCO for a PC might run up to three times the original purchase price of the equipment. "Hidden costs" for support staff, downtime, and additional network management can make distributed client/server architectures—especially those incorporating handheld computers and wireless devices—more expensive than centralized mainframe architectures.

Many large firms are saddled with redundant, incompatible hardware and software because their departments and divisions have been allowed to make their own technology purchases. These firms could reduce their TCO through greater centralization and standardization of their hardware and software resources. Companies could reduce the size of the information systems staff required to support their infrastructure if the firm minimized the number of different computer models and pieces of software that employees are allowed to use.

## Using Technology Service Providers

Some of the most important questions facing managers are "How should we acquire and maintain our technology assets? Should we build software applications ourselves or outsource them to an external contractor? Should we purchase and run them ourselves or rent them from external service providers?" In the past, most companies ran their own computer facilities and developed their own software. Today, more and more companies are obtaining their hardware and software technology from external service vendors.

### Outsourcing

A number of firms are **outsourcing** the maintenance of their IT infrastructures and the development of new systems to external vendors. They may contract with an external service provider to run their computer center and networks, to develop new software, or to manage all of the components of their IT infrastructures, as did Procter & Gamble (P&G). P&G agreed to pay Hewlett-Packard (HP) $3 billion to manage its IT infrastructure, computer center operations, desktop and end-user support, network management, and applications development and maintenance for global operations in 160 countries. For another perspective on outsourcing, see the chapter-ending case, which describes why JP Morgan Chase terminated its outsourcing arrangement with IBM when its infrastructure requirements changed after it acquired Bank One.

Specialized Web hosting services are available for companies that lack the financial or technical resources to operate their own Web sites. A **Web hosting service** maintains a large Web server, or a series of servers, and provides fee-paying subscribers with space to maintain their Web sites. The subscribing companies may create their own Web pages or have the hosting service, or a Web design firm, create them. Some services offer **co-location**, in which the firm actually purchases and owns the server computer housing its Web site but locates the server in the physical facility of the hosting service.

Firms often will retain control over their hardware resources but outsource custom software development or maintenance to outside firms, frequently firms that operate offshore in low-wage areas of the world. When firms outsource software work outside their national borders, the practice is called **offshore software outsourcing**. Offshore firms provided about $8 billion in software services to the United States in 2004, which is about 2 percent of the combined U.S. software plus software services budget (about $400 billion). Until recently, this type of software development involved lower-level maintenance, data entry, and call center operations, but with the growing sophistication and experience of offshore firms, particularly in India, more and more new program development is taking place offshore. Chapter 11 discusses offshore software outsourcing in greater detail.

### On-Demand Computing

Even if firms continue to run their own IT infrastructures, they now have the option to rent additional infrastructure capacity on an as-needed basis. **On-demand computing** refers to firms off-loading peak demand for computing power to remote, large-scale data processing centers. In this manner, firms can reduce their technology expenditures by investing just enough to handle average processing loads and paying for only as much additional computing power as the market demands. Another term for on-demand computing is **utility computing**, which suggests that firms purchase computing power from central computing utilities and pay only for the amount of computing power they use, much as they would pay for electricity.

IBM is investing $10 billion to bring this vision to reality and has created four on-demand computing centers around the United States where businesses can experiment with the concepts. HP's Adaptive Enterprise offers similar capabilities.

In addition to lowering the cost of owning hardware resources, on-demand computing gives firms greater agility to use technology. On-demand computing shifts firms from having a fixed infrastructure capacity toward a highly flexible infrastructure, some of it owned by the firm, and some of it rented from giant computer centers run by technology specialists. This arrangement frees firms to launch entirely new business processes that they would never attempt with a fixed infrastructure.

For example, Exa Corp, a provider of fluid flow simulation software, has found that IBM's on-demand computing enables it to serve large markets, such as the automobile industry, quickly and effectively by reducing its computing costs by as much as a factor of five to ten. Exa has a contract with IBM to provide it with millions of hours of computer processing per year, delivered through IBM's Poughkeepsie computing facility. Exa can also order extra processing time for specific workloads, such as testing additional simulations over a weekend (Dunn, 2005).

### Application Service Providers (ASPs)

It is clear that software will be increasingly delivered and used over networks as a service. According to an International Data Corporation study, worldwide spending on software as a service reached $4.2 billion in 2004 and is expected to reach $10.7 billion by 2009 (Traudt and Konary, 2005).

Online application service providers are springing up to provide these software services over the Web and over private networks. An **application service provider (ASP)** is a business that delivers and manages applications and computer services from remote computer centers to multiple users via the Internet or a private network. Instead of buying and installing software programs, subscribing companies can rent the same functions from these services. Users pay for the use of this software either on a subscription or per transaction basis.

The ASP's solution combines package software applications and all of the related hardware, system software, network, and other infrastructure services that the customer otherwise would have to purchase, integrate, and manage independently. The ASP customer interacts with a single entity instead of an array of technologies and service vendors.

The "time-sharing" services of the 1970s, which ran applications such as payroll on their computers for other companies, were an earlier version of this application hosting. But today's ASPs run a wider array of applications than these earlier services and deliver many of these software services over the Web. At Web-based services, servers perform the bulk of the processing and the only essential program needed by users is client software running on a desktop computer or a Web browser. Figure 4-11 illustrates one model of an ASP. The ASP hosts applications at its own site, often on servers in a server farm. (A server farm consists of a large group of servers maintained by a commercial vendor and made available to subscribers.) Servers are not dedicated to specific customers but are assigned applications based on available capacity. The application is then transmitted to the customer via the Internet or a private network.

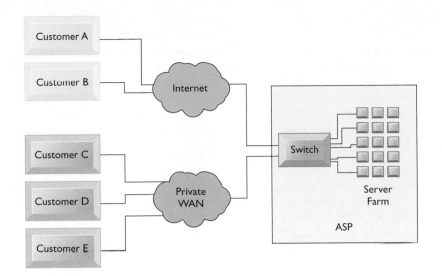

**Figure 4-11**

Model of an Application Service Provider (ASP)

*ASPs provide economies of scale by remotely running software applications for many subscribing companies. Applications are transmitted over the Internet or a private network to user client computers.*

Large and medium-size businesses are using ASPs for enterprise systems, sales force automation, or financial management, and small businesses are using them for functions such as invoicing, tax calculations, electronic calendars, and accounting. ASP vendors are starting to provide tools to integrate the applications they manage with clients' internal systems or with applications hosted by different vendors.

Some companies will find it much easier to "rent" software from another firm and avoid the expense and difficulty of installing, operating, and maintaining the hardware and software for complex systems, such as enterprise resource planning (ERP) systems. The ASP contracts guarantee a level of service and support to ensure that the software is available and working at all times. Today's Internet-driven business environment is changing so rapidly that getting a system up and running in three months instead of six could mean the difference between success and failure. Application service providers also enable small and medium-size companies to use applications that they otherwise could not afford.

Companies considering the software service model need to carefully assess application service provider costs and benefits, weighing all management, organizational, and technology issues, including the ASP's ability to integrate with existing systems and deliver the level of service and performance it has promised. In some cases, the cost of renting software can add up to more than purchasing and maintaining the application in-house. Yet there may be benefits to paying more for software through an ASP if this decision allows the company to focus on core business issues instead of technology challenges.

**LEARNING TRACKS**

1. If you want to learn more about the evolution of IT infrastructure, you will find a Learning Track on this topic at the Laudon Web site for this chapter.
2. If you want to learn more about the developments in computer processing, storage, and networking that have transformed IT infrastructure, you will find a Learning Track on technology drivers of infrastructure evolution on the Laudon Web site for this chapter.
3. If you want to learn more about the management of IT infrastructure, you will find a Learning Track on Management Opportunities, Challenges, and Solutions at the Laudon Web site for this chapter.
4. If you want a more detailed description of how computer hardware and software work, you will find a Learning Track on this topic at the Laudon Web site for this chapter.

## Summary

**1** **Identify and describe the components of IT infrastructure.** IT infrastructure is the shared technology resources that provide the platform for the firm's specific information system applications. IT infrastructure includes hardware, software, and services that are shared across the entire firm. Major IT infrastructure components include computer hardware, software, data management technology, networking and telecommunications technology, and technology services.

**2** **Identify and describe the major types of computer hardware, data storage, and input and output technology.** Computers are categorized as mainframes, midrange computers, PCs, workstations, or supercomputers. Mainframes are the largest computers; midrange computers can be minicomputers used in factory, university, or research lab systems, or servers providing software and other resources to computers on a network. PCs are desktop or laptop machines; workstations are desktop machines with powerful mathematical and graphic capabilities; and supercomputers are sophisticated, powerful computers that can perform massive and complex computations rapidly. Computing power can be further increased by connecting geographically remote computers into a single network to create a computational grid that combines the computing power of all the computers on the network.

Computers can be networked together to distribute processing among different machines. In the client/server model of computing, computer processing is split between "clients" and "servers" connected via a network. The exact division of tasks between client and server depends on the application. An N-tier client/server architecture balances the work of the entire network over several different levels of servers, such as a Web server and an application server.

The principal secondary storage technologies are magnetic disk, optical disk, and magnetic tape. Optical CD-ROM and DVD disks can store vast amounts of data compactly and some types are rewritable. Storage area networks (SANs) connect multiple storage devices on a separate high-speed network dedicated to storage. The principal input devices are keyboards, computer mice, touch screens, magnetic ink and optical character recognition devices, pen-based instruments, digital scanners, sensors, and audio input devices. The principal output devices are cathode ray tube terminals, printers, and audio output devices. In batch processing, transactions are accumulated and stored in a group until the time when it is efficient or necessary to process them. In online processing, the user enters transactions into a device that is directly connected to the computer system and the transactions are usually processed immediately.

**3** **Identify and describe the major types of computer software used in business.** There are two major types of software: system software and application software. System software coordinates the various parts of the computer system and mediates between application software and computer hardware. Application software is used to develop specific business applications.

The system software that manages and controls the activities of the computer is called the operating system. The operating system acts as the chief manager of the information system, allocating, assigning, and scheduling system resources, and monitoring the use of the computer. Other system software includes computer-language translation programs, which convert programming languages into machine language, and utility programs that perform common processing tasks.

PC operating systems have developed sophisticated capabilities, such as multitasking and support for multiple users on networks. Leading PC operating systems include Windows Vista, Windows XP, Windows Server 2003, Windows CE, UNIX, Linux, and the Macintosh operating system. Linux is a powerful, resilient, open-source operating system that can run on multiple hardware platforms and is used widely to run Web servers. PC operating systems and many kinds of applications software now use graphical user interfaces.

The principal programming languages used in business application software include COBOL, C, C++, and Visual Basic, and each is designed to solve specific types of problems. Fourth-generation languages are less procedural than conventional programming languages and enable end users to perform many software tasks that previously required technical specialists. They include popular PC software tools, such as word processing, spreadsheet, data management, presentation graphics, and e-mail software, along with Web browsers and groupware. Java is an operating-system- and hardware-independent programming language that is the leading interactive programming environment for the Web. HTML is a page description language for creating Web pages.

Software for enterprise integration includes enterprise applications and middleware, such as enterprise application integration (EAI) software and Web services. Web services are loosely coupled software components based on XML and open Web standards that are not product specific and can work with any application software and operating system. They can be used as components of Web-based applications linking the systems of two different organizations or to link disparate systems of a single company.

4 **Assess contemporary computer hardware and software trends.** Contemporary hardware and software trends demonstrate that, increasingly, computing is taking place over a network. Computing and telecommunications platforms are becoming integrated. Edge computing balances the processing load for Web-based applications by distributing parts of the Web content, logic, and processing among multiple servers. In autonomic computing, computer systems have capabilities for automatically configuring and repairing themselves. Mashups are new software applications and services based on combining different online software applications using high-speed data networks, universal communication standards, and open-source code.

5 **Evaluate the principal issues in managing hardware and software technology.** Electronic commerce and electronic business have put new strategic emphasis on technologies that can store vast quantities of transaction data and make them immediately available online. Managers and information systems specialists need to pay special attention to hardware capacity planning and scalability to ensure that the firm has enough computing power for its current and future needs.

Businesses also need to balance the costs and benefits of building and maintaining their own hardware and software versus outsourcing these assets to external service providers. Companies may outsource custom software application development to an external vendor (that may be offshore) or rent software services from an application service provider (ASP). ASPs rent out software applications and computer services from remote computer centers to subscribers over the Internet or private networks. In an on-demand (utility) computing model, companies pay technology service providers only for the amount of computing power and services that they actually use.

Calculating the total cost of ownership (TCO) of the organization's technology assets can help provide managers with the information they need to manage these assets and decide whether to rent or own these assets. The total cost of owning technology resources includes not only the original cost of computer hardware and software but also costs for hardware and software upgrades, maintenance, technical support, and training.

# Key Terms

Application server, 116
Application service provider (ASP), 138
Application software, 113
Autonomic computing, 120
Batch processing, 119
C, 124
C++, 124
Capacity planning, 136
CD-ROM (compact disk read-only memory), 118
CD-RW (CD-ReWritable), 118
Centralized processing, 116
Client, 116
Client/server computing, 116
COBOL (COmmon Business Oriented Language), 124
Co-location, 137
Data management software, 113
Desktop publishing, 127
Digital video disk (DVD), 118
Distributed processing, 116
Downsizing, 117
Edge computing, 120

Electronic mail (e-mail), 129
Enterprise application integration (EAI) software, 131
Fourth-generation languages, 124
Graphical user interface (GUI), 122
Grid computing, 116
Groupware, 129
Hard drives, 117
Hypertext markup language (HTML), 130
Input devices, 118
Integrated software packages, 127
Java, 129
Legacy systems, 113
Linux, 123
Magnetic disk, 117
Magnetic tape, 118
Mainframe, 115
Mashups, 133
Middleware, 131
Midrange computers, 115
Minicomputers, 115

Natural languages, 126
Multitiered (N-tier) client/server architecture, 116
Object, 124
Office 2003, 129
Office XP, 129
Offshore software outsourcing, 137
On-demand computing, 137
Online processing, 119
Open-source software, 124
Operating system, 121
Output devices, 118
Outsourcing, 137
Personal computer (PC), 114
Presentation graphics, 127
Query languages, 126
RAID (Redundant Array of Inexpensive Disks), 117
Scalability, 136
Server, 115
Service-oriented architecture (SOA), 132
Simple Object Access Protocol (SOAP), 132
Software package, 126

## Review Questions

**4.1** What is information technology (IT) infrastructure? List and describe each of its components.

**4.2** List and describes the various types of computers available to businesses today.

**4.3** What is the client/server model of computing? Describe the difference between a two-tiered and N-tier client/server architecture.

**4.4** List the most important secondary storage media. What are the strengths and limitations of each?

**4.5** List and describe the major computer input and output devices.

**4.6** What is the difference between batch and online processing?

**4.7** Define and describe grid computing, edge computing, and autonomic computing.

**4.8** What is the difference between application software and system software? What role does each play?

**4.9** What is the operating system of a computer? What does it do?

**4.10** List and describe the major PC operating systems.

**4.11** Why are open-source software and Linux so important today? How can they benefit businesses?

**4.12** How do fourth-generation languages differ from conventional application programming languages? Name and describe each category of fourth-generation software tools.

**4.13** Name and describe the major desktop productivity software tools.

**4.14** How are Java and HTML used in building applications for the Web?

**4.15** Name and describe the kinds of software that can be used for enterprise integration.

**4.16** Describe the technologies used in Web services. How do Web services benefit business?

**4.17** What are Web mashups? How do they benefit businesses?

**4.18** List and describe the principal issues in managing hardware and software assets.

## Discussion Questions

**4.1** Why is selecting computer hardware and software for the organization an important business decision? What people, organization, and technology issues should be considered when selecting computer hardware and software?

**4.2** Should organizations use application service providers (ASPs) for all their software needs? Why or why not? What people, organization, and technology factors should be considered when making this decision?

## Application Software Exercise

### Spreadsheet Exercise: Evaluating Computer Hardware and Software Options

Software skills: Spreadsheet formulas

Business skills: Technology pricing

You have been asked to obtain pricing information on hardware and software for an office of 30 people. Using the Internet, get pricing for 30 PC desktop systems (monitors, computers, and keyboards) manufactured by IBM, Dell, and Compaq as listed at their respective corporate Web sites. (For the purposes of this exercise, ignore the fact that desktop systems usually come with preloaded software packages.) Also obtain pricing on 15 monochrome desktop printers manufactured by Hewlett-Packard and by Xerox. Each desktop system must satisfy the minimum specifications shown in the following table:

| Minimum Desktop Specifications | |
| --- | --- |
| Processor speed | 2 GHz |
| Hard drive | 80 GB |
| RAM | 512 MB |
| CD-ROM speed | 48 speed |
| Monitor (diagonal measurement) | 17 inches |

Each desktop printer must satisfy the minimum specifications shown in the following table:

| Minimum Monochrome Printer Specifications | |
| --- | --- |
| Print speed | 12 pages per minute |
| Print resolution | 600 × 600 |
| Network ready? | Yes |
| Maximum price/unit | $1,000 |

After pricing the desktop systems and printers, obtain pricing on 30 copies of Microsoft's Office XP or Office 2003, the most recent versions of Corel's WordPerfect Office and IBM's Lotus SmartSuite application packages, and on 30 copies of Microsoft Windows XP Professional Edition. The application software suite packages come in various versions, so be sure that each package contains programs for word processing, spreadsheet analysis, database analysis, graphics preparation, and e-mail.

Prepare a spreadsheet showing your research results for the desktop systems, for the printers, and for the software. Use your spreadsheet software to determine the desktop system, printer, and software combination that will offer both the best performance and pricing per worker. Because every two workers will share one printer (15 printers/30 systems), assume only half a printer cost per worker in the spreadsheet. Assume that your company will take the standard warranty and service contract offered by each product's manufacturer.

## Analyzing the Total Cost of Ownership (TCO) of Desktop Software Assets

Software skills: Spreadsheet formulas

Business skills: Total cost of ownership (TCO) analysis

Dirt Bikes would like to replace the desktop office productivity software used by its corporate administrative staff, including the controller, accountant, administrative assistant, two human resources specialists, and three secretaries—a total of eight users. These employees need a suite that has word processing, spreadsheet, database, electronic presentation, and e-mail software tools. Occasionally, they would like to use these software tools to publish Web pages or to access data from the Internet. Use the Web to research and compare the pricing and capabilities of either Microsoft Office 2003 or Office XP versus Sun StarOffice.

1. Use your spreadsheet software to create a matrix comparing the prices of each software suite as well as their functionality. Identify the lowest-price system that meets Dirt Bikes's requirements.
2. You have learned that hardware and software purchase costs represent only part of the total cost of ownership (TCO) of technology assets and that there are additional cost components to consider. For this particular software system, assume that one-time installation costs $25 per user, one-time training costs $100 per user, annual technical support costs 30 percent of the initial purchase costs, and annual downtime costs another 15 percent of the purchase costs. What is the total cost of ownership of Dirt Bikes's new desktop productivity systems over a three-year period?
3. (Optional) If possible, use electronic presentation software to summarize your findings for management.

## Building Internet Skills

### Planning and Budgeting for a Sales Conference

This project will help develop your Internet skills in using online travel sites.

The Foremost Composite Materials Company is planning a two-day sales conference for October 15–16, starting with a reception on the evening of October 14. The conference consists of all-day meetings that the entire sales force, numbering 125 sales representatives and their 16 managers, must attend. Each sales representative requires his or her own room, and the company needs two common meeting rooms, one large enough to hold the entire sales force plus a few visitors (200) and the other able to hold half the force. Management has set a budget of $85,000 for the representatives' room rentals. The hotel must also have such services as overhead and computer projectors as well as business center and banquet facilities. It also should have facilities for the company reps to be able to work in their rooms and to enjoy themselves in a swimming pool or gym facility. The company would like to hold the conference in either Miami or Marco Island, Florida.

Foremost usually likes to hold such meetings in Hilton- or Marriott-owned hotels. Use the Hilton and Marriott Web sites to select a hotel in whichever of these cities that would enable the company to hold its sales conference within its budget.

Link to the two sites' home pages, and search them to find a hotel that meets Foremost's sales conference requirements. Once you have selected the hotel, locate flights arriving the afternoon prior to the conference because the attendees will need to check in the day before and attend your reception the evening prior to the conference. Your attendees will be coming from Los Angeles (54), San Francisco (32), Seattle (22), Chicago (19), and Pittsburgh (14). Determine costs of each airline ticket from these cities. When you are finished, create a budget for the conference. The budget will include the cost of each airline ticket, the room cost, and $60 per attendee per day for food.

What was your final budget? Which did you select as the best hotel for the sales conference and why?

## Video Case

You will find a video case illustrating some of the concepts in this chapter on the Laudon Web site at **www.prenhall.com/laudon** along with questions to help you analyze the case.

## Teamwork

### Evaluating Server Operating Systems

Form a group with three or four of your classmates. One group should research and compare the capabilities and costs of Linux versus the most recent version of the Windows operating system for servers. Another group should research and compare the capabilities and costs of Linux versus UNIX. Each group should present its findings to the class, using electronic presentation software if possible.

# BUSINESS PROBLEM-SOLVING CASE

## JP Morgan Chase Shifts IT Outsourcing into Reverse

JP Morgan Chase is a financial holding company with $1.2 trillion in assets and $106 billion in stockholders' equity. It is the second-largest financial services firm in the United States with $56.9 billion in revenue and more than 160,000 employees. The firm operates in more than 50 countries. Its principal banking subsidiaries include JP Morgan Chase Bank National Association, which is a national banking association with locations in 17 states; and Chase Bank USA, National Association, which issues credit cards for the firm. JP Morgan Chase also operates a principal nonbanking subsidiary, JP Morgan Securities Inc., which is an investment banking firm in the United States.

Under the corporate umbrella, the firm runs an additional set of businesses, including its Private Equity and Treasury businesses, corporate support companies, automobile financing companies, leasing companies, e-commerce companies, and a host of other financial services businesses. On some endeavors, JP Morgan Chase competes in a global market; on others, it competes regionally. The firm points to a number of factors that determine how well it can compete in either arena. Among these factors are the performance of its products, the appeal of its products to customers, its ability to meet the objectives and needs of clients, its reputation, and its ability to attract and retain its personnel. JP Morgan Chase competes with banks, brokerage firms, investment banking companies, insurance companies, credit card companies, and mutual fund companies.

To position itself better in its various markets, JP Morgan Chase made a major strategic decision in 2002. The firm struck a deal with IBM to outsource a significant portion of its IT infrastructure to the computing giant. According to JP Morgan Chase management, this agreement would create "significant value" for clients, shareholders, and employees by creating capacity for "efficient growth" while reducing costs and increasing quality.

The agreement called for a seven-year relationship and bore a price tag of more than $5 billion. It was, at the time, the largest contract to which JP Morgan Chase had ever agreed. It was also the largest outsourcing deal in terms of dollars that IBM had ever secured, surpassing a seven-year, $4 billion pact with American Express.

For IBM, the contract was an opportunity to demonstrate the power of its new on-demand services on a stage provided by a relationship with a major corporation. IBM hoped that a successful venture with JP Morgan Chase would usher in a new era of corporate client relationships based on a pay-as-you-go strategy for computing services and IT infrastructure. JP Morgan Chase was to be the poster child for this sort of arrangement. Under the agreement, IBM took over much of the bank's data processing infrastructure. JP Morgan Chase turned over such tasks as hosting computer centers, running help desks, distributing applications, and maintaining data and voice networks. IBM also lent its resources to key components of the bank's business, such as hosting trading applications for JP Morgan Securities.

The on-demand aspect of the relationship between the two companies originated from what was being called a "virtual pool" of computing resources. The resources, supplied by both JP Morgan Chase and IBM's global services division, were set up to be accessible on an as-needed basis. IBM referred to the technology that supports this setup as the Utility Management Infrastructure (UMI). The technology used open architecture standards that enabled different components, such as storage devices and servers, to work together. This approach to architecture eliminated the need to write new applications for each system that the client required to run its business. IBM made on-demand services a major focus of its business strategy and planned to spend $10 billion during a 10-year period to continue developing such services. The initiative incorporated generous support of the Linux operating system, then a rising star in open-source computing.

Senior analyst Ronald Schmelzer of the tech research firm ZapThink viewed this gravitation toward utility computing as a positive sign for the IT infrastructure services industry. He did question, however, whether IBM would be able supply such services for multiple companies the size of JP Morgan Chase. Absorbing the costs of IT for those companies was feasible, but scaling up the on demand infrastructure to such a degree was another issue. IBM was confident in its ability to provide its clients with flexible IT costs. JP Morgan Chase, in turn, was enthusiastic about the prospect of scaling its IT expenditures according to its actual needs rather than paying full costs based on projections up front.

In the first half of 2003, JP Morgan Chase transferred approximately 4,000 employees to IBM's payroll as part of the outsourcing agreement. The bank retained a few of its IT functions, including application delivery and development, desktop support, and other core functions.

For some JP Morgan Chase employees, the realities of this arrangement were not nearly as rosy as promised. David Rosario was one of the IT workers whose employment was transferred to IBM. However, instead of going through an easy transition, he had to interview again for his job. Some of his colleagues learned that their positions would likely be eliminated within as few as 12 months.

Scott Kirwin, an independent consultant who worked for JP Morgan Chase from mid-2002 until spring 2003, witnessed not only a dip in morale as a result of the reapplication process and salary reductions but also a drop in productivity caused by the distractions of coordinating the outsourcing. Managers and staff had to devote time to documenting procedures, staffing levels, skill sets, budgets, day-to-day responsibilities, and work allocations while still performing their regular duties. The extra workload persisted from the conception of the outsourcing deal into its execution. According to Kirwin, "The minute you start talking about outsourcing, you lose productivity, not just among us employees but managers and directors who have to set aside what they're hired to do to talk about this significant business change."

Kirwin speculated that JP Morgan Chase might not have signed such an outsourcing deal if the company knew how much the loss of productivity would cost. The outsourcing process incurs additional expenses from investments in consultants who assist in outsourcing strategy and reengineering, in human resources efforts to assist employees in the process, and in retention bonuses to mollify employees during the arduous transition. In this case, some of these expenses were passed back to the bank. A consultant who worked for JP Morgan Chase at the time said, "IBM caused tremendous headaches for JP Morgan and the company's infrastructure, nickel-and-diming to control their own costs. A data management specialist outsourced to IBM added, "Things that used to get done no longer got done."

Rosario's recollections supported the comments of the consultants. He reported that the organizational infrastructure at IBM at times made it difficult to procure even the most basic office supplies, such as pager batteries and copier batteries. Project managers resorted to buying their own supplies. Only with knowledge of these negative experiences does the announcement by JP Morgan Chase in September 2004 that it was canceling the remainder of its outsourcing deal with IBM after only 21 months seem expected.

At the time, the decision sent ripples through the business and IT communities. IBM lost one of its most high-profile clients, fueling speculation that its ability to produce returns for its customers was in doubt. Analyst Anthony Miller of Ovum Holway forecasted a significant hit for IBM. Miller noted that postinvestment phase earnings are key to this type of deal and that IBM was going to miss out on much of this portion of the relationship. He went on to say, "The cancellation of the JP Morgan Chase deal could stem the tide of future banking megadeals, a sector we had expected to be one of the major drivers for outsourcing in coming years."

Statements from both sides absolved IBM of any fault and pointed instead to a change in business strategy on the part of JP Morgan Chase. IBM stated publicly that the cancellation of the contract would have a positive effect on its earnings per share. A spokesman reasoned that the early stages of the outsourcing arrangement necessitated large expenditures up front and IBM would suddenly be relieved of those expenses. The separation did not spark an exodus of major IBM outsourcing customers. Qwest Communications International and American Express planned to proceed with their multibillion-dollar long-term deals.

JP Morgan Chase's decision to reverse its IT strategy, "backsourcing" its information technology, was triggered by a merger with Bank One Corp. in July 2004. In the $58.5 billion deal, JP Morgan Chase acquired a larger retail banking presence and an increased capacity to manage its technology infrastructure. Bank One's approach to IT was based on consolidation, cost cutting,

and self-sufficiency. Bank One's CIO Austin Adams preached a do-it-yourself philosophy. He remained CIO of the merged company and proclaimed, "We believe managing our own technology infrastructure is best for the long-term growth and success of our company, as well as our shareholders. Our new capabilities will give us competitive advantages, accelerate innovation, and enable us to become more streamlined and efficient."

Adams's history supported the strategy. Under his supervision, Bank One had pulled out of its own outsourcing deal with IBM a few years earlier. Then, between 2000 and 2003, Bank One cut staff by 12 percent and raised its revenue 17 percent. (For the same period, JP Morgan Chase cut its staff by 6 percent and increased revenue only 1 percent.) The average salary of Bank One employees in 2003 was just under $67,000, whereas JP Morgan Chase employees averaged more than $125,000. In comparison with other banks, JP Morgan Chase was spending more than twice as much on technology per employee, approximately $28,000 compared to $13,000. JP Morgan Chase's spending was too high. Overall, the purpose of bringing IT back in-house from IBM was to fix the poor economics of JP Morgan Chase. However, even if with the strength of a recognized consolidation expert such as Bank One in the fold, backsourcing was not a guaranteed success.

Ralph Schonenbach, CEO of the Trestle Group, a Swiss outsourcing consultancy, described backsourcing as difficult and painful for an organization. In fact, he said, "Bringing outsourced work back in-house can cause such disruption to an organization that most people don't do it." A Deloitte Consulting study found that 70 percent of senior executives were unhappy with outsourcing initiatives, but only 25 percent reversed their decisions. Although most experts and analysts agree with management that backsourcing was the correct move, the suggestion that the transition was entirely smooth deserves some examination. Some employees, even those who agreed that the strategy was sound, experienced more than a change in ID badge and company imprint on their checks. Many of the troubles associated with the outsourcing repeated themselves.

Morale suffered again as employees wondered why they were being shuffled back to JP Morgan Chase for the same reasons they were shuffled out to IBM in the first place. Some employees lost their jobs on the way back in. The merger will create 12,000 layoffs by 2007; the company insisted that these would not be IT jobs. The company reported that 97 percent of the outsourced workforce accepted offers to return to JP Morgan Chase. But David Rosario claimed that many of these workers still feared that their jobs would be eliminated as a result of the merger. In some cases they were right.

In addition to turmoil in the workforce, the backsourcing was a drag on productivity just as the outsourcing had been. Mission-critical tasks once again gave way for those associated with reorganization. At the same time, JP Morgan discovered the extent to which projects had lagged at IBM. A systems engineer who survived both moves pointed to vague language in the agreement between the companies as a source of stagnation. IBM wanted to charge additional fees for any projects that were not ongoing when the contract began. If the bank did not pay, the projects were not approved even if they were worthwhile.

Despite what appeared to be a second complicated reorganization, officials of JP Morgan Chase maintained that the disruption was minimal. Spokesperson Charlotte Gilbert-Biro explained that the relatively short duration of the contract never enabled the bank to move the bulk of its work to IBM's computer centers. JP Morgan Chase also said that IBM would remain a "key technology partner" and would continue to provide hardware, software, and services to a number of the bank's business units. Neither company would say how much the "divorce" cost them, but industry analysts believe JP Morgan Chase had to pay IBM millions of dollars—and perhaps many millions of dollars to terminate the outsourcing contract.

James Dimon, the former CEO of Bank One, became CEO of JP Morgan Chase. With Dimon and Adams at the helm, the merged company was expected to maintain its reliance on in-house technology work. Analysts predicted that JP Morgan Chase would look offshore for outsourcing arrangements in the future but would follow a diverse multisource model rather than agree to a megadeal with a single vendor.

*Sources:* Stephanie Overby, "Backsourcing Pain," *CIO Magazine*, September 1, 2005; Stacy Cowley, "Update: J.P. Morgan Cancels $5B IBM Outsourcing Deal," *Computerworld*, September 15, 2004; Erin Joyce, "JP Morgan, IBM Finalize $5 Billion IT Deal," atnewyork.com, accessed December 30, 2002; Paul A. Strassmann, "Why JP Morgan Chase Really Dropped IBM," *Baseline*, January 13, 2005; Matthew Goldstein, "J.P. Morgan Cancels IBM Pact," TheStreet.com, accessed September 15, 2004; Andy McCue, "Bank Ditches $5bn IBM Deal and Brings IT Back In-House," Silicon.com, accessed September 16, 2004; Thomas Hoffman, "J.P. Morgan Chase to Scale Back Outsourcing Pact," *Computerworld*, June 14, 2004; JP Morgan Chase & Co. Annual Report on Form 10-K, jpmorganchase.com, accessed September 22, 2005.

## Case Study Questions

1. Why did JP Morgan Chase want to outsource its infrastructure to IBM? What problems did it have that it thought outsourcing would solve?
2. What technology functions was IBM supposed to perform for JP Morgan Chase?
3. What problems arose during the outsourcing contract?
4. How did management handle these problems? Could management have handled them better?
5. Was canceling the contract and bringing IT back in-house the best solution for JP Morgan Chase? How could this case be considered a cautionary tale for executives of major corporations who are considering large outsourcing deals?

# Foundations of Business Intelligence: Databases and Information Management

**CHAPTER 5**

## STUDENT OBJECTIVES

After completing this chapter, you will be able to:

1. Describe how a relational database organizes data and compare its approach to an object-oriented database.

2. Identify and describe the principles of a database management system.

3. Evaluate tools and technologies for providing information from databases to improve business performance and decision making.

4. Assess the role of information policy and data administration in the management of organizational data resources.

5. Assess the importance of data quality assurance for the business.

## CHAPTER OUTLINE

## SEVEN-ELEVEN STORES ASK THE CUSTOMER BY ASKING THE DATA

**There is probably a Seven-Eleven** store in your neighborhood, and it's a convenient place for picking up a can of Coke or a quick ham-and-cheese sandwich. It's the number one convenience store chain in the United States, with 3,300 franchise-owned stores and 2,500 company-owned stores. This company started out about 75 years ago as an ice-dock operator. When refrigerators started replacing iceboxes, the manager of each store asked customers one by one what items they'd like to stock in their new appliances. By asking customers directly and stocking only the items customers most wanted, the company grew and prospered.

Over time, the company moved away from its roots, losing touch with customers along the way. It had no means of knowing what sold in each store and allowed vendors, such as Coke and Frito-Lay, to decide what to stock on its shelves. But Seven-Eleven stores are not all alike. What their customers want depends a great deal on the

149

neighborhood and region of the country where they are located. What sells well in Boston may not work in Texas. Profit margins are very thin in the convenience store business, so a quarter-point increase in sales volume can spell the difference between success and failure. Precise information on what to sell in each store makes a big difference.

In 2004, Seven-Eleven installed Hewlett-Packard servers and networking switches in all of its franchise-owned and company-owned stores to implement a Retail Information System. This system collects data from point-of-sale terminals in each store about each daily purchase made by its six million U.S. customers and transmits the information in real time to a 7-terabyte Oracle database operated by Electronic Data Systems (EDS). With this database, Seven-Eleven keeps track of its purchase transactions and also analyzes them to find patterns for customer demand, pricing, and interest in new products, such as the Diet Pepsi Slurpee. The system provides store managers with information on daily, weekly, and monthly sales of each item to help them determine which items to order and the exact quantities they will need for their stores. Managers use this information, plus their on-the-spot knowledge of the neighborhood, to make final ordering decisions.

Store managers enter orders into workstations or handheld computers by 10 A.M. each day. The system consolidates these orders and transmits them to Seven-Eleven's suppliers. Orders are consolidated four times a day, one for each U.S. time zone in which Seven-Eleven stores operate. Seven-Eleven's orders for fresh food items are aggregated at Seven-Eleven headquarters and transmitted to fresh food suppliers and bakeries for preparation and delivery the next day.

Thanks to information technology, Seven-Eleven has come full circle in its ability to respond to the needs of the customer. By tracking and analyzing its data, it knows its customers as intimately as it did when store owners talked to each customer who walked through the door. ▧

*Sources*: Christopher Koch, "Who's Mining the Store?" *CIO*, May 15, 2005; James Keyes, "Data on the Fly," *Baseline*, August 2005; Laurie Sullivan, "Fine-Tuned Pricing," *InformationWeek*, August 15/22, 2005; and Steven Marlin, "The 24-Hour Supply Chain," *InformationWeek*, January 26, 2004.

**S**even-Eleven stores' experience illustrates the importance of data and database systems for success in business. Seven-Eleven used to know exactly what its customers wanted many years ago when it was a much smaller company and managers had more face-to-face relationships with their customers. But the company expanded and grew too big for this approach. It needed to find a way to analyze what was being sold in each store and neighborhood and stock its stores accordingly.

Before the company implemented its Retail Information System it could not determine which items were selling well, or which items were most profitable to sell in the first place. This made a difference to the company's bottom line because of missed sales opportunities, lower profits, and excess store inventory, some of which consisted of perishable goods that had a very short shelf life. Profit margins in this industry are exceedingly thin, so any way to reduce unwanted inventory and increase sales would provide a great boost to profits. Briefly, Seven-Eleven had lost the ability to rationally decide what inventory to put on its shelves.

One solution tried by Seven-Eleven was to rely on its vendors' knowledge of what they were selling in its stores and let the vendors make the stocking decisions. These vendors, such as Frito-Lay and Coca-Cola, had powerful information systems for analyzing what they sold in individual stores. But other vendors didn't have such systems, and these vendor's systems were designed to maximize opportunities for their businesses, not for Seven-Eleven. Another alternative was to have store managers keep track on their own of what each customer purchased. This was definitely too time-consuming to work.

The solution that worked best was for Seven-Eleven to develop its own Retail Information System, which captured point-of-sale data, stored them in a large database, and then analyzed the data to show store managers what was selling in each of their stores. Managers could then make the final stocking decisions, supplementing the information from the system with their own personal knowledge of their customers and neighborhood.

It's easy to see how Seven-Eleven's Retail Information System helps it increase profitability and even competitive advantage. The database improves operational efficiency and

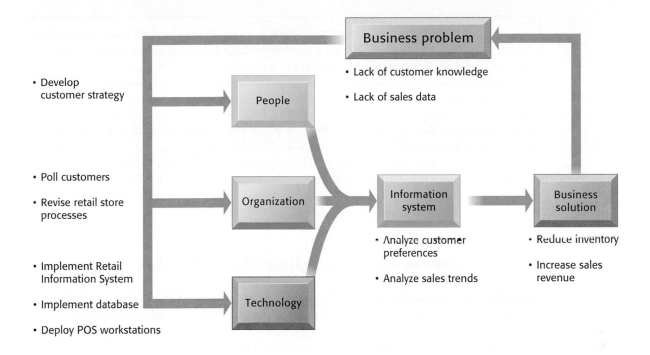

decision making, helps the company understand its own consumers better, increases the chances that new successful products and services will flourish (while unpopular items will disappear quickly), and may help the company respond more efficiently to requests for information (such as how many units of a defective product were sold at each store, and when).

**HEADS UP**

This chapter focuses on databases and how businesses use databases to achieve their objectives. Small and large companies alike use databases to record business transactions, control inventories, manage employees, and achieve customer and supplier intimacy. Once these data are properly organized in database management systems, the data can be analyzed, and the resulting information can be used to develop new businesses, achieve operational excellence, inform management decision making, and help the firm fulfill its reporting requirements to higher authorities. Entire businesses, such as UPS, credit card companies, and Google, are based on databases. It would not be an overstatement to say that databases are the foundation of business today and that most businesses would fail should their databases cease to exist.

•   If your career is in finance and accounting, you will be working with databases of financial transactions, such as payments, invoices, or credit history. If your job is in finance, you will work with massive databases housing data about securities prices, investment portfolios, and economic statistics.

•   If your career is in human resources, you will work with databases maintaining data on employees, benefits plans, compensation plans, training programs, and compliance with governmental regulations on health, safety, and equal employment opportunity.

•   If your career is in manufacturing, production, or operations management, you will be working with large databases with data on finished goods, raw materials in inventory, suppliers, product components, product quality, and goods in transit that can be used for supply chain management.

*(continued)*

> •   If your career is in sales and marketing, you will be using databases for track-
> ing customer purchases, analyzing customer data for targeted marketing cam-
> paigns, or identifying profitable customers and products.

In this chapter, we'll be looking at important applications of database technology so that you can see the critical role it plays in business. We'll start by looking at how businesses organize data and the database approach to data management. Next, we'll learn how database management software works and exactly how this technology helps businesses operate efficiently and make better decisions. Finally, we'll look at the policies and procedures businesses need to manage their data effectively.

## 5.1 The Database Approach to Data Management

A **database** is a collection of related files containing records on people, places, or things. One of the most successful databases in modern history is the telephone book. The telephone book is a collection of records on people and businesses who have telephones. The telephone book lists four pieces of information for each phone user: last name, first name, address, and phone number. It also contains information on businesses and business categories, such as auto dealers or plumbing suppliers. The telephone book draws its information from a database with files for customers, business classifications, and area codes and geographic regions.

Prior to the development of digital databases, a business would use large filing cabinets filled with paper files to store information on transactions, customers, suppliers, inventory, and employees. They would also use lists, laboriously collated and typed by hand, to quickly summarize the information in paper files. You can still find paper-based manual databases in most doctors' offices where patient records are stored in thousands of paper files.

Needless to say, paper-based databases are extremely inefficient and costly to maintain, often contain inaccurate data, are slow, and make it difficult to access the data in a timely fashion. Paper-based databases are also extremely inflexible. For instance, it would be extremely difficult for a paper-based doctor's office to combine its files on prescriptions with its files on patients in order to produce a list of all people for whom they had prescribed a specific drug. For a modern computer database, this would be very easy. In fact, a powerful feature of computer databases is the ability to quickly relate one set of files to another.

### Entities and Attributes

How do you start thinking about the data for your business and how to manage them? If you're starting up or running a business, you'll have to identify the data you'll need to run your business. Typically, you'll be using data on categories of information, such as customers, suppliers, employees, orders, products, shippers, and perhaps parts. Each of these generalized categories representing a person, place, or thing on which we store and maintain information is called an **entity**. Each entity has specific characteristics, called **attributes**. For example, the entity SUPPLIER has specific attributes, such as the supplier's name and address, which would most likely include street, city, state, and ZIP code. The entity PART typically has attributes such as part description, price of each part (unit price), and supplier who produced the part.

### Organizing Data in a Relational Database

If you stored this information in paper files, you would probably have a file on each entity and its attributes. In an information system, a database organizes the data much the same way, grouping related pieces of data together. The **relational database** is the most common type of database today. Relational databases organize data into two-dimensional tables (called relations) with columns and rows. Each table contains data on an entity and its attrib-

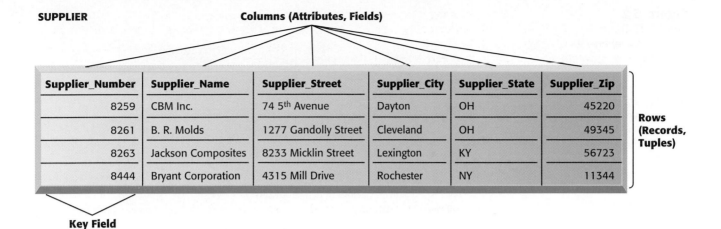

**Figure 5-1**
A Relational Database Table
*A relational database organizes data in the form of two-dimensional tables. Illustrated here is a table for the entity SUPPLIER showing how it represents the entity and its attributes. Supplier_Number is the key field.*

utes. For the most part, there is one table for each business entity. So, at the most basic level, you will have one table for customers, and a table each for suppliers, parts, employees, and sales transactions.

Let's look at how a relational database would organize data about suppliers and parts. Take the SUPPLIER table, which is illustrated in Figure 5-1. It consists of a grid of columns and rows of data. Each individual element of data about a supplier, such as the supplier name, street, city, state, and ZIP code, is stored as a separate **field** within the SUPPLIER table. Each field represents an attribute for the entity SUPPLIER. Fields in a relational database are also called **columns**.

The actual information about *a single supplier* that resides in a table is called a row. Rows are commonly referred to as **records**, or, in very technical terms, as **tuples**.

Note that there is a field for Supplier_Number in this table. This field uniquely identifies each record so that the record can be retrieved, updated, or sorted and it is called a **key field**. Each table in a relational database has one field that is designated as its **primary key**. This key field is the unique identifier for all the information in any row of the table and this primary key cannot be duplicated.

We could use the supplier's name as a key field. However, if two different suppliers had the same name (which does happen from time to time), supplier name would not uniquely identify each, so it is necessary to assign a special identifier field for this purpose. For example, if you had two suppliers, both named "CBM," but one is based in Dayton and another in St. Louis, it would be easy to confuse them. However, if each has a unique Supplier_Number, such confusion is prevented.

We also see that the address information has been separated into four separate fields: Supplier_Street, Supplier_City, Supplier_State, and Supplier_Zip. Data are separated into the smallest elements that one would want to access separately to make it easy to select only the rows in the table that match the contents of one field, such as all the suppliers in Ohio (OH). The rows of data can also be sorted by the contents of the State field to get a list of suppliers by state regardless of their cities.

So far the SUPPLIER table doesn't have any information about the parts that a particular supplier provides for your company. PART is a separate entity from SUPPLIER, and fields with information about parts should be stored in a separate PART table (see Figure 5-2).

Why not keep information on parts in the same table as suppliers? If we did that, each row of the table would contain the attributes of both PART and SUPPLIER. Because one supplier could supply more than one part, the table would need many extra rows for a single

**Figure 5-2**
The PART Table
*Data for the entity PART
have their own separate
table. Part_Number is
the primary key and
Supplier_Number is the
foreign key, enabling
users to find related
information from the
SUPPLIER table about
the supplier for each
part.*

**PART**

| Part_Number | Part_Name | Unit_Price | Supplier_Number |
|---|---|---|---|
| 137 | Door latch | 22.00 | 8259 |
| 145 | Side mirror | 12.00 | 8444 |
| 150 | Door molding | 6.00 | 8263 |
| 152 | Door lock | 31.00 | 8259 |
| 155 | Compressor | 54.00 | 8261 |
| 178 | Door handle | 10.00 | 8259 |

**Primary Key**                                          **Foreign Key**

supplier to show all the parts that supplier provided. We would be maintaining a great deal of redundant data about suppliers, and it would be difficult to search for the information on any individual part because you would not know whether this part is the first or fiftieth part in this supplier's record. A separate table, PART, should be created to store these three fields and solve this problem.

The PART table would also have to contain another field, Supplier_Number, so that you would know the supplier for each part. It would not be necessary to keep repeating all the information about a supplier in each PART record because having a Supplier_ Number field in the PART table allows you to "look up" the data in the fields of the SUPPLIER table.

Notice that Supplier_Number appears in both the SUPPLIER and PART tables. In the SUPPLIER table, Supplier_Number is the primary key. When the field Supplier_Number appears in the PART table it is called a **foreign key** and is essentially a look-up field to look up data about the supplier of a specific part. Note that the PART table would itself have its own primary key field, Part_Number, to uniquely identify each part. This key is not used to link PART with SUPPLIER but might be used to link PART with a different entity.

As we organize data into tables, it's important to make sure that all the attributes for a particular entity apply only to that entity. If you were to keep the supplier's address with the PART record, that information would not really relate to only the PART; it would relate to both the PART and the SUPPLIER. If the supplier's address were to change, it would be necessary to alter the data in every PART record rather than only once in the SUPPLIER record.

## Establishing Relationships

Now that we've broken down our data into a SUPPLIER table and a PART table, we must make sure we understand the relationship between them. A schematic called an **entity-relationship diagram** is used to clarify table relationships in a relational database. The most important piece of information provided by an entity-relationship diagram is the manner in which two tables are related to each other. Tables in a relational database may have one-to-one, one-to-many, and many-to-many relationships.

An example of a one-to-one relationship might be a situation where a human resources system must store confidential data about employees. It might store data, such as the employee name, date of birth, address, and job position in one table, and confidential data about that employee, such as salary or pension benefits, in another table. These two tables pertaining to a single employee would have a one-to-one relationship because each record in the EMPLOYEE table with basic employee data has only one related record in the table storing confidential data.

The relationship between the SUPPLIER and PART entities in our database is a one-to-many relationship: Each supplier can supply more than one part, but each part has only one

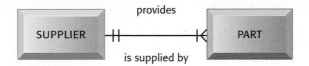

**Figure 5-3**
A Simple Entity-Relationship Diagram
*This diagram shows the relationship between the entities SUPPLIER and PART.*

supplier. For every record in the SUPPLIER table there may be many related records in the PART table.

Figure 5-3 illustrates how an entity-relationship diagram would depict this one-to-many relationship. The boxes represent entities. The lines connecting the boxes represent relationships. A line connecting two entities that ends in two short marks designates a one-to-one relationship. A line connecting two entities that ends with a crow's foot topped by a short mark indicates a one-to-many relationship. Figure 5-3 shows that each PART has only one SUPPLIER but many PARTs can be provided by the same SUPPLIER.

We would also see a one-to-many relationship if we wanted to add a table about orders to our database because one supplier services many orders. The ORDER table would only contain the Order_Number and Order_Date. Figure 5-4 illustrates a report showing an order of parts from a supplier. If you look at the report, you can see that the information on the top right portion of the report comes from the ORDER table. The actual line items ordered are listed in the lower portion of the report.

Because one ORDER can be for many parts from a supplier and a single PART can be ordered many times on different orders, this creates a many-to-many relationship between the PART and ORDER tables. Whenever a many-to-many relationship exists between two tables, it is necessary to link these two tables in a table that joins this information. Creating a separate table for a LINE_ITEM in the order would serve this purpose. This table is often called a *join table* or an *intersection relation*. This join table contains only three fields (two of which, Order_Number and Part_Number, are only used to link the ORDER and PART tables) and the Part_Quantity. If you look at the bottom left part of the report, this is the information coming from the LINE_ITEM table.

We would thus wind up with a total of four tables in our database. Figure 5-5 illustrates the final set of tables, and Figure 5-6 shows what the entity-relationship diagram for this set of tables would look like. Note that the ORDER table does not contain data on the extended price because that value could be calculated by multiplying Unit_Price by Part_Quantity. This data element can be *derived* when needed using information that already exists in the PART and LINE_ITEM tables. Order Total is another derived field calculated by totaling the extended prices for items ordered.

The process of streamlining complex groups of data to minimize redundant data elements and awkward many-to-many relationships, and increase stability and flexibility is

**Figure 5-4**
Sample Order Report
*The shaded areas show which data came from the SUPPLIER, ORDER, and LINE_ITEM tables. The database does not maintain data on Extended Price or Order Total because they can be derived from other data in the tables.*

Order Number:  3502
Order Date:    1/15/2006

Supplier Number: 8259
Supplier Name:   CBM Inc.
Supplier Address: 74 5th Avenue, Dayton, OH 45220

| Order_Number | Part_Number | Part_Quantity | Part_Name | Unit_Price | Extended Price |
|---|---|---|---|---|---|
| 3502 | 137 | 10 | Door latch | 22.00 | $220.00 |
| 3502 | 152 | 20 | Door lock | 31.00 | 620.00 |
| 3502 | 178 | 5 | Door handle | 10.00 | 50.00 |
| | | | Order Total: | | $890.00 |

**PART**

| Part_Number | Part_Name | Unit_Price | Supplier_Number |
|---|---|---|---|
| 137 | Door latch | 22.00 | 8259 |
| 145 | Side mirror | 12.00 | 8444 |
| 150 | Door molding | 6.00 | 8263 |
| 152 | Door lock | 31.00 | 8259 |
| 155 | Compressor | 54.00 | 8261 |
| 178 | Door handle | 10.00 | 8259 |

**LINE_ITEM**

| Order_Number | Part_Number | Part_Quantity |
|---|---|---|
| 3502 | 137 | 10 |
| 3502 | 152 | 20 |
| 3502 | 178 | 5 |

**ORDER**

| Order_Number | Order_Date |
|---|---|
| 3502 | 1/15/2006 |
| 3502 | 1/15/2006 |
| 3502 | 1/15/2006 |

**SUPPLIER**

| Supplier_Number | Supplier_Name | Supplier_Street | Supplier_City | Supplier_State | Supplier_Zip |
|---|---|---|---|---|---|
| 8259 | CBM Inc. | 74 5th Avenue | Dayton | OH | 45220 |
| 8261 | B. R. Molds | 1277 Gandolly Street | Cleveland | OH | 49345 |
| 8263 | Jackson Components | 8233 Micklin Street | Lexington | KY | 56723 |
| 8444 | Bryant Corporation | 4315 Mill Drive | Rochester | NY | 11344 |

**Figure 5-5**
The Final Database Design with Sample Records
*The final design of the database for suppliers, parts, and orders has four tables. The LINE_ITEM table is a join table that eliminates the many-to-many relationship between ORDER and PART.*

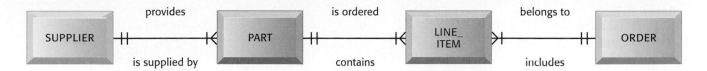

**Figure 5-6**
Entity-Relationship Diagram for the Database with Four Tables
*This diagram shows the relationship between the entities SUPPLIER, PART, LINE_ITEM, and ORDER.*

called **normalization**. A database that has been properly designed and normalized will be easy to maintain, and will minimize duplicate data. The Learning Tracks at the end of this chapter directs you to more detailed discussions of normalization, entity-relationship diagramming, and database design on the Laudon Web site.

The example provided here is a very simple one. Even in a very small business, you'll have tables for other important entities, such as customers, shippers, and employees. A very large corporation might have databases with thousands of entities (tables) to maintain. What is important for any business, large or small, is to have a good data model that includes all of its entities and the relationships among them, one that is organized to minimize redundancy, maximize accuracy, and make data easily accessible for reporting and analysis.

It can't be emphasized enough: If the business doesn't get its data model right, the system won't be able to serve the business right. The company's systems will not be as effective as they could be because they'll have to work with data that may be inaccurate, incomplete, or difficult to retrieve. Understanding the organization's data and how they should be represented in a database is perhaps the most important lesson you can learn from this course.

For example, Famous Footwear, a shoe store chain with more than 800 locations in 49 states, could not achieve its goal of having "the right style of shoe in the right store for sale at the right price" because its database was not properly designed for rapidly adjusting store inventory. The company had an Oracle relational database running on an IBM AS/400 midrange computer, but the database was designed primarily for producing standard reports for management rather than for reacting to marketplace changes. Management could not obtain precise data on specific items in inventory in each of its stores. The company had to work around this problem by building a new database where the sales and inventory data could be better organized for analysis and inventory management.

## 5.2 Database Management Systems

Now that you've started creating the files and identifying the data required by your business, you'll need a database management system to help you manage and use the data. A **database management system (DBMS)** is a specific type of software for creating, storing, organizing, and accessing data from a database. Microsoft Access is a DBMS for desktop systems, whereas DB2, Oracle Database, and Microsoft SQL Server are DBMS for large mainframes and midrange computers. MYSQL is a popular open-source DBMS, and Oracle Database Lite is a DBMS for small handheld computing devices. All of these products are relational DBMS that support a relational database.

The DBMS relieves the end user or programmer from the task of understanding where and how the data are actually stored by separating the logical and physical views of the data. The *logical view* presents data as end users or business specialists would perceive them, whereas the *physical view* shows how data are actually organized and structured on physical storage media, such as a hard disk.

The database management software makes the physical database available for different logical views required by users. For example, for the human resources database illustrated in

**Figure 5-7**
Human Resources
Database with
Multiple Views
*A single human
resources database pro-
vides many different
views of data, depend-
ing on the information
requirements of the
user. Illustrated here
are two possible views,
one of interest to a ben-
efits specialist and one
of interest to a member
of the company's pay-
roll department.*

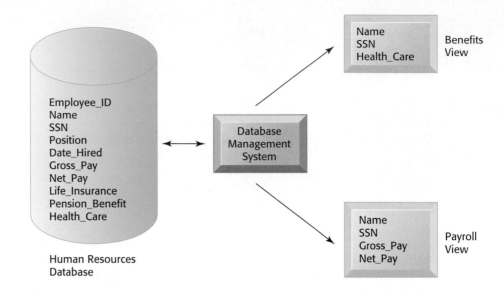

Figure 5-7, a benefits specialist might require a view consisting of the employee's name, social security number, and health insurance coverage. A payroll department member might need data such as the employee's name, social security number, gross pay, and net pay. The data for all of these views are stored in a single database, where it can be more easily managed by the organization.

### Operations of a Relational DBMS

In a relational database, tables can easily be combined to deliver data required by users, provided that any two tables share a common data element. Let's return to the database we set up earlier with the PART and SUPPLIER tables illustrated in Figures 5-1 and 5-2.

Suppose we wanted to find in this database the names of suppliers who could provide us with part number 137 or part number 150. We would need information from two tables: the SUPPLIER table and the PART table. Note that these two tables have a shared data element: Supplier_Number.

In a relational database, three basic operations, as shown in Figure 5-8, are used to develop useful sets of data: select, project, and join. The *select* operation creates a subset consisting of all records (rows) in the table that meet stated criteria. In our example, we want to select records (rows) from the PART table where the Part_Number equals 137 or 150. The *join* operation combines relational tables to provide the user with more information than is available in individual tables. In our example, we want to join the now-shortened PART table (only parts 137 or 150 will be presented) and the SUPPLIER table into a single new table.

The *project* operation creates a subset consisting of columns in a table, permitting the user to create new tables that contain only the information required. In our example, we want to extract from the new table only the following columns: Part_Number, Part_Name, Supplier_Number, and Supplier_Name (see Figure 5-8).

### Capabilities of Database Management Systems

A DBMS includes capabilities and tools for organizing, managing, and accessing the data in the database. The most important are its data definition capability, data dictionary, and data manipulation language.

DBMS have a **data definition** capability to specify the structure of the content of the database. It would be used to create database tables and to define the characteristics of the fields in each table. This information about the database would be documented in a **data**

**PART**

| Part_Number | Part_Name | Unit_Price | Supplier_Number |
|---|---|---|---|
| 137 | Door latch | 22.00 | 8259 |
| 145 | Side mirror | 12.00 | 8444 |
| 150 | Door molding | 6.00 | 8263 |
| 152 | Door lock | 31.00 | 8259 |
| 155 | Compressor | 54.00 | 8261 |
| 178 | Door handle | 10.00 | 8259 |

Select Part_Number = 137 or 150

**SUPPLIER**

| Supplier_Number | Supplier_Name | Supplier_Street | Supplier_City | Supplier_State | Supplier_Zip |
|---|---|---|---|---|---|
| 8259 | CBM Inc. | 74 5th Avenue | Dayton | OH | 45220 |
| 8261 | B. R. Molds | 1277 Gandolly Street | Cleveland | OH | 49345 |
| 8263 | Jackson Components | 8233 Micklin Street | Lexington | KY | 56723 |
| 8444 | Bryant Corporation | 4315 Mill Drive | Rochester | NY | 11344 |

Join by Supplier_Number

| Part_Number | Part_Name | Supplier_Number | Supplier_Name |
|---|---|---|---|
| 137 | Door latch | 8259 | CBM Inc. |
| 150 | Door molding | 8263 | Jackson Components |

Project selected columns

**Figure 5-8**

The Three Basic Operations of a Relational DBMS

*The select, project, and join operations enable data from two different tables to be combined and only selected attributes to be displayed.*

**Figure 5-9**
Access Data
Dictionary Features
*Microsoft Access has a
rudimentary data dictio-
nary capability that dis-
plays information about
the size, format, and
other characteristics of
each field in a data-
base. Displayed here is
the information main-
tained in the SUPPLIER
table. The small key
icon to the left of
Supplier_Number indi-
cates that it is a key
field.*

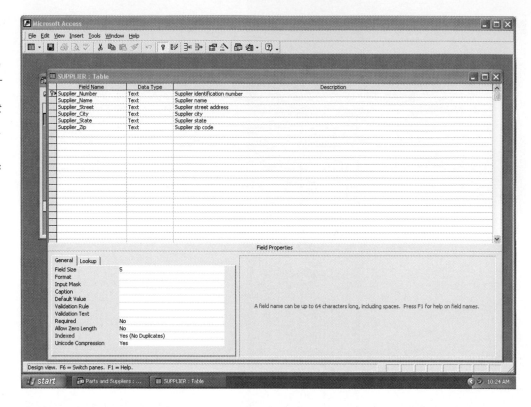

**dictionary**. A data dictionary is an automated or manual file that stores definitions of data elements and their characteristics. Microsoft Access has a built-in rudimentary data dictionary capability that displays information about the name, description, size, type, and format of each field in a table when it is in Design view (see Figure 5-9), as well as other properties of the field when the Documenter capability is employed. Data dictionaries for large corporate databases may capture additional information, such as usage; ownership (who in the organization is responsible for maintaining the data); authorization; security; and the individuals, business functions, programs, and reports that use each data element.

### Querying and Reporting

DBMS include tools for accessing and manipulating information in databases. Most DBMS have a specialized language called a **data manipulation language** that is used to add, change, delete, and retrieve the data in the database. This language contains commands that permit end users and programming specialists to extract data from the database to satisfy information requests and develop applications. The most prominent data manipulation language today is **Structured Query Language**, or **SQL**. Figure 5-10 illustrates the SQL query that would produce the new resultant table in Figure 5-8. You can find out more about how to perform SQL queries in our Learning Tracks for this chapter, which can be found on the Laudon Web site.

SELECT PART.Part_Number, PART.Part_Name, SUPPLIER.Supplier_Number,
SUPPLIER.Supplier_Name
FROM PART, SUPPLIER
WHERE PART.Supplier_Number = SUPPLIER.Supplier_Number AND
Part_Number = 137 OR Part_Number = 150;

**Figure 5-10**
Example of an SQL Query
*Illustrated here are the SQL statements for a query to select suppliers for parts 137 or 150.
They produce a list with the same results as Figure 5-8.*

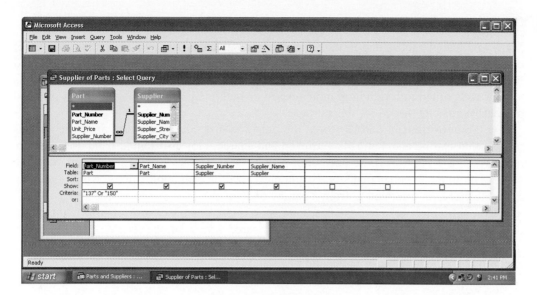

**Figure 5-11**
An Access Query
*Illustrated here is how the query in Figure 5-10 would be constructed using query-building tools in the Access Query Design View. It shows the tables, fields, and selection criteria used for the query.*

Users of DBMS for large and midrange computers, such as DB2, Oracle Database, or SQL Server, would employ SQL to retrieve information they needed from the database. Microsoft Access also uses SQL, but it provides its own set of user-friendly tools for querying databases and for organizing data from databases into more polished reports.

In Microsoft Access, you will find the Query Wizard and Query Design View features that enable users to create queries by identifying the tables and fields they want and the results, and then selecting the rows from the database that meet particular criteria. These actions in turn are translated into SQL commands. Figure 5-11 illustrates how the same query as the SQL query to select parts and suppliers in Figure 5-10 would be constructed using the Query Design View.

DBMS typically include capabilities for report generation so that the data of interest can be displayed in a more structured and polished format than would be possible just by querying. Figure 5-12 illustrates how the Access Report Writer would build a report using the same data from the query illustrated in Figure 5-11. Crystal Reports is a popular report generator for large corporate DBMS, although it can also be used with Access.

Access also has capabilities for developing desktop system applications. These include tools for creating data entry screens, reports, and developing the logic for processing transactions.

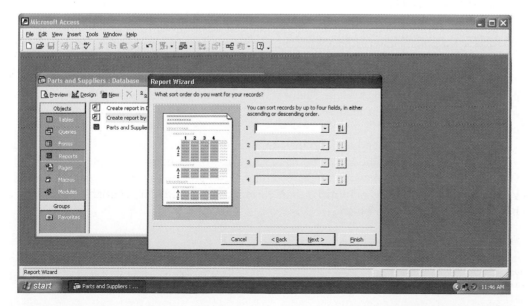

**Figure 5-12**
Access Report Writer
*The Access Report Writer enables users to specify the fields, format, and order of display for polished reports that use data from the database.*

## Object-Oriented Databases

Many applications today and in the future require databases that can store and retrieve not only structured numbers and characters but also drawings, images, photographs, voice, and full-motion video. DBMS designed for organizing structured data into rows and columns are not well suited to handling graphics-based or multimedia applications. Object-oriented databases are better suited for this purpose.

An **object-oriented DBMS** stores the data and procedures that act on those data as objects that can be automatically retrieved and shared. Object-oriented database management systems (OODBMS) are becoming popular because they can be used to manage the various multimedia components or Java applets used in Web applications, which typically integrate pieces of information from a variety of sources.

Although object-oriented databases can store more complex types of information than relational DBMS, they are relatively slow compared with relational DBMS for processing large numbers of transactions. Hybrid **object-relational DBMS** are now available to provide capabilities of both object-oriented and relational DBMS.

## 5.3 Using Databases to Improve Business Performance and Decision Making

Businesses use their databases to keep track of basic transactions, such as paying suppliers, processing orders, serving customers, and paying employees. But they also need databases to provide information that will help the company run the business more efficiently, and help managers and employees make better decisions. If a company wants to know which product is the most popular or who is its most profitable customer, the answer lies in the data.

For example, by analyzing data from customer credit card purchases, Louise's Trattoria, a Los Angeles restaurant chain, learned that quality was more important than price for most of its customers, who were college-educated and liked fine wine. Acting on this information, the chain introduced vegetarian dishes, more seafood selections, and more expensive wines, raising sales by more than 10 percent.

In a large company, with large databases or large systems for separate functions, such as manufacturing, sales, and accounting, special capabilities and tools are required for analyzing vast quantities of data and for accessing data from multiple systems. These capabilities include data warehousing, data mining, and tools for accessing internal databases through the Web.

## Data Warehouses

What if you wanted concise, reliable information about current operations, trends, and changes across the entire company? If you worked in a large company, this might be difficult because data are often maintained in separate systems, such as sales, manufacturing, or accounting. Some of the data you needed might be found in the sales system, and other pieces in the manufacturing system. Many of these systems are older legacy systems that use outdated data management technologies or file systems where information is difficult for users to access.

You might have to spend an inordinate amount of time locating and gathering the data you needed, or you would be forced to make your decision based on incomplete knowledge. If you wanted information about trends, you might also have trouble finding data about past events because most firms only make their current data immediately available. Data warehousing addresses these problems.

### What Is a Data Warehouse?

A **data warehouse** is a database that stores current and historical data of potential interest to decision makers throughout the company. The data originate in many core operational

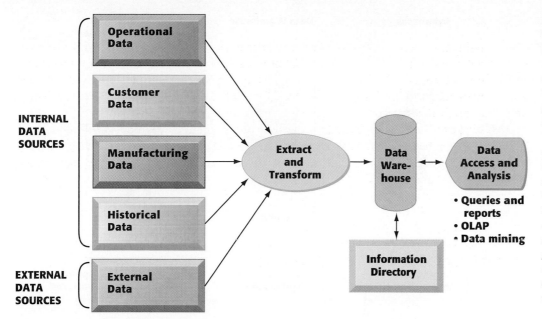

**Figure 5-13**
Components of a
Data Warehouse
*The data warehouse
extracts current and historical data from multiple operational systems
inside the organization.
These data are combined with data from
external sources and
reorganized into a central database designed
for management reporting and analysis. The
information directory
provides users with
information about the
data available in the
warehouse.*

transaction systems, such as systems for sales, customer accounts, and manufacturing, and may include data from Web site transactions. The data warehouse consolidates and standardizes information from different operational databases so that the information can be used across the enterprise for management analysis and decision making.

Figure 5-13 illustrates how a data warehouse works. The data warehouse makes the data available for anyone to access as needed, but it cannot be altered. A data warehouse system also provides a range of ad hoc and standardized query tools, analytical tools, and graphical reporting facilities. Many firms use intranet portals to make the data warehouse information widely available throughout the firm.

### Data Marts

Companies often build enterprise-wide data warehouses, where a central data warehouse serves the entire organization, or they create smaller, decentralized warehouses called data marts. A **data mart** is a subset of a data warehouse in which a summarized or highly focused portion of the organization's data is placed in a separate database for a specific population of users. For example, a company might develop marketing and sales data marts to deal with customer information. A data mart typically focuses on a single subject area or line of business, so it usually can be constructed more rapidly and at lower cost than an enterprise-wide data warehouse.

## Business Intelligence, Multidimensional Data Analysis, and Data Mining

Once data have been captured and organized in data warehouses and data marts, they are available for further analysis. A series of tools enables users to analyze these data to see new patterns, relationships, and insights that are useful for guiding decision making. These tools for consolidating, analyzing, and providing access to vast amounts of data to help users make better business decisions are often referred to as **business intelligence (BI)**. Principal tools for business intelligence include software for database query and reporting, tools for multidimensional data analysis (online analytical processing), and data mining.

When we think of *intelligence* as applied to humans, we typically think of people's ability to combine learned knowledge with new information and change behaviors in such a way that they succeed at their task or adapt to a new situation. Likewise, business intelligence provides firms with the capability to amass information; develop knowledge about customers, competitors, and internal operations; and change decision-making behavior to achieve higher profitability and other business goals.

**Figure 5-14**
Business Intelligence
*A series of analytical tools works with data stored in databases to find patterns and insights for helping managers and employees make better decisions to improve organizational performance.*

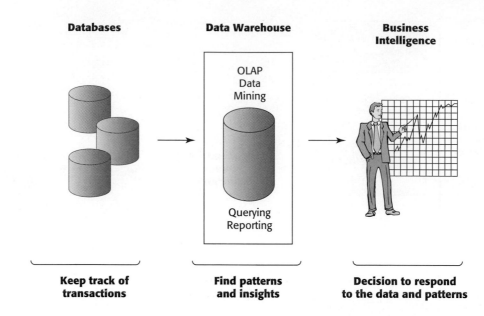

For instance, Harrah's Entertainment, the second-largest gambling company in its industry, continually analyzes data about its customers that's gathered when people play its slot machines or use Harrah's casinos and hotels. Harrah's marketing department uses this information to build a detailed gambling profile, based on a particular customer's ongoing value to the company. This information guides management decisions about how to cultivate the most profitable customers, encourage those customers to spend more, and attract more customers with high revenue-generating potential. Business intelligence has improved Harrah's profits so much that it has become the centerpiece of the firm's business strategy.

Figure 5-14 illustrates how business intelligence works. The firm's operational databases keep track of the transactions generated by running the business. These databases feed data to the data warehouse. Managers use business intelligence tools to find patterns and meanings in the data. Managers then act on what they have learned from analyzing the data by making more informed and intelligent business decisions.

This section will introduce you to the most important business intelligence technologies and tools. We'll provide more detail about business intelligence applications in the Chapter 10 discussion of decision making.

### Online Analytical Processing (OLAP)

Suppose your company sells four different products—nuts, bolts, washers, and screws—in the East, West, and Central regions. If you wanted to ask a fairly straightforward question, such as how many washers sold during the past quarter, you could easily find the answer by querying your sales database. But what if you wanted to know how many washers sold in each of your sales regions and compare actual results with projected sales?

To obtain the answer, you would need **online analytical processing (OLAP)**. OLAP supports multidimensional data analysis, enabling users to view the same data in different ways using multiple dimensions. Each aspect of information—product, pricing, cost, region, or time period—represents a different dimension. So, a product manager could use a multidimensional data analysis tool to learn how many washers were sold in the East in June, how that compares with the previous month and the previous June, and how it compares with the sales forecast. OLAP enables users to obtain online answers to ad hoc questions such as these in a fairly rapid amount of time, even when the data are stored in very large databases, such as sales figures for multiple years.

Figure 5-15 shows a multidimensional model that could be created to represent products, regions, actual sales, and projected sales. A matrix of actual sales can be stacked on top of a matrix of projected sales to form a cube with six faces. If you rotate the cube 90 degrees one way, the face that's showing will be product versus actual and projected sales. If you

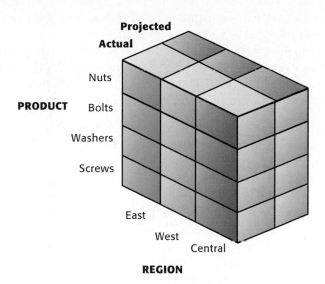

**Figure 5-15**
Multidimensional
Data Model
*The view that is show-
ing is product versus
region. If you rotate the
cube 90 degrees, the
face that will show is
product versus actual
and projected sales. If
you rotate the cube 90
degrees again, you will
see region versus
actual and projected
sales. Other views are
possible.*

rotate the cube 90 degrees again, you will see region versus actual and projected sales. If you rotate 180 degrees from the original view, you will see projected sales and product versus region. Cubes can be nested within cubes to build complex views of data. A company would use either a specialized multidimensional database or a tool that creates multidimensional views of data in relational databases.

## Data Mining

Traditional database queries answer such questions as, "How many units of product number 403 were shipped in February 2006?" OLAP supports much more complex requests for information, such as, "Compare sales of product 403 relative to plan by quarter and sales region for the past two years." With OLAP and query-oriented data analysis, users need to have a good idea about the information for which they are looking.

**Data mining** is more discovery driven. Data mining provides insights into corporate data that cannot be obtained with OLAP by finding hidden patterns and relationships in large databases and inferring rules from them to predict future behavior. The patterns and rules are used to guide decision making and forecast the effect of those decisions. The types of information obtainable from data mining include associations, sequences, classifications, clusters, and forecasts.

- *Associations* are occurrences linked to a single event. For instance, a study of supermarket purchasing patterns might reveal that, when corn chips are purchased, a cola drink is purchased 65 percent of the time, but when there is a promotion, cola is purchased 85 percent of the time. This information helps managers make better decisions because they have learned the profitability of a promotion.
- In *sequences*, events are linked over time. We might find, for example, that if a house is purchased, a new refrigerator will be purchased within two weeks 65 percent of the time, and an oven will be bought within one month of the home purchase 45 percent of the time.
- *Classification* recognizes patterns that describe the group to which an item belongs by examining existing items that have been classified and by inferring a set of rules. For example, businesses such as credit card or telephone companies worry about the loss of steady customers. Classification helps discover the characteristics of customers who are likely to leave and can provide a model to help managers predict who those customers are so that the managers can devise special campaigns to retain such customers.
- *Clustering* works in a manner similar to classification when no groups have yet been defined. A data mining tool can discover different groupings within data, such as finding

affinity groups for bank cards or partitioning a database into groups of customers based on demographics and types of personal investments.

- Although these applications involve predictions, *forecasting* uses predictions in a different way. It uses a series of existing values to forecast what other values will be. For example, forecasting might find patterns in data to help managers estimate the future value of continuous variables, such as sales figures.

These systems perform high-level analyses of patterns or trends, but they can also drill down to provide more detail when needed. There are data mining applications for all the functional areas of business, and for government and scientific work. One popular use for data mining is to provide detailed analyses of patterns in customer data for one-to-one marketing campaigns or for identifying profitable customers.

For example, Virgin Mobile Australia uses a data warehouse and data mining to increase customer loyalty and roll out new services. The company created a data warehouse that consolidated data from its enterprise system, customer relationship management system, and customer billing systems in a massive database. Data mining has enabled management to determine the demographic profile of new customers and relate it to the handsets they purchased as well as the performance of each store and point-of-sale campaigns, consumer reactions to new products and services, customer attrition rates, and the revenue generated by each customer.

**Predictive analysis** uses data mining techniques, historical data, and assumptions about future conditions to predict outcomes of events, such as the probability a customer will respond to an offer or purchase a specific product. For example, the U.S. division of The Body Shop International plc used predictive analysis with its database of catalog, Web, and retail store customers to identify customers who were more likely to make catalog purchases. That information helped the company build a more precise and targeted mailing list for its catalogs, improving the response rate for catalog mailings and catalog revenues.

The Focus on Organizations describes how Peru's Banco de Credito used data warehouses and data mining to learn more about its customers to improve marketing and customer service. The bank implemented an Oracle data warehouse to replace outdated data warehousing technology. As you read this case, try to identify the problem this company was facing; what alternative solutions were available to management; how well the chosen solution worked; and the people, organization, and technology issues that had to be addressed when developing the solution.

Data mining is both a powerful and profitable tool, but it poses challenges to the protection of individual privacy. Data mining technology can combine information from many diverse sources to create a detailed "data image" about each of us—our income, our driving habits, our hobbies, our families, and our political interests. The question of whether companies should be allowed to collect such detailed information about individuals is explored in Chapter 12.

## Databases and the Web

Many companies are using the Web to make some of the information in their internal databases available to customers and business partners. Prospective customers might use a company's Web site to view the company's product catalog or to place an order. The company in turn might use the Web to check inventory availability for that product from its supplier. That supplier, in turn, may have to check with its own suppliers as well as delivery firms needed to ship the products on time.

These actions involve accessing and (in the case of ordering) updating corporate databases through the Web. A series of middleware and other software products make this possible. Suppose, for example, a customer with a Web browser wants to search an online retailer's database for pricing information. Figure 5-16 illustrates how that customer might access the retailer's internal database over the Web. The user would access the retailer's Web site over the Internet using Web browser software on his or her client PC. The user's Web

## FOCUS ON ORGANIZATIONS   Peru's Banco de Credito Scores with a New Data Warehouse

Banco de Credito Peru (BCP) is Peru's oldest bank, with more than U.S. $6 billion in assets, 210 branches worldwide (including one in Miami, Florida), and more than two million customers. It accounts for about 25 percent of all loans in Peru's banking system, 48 percent of the country's corporate banking market, and between 35 and 38 percent of its consumer banking market.

As Peru's economy opened up to foreign banks, BCP had more trouble keeping old customers and attracting new ones. The bank responded to the challenge by focusing on customer services. It added electronic banking services so that customers could perform more of their transactions themselves at ATMs and in their homes. It established Internet banking links with corporate clients. It also increased the number of tellers at all of its branches by 40 percent and invested in additional employee training programs.

Although paying for a banking professional's salary cost more than maintaining an AIM, bank management believed that spending for more employees interacting with customers represented a good investment. According to Guillermo Bustamante, BCP's chief information officer, every time a customer comes to a bank branch and makes contact with a bank employee represents an opportunity for selling that customer additional financial products and services.

When a customer enters a bank branch, BCP needs to provide bank employees with as much information as possible about that customer so that staff can market to them more intelligently. Several years ago, it did not have this information available. The bank had a data warehouse with information on all its customers, but it was inefficient and could not scale to handle the bank's swelling customer base. Segmenting customers was a very laborious task. It took so long to analyze customer data that, by the time results were tabulated, they were no longer accurate. The database housed information about the results of specific marketing campaigns, but there was no way to correlate these results with customer segments to find out on which customer groups the campaign had the greatest impact. In other words, the data were essentially useless.

Purchasing new hardware was not an issue because hardware had become a commodity and was relatively inexpensive. Management could choose to upgrade the same database management software for the warehouse that BCP had been using, but costs would be considerable (U.S. $3 million) because the database software was expensive and needed to be constantly updated and maintained.

Instead, management chose to migrate to a data warehouse based on Oracle DBMS software. Implementing these data management tools amounted to half of the upgrade costs for the bank's existing database management software, and the subsequent annual costs to maintain this software were also half the cost of the other option.

Besides reducing information system costs, the new Oracle data warehouse changed the way the bank analyzed and segmented its customer data. The data warehouse includes information about what products customers use, the nature of their business relationships with the bank, and how often they interact with the bank. This information enables BCP to create profiles for every customer, and market and identify customer segments more accurately.

BCP's marketing can now see the impact of new campaigns immediately and also monitor the results of older campaigns. For example, if the bank markets a new credit card product, it can now track the results of the marketing campaign throughout the life of that credit card to see which customers are generating revenue with the card and which are delinquent. These results, in turn, help the bank act more intelligently when creating new marketing campaigns.

Another benefit: The new data warehouse enables BCP to stage more marketing campaigns with fewer employees. Before migrating to the Oracle data warehouse, it took 5 to 10 employees to stage 20 new marketing campaigns each year. Today, three employees can create and run more than 200 campaigns annually.

BCP also uses the data warehouse to pursue new opportunities for generating revenue. For example, information gleaned from the warehouse alerted management to the possibility of generating revenue by charging for use of debit cards. After analyzing other fee-based products in the data warehouse, management found that customers would not object if the bank charged a U.S. $1 monthly for this service. This single initiative pulls in more than U.S. $12 million each year.

*Sources*: Karen J. Bannan, "Customer Credit," Oracle Profit Special Edition for Financial Services, accessed May 23, 2005; "Banco de Credito Expects to Save US $1 Million Each Year with Oracle Data Warehouse," http://www.oracle.com, accessed May 23, 2005; and Lucien Chauvin, "Surviving the Storm: Peru's Largest Bank Rises and Falls with Country's Economy-But Remains Independent," http://www.looksmart.com, accessed May 23, 2005.

**To Think About:**
What problems does Banco de Credito Peru face? How do the problems affect the bank's strategy and business performance? How did management choose to solve these problems? Analyze the people, organization, and technology dimensions of its solution. What alternatives were available to management? Did management choose the best alternative? Explain your answer.

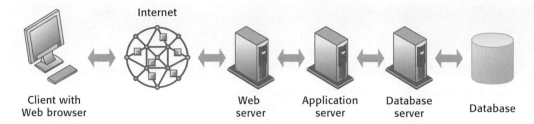

**Figure 5-16**
Linking Internal Databases to the Web
*Users access an organization's internal database through the Web using their desktop PCs and Web browser software.*

browser software would request data from the organization's database, using HTML commands to communicate with the Web server.

Because many "back-end" databases cannot interpret commands written in HTML, the Web server would pass these requests for data to software that translates HTML commands into SQL so that they can be processed by the DBMS working with the database. In a client/server environment, the DBMS often resides on a dedicated computer called a **database server**. The DBMS receives the SQL requests and provides the required data. The middleware transfers information from the organization's internal database back to the Web server for delivery in the form of a Web page to the user.

Figure 5-16 shows that the middleware working between the Web server and the DBMS could be an application server running on its own dedicated computer (see Chapter 4). The application server software handles all application operations, including transaction processing and data access, between browser-based computers and a company's back-end business applications or databases. The application server takes requests from the Web server, runs the business logic to process transactions based on those requests, and provides connectivity to the organization's back-end systems or databases. Alternatively, the software for handling these operations could be a custom program or a CGI script. A CGI script is a compact program using the *Common Gateway Interface (CGI)* specification for processing data on a Web server.

There are a number of advantages to using the Web to access an organization's internal databases. First, everyone knows how to use Web browser software, and employees require much less training than if they used proprietary query tools. Second, the Web interface requires few or no changes to the internal database. Companies leverage their investments in older systems because it costs much less to add a Web interface in front of a legacy system than to redesign and rebuild the system to improve user access. For this reason, most large Fortune 500 firms have back-end legacy databases running on mainframe computers that are linked to "front-end" software that makes the information available in the form of a Web page to users on request.

Accessing corporate databases through the Web is creating new efficiencies and opportunities, and, in some cases, it is even changing the way business is being done. ThomasNet.com provides an up-to-date directory of information from more than 650,000 suppliers of industrial products, such as chemicals, metals, plastics, rubber, and automotive equipment. Formerly called Thomas Register, the company used to send out huge paper catalogs with this information. Now, it provides this information to users online via its Web site and has become a smaller, leaner company.

Other companies have created entirely new businesses based on access to large databases through the Web. For example, Igo.com is a new Internet-based business that sells batteries and accessories for mobile phones and computing devices. Its Web site is linked to a giant relational database housing information about batteries and peripherals for nearly every brand and model of mobile computer and portable electronic device. Visitors can use the Web site to query the database online about each electronic device and the batteries and parts it uses, and can place orders for these parts over the Web.

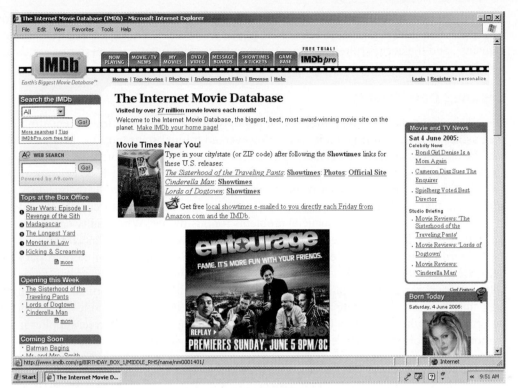

The Internet Movie Database Web site is linked to a massive database that includes summaries, cast information, and actor biographies for almost every film ever released.

## 5.4 Managing Data Resources

Setting up a database is only a start. In order to make sure that the data for your business remain accurate, reliable, and readily available to those who need them, your business will need special policies and procedures for data management.

### Establishing an Information Policy

Every business, large and small, needs an information policy. Your firm's data are an important resource, and you don't want people doing whatever they want with them. You need to have rules on how the data are to be organized and maintained, and who is allowed to view the data or change them.

An **information policy** specifies the organization's rules for sharing, disseminating, acquiring, standardizing, classifying, and inventorying information. Information policy lays out specific procedures and accountabilities, identifying which users and organizational units can share information, where information can be distributed, and who is responsible for updating and maintaining the information. For example, a typical information policy would specify that only selected members of the payroll and human resources department would have the right to change and view sensitive employee data, such as an employee's salary or social security number, and that these departments are responsible for making sure that such employee data are accurate.

If you are in a small business, the information policy would be established and implemented by the owners or managers. In a large organization, managing and planning for information as a corporate resource often requires a formal data administration function. **Data administration** is responsible for the specific policies and procedures through which data can be managed as an organizational resource. These responsibilities include developing information policy, planning for data, overseeing logical database design and data dictionary development, and monitoring how information systems specialists and end-user groups use data.

A large organization will also have a database design and management group within the corporate information systems division that is responsible for defining and organizing the structure and content of the database, and maintaining the database. In close cooperation with users, the design group establishes the physical database, the logical relations among elements, and the access rules and security procedures. The functions it performs are called **database administration**.

## Ensuring Data Quality

A well-designed database and information policy will go a long way toward ensuring that the business has the information it needs. However, additional steps must be taken to ensure that the data in organizational databases are accurate and remain reliable.

What would happen if a customer's telephone number or account balance were incorrect? What would be the impact if the database had the wrong price for the product you sold? Data that are inaccurate, untimely, or inconsistent with other sources of information create serious operational and financial problems for businesses. When faulty data go unnoticed, they often lead to incorrect decisions, product recalls, and even financial losses.

According to Forrester Research, 20 percent of U.S. mail and commercial package deliveries were returned because of incorrect names or addresses. The Gartner Group consultants reported that more than 25 percent of the critical data in large Fortune 1000 companies' databases is inaccurate or incomplete, including bad product codes and product descriptions, faulty inventory descriptions, erroneous financial data, incorrect supplier information, and incorrect employee data. Gartner believes that customer data degrade at a rate of 2 percent per month, making poor data quality a major obstacle to successful customer relationship management (Gage and McCormick, 2005; Klau, 2003).

Some of these data quality problems are caused by redundant and inconsistent data produced by multiple systems. For example, the sales ordering system and the inventory management system might both maintain data on the organization's products. However, the sales ordering system might use the term *Item Number* and the inventory system might call the same attribute *Product Number*. The sales, inventory, or manufacturing systems of a clothing retailer might use different codes to represent values for an attribute. One system might represent clothing size as "extra large," whereas the other system might use the code "XL" for the same purpose. During the design process for a database, data describing entities, such as a customer, product, or order, should be named and defined consistently for all business areas using the database.

When you download a song from an online music site, you are actually accessing it from a massive database of digital song data. If you ever had a problem downloading one of these songs, it could be the result of data quality problems. The Focus on Technology explores this topic. As you read this case, try to identify the problem and the scope of the problem. Does it primarily affect individuals using digital music services or the music services themselves? What solutions are available for dealing with the problem? What people, organization, and technology issues have to be addressed?

If a database is properly designed and enterprise-wide data standards established, duplicate or inconsistent data elements should be minimal. Most data quality problems, however, such as misspelled names, transposed numbers, or incorrect or missing codes, stem from errors during data input. The incidence of such errors is rising as companies move their businesses to the Web and allow customers and suppliers to enter data into their Web sites that directly update internal systems.

Think of all the times you've received several pieces of the same direct mail advertising on the same day. This is very likely the result of having your name maintained multiple times in a database. Your name may have been misspelled or you used your middle initial on one occasion and not on another or the information was initially entered onto a paper form and not scanned properly into the system. Because of these inconsistencies, the database would treat you as different people! We often receive redundant mail addressed to Laudon, Lavdon, Lauden, or Landon.

Before a new database is in place, organizations need to identify and correct their faulty data and establish better routines for editing data once their database is in operation. Analysis of data quality often begins with a **data quality audit**, which is a structured survey

## FOCUS ON TECHNOLOGY  Downloading Digital Music—When You're on the Wrong Track

Have you ever had trouble downloading a song to your iPod or other handheld music player? If you have, the reason may be because of bad data.

Digital songs contain more than the data for the tune itself. Every song file also contains data about the song, such as the artist's name, album, genre, or date of release. Such data describing digital data are called "metadata" or "tags," and they are used by portable music players and music software to categorize, organize, and search music in a number of different ways. In an iPod, the metadata enables users to find tracks either by alphabetical order or by artist or song title.

However, these tags are not automatically built into music CDs. When you copy music onto your computer, your music software has to search for all that information in an online database. These databases are full of errors and omissions, such as misspelled artist names and missing song and album titles.

Apple's iTunes Music Store obtains its metadata for its songs from record labels and information providers, such as Muze Inc. For example, iTunes sells "The Cosmic Game," an album released by the electronic groove band Thievery Corporation, for $9.99. Those who purchase it are allowed to download all 16 tracks, which supposedly contain standard metadata about the artist's name, album title, song name, and album release year. Although all 16 songs are from the same band, the tag for almost every song is different. There are tags for "Thievery Corporation," "Gunjan, Sleeping Wonder & Thievery Corporation," "Thievery Corporation & The Flaming Lips," and 10 other variations, each reflecting a different collaborator with the band. So the album appears to be split into 13 different artist entries because of the differing tags on the songs.

When you transfer this information to an iPod music player, the problems begin. Because the tags show 13 different artist listings for "The Cosmic Game," your iPod will have 13 different folders instead of a single folder for the album. Each folder contains the individual tracks labeled with the name of each particular artist. This situation can be likened to a cluttered filing cabinet that separately includes every page of a report or tax return.

According to Paul Zullo, chief executive of Muze of New York, which supplies the metadata for iTunes and other music sites, the company could eliminate problems, such as the varying artist tags on the Thievery Corporation album, but "then we're giving less information" about the music users purchased.

The biggest tagging problems arise when people "rip" CDs, copying and transferring digital songs from a compact disk to a computer hard drive. When you insert a music CD into your computer drive, software, such as iTunes or Microsoft's Windows Media player, scans the disk for a digital directory that shows where each song starts and stops on the CD. Because there is only limited metadata on the CD, the software connects to an online song database to search for a profile of the song. If it finds a match, the software automatically retrieves all the metadata from the database and attaches it to the copy of the album it has just created on the user's computer hard drive.

Some of the data in these online song databases are not accurate. For example, CDDB (compact disk database) originally relied on Internet users to contribute missing CD information. Because this started out as a grassroots effort, no one initially spent much time editing the entries. The data quality was highly variable. A user who wanted to submit tags for "21 Questions" by rapper 50 Cent might spell the rapper's name 50 Cent, 50 Cents, or Fifty Cent. This would affect how the song was displayed in most portable music players and music software.

Digital music companies have been trying to improve the accuracy and comprehensiveness of their databases. Microsoft maintains its own database of music metadata. Gracenote, which now owns CDDB, catalogs more than 44.8 million songs and 3.5 million CDs with close editorial attention to the quality of the information submitted by users.

Most music software on PCs requires users to manually correct song tags. Software makers are working on automated tools for correcting bad metadata. Windows Media Player can scan existing tags on digital songs, even if they are incomplete. It will look for the best matches in its online catalog and then retag the songs. A newer software tool analyzes the unique acoustic properties of each digital song and matches the sound properties on a user's PC with a record in an online database. Gracenote is rolling out this technology, as is metadata Web site MusicBrainz.org.

*Sources*: Nick Wingfield, "On the Wrong Track," *The Wall Street Journal*, March 21, 2005; and Graham Stewart, "Digital Music & Metadata," http://www.grahamstewart.com, accessed May 22, 2005.

**To Think About:**

What data management and data quality problems are posed by digital music services? What is the impact of these problems on individuals and the digital music industry? What people, organization, and technology factors were involved? What alternative solutions are available?

of the accuracy and level of completeness of the data in an information system. Data quality audits can be performed by surveying entire data files, surveying samples from data files, or surveying end users for their perceptions of data quality.

**Data cleansing**, also known as *data scrubbing*, consists of activities for detecting and correcting data in a database that are incorrect, incomplete, improperly formatted, or redundant. Data cleansing not only corrects data but also enforces consistency among different sets of data that originated in separate information systems. Specialized data-cleansing software is available to automatically survey data files, correct errors in the data, and integrate the data in a consistent company-wide format.

---

**LEARNING TRACKS**

1. If you want to learn more about entity-relationship diagramming and normalization, you will find a Learning Track on Database Design, Normalization, and Entity-Relationship Diagramming at the Laudon Web site for this chapter.
2. If you want to learn more about using SQL to query a database, you will find a Learning Track on SQL at the Laudon Web site for this chapter.

---

## Summary

**1** **Describe how a relational database organizes data and compare its approach to an object-oriented database.** The relational database is the primary method for organizing and maintaining data today in information systems. It organizes data in two-dimensional tables with rows and columns called relations. Each table contains data about an entity and its attributes. Each row represents a record and each column represents an attribute or field. Each table also contains a key field to uniquely identify each record for retrieval or manipulation. An entity-relationship diagram graphically depicts the relationship between entities (tables) in a relational database. A well-designed relational database will not have many-to-many relationships, and all attributes for a specific entity will only apply to that entity. The process of breaking down complex groupings of data and streamlining them to minimize redundancy and awkward many-to-many relationships is called normalization.

An object-oriented database stores data and procedures that act on the data as objects, and it can handle multimedia as well as characters and numbers.

**2** **Identify and describe the principles of a database management system.** A database management system (DBMS) consists of software that permits centralization of data and data management so that businesses have a single consistent source for all their data needs. A single database services multiple applications. The most important feature of the DBMS is its ability to separate the logical and physical views of data. The user works with a logical view of data. The DBMS retrieves information so that the user does not have to be concerned with its physical location.

The principal capabilities of a DBMS includes a data definition capability, a data dictionary capability, and a data manipulation language. The data definition capability specifies the structure and content of the database. The data dictionary is an automated or manual file that stores information about the data in the database, including names, definitions, formats, and descriptions of data elements. The data manipulation language, such as SQL, is a specialized language for accessing and manipulating the data in the database.

**3** **Evaluate tools and technologies for providing information from databases to improve business performance and decision making.** Powerful tools are available to analyze and access the information in databases. A data warehouse consolidates current and historical data from many different operational systems in a central database designed for reporting and analysis. Data warehouses support multidimensional data analysis, also known as online analytical processing (OLAP). OLAP represents relationships among data as a multidimensional structure, which can be visualized as cubes of data and cubes within cubes of data, enabling more sophisticated data analysis. Data mining analyzes large pools of data, including the contents of data warehouses, to find patterns and rules that can be used to predict future behavior and guide decision making. Conventional databases can be linked via middleware to the Web or a Web interface to facilitate user access to an organization's internal data.

4 **Assess the role of information policy and data administration in the management of organizational data resources.** Developing a database environment requires policies and procedures for managing organizational data as well as a good data model and database technology. A formal information policy governs the maintenance, distribution, and use of information in the organization. In large corporations, a formal data administration function is responsible for information policy, as well as for data planning, data dictionary development, and monitoring data usage in the firm.

5 **Assess the importance of data quality assurance for the business.** Data that are inaccurate, incomplete, or inconsistent create serious operational and financial problems for businesses because they may create inaccuracies in product pricing, customer accounts, and inventory data, and lead to inaccurate decisions about the actions that should be taken by the firm. Firms must take special steps to make sure they have a high level of data quality. These include using enterprise-wide data standards, databases designed to minimize inconsistent and redundant data, data quality audits, and data cleansing software.

## Key Terms

Attributes, 152
Business intelligence (BI), 163
Data administration, 169
Data cleansing, 172
Data definition, 158
Data dictionary, 158
Data manipulation language, 160
Data mart, 163
Data mining, 165
Data quality audit, 170
Data warehouse, 162

Database, 152
Database administration, 170
Database management system (DBMS), 157
Database server, 168
Entity, 152
Entity-relationship diagram, 154
Field, 153
Foreign key, 154
Information policy, 169
Key field, 153

Normalization, 157
Object-oriented DBMS, 162
Object-relational DBMS, 162
Online analytical processing (OLAP), 164
Predictive analysis, 166
Primary key, 153
Records, 153
Relational database, 152
Structured Query Language (SQL), 160
Tuples, 153

## Review Questions

**5.1** Define and explain the significance of entities, attributes, and key fields.

**5.2** What is a relational database? How does it organize and store information?

**5.3** What is the role of entity-relationship diagrams and normalization in database design?

**5.4** What is a database management system (DBMS)? How does it work? What benefits does it provide?

**5.5** What is the difference between a logical and a physical view of data?

**5.6** Define and describe the three operations of a relational database management system.

**5.7** Name and describe the three major capabilities of a DBMS.

**5.8** What is an object-oriented database? How does it differ from a relational database?

**5.9** What is a data warehouse? What problems does it solve for a business?

**5.10** What is business intelligence? How is it related to database technology?

**5.11** Describe the capabilities of online analytical processing (OLAP).

**5.12** What is data mining? How does it differ from OLAP? What types of information can be obtained from data mining?

**5.13** How can users access information from a company's internal databases through the Web?

**5.14** What are the roles of information policy and data administration in data management?

**5.15** Why are data quality audits and data cleansing essential?

## Discussion Questions

**5.1** It has been said that you do not need database management software to create a database environment. Discuss.

**5.2** To what extent should end users be involved in the selection of a database management system and database design?

## Application Software Exercise

### Database Exercise: Building a Relational Database for a Small Business

Software skills: Database design; querying and reporting

Business skills: Inventory management

Sylvester's Bike Shop, located in San Francisco, California, sells road, mountain, hybrid, leisure, and children's bicycles. Currently, Sylvester's purchases bikes from three suppliers but plans to add new suppliers in the near future. This rapidly growing business needs a database system to manage this information.

Initially, the database should house information about suppliers and products. The database will contain two tables: a supplier table and a product table. The reorder level refers to the number of items in inventory that triggers a decision to order more items to prevent a stockout. (In other words, if the number of units of a particular inventory item falls below the reorder level, the item should be reordered.) The user should be able to perform several queries and produce several managerial reports based on the data contained in the two tables.

Using the information found in the tables on the Laudon Web site for Chapter 5, build a simple relational database for Sylvester's. Once you have built the database, perform the following activities:

1. Prepare a report that identifies the five most expensive bicycles. The report should list the bicycles in descending order from most expensive to least expensive, the quantity on hand for each, and the markup percentage for each.
2. Prepare a report that lists each supplier, its products, the quantities on hand, and associated reorder levels. The report should be sorted alphabetically by supplier. Within each supplier category, the products should be sorted alphabetically.
3. Prepare a report listing only the bicycles that are low in stock and need to be reordered. The report should provide supplier information for the items identified.
4. Write a brief description of how the database could be enhanced to further improve management of the business. What tables or fields could be added? What additional reports would be useful?

## Redesigning the Customer Database

Software skills: Database design; querying and reporting

Business skills: Customer profiling

Dirt Bikes U.S.A. sells primarily through its distributors. It maintains a small customer database with the following data: customer name, address, telephone number, model purchased, date of purchase, and distributor. You can find this database on the Laudon Web site for Chapter 5. These data are collected by its distributors when they make a sale and are then forwarded to Dirt Bikes. Dirt Bikes would like to be able to market more aggressively to its customers. The Marketing Department would like to be able to send customers e-mail notices of special racing events and of sales on parts. It would also like to learn more about customers' interests and tastes: their ages, years of schooling, another sport in which they are interested, and whether they attend dirt bike racing events. Additionally, Dirt Bikes would like to know whether customers own more than one motorcycle. (Some Dirt Bikes customers own two or three motorcycles purchased from Dirt Bikes U.S.A. or another manufacturer.) If a motorcycle was purchased from Dirt Bikes, the company would like to know the date of purchase, model purchased, and distributor. If the customer owns a non–Dirt Bikes motorcycle, the company would like to know the manufacturer and model of the other motorcycle (or motorcycles) and the distributor from whom the customer purchased that motorcycle.

1. Redesign Dirt Bikes's customer database so that it can store and provide the information needed for marketing. You will need to develop a design for the new customer database and then implement that design using database software. Consider using multiple tables in your new design. Populate each new table with 10 records.
2. Develop several reports that would be of great interest to Dirt Bikes's marketing and sales department (for example, lists of repeat Dirt Bikes customers, Dirt Bikes customers who attend racing events, or the average ages and years of schooling of Dirt Bikes customers) and print them.

## Building Internet Skills

### Searching Online Databases

This project will help develop your Internet skills in searching online databases.

The Internet is a valuable source of databases where users can search for services and products in areas or countries that are far from their own locations. Your company is located in Greensboro, North Carolina, and manufactures office furniture of various types. You have recently acquired several new customers in Australia, and a study you commissioned indicates that, with a presence there, you could greatly increase your sales. Moreover, your study indicates that you could do even better if you actually manufactured many of your products locally (in Australia). First, you need to set up an office in Melbourne to establish a presence, and then you need to begin importing from the United States. You can then plan to start producing locally.

You will soon be traveling to the area to make plans to actually set up an office, and you want to meet with organizations that can help you with your operation. You will need to engage people or organizations that offer many services necessary for you to open your office, including lawyers, accountants, import–export experts, telecommunications equipment and support, and even trainers who can help you to prepare your future employees to work for you. List the companies you would contact to interview on your trip to determine whether they can help you with these and any other functions you think are vital to establishing your office. Start by searching for the U.S. Department of Commerce advice on doing business in Australia. Then try the following online databases to locate companies that you would like to meet with during your upcoming trip: Australian Business Register (abr.business.gov.au/), Australia Trade Now (australiatradenow.com/), and the Nationwide Business Directory of Australia (www.nationwide.com.au). If necessary, you could also try search engines such as Yahoo! and Google.

Rate the databases you used for accuracy of name, completeness, ease of use, and general helpfulness. What does this exercise tell you about the design of databases?

## Video Case

You will find a video case illustrating some of the concepts in this chapter on the Laudon Web site at **www.prenhall.com/laudon** along with questions to help you analyze the case.

## Teamwork

### Identifying Entities and Attributes in an Online Database

With a group of two or three of your fellow students, select an online database to explore, such as AOL Music, Gracenote.com, or the Internet Movie Database. Explore these Web sites to see what information they provide. Then list the entities and attributes that they must keep track of in their databases. If possible, diagram the relationship between the entities you have identified. If possible, use electronic presentation software to present your findings to the class.

# BUSINESS PROBLEM-SOLVING CASE

## The FBI Abandons Its Virtual Case System

The World Trade Center and Pentagon terrorist attacks on September 11, 2001, have focused attention on the need for accurate information about terrorist activities to prevent similar catastrophes in the future. Much of the information necessary to combat future terrorist attacks, as well as to fight domestic crime, is stored in databases of literally thousands of federal, state, and local government agencies. Bringing together this information to make it useful for fighting terrorism and crime is proving to be an immense task.

The Federal Bureau of Investigation (FBI) was singled out for special scrutiny because its inefficient file and record systems created impediments to information sharing that may have contributed to its inability to detect the al Qaeda hijacking plot. Although other intelligence agencies, such as the Central Intelligence Agency (CIA) and National Security Agency, implemented powerful and secure information systems long ago, the FBI's systems remained cumbersome and woefully out of date.

The FBI had no enterprise-wide information architecture but rather hundreds of applications written in various languages and running on disparate systems and databases. Many special agents were still using personal computers and software applications that were at least 10 years old. There was no way agents could simultaneously access the dozens of databases they used every day. Antiquated equipment and patchwork communications made it virtually impossible to access and share information while working cases.

The bulk of the internal reports and documents produced at the FBI had to be printed, signed, and scanned by hand into computer format each day. The FBI continued to rely on paper as its chief information management tool.

Over the years, the FBI had created five critical but independent investigative application systems, each storing its data differently, with different data names, codes, and formats. These databases are considered the backbone of the FBI systems. Each of these five investigative application systems could be viewed only by using very old-fashioned green IBM 3270 terminals. Many agents could not access the Internet from their desks because of security concerns.

When the FBI tried to create the huge Integrated Automated Fingerprint Identification System (IAFIS) in the late 1990s, it had to integrate two already-existing but dissimilar systems, the FBI's IAFIS and the Immigration and Naturalization Service's Automated Biometric Identification (IDENT) System. Whereas the IAFIS stored 10 rolled prints for each person, IDENT stored only two flat prints. For an interim solution, the FBI first had to develop custom software to exchange fingerprinting data between the two systems. Two fingerprints from IAFIS were added to IDENT, while workstations for using 10 rolled prints were also being designed. Second, a study had to be undertaken to determine how to capture the 10 prints more rapidly. Ultimately, the FBI developed a fast transaction type that retrieves an individual's criminal history without displaying the fingerprints. Fingerprint matching could be done later if needed.

Agents required security clearances to access much of the data, but security clearance often took up to eight months to obtain. Because of the secretive FBI culture, it has had a mind-set to keep information to itself, a problem highlighted by the events of September 11.

In November 2000, Congress allocated $379 million to update the FBI's systems. The project, dubbed Trilogy, involved upgrading the FBI's hardware and networking infrastructure and linking 622 field offices. The centerpiece of the project was a massive data warehouse that would integrate more than 180 different FBI databases through a single Web portal and enable agents and analysts to share case information. This portion of the project was called the Virtual Case File (VCF) system. The information in the data warehouse would come from thousands of transaction records and files generated in local and national FBI offices. The idea was to combine all this transaction data into a single data warehouse where it could be analyzed, searched for patterns, and, hopefully, used to identify suspicious people and circumstances.

Instead of faxing or mailing information about a suspected terrorist from one field office to another, FBI field agents would be able to access the VCF system using a standard Web browser. VCF also could be shared with the CIA, the National Security Agency, and local police departments. With proper security clearance, FBI agents would be able to add information to the system at any time. A related system would automate and scan all paper-based information, amounting to 31 million documents, into a relational database that could be mined. The bureau's nearly 12,000 agents would have instant access to FBI databases, allowing speedier investigations and more integration of information within the bureau and with other intelligence agencies coordinating national security. Information would flow to the warehouse from telephone records; Joint Terrorism Task Force data; the Drug Enforcement Administration; the Bureau of Alcohol, Tobacco, Firearms and Explosives; the State Department's visa database; and from other agencies.

The FBI hired the information systems consultancy firm Science Applications International Corporation (SAIC) to develop the Virtual Case File. The project was supposed to be completed by the end of 2003.

By that time, the FBI had installed 21,000 Dell desktop computers, more than 3,000 printers, and nearly 1,500 scanners. In addition, it linked 622 FBI offices with high-speed data connections and implemented an Investigative Data Warehouse (IDW), which provides a single access point to more than 47 sources of counterterrorism data, including FBI files, other government agency data, and open source news feeds that were previously available only through separate stove-piped systems. Users could rapidly search up to 100 million pages of international terrorism-related documents and photos and more easily identify relationships across cases.

What was missing was the capability for agents to directly input investigative and intelligence information into their computers, receive electronic approval for entering this information, and upload the new information into the database, where it could be immediately available to others who need it—other agents, and federal, state, and local employees. Very little work had been accomplished on the Virtual Case File, which was supposed to provide those capabilities. As deadlines were pushed back, costs mounted. By the end of 2004, a year after the original deadline for VCF had passed, the FBI had spent $170 million on the Virtual Case File project, and only one-tenth of the work had been completed.

The FBI had done such a poor job of documenting its databases that it had to catalog information on each database while the Trilogy project was under way, adding to the delays. Many of the bureau's legacy systems were not designed to communicate with other systems and had various levels of security clearance. Some are highly secure and accessible only to a very small number of people; others are available to larger numbers of agents. The new system had to be both secure and accessible.

The FBI lacked staff experienced in project management, contract management, and software development. It underestimated the complexity of interfacing with its legacy systems, addressing security needs, and establishing an enterprise-wide application framework. The VCF system was developed without any testing or contingency plan for handling "mission disruptive features" if the old system were directly cut over to the new one.

The initial inflexible design of VCF contributed to the delays. VCF was originally designed before the September 11 terrorist attacks to support criminal investigations and prosecutions rather than terrorism and intelligence-gathering and analysis. SAIC chose to write the required software itself, rather than relying on off-the-shelf software and tools. As it was designed, the system lacked the flexibility to accommodate future needs, such as the ability to create or transmit electronic signatures.

The project proceeded so slowly that it could not keep pace with changes in information technology that would have made the Virtual Case File easier to develop. The FBI acknowledged, "there are now existing products to suit our purposes that did not exist when Trilogy began." Bureau officials considered the prototype of the Virtual Case File completed by SAIC in December 2004 to be inadequate and already outdated. They used it mainly on a trial basis to glean information from users that might be useful when designing a future system. The prototype's main feature allows users to prepare documents and forward them in a usable form.

SAIC refused to accept all the blame for Virtual Case File problems. "The FBI modernization effort involved a massive technological and cultural change, agencywide," stated Duane Andrews, SAIC chief operating officer. SAIC said the FBI changed CIOs four times and had 14 different managers during the Trilogy project since its inception in 2001. These changes in management made it difficult to finalize design requirements. FBI officials submitted change requests at a rate of 1.3 per day and revised the contract for VCF 26 times. In May 2004, a National Research Council report recommended that the FBI change its implementation strategy from all at once to a less risk incremental phase-in of VCF functions.

On March 8, 2005, FBI director Robert Mueller announced that the agency was scrapping the Virtual Case File project. A report by Justice Department Inspector General Glenn A. Fine found that "the F.B.I's operations remain significantly hampered due to the poor functionality and lack of information-sharing capabilities of its current systems." It concluded that the VCF system as it had been designed and conceived would not work and could not be put into use. The report noted that these problems raise "national security implications" because FBI agents and analysts are still unable to adequately share and search for information.

As it stands now, the FBI's counterterrorism files are largely online, but the system does not provide immediate access to data from other parts of the organization. With these limited capabilities, an agent investigating terrorism might not be immediately aware of relevant information from a credit card fraud case. The majority of internal reports and documents produced by the FBI must still be printed, signed, and scanned by hand into computer format each day.

In May 2005, FBI Director Robert Mueller announced plans for a new system called Sentinel to replace the failed Virtual Case File system. About 80 to 90 percent of Sentinel will use off-the-shelf software.

*Sources*: Larry Greenemeier, "Tech vs. Terrorism," *InformationWeek*, June 6, 2005, "Snafus Cause FBI to Try Packaged Software," *InformationWeek*, May 30, 2005, and "FBI Not Getting Results in File-Sharing Project," *InformationWeek*, January 17, 2005; Eric Lichtblau, "F.B.I. May Scrap Virtual Overhaul for Computers," *The New York Times*, January 14, 2005; Alan Holmes, "Why the G-Men Aren't IT Men," *CIO Magazine*, June 15, 2005; Seth Grims, "FBI Virtual Case File System Marked for Termination," *Systems Management Pipeline*, March 1, 2005; Dan Eggen, "Computer Woes Hinder FBI's Work, Report Says," *Washington Post*, February 4, 2005; Robert S. Mueller, III, "Congressional Testimony before the United States Senate Committee on Appropriations Subcommittee on Commerce, Justice, State and the Judiciary," February 3, 2005; Arik Johnson, "Competitive Intelligence: FBI Virtual Case File = Total Disaster," January 13, 2005; http://www.aurorawdc.com, accessed May 18, 2005; David Perera, "FBI Picking Up IT Pieces," *Federal Computer Week*, February 7, 2005 and "Virtual Case File a Virtual Bust," *Federal Computer Week*, January 14, 2005; Susan Kuchinskas, "FBI's Virtual Case File Flops," *Internet News*, January 14, 2005; Linda Rosencrance, "It's Official: FBI Scraps $170M Virtual Case File Project," *Computerworld*, March 9, 2005; Wilsom P. Dizard III, "New System to Replace FBI Virtual Case File," *PostNewsweek Tech Media*, May 13, 1005; Larry Barrett, "FBI: Under the Gun," *Baseline*, September 1, 2003; and Sara Michael, "FBI Boosting Virtual Case Database," *Federal Computer Week*, April 14, 2003.

## Case Study Questions

1. Describe the problem raised by this case. What caused this problem? What was its impact?
2. Did FBI management correctly identify the problem and its people, organizational, and technology issues?
3. What solutions did FBI management consider? Did they choose the correct solution?
4. Did the FBI implement the solution effectively? Did they deal successfully with people, organizational, and technology issues during implementation?
5. Do you think Sentinel will succeed where the Virtual Case File system failed? Explain your answer.

# Telecommunications, the Internet, and Wireless Technology

CHAPTER 6

## STUDENT OBJECTIVES

After reading this chapter, you will be able to:

1. Describe the features of telecommunications networks and identify key networking technologies.

2. Evaluate alternative transmission media, types of networks, and network services.

3. Demonstrate how the Internet and Internet technology work and how they support communication and e-business.

4. Identify and describe the principal technologies and standards for wireless networking, communication, and Internet access.

5. Assess the business value of wireless technology and important wireless applications in business.

## DARTMOUTH: AN OLD COLLEGE BECOMES A NEW NETWORKING INNOVATOR

**Founded in 1769, Dartmouth College** is one of the oldest colleges in the United States, but in terms of technology, it is new and leading edge. Dartmouth is a pioneer in wireless networking, and boasts one of the most powerful and advanced Wi-Fi wireless networks in operation. The network provides 6,000 students and 2,500 faculty and staff with always-on high-speed Internet access and capabilities for transmitting voice, video, and data from any campus location.

Dartmouth has always been known for a high-quality learning environment that brings students in close contact with faculty dedicated to outstanding teaching and scholarship. But it is also a nonprofit organization that is concerned with costs like any other business. Its costs for operating its campuswide information systems linking 161 buildings with 1,000 rooms were high because it had to manage separate networks for voice, data, and video transmission that were out of date.

In 2001, Brad Noblet, director of Dartmouth's technical services, decided to replace this aging telecommunications infrastructure with a single IP network based on Internet technology standards capable of transmitting voice, video, and data. This converged network saved two-thirds the cost to rebuild three separate networks and saves nearly $1 million per year in network maintenance, cabling, and personnel costs.

Dartmouth used these savings to implement a wireless 802.11b Wi-Fi network linking the entire campus, becoming one of the first colleges in the United States to completely integrate its systems into a wireless infrastructure. Dartmouth upgraded the network four years later to add more wired and wireless access points, and to boost transmission capacity so that it could deliver cable television programming as well as data and voice over its wireless infrastructure. The Dartmouth campus has no conventional cell phone service, but the network provides some capability for wireless voice service based on Internet telephony (voice over Wi-Fi).

Nearly every Dartmouth student has a Wi-Fi enabled computer, and more than 9,000 PCs are in use campuswide. Students use the network to submit their course work, watch streaming video, listen to Internet radio, and communicate with each other via instant messaging. Professors transmit class assignments, lecture notes, or reference materials to students wirelessly.

According to Noblet, "This really improves our ability to deliver types of information services that enhance teaching and learning." For example, students in Professor Thomas H. Luxon's Shakespeare class can view filmed scenes from Macbeth on their PCs in their dorm rooms or on the campus lawn on their own time and pace instead of having to go to the classroom or media center. Students will still need to write papers, but they could annotate their papers with video clips from a Shakespeare play as if they were quotations and transmit them over the network for Professor Luxon to review. ■

*Sources:* Katie Zezima, "At Dartmouth, Advanced Wi-Fi," *The New York Times,* May 4, 2005; "Dartmouth: Creating a Wi-Fi Monster," *Wi-Fi Planet,* April 20, 2005; Aruba Networks, "Dartmouth College Nation's Largest University Wi-Fi System," *TMCnet News,* February 28, 2005; and www.dartmouth.edu, accessed July 3, 2005.

**D**artmouth College illustrates some of the new capabilities—and opportunities—provided by contemporary networking technology. Although some of Dartmouth's applications are leading edge for a higher educational institution, much of the technology described here—wireless Wi-Fi networks, Internet standards, and Internet telephony—is widely used in businesses of all sizes.

Dartmouth was looking for new ways to fulfill its mission of maintaining a high-quality, vital learning environment while lowering its operating costs. It was also on the lookout for creative ways to harness the opportunities opened up by new technology. Dartmouth's networking costs were higher than necessary because it had been maintaining three separate networks to handle voice, data, and video transmission, and these networks were out of date.

Dartmouth could have replaced its outdated voice, data, and video networks with more up-to-date individual networks for each of these services. Instead, it implemented a single converged IP network based on Internet technology standards that could handle all of these services. Dartmouth also installed a high-capacity wireless Wi-Fi network that was accessible throughout the campus. This solution eliminated the need for fixed network cabling, reduced network administration costs, and created a much more flexible technology platform than it previously had to support innovations in learning.

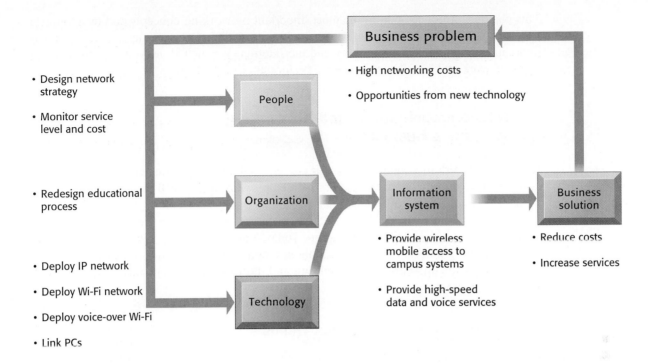

- Design network strategy
- Monitor service level and cost

- Redesign educational process

- Deploy IP network
- Deploy Wi-Fi network
- Deploy voice-over Wi-Fi
- Link PCs

**People**

**Organization**

**Technology**

**Business problem**
- High networking costs
- Opportunities from new technology

**Information system**
- Provide wireless mobile access to campus systems
- Provide high-speed data and voice services

**Business solution**
- Reduce costs
- Increase services

## HEADS UP

This chapter focuses on networks and how business firms use networks to achieve operational excellence, strategic advantage, and close relationships with suppliers and customers. Both small and large companies use networks of various kinds to link together the diverse groups that make up a business enterprise. Networks provide the communication highway linking together suppliers, customers, employees, and strategic partners. Businesses today could not survive without their computer and telecommunications networks.

• If your career is in finance or accounting, you will be working with networked systems and the Internet for accessing and updating account information, researching financial markets, trading securities, and transferring funds.

• If your career is in human resources, you will be using private corporate networks and intranets to access employee records and the Internet to research benefits and compensation plans.

• If your career is in manufacturing, production, or operations management, you will be working with networked systems for monitoring the factory floor, for scheduling work, for supply chain management, and for warehousing and delivery. Some of these systems will be based on intranets and extranets.

• If your career is in sales and marketing, you will be working with online sales systems that obtain order transactions from private networks or the Web and with marketing systems that use data generated by Web sites.

This chapter introduces you to the most important networking concepts and technologies used in business. We identify the key technologies for digital networking and communications, including wireless technology and the Internet. We then show you how these technologies work and how they enhance the performance of the firm.

## 6.1 Telecommunications and Networking in Today's Business World

If you run or work in a business, you can't do without networks. You need to communicate rapidly with your customers, suppliers, and employees, and you'll need to transmit data immediately to process orders, purchase from suppliers, or respond to service requests. Until about 1990, you would have used the postal system or telephone system with voice or fax for your business communication. Today, however, you and your employees use computers and e-mail, the Internet, cell phones, and mobile computers connected to wireless networks for this purpose. Networking and the Internet are now nearly synonymous with doing business.

### Networking and Communication Trends

Firms in the past used two fundamentally different types of networks: telephone networks and computer networks. Telephone networks historically handled voice communication, and computer networks handled data traffic. Telephone networks were built by telephone companies throughout the twentieth century using voice transmission technologies (hardware and software), and these companies almost always operated as regulated monopolies throughout the world. Computer networks were originally built by computer companies seeking to transmit data between computers in different locations.

Thanks to continuing telecommunications deregulation and information technology innovation, telephone and computer networks are slowly merging into a single digital network using shared Internet-based standards and equipment. Although this transformation is not yet complete, the general trend is toward the convergence of computer and telephone networks. Telecommunications providers, such as AT&T and Verizon, today offer data transmission, Internet access, wireless telephone service, and television programming as well as voice service. Cable companies, such as Cablevision and Comcast, now offer voice service and Internet access. Computer networks have expanded to include Internet telephone and limited video services. Increasingly, all of these voice, video, and data communications are based on Internet technology.

Both voice and data communication networks have also become more powerful (faster), more portable (smaller and mobile), and less expensive. For instance, the typical Internet connection speed in 2000 was 56 kilobits per second, but today more than 60 percent of U.S. Internet users have high-speed **broadband** connections provided by telephone and cable TV companies running at one million bits per second. The cost per kilobit of communication has fallen exponentially, from 25 cents in 2000, to less than 1 cent in 2005.

Increasingly, voice and data communication as well as Internet access are taking place over broadband wireless platforms, such as cell phones, handheld digital devices, and PCs in wireless networks (eMarketer, 2005a). In fact, wireless broadband access is the fastest-growing form of Internet access, growing at 28 percent a year.

### What Is a Computer Network?

If you had to connect the computers for two or more employees together in the same office, you would need a computer network. Exactly what is a network? In its simplest form, a network consists of two or more connected computers. Figure 6-1 illustrates the

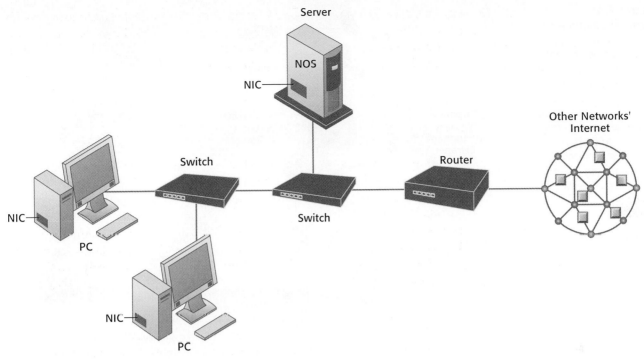

**Figure 6-1**
Components of a Simple Computer Network
*Illustrated here is a very simple computer network, consisting of computers, a network operating system residing on a dedicated server computer, cable (wiring) connecting the devices, network interface cards (NIC), switches, and a router.*

major hardware, software, and transmission components used in a simple network: a client computer and a dedicated server computer, network interfaces, a connection medium, network operating system software, and either a hub or a switch. Each computer on the network contains a network interface device called a **network interface card (NIC)**. Most personal computers today have this card built into the motherboard. The connection medium for linking network components can be a telephone wire, coaxial cable, or radio signal in the case of cell phone and wireless local-area networks (Wi-Fi networks).

The **network operating system (NOS)** routes and manages communications on the network and coordinates network resources. It can reside on every computer in the network, or it can reside primarily on a dedicated server computer for all the applications on the network. A server computer is a computer on a network that performs important network functions for client computers, such as serving up Web pages, storing data, and storing the network operating system (and hence controlling the network). Server software, such as Microsoft Windows Server 2003, along with the server versions of Windows 2000, Linux, and Novell NetWare, are the most widely used network operating systems.

Most networks also contain a switch or a hub acting as a connection point between the computers. **Hubs** are very simple devices that connect network components, sending a packet of data to all other connected devices. A **switch** has more intelligence than a hub and can filter and forward data to a specified destination. Switches are used within individual networks. To communicate with another network, the network would use a device called a router. A **router** is a special communications processor used to route packets of data through different networks, ensuring that the message sent gets to the correct address.

**Figure 6-2**
Corporate Network
Infrastructure
*Today's corporate net-*
*work infrastructure is a*
*collection of many dif-*
*ferent networks from*
*the public switched tele-*
*phone network; to the*
*Internet; to corporate*
*local-area networks link-*
*ing workgroups, depart-*
*ments, or office floors.*

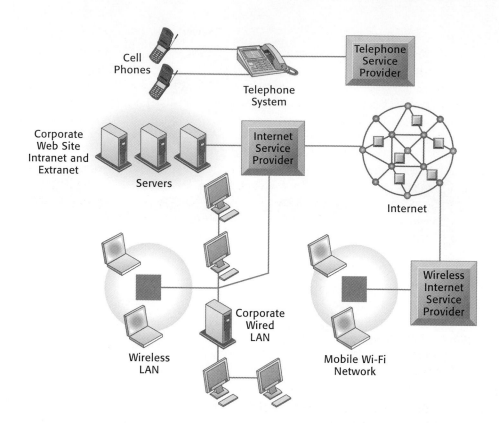

## Networks in Large Companies

The network we've just described might be suitable for a small business. But what about large companies with many different locations and thousands of employees? As a firm grows, and collects hundreds of small local-area networks (LANs), these networks can be tied together easily into a corporate-wide networking infrastructure. The network infrastructure for a large corporation consists of a large number of these small local-area networks linked to other local-area networks and to firmwide corporate networks. A number of powerful servers are used to support a corporate Web site, a corporate intranet, and perhaps an extranet. Some of these servers link to other large computers supporting backend systems.

Figure 6-2 provides an illustration of these more complex, larger scale corporate-wide networks. Here you can see that the corporate network infrastructure supports a mobile sales force using cell phones; mobile employees linking to the company Web site, or internal company networks using mobile wireless local-area networks (Wi-Fi networks); and a video-conferencing system to support managers across the world. In addition to these computer networks, the firm's infrastructure usually includes a separate telephone network that handles most voice data. Many firms are dispensing with their traditional telephone networks and using Internet telephones that run on their existing data networks (described later).

This infrastructure uses a wide variety of technologies, everything from ordinary telephone service and corporate data networks to Internet service, wireless Internet, and wireless cell phones. One of the major problems facing corporations today is how to integrate all the different communication networks and channels into a coherent system that enables information to flow from one part of the corporation to another, from one system to another. As more and more communication networks become digital, and based on Internet technologies, it will become easier to integrate them.

## Key Digital Networking Technologies

Contemporary digital networks and the Internet are based on three key technologies: client/server computing, the use of packet switching, and the development of widely used communications standards (the most important of which is Transmission Control Protocol/Internet Protocol [TCP/IP]) for linking disparate networks and computers.

## Client/Server Computing

In Chapter 4, we introduced client/server computing in which client computers are connected in a network with one or more server computers. Client/server computing is a distributed computing model in which some of the processing power is located within small, inexpensive client computers under user control, and resides literally on desktops, laptops, or in handheld devices. These powerful clients are linked to one another through a network that is controlled by a network server computer. The server sets the rule of communication for the network and provides every client with an address so others can find it on the network.

Client/server computing has largely replaced centralized mainframe computing in which nearly all of the processing takes place on a central large mainframe computer. Client/server computing has extended computing to departments, workgroups, factory floors, and other parts of the business that could not be served by a centralized architecture. The Internet is the largest implementation of client/server computing.

## Packet Switching

**Packet switching** is a method of slicing digital messages into parcels called packets, sending the packets along different communication paths as they become available, and then reassembling the packets once they arrive at their destinations (see Figure 6-3). Prior to the development of packet switching, computer networks used leased, dedicated telephone circuits to communicate with other computers in remote locations. In circuit-switched networks, such as the telephone system, a complete point-to-point circuit is assembled, and then communication can proceed. These dedicated circuit-switching techniques were expensive and wasted available communications capacity—the circuit was maintained regardless of whether any data were being sent.

Packet switching makes much more efficient use of the communications capacity of a network. In packet-switched networks, messages are first broken down into small fixed bundles of data called packets. There are many different packet sizes, depending on the communications standard being used. The packets include information for directing the packet to the right address and for checking transmission errors along with the data.

Data are gathered from many users, divided into small packets, and transmitted over various communications channels using routers. Each packet travels independently through these networks. Packets of data originating at one source can be routed through many different paths and networks before being reassembled into the original message when they reach their destinations.

Packet switching does not require a dedicated circuit but can make use of any available spare capacity. If some lines are disabled or too busy, the packets can be sent over any available line that eventually leads to the destination point.

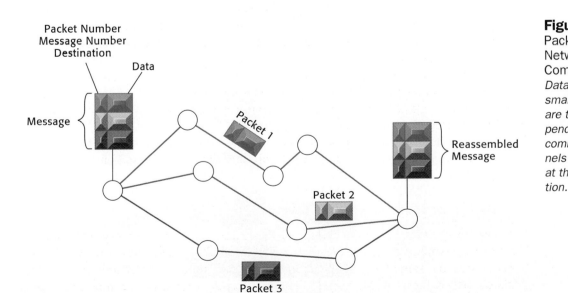

**Figure 6-3**
Packet-Switched Networks and Packet Communications
*Data are grouped into small packets, which are transmitted independently over various communications channels and reassembled at their final destination.*

## TCP/IP and Connectivity

In a typical telecommunications network, diverse hardware and software components need to work together to transmit information. Different components in a network communicate with each other only by adhering to a common set of rules called protocols. A **protocol** is a set of rules and procedures governing transmission of information between two points in a network. In the past, many diverse proprietary and incompatible protocols often forced business firms to purchase computing and communications equipment from a single vendor. But today corporate networks are increasingly using a single, common, worldwide standard called **Transmission Control Protocol/Internet Protocol (TCP/IP)**.

TCP/IP provides a universally agreed-on method for breaking up digital messages into packets, routing them to the proper addresses, and then reassembling them into coherent messages. TCP/IP was developed during the early 1970s to support U.S. Department of Defense Advanced Research Projects Agency (DARPA) efforts to help scientists transmit data among different types of computers over long distances.

TCP/IP uses a suite of protocols, the main ones being TCP and IP. *TCP* refers to the Transmission Control Protocol (TCP), which handles the movement of data between computers. TCP establishes a connection between the computers, sequences the transfer of packets, and acknowledges the packets sent. *IP* refers to the Internet Protocol (IP), which is responsible for the delivery of packets and includes the disassembling and reassembling of packets during transmission. Figure 6-4 illustrates the four-layered Department of Defense reference model for TCP/IP.

1. *Application layer.* The application layer enables client application programs to access the other layers and defines the protocols that applications use to exchange data. One of these application protocols is the Hypertext Transfer Protocol (HTTP), which is used to transfer Web page files.
2. *Transport layer.* The transport layer is responsible for providing the application layer with communication and packet services. This layer includes TCP and other protocols.
3. *Internet layer.* The Internet layer is responsible for addressing, routing, and packaging data packets called IP datagrams. The Internet Protocol is one of the protocols used in this layer.
4. *Network interface layer.* At the bottom of the reference model, the network interface layer is responsible for placing packets on and receiving them from the physical network medium, which could be any networking technology.

Two computers using TCP/IP can communicate even if they are based on different hardware and software platforms. Data sent from one computer to the other passes downward through all four layers, starting with the sending computer's application layer and passing through the network interface layer. After the data reach the recipient host computer, they travel up the layers and are reassembled into a format the receiving computer can use. If the

**Figure 6-4**
The Transmission Control Protocol/Internet Protocol (TCP/IP) Reference Model
*This figure illustrates the four layers of the TCP/IP reference model for communications.*

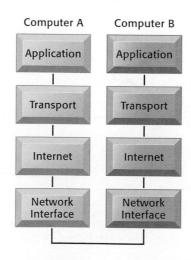

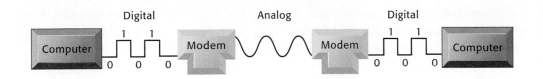

**Figure 6-5**
Functions of the Modem
*A modem is a device that translates digital signals from a computer into analog form so that they can be transmitted over analog telephone lines. The modem also translates analog signals back into digital form for the receiving computer.*

receiving computer finds a damaged packet, it asks the sending computer to retransmit it. This process is reversed when the receiving computer responds.

## 6.2 Communications Networks

Let's look more closely at the alternative networking technologies and arrangements available to businesses.

### Physical Transmission Media

Networks use different kinds of physical transmission media, including twisted wire, coaxial cable, fiber optics, and media for wireless transmission. Each has advantages and limitations. A wide range of speeds is possible for any given medium depending on the software and hardware configuration.

#### Twisted Wire

**Twisted wire** consists of strands of copper wire twisted in pairs and is an older type of transmission medium. Many of the telephone systems in buildings had twisted wires installed for analog communication, but they can be used for digital communication as well.

An *analog signal* is represented by a continuous waveform that passes through a communications medium and has been used for voice communication. A *digital signal* is a discrete, rather than a continuous, waveform. It transmits data coded into two discrete states: one bit and zero bits, which are represented as on–off electrical pulses. Computers use digital signals, so if one wants to use the analog telephone system to send digital data, a device called a **modem** is required to translate digital signals into analog form (see Figure 6-5). *Modem* stands for modulation/demodulation.

Although twisted wire is low in cost and usually is already in place, it can be relatively slow and noisy for transmitting data. There are limits to the amount of data that ordinary twisted wire can carry, but new software and hardware used by local telephone companies have raised twisted-wire transmission capacity to make it useful for high-speed connectivity to the Internet at speeds up to one megabit per second (Mbps), or one million bits per second.

#### Coaxial Cable

**Coaxial cable**, similar to that used for cable television, consists of thickly insulated copper wire, which can transmit a larger volume of data than twisted wire. Cable is commonly used for local-area networks because it is a faster, more interference-free transmission medium, capable of speeds up to 200 Mbps.

#### Fiber Optics and Optical Networks

**Fiber-optic cable** consists of strands of clear glass fiber, each the thickness of a human hair, which are bound into cables. Data are transformed into pulses of light, which are sent through the fiber-optic cable by a laser device at rates varying from 500 kilobits to several trillion bits per second in experimental settings. Fiber-optic cable is considerably faster, lighter, and more durable than wire media, and is well suited to systems requiring transfers of large volumes of data. However, fiber-optic cable is more difficult to work with, more expensive, and harder to install.

Until recently, fiber-optic cable had been used primarily as the high-speed network backbone, whereas twisted wire and coaxial cable were used to connect the backbone to individual businesses and households. A **backbone** is the part of a network that handles the major traffic. It acts as the primary path for traffic flowing to or from other networks. Now, local cable companies are bringing fiber all the way into the basements of buildings so they can provide a variety of new services to businesses and eventually residential customers.

These **optical networks** can transmit all types of traffic—voice, data, and video—over fiber cables and provide the massive bandwidth for new types of services and software. Using optical networks, on-demand video, software downloads, and high-quality digital audio can be accessed using set-top boxes and other information appliances without severe degradation in quality or delays.

Optical networks can boost capacity by using **dense wavelength division multiplexing (DWDM)**. **Multiplexing** enables a single communications channel to carry simultaneous data transmissions from multiple sources. (This can be accomplished by dividing a high-speed channel into multiple channels of slower speeds or by assigning each transmission source a very small slice of time for using a high-speed channel.) DWDM boosts transmission capacity by using many different colors of light, or different wavelengths, to carry separate streams of data over the same fiber strand at the same time. DWDM combines up to 160 wavelengths per strand and can transmit up to 6.4 terabits per second (Tbps) over a single fiber. This technology will enable communications service providers to add transmission capacity to an existing fiber-optic network without having to lay more fiber-optic cable. Before wavelength division multiplexing, optical networks could use only a single wavelength per strand.

### Wireless Transmission Media and Devices

Wireless transmission is based on radio signals of various frequencies. **Microwave** systems, both terrestrial and celestial, transmit high-frequency radio signals through the atmosphere and are widely used for high-volume, long-distance, point-to-point communication. Microwave signals follow a straight line and do not bend with the curvature of the earth; therefore, long-distance terrestrial transmission systems require that transmission stations be positioned about 37 miles apart, adding to the expense of microwave systems.

This problem can be solved by bouncing microwave signals off communication **satellites**, enabling them to serve as relay stations for microwave signals transmitted from terrestrial stations. Satellites are typically used for communications in large, geographically dispersed organizations that would be difficult to tie together through cabling media or terrestrial microwave transmission.

For instance, BP Amoco uses satellites for real-time data transfer of oil field exploration data gathered from searches of the ocean floor. Using geosynchronous satellites, exploration ships transfer these data to central computing centers in the United States for use by researchers in Houston, Tulsa, and suburban Chicago. Figure 6-6 illustrates how this system works.

**Figure 6-6**
BP Amoco's Satellite Transmission System
*Satellites help BP Amoco transfer seismic data between oil exploration ships and research centers in the United States.*

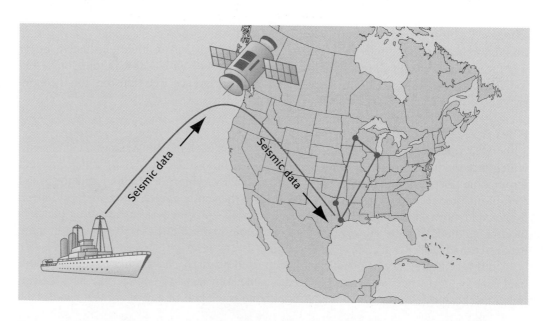

**Cellular telephones (cell phones)** work by using radio waves to communicate with radio antennas (towers) placed within adjacent geographic areas called *cells*. A telephone message is transmitted to the local cell by the cellular telephone and then is passed from antenna to antenna—cell to cell—until it reaches its destination cell, where it is transmitted to the receiving telephone. As a cellular signal travels from one cell into another, a computer that monitors signals from the cells switches the conversation to a radio channel assigned to the next cell.

Older cellular systems are analog and used primarily for voice transmission. Contemporary cellular systems are digital, supporting data transmission as well as voice transmission.

Wireless transmission technology has matured to the point where wireless networks are supplanting traditional wired networks for many applications and creating new applications, services, and business opportunities. In Section 6.4 we provide a detailed description of the applications and technology standards driving the "wireless revolution."

## Transmission Speed

The total amount of digital information that can be transmitted through any telecommunications medium is measured in bits per second (bps). One signal change, or cycle, is required to transmit one or several bits; therefore, the transmission capacity of each type of telecommunications medium is a function of its frequency. The number of cycles per second that can be sent through that medium is measured in **hertz**—one hertz is equal to one cycle of the medium.

The range of frequencies that can be accommodated on a particular telecommunications channel is called its **bandwidth**. The bandwidth is the difference between the highest and lowest frequencies that can be accommodated on a single channel. The greater the range of frequencies, the greater the bandwidth and the greater the channel's transmission capacity. Table 6.1 compares the transmission speeds of the major types of media.

## Types of Networks

There are many different kinds of networks and ways of classifying them. One way of looking at networks is in terms of their geographic scope (see Table 6.2).

### Local-Area Networks

The first computer networks appeared in the early 1960s and consisted of display terminals linked to a mainframe computer within the same building. Researchers at Xerox Palo Alto Research Center (PARC) invented the first local-area network late in that decade to connect desktop machines into a coherent computing facility. These networks enabled desktop machines to share printers, communicate with one another, and store files on a central desktop machine called a server.

Today, most people in corporations connect to other employees and groups using local-area networks. A **local-area network (LAN)** is designed to connect personal computers and

| Medium | Speed |
|---|---|
| Twisted wire (unshielded) | Up to 100 Mbps |
| Microwave | Up to 600+ Mbps |
| Satellite | Up to 600+ Mbps |
| Coaxial cable | Up to 1 Gbps |
| Fiber-optic cable | Up to 6+ Tbps |

**TABLE 6.1**

**Typical Speeds and Costs of Telecommunications Transmission Media**

Mbps = megabits per second
Gbps = gigabits per second
Tbps = terabits per second

**TABLE 6.2**

**Types of Networks**

| Type | Area |
|---|---|
| Local-area network (LAN) | Up to 500 meters (half a mile); an office or floor of a building |
| Campus-area network (CAN) | Up to 1,000 meters (a mile); a college campus or corporate facility |
| Metropolitan-area network (MAN) | A city or metropolitan area |
| Wide-area network (WAN) | A transcontinental or global area |

other digital devices within a half-mile or 500-meter radius. LANs typically connect a few computers in a small office, all the computers in one building, or all the computers in several buildings in close proximity. LANs interconnected within multiple buildings or a geographic area, such as a school campus or military base, create a **campus-area network (CAN)**. LANs can link to long-distance wide-area networks (WANs, described later in this section) and other networks around the world using the Internet.

Review Figure 6-1, which could serve as a model for a small LAN that might be used in an office. One computer is a dedicated network file server, providing users with access to shared computing resources in the network, including software programs and data files. The server determines who gets access to what and in which sequence. The router connects the LAN to other networks, which could be the Internet or another corporate network, so that the LAN can exchange information with networks external to it. The most common LAN operating systems are Windows, Linux, and Novell. Each of these network operating systems supports TCP/IP as their default networking protocol.

Ethernet is the dominant LAN standard at the physical network level, specifying the physical medium to carry signals between computers; access control rules; and a standardized frame, or set of bits used to carry data over the system. Originally, Ethernet supported a data transfer rate of 10 Mbps. Newer versions, such as Fast Ethernet and Gigabit Ethernet, support data transfer rates of 100 Mbps and 1 Gbps, respectively, and are used in network backbones.

The LAN illustrated in Figure 6-1 uses a client/server architecture where the network operating system resides primarily on a single file server, and the server provides much of the control and resources for the network. Alternatively, LANs may use a **peer-to-peer** architecture. A peer-to-peer network treats all processors equally and is used primarily in small networks with 10 or fewer users. The various computers on the network can exchange data by direct access and can share peripheral devices without going through a separate server.

In LANs using the Windows family of operating systems, the peer-to-peer architecture is called the *workgroup network model* in which a small group of computers can share resources, such as files, folders, and printers, over the network without a dedicated server. The Windows *domain network model,* in contrast, uses a dedicated server to manage the computers in the network.

Larger LANs have many clients and multiple servers, with separate servers for specific services, such as storing and managing files and databases (file servers or database servers), managing printers (print servers), storing and managing e-mail (mail servers), or storing and managing Web pages (Web servers).

Sometimes LANs are described in terms of the way their components are connected together, or their **topology**. There are three major LAN topologies: star, bus, and ring (see Figure 6-7).

In a star topology, all devices on the network connect to a single hub. Figure 6-7 illustrates a simple **star network** in which all network components connect to a single hub. All network traffic flows through the hub. In an *extended star network,* multiple layers or hubs are organized into a hierarchy.

In a bus topology, one station transmits signals, which travel in both directions along a single transmission segment. All of the signals are broadcast in both directions to the entire network. All machines on the network receive the same signals, and software installed on the

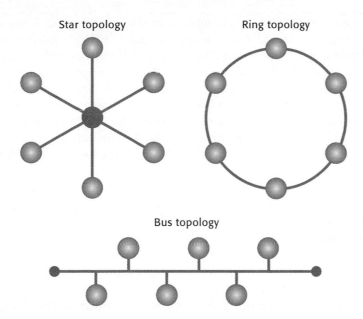

Star topology          Ring topology

Bus topology

clients enables each client to listen for messages addressed specifically to it. **Bus networks** are the most common Ethernet topology.

A ring topology connects network components in a closed loop. Messages pass from computer to computer in only one direction around the loop, and only one station at a time may transmit. **Ring networks** are used primarily in older LANs using Token Ring networking software.

### Metropolitan and Wide-Area Networks

**Wide-area networks (WANs)** span broad geographical distances—entire regions, states, continents, or the entire globe. The most universal and powerful WAN is the Internet. Computers connect to a WAN through public networks, such as the telephone system, private cable systems, or through leased lines or satellites. A **metropolitan-area network (MAN)** is a network that spans a metropolitan area, usually a city and its major suburbs. Its geographic scope falls between a WAN and a LAN. MANs sometimes provide Internet connectivity for local-area networks in a metropolitan region.

### Broadband Network Services and Technologies

A number of network services and technologies are available to companies that need high-speed transmission or access to the Internet.

**Frame relay** is a shared network service that is faster and less expensive than packet switching and can achieve transmission speeds ranging from 56 kilobits per second (Kbps) to more than 40 Mbps. Frame relay packages data into frames similar to packets but takes advantage of higher-speed, more reliable digital circuits that require less error checking than packet switching. The major telecommunications carriers provide frame relay services. Many organizations use frame relay services in their international data communication networks.

A technology called **Asynchronous Transfer Mode (ATM)** can handle many types of network traffic and provides transmission speeds ranging from 1.5 Mbps to more than 9 Gbps. Like frame relay, ATM takes advantage of high-bandwidth digital circuits, parceling information into fixed 53-byte cells, of which 48 bytes are for data and 5 are for header information. ATM can pass data among computers from different vendors and is popular for transmitting data, video, and audio over the same network. Many telecommunications carriers and large enterprise backbone networks use ATM.

**Integrated Services Digital Network (ISDN)** is an older, international telephone standard for network access that integrates voice, data, image, and video services. Although ISDN cannot match the transmission capacity of frame relay or ATM, it is a service working on prepared local telephone lines, where subscribers pay a monthly fee. There are two levels of ISDN service: basic rate ISDN (which can transmit 128 Kbps) and primary rate ISDN (which can transmit at 1.5 Mbps). In 2005, most small businesses have converted from ISDN to either cable or DSL Internet services, which are cheaper and more powerful.

Other high-capacity services include digital subscriber line technologies, cable, and T lines. Like ISDN, **digital subscriber line (DSL)** technologies also operate over existing telephone lines to carry voice, data, and video, but they have higher transmission capacities than ISDN. There are several categories of DSL. Asymmetric digital subscriber lines (ADSLs) support a transmission rate of 1.5 to 9 Mbps when receiving data and over 700 Kbps when sending data. Symmetric digital subscriber lines (SDSLs) support the same transmission rate for sending and receiving data of up to 3 Mbps.

**Cable Internet connections** provided by cable television vendors use digital cable coaxial lines to deliver high-speed Internet access to homes and businesses. They can provide high-speed access to the Internet of up to 10 Mbps. In 2005, more than 60 percent of U.S. broadband households used cable (eMarketer, 2005b).

Firms that have large amounts of data to move across the continent, or around the world, or that have high-security or guaranteed service level requirements, often lease high-speed data lines from communication providers, typically long-distance telephone companies. These lines are designated as **T lines**. T1 lines offer up to twenty-four 64-Kbps channels that can support a total data transmission rate of 1.544 Mbps. Each of these 64-Kbps channels can be configured to carry voice or data traffic. A T3 line is a very high-speed connection capable of transmitting data at a whopping rate of 45 Mbps. You will rarely encounter a T3 line unless you work in the networking department of a major corporation or university. For instance, the Internet backbone operates using multiple T3 lines. Leasing a T1 line costs about $1,000 per month, whereas T3 line costs start around $10,000 per month. Table 6.3 summarizes these network services.

**TABLE 6.3**

**Broadband Network Services**

| Service | Description | Bandwidth |
|---------|-------------|-----------|
| Frame relay | Packages data into frames for high-speed transmission over reliable circuits that require less error checking than packet switching | 56 Kbps to 40+ Mbps |
| Asynchronous Transfer Mode (ATM) | Parcels data into uniform 53-byte cells for high-speed transmission; can transmit data, video, and audio over the same network | 1.5 Mbps to 9+ Gbps |
| Integrated Services Digital Network (ISDN) | Dial-up network access standard that can integrate voice, data, and video services | Basic rate ISDN: 128 Kbps
Primary rate ISDN: 1.5 Mbps |
| Digital subscriber line (DSL) | Dedicated telephone network broadband Internet access | ADSL: Up to 9 Mbps for receiving and over 700 Kbps for sending data
SDSL: Up to 3 Mbps for both sending and receiving |
| Cable Internet connection | Dedicated cable network broadband access | Up to 10 Mbps |
| T lines | Dedicated lines for high-speed data transmission and Internet connection | T1: 1.544 Mbps
T3: 45 Mbps |

## 6.3 The Internet

If you ran or owned a small business with salespeople spread out over a regional or national area, you would quickly discover how useful it would be if each salesperson had remote access to your company's internal systems through its Web site to obtain the latest information on pricing, availability, and shipping information. Without near instant access to this information, your sales team could not answer customer questions (such as, "When can you ship and how much will it cost?") and would have to rely on much slower technologies (such as the telephone and fax machines) to find answers. In short, you would need to provide remote Internet access to your sales force in order to achieve customer and supplier intimacy and strong operational performance.

We all use the Internet, and many of us believe we can't do without it. It's become an indispensable personal and business tool. But what exactly is the Internet? How does it work, and what does Internet technology have to offer for business? Let's look at the most important features of the Internet for business.

### What Is the Internet?

In 2005, there were an estimated 958 million Internet users worldwide, representing 14.5 percent of the world's population. In the past decade, the Internet has become the world's most extensive public communication system that now rivals the global telephone system in reach and range. It's also the world's largest implementation of client/server computing and internetworking, linking hundreds of thousands of individual networks all over the world. The word *Internet* derives from the word **internetworking**, or the linking of separate networks, each of which retains its own identity, into an interconnected network. This gigantic network of networks began in the early 1970s as a U.S. Department of Defense network to link scientists and university professors around the world.

Individuals connect to the Internet in two ways. Most homes connect to the Internet by subscribing to an Internet service provider. An **Internet service provider (ISP)** is a commercial organization with a permanent connection to the Internet that sells temporary connections to retail subscribers. Telephone lines, cable lines, or wireless services can provide these connections. America Online, Yahoo!, and Microsoft Network (MSN) are ISPs in addition to being content portals. Individuals also connect to the Internet through their business firms, universities, or research centers that have designated Internet domains, such as www.ibm.com.

### Internet Addressing and Architecture

The Internet is based on the TCP/IP networking protocol suite described earlier in this chapter. Every computer on the Internet is assigned a unique **Internet Protocol (IP) address**, which currently is a 32-bit number represented by four strings of numbers ranging from 0 to 255 separated by periods. For instance, the IP address of www.microsoft.com is 207.46.250.119.

When a user sends a message to another user on the Internet, the message is first decomposed into packets using the TCP protocol. Each packet contains its destination address. The packets are then sent from the client to the network server and from there on to as many other servers as necessary to arrive at a specific computer with a known address. At the destination address, the packets are reassembled into the original message.

#### The Domain Name System

Because it would be incredibly difficult for Internet users to remember strings of 12 numbers, a **Domain Name System (DNS)** converts IP addresses to domain names. The **domain name** is the English-like name that corresponds to the unique 32-bit numeric IP address for each computer connected to the Internet. DNS servers maintain a database containing IP addresses mapped to their corresponding domain names. To access a computer on the Internet, users need only specify its domain name.

**Figure 6-8**
The Domain Name
System
*The Domain Name*
*System is a hierarchi-*
*cal system with a*
*root domain, top-level*
*domains, second-level*
*domains, and host*
*computers at the third*
*level.*

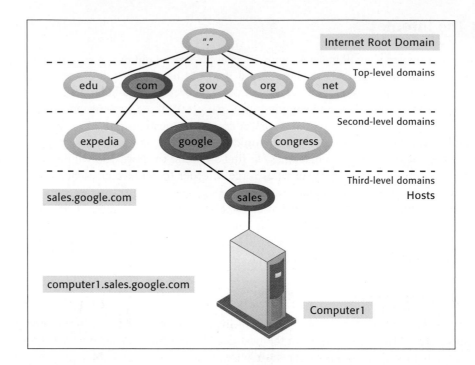

DNS has a hierarchical structure (see Figure 6-8). At the top of the DNS hierarchy is the root domain. The child domain of the root is called a top-level domain, and the child domain of a top-level domain is called a second-level domain. Top-level domains are two- and three-character names you are familiar with from surfing the Web, for example, .com, .edu, .gov, and the various country codes such as .ca for Canada or .it for Italy. Second-level domains have two parts, designating a top-level name and a second-level name—such as buy.com, nyu.edu, or amazon.ca. A host name at the bottom of the hierarchy designates a specific computer on either the Internet or a private network.

The most common domain extensions currently available and officially sanctioned are shown in the following list. Countries also have domain names such as .uk, .au, and .fr (United Kingdom, Australia, and France, respectively). Included in the following list are recently approved top-level domains, .biz and .info. In the future, this list will expand to include many more types of organizations and industries.

.com Commercial organizations/businesses

.edu Educational institutions

.gov U.S. government agencies

.mil U.S. military

.net Network computers

.org Nonprofit organizations and foundations

.biz Business firms

.info Information providers

## Internet Architecture and Governance

Internet data traffic courses over transcontinental high-speed backbone networks that generally operate today in the range of 45 Mbps to 2.5 Gbps (see Figure 6-9). These trunk lines are typically owned by long-distance telephone companies (called *network service providers*) or by national governments. Local connection lines are owned by regional telephone and cable television companies in the United States that connect retail users in homes and businesses to the Internet. The regional networks lease access to ISPs, private companies, and government institutions.

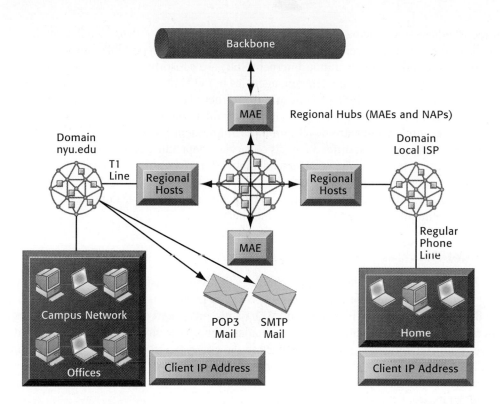

**Figure 6-9**
Internet Network
Architecture
*The Internet backbone
connects to regional
networks, which in turn
provide access to
Internet service
providers, large firms,
and government institu-
tions. Network access
points (NAPs) and met-
ropolitan-area
exchanges (MAEs) are
hubs where the back-
bone intersects regional
and local networks and
where backbone owners
connect with one
another.*

No one "owns" the Internet, and it has no formal management. However, worldwide Internet policies are established by a number of professional organizations and government bodies, including the Internet Architecture Board (IAB), which helps define the overall structure of the Internet; the Internet Corporation for Assigned Names and Numbers (ICANN), which assigns IP addresses; and the World Wide Web Consortium (W3C), which sets hypertext markup language (HTML) and other programming standards for the Web.

Although none of these organizations has actual control over the Internet and how it functions, they can and do influence government agencies, major network owners, ISPs, corporations, and software developers with the goal of keeping the Internet operating as efficiently as possible. In addition to these professional bodies, the Internet must also conform to the laws of the sovereign nation-states in which it operates, as well as the technical infrastructures that exist within the nation-states. Although in the early years of the Internet and the Web there was very little legislative or executive interference, this situation is changing as the Internet plays a growing role in the distribution of information and knowledge, including content that some find objectionable.

The Internet is not "free," even though some college students believe they do not pay for their access. In fact, everyone who uses the Internet pays some fee—hidden or otherwise—to maintain the network. Each organization pays for its own networks and its own local Internet connection services, a part of which is paid to the long-distance trunk line owners through monthly charges for telephone and Internet services. The costs of e-mail and other Internet connections tend to be far lower than equivalent voice, postal, or overnight delivery costs, making the Internet a very inexpensive communications medium. It is also a very fast method of communication, with messages arriving anywhere in the world in a matter of seconds, or a minute or two at most.

## The Future Internet: IPv6 and Internet2

The Internet was not originally designed to handle the transmission of massive quantities of data and mushrooming numbers of users. Because many corporations and governments have been given large blocks of millions of IP addresses to accommodate current and future workforces, and because of sheer Internet population growth, the world is running out of available IP addresses using the existing addressing convention. Under development is a new version of the IP addressing schema called *Internet Protocol version 6 (IPv6),* which contains 128-bit addresses (2 to the power of 128), or more than a quadrillion possible unique addresses.

**Internet2** and Next-Generation Internet (NGI) are consortia representing 200 universities, private businesses, and government agencies in the United States that are working on a new, robust, high-bandwidth version of the Internet. They have established several new high-performance backbone networks with bandwidths ranging from 2.5 Gbps to 9.6 Gbps. Internet2 research groups are developing and implementing new technologies for more effective routing practices; different levels of service, depending on the type and importance of the data being transmitted; and advanced applications for distributed computation, virtual laboratories, digital libraries, distributed learning, and tele-immersion. These networks do not replace the public Internet, but they do provide test beds for leading-edge technology that may eventually migrate to the public Internet.

## Internet Services

The Internet is based on client/server technology. Individuals using the Internet control what they do through client applications on their computers, such as Web browser software. All the data, including e-mail messages and Web pages, are stored on servers. A client uses the Internet to request information from a particular Web server on a distant computer, and the server sends the requested information back to the client over the Internet. Chapters 4 and 5 describe how Web servers work with application servers and database servers to access information from an organization's internal information systems applications and their associated databases.

Client platforms today include not only PCs and other computers but also cell phones, small handheld digital devices, and other information appliances. An **information appliance** is a device, such as an Internet-enabled cell phone or a TV Internet receiver for Web access and e-mail, that has been customized to perform a few specialized computing tasks well with minimal user effort. People are increasingly relying on these easy-to-use specialized information appliances to connect to the Internet.

A client computer connecting to the Internet has access to a variety of services. These services include e-mail, electronic discussion groups (Usenet newsgroups and LISTSERVs), chatting and instant messaging, **Telnet**, **File Transfer Protocol (FTP)**, and the World Wide Web. Table 6.4 provides a brief description of these services.

Each Internet service is implemented by one or more software programs. All of the services may run on a single server computer, or different services may be allocated to different machines. Figure 6-10 illustrates one way that these services might be arranged in a multitiered client/server architecture.

| **TABLE 6.4** | Capability | Functions Supported |
|---|---|---|
| **Major Internet Services** | E-mail | Person-to-person messaging; document sharing |
| | Usenet newsgroups | Discussion groups on electronic bulletin boards |
| | LISTSERVs | Discussion groups using e-mail mailing list servers |
| | Chatting and instant messaging | Interactive conversations |
| | Telnet | Logging on to one computer system and doing work on another |
| | File Transfer Protocol (FTP) | Transferring files from computer to computer |
| | World Wide Web | Retrieving, formatting, and displaying information (including text, audio, graphics, and video) using hypertext links |

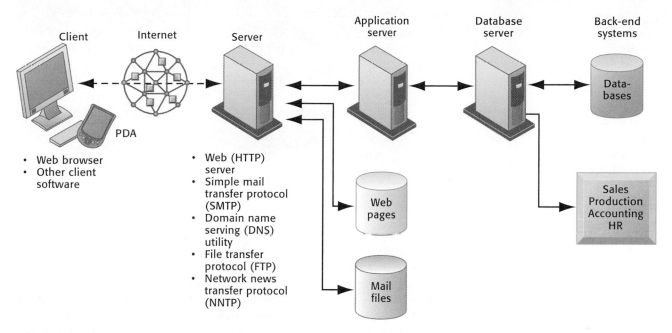

**Figure 6-10**
Client/Server Computing on the Internet
*Client computers running Web browser and other software can access an array of services on servers over the Internet. These services may all run on a single server or on multiple specialized servers.*

## The World Wide Web

The World Wide Web (the Web) is the most popular Internet service. It is a system with universally accepted standards for storing, retrieving, formatting, and displaying information using a client/server architecture. Web pages are formatted using hypertext with embedded links that connect documents to one another and that also link pages to other objects, such as sound, video, or animation files. When you click a graphic and a video clip plays, you have clicked a hyperlink.

### Hypertext

Web pages are based on a standard hypertext markup language (HTML), which formats documents and incorporates dynamic links to other documents and pictures stored in the same or remote computers (see Chapter 4). Web pages are accessible through the Internet because Web browser software operating on your computer can request Web pages stored on an Internet host server using the **Hypertext Transfer Protocol (HTTP)**. HTTP is the communications standard used to transfer pages on the Web. For example, when you type a Web address in your browser, such as www.sec.gov, your browser sends an HTTP request to the sec.gov server requesting the home page of sec.gov.

HTTP is the first set of letters at the start of every Web address, followed by the domain name, which specifies the organization's server computer that is storing the document. Most companies have a domain name that is the same as or closely related to their official corporate name. The directory path and document name are two more pieces of information within the Web address that help the browser track down the requested page. Together, the address is called a **uniform resource locator (URL)**. When typed into a browser, a URL tells the browser software exactly where to look for the information. For example, in the following URL, http://www.megacorp.com/content/features/082602.html *http* names the protocol used to display Web pages, *www.megacorp.com* is the domain name, *content/features* is the directory path that identifies where on the domain Web server the page is stored, and *082602.html* is the document name and the name of the format it is in (it is an HTML page).

**Figure 6-11**
Major Web Search
Engines
*Google is the most pop-
ular search engine on
the Web, handling
nearly 50 percent of all
Web searches.*

*Sources:*
http://searchenginewatch.
com/reports/article.php/
2156451, accessed July
2005; www.seoconsultants.
com, accessed August 3,
2005; the Pre-Commerce
Group, "At 47% of Online
Searches, Google's Share
Tops Yahoo's and MSN's
Combined," *Internet
Retailer,* March 1, 2005.

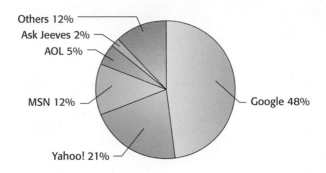

## Web Servers

A Web server is software for locating and managing stored Web pages. It locates the Web pages requested by a user on the computer where they are stored and delivers the Web pages to the user's computer. Server applications usually run on dedicated computers, although they can all reside on a single computer in small organizations.

The most common Web server in use today is Apache HTTP Server, which controls 70 percent of the market. Apache is an open source product that is free of charge and can be downloaded from the Web. Microsoft's product Internet Information Services is the second most commonly used Web server, with a 21 percent market share.

A typical **Web site** is a collection of Web pages linked to a **home page**—a text and graphical screen display that usually welcomes the user and provides a brief description of the organization that has established the Web site. Most home pages offer a way to contact the organization or individual. The person in charge of an organization's Web site is called a **Webmaster**.

## Searching for Information on the Web

No one knows for sure how many Web pages there really are. The surface Web is the part of the Web that search engines visit and about which information is recorded. For instance, Google visited about eight billion pages in 2005 and stored information about those pages in its massive collection of more than 100,000 PCs located throughout California and surrounding states. Microsoft indexes five billion; Yahoo indexes four billion; and Ask Jeeves another 2.3 billion (Fallows, 2005). But there is a "deep Web" that contains an estimated 800 billion additional pages, many of them proprietary (such as the pages of *The Wall Street Journal* Online, which cannot be visited without an access code) or behind corporate firewalls (Zillman, 2005).

**Search Engines** Obviously, with so many Web pages, finding specific Web pages that can help you or your business, nearly instantly, is an important problem. The question is, How can you find the one or two pages you really want and need out of the eight billion indexed Web pages? **Search engines** solve the problem of finding useful information on the Web nearly instantly, and, arguably, they are the "killer app" of the Internet era. About 40 million Americans use search engines each day, generating four billion queries a month. There are hundreds of different search engines in the world, but the vast majority of search results are supplied by three top providers (see Figure 6-11).

Web search engines started out in the early 1990s as relatively simple software programs that roamed the nascent Web, visiting pages, and gathering information about the content of each page. These early programs were called variously crawlers, spiders, and wanderers. AltaVista, launched in 1995, was the first to allow "natural language" queries, such as "history of web search engines" rather than "history + web search + search engine."

The first search engines were simple keyword indexes of all the pages they visited. They would count the number of times a word appeared on the pages and store this information in an index, leaving the user with lists of pages that may not have been truly relevant to their search.

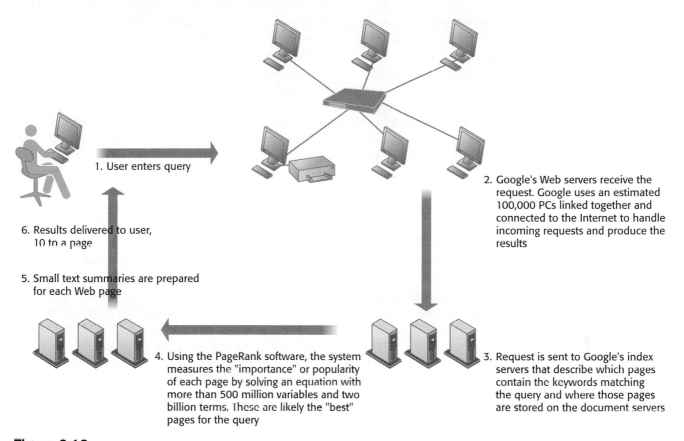

1. User enters query

6. Results delivered to user, 10 to a page

5. Small text summaries are prepared for each Web page

4. Using the PageRank software, the system measures the "importance" or popularity of each page by solving an equation with more than 500 million variables and two billion terms. These are likely the "best" pages for the query

2. Google's Web servers receive the request. Google uses an estimated 100,000 PCs linked together and connected to the Internet to handle incoming requests and produce the results

3. Request is sent to Google's index servers that describe which pages contain the keywords matching the query and where those pages are stored on the document servers

**Figure 6-12**
How Google Works
*The Google search engine is continuously crawling the Web, indexing the content of each page, calculating its popularity, and storing the pages so that it can respond quickly to user requests to see a page. The entire process takes about one-half second.*

In the mid-1990s, Stanford, Berkeley, and three other universities became hotbeds of Web search innovations. In 1994, Stanford University computer science students David Filo and Jerry Yang created a hand-selected list of their favorite Web pages and called it "Yet Another Hierarchical Officious Oracle," or Yahoo!. Yahoo! was never a real search engine but rather an edited selection of Web sites organized by categories the editors found useful. Yahoo! has since developed its own search engine capabilities.

In 1998, Larry Page and Sergey Brin, two other Stanford computer science students, released their first version of Google. This search engine was different: Not only did it index each Web page's words but it also ranked search results based on the relevance of each page. Page patented the idea of a page ranking system (PageRank System), which essentially measures the popularity of a Web page by calculating what other sites link to that page. Brin contributed a unique Web crawler program that indexed not only keywords on a page but also combinations of words (such as authors and the titles of their articles). These two ideas became the foundation for the Google search engine (Brandt, 2004). Figure 6-12 illustrates how Google works.

Web sites for locating information such as Yahoo!, Google, and MSN have become so popular and easy to use that they also serve as major portals for the Internet (see Chapter 9). The search marketplace has become very competitive. Yahoo! has transformed its edited collection of Web pages into a true search engine; Microsoft has unleashed its search tool MSN Search; Amazon.com has entered the fray with A9; and Overture.com (now owned by Yahoo!) transformed the search world by charging advertisers for placement and ranking.

The spectacular increase in Internet advertising revenues has helped search engines transform themselves into major shopping tools by offering what is now called **search engine marketing**. When users enter a search term at Google, MSN Search, Yahoo!, or any of the other sites serviced by these search engines, they receive two types of listings: sponsored links, for which advertisers have paid to be listed (usually at the top of the search results page) and unsponsored "organic" search results. In addition, advertisers can purchase tiny text boxes on the right side of the Google and MSN search results page. The paid, sponsored advertisements are the fastest-growing form of Internet advertising and are powerful new marketing tools that precisely match consumer interests with advertising messages at the right moment.

Search engines have also become crucial tools within individual e-commerce sites. Customers can search easily for the product information they want with the help of an internal search program. However, within Web sites, the search engine is limited to finding matches from that one site.

**Intelligent Agent Shopping Bots**  Chapter 10 describes the capabilities of software agents with built-in intelligence that can gather or filter information and perform other tasks to assist users. **Shopping bots** use intelligent agent software for searching the Internet for shopping information. Shopping bots such as MySimon or Froogle can help people interested in making a purchase filter and retrieve information about products of interest, evaluate competing products according to criteria the users have established, and negotiate with vendors for price and delivery terms. Many of these shopping agents search the Web for pricing and availability of products specified by the user and return a list of sites that sell the item along with pricing information and a purchase link.

**RSS**  Instead of spending hours surfing the Web, users now have special tools to deliver the information in which they are interested automatically to their desktops. One that is growing in popularity is RSS. **RSS** is short for Rich Site Summary or Really Simple Syndication. RSS is a simple way for people to have content they want pulled from Web sites and fed automatically to their computers, where it can be stored for later viewing. For example, if you're interested in local weather reports, RSS would let you receive updated forecasts at your computer without having to visit a particular Web site.

To receive an RSS information feed, you need to install aggregator or news reader software that can be downloaded from the Web. Alternatively, you can establish an account with an aggregator Web site. You then tell the aggregator to collect all updates from a given Web page, or list of pages, or gather information on a given subject by conducting Web searches at regular intervals. Once subscribed, you automatically receive new content as it is posted to the specified Web site.

RSS first became popular in blogs (Weblogs), which we discuss in Chapter 9. It provided a way for users to keep up with their favorite blogs without constantly checking them for updates. Now thousands of sites have put their content in XML format that is readable by RSS software. For example, you can receive regular updates on topics of your choosing from Web sites for *The New York Times, The Washington Post,* the British Broadcasting Company (BBC), Amazon.com, or craigslist.com. A number of businesses are using RSS internally to distribute updated corporate information.

## Intranets and Extranets

Organizations use Internet networking standards and Web technology to create private networks called *intranets*. We introduced intranets in Chapter 1, explaining that an intranet is an internal organizational network that provides access to data across the enterprise. It uses the existing company network infrastructure along with Internet connectivity standards and software developed for the World Wide Web. Intranets create networked applications that can run on many different kinds of computers throughout the organization, including mobile handheld computers and wireless remote access devices.

Whereas the Web is available to anyone, an intranet is private and is protected from public visits by **firewalls**—security systems with specialized software to prevent outsiders from entering private networks. Intranet software technology is the same as that of the World Wide Web. Intranets use HTML to program Web pages and to establish dynamic, point-and-click hypertext links to other pages. The Web browser and Web server software used for intranets are the same as those on the Web. A simple intranet can be created by linking a client computer with a Web browser to a computer with Web server software using a TCP/IP network with software to keep unwanted visitors out.

### Extranets

A firm creates an extranet to allow authorized vendors and customers to have limited access to its internal intranet. For example, authorized buyers could link to a portion of a company's intranet from the public Internet to obtain information about the costs and features of the company's products. The company uses firewalls to ensure that access to its internal data is limited and remains secure; firewalls also authenticate users, making sure that only authorized users access the site.

Both intranets and extranets reduce operational costs by providing additional connectivity for coordinating disparate business processes within the firm and for linking electronically to customers and suppliers. Extranets often are employed for collaborating with other companies for supply chain management, product design and development, and training efforts.

## Technologies and Tools for Communication and E-Business

Internet technology is the source of the principal tools used today in business for communication and coordination.

### E-Mail, Chat, Instant Messaging, and Electronic Discussions

**E-mail** enables messages to be exchanged from computer to computer, eliminating costly long-distance telephone charges while expediting communication among different parts of the organization. In addition to providing electronic messaging, e-mail software has capabilities for routing messages to multiple recipients, forwarding messages, and attaching text documents or multimedia files to messages. Although some organizations operate their own internal electronic mail systems, a great deal of e-mail today is sent through the Internet.

Nearly 90 percent of U.S. workplaces have employees communicating interactively using **chat** or instant messaging tools. Chatting enables two or more people who are simultaneously connected to the Internet to hold live, interactive conversations. Chat groups are divided into channels, and each is assigned its own topic of conversation. The first generation of chat tools was for written conversations in which participants typed their remarks using their keyboard and read responses on their computer screens. Chat systems now feature voice and video chat capabilities.

**Instant messaging** is a type of chat service that enables participants to create their own private chat channels. The instant messaging system alerts the user whenever someone on his or her private list is online so that the user can initiate a chat session with other individuals. A number of competing instant messaging systems exist for consumers, including Yahoo! Messenger, MSN Messenger, and AOL Instant Messenger. Companies concerned with security are building proprietary instant messaging systems using tools such as Lotus Sametime. Many online retail businesses offer chat services on their Web sites to attract visitors, to encourage repeat purchases, and to improve customer service. Instant messaging has been migrating to cell phones and wireless handhelds.

**Usenet** newsgroups are worldwide discussion groups posted on Internet electronic bulletin boards on which people share information and ideas on a defined topic, such as radiology or rock bands. Anyone can post messages on these bulletin boards for others to read. Many thousands of groups exist that discuss almost all conceivable topics.

Another type of forum, **LISTSERV**, enables discussions to be conducted through predefined groups but uses e-mail mailing list servers instead of bulletin boards for communications. If you find a LISTSERV topic in which you are interested, you can subscribe. From then on, through e-mail, you will receive all messages sent by other subscribers concerning that topic. You can, in turn, send a message to your LISTSERV and it will automatically be broadcast to the other subscribers.

Employee use of e-mail, instant messaging, and the Internet is supposed to increase worker productivity, but the accompanying Focus on People shows that this may not always be the case. Many companies now believe they need to monitor their employees' online activity. But is this ethical? Although there are some strong business reasons why companies may need to monitor their employees' e-mail and Web activities, what does this mean for employee privacy? As you read this case, try to identify the problems created by employee e-mail and Web use in the workplace; what alternative solutions are available to management; and the people, organization, and technology issues that should be addressed when developing the solution.

### Groupware and Electronic Conferencing

**Groupware** provides capabilities for supporting enterprise-wide communication and collaborative work. Individuals, teams, and workgroups at different locations in the organization use groupware for writing and commenting on group projects, sharing ideas and documents, conducting electronic meetings, tracking the status of tasks and projects, scheduling, and sending e-mail. Any group member can review the ideas of other group members at any time and add to them, or an individual can post a document for others to comment on or edit. Commercial groupware products, such as Lotus Notes and OpenText's LiveLink, integrate with the Internet or private intranets. Groove is a groupware tool based on peer-to-peer technology that enables people to work directly with other people over the Internet without going through a central server.

A growing number of companies are using Internet conferencing tools to stage meetings, conferences, and presentations online. Web conferencing and collaboration software provides virtual conference tables where participants view and modify documents and slides, write or draw on an electronic whiteboard, or share their thoughts and comments using chat or voice conferencing. The current generation of such tools from Lotus, Microsoft, and WebEx work through a standard Web browser. Web videoconferencing tools enable meeting participants equipped with Web cameras to see and talk to each other using their PCs and Web browsers. These forms of electronic conferencing are growing in popularity because they reduce the need for face-to-face meetings, saving travel time and cost.

### Internet Telephony

**Internet telephony** enables companies to use Internet technology for telephone voice transmission over the Internet or private networks. (Internet telephony products sometimes are called *IP telephony* products.) **Voice over IP (VoIP)** technology uses the Internet Protocol (IP) to deliver voice information in digital form using packet switching, avoiding the tolls charged by local and long-distance telephone networks (see Figure 6-13). Calls that would ordinarily be transmitted over public telephone networks would travel over the corporate network based on the Internet Protocol, or the public Internet. IP telephony calls can be made and received with a desktop computer equipped with a microphone and speakers or with a VoIP-enabled telephone.

VoIP is the fastest-growing form of telephone service in the United States. In 2005, there were four million residential VoIP lines, and 5.9 million commercial lines. The number of lines is roughly doubling each year and is expected to reach 30 million lines by 2008

## FOCUS ON PEOPLE    Monitoring Employees on Networks: Unethical or Good Business?

As e-mail use has exploded worldwide, so has the use of e-mail and the Web for personal business at the workplace. A number of studies have concluded that at least 25 percent of employee online time is spent on non–work-related Web surfing, and perhaps as many as 90 percent of employees receive or send personal e-mail at work.

Many companies have begun monitoring their employees' use of e-mail and the Internet, often without the knowledge of the employees. A study by the American Management Association and the ePolicy Institute concluded that 76 percent of U.S. employers monitor their Web connections. The study also reported that 65 percent of companies block connections to Web sites considered inappropriate, and 55 percent retain and review employee e-mail messages. Although U.S. companies have the legal right to monitor employee Internet and e-mail activity, is such monitoring unethical, or is it simply good business?

Managers worry about the loss of time and employee productivity when employees are focusing on personal rather than company business. A recent survey by America Online and Salary.com found that the average U.S. worker wastes more than two hours per day on non–work-related business, and 45 percent of respondents cited personal Internet use as their primary time-wasting activity at work.

If personal traffic on company networks is too high, it can also clog the company's network so that business work cannot be performed. Some employees at Xerox had sent so much junk and pornographic e-mail while on the job that the company's e-mail system shut down. Too much time on personal business, on the Internet or not, can mean lost revenue or overcharges to clients. Some employees may be charging time they spend trading their personal stocks online or pursuing other personal business to clients, thus overcharging the clients.

When employees use e-mail or the Web at employer facilities or with employer equipment, anything they do, including anything illegal, carries the company's name. Therefore, the employer can be traced and held liable. Management in many firms fear that racist, sexually explicit, or other potentially offensive material accessed or traded by their employees could result in adverse publicity and even lawsuits for the firm. Even if the company is found not to be liable, responding to lawsuits could cost the company tens of thousands of dollars. Companies also fear e-mail leakage of trade secrets.

Companies that allow employees to use personal e-mail accounts at work could face legal and regulatory trouble if they do not retain those messages. E-mail today is an important source of evidence for lawsuits, and companies are now required to retain all of their e-mail messages for longer periods than in the past. Courts do not discriminate about whether e-mails involved in lawsuits were sent via personal or business e-mail accounts. Not producing those e-mails could result in a five- to six-figure fine. Companies have the legal right to monitor what employees are doing with company equipment during business hours. The question is whether electronic surveillance is an appropriate tool for maintaining an efficient and positive workplace. Some companies try to ban all personal activities on corporate networks—zero tolerance. Others block employee access to specific Web sites or limit personal time on the Web using software that enables IT departments to track the Web sites employees visit, the amount of time employees spend at these sites, and the files they download. Some firms have fired employees who have stepped out of bounds.

No solution is problem free, but many consultants believe companies should write corporate policies on employee e-mail and Internet use. The policies should include explicit ground rules that state, by position or level, under what circumstances employees can use company facilities for e-mail or Internet use. The policies should also inform employees whether these activities are monitored and explain why.

The rules should be tailored to specific business needs and organizational cultures. For example, although some companies may exclude all employees from visiting sites that have explicit sexual material, law firm or hospital employees may require access to these sites. Investment firms will need to allow many of their employees access to other investment sites. A company dependent on widespread information sharing, innovation, and independence could very well find that monitoring creates more problems than it solves.

Sources: Solomon D. Leach, "Surfing the Net at Work? The Boss May Be Watching," Delcotimes.com, accessed June 30, 2005; Sandra Gittlen, "Personal Web-Based Email Puts Enterprise at Risk," July 6, 2005, www.itmanagement.earthweb.com, accessed July 7, 2005; "Americans Waste More Than 2 Hours a Day at Work, Costing Companies $570 billion a Year, According to Salary.com and America Online Survey," www.businesswire.com, accessed July 18, 2005; Riva Richmond, "It's 10 A.M. Do You Know Where Your Workers Are?" *The Wall Street Journal*, January 12, 2004; and Eric Zoeckler, "Issues to Ponder Before E-Monitoring Workers," *Snohomish County Business Journal*, July 2004.

### To Think About:

What problems arise from giving employees access to e-mail and the Internet during working hours? Should managers monitor employee e-mail and Internet usage? Why or why not? Describe an effective e-mail and Web use policy for a company.

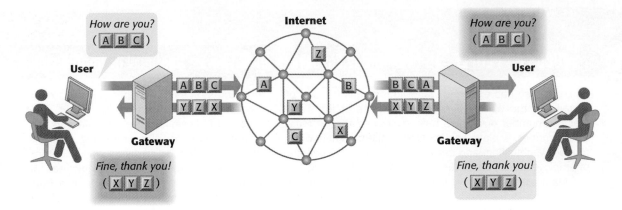

**Figure 6-13**
How IP Telephony Works
*An IP phone call digitizes and breaks up a voice message into data packets that may travel along different routes before being reassembled at the final destination. A processor nearest the call's destination, called a gateway, arranges the packets in the proper order and directs them to the telephone number of the receiver or the IP address of the receiving computer.*

(eMarketer, 2005c). The early mover in VoIP was Vonage. This firm is increasingly in competition with major telecommunications service providers (such as Verizon) and cable firms (such as Time Warner and Cablevision). Skype, which offers free VoIP worldwide using a peer-to-peer network was acquired by eBay.

Although there are up-front investments required for an IP phone system, VoIP can reduce communication and network management costs by 20 to 30 percent. In addition to lowering long-distance costs and eliminating monthly fees for private lines, an IP network provides a single voice-data infrastructure that provides both telecommunications and computing services. Companies no longer have to maintain separate networks or provide support services and personnel for each different type of network. Businesses can use this technology for applications, such as Internet conference calls using video or for Web sites that enable users to reach a live customer service representative by clicking a link on a Web page.

Another advantage of VoIP is its flexibility. Unlike the traditional telephone network, phones can be added or moved to different offices without rewiring or reconfiguring the network. With VoIP, a conference call is arranged by a simple click-and-drag operation on the computer screen to select the names of the conferees. Voice mail and e-mail can be combined into a single directory.

### Virtual Private Networks

What if you had a marketing group charged with developing new products and services for your firm with members spread across the United States. You would want to be able to e-mail each other and communicate with the home office without any chance that outsiders could intercept the communications. In the past, one answer to this problem was to work with large, private networking firms who offered secure, private, dedicated networks to customers. But this was an expensive solution. A much less expensive solution is to create a virtual private network within the public Internet.

A **virtual private network (VPN)** is a secure, encrypted, private network that has been configured within a public network to take advantage of the economies of scale and management facilities of large networks, such as the Internet (see Figure 6-14). A VPN provides your firm with secure, encrypted communications at a much lower cost than the same capabilities offered by traditional non-Internet providers who use their private networks to secure communications. VPNs also provide a network infrastructure for combining voice and data networks.

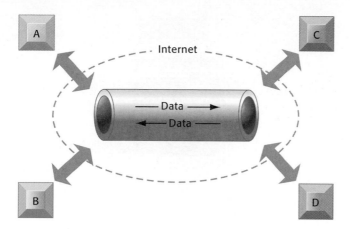

**Figure 6-14**
A Virtual Private Network Using the Internet
*This VPN is a private network of computers linked using a secure "tunnel" connection over the Internet. It protects data transmitted over the public Internet by encoding the data and "wrapping" them within the Internet Protocol (IP). By adding a wrapper around a network message to hide its content, organizations can create a private connection that travels through the public Internet.*

Several competing protocols are used to protect data transmitted over the public Internet, including Point-to-Point Tunneling Protocol (PPTP). In a process called *tunneling,* packets of data are encrypted and wrapped inside IP packets. By adding this wrapper around a network message to hide its content, business firms create a private connection that travels through the public Internet.

## 6.4 The Wireless Revolution

If you have a cell phone, do you use it for taking and sending photos, sending text messages, or downloading music clips? Do you take your laptop to class or to the library to link up to the Internet? If so, you're part of the wireless revolution! Cell phones, laptops, and small handheld devices have morphed into portable computing platforms that let you perform some of the computing tasks you used to do at your desk.

Wireless communication helps businesses more easily stay in touch with customers, suppliers, and employees and provides more flexible arrangements for organizing work. Companies save on wiring offices and conference rooms by using wireless networks because they do not have to pull cables through walls, making additions, moves, and changes much easier. Wireless technology has also created new products, services, and sales channels, which we discuss in Chapter 9.

### Wireless Devices

If you require mobile communication and computing power or remote access to corporate systems, you can work with an array of wireless devices: cell phones, personal digital assistants (PDAs), e-mail handhelds, and smart phones. Personal computers are also starting to be used in wireless transmission.

We introduced cell phones in Section 6.2. **Personal digital assistants (PDAs)** are small, handheld computers featuring applications such as electronic schedulers, address books, memo pads, and expense trackers. High-end models display, compose, send, and receive e-mail messages and provide wireless access to the Internet. Some have built-in digital cameras and voice communication capabilities. **E-mail handhelds**, such as the BlackBerry Handheld, are a special type of handheld that is optimized for wireless text messaging. Hybrid devices combining the functionality of a PDA with that of a digital cell phone are called **smart phones.**

### Cellular Systems

Today's mobile phones are not only for voice communication—they have become mobile platforms for delivering digital data. Many are able to navigate the Web; download music,

The LG VX-8100 mobile phone uses broadband wireless technology to provide video and music on demand as well as video and picture messaging and mobile access to the Web. It has a digital camera, dual speakers for stereo sound, and a personal organizer with a calendar, scheduler, alarm clock, and notepad.

games, and video; and transmit photos, e-mail, and short text messages. Some have embedded digital cameras, and may be able to record and transmit video clips. Recent models are equipped to download, store, and play MP3 music files similar to an iPod. Mobile phones enable many millions of people to communicate and access the Internet in Africa and other countries where conventional telephone or Internet service is expensive or unavailable.

### Cellular Network Standards and Generations

Digital cellular service uses several competing standards that are incompatible. This means that digital cellular handsets cannot work on networks that use another wireless standard.

In Europe and much of the rest of the world outside the United Sates, the standard is **Global System for Mobile Communication (GSM)**. GSM's strength is its international roaming capability. Users have seamless same-number roaming in more than 170 countries. Most GSM systems outside North America operate in the 900-megahertz (MHz) and 1.8-gigahertz (GHz) frequency bands. (In North America they operate in the 1.9 GHz band.)

There are GSM cell phone systems in the United States, including T-Mobile, VoiceStream, Cingular, and AT&T. However, the major standard in the United States is **Code Division Multiple Access (CDMA)**, which is the system used by Verizon, MCI, and Sprint. CDMA was developed by the military during World War II. It transmits over several frequencies, occupies the entire spectrum, and randomly assigns users to a range of frequencies over time. In general, CDMA is cheaper to implement, is more efficient in its use of spectrum, and provides higher quality throughput of voice and data than GSM.

### Cellular Generations

Most digital cellular systems today are used primarily for voice, but they are able to transmit data at rates ranging from 9.6 to 14.4 Kbps. This transmission speed is still too slow for comfortable Internet access, but it is useful for sending and receiving short text messages. **Short message service (SMS)** is a text message service used by a number of digital cell phone systems to send and receive short alphanumeric messages less than 160 characters in length. Like e-mail, SMS messages can be forwarded and stored for later retrieval.

More powerful cellular networks called **third-generation (3G) networks** have transmission speeds ranging from 144 Kbps for mobile users in, say, a car, to more than 2 Mbps for stationary users. This is sufficient transmission capacity for video, graphics, and other rich media, in addition to voice, making 3G networks suitable for wireless broadband Internet access and always-on data transmission.

Although wireless carriers have invested in 3G technology, they have just begun rolling out their 3G services. In the meantime, those interested in high-speed Internet access and data transmission where 3G is unavailable are relying on an interim solution called **2.5G networks**. 2.5G networks use upgrades to the existing cellular infrastructure and feature data transmission rates ranging from 50 to 144 Kbps.

### Mobile Wireless Standards for Web Access

There are also multiple standards and technologies governing how cellular phones access the Internet and the World Wide Web. **Wireless Application Protocol (WAP)** is a system of protocols and technologies that enables cell phones and other wireless devices with tiny display screens, low-bandwidth connections, and minimal memory to access Web-based information and services. WAP uses Wireless Markup Language (WML), which is based on XML (see Chapter 4) and is optimized for tiny displays.

A person with a WAP-compliant phone uses the built-in microbrowser to make a request in WML. A **microbrowser** is an Internet browser with a small file size that works with the low-memory constraints of handheld wireless devices and the low bandwidth of wireless networks. The request is passed to a WAP gateway, which retrieves the information from an Internet server in either standard HTML format or WML. The gateway translates HTML content back into WML for the WAP client to receive it. WAP supports most wireless network standards and operating systems for handheld computing devices.

**I-mode** is a wireless service offered by Japan's NTT DoCoMo mobile phone network that uses a different set of standards. Instead of using WAP, I-mode uses compact HTML to deliver content, making it easier for businesses to convert their HTML Web sites to mobile service. I-mode uses packet switching, which enables users to be connected constantly to the network and content providers to broadcast relevant information to users. (WAP users have to dial in to see if a site has changed.) I-mode can handle color graphics not available on WAP handsets as well as video, although WAP is being modified to handle color graphics (see Figure 6-15).

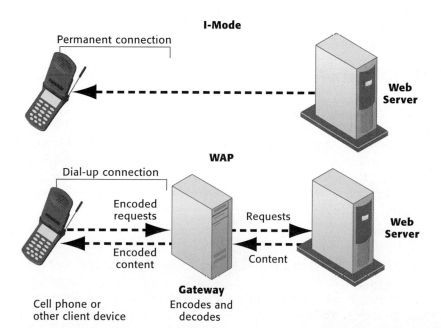

### Figure 6-15
Wireless Application Protocol (WAP) Versus I-Mode
*WAP and I-mode use alternative standards for accessing information from the wireless Web.*

## Wireless Computer Networks and Internet Access

If you have a laptop computer, you might be able to use it to access the Internet as you move from room to room in your dorm, or table to table in your university library. An array of technologies has emerged to provide high-speed wireless access to the Internet for PCs and other wireless handheld devices as well as for cell phones. These new high-speed services have extended Internet access to numerous locations that could not be covered by traditional wired Internet services.

The Institute of Electrical and Electronics Engineers (IEEE) has established a hierarchy of complementary standards for wireless computer networks. These standards include IEEE 802.15 for the personal-area network (Bluetooth), IEEE 802.11 for the local-area network (LAN; Wi-Fi), and 802.16 for the metropolitan-area network (MAN; WiMax).

### Bluetooth

**Bluetooth** is the popular name for the 802.15 wireless networking standard, which is useful for creating small **personal-area networks (PANs)**. It links up to eight devices within a 10-meter area using low-power, radio-based communication and can transmit up to 722 Kbps in the 2.4-GHz band.

Wireless phones, pagers, computers, printers, and computing devices using Bluetooth communicate with each other and even operate each other without direct user intervention (see Figure 6-16). For example, a person could highlight a telephone number on a wireless PDA and automatically activate a call on a digital phone, or that person could direct a notebook computer to send a document file wirelessly to a printer. Bluetooth connects wireless keyboards and mice to PCs or cell phones to earpieces without wires. Bluetooth has low power requirements, making it appropriate for battery-powered handheld computers, cell phones, or PDAs.

Although Bluetooth lends itself to personal networking, it has uses in large corporations. A Coca-Cola bottling company in Australia equipped field sales and marketing staff with Bluetooth-enabled laptop computers and Bluetooth-enabled phones. Bluetooth enabled the laptop to connect to the mobile phone's data network, enabling employees to connect to the Internet, company network, e-mail, and client information anywhere and anytime.

**Figure 6-16**

A Bluetooth Network (PAN)

*Bluetooth enables a variety of devices, including cell phones, PDAs, wireless keyboards and mice, PCs, and printers, to interact wirelessly with each other within a small 30-foot (10-meter) area. In addition to the links shown, Bluetooth can be used to network similar devices to send data from one PC to another, for example.*

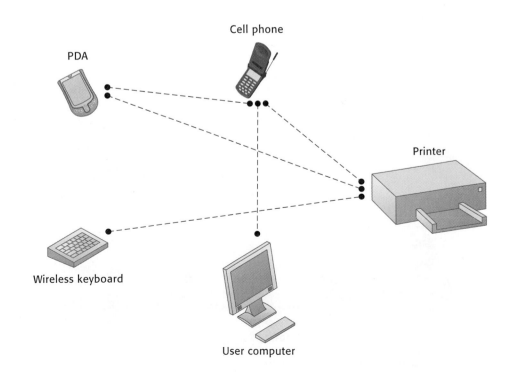

## Wi-Fi

The IEEE set of standards for wireless LANs is the 802.11 family, also known as **Wi-Fi** (for Wireless Fidelity). There are three standards in this family: 802.11a, 802.11b, and 802.11g. 802.11n is an emerging standard for increasing the speed and capacity of wireless networking scheduled to be finalized in 2006.

The 802.11a standard can transmit up to 54 Mbps in the unlicensed 5-GHz frequency range and has an effective distance of 10 to 30 meters. The 802.11b standard can transmit up to 11 Mbps in the unlicensed 2.4-GHz band and has an effective distance of 30 to 50 meters, although this range can be extended outdoors by using tower-mounted antennas. The 802.11g standard can transmit up to 54 Mbps in the 2.4-GHz range. Once finalized, 802.11n will transmit at more than 100 Mbps.

Because 802.11b and 802.11g operate in the 2.4-GHz frequency, products built for either of these two standards are compatible. Products designed for the 802.11a specification won't work with either 802.11b or 802.11g because 802.11a uses a different frequency band.

The 802.11b standard has been the most widely used standard for creating wireless LANs and providing wireless Internet access. However, 802.11g may become more popular in the next few years, and dual-band systems capable of handling 802.11b and 802.11g are expected to proliferate.

A Wi-Fi system can operate in two different modes. In infrastructure mode, wireless devices communicate with a wired LAN using access points. An **access point** is a box consisting of a radio receiver/transmitter and antennas that link to a wired network, router, or hub. Each access point and its wireless devices are known as a basic service set (BSS).

In ad hoc mode, also known as peer-to-peer mode, wireless devices communicate with each other directly and do not use an access point. Most Wi-Fi communication uses infrastructure mode. (Ad hoc mode is used for very small LANs in the home or small business offices.)

Figure 6-17 illustrates an 802.11 wireless LAN operating in infrastructure mode that connects a small number of mobile devices to a larger wired LAN. Most wireless devices are client machines. The servers that the mobile client stations need to use are on the wired LAN. The access point controls the wireless stations and acts as a bridge between the main wired LAN and the wireless LAN. (A bridge connects two LANs based on different technologies.)

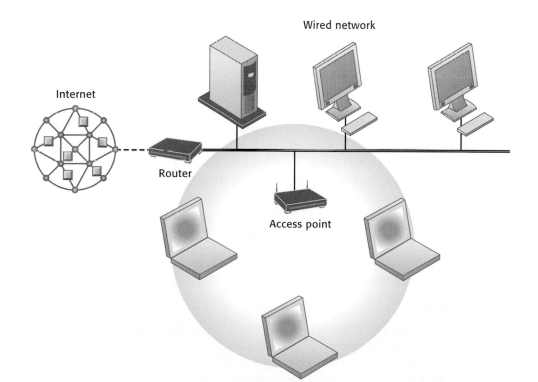

**Figure 6-17**
An 802.11 Wireless LAN
*Mobile laptop computers equipped with network interface cards link to the wired LAN by communicating with the access point. The access point uses radio waves to transmit network signals from the wired network to the client adapters, which convert them into data that the mobile device can understand. The client adapter then transmits the data from the mobile device back to the access point, which forwards the data to the wired network.*

Mobile wireless stations often need an add-in card called a *wireless network interface card (NIC)* that has a built-in radio and antenna. **Wireless NICs** can be credit card–size cards that snap into the PCMCIA card slot on a PC or external adapters that plug into the PC's universal serial bus (USB) port. Newer laptop PCs come equipped with chips that can receive Wi-Fi signals.

### Wi-Fi and Wireless Internet Access

The 802.11 standard also provides wireless access to the Internet using a broadband connection. In this instance, an access point plugs into an Internet connection, which could come from a cable TV line or DSL telephone service. Computers within a range of the access point would be able to use it to link wirelessly to the Internet.

Wi-Fi networking costs have declined so that a simple wireless Wi-Fi network can be set up for a few hundred dollars. Computer makers are making wireless capability a standard feature of their hardware. Intel now sells Centrino microprocessor and accessory chips for notebook computers that have specialized Wi-Fi capabilities (the accessory chips include a Wi-Fi transmitter) and smaller power consumption requirements. Wi-Fi technology has been further enhanced to support wireless voice calls over the Internet.

Large corporations and small businesses are using Wi-Fi networks to provide low-cost wireless LANs and Internet access. Wi-Fi hotspots are springing up in hotels, airport lounges, libraries, and college campuses to provide mobile access to the Internet. Dartmouth College, described in the chapter-opening case, is one of many campuses where students now use Wi-Fi for research, course work, and entertainment.

**Hotspots** typically consist of one or more access points positioned on a ceiling, wall, or other strategic spot in a public place to provide maximum wireless coverage for a specific area. Users in range of a hotspot are able to access the Internet from their laptops. Some hotspots are free or do not require any additional software to use; others may require activation and the establishment of a user account by providing a credit card number over the Web.

American Airlines has installed Wi-Fi in its Admiral's Clubs and is partnering with T-Mobile, along with Delta Airlines and United Airlines, to install Wi-Fi services at the gates of several major airports. Lufthansa Airlines and other airlines are starting to equip their jet airplanes with a Wi-Fi service called Connexion supplied by Boeing so that passengers with laptop computers can log onto the Internet while they are in flight.

Companies such as Starbucks and McDonald's are offering customers Wi-Fi services in many of their retail outlets. They receive some revenue from their fees for Wi-Fi services, but their primary motivation for deploying the technology is to encourage customers to spend more time in their stores, purchase more food, or select their establishments over competitors'.

Wi-Fi technology poses several challenges, however. Right now, users cannot freely roam from hotspot to hotspot if these hotspots use different Wi-Fi network services. Unless the service is free, users would need to log on to separate accounts for each service, each with its own fees.

One major drawback of Wi-Fi is its weak security features, which make these wireless networks vulnerable to intruders. We provide more detail about Wi-Fi security issues in Chapter 7.

Another drawback of Wi-Fi networks is susceptibility to interference from nearby systems operating in the same spectrum, such as wireless phones, microwave ovens, or other wireless LANs. Wireless networks based on the 802.11n specification will solve this problem by using multiple wireless antennas in tandem to transmit and receive data and technology called *MIMO* (multiple input multiple output) to coordinate multiple simultaneous radio signals.

### WiMax

A surprisingly large number of areas in the United States and throughout the world do not have access to Wi-Fi or fixed broadband connectivity. The range of Wi-Fi systems is no more than 300 feet from the base station, making it difficult for rural groups that don't have cable or DSL service to find wireless access to the Internet.

The IEEE developed a new family of standards known as WiMax to deal with these problems. **WiMax**, which stands for Worldwide Interoperability for Microwave Access, is the popular term for IEEE Standard 802.16, known as the "Air Interface for Fixed Broadband Wireless Access Systems." WiMax has a wireless access range of up to 31 miles, compared to 300 feet for Wi-Fi and 30 feet for Bluetooth, and a data transfer rate of up to 75 Mbps. The 802.16 specification also has robust security and quality-of-service features to support voice and video.

WiMax antennas are powerful enough to beam high-speed Internet connections to rooftop antennas of homes and businesses that are miles away. The technology thus provides long-distance broadband wireless access to rural areas and other locations that are not currently served, while avoiding the steep installation costs of the traditional wired infrastructure. The 802.16a standard supports use of frequencies ranging from 2 to 11 GHz, which include both licensed and unregulated bands.

### Broadband Cellular Wireless

Suppose your sales force needs to access the Web or use e-mail but can't always find a convenient Wi-Fi hotspot. Major cellular telephone carriers have come up with a solution. They have configured their 3G networks to provide anytime, anywhere broadband access for PCs and other handheld devices. Cingular offers a service called EDGE. Verizon's service is called BroadBand Access and is based on a technology called **EV-DO**, which stands for Evolution Data Optimized. EV-DO provides wireless access to the Internet over a cellular network at an average speed of 300 to 500 Kbps. Although it has a wider range of coverage than Wi-Fi, it won't work in "dead spots" where regular cell phone systems have weak signals, including deep inside buildings.

To use this service, Verizon subscribers install software and insert a network card into their laptops. The card has a miniantenna that connects the laptop to the Verizon wireless network and establishes an Internet connection. Sprint offers a similar broadband wireless service based on EV-DO.

Over time, cell phones, wireless PDAs, and laptops will be able to switch from one type of network to another, moving from Wi-Fi to WiMax to cellular networks. Cell phone makers Nokia, LG Electronics, and Samsung now offer handsets with Wi-Fi and Bluetooth capabilities.

## RFID and Wireless Sensor Networks

Mobile technologies are creating new efficiencies and ways of working throughout the enterprise. In addition to the wireless systems we have just described, radio frequency identification (RFID) systems and wireless sensor networks are having a major impact.

### Radio Frequency Identification (RFID)

**Radio frequency identification (RFID)** systems provide a powerful technology for tracking the movement of goods throughout the supply chain. RFID systems use tiny tags with embedded microchips containing data about an item and its location to transmit radio signals over a short distance to special RFID readers. The RFID readers then pass the data over a network to a computer for processing. Unlike bar codes, RFID tags do not need line-of-sight contact to be read.

The transponder, or RFID tag, is electronically programmed with information that can uniquely identify an item, such as an electronic identification code, plus other information about the item, such as its location, where and when it was made, or its status during production. Embedded in the tag is a microchip for storing the data. The rest of the tag is an antenna that transmits data to the reader.

The reader unit consists of an antenna and radio transmitter with a decoding capability attached to a stationary or handheld device. The reader emits radio waves in ranges anywhere from 1 inch to 100 feet, depending on its power output, the radio frequency employed, and surrounding environmental conditions. When an RFID tag comes within the range of the reader, the tag is activated and starts sending data. The reader captures these data, decodes them, and sends them back over a wired or wireless network to a host

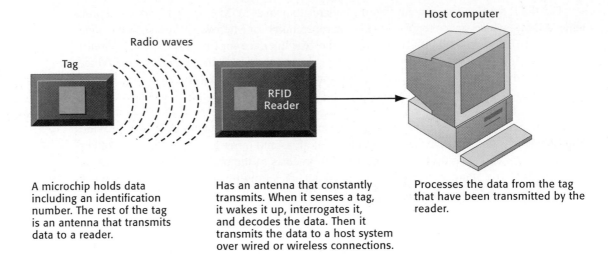

A microchip holds data including an identification number. The rest of the tag is an antenna that transmits data to a reader.

Has an antenna that constantly transmits. When it senses a tag, it wakes it up, interrogates it, and decodes the data. Then it transmits the data to a host system over wired or wireless connections.

Processes the data from the tag that have been transmitted by the reader.

**Figure 6-18**
How RFID Works
*RFID uses low-powered radio transmitters to read data stored in a tag at distances ranging from 1 inch to 100 feet. The reader captures the data from the tag and sends them over a network to a host computer for processing.*

computer for further processing (see Figure 6-18). Both RFID tags and antennas come in a variety of shapes and sizes.

RFID systems operate in a number of unlicensed frequency bands worldwide. Low-frequency systems (30 to 500 kilohertz) have short reading ranges (inches to a few feet); lower system costs; and are often used in security, asset tracking, or animal identification applications. High-frequency RFID systems (850 to 950 MHz and 2.4 to 2.5 GHz) offer reading ranges that can extend beyond 90 feet and are useful for applications such as railroad car tracking or automated toll collection for highways or bridges.

In inventory control and supply chain management, RFID systems capture and manage more detailed information about items in warehouses or in production than bar coding systems. If a large number of items are shipped together, RFID systems track each pallet, lot, or even unit item in the shipment. Manufacturers using RFID will be able to track the production history of each product for a better understanding of product defects and successes. RFID could change the way invoices are paid by triggering an electronic payment to the shipper once a tagged pallet enters a retailer's warehouse.

RFID has been available for decades, but widespread use was held back by the expense of the tags, which ranged from just under $1.00 to $20.00 each. Now the cost of a tag has dropped to about 19 cents and will shortly drop to 5 cents. At these prices for tags, RFID becomes cost-effective for many companies, including Wal-Mart, Home Depot, Delta Airlines, Federal Express, and Unilever.

The top 100 suppliers to Wal-Mart stores and thousands of suppliers to the U.S. Department of Defense are required to use passive RFID tags on cases and pallets they ship to these organizations. Wal-Mart expects RFID-tagged shipments to help it track and record inventory flow.

Coors UK, Scottish & Newcastle, and other large British brewing companies are using RFID to improve tracking of kegs that are shipped out and returned. Breweries lose on average 5 to 6 percent of their kegs each year, and RFID tracking has cut those losses in half.

Steep costs and extensive preparation are required for successful deployment of RFID. In addition to installing RFID readers and tagging systems, companies may need to upgrade their hardware and software to process the massive amounts of data produced by RFID systems—transactions that could add up to tens or hundreds of terabytes.

Special middleware is required to filter, aggregate, and prevent RFID data from overloading business networks and system applications. Applications will need to be redesigned

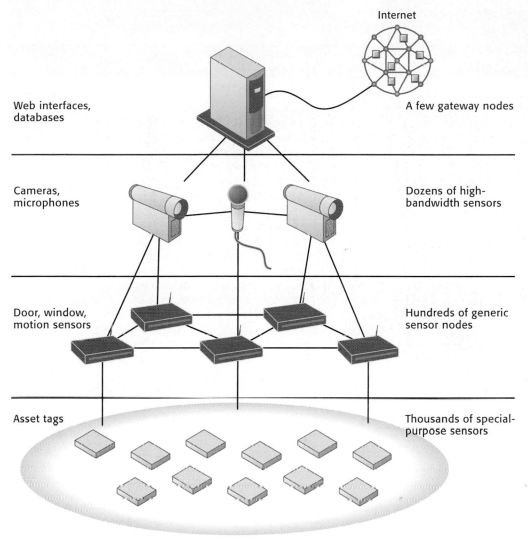

**Figure 6-19**
A Wireless Sensor Network
*This wireless sensor network for a security system illustrates the hierarchical organization of wireless sensor networks. Each level handles different types of sensing.*

*Source:* From Jason Hill, Mike Horton, Ralph Kling, and Lakshman Krishamurthy, "The Platforms Enabling Wireless Sensor Networks," *Communications of the ACM* 47, no. 6 (June 2004).

to accept massive volumes of RFID-generated data frequently and to share those data with other applications. Major enterprise software vendors, including SAP and Oracle, now offer RFID-ready versions of their supply chain management applications.

### Wireless Sensor Networks

If your company wanted state-of-the art technology to monitor building security or detect hazardous substances in the air, it might deploy a wireless sensor network. **Wireless sensor networks (WSNs)** are networks of interconnected wireless devices that are embedded into the physical environment to provide measurements of many points over large spaces. They are based on devices with built-in processing, storage, and radio frequency sensors and antennas. The devices are linked into an interconnected network that routes the data they capture to a computer for analysis.

These networks range from hundreds to thousands of nodes. Because wireless sensor devices are placed in the field for years at a time without any maintenance or human intervention, they must have very low power requirements and batteries capable of lasting for long periods of time—years.

Sensor networks typically have a tiered architecture, such as that used by the wireless security system illustrated in Figure 6-19. This particular wireless sensor network consists of a hierarchy of nodes, starting with low-level sensors and progressing toward nodes for high-level data aggregation, analysis, and storage. Lower-level sensors for monitoring events, such as doors opening and closing, motion, and breakage of windows

# FOCUS ON TECHNOLOGY   TransAlta: New Power from Wireless Technology

TransAlta, based in Calgary, Alberta, Canada, generates and sells wholesale electricity using 51 gas, coal, and hydroelectric plants in Canada, the United States, Mexico, and Australia. It also mines the coal it burns and conducts energy trading.

When the electricity industry underwent deregulation, TransAlta was transformed from an integrated, regulated Alberta-based coal and hydroelectric utility into Canada's largest nonregulated power generator. The company has approximately 10,000 megawatts of generation capacity.

Now that TransAlta is deregulated, it no longer has to worry about following the rules of a regulatory bureaucracy. But it does have to worry about competition and finding ways to keep its level of service high and its prices low. TransAlta has a clear-cut set of business objectives: Focus on operational excellence, maintain a strong balance sheet, carefully manage its risk profile, and methodically increase its capacity as a low-cost power plant operator. RFID, Wi-Fi, and Bluetooth technology are helping TransAlta achieve these objectives.

When power plants experience forced outages, they can lose a substantial amount of revenue. TransAlta is using RFID to help maintain equipment more efficiently in several of its 600-foot-long power plants. Equipment tagged with RFID labels triggers a mobile application to call up repair histories and maintenance guides on a field service technician's handheld device.

Paul Kurchina, TransAlta's program director for information technology, wanted to link field maintenance workers directly to the company's SAP ERP suite and Oracle databases through a wireless handheld device and mobile field service software. He worked with the company's field service technicians to design a field service application based on RFID that enables a field technician to access the repair history of a pump or motor from a wireless handheld, prompts the technician to input data, and then guides the technician through a series of steps for maintenance or troubleshooting.

The field service technicians identified what they needed from the company's back-end systems and databases, the sequence of steps to be performed in the client part of the application and in the screen displays, and the hardware requirements for the handheld computer and peripherals. Kurchina and his team researched what other industries with expensive equipment and assets requiring more cost-effective and efficient maintenance were doing. Kurchina's group found that other companies had found solutions in wireless networks and mobile applications.

TransAlta selected SAT's IntellaTrack mobile workflow software and a wireless handheld computer from Symbol Technologies. The Symbol handheld incorporates an RFID reader and provides wireless transmission using 802.11b (Wi-Fi) and Bluetooth. "Bluetooth let us use all these other capabilities in portable handheld devices without bulking up the handheld itself," Kurchina noted. TransAlta's previ-

ous handhelds had to be connected physically to other peripheral devices to gather data.

When a field technician reads the RFID tag on a pump, the information on the tag triggers a series of steps, including guidance if needed. The IntellaTrack software accesses information from the company's back-end systems about the pump's maintenance history. The system uses data from these internal corporate systems to automatically fill in simple work orders, which are updated by the technician's input.

The system's costs were not made public, but Kurchina said that the system paid for itself in less than four months. It cut job times in half for routine tasks for both experienced and inexperienced workers.

TransAlta headquarters, three of its generating plants, and several warehouses use wireless LANs, and the company operates a vehicle-mounted wireless LAN at its coal mine. Sensors on Caterpillar dump trucks and vehicles collect data on loads, temperature, and other variables. The data are collected centrally over a wireless LAN and analyzed, providing information to schedule and route the big trucks in the mine to prevent bottlenecks.

The company is rolling out more sensor applications. One suggested by TransAlta workers attaches an 802.11b sensor to an aging machine. Data captured by the sensor enable TransAlta to extend the life of the equipment by six months, increasing the return on its investment.

Also in the works is a project to add RFID capabilities to TransAlta's existing Wi-Fi networks at three Alberta power plants. The company is investigating software, such as AeroScout's Visibility System, which supports RFID, real-time location tracking, telemetry, and choke-point detection. (Choke-point detection systems detect tagged items or people as they pass through gates or other defined spaces.) According to Kurchina, locating an expensive calibration tool in a 600-foot-long power plant is often very difficult. TransAlta wants to be able to locate the equipment while it's mobile. By using active RFID and a Wi-Fi network, the company will know the exact location of a specific calibration tool in the plant, or if the tool is leaving the premises.

*Sources:* John Cox, "TransAlta Uses Wireless Technology to Get More Competitive," *Network World,* April 13, 2005, and "Wireless Sparks Enterprise Network Innovation," *Network World,* April 15, 2005; Elena Malykhina, "Active RFID Meets Wi-Fi to Ease Asset Tracking," *InformationWeek,* January 17, 2005; and www.transalta.com, accessed July 10, 2005.

**To Think About:**

What problems and challenges did TransAlta face? How did these problems affect its business? How did wireless technology help the company solve these problems? What other solutions might the company have tried? Did TransAlta choose the best solution? Explain your answer.

and doors, are complemented by a small group of more advanced sensors placed in key locations, such as cameras and acoustic and chemical detectors. Both simple and complex data are routed over a network to an automated facility that provides continuous building monitoring and control.

Wireless sensor networks are valuable in areas such as monitoring environmental changes; monitoring traffic or military activity; protecting property; efficiently operating and managing machinery and vehicles; establishing security perimeters; monitoring supply chain management; or detecting chemical, biological, or radiological material.

The Focus on Technology describes how TransAlta, a leading Canadian power provider benefited from RFID, wireless sensor networks, Bluetooth, and other wireless technology. This company must compete on a deregulated playing field where profitability and the survival of the firm depend on efficiency, quality of service, and keeping costs low. As you read this case, try to identify the problems TransAlta faced; the business impact of these problems; what alternative solutions were available to management; how well the chosen solutions worked; and the people, organization, and technology issues that had to be addressed when developing the solutions.

---

**LEARNING TRACKS**

1. If you want to learn more about the range of computing and communications services available from commercial telecommunications vendors, you will find a Learning Track on services provided by telephone industry firms at the Laudon Web site for this chapter.
2. If you want to learn more about generations of cellular systems, you will find a Learning Track on this topic at the Laudon Web site for this chapter.
3. If you want to learn more about wireless applications for customer relationship management (CRM), supply chain management (SCM), and healthcare, you will find a Learning Track on this topic at the Laudon Web site for this chapter.

---

## Summary

1 **Describe the features of telecommunications networks and identify key networking technologies.** A simple network consists of two or more connected computers. Basic network components include computers, network interfaces, a connection medium, network operating system software, and either a hub or a switch. The networking infrastructure for a large company relies on both public and private infrastructures to support the movement of information across diverse technological platforms. It includes the traditional telephone system, mobile cellular communication, wireless local-area networks, videoconferencing systems, a corporate Web site, intranets, extranets, and an array of local- and wide-area networks, including the Internet. This collection of networks evolved from two fundamentally different types of networks: telephone networks and computer networks.

Contemporary networks have been shaped by the rise of client/server computing, the use of packet switching, and the adoption of Transmission Control Protocol/Internet Protocol (TCP/IP) as a universal communications standard for linking disparate networks and computers. Client/server networks have distributed much of the organization's computing power to the desktop and factory floor. Packet switching makes more efficient use of network communications capacity by breaking messages into small packets that are sent independently along different paths in a network and then reassembled at their destinations. Protocols provide a common set of rules that enable communication among diverse components in a telecommunications network. TCP/IP is a suite of protocols that has become the dominant model of achieving connectivity among different networks and computers. It is the connectivity model used in the Internet.

2 **Evaluate alternative transmission media, types of networks, and network services.** The principal physical transmission media are twisted copper telephone wire, coaxial copper cable, fiber-optic cable, and wireless transmission. The choice of transmission medium depends on the distance and volume of communication required by the organization and its financial resources. Twisted wire enables companies to use existing wiring for telephone systems for digital communication, although it is relatively slow. Fiber-optic and coaxial cable are used for high-volume transmission but are expensive to install. Microwave and satellite are used for wireless communication over long distances. The transmission capacity of a medium, known as the bandwidth, is determined by the range of frequencies it can accommodate.

There are different types of networks and network services available to organizations. Network selection and design should be based on the organization's information requirements and the distance required for transmission. Local-area networks (LANs) connect PCs and other digital devices together within a 500-meter radius and are used today for many corporate computing tasks. Network components may be connected together using a star, bus, or ring topology. Wide-area networks (WANs) span broad geographical distances, ranging from several miles to continents, and are private networks that are independently managed. Metropolitan-area networks (MANs) span a single urban area, whereas campus-area networks (CANs) span a campus of buildings or a military base.

A number of network services are available to organizations requiring high-bandwidth transmission. Frame relay is a shared network service with transmission speeds ranging from 56 Kbps to more than 40 Mbps; it relies on digital circuits that require less error checking than packet switching. Asynchronous Transfer Mode (ATM) provides transmission speeds of 1.5 Mbps to more than 9 Gbps, parceling data into fixed 53-byte cells. ATM can pass data between computers from different vendors and is popular for transmitting data, video, and audio over the same network. Integrated Services Digital Network (ISDN) is an international standard for dial up network access that uses existing local telephone lines to integrate voice, data, image, and video services. Basic rate ISDN can transmit data at a rate of 128 Kbps.

Digital subscriber line (DSL) technologies, cable Internet connections, and T1 lines are often used for high-capacity Internet connections. Like ISDN, DSL technologies also operate over existing copper telephone lines to carry voice, data, and video, but they have higher transmission capacities than ISDN. Asymmetric Digital Subscriber Line (ADSL) supports a transmission rate of 1.5 to 9 Mbps when receiving data and over 700 Kbps when sending data. Symmetric Digital Subscriber Line (SDSL) supports the same transmission rate for sending and receiving data of up to 3 Mbps.

Cable Internet connections provide high-speed access to the Web or corporate intranets at speeds of up to 10 Mbps. T lines are high-speed data lines leased from communications providers. A T1 line supports a data transmission rate of 1.544 Mbps.

3 **Demonstrate how the Internet and Internet technology work and how they support communication and e-business.** The Internet is a worldwide network of networks that uses the client/server model of computing and the TCP/IP network reference model. Every computer on the Internet is assigned a unique numeric IP address. The Domain Name System (DNS) converts IP addresses to domain names so that users only need to specify a domain name to access a computer on the Internet instead of typing in the numeric IP address. No one owns the Internet and it has no formal management organization. However, worldwide Internet policies are established by organizations and government bodies, such as the Internet Architecture Board and the World Wide Web Consortium. The Internet must also conform to the laws of the sovereign nation-states in which it operates, as well as the technical infrastructures that exist within the nation-state.

Major Internet services include e-mail, Usenet, LISTSERV, chatting, instant messaging, Telnet, FTP, and the World Wide Web. Web pages are based on hypertext markup language (HTML) and can display text, graphics, video, and audio. Web site directories, search engines, and RSS technology help users locate the information they need on the Web. Web technology and Internet networking standards provide the connectivity and interfaces for internal private intranets and private extranets that be accessed by many different kinds of computers inside and outside the organization.

Internet-based groupware and electronic conferencing software provide tools to support communication and collaboration when people work together in groups or work teams, often in different locations. Firms are also starting to realize economies by using Internet telephony, which enables

Internet technology to be used for telephone voice transmission. Internet technology can also reduce communication costs by enabling companies to create virtual private networks (VPNs) as low-cost alternatives to private WANs.

**4** **Identify and describe the principal technologies and standards for wireless networking, communication, and Internet access.** Cellular networks have evolved from slow-speed (1G) analog networks to high-speed, high-bandwidth, digital, packet-switched, third-generation (3G) networks with speeds ranging from 144 Kbps to more than 2 Mbps for data transmission. Second-generation (2G) cellular networks are digital networks used primarily for voice transmission, but they can also transmit data at rates ranging from 9.6 to 14.4 Kbps. 2.5G networks are packet-switched, use many existing infrastructure elements, and have data transmission rates ranging from 50 to 144 Kbps.

Major cellular standards include Code Division Multiple Access (CDMA), which is used primarily in the United States, and Global System for Mobile Communication (GSM), which is the standard in Europe and much of the rest of the world.

Alternative standards governing the way wireless mobile devices access the Internet and the World Wide Web include Wireless Application Protocol (WAP) and I-mode.

Standards for wireless computer networks include Bluetooth (802.15) for small personal-area networks (PANs), Wi-Fi (802.11) for local-area networks (LANs), and WiMax (802.16) for metropolitan-area networks (MANs). Bluetooth can link up to eight devices within a 10-meter area using low-power, radio-based communication and can transmit up to 722 Kbps in the 2.4-GHz band. Wireless phones, keyboards, computers, printers, and PDAs using Bluetooth can communicate with each other and even operate each other without direct user intervention.

The most popular of the 802.11 standards is currently 802.11b, which can transmit up to 11 Mbps in the unlicensed 2.4-GHz band and has an effective distance of 30 to 50 meters, although this range can be extended outdoors by using tower-mounted antennas. The 802.11b standard has been the most widely used standard for creating wireless LANs and providing broadband wireless Internet access. However, 802.11b is vulnerable to penetration by outsiders and interference from other wireless devices in the same frequency spectrum.

WiMax has a wireless access range of up to 31 miles and a data transfer rate of up to 75 Mbps, making it suitable for providing broadband Internet access in areas lacking DSL and cable lines. The 802.16 specification also has robust security and quality of service features to support voice and video.

Major cellular carriers are also upgrading their networks to provide wireless broadband access to the Internet at an average speed of 300 to 500 Kbps. Verizon's service, called BroadBand Access, uses a technology called EV-DO to provide Internet access over a cellular network.

**5** **Assess the business value of wireless technology and important wireless applications in business.** Wireless technology increases productivity and worker output by providing any-time, anywhere communication and access to information, including the information resources of the Internet. Wireless communication helps businesses stay more easily in touch with customers, suppliers, and employees and provides more flexible arrangements for organizing work.

Mobile wireless technology facilitates supply chain management by capturing data on the movement of goods as these events take place and by providing detailed, immediate information as goods move among supply chain partners. Radio frequency identification (RFID) systems provide a powerful technology for this purpose. These systems use tiny tags that have embedded microchips that contain data about an item and its location. The tags transmit radio signals over a short distance to special RFID readers. The RFID readers then pass the data over a network to a computer for processing.

Wireless sensor networks (WSNs) are networks of interconnected wireless devices with some processing and radio-transmitting capability that are embedded into the physical environment to provide measurements of many points over large spaces. Wireless sensor networks are valuable for monitoring environmental changes, traffic patterns, security incidents, or supply chain events.

## Key Terms

2.5G networks, 207
Access point, 209
Asynchronous Transfer Mode
(ATM), 191
Backbone, 187
Bandwidth, 189
Bluetooth, 208
Broadband, 182
Bus networks, 191
Cable Internet
connections, 192
Campus-area network
(CAN), 190
Cellular telephones (cell
phones), 189
Chat, 201
Coaxial cable, 187
Code Division Multiple
Access (CDMA), 206
Dense wavelength division
multiplexing (DWDM), 188
Digital subscriber line
(DSL), 192
Domain name, 193
Domain Name System
(DNS), 193
E-mail, 201
E-mail handhelds, 205
EV-DO, 211
Fiber-optic cable, 187
File Transfer Protocol
(FTP), 196
Firewalls, 201
Frame relay, 191
Global System for Mobile
Communication (GSM), 206
Groupware, 202
Hertz, 189
Home page, 198

Hotspots, 210
Hubs, 183
Hypertext Transfer Protocol
(HTTP), 197
I-mode, 207
Information appliance, 196
Instant messaging, 201
Integrated Services Digital
Network (ISDN), 191
Internet Protocol (IP)
address, 193
Internet service provider
(ISP), 193
Internet telephony, 202
Internet2, 196
Internetworking, 193
LISTSERV, 202
Local-area network
(LAN), 189
Metropolitan-area network
(MAN), 191
Microbrowser, 207
Microwave, 188
Modem, 187
Multiplexing, 188
Network interface card
(NIC), 183
Network operating system
(NOS), 183
Optical networks, 188
Packet switching, 185
Peer-to-peer, 190
Personal-area networks
(PANs), 208
Personal digital assistants
(PDAs), 205
Protocol, 186
Radio frequency
identification (RFID), 211

Ring networks, 191
Router, 183
RSS, 200
Satellites, 188
Search engine marketing, 200
Search engines, 198
Shopping bots, 200
Short message service
(SMS), 206
Smart phones, 205
Star network, 190
Switch, 183
T lines, 192
Telnet, 196
Third-generation (3G)
networks, 207
Topology, 190
Transmission Control
Protocol/Internet Protocol
(TCP/IP), 186
Twisted wire, 187
Uniform resource locator
(URL), 197
Usenet, 201
Virtual private network
(VPN), 204
Voice over IP (VoIP), 202
Web site, 198
Webmaster, 198
Wide-area networks
(WANs), 191
Wi-Fi, 209
WiMax, 211
Wireless Application
Protocol (WAP), 207
Wireless NICs, 210
Wireless sensor networks
(WSNs), 213

## Review Questions

**6.1** Describe the features of a simple network and the network infrastructure for a large company.

**6.2** Name and describe the principal technologies and trends that have shaped contemporary telecommunications systems.

**6.3** Name the different types of physical transmission media and compare them in terms of speed and cost.

**6.4** What is a local-area network (LAN)? What are the components of a typical LAN? What are the functions of each component?

**6.5** Name and describe the principal network topologies.

**6.6** Define the following: WAN, MAN, 3G, modem, protocol, optical network, bandwidth, and Internet2.

**6.7** List and describe the various broadband network services.

**6.8** What is the Internet? How does it work?

**6.9** Explain how the domain name and IP addressing systems work.

**6.10** List and describe the principal Internet services.

**6.11** List and describe alternative ways of locating information on the Web.

**6.12** What are intranets and extranets? How do they provide value to businesses?

**6.13** Name and describe the principal technologies and tools that support communication and electronic business.

**6.14** What are Internet telephony and virtual private networks? How do they provide value to businesses?

**6.15** Compare Bluetooth, Wi-Fi, WiMax, and EV-DO. What are their capabilities? For what types of applications is each best suited?

**6.16** Compare the WAP and I-mode standards for wireless access to the Web.

**6.17** What is RFID? How does it work? How does it provide value to businesses?

**6.18** What are wireless sensor networks? How do they work? What applications use them?

## Discussion Questions

**6.1** Network design is a key business decision as well as a technology decision. Why?

**6.2** Should all major retailing and manufacturing companies switch to RFID? Why or why not?

## Application Software Exercise

## Spreadsheet Exercise: Comparing Wireless Services

Software skills: Spreadsheet formulas, formatting

Business skills: Analyzing telecommunications services and costs

You would like to equip your sales force of 35 based in Cincinnati, Ohio, with mobile phones that have capabilities for voice transmission, text messaging, and taking and sending photos. Use the Web to select a wireless service provider that provides nationwide service as well as good service in your home area. Examine the features of the mobile handsets offered by each of these vendors. Assume that each of the 35 salespeople will need to spend three hours per day during business hours (8 A.M. to 6 P.M.) on mobile voice communication, send 30 text messages per day, and five photos per week. Use your spreadsheet software to determine the wireless service and handset that will offer the best pricing per user over a two-year period. For the purposes of this exercise, you do not need to consider corporate discounts.

## Using Internet Tools to Increase Efficiency and Productivity

Business skills: Employee productivity analysis

Dirt Bikes's management is concerned about how much money is being spent communicating with people inside and outside the company and on obtaining information about developments in the motorcycle industry and the global economy. You have been asked to investigate how Internet tools and technology could be used to help Dirt Bikes employees communicate and obtain information more efficiently. Dirt Bikes provides Internet access to all of its employees who use desktop computers.

1. How could the various Internet tools help employees at Dirt Bikes? Create a matrix showing what types of employees and business functions would benefit from using each type of tool and why.
2. How could Dirt Bikes benefit from intranets for its sales and marketing, human resources, and manufacturing and production departments? Select one of these departments and describe the kind of information that could be provided by an intranet for that department. How could this intranet increase efficiency and productivity for that department?
3. (Optional) If possible, use electronic presentation software to summarize your findings for management.

## Building Internet Skills

### Using Web Search Engines for Business Research

This project will help develop your Internet skills in using Web search engines for business research.

You have heard that fuel cells are new and might be an inexpensive way to provide electricity for your house, but you do not know anything about fuel cells. You decide that you want to research the topic to learn what fuel cells are and how they can be used for generating electricity for your house. Use the following four search engines to obtain that information: Yahoo!, AltaVista, Google, and Ask Jeeves. If you wish, try some other search engines as well. Compare the volume and quality of information you find with each search tool. Which tool is the easiest to use? Which produced the best results for your research? Why?

## Video Case

You will find a video case illustrating some of the concepts in this chapter on the Laudon Web site at **www.prenhall.com/laudon** along with questions to help you analyze the case.

## Teamwork

### Comparing Mobile Internet Access Systems

Form a group with three or four of your classmates. Evaluate mobile devices with Internet access from two different vendors, such as Palm, BlackBerry, Nokia, Samsung, or Motorola. Your analysis should consider the purchase cost of each device, the wireless networks where each device can operate, the cost of wireless Internet services, and what other services are available for each device. You should also consider other capabilities of each device, including the ability to integrate with existing corporate or PC applications. Which device would you select? What criteria would you use to guide your selection? If possible, use electronic presentation software to present your findings to the class.

# BUSINESS PROBLEM-SOLVING CASE

## Google Takes on the World

What's the easiest way to measure the success of a brand name? Perhaps it's when the name itself replaces the purpose for which it is used. Five years ago, if you asked the average Web surfer how to find the address of a particular site, he or she would likely tell you to use a search engine. Today, the answer would be simply, "Google it."

The rise of Google has been fast and fierce. The founders of the company, Sergey Brin and Larry Page, met as graduate students in 1995 at Stanford University, where they were Ph.D. candidates in computer science. They found a common interest in the challenge of filtering relevant information from large data sets. Their collaboration resulted in a search engine, run out of their dorm rooms, that they called BackRub because it produced search results based on back links, or links that pointed back to a particular Web page. The engine combines the technologies of Page's PageRank system, which evalu-

ates a page's importance based on the external links to it, and Brin's Web crawler, which visits Web sites and records a summary of their content.

Brin and Page incorporated their venture under the Google name in 1998 after raising $1 million from friends, family, and angel investors. Google's first office outside of the Stanford dorms was a garage in Menlo Park, California. By the end of 1998, Google, which was still in beta testing, was fielding 10,000 search queries per day. The reputation of Google as an effective search engine spread quickly by word of mouth, and in the first half of 1999, the site was receiving 500,000 queries per day having done no advertising.

During the next few years, Google continued to expand and hired the best information technology experts it could find, many of them graduate students from Stanford's Computer Science Department. AOL/Netscape chose the award-winning service for its hosted searches, increasing usage to three million searches per day. By the second half of 1999, the company moved its 39 employees into its new Googleplex headquarters in Mountain View, California. The search engine also officially moved out of the beta stage. In 2000, the Google index included one billion Web pages. Yet, its scope and popularity were really just getting started.

As of mid-2005, Google searches an index of more than eight billion Web pages. The index also includes one billion images and one billion Usenet newsgroup messages. In addition to searching for Web pages, users of Google.com can search for PDF, PostScript, text, Microsoft Office, Lotus, PowerPoint, and Shockwave files. Google claims to be one of the five most popular sites on the Internet with more than 80 million unique users per month and more than 50 percent of its traffic now coming from outside the United States. The company employs more than 3,000 workers to carry out its mission of "organizing the world's information and making it universally accessible and useful."

To find potential weaknesses in Google's business approach, it is necessary to examine the company's strengths. Two main sources account for most of Google's revenue: online advertising and online search services. Google Search Services enable organizations to include the Google search engine on their own Web pages. This is a straightforward technology licensing arrangement—not groundbreaking, but profitable, considering that the search engine is thought by many to be the best available.

The side of Google that has driven its phenomenal growth and profits is its advertising program. In a fraction of a second, Google's technology can evaluate millions of variables about its users and advertisers, correlate them with millions of potential ads, and deliver the message to which each user is most likely to respond. Because this technology makes ads more relevant, users click on ads 50 to 100 percent more often on Google than on Yahoo!, creating a better return for advertisers. Google sold over $6 billion in ads in 2005.

In 2000, Google launched AdWords, a self-service advertising program in which vendors enroll online using a credit card. Advertisers bid to have their ads placed alongside the search results for specific keyword queries. In 2002, AdWords Select introduced cost-per-click (CPC) pricing so that advertisers only pay for their ads when users actually click on them. Google determines the placement of ads through a combination of the CPC and click-through (total number of clicks) rates so that the most relevant ads for a keyword string appear in the most prominent positions. AdWords provides extensive exposure because the keyword-targeted ads appear throughout the Google Network, which includes America Online, Netscape Netcenter, Shopping.com, Ask Jeeves, *The New York Times* on the Web, and more than a dozen more high-profile sites on the Internet.

The number of active advertisers in the AdWords program surpassed 100,000 in the spring of 2003. However, the program has come under some fire recently for being vulnerable to malicious forms of manipulation. Specifically, unscrupulous businesses can use a practice known as click-fraud to drive up the costs of their competitors' ads. A business whose ad receives thousands of clicks from sources that have no intention of making a purchase may run through its marketing budget quickly and have to drop out of the ad game altogether, leaving the business at a competitive disadvantage.

The problem has grown large enough to give rise to firms that are in the business of detecting fraudulent clicks. Companies who sell keyword-targeted advertising, such as Google and its competitor Yahoo!, acknowledge the problem but are vague in their response to it. Google does credit customers for invalid clicks. It also has a system in place to detect click-fraud before customers are charged. Google does not disclose details about its antifraud methods to advertisers because of concerns about security. The company also does not want to expose the surveillance technology in use because perpetrators could gain a further advantage. Neither Google nor Yahoo! comment on specific cases of fraud. Both companies express a willingness to work with third-party fraud detectors, but they are still criticized for being unresponsive and ineffective when they do respond.

Although advertising customers are worried about fraud attacks from their competitors, Google must be concerned with legitimate offensives from its rivals. And there is no shortage of rivals. Companies large and small are poised to take a run at Google's supremacy in the search engine market. Leading the charge is none other than the world's leading software developer, Microsoft. Microsoft has a history of diminishing or destroying its competitors by exploiting the fact that its operating system Microsoft Windows can be found on 95 percent of the world's six billion personal computers. Netscape Navigator, Lotus 1–2–3, and WordPerfect have all been defeated in this manner. However, Google has proven to be such a formidable foe that a frustrated Bill Gates himself is steering his company's strategic responses. Gates has watched as Google has supplanted Microsoft as the hot tech name and the hot tech stock. There has even been a significant migration of Microsoft employees to Google.

For most of its existence, MSN, Microsoft's Web portal, has outsourced its search features. Search technology was never considered a moneymaker until Google developed its profitable target ad program to go along with its well-regarded search engine. In 2003, Microsoft employee Chris Payne convinced Gates to approve a $100 million, 18-month project to build Microsoft's own search engine. MSN Search launched in November 2004, buoyed by a $150 million promotional campaign. However, in its first six months, MSN Search made only a marginal dent in the market, accounting for 13 percent of worldwide search requests. Still, that 13 percent could easily grow to 25 percent with the introduction of the new Windows Vista operating system, due out in 2006.

Microsoft plans to integrate search technology into Windows Vista and into future versions of Office. The company believes that these enhancements will make the idea of going to a Web page to enter a query and receiving thousands of possible matches seem antiquated. Two other areas in which Microsoft can vault ahead of Google are context-aware searches and Deep Web searches. By personalizing search technology, a search engine can return results that accurately match the context of the user's query. Google has launched a personalized search tool that takes into account a user's previous searches when returning results. The cumulative effect is more relevant results.

The Deep Web refers to the massive quantity of documents and data that exists on the world's servers but is not available to the general public and cannot be indexed by search engines. Some of these data are copyright protected and some are simply stored several layers down in databases, only surfacing when requested specifically through a Web site form. One estimate puts the size of the Deep Web at 500 times that of the surface Web. Because Gates has the capital to purchase the rights to copyrighted material and his company owns powerful digital rights management software, Microsoft is viewed as a good candidate to become the gateway to the Deep Web. A search engine developed by the Chicago-based company Dipsie claims to crawl a larger portion of the 99 percent of the Web that most search engines cannot access.

The list of contenders for Google's search engine throne also includes smaller players like Teoma and Mooter. Teoma, owned by Ask Jeeves, does not rank sites based on the number of links leading to them. Instead, it analyzes the naturally occurring communities that develop around a particular subject on the Web and then bases its rankings on the number of same-subject pages that link to a site. Teoma believes that this technique makes its search results more authoritative, whereas Google's are more of a popularity contest. Computer scientists at Rutgers University, lead by Apostolos Gerasoulis, created Teoma, which is the Gaelic word for "expert."

Mooter, an Australian start-up founded by Liesl Capper, uses principles of psychology, software, and neural network technology (see Chapter 10) to make Web searches more personal. Capper and her associates, Jondarr Gibb and John Zakos, created a ranking algorithm that learns from the choices a user makes when working with search results. The results are first displayed as clusters so that the user can immediately narrow the scope of the search to her or his intended category of interest. Mooter remembers which clusters the user clicks and then adjusts future results to match the pattern of interest.

Microsoft differs from these smaller ventures in that its battle for Google's market share goes beyond search engines. To Microsoft, Google has ceased being a search technology company and is now a software company, capable of infringing on the markets that Microsoft dominates, such as operating systems and office productivity. In the past, Microsoft has thwarted competition through strategic pricing and feature enhancements, as well as by tying its products together so that they are the most convenient to use. Integrating the Internet Explorer Web browser into the Windows operating system was a Netscape killer. Microsoft may not find it so easy to develop a Google killer. Other software manufacturers have had to rely on Windows as a platform on which to run their products. Google is giving away its Linux-based programs over the Internet for free.

Google is constantly looking for new ways to grow. Its AdSense program scans Web pages for target words and displays appropriate advertisements, enabling Web site operators to generate revenue from their sites. Google introduced the Google Toolbar, which enables Web surfers to search the Google index without visiting the Google home page. The toolbar also provided one of the Web's earliest defenses against pop-up ads. Google's image search index launched in 2001 with 250 million images archived (now more than one billion). In 2002, Google Labs was born, enabling curious users to test out the company's newest initiatives online while they are still in development. Later that year, Google News appeared, becoming the first Internet news service compiled completely by computer algorithms. Google News Alerts followed later, enabling subscribers to receive customized news alerts by e-mail.

In April 2004, Google announced its Gmail, Web-based e-mail service, offering one gigabyte of free online storage to users, which was an unprecedented amount of space at the time. Gmail became a desired commodity as a result of a viral marketing campaign. While Gmail was in beta version, the only way to obtain a Gmail account was to have a current user send an invitation. Google made big news later in 2004 when it released Google Desktop Search, a downloadable program for searching personal files on a computer, including e-mail, productivity files, browsing history, and instant message conversations. This release was a particular affront to Microsoft, which wasn't able to offer its competing desktop search tool for another two months. Other popular services that Google has introduced include Froogle, a consumer product locator, and Google Maps, which includes dynamic online mapping and satellite pictures of searchable addresses. Google also acquired and improved Picasa digital photo management software, which is downloadable free of charge and introduced a free instant messaging and voice communication service for personal computers called Google Talk.

Not all of Google's products have been met with unanimous enthusiasm. Gmail, for instance, raised the ire of privacy advocates because it uses the same technology as AdSense to place advertisements alongside messages. The selection of ads is based on the actual text of the messages, meaning that every Gmail message is read by an automated scanner. In 2005, Google angered some members of the entertainment industry by archiving still images from television shows to test its new Google Video search service. Entertainment executives believed that Google was being disrespectful in not asking permission to use the copyrighted content. Google has faced similar criticism in planning to digitize the contents of millions of books. The company has also been sued by a French news agency for possible copyright violations on Google News.

Plans to start an online electronic payment service indicate that Google's next goal may be to become a major media outlet. Allowing users to search for and then play TV shows, sports broadcasts, film clips, and music videos would require business strategies that the company has not had to employ in dealing with free information. Yahoo! and Microsoft already have years of experience in negotiating with content providers, who are particularly concerned with piracy in the digital age. Eric Schmidt, Google's CEO, says that video search and its corresponding rights issues "will be a major story for Google for years." In the meantime, Google will continue to innovate in its core business. Schmidt estimates that Google will need 300 years to organize all of the information in the world.

*Sources:* Saul Hansell, "Your Ads Here (All of Them)," *New York Times,* October 30, 2005; John Markoff, "Google to Offer Instant Messaging and Voice Communications on Web," *The New York Times,* August 24, 2005; Fred Vogelstein, "Search and Destroy," *Fortune,* May 2, 2005; Kevin J. Delaney, "Web Start-Ups Vie to Detect 'Click Fraud,'" *The Wall Street Journal,* June 9, 2005; Kevin J. Delaney and Mylene Mangalindan, "Google Plans Online-Payment Service," *The Wall Street Journal,* June 20, 2005; Walter S. Mossberg, "Google Thrills with Photos, Stunts, But How Practical Is It?" *The Wall Street Journal,* July 7, 2005; Kevin J. Delaney and Brooks Barnes, "For Soaring Google, Next Act Won't Be as Easy as the First," *The Wall Street Journal,* June 30, 2005; www.google.com; Richard Brandt, "Net Assets," *Stanford Magazine,* November/December 2004; and Wade Roush, "Search Beyond Google," *Technology Review,* March 2004.

## Case Study Questions

1. What problems and challenges does Google face in this case? What is the source of these problems and challenges?
2. Has Google correctly identified the challenges it faces? How has the company chosen to approach these challenges? What solutions has it chosen? Are there any solutions that the company hasn't considered?
3. Has Google implemented its solutions successfully?
4. Has Google identified the people, organization, and technology issues associated with its problem and solutions? What are these issues?
5. What other factors should Google examine in addressing its current and future challenges? Do you think Google will be successful with the strategies it has adopted?

# Securing Information Systems

CHAPTER 7

## STUDENT OBJECTIVES

**After completing this chapter, you will be able to:**

1. Analyze why information systems need special protection from destruction, error, and abuse.

2. Assess the business value of security and control.

3. Design an organizational framework for security and control.

4. Evaluate the most important tools and technologies for safeguarding information resources.

## CHAPTER OUTLINE

## PHISHING: A COSTLY NEW SPORT FOR INTERNET USERS

**Elizabeth Owen almost lost her** identity. A frequent eBay user, she received an e-mail that appeared to come from eBay's payment service PayPal asking her to update her credit information or be barred from future purchases. She immediately started assembling the data. Right before she was to transmit it, she stopped. Her office, the National Association of Consumer Agency Administrators, had received constant complaints of e-mail scams. Even with this knowledge, she had almost become a victim of a special type of identify theft called phishing.

A phishing attack sends e-mail that claims to be from a bank, credit card company, retailer, or other company directing the recipient to a Web site where that person is asked to enter vital information, such as bank account numbers, social security numbers, credit card details, or online passwords. The Web site appears to be legitimate, but it's actually bogus. Scam artists use information obtained through phishing to drain bank or credit card accounts or sell the information to others to do the same.

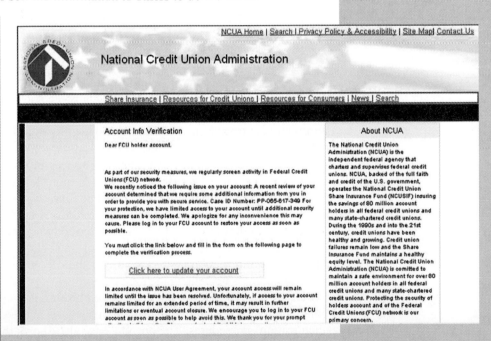

According to the Anti-Phishing Working Group, Citibank, U.S. Bank, and Visa topped the list of financial brand names hijacked by phishers. Phishers are also taking advantage of bank mergers, such as that between Wachovia and Sun Trust, hoping to lure customers into providing their account numbers by claiming they need this information to migrate to new accounts after the merger.

Phishing is growing at an explosive pace. Gartner Research reported in May 2005 that 73 million Americans had received phishing e-mails and 2.4 million of them were duped during the 12 months preceding its survey. Most of these losses were absorbed by the banks and credit card companies, but fear of identity theft has discouraged a significant number of people from using online financial services.

What can be done to combat phishing and prevent confidence from disappearing? A number of approaches are helpful. First, companies can educate their consumers about phishing scams. Citigroup's Citibank unit warns its Web site visitors about the dangers of phishing along with providing warning signs of potentially fraudulent e-mails. Citibank asserts that it won't ever send customers e-mail requesting sensitive information.

Individual Web sites and Internet service providers (ISPs) have started using antiphishing products and services. Some services sift through junk e-mail. Others scour the Web for bogus sites, issuing blacklists of known phishing sites to warn consumers about them. Some monitor online banking sites for signs the sites are being cased as possible targets and even contact Internet service providers to remove offending sites.

EBay has integrated Web Caller-ID from WholeSecurity Inc. of Austin, Texas, into the Account Guard feature of its downloadable toolbar used by customers to keep track of their eBay activities. Account Guard displays an icon that is green when users enter authentic eBay and PayPal addresses but turns red when blacklisted or suspicious Web sites are requested.

Banks are starting to blunt phishing attacks by requiring multilevel authentication of online customers—their user names and passwords plus something extra, such as a tiny, unique photo. Bank of America now requires Internet customers to register their computers and assign a digital image, such as the photo of a cat, to their account. When a customer accesses the bank's online site, the image is displayed before the customer enters his or her password to assure the customer the site is legitimate. However, other banks are hesitant to adopt such measures, for fear that they will make Internet banking too difficult. ■

*Sources:* Kimberly Morrison, "Internet Sees Increase in 'Phishing' for Online Victims," *Knight Ridder Newspapers,* February 28, 2005; Marshall Lager, "Online Insecurity Is Eroding Consumer Confidence," www.destinationcrm.com, accessed June 30, 2005; Vauhini Vara, "Banks Turn to Photos, Other Tactics to Boost Online Security, *The Wall Street Journal,* May 21, 2005; Brian Krebs, "New Industry Helps Banks Fight Back," *Washington Post,* March 4, 2005; and Rich Miller, "Bank Mergers Provide Opportunity for Phishing," *Netcraft,* June 9, 2005.

The problems created by phishing for companies such as eBay and Citigroup and for individual consumers illustrate some of the reasons why businesses need to pay special attention to information system security. Phishing and identity theft have flourished because so many people and businesses use the Internet for online commerce and financial transactions. These crimes have cost banks and financial services billions of dollars and individual victims much agony and worry. They also have a more far-reaching impact by discouraging individuals from making Internet purchases or from using online banking and other financial services, thereby lowering revenues and profits. A study by Gartner Group consultants reported that 33 percent of online shoppers are buying fewer items and cutting down on online financial transactions because of fear of fraud (Lager, 2005). So combating phishing and promoting information system security help prevent losses from fraud in the short term and loss of business revenue in the long term.

The opening case shows that combating phishing is a complex endeavor that involves multiple approaches, including education, new tools and technologies, and better security (authentication) procedures. The opening case also shows that no single approach is sufficient. Moreover, some approaches, such as multistep authentication procedures for accessing online systems, are helpful, but they are not always effective if they discourage people from visiting a Web site or using a system because it is too complicated.

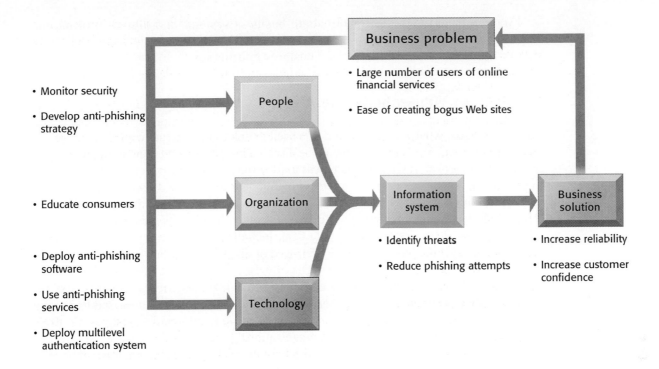

- Monitor security
- Develop anti-phishing strategy

**People**

**Business problem**
- Large number of users of online financial services
- Ease of creating bogus Web sites

- Educate consumers

**Organization**

**Information system**
- Identify threats
- Reduce phishing attempts

**Business solution**
- Increase reliability
- Increase customer confidence

- Deploy anti-phishing software
- Use anti-phishing services
- Deploy multilevel authentication system

**Technology**

This is not only true of antiphishing efforts but for information system security as a whole. Securing information systems from unauthorized access, abuse, destruction, or tampering of assets requires a combination of training, procedures, and technologies. The cost and difficulty of using all of these must be balanced with the net benefits they provide the business in the form of greater customer trust, uninterrupted operations, compliance with government regulations, and protection of financial assets.

---

**HEADS UP**

This chapter focuses on how to secure your information systems and the information inside them. As e-commerce and e-business have grown to encompass so much of our lives, we have all become much more aware of the importance of securing digital information. Your customers expect you to keep their digital private information secure and confidential. As your business increasingly relies on the Internet, you will become vulnerable to a variety of attacks against your systems that could, if successful, put you out of business in a very short time. To protect your business, you'll need to pay more attention to security and control than ever before.

• If your career is in finance or accounting, you will need to work with information system controls to prevent errors, fraud, and disruption of services that lead to large monetary losses and the erosion of customer confidence.

• If your career is in human resources, you will be dealing with "people factors," which are as important as technology in establishing the security and reliability of the firm's information systems. Many security breaches and system errors are caused by legitimate company insiders, and the human resources function is responsible for training programs and establishing security awareness among employees.

• If your career is in manufacturing and production or operations management, you will be concerned with preventing security breaches and downtime as your firm links with the systems of other firms for supply chain management.

• If your career is in sales and marketing, you will be concerned with secure payment systems for online purchases, as well as measures for ensuring that customer data are secure and properly used.

First we describe the major threats to business systems and digital information. Next, we describe the business benefits of protecting information systems. Then we show what steps to take to secure your business information.

## 7.1 System Vulnerability and Abuse

Can you imagine what would happen if you tried to link to the Internet without a firewall or antivirus software? Your computer would be disabled in a few seconds, and it might take you many days to recover. If your computer was used to run your business, you might not be able to sell to your customers or place orders with your suppliers while it was down. You might need to hire high-priced systems specialists to get your computer working again. And you might find that during this time, your computer system had been penetrated by outsiders, who perhaps stole or destroyed valuable data, including confidential payment data from your customers. If too much data were destroyed or divulged, your business might never be able to recover!

In short, if you operate a business today, you need to make security and control a top priority. **Security** refers to the policies, procedures, and technical measures used to prevent unauthorized access, alteration, theft, or physical damage to information systems. **Controls** consist of all the methods, policies, and organizational procedures that ensure the safety of the organization's assets; the accuracy and reliability of its accounting records; and operational adherence to management standards.

### Why Systems Are Vulnerable

When large amounts of data are stored in electronic form they are vulnerable to many more kinds of threats than when they existed in manual form. Through communications networks, information systems in different locations are interconnected. The potential for unauthorized access, abuse, or fraud is not limited to a single location but can occur at any access point in the network.

Figure 7-1 illustrates the most common threats against contemporary information systems. They can stem from technical, organizational, and environmental factors compounded by poor management decisions. In the multitier client/server computing environment illustrated here,

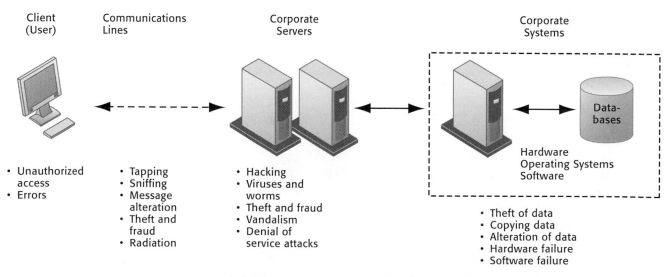

## Figure 7-1
Contemporary Security Challenges and Vulnerabilities
*The architecture of a Web-based application typically includes a Web client, a server, and corporate information systems linked to databases. Each of these components presents security challenges and vulnerabilities. Floods, fires, power failures, and other electrical problems can cause disruptions at any point in the network.*

vulnerabilities exist at each layer and in the communications between the layers. Users at the client layer can cause harm by introducing errors or by accessing systems without authorization. It is possible to access data flowing over networks, steal valuable data during transmission, or alter messages without authorization. Radiation may disrupt a network at various points as well. Intruders can launch denial-of-service attacks or malicious software to disrupt the operation of Web sites. Those capable of penetrating corporate systems can destroy or alter corporate data stored in databases or files.

Systems malfunction if computer hardware breaks down, is not configured properly, or is damaged by improper use or criminal acts. Errors in programming, improper installation, or unauthorized changes cause computer software to fail. Power failures, floods, fires, or other natural disasters can also disrupt computer systems.

Domestic or offshore partnering with another company adds to system vulnerability if valuable information resides on networks and computers outside the organization's control. Without strong safeguards, valuable data could be lost, destroyed, or could fall into the wrong hands, revealing important trade secrets or information that violates personal privacy.

## Internet Vulnerabilities

Large public networks, such as the Internet, are more vulnerable than internal networks because they are virtually open to anyone. The Internet is so huge that when abuses do occur, they can have an enormously widespread impact. When the Internet becomes part of the corporate network, the organization's information systems are even more vulnerable to actions from outsiders.

Computers that are constantly connected to the Internet by cable modems or digital subscriber line (DSL) lines are more open to penetration by outsiders because they use fixed Internet addresses where they can be easily identified. (With dial-up service, a temporary Internet address is assigned for each session.) A fixed Internet address creates a fixed target for hackers.

Telephone service based on Internet technology (see Chapter 6) can be more vulnerable than the switched voice network if it does not run over a secure private network. Most Voice-over IP (VoIP) traffic over the public Internet is not encrypted, so anyone with a network can listen in on conversations. Hackers can intercept conversations to obtain credit card and other confidential personal information or shut down voice service by flooding servers supporting VoIP with bogus traffic.

Vulnerability has also increased from widespread use of e-mail and instant messaging (IM). E-mail may contain attachments that serve as springboards for malicious software or unauthorized access to internal corporate systems. Employees may use e-mail messages to transmit valuable trade secrets, financial data, or confidential customer information to unauthorized recipients. Popular instant messaging applications for consumers do not use a secure layer for text messages, so they can be intercepted and read by outsiders during transmission over the public Internet. IM activity over the Internet can in some cases be used as a back door to an otherwise secure network. (IM systems designed for corporations, such as IBM's SameTime, include security features.)

## Wireless Security Challenges

Wireless networks using radio-based technology are even more vulnerable to penetration because radio frequency bands are easy to scan. Both Bluetooth and Wi-Fi networks are susceptible to hacking by eavesdroppers.

Although the range of Wireless Fidelity (Wi-Fi) networks is only several hundred feet, it can be extended up to one-fourth of a mile using external antennae. Local-area networks (LANs) that use the 802.11b (Wi-Fi) standard can be easily penetrated by outsiders armed with laptops, wireless cards, external antennae, and freeware hacking software. Hackers can use these tools to detect unprotected networks, monitor network traffic, and, in some cases, gain access to the Internet or to corporate networks.

Wi-Fi transmission technology uses spread spectrum transmission in which a signal is spread over a wide range of frequencies, and the particular version of spread spectrum transmission used in the 802.11 standard was designed to make it easier for stations to find

**Figure 7-2**
Wi-Fi Security
Challenges
*Many Wi-Fi networks
can be penetrated eas-
ily by intruders using
sniffer programs to
obtain an address to
access the resources of
a network without
authorization.*

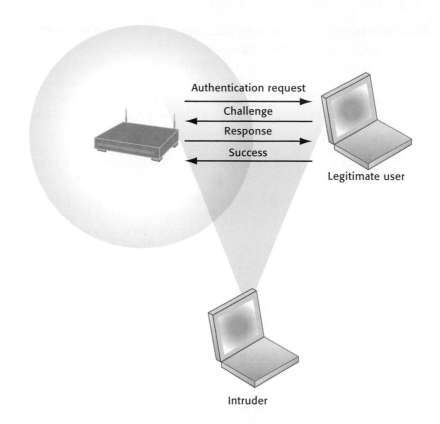

and hear one another. The *service set identifiers (SSID)* identifying the access points in a Wi-Fi network are broadcast multiple times and can be picked up fairly easily by intruders' sniffer programs (see Figure 7-2). Wireless networks in many locations do not have basic protections against **war driving**, in which eavesdroppers drive by buildings or park outside and try to intercept wireless network traffic.

The 802.11 standard specifies the SSID as a form of password for a user's radio network interface card (NIC) to join a particular wireless network. The user's radio NIC must have the same SSID as the access point to enable association and communication. Most access points broadcast the SSID multiple times per second. A hacker can employ an 802.11 analysis tool to identify the SSID. (Windows XP has capabilities for detecting the SSID used in a network and automatically configuring the radio NIC within the user's device.) An intruder that has associated with an access point by using the correct SSID can then obtain a legitimate Internet Protocol (IP) address to access other resources on the network because many wireless LANs automatically assign IP addresses to users as they become active. This enables an intruder who has illicitly associated with a wireless LAN to use the Windows operating system to determine which other users are connected to the network, and even to click on other users' devices, locate their documents folders, and open or copy their files. This is a serious problem many end users overlook when connecting to access points at airports or other public locations.

Intruders can also use the information they have gleaned about IP addresses and SSIDs to set up rogue access points on a different radio channel in physical locations close to users to force a user's radio NIC to associate with the rogue access point. Once this association occurs, hackers using the rogue access point can capture the names and passwords of unsuspecting users.

The initial security standard developed for Wi-Fi, called *Wired Equivalent Privacy (WEP),* is not very effective. WEP is built into all standard 802.11 products, but its use is optional. Users must turn it on, and many neglect to do so, leaving many access points unprotected. The basic WEP specification calls for an access point and all of its users to share the same 40-bit encrypted password, which can be easily decrypted by hackers from a small amount of traffic. Manufacturers of wireless networking products are now beefing up their security by offering stronger encryption and authentication systems.

## Malicious Software: Viruses, Worms, Trojan Horses, and Spyware

Malicious software programs are referred to as **malware** and include a variety of threats, such as computer viruses, worms, and Trojan horses. A **computer virus** is a rogue software program that attaches itself to other software programs or data files in order to be executed, usually without user knowledge or permission. Most computer viruses deliver a "payload." The payload may be relatively benign, such as the instructions to display a message or image, or it may be highly destructive—destroying programs or data, clogging computer memory, reformatting a computer's hard drive, or causing programs to run improperly. Viruses typically spread from computer to computer when humans take an action, such as sending an e-mail attachment or copying an infected file.

Most recent attacks have come from **worms**, which are independent computer programs that copy themselves from one computer to other computers over a network. (Unlike viruses, they can operate on their own without attaching to other computer program files and rely less on human behavior in order to spread from computer to computer. This explains why computer worms spread much more rapidly than computer viruses.) Worms destroy data and programs as well as disrupt or even halt the operation of computer networks.

Worms and viruses are often spread over the Internet from files of downloaded software, from files attached to e-mail transmissions, or from compromised e-mail messages or instant messaging. Viruses have also invaded computerized information systems from "infected" disks or infected machines. E-mail worms are currently the most problematic. IBM reported that more than 30 percent of e-mails in May 2005 contained some form of malware (IBM, 2005; Leyden, 2005).

Now viruses and worms are spreading to wireless computing devices. For example, the Cabir worm, which first appeared in early 2005, targets mobile devices running the popular Symbian mobile operating system and spreads through Bluetooth wireless networks. Cabir continually seeks other Bluetooth devices and eventually runs down a device's battery (Bank, 2004, Hulme, 2005). Mobile device viruses could pose serious threats to enterprise computing because so many wireless devices are now linked to corporate information systems. Table 7.1 describes the characteristics of some of the most harmful worms and viruses that have appeared.

Over the past decade, worms and viruses have caused billions of dollars of damage to corporate networks, e-mail systems, and data. Among the companies surveyed in the ICSA Labs Tenth Annual Virus Prevalence Survey, recovering from virus and malware attacks

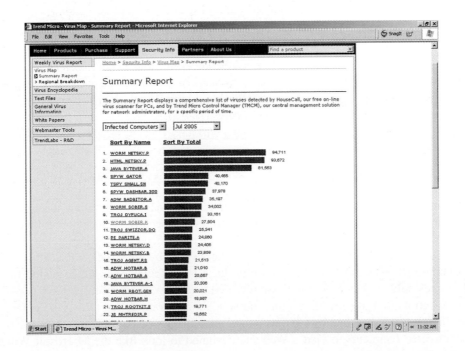

This Trend Micro chart lists the most prevalent computer worms and viruses worldwide in July 2005 and the number of computers infected by each worm or virus.

**TABLE 7.1**

**Examples of Malicious Code**

| Name | Type | Description |
|---|---|---|
| MyDoom.A | Worm | First appeared January 26, 2004. Spreads as an attachment to e-mail, affecting systems running Microsoft Windows. Sends e-mail to addresses harvested from infected machines, forging the sender's address. Considered the "fastest-spreading mass-mailer ever." |
| Sasser.ftp | Worm | First appeared May 2004. Spreads over the Internet by attacking random IP addresses. Causes computers to continually crash and reboot, and infected computers to search for more victims. |
| Klez | E-mail worm | Delivered in an e-mail containing a random subject line and message body targeting all addresses in the Windows address book, the database of instant messaging program ICQ, and local files. A file from the user's system is randomly selected and sent along with the worm. Klez also attempts to disable antivirus software and drops another virus in the user's system that tries to infect executable files there and across network filing systems. |
| StartPage.FH | Trojan Horse | First appeared June 15, 2004. Transmitted through infected floppy disks, CD-ROMs, Internet downloads, and peer-to-peer (P2P) file sharing. Changes Microsoft Internet Explorer's home page to display fake messages warning users of spyware infection. Attempts to entice users to visit a Web site where additional malware can be installed. |
| Netsky.P | Worm | First appeared March 21, 2004. Spreads through e-mail and through P2P file sharing. Deletes entries belonging to several other worms, including MyDoom and Bagle. Activated when the message is viewed in Microsoft Outlook's preview pane. |
| Sobig.F | Worm | First detected on August 19, 2003. Sends massive amounts of mail with forged sender information. Payload activates on Fridays or Sundays, when it downloads a program and runs it on the infected computer. |
| Melissa | Macro virus/ worm | First appeared in March 1999. At the time, it was the fastest-spreading infectious program ever discovered. Attacked Microsoft Word's Normal.dot global template, ensuring infection of all newly created documents. Mailed infected Word file to first 50 entries in user's Microsoft Outlook address book. |

took respondents an average of seven person days and cost an average of $130,000 (ICSA Labs, 2005).

A **Trojan horse** is a software program that appears to be benign but then does something other than expected. The Trojan horse is not itself a virus because it does not replicate but is often a way for viruses or other malicious code to be introduced into a computer system. The term *Trojan horse* is based on the huge wooden horse used by the Greeks to trick the Trojans into opening the gates to their fortified city during the Trojan War. Once inside the city walls, Greek soldiers hidden in the horse revealed themselves and captured the city.

An example of a modern-day Trojan horse is the program called DSNX-05 detected in early 2005. It was unleashed by a bogus e-mail message appearing to come from Microsoft, which directed recipients to visit a Web site designed to look like the Microsoft Windows

Update page. The Web site downloaded and installed malicious code on the compromised computer. Once this Trojan horse was installed, hackers could access the computer remotely without detection and use it for their own purposes.

Some types of **spyware** also act as malicious software. These small programs install themselves on computers to monitor user Web surfing activity and serve up advertising. Some Web advertisers use spyware to obtain information about users' buying habits and to serve tailored advertisements. Many users find such spyware annoying and some critics worry about its infringement on computer users' privacy.

Other forms of spyware, however, are much more nefarious. **Key loggers** record every keystroke made on a computer to steal serial numbers for software, to launch Internet attacks, to gain access to e-mail accounts, to obtain passwords to protected computer systems, or to pick up personal information such as credit card numbers. Other spyware programs reset Web browser home pages, redirect search requests, or slow computer performance by taking up too much memory. Nearly 1,000 forms of spyware have been documented.

## Hackers and Cybervandalism

A **hacker** is an individual who intends to gain unauthorized access to a computer system. Within the hacking community, the term **cracker** is typically used to denote a hacker with criminal intent, although in the public press, the terms *hacker* and *cracker* are used interchangeably. Hackers and crackers gain unauthorized access by finding weaknesses in the security protections employed by Web sites and computer systems, often taking advantage of various features of the Internet that make it an open system that is easy to use.

Hacker activities have broadened beyond mere system intrusion to include theft of goods and information, as well as system damage and **cybervandalism**, the intentional disruption, defacement, or even destruction of a Web site or corporate information system. In May of 2004, the Sasser worm appeared, eventually affecting millions of computers belonging to individuals and businesses worldwide. Sasser targeted a flaw in the Microsoft Windows operating system. Sasser disrupted British Airways flight check-ins, operations of British coast guard stations, Hong Kong hospitals, Taiwan post office branches, and Australia's Westpac Bank. Sasser and its variants caused an estimated $14.8 billion to $18.6 billion in damages worldwide (Associated Press, 2005; Cox, 2005).

### Spoofing and Sniffing

Hackers attempting to hide their true identities often spoof, or misrepresent, themselves by using fake e-mail addresses or masquerading as someone else. **Spoofing** also may involve redirecting a Web link to an address different from the intended one, with the site masquerading as the intended destination. Links that are designed to lead to one site can be reset to send users to a totally unrelated site, one that benefits the hacker. For example, if hackers redirect customers to a fake Web site that looks almost exactly like the true site, they can then collect and process orders, effectively stealing business as well as sensitive customer information from the true site. We provide more detail on other forms of spoofing in our discussion of computer crime.

A **sniffer** is a type of eavesdropping program that monitors information traveling over a network. When used legitimately, sniffers can help identify potential network trouble spots or criminal activity on networks, but when used for criminal purposes, they can be damaging and very difficult to detect. Sniffers enable hackers to steal proprietary information from anywhere on a network, including e-mail messages, company files, and confidential reports.

### Denial-of-Service Attacks

In a **denial-of-service (DoS) attack**, hackers flood a network server or Web server with many thousands of false communications or requests for services to crash the network. The network receives so many queries that it cannot keep up with them and is thus unavailable to service legitimate requests. A **distributed denial-of-service (DDoS) attack** uses numerous computers to inundate and overwhelm the network from numerous launch points.

For example, on June 15, 2004, Web infrastructure provider Akamai Technology was hit by a distributed denial-of-service attack that slowed some of its customers' Web sites for more than two hours. Akamai provides Web server capacity for more than 1,000 Web sites, and Microsoft, Apple, and Yahoo! were among the sites affected.

The attack on Akamai used thousands of "zombie" PCs, which had been infected by malicious software without their owners' knowledge and organized into a **botnet**. Hackers create these botnets by infecting other people's computers with bot malware that opens a back door through which an attacker can give instructions. The infected computer then becomes a slave, or zombie, serving a master computer belonging to someone else. Once a hacker infects enough computers, her or she can use the amassed resources of the botnet to launch distributed denial-of-service attacks, phishing campaigns, or unsolicited "spam" e-mail (see Chapter 12).

Although DoS attacks do not destroy information or access restricted areas of a company's information systems, they often cause a Web site to shut down, making it impossible for legitimate users to access the site. For busy e-commerce sites, such as those described in the Focus on Organizations, these attacks are costly; while the site is shut down, customers cannot make purchases. Companies whose business relies heavily on the Internet, such as gambling Web sites, financial services sites, and online payment processors, are typical targets. Especially vulnerable are small and midsize businesses whose networks tend to be less protected than those of large corporations.

As you read the Focus on Organizations, try to identify the problems created by botnets; their causes and impact; what alternative solutions were available to targeted businesses; how well the chosen solution worked; and the people, organization, and technology issues that had to be addressed when developing the solution.

Figure 7-3 illustrates the estimated worldwide damage from all forms of digital attack, including hacking, malware, and spam between 1999 and 2004.

## Computer Crime and Cyberterrorism

Most hacker activities are criminal offenses, and the vulnerabilities of systems we have just described make them targets for other types of computer crime as well. The U.S. Department of Justice defines **computer crime** as "any violations of criminal law that involve a knowledge of computer technology for their perpetration, investigation, or prosecution." The computer can be a target of a crime or an instrument of a crime. Table 7.2 provides examples of both categories of computer crime.

No one knows the magnitude of the computer crime problem—how many systems are invaded, how many people engage in the practice, or the total economic damage. According

**Figure 7-3**
Worldwide Damage from Digital Attacks
*This chart shows estimates of the average annual worldwide damage from hacking, malware, and spam since 1998. These figures are based on data from mi2G and the authors.*

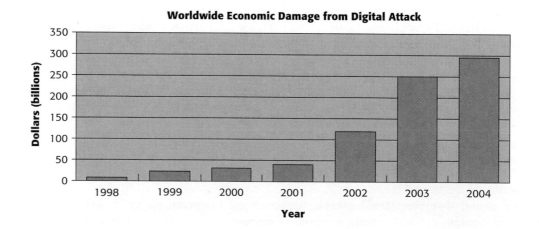

# FOCUS ON ORGANIZATIONS    Cyber Blackmail and Network Zombies: New Threats from DoS Attacks

Gary Chiacco owns an online sports apparel store named Jersey Joe. On July 7, 2004, Chiacco reported to federal authorities that customers had been having trouble accessing his store's Web site, jersey-joe.com, for several days. Unable to conduct business, Jersey Joe lost hundreds of thousands of dollars in sales. Jersey Joe had become the victim of a denial-of-service attack, in which the Web site was bombarded by so many requests that the site overloaded and went offline. As investigators worked on the case into the fall of 2004, the attacks worsened to such a degree that the company hosting jersey-joe.com asked Chiacco to take his site elsewhere because the attacks were affecting service to other Web sites hosted by the company. Chiacco received the same request from two other hosting companies.

Investigators discovered that computers belonging to college students in Massachusetts and Pennsylvania were infected with software that made them zombies. The computers were receiving instructions from a user named pherk, whose IP address was traced to a high school student in Edison, New Jersey, named Jasmine Singh. The teenager had been hired to launch these attacks by 18 year-old Jason Arabo, another online seller of sports apparel who wanted to harm his competition. Arabo was caught in an FBI sting in which he attempted to hire an undercover agent to inflict more damage to his competitors than Singh was able to inflict with his attacks. Arabo could be sentenced to five years in prison, whereas Singh will likely receive probation for his role.

Although the attacks on Jersey Joe caused considerable financial loss, and, undoubtedly, significant anguish, Chiacco may be grateful that he wasn't the target of an even more sinister type of cyberattack. Michael Alculumbre is the head of Protx Ltd., a British company that provides e-commerce payments and security services. Protx received an e-mail that threatened attacks on the company's Web site. The perpetrator challenged Protx to fight off the attacks, which would cost hundreds of thousands of dollars, or simply pay the sum of $10,000 to have the site left alone for a year. Within a few days of receiving the e-mail, Protx experienced disabling attacks on its servers, preventing retailers, who use the site to process client payments, from doing business. During one phase of the attack, Protx servers were being flooded with five times the amount of data that a large Internet service provider usually handles. Alculumbre considered paying the extortion fee but instead invested nearly half a million dollars in network security that was a better guarantee of protection.

Having a strategy in place before a bot attack hits is crucial to mitigating the damage of the attack. When DNS

servers that keep track of Internet addresses and domain names at Akamai Technologies were flooded in June 2004 with bogus requests for connections from a zombie army, the damage to Akamai's business could have been severe. However, the staff at Akamai was prepared to respond.

Andy Ellis, Akamai's director of information security, noticed a bottleneck when he made a request for a customer's Web site. Nearby, at the company's Network Operations Command Center (NOCC), displays showed spikes in traffic volume on Akamai's DNS servers. Akamai's first response team, known as the White Hat team, mobilized immediately and initiated its emergency response procedure. The team made its initial diagnosis of who and what was under attack and then the team split into subgroups. One group was put in charge of capturing the incoming requests, decoding their patterns, creating a profile of the attack, and recommending countermeasures. A second group began notifying federal law enforcement officials and Internet service providers, who could offer guidance and help shut down secondary attacks. Another group measured the impact of the attack on customers. Still another group deployed a custom-built application to identify and filter the bogus incoming data packets.

A colleague at a university data center, alerted about the Akamai attack, realized that the commandeered computers were carrying out the attack from his own university. With that additional information, Akamai was able to suppress the attack within 90 minutes.

Experts doubt that it is possible to completely secure oneself from a bot attack. The real problem is that so many unsuspected users have compromised computers. En masse, these computers can cause problems for any company no matter how secure its network is. The best defense for individuals is to use updated antivirus, antispam, and antispyware software so that the bot programs are eliminated or disabled before they can turn over control of a computer to a hacker.

*Sources:* Cassell Bryan-Low, "Tech-Savvy Blackmailers Hone a New Form of Extortion," *The Wall Street Journal,* May 5, 2005; Stephen Labaton, "An Army of Soulless 1's and 0's," *The New York Times,* June 24, 2005; and Kevin Fogarty, "Your Money or Your Network," *Baseline,* February 9, 2005.

**To Think About:**

What problem faced the companies in this discussion? How did they detect the problem? How did the problem affect their businesses? What solutions were available to the companies to help solve the problem? What other solutions might they have considered? How did people, organization, and technology issues factor into the problem?

**TABLE 7.2**

**Examples of
Computer Crime**

**COMPUTERS AS TARGETS OF CRIME**

Breaching the confidentiality of protected computerized data

Accessing a computer system without authority

Knowingly accessing a protected computer to commit fraud

Intentionally accessing a protected computer and causing damage, negligently or deliberately

Knowingly transmitting a program, program code, or command that intentionally causes damage
to a protected computer

Threatening to cause damage to a protected computer

**COMPUTERS AS INSTRUMENTS OF CRIME**

Theft of trade secrets

Unauthorized copying of software or copyrighted intellectual property, such as articles, books,
music, and video

Schemes to defraud

Using e-mail for threats or harassment

Intentionally attempting to intercept electronic communication

Illegally accessing stored electronic communications, including e-mail and voice mail

Transmitting or possessing child pornography using a computer

to one study by the Computer Crime Research Center, U.S. companies lose approximately $14 billion annually to cybercrimes. Many companies are reluctant to report computer crimes because the crimes may involve employees or the company fears that publicizing its vulnerability will hurt its reputation.

The most economically damaging kinds of computer crime are DoS attacks, introducing viruses, theft of services, and disruption of computer systems. Traditionally, employees—insiders—have been the source of the most injurious computer crimes because they have the knowledge, access, and, frequently, job-related motives to commit such crimes. However, the Internet's ease of use and accessibility has created new opportunities for computer crime and abuse by outsiders.

### Identity Theft

With the growth of the Internet and electronic commerce, identity theft has become especially troubling. **Identity theft** is a crime in which an imposter obtains key pieces of personal information, such as social security identification numbers, driver's license numbers, or credit card numbers, to impersonate someone else. The information may be used to obtain credit, merchandise, or services in the name of the victim or to provide the thief with false credentials. According to the U.S. Federal Trade Commission, about 3.2 million U.S. consumers are falling victim to identity theft each year (Rivlin, 2005).

The Internet has made it easy for identity thieves to use stolen information because goods can be purchased online without any personal interaction, and the Internet has also inspired new tactics for stealing personal information. Credit card files are a major target of Web site hackers. Moreover, e-commerce sites are wonderful sources of customer personal information—name, address, and phone number. Armed with this information, criminals can assume new identities and establish new credit for their own purposes.

One increasingly popular tactic is a form of spoofing called **phishing**, which we described in the chapter-opening case. Phishing involves setting up fake Web sites or sending e-mail messages that look like those of legitimate businesses to ask users for confidential personal data. The e-mail message instructs recipients to update or confirm records by providing social security numbers, bank and credit card information, and other confidential data either by responding to the e-mail message or by entering the information at a bogus Web site.

Phishing scams have posed as PayPal, the online payment service; online service provider America Online (AOL); Citibank; Fleet Bank; American Express; the Federal Deposit Insurance Corporation; the Bank of England; and other banks around the world. British security firm mi2g estimated the worldwide economic damage from phishing scams exceeded $13.5 billion in customer and productivity losses, business interruptions, and efforts to repair damage to brand reputation (Barrett, 2004).

New phishing techniques called evil twins and pharming are even harder to detect. **Evil twins** are wireless networks that pretend to offer trustworthy Wi-Fi connections to the Internet, such as those in airport lounges, hotels, or coffee shops. The bogus network looks identical to a legitimate public network. Fraudsters try to capture passwords or credit card numbers of unwitting users who log on to the network.

**Pharming** redirects users to a bogus Web page, even when the individual types the correct Web page address into his or her browser. This is possible if pharming perpetrators gain access to the Internet address information stored by Internet service providers to speed up Web browsing and the ISP companies have flawed software on their servers that allows the fraudsters to hack in and change those addresses.

The U.S. Congress responded to the threat of computer crime in 1986 with the Computer Fraud and Abuse Act. This act makes it illegal to access a computer system without authorization. Most states have similar laws, and nations in Europe have similar legislation. Congress also passed the National Information Infrastructure Protection Act in 1996 to make virus distribution and hacker attacks to disable Web sites federal crimes. U.S. legislation, such as the Wiretap Act, Wire Fraud Act, Economic Espionage Act, Electronic Communications Privacy Act, E-Mail Threats and Harassment Act, and Child Pornography Act, covers computer crimes involving intercepting electronic communication, using electronic communication to defraud, stealing trade secrets, illegally accessing stored electronic communications, using e-mail for threats or harassment, and transmitting or possessing child pornography.

Some harmful acts committed with computers are not necessarily illegal but may still be unethical. **Computer abuse** is the commission of acts involving a computer that may not be illegal but that are considered unethical. One widespread form of abuse is **spamming**, in which thousands and even hundreds of thousands of unsolicited e-mail and electronic messages are sent out, creating a nuisance for both businesses and individual users. We discuss computer abuse and spamming in greater detail in Chapter 12.

### Cyberterrorism and Cyberwarfare

Concern is mounting that the vulnerabilities of the Internet or other networks could be exploited by terrorists, foreign intelligence services, or other groups to create widespread disruption and harm. Such cyberattacks might target the software that runs electrical power grids, air traffic control systems, or networks of major banks and financial institutions. Hackers from a number of countries, including China, have been probing and mapping U.S. networks, and at least 20 countries are believed to be developing offensive and defensive cyberwarfare capabilities. U.S. military networks and U.S. government agencies suffer hundreds of hacker attacks each year.

The U.S. government has taken some steps to deal with the potential threat. The Department of Homeland Security has an Information Analysis and Infrastructure Protection Directorate to coordinate cybersecurity. The directorate's National Cyber Security Division is responsible for protecting critical infrastructure. It conducts cyberspace analysis, promotes information sharing, issues alerts, and aids in national recovery efforts. The U.S. Department of Defense has joint task forces for computer network defense and for managing computer network attacks. Congress has approved a Cybersecurity Research and Development Act to fund universities that are researching ways to protect computer systems.

## Internal Threats: Employees

We tend to think the security threats to a business originate outside the organization. In fact, the largest financial threats to business institutions come not from robberies, but from embezzlement by insiders. Some of the largest disruptions to service, destruction of e-commerce sites, and diversion of customer credit data and personal information have come from insiders—once trusted employees. Employees have access to privileged information, and in the presence of sloppy internal security procedures, they are often able to roam throughout an organization's systems without leaving a trace.

Studies have found that users' lack of knowledge is the single greatest cause of network security breaches. Many employees forget their passwords to access computer systems or allow co-workers to use them, which compromises the system. Malicious intruders seeking system access sometimes trick employees into revealing their passwords by pretending to be legitimate members of the company in need of information. This practice is called **social engineering**.

Employees—both end users and information systems specialists—are also a major source of errors introduced into an information system. Employees can introduce errors by entering faulty data or by not following the proper instructions for processing data and using computer equipment. Information systems specialists can also create software errors as they design and develop new software or maintain existing programs.

## Software Vulnerability

Software errors also pose a constant threat to information systems, causing untold losses in productivity. The U.S. Department of Commerce National Institute of Standards and Technology (NIST) reports that software flaws (including vulnerabilities to hackers and malware) cost the U.S. economy $59.6 billion each year (NIST, 2005).

Commercial software often contains flaws that create not only performance problems but also security vulnerabilities that open networks to intruders. These vulnerabilities enable malware to slip past antivirus defenses. A great deal of malware has been trying to exploit vulnerabilities in the Microsoft Windows operating system and other Microsoft products, but malware targeting the Linux operating system is on the rise as well.

To correct software flaws once they are identified, the software vendor creates small pieces of software called **patches** to repair the flaws without disturbing the proper operation of the software. An example is Microsoft's XP Service Pack 2 (SP2) introduced in 2004, which features added firewall protection against viruses and intruders, capabilities for automatic security updates, and an easy-to-use interface for managing the security applications on the user's computer. It is up to users of the software to track these vulnerabilities, test, and apply all patches. This process is called *patch management*.

Because a company's IT infrastructure is typically laden with multiple business applications, operating system installations, and other system services, the process of maintaining patches on all devices and services used by a company can be very time-consuming and costly. Malware is being created so rapidly that companies have very little time to respond between the time a vulnerability and a patch are announced and the time malicious software appears to exploit the vulnerability. This is one reason why Sasser, SQL Slammer, SoBig.F, and other worms and viruses have been able to infect so many computer systems.

## 7.2 Business Value of Security and Control

Many firms are reluctant to spend heavily on security because it is not directly related to sales revenue. However, protecting information systems is so critical to the operation of the business that it deserves a second look. When computer systems fail to run or work as required, firms that depend heavily on computers experience a serious loss of business function. The longer computer systems are down, the more serious the consequences for the firm. Some firms relying on computers to process their critical business transactions might experience a total loss of business function if they lose computer capability for more than a few days. And with so much business now dependent on the Internet and networked systems, firms are more vulnerable than ever to disruption and harm.

Companies have very valuable information assets to protect. Systems often house confidential information about individuals' taxes, financial assets, medical records, and job performance reviews. They also can contain information on corporate operations, including trade secrets, new product development plans, and marketing strategies. Government systems may store information on weapons systems, intelligence operations, and military targets. These information assets have tremendous value, and the repercussions can be devastating if they are lost, destroyed, or placed in the wrong hands. A recent study estimated that when the security of a large firm is compromised, the company loses approximately 2.1 percent of its market value within two days of the security breach, which translates into an average loss of $1.65 billion in stock market value per incident (Cavusoglu, Mishra, and Raghunathan, 2004).

Inadequate security and control can also create serious legal liability. Businesses must protect not only their own information assets but also those of customers, employees, and business partners. Failure to do so may open the firm to costly litigation for data exposure or theft. An organization can be held liable for needless risk and harm created if the organization fails to take appropriate protective action to prevent loss of confidential information, data corruption, or breach of privacy. A sound security and control framework that protects business information assets can thus produce a high return on investment.

## Legal and Regulatory Requirements for Electronic Records Management

Recent U.S. government regulations are forcing companies to take security and control more seriously by mandating the protection of data from abuse, exposure, and unauthorized access. Firms face new legal obligations for electronic records management and document retention as well as for privacy protection. **Electronic records management (ERM)** consists of policies, procedures, and tools for managing the retention, destruction, and storage of electronic records.

If you work in the healthcare industry, your firm will need to comply with the Health Insurance Portability and Accountability Act (HIPAA) of 1996. **HIPAA** outlines medical security and privacy rules and procedures for simplifying the administration of healthcare billing and automating the transfer of healthcare data between healthcare providers, payers, and plans. It requires members of the healthcare industry to retain patient information for six years and ensure the confidentiality of those records. It specifies privacy, security, and electronic transaction standards for healthcare providers handling patient information, providing penalties for breaches of medical privacy, disclosure of patient records by e-mail, or unauthorized network access.

If you work in a firm providing financial services, your firm will need to comply with the **Gramm–Leach–Bliley Act**. The Financial Services Modernization Act of 1999, better known as the Gramm–Leach–Bliley Act after its congressional sponsors, requires financial institutions to ensure the security and confidentiality of customer data. Data must be stored on a secure medium. Special security measures must be enforced to protect such data on storage media and during transmittal.

If you work in a publicly traded company, your company will need to comply with the **Sarbanes–Oxley Act**. The Public Company Accounting Reform and Investor Protection Act of 2002, better known as Sarbanes–Oxley after its sponsors Senator Paul Sarbanes of Maryland and Representative Michael Oxley of Ohio, was designed to protect investors after the financial scandals at Enron, WorldCom, and other public companies. It imposes responsibility on companies and their management to safeguard the accuracy and integrity of financial information that is used internally and released externally.

Sarbanes–Oxley is fundamentally about ensuring that internal controls are in place to govern the creation and documentation of information in financial statements. Because information systems are used to generate, store, and transport such data, the legislation requires firms to consider information systems security and other controls required to ensure the integrity, confidentiality, and accuracy of their data. Each system application that deals with critical financial reporting data requires controls to make sure the data are accurate. Controls to secure the corporate network, prevent unauthorized access to systems and data, and ensure data integrity and availability in the event of disaster or other disruption of service are essential as well.

### Electronic Evidence and Computer Forensics

Security, control, and electronic records management have become essential for responding to legal actions. Much of the evidence today for stock fraud, embezzlement, theft of company trade secrets, computer crime, and many civil cases is in digital form. In addition to information from printed or typewritten pages, legal cases today increasingly rely on evidence represented as computer data stored on portable floppy disks, CDs, and computer hard disk drives, as well as in e-mail, instant messages, and e-commerce transactions over the Internet. E-mail is currently the most common type of electronic evidence.

In a legal action, a firm may have to submit to a discovery request for access to information that may be used as evidence, and the company is required by law to produce those data. The cost of responding to a discovery request can be enormous if the company has trouble assembling the required data or the data have been corrupted or destroyed. Courts now impose severe financial and even criminal penalties for improper destruction of electronic documents.

An effective electronic document retention policy ensures that electronic documents, e-mail, and other records are well organized, accessible, and neither retained too long nor discarded too soon. It also reflects an awareness of how to preserve potential evidence for computer forensics. **Computer forensics** is the scientific collection, examination, authentication, preservation, and analysis of data held on or retrieved from computer storage media in such a way that the information can be used as evidence in a court of law. It deals with the following problems:

- Recovering data from computers while preserving evidential integrity
- Securely storing and handling recovered electronic data
- Finding significant information in a large volume of electronic data
- Presenting the information to a court of law

Electronic evidence may reside on computer storage media in the form of computer files and as *ambient data,* which are not visible to the average user. An example might be a file that has been deleted on a PC hard drive. Data that a computer user may have deleted on computer storage media can be recovered through various techniques. Computer forensics experts try to recover such hidden data for presentation as evidence.

An awareness of the need for computer forensics should be incorporated into a firm's contingency planning process. The CIO, security specialists, information systems staff, and corporate legal counsel should all work together to have a plan in place that can be executed if a legal need arises.

## 7.3 Establishing a Framework for Security and Control

Technology is not the key issue in information systems security and control. The technology provides a foundation, but in the absence of intelligent management policies, even the best technology is easily defeated. For instance, experts believe that more than 90 percent of successful cyberattacks could have been prevented by technology available at the time. Inadequate human attention made these attacks so prevalent.

Protection of information resources requires a sound security policy and set of controls. **ISO 17799**, an international set of standards for security and control, provides helpful guidelines. It specifies best practices in information systems security and control, including security policy, business continuity planning, physical security, access control, compliance, and creating a security function within the organization.

## Risk Assessment

Before your company commits resources to security, it must know which assets require protection and the extent to which these assets are vulnerable. A risk assessment helps answer these questions and determines the most cost-effective set of controls for protecting assets.

A **risk assessment** determines the level of risk to the firm if a specific activity or process is not properly controlled. Business managers working with information systems specialists can determine the value of information assets, points of vulnerability, the likely frequency of a problem, and the potential for damage. For example, if an event is likely to occur no more than once a year, with a maximum of a $1,000 loss to the organization, it is not feasible to spend $20,000 on the design and maintenance of a control to protect against that event. However, if that same event were to occur at least once a day, with a potential loss of more than $300,000 a year, $100,000 spent on a control might be entirely appropriate.

Table 7.3 illustrates sample results of a risk assessment for an online order processing system that processes 30,000 orders per day. The likelihood of each exposure occurring over a one-year period is expressed as a percentage. The next column shows the highest and lowest possible loss that could be expected each time the exposure occurred and an average loss calculated by adding the highest and lowest figures together and dividing by two. The expected annual loss for each exposure can be determined by multiplying the average loss by its probability of occurrence.

This risk assessment shows that the probability of a power failure occurring in a one-year period is 30 percent. Loss of order transactions while power is down could range from $5,000 to $200,000 (averaging $102,500) for each occurrence, depending on how long processing is halted. The probability of embezzlement occurring over a yearly period is about 5 percent, with potential losses ranging from $1,000 to $50,000 (and averaging $25,500) for each occurrence. User errors have a 98 percent chance of occurring over a yearly period, with losses ranging from $200 to $40,000 (and averaging $20,100) for each occurrence.

Once the risks have been assessed, system builders will concentrate on the control points with the greatest vulnerability and potential for loss. In this case, controls should focus on ways to minimize the risk of power failures and user errors because anticipated annual losses are highest for these areas.

## Security Policy

Once you've identified the main risks to your systems, your company will need to develop a security policy for protecting the company's assets. A **security policy** consists of statements ranking information risks, identifying acceptable security goals, and identifying the mechanisms for achieving these goals. What are the firm's most important information assets? Who generates and controls this information in the firm? What existing security policies are

**TABLE 7.3**

**Online Order Processing Risk Assessment**

| Exposure | Probability of Occurrence (%) | Loss Range/ Average ($) | Expected Annual Loss ($) |
|---|---|---|---|
| Power failure | 30% | $5,000–$200,000 ($102,500) | $30,750 |
| Embezzlement | 5% | $1,000–$50,000 ($25,500) | $1,275 |
| User error | 98% | $200–$40,000 ($20,100) | $19,698 |

in place to protect the information? What level of risk is management willing to accept for each of these assets? Is it willing, for instance, to lose customer credit data once every 10 years? Or will it build a security system for credit card data that can withstand the once-in-a-hundred-year disaster? Management must estimate how much it will cost to achieve this level of acceptable risk.

In larger firms, you may see a formal corporate security function headed by a **chief security officer (CSO)**. The security group educates and trains users, keeps management aware of security threats and breakdowns, and maintains the tools chosen to implement security. The chief security officer is responsible for enforcing the firm's security policy.

The security policy drives policies determining acceptable use of the firm's information resources and which members of the company have access to its information assets. An **acceptable use policy (AUP)** defines acceptable uses of the firm's information resources and computing equipment, including desktop and laptop computers, wireless devices, telephones, and the Internet. The policy should clarify company policy regarding privacy, user responsibility, and personal use of company equipment and networks. A good AUP defines unacceptable and acceptable actions for every user and specifies consequences for noncompliance.

**Authorization policies** determine differing levels of access to information assets for different levels of users. **Authorization management systems** establish where and when a user is permitted to access certain parts of a Web site or a corporate database. Such systems allow each user access only to those portions of a system that person is permitted to enter, based on information established by a set of access rules.

The authorization management system knows exactly what information each user is permitted to access, as shown in Figure 7-4. This figure illustrates the security allowed for two sets of users of an online personnel database containing sensitive information, such as employees' salaries, benefits, and medical histories. One set of users consists of all employees who perform clerical functions, such as inputting employee data into the system. All individuals with this type of profile can update the system but can neither read nor update sensitive fields, such as salary, medical history, or earnings data. Another profile applies to a divisional

**Figure 7-4**
Security Profiles for a Personnel System
*These two examples represent two security profiles or data security patterns that might be found in a personnel system. Depending on the security profile, a user would have certain restrictions on access to various systems, locations, or data in an organization.*

**SECURITY PROFILE 1**

User: Personnel Dept. Clerk

Location: Division 1

Employee Identification
Codes with This Profile:                    00753, 27834, 37665, 44116

| Data Field Restrictions | Type of Access |
|---|---|
| All employee data for Division 1 only | Read and Update |
| • Medical history data | None |
| • Salary | None |
| • Pensionable earnings | None |

**SECURITY PROFILE 2**

User: Divisional Personnel Manager

Location: Division 1

Employee Identification
Codes with This Profile:        27321

| Data Field Restrictions | Type of Access |
|---|---|
| All employee data for Division 1 only | Read Only |

manager, who cannot update the system but who can read all employee data fields for his or her division, including medical history and salary. These profiles are based on access rules supplied by business groups. The system illustrated in Figure 7-4 provides very fine-grained security restrictions, such as allowing authorized personnel users to inquire about all employee information except that in confidential fields, such as salary or medical history.

## Ensuring Business Continuity

As companies increasingly rely on digital networks for their revenue and operations, they need to take additional steps to ensure that their systems and applications are always available. Many factors can disrupt the performance of a Web site, including denial-of-service attacks, network failure, heavy Internet traffic, and exhausted server resources. Computer failures, interruptions, and downtime translate into disgruntled customers, millions of dollars in lost sales, and the inability to perform critical internal transactions. **Downtime** refers to periods of time in which a system is not operational.

Firms such as those in the airline and financial services industries with critical applications requiring online transaction processing have used fault-tolerant computer systems for many years to ensure 100 percent availability. In **online transaction processing**, transactions entered online are immediately processed by the computer. Multitudinous changes to databases, reporting, and requests for information occur each instant.

**Fault-tolerant computer systems** contain redundant hardware, software, and power supply components that create an environment that provides continuous, uninterrupted service. Fault-tolerant computers contain extra memory chips, processors, and disk storage devices to back up a system and keep it running to prevent failure. They use special software routines or self-checking logic built into their circuitry to detect hardware failures and automatically switch to a backup device. Parts from these computers can be removed and repaired without disruption to the computer system.

Fault tolerance should be distinguished from **high-availability computing**. Both fault tolerance and high-availability computing are designed to maximize application and system availability. Both use backup hardware resources. However, high-availability computing helps firms recover quickly from a system crash, whereas fault tolerance promises continuous availability and the elimination of recovery time altogether. High-availability computing environments are a minimum requirement for firms with heavy electronic commerce processing or for firms that depend on digital networks for their internal operations.

High-availability computing requires backup servers, distribution of processing across multiple servers, high-capacity storage, and good disaster recovery and business continuity plans. The firm's computing platform must be extremely robust with scalable processing power, storage, and bandwidth.

Researchers are exploring ways to make computing systems recover even more rapidly when mishaps occur, an approach called **recovery-oriented computing**. This work includes designing systems that recover quickly, and implementing capabilities and tools to help operators pinpoint the sources of faults in multicomponent systems and easily correct their mistakes (Fox and Patterson 2003).

### Disaster Recovery Planning and Business Continuity Planning

**Disaster recovery planning** devises plans for the restoration of computing and communications services after they have been disrupted by an event such as an earthquake, flood, or terrorist attack. Disaster recovery plans focus primarily on the technical issues involved in keeping systems up and running, such as which files to back up and the maintenance of backup computer systems or disaster recovery services.

For example, MasterCard maintains a duplicate computer center in Kansas City, Missouri, to serve as an emergency backup to its primary computer center in St. Louis. Rather than build their own backup facilities, many firms contract with disaster recovery firms, such as Comdisco Disaster Recovery Services in Rosemont, Illinois, and SunGard

Recovery Services, headquartered in Wayne, Pennsylvania. These disaster recovery firms provide hot sites housing spare computers at locations around the country where subscribing firms can run their critical applications in an emergency.

**Business continuity planning** focuses on how the company can restore business operations after a disaster strikes. The business continuity plan identifies critical business processes and determines action plans for handling mission-critical functions if systems go down.

Business managers and information technology specialists need to work together on both types of plans to determine which systems and business processes are most critical to the company. They must conduct a business impact analysis to identify the firm's most critical systems and the impact a systems outage would have on the business. Management must determine the maximum amount of time the business can survive with its systems down and which parts of the business must be restored first.

### Security Outsourcing

Many companies, especially small businesses, lack the resources or expertise to provide a secure high-availability computing environment on their own. They can outsource many security functions to **managed security service providers (MSSPs)** that monitor network activity and perform vulnerability testing and intrusion detection. Counterpane, VeriSign, and Symantec are leading providers of MSSP services.

## The Role of Auditing

How does management know that information systems security and controls are effective? To answer this question, organizations must conduct comprehensive and systematic audits. An **MIS audit** identifies all of the controls that govern individual information systems and assesses their effectiveness. To accomplish this, the auditor must acquire a thorough understanding of operations, physical facilities, telecommunications, security systems, security objectives, organizational structure, personnel, manual procedures, and individual applications.

The auditor usually interviews key individuals who use and operate a specific information system concerning their activities and procedures. Security, application controls, overall integrity controls, and control disciplines are examined. The auditor should trace the flow of sample transactions through the system and perform tests, using, if appropriate, automated audit software.

Security audits should review technologies, procedures, documentation, training, and personnel. A thorough audit will even simulate an attack or disaster to test the response of the technology, information systems staff, and business employees.

An auditor often traces the flow of sample transactions through an information system and may perform tests using automated audit software. MIS audits help management identify security vulnerabilities and determine whether information system controls are effective.

| Function: Loans<br>Location: Peoria, IL | Prepared by: J. Ericson<br>Date: June 16, 2006 | | Received by: T. Benson<br>Review date: June 28, 2006 | |
|---|---|---|---|---|
| Nature of Weakness and Impact | Chance for Error/Abuse | | Notification to Management | |
| | Yes/No | Justification | Report date | Management response |
| User accounts with missing passwords | Yes | Leaves system open to unauthorized outsiders or attackers | 5/10/06 | Eliminate accounts without passwords |
| Network configured to allow some sharing of system files | Yes | Exposes critical system files to hostile parties connected to the network | 5/10/06 | Ensure only required directories are shared and that they are protected with strong passwords |
| Software patches can update production programs without final approval from Standards and Controls group | No | All production programs require management approval; Standards and Controls group assigns such cases to a temporary production status | | |

**Figure 7-5**
Sample Auditor's List of Control Weaknesses
*This chart is a sample page from a list of control weaknesses that an auditor might find in a loan system in a local commercial bank. This form helps auditors record and evaluate control weaknesses and shows the results of discussing those weaknesses with management, as well as any corrective actions taken by management.*

The audit lists and ranks all control weaknesses and estimates the probability of their occurrence. It then assesses the financial and organizational impact of each threat. Figure 7-5 is a sample auditor's listing of control weaknesses for a loan system. It includes a section for notifying management of such weaknesses and for management's response. Management is expected to devise a plan for countering significant weaknesses in controls.

## 7.4 Technologies and Tools for Security

An array of tools and technologies can help firms secure their systems and data. They include tools for authentication, firewalls, intrusion detection systems, antivirus and anti-spyware software, and encryption.

### Access Control

**Access control** consists of all the policies and procedures a company uses to prevent improper access to systems by unauthorized insiders and outsiders. To gain access, a user must be authorized and authenticated. **Authentication** refers to the ability to know that a person is who he or she claims to be. Access control software is designed to allow only authorized users to use systems or to access data using some method for authentication.

Authentication is often established by using passwords known only to authorized users. An end user uses a password to log on to a computer system and may also use passwords for accessing specific systems and files. However, users often forget passwords, share them, or choose poor passwords that are easy to guess, which compromises security. Password systems that are too rigorous hinder employee productivity. When employees must change complex passwords frequently, they often take shortcuts, such as choosing passwords that are easy to guess or writing down their passwords at their workstations in plain view. Passwords can also be "sniffed" if transmitted over a network or stolen through social engineering.

E-commerce has caused the proliferation of password-protected Web sites. If users employ passwords to access multiple systems and they reuse a password for more than one system, a hacker gaining access to one user account may be able to gain access to others (Ives, Walsh, and Schneider, 2004).

New authentication technologies, such as tokens, smart cards, and biometric authentication, overcome some of these problems. A **token** is a physical device, similar to an identification

Biometric identification uses technologies that read and interpret individual human traits, such as fingerprints, voices, or facial images, in order to grant or deny access to systems.

card, that is designed to prove the identity of a single user. Tokens are small gadgets that typically fit on key rings and display passcodes that change frequently. A **smart card** is a device about the size of a credit card that contains a chip formatted with access permission and other data. (Smart cards are also used in electronic payment systems.) A reader device interprets the data on the smart card and allows or denies access.

**Biometric authentication** is based on the measurement of a physical or behavioral trait that makes each individual unique. It compares a person's unique characteristics, such as the fingerprints, face, or retinal image, against a stored set profile of these characteristics to determine whether there are any differences between these characteristics and the stored profile. If the two profiles match, access is granted. The technology is expensive, and fingerprint and facial recognition technologies are just beginning to be used for security applications.

The Focus on Technology describes how Monsanto, GM, and other companies implemented some of these technologies to improve access control and identity management. These companies wanted to replace ineffective password-based systems that drained worker productivity and prevented them from having enough control over their financial data to meet security standards for the Sarbanes–Oxley Act. As you read this case, try to identify the problems these companies were facing; what alternative solutions were available to management; how well the chosen solution worked; and the people, organization, and technology issues that had to be addressed when developing the solution.

## Firewalls, Intrusion Detection Systems, and Antivirus Software

As growing numbers of businesses expose their networks to Internet traffic, firewalls, intrusion detection systems, and antivirus software have become essential.

### Firewalls

Chapter 6 describes the use of *firewalls* to prevent unauthorized users from accessing private networks. A firewall is a combination of hardware and software that controls the flow of incoming and outgoing network traffic. It is generally placed between the organization's private internal networks and external networks, such as the Internet, although firewalls can

# FOCUS ON TECHNOLOGY   New Solutions for Identity Management

Many companies are discovering that defending against unauthorized employee access to systems requires at least as much attention as protecting against outside intruders. It is not simply the case that disgruntled employees may attempt to harm the company by committing malicious acts. Companies, especially those subject to the requirements of the Sarbanes–Oxley Act or HIPAA, have a legal obligation to demonstrate the security of their networks and data files. If employees have access to sensitive data that do not pertain to their job responsibilities, their employers may not be in compliance with the law. Companies are also combating programs that are used to steal passwords, account data, and other sensitive information that is stored online.

Fortunately, a number of new technologies are available for authenticating users who are attempting to access a system. Among the new technologies for authenticating users are tokens, smart cards, and biometrics, which we have just described. These advanced technologies provide enhanced security at a price. However, the alternative is often nothing better than asking employees to change their passwords more often and make them more complex by adding numbers, uppercase letters, and special characters. Most companies who take this approach are not managing their passwords effectively, are spending too much on the systems they do have, and are frustrating their users. Gartner Inc., the Stamford, Connecticut, research group says that nearly one-third of calls to IT help desks are from employees who are having password problems.

Monsanto Co. is one company that made the leap to overhaul a poor password system. The St. Louis agriculture and biotech company invested several hundred thousand dollars in a token-based system created by ActivCard Corporation in order to demonstrate control of its financial data to auditors. Monsanto was especially concerned about its approximately 6,700 employees who log on to the corporate network remotely while they are traveling. Remote access always presents security risks by itself, but in this case, there was a secondary risk: Monsanto contracted with its ISP, MCI Inc., to manage its user names and passwords. The employees found it difficult to change their passwords, so they rarely did. Furthermore, MCI did not always delete the user accounts of employees when they left Monsanto, so those employees could still access the company's network.

Monsanto invested several hundred thousand dollars to switch to a token-based authentication system from ActivCard Corporation. The tokens, built into most workers' computers, transmit a numerical passcode as they try to access Monsanto's network. All each worker has to remember is his or her personal identification number (PIN). The tokens generate new numerical passcodes

each time a user connects, thereby blunting the effect of malicious spyware programs trying to capture personal information. The several hundred Monsanto employees who use multiple computers to access the Monsanto network carry separate ActivCard tokens, which they use to type in passcodes for each computer they use. By implementing its own token system, Monsanto made its network more secure and saves itself nearly half a million dollars annually in costs related to outsourcing its password management system.

Clarian Health Partners is another example of a company that addressed identity management system problems with innovative technology. Clarian runs three hospitals in Indianapolis where employees have had to use multiple log-in names and passwords to access the company's resources. As a result, many employees wasted time trying to remember their log-in information and some even resorted to writing down passwords, presenting a serious risk to network security. Clarian has replaced this system for accessing sensitive medical and financial data with one that requires a single log-in and password combination as well as a fingerprint scan. The company may replace fingerprint technology with iris scanning in operating rooms because the employees there wear gloves, handle body fluids, and work in a sterile environment. Clarian purchased the password technology and the biometrics component from different vendors. Phil Canada, director of business innovations for Clarian, believes that the company will recoup its half-million-dollar investment inside of a few years if the help desk receives fewer calls about forgotten passwords while saving employees valuable time.

General Motors Corp. (GM) has also learned that addressing identity and access management issues cuts administrative costs and enables its employees to work more efficiently. GM plans to streamline its end-user identity management services into a single global system that will eliminate "silos of identity [data]." The automobile manufacturer will be able to leverage this centralized system toward its goal of a global supply chain and manufacturing model that truly operates as an enterprise.

*Sources:* Riva Richmond, "Who Goes There?" *The Wall Street Journal,* March 21, 2005; Larry Poneman, "The Seven Deadly Sins of Identity Management," *Computerworld,* May 20, 2005; and Jaikumar Viyanan, "GM, Boeing Push Identity Management," *Computerworld,* November 1, 2004.

**To Think About:**
What problems were Monsanto, Clarian, and others having with identity management? What was the impact of those problems? How did they solve these problems? What alternative solutions were available? What people, organization, and technology issues had to be addressed in developing solutions? Do you think the solutions chosen are effective? Why or why not?

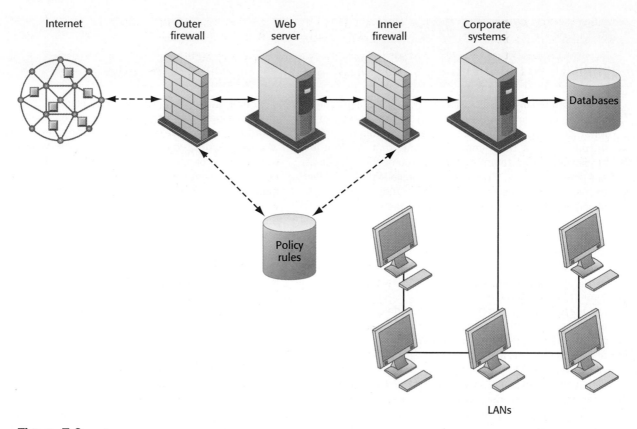

**Figure 7-6**
A Corporate Firewall
*The firewall is placed between the firm's private network and the public Internet or another distrusted network to protect against unauthorized traffic.*

also be used to protect one part of a company's network from the rest of the network (see Figure 7-6).

The firewall acts like a gatekeeper who examines each user's credentials before access is granted to a network. The firewall identifies names, IP addresses, applications, and other characteristics of incoming traffic. It checks this information against the access rules that have been programmed into the system by the network administrator. The firewall prevents unauthorized communication into and out of the network, allowing the organization to enforce a security policy on traffic flowing between its network and other networks, including the Internet.

In large organizations, the firewall often resides on a specially designated computer separate from the rest of the network, so no incoming request can directly access private network resources. There are a number of firewall screening technologies, including static packet filtering, stateful inspection, Network Address Translation, and application proxy filtering. The following techniques are used in combination to provide firewall protection.

**Packet filtering** examines selected fields in the headers of data packets flowing back and forth between the trusted network and the Internet, examining individual packets in isolation. This filtering technology can miss many types of attacks. **Stateful inspection** provides additional security by determining whether packets are part of an ongoing dialogue between a sender and a receiver. It sets up state tables to track information over multiple packets. Packets are accepted or rejected based on whether they are part of an approved conversation or whether they are attempting to establish a legitimate connection.

**Network Address Translation (NAT)** can provide another layer of protection when static packet filtering and stateful inspection are employed. NAT conceals the IP addresses of the organization's internal host computer(s) to prevent sniffer programs outside the firewall from ascertaining them and using that information to penetrate internal systems.

**Application proxy filtering** examines the application content of packets. A proxy server stops data packets originating outside the organization, inspects them, and passes a proxy to the other side of the firewall. If a user outside the company wants to communicate with a user inside the organization, the outside user first "talks" to the proxy application and the proxy application communicates with the firm's internal computer. Likewise, a computer user inside the organization goes through the proxy to talk with computers on the outside.

To create a good firewall, an administrator must write in very fine detail and maintain the internal rules identifying the people, applications, or addresses that are allowed or rejected. Firewalls can deter, but not completely prevent, network penetration by outsiders and should be viewed as one element in an overall security plan. To deal effectively with Internet security, broad corporate policies and procedures, user responsibilities, and security awareness training may be required.

## Intrusion Detection Systems

In addition to firewalls, commercial security vendors now provide intrusion detection tools and services to protect against suspicious network traffic and attempts to access files and databases. **Intrusion detection systems** feature full-time monitoring tools placed at the most vulnerable points or "hot spots" of corporate networks to detect and deter intruders continually. The system generates an alarm if it finds a suspicious or anomalous event. Scanning software looks for patterns indicative of known methods of computer attacks, such as bad passwords, checks to see if important files have been removed or modified, and sends warnings of vandalism or system administration errors. Monitoring software examines events as they are happening to discover security attacks in progress. The intrusion detection tool can also be customized to shut down a particularly sensitive part of a network if it receives unauthorized traffic.

## Antivirus and Antispyware Software

Defensive technology plans for both individuals and businesses must include antivirus protection for every computer. **Antivirus software** is designed to check computer systems and drives for the presence of computer viruses. Often, the software can eliminate the virus from the infected area. However, most antivirus software is effective only against viruses already known when the software was written. To remain effective, the antivirus software must be continually updated. Leading antivirus software vendors include McAfee and Symantec. Software products explicitly designed to eliminate spyware, such as Ad-Aware SE Personal, Spybot Search and Destroy, and Spy Sweeper, are also very helpful.

McAfee is a leading provider of antivirus software and other tools for protecting home and corporate Internet users. An index color of green shows that protective tools are active.

## Securing Wireless Networks

Despite its flaws, WEP provides some margin of security if Wi-Fi users remember to acti-vate it. Corporations can further improve WEP security by using it in conjunction with virtual private network (VPN) technology when a wireless network has access to internal corporate data.

Vendors of Wi-Fi equipment have developed new and stronger security standards. The Wi-Fi Alliance industry trade group issued a Wi-Fi Protected Access (WPA) specification that will work with future wireless LAN products and can update equipment that uses 802.11b. WPA improves data encryption by replacing the static encryption keys used in WEP with longer, 128-bit keys that continually change, making them harder to crack. To strengthen user authentication, WPA provides a mechanism based on the Extensible Authentication Protocol (EAP) that works with a central authentication server to authenti-cate each user on the network before the user can join it. It also employs mutual authentica-tion so that a wireless user does not get pulled into a rogue network that might steal the user's network credentials. Data packets can be checked to make sure they are part of a cur-rent network session and not repeated by hackers to fool network users.

## Encryption and Public Key Infrastructure

Many businesses use encryption to protect digital information that they store, physically transfer, or send over the Internet. **Encryption** is the process of transforming plain text or data into cipher text that cannot be read by anyone other than the sender and the intended receiver. Data are encrypted by using a secret numerical code, called an encryption key, that transforms plain data into cipher text. The message must be decrypted by the receiver.

Two methods for encrypting network traffic on the Web are SSL and S-HTTP. **Secure Sockets Layer (SSL)** and its successor **Transport Layer Security (TLS)** enable client and server computers to manage encryption and decryption activities as they communicate with each other during a secure Web session. **Secure Hypertext Transfer Protocol (S-HTTP)** is another protocol used for encrypting data flowing over the Internet, but it is limited to indi-vidual messages, whereas SSL and TLS are designed to establish a secure connection between two computers.

The capability to generate secure sessions is built into Internet client browser software and servers, and occurs automatically with little user intervention. The client and the server negotiate what key and what level of security to use. Once a secure session is established between the client and the server, all messages in that session are encrypted.

There are two alternative methods of encryption: symmetric key encryption and public key encryption. In symmetric key encryption, the sender and receiver establish a secure Internet session by creating a single encryption key and sending it to the receiver so both the sender and receiver share the same key. The strength of the encryption key is measured by its bit length. Today, a typical key will be 128 bits long (a string of 128 binary digits).

The problem with all symmetric encryption schemes is that the key itself must be shared somehow among the senders and receivers, which exposes the key to outsiders who might just be able to intercept and decrypt the key. A more secure form of encryption called **public key encryption** uses two keys: one shared (or public) and one totally pri-vate, as shown in Figure 7-7. The keys are mathematically related so that data encrypted with one key can be decrypted using only the other key. To send and receive messages, communicators first create separate pairs of private and public keys. The public key is kept in a directory and the private key must be kept secret. The sender encrypts a message with the recipient's public key. On receiving the message, the recipient uses his or her private key to decrypt it.

Digital signatures and digital certificates further help with authentication. A **digital signature** is an encrypted message (such as the sender's name) that only the sender using his or her private key can create. A digital signature is used to verify the origin and contents of a message. It provides a way to associate a message with a sender, performing a function similar to a written signature.

**Figure 7-7**
Public Key Encryption
*A public key encryption system can be viewed as a series of public and private keys that lock data when they are transmitted and unlock the data when they are received. The sender locates the recipient's public key in a directory and uses it to encrypt a message. The message is sent in encrypted form over the Internet or a private network. When the encrypted message arrives, the recipient uses his or her private key to decrypt the data and read the message.*

**Digital certificates** are data files used to establish the identity of users and electronic assets for protection of online transactions (see Figure 7-8). A digital certificate system uses a trusted third party, known as a certificate authority (CA), to validate a user's identity. There are many CAs in the United States and around the world, such as the Federal Reserve System, Microsoft, and the largest issuer of certificates, VeriSign. The CA verifies a digital certificate user's identity offline. This information is put into a CA server, which generates an encrypted digital certificate containing owner identification information and a copy of the owner's public key. The certificate authenticates that the public key belongs to the designated owner. The CA makes its own public key available publicly either in print or perhaps on the Internet. The recipient of an encrypted message uses the CA's public key to decode the digital certificate attached to the message, verifies it was issued by the CA, and then obtains the sender's public key and identification information contained in the certificate. Using this information, the recipient can send an encrypted reply. The digital certificate system would enable, for example, a credit card user and a merchant to validate that their digital certificates were issued by an authorized and trusted third party before they exchange data.

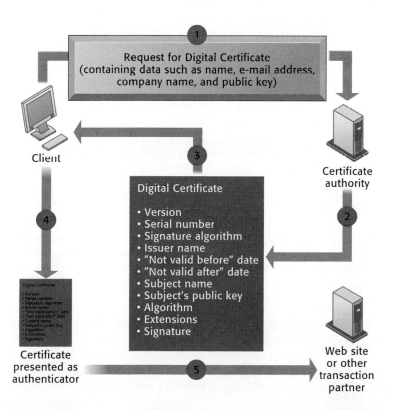

**Figure 7-8**
Digital Certificates
*Digital certificates help establish the identity of people or electronic assets. They protect online transactions by providing secure, encrypted, online communication.*

**Public key infrastructure (PKI)**, the use of public key cryptography working with a certificate authority, is becoming one of the major security technologies for business-to-business commerce on the Internet. Generally, individual consumers do not have digital certificates or public and private keys.

---

### LEARNING TRACKS

1. If you want to learn more about the various types of controls used in information systems, you will find a Learning Track on general and application controls at the Laudon Web site for this chapter.
2. If you want to learn more about management challenges and decisions concerning security and control, you will find a Learning Track on that topic at the Laudon Web site for this chapter.
3. If you want to learn more about software vulnerability and measures to ensure software reliability, you will find a Learning Track on these topics at the Laudon Web site for this chapter.

---

## Summary

**1 Analyze why information systems need special protection from destruction, error, and abuse.** With data concentrated into electronic form and many procedures invisible through automation, computerized information systems are vulnerable to destruction, misuse, error, fraud, and hardware or software failures. Corporate systems using the Internet are especially vulnerable because the Internet is designed to be an open system and makes internal corporate systems more vulnerable to actions from outsiders. Hackers can unleash denial-of-service (DoS) attacks or penetrate corporate networks, causing serious system disruptions. Wi-Fi networks can easily be penetrated by intruders using sniffer programs to obtain an address to access the resources of the network. Computer viruses and worms can spread rampantly from system to system, clogging computer memory or destroying programs and data. Software presents problems because software bugs may be impossible to eliminate and because software vulnerabilities can be exploited by hackers and malicious software. End users can introduce errors.

**2 Assess the business value of security and control.** Security and control are important but often-neglected areas for information systems investment. Firms relying on computer systems for their core business functions can lose sales and productivity. Information assets, such as confidential employee records, trade secrets, or business plans, lose much of their value if they are revealed to outsiders or if they expose the firm to legal liability. New laws, such as HIPAA, the Sarbanes–Oxley Act, and the Gramm–Leach–Bliley Act, require companies to practice stringent electronic records management and adhere to strict standards for security, privacy, and control. Legal actions requiring electronic evidence and computer forensics also require firms to pay more attention to security and electronic records management.

**3 Design an organizational framework for security and control.** Firms need to establish an appropriate organizational and managerial framework for security and control to use technologies effectively to protect their information resources. A risk assessment evaluates information assets, identifies control points and control weaknesses, and determines the most cost-effective set of controls.

Firms must also develop a coherent corporate security policy and plans for continuing business operations in the event of disaster or disruption. The security policy includes policies for acceptable use and authorization. A disaster recovery plan provides procedures and facilities for restoring computing and communication services after they have been disrupted, whereas a business continuity plan focuses on how the company can restore business operations.

Comprehensive and systematic MIS auditing helps organizations determine the effectiveness of security and controls for their information systems.

**4 Evaluate the most important tools and technologies for safeguarding information resources.** Companies require special measures to support electronic commerce and digital business processes. They can use fault-tolerant computer systems or create high-availability computing environments to make sure that their information systems are always available and performing without interruptions. Firewalls are placed between an organization's private network and external networks, such as the Internet, to prevent unauthorized users from accessing the private network. Intrusion detection systems monitor private networks for suspicious network traffic and attempts to access corporate systems. Passwords, tokens, smart cards, and biometric authentication are used to authenticate system users. Antivirus software checks computer systems for infections by viruses and worms and often eliminates the malicious software, whereas antispyware software combats intrusive and harmful spyware programs. Encryption, the coding and scrambling of messages, is a widely used technology for securing electronic transmissions over the Internet and over Wi-Fi networks. Digital certificates combined with public key encryption provide further protection of electronic transactions by authenticating a user's identity.

## Key Terms

Acceptable use policy (AUP), 242
Access control, 245
Antivirus software, 249
Application proxy filtering, 249
Authentication, 245
Authorization management systems, 242
Authorization policies, 242
Biometric authentication, 246
Botnet, 234
Business continuity planning, 244
Chief security officer (CSO), 242
Computer abuse, 237
Computer crime, 234
Computer forensics, 240
Computer virus, 231
Controls, 228
Cracker, 233
Cybervandalism, 233
Denial-of-service (DoS) attack, 233
Digital certificates, 251
Digital signature, 250
Disaster recovery planning, 243

Distributed denial-of-service (DDoS) attack, 233
Downtime, 243
Electronic records management (ERM), 239
Encryption, 250
Evil twins, 237
Fault-tolerant computer systems, 243
Gramm–Leach–Bliley Act, 239
Hacker, 233
High-availability computing, 243
HIPAA, 239
Identity theft, 236
Intrusion detection systems, 249
ISO 17799, 240
Key loggers, 233
Malware, 231
Managed security service providers (MSSPs), 244
MIS audit, 244
Network Address Translation (NAT), 248
Online transaction processing, 243
Packet filtering, 248
Patches, 238

Pharming, 237
Phishing, 236
Public key encryption, 250
Public key infrastructure (PKI), 252
Recovery-oriented computing, 243
Risk assessment, 241
Sarbanes–Oxley Act, 239
Secure Hypertext Transfer Protocol (S-HTTP), 250
Secure Sockets Layer (SSL), 250
Security, 228
Security policy, 241
Smart card, 246
Sniffer, 233
Social engineering, 238
Spamming, 237
Spoofing, 233
Spyware, 233
Stateful inspection, 248
Token, 245
Transport Layer Security (TLS), 250
Trojan horse, 232
War driving, 230
Worms, 231

## Review Questions

**7.1** Why are computer systems so vulnerable? Describe the most common threats against contemporary information systems.

**7.2** Why are the Internet and Wi-Fi networks so difficult to secure?

**7.3** What is malware? Distinguish among a virus, a worm, and a Trojan horse.

**7.4** What is a hacker? How do hackers create security problems and damage systems?

**7.5** How can software affect system reliability and security?

**7.6** What is computer crime? Provide two examples of crime in which computers are targets and two examples in which computers are used as instruments of crime.

**7.7** What is identity theft? Why is it such a big problem today? How does phishing promote identity theft?

**7.8** How can computer systems and networks be used for cyberterrorism and cyberwarfare?

**7.9** What security problems are created by employees?

**7.10** Define security and control. How do they provide business value? How are security and control related to recent U.S. government regulatory requirements and to computer forensics?

**7.11** What is the function of risk assessment? How is it conducted for information systems?

**7.12** Define and describe the following: security policy, acceptable use policy, and authorization policy.

**7.13** Distinguish between fault-tolerant and high-availability computing, and between disaster recovery planning and business continuity planning.

**7.14** How does MIS auditing enhance the control process?

**7.15** Name and describe three authentication methods.

**7.16** Describe the roles of firewalls, intrusion detection systems, and antivirus software in promoting security.

**7.17** How can encryption be used to protect information? Describe the role of encryption and digital certificates in a public key infrastructure.

## Discussion Questions

**7.1** Security isn't simply a technology issue, it's a business issue. Discuss.

**7.2** If you were developing a business continuity plan for your company, where would you start? What aspects of the business would the plan address?

## Application Software Exercise

## Spreadsheet Exercise: Performing a Security Risk Assessment

Software skills: Spreadsheet formulas and charts

Business skills: Risk assessment

Mercer Paints is a small but highly regarded paint manufacturing company located in Alabama. The company has a network in place linking many of its business operations. Although the firm believes that its security is adequate, the recent addition of a Web site has become an open invitation to hackers. Management requested a risk assessment. The risk assessment identified a number of potential exposures. These exposures, their associated probabilities, and average losses are summarized in the following table.

**Mercer Paints Risk Assessment**

| Exposure | Probability of Occurrence (%) | Average Loss ($) |
|---|---|---|
| Malware attack | 60% | $75,000 |
| Data loss | 12% | $70,000 |
| Embezzlement | 3% | $30,000 |
| User errors | 95% | $25,000 |
| Threats from hackers | 95% | $90,000 |
| Improper use by employees | 5% | $5,000 |
| Power failure | 15% | $300,000 |

In addition to the potential exposures listed, you should identify at least three other potential threats to Mercer Paints, assign probabilities, and estimate a loss range. Using spreadsheet software and the risk assessment data, calculate the expected annual loss for each exposure. Present your findings in the form of a chart. Which control points have the greatest vulnerability? What recommendations would you make to Mercer Paints? Prepare a written report that summarizes your findings and recommendations.

## Developing a Disaster Recovery Plan

Business skills: Disaster recovery planning

Management is concerned that Dirt Bikes's computer systems could be vulnerable to power outages, vandalism, computer viruses, natural disasters, or telecommunications disruptions. You have been asked to perform an analysis of system vulnerabilities and disaster recovery planning for the company. Your report should answer the following questions:

1. What are the most likely threats to the continued operation of Dirt Bikes's systems?
2. What would you identify as Dirt Bikes's most critical systems? What is the impact on the company if these systems cannot operate? How long could the company survive if these systems were down? Which systems are the most important to back up and restore in the event of a disaster?
3. Use the Web to locate two disaster recovery services that could be used by a small business such as Dirt Bikes. Compare them in terms of the services they offer. Which should Dirt Bikes use? Exactly how could these services help Dirt Bikes recover from a disaster?
4. (Optional) If possible, use electronic presentation software to summarize your findings for management.

## Building Internet Skills

### Evaluating Security Outsourcing Services

This project will help develop your Internet skills in using the Web to research and evaluate business outsourcing services.

Data and network security are major challenges, and many companies have taken actions to protect their equipment and access to their data. Some of those companies have chosen to outsource the security function rather than train their own staff or hire specialists from outside the company. Finding security outsourcing services can be difficult, although finding sources that help you decide whether to outsource is much easier. In both cases, use several search engines to find sources that can help you decide whether to outsource and to locate companies that offer outsourcing of computer security.

As an information systems expert in your firm, you have been assigned the following tasks. First, present a brief summary of the arguments for and against outsourcing computer security. Second, select two firms that offer computer security outsourcing services, and compare them and their services. Third, prepare a written recommendation to management on whether you believe they should opt for outsourcing computer security and on which of the two firms you believe they should select if they do decide to outsource.

## Video Case

You will find a video case illustrating some of the concepts in this chapter on the Laudon Web site at **www.prenhall.com/laudon** along with questions to help you analyze the case.

## Teamwork

### Evaluating Security Software Tools

With a group of three or four students, use the Web to research and evaluate security products from two competing vendors, such as antivirus software, firewalls, or antispyware software. For each product, describe its capabilities, for what types of businesses it is best suited, and its cost to purchase and install. Which is the best product? Why? If possible, use electronic presentation software to present your findings to the class.

## BUSINESS PROBLEM-SOLVING CASE

### MasterCard and CardSystems: The Worst Data Theft Ever?

Picture yourself making a purchase at your local super-market or electronics store. The cashier rings up your total and you swipe your credit card in the checkout terminal. In less than a minute, sometimes mere seconds, the transaction is approved and you are signing the sales receipt. But have you ever thought about what exactly is happening during those moments while you wait for your credit card to be approved? The checkout terminal converts the cardholder's data into a digital message and routes it to a payment processing company that is employed by the merchant's bank. This processing center uses the account number to record the payment at the merchant's terminal and to route the transaction to the appropriate card payment network (MasterCard, Visa, American Express, etc.). Then a processing company contracted by the cardholder's bank identifies the account and authorizes the payment. The cardholder's bank then issues a credit for the sale. A message authorizing the payment flows back to the merchant over the same pathway. Finally, the merchant's terminal accepts the authorization and prints the sales receipt. A similar process is responsible for the settlement of the transaction, during which funds are transferred from the cardholder's bank to the merchant's bank.

In the short time that you are waiting at the checkout register, your credit card data bounces around quite a bit. Many credit card customers may take it for granted that these transactions are secure. However, on June 17, 2005, MasterCard International announced what could be the largest breach of data security ever made public: Data from as many as 40 million credit card accounts had been exposed in a hacking incident. The breach occurred not at a MasterCard facility, but at the Tucson, Arizona, location of a payment processing company named CardSystems Solutions. The exposed accounts included 22 million Visa cards, 13.9 million MasterCards, and smaller numbers of American Express and Discover cards. According to James Van Dyke, principal analyst at Javelin Strategy & Research in Pleasanton, California, "In sheer numbers, this is probably one of the largest data security breaches."

The breach occurred when a hacker exploited security vulnerabilities in the CardSystems network by placing a small computer program, or script, on CardSystems's network that made it possible to gain access to cardholder data. The data were not encrypted. Encryption would not have prevented the theft but would have made the stolen data less valuable and, perhaps, useless. MasterCard security analysts worked with law enforcement officials to trace a pattern of fraudulent charges to the intrusion. The credit card company says that it began the investigation when a number of banks reported unusually high levels of fraudulent charges. According to CardSystems, the security incident happened on May 22, 2005, and the company notified the FBI, as well as Visa and MasterCard, the next day. Initially, Visa did not comment on the breach at the request of the investigators.

In the early days of the investigation, the FBI was still trying to determine the scope of the breach. CardSystems admits that of the 40 million credit and debit card accounts that were exposed, the data for 200,000 of the cards was actually stolen. The card brands affected were Visa, MasterCard, and American Express. Both CardSystems and the credit card companies moved to comfort customers whose data might have been stolen. The credit card companies assured their customers that they would not be held responsible for any fraudulent charges. CardSystems revealed that the exposed data consisted of names, credit card numbers, expiration dates, and security codes, but not dates of birth or social security numbers. Therefore, the stolen accounts could be used for credit card fraud but likely not identify theft.

Although the consequences of this incident are certainly worthy of consideration, the more important questions are, "How did this happen?" and "How could it have been prevented?" One explanation is that credit card companies lack the financial incentive to protect consumer data because neither the companies nor their customers suffer losses. The damage from credit card fraud falls on merchants who lose inventory and must pay fees to reverse authorized charges.

Credit card companies use elaborate security measures to protect their data. Moreover, MasterCard does have rules for the handling of its data by third-party processing companies such as CardSystems. For example, the processing companies are supposed to transfer credit card information to the appropriate banks, but the processors are not supposed to retain that information. CardSystems acknowledged it was storing transaction records of thousands of cardholders, including data on their names, account numbers, expiration dates, and security codes, in violation of both MasterCard and Visa's rules. The company explained it was doing so for research purposes, specifically to analyze why certain transactions were not authorized or completed. Laws do not govern the security requirements that credit cards companies set up for their payment processors, but Visa and MasterCard can levy six-figure fines against processors who fail to comply with the rules. CardSystems stopped the practice of storing cardholder data soon after the discovery of the security breach. Of course, by that time, it was apparent that an intruder had exported a file containing the account information for 68,000 MasterCard customers and 100,000 Visa customers.

In addition to the criminal investigation launched by the FBI, federal banking regulators initiated an investigation into the security systems of CardSystems, the major credit card companies, and the banks that were connected to the attack. However, the Federal Financial Institutions Examination Council, an interagency group of the five federal banking regulators, does not have direct enforcement powers over payment processors such as CardSystems. The council's investigation intended to review CardSystems's financial and security audits as well as to determine whether their systems and controls met government security deadlines. Ultimately, though, the banks and credit card companies are responsible for ensuring that the payment processors follow their security guidelines. The council does have enforcement power over these financial institutions. The banks and payment associations must submit to an IT and security assessment by the council every 18 to 36 months. However, the council investigates the processing companies only when an issue or risk makes it necessary.

According to some, this wait-and-see approach seems to be true of the credit card companies, too. Avivah Litan, an analyst with Gartner Inc., says that banks and credit card companies are not watching their payment processors closely enough. Instead, the financial institutions "just sort of wait for them to have a breach" and their enforcement of security requirements is vague. It may be cheaper for banks to pay for fraud losses when they occur than to reissue hundreds of thousands of credit cards at a cost of $10 to $20 per card. Litan goes on to say that breaches, such as the one at CardSystems, have happened previously but were not made public. Jessica Antle, a spokeswoman for MasterCard, said that CardSystems had never demonstrated compliance with MasterCard's security guidelines. MasterCard put CardSystems on notice after the breach. A Visa spokeswoman, Rosetta Jones, also admitted that CardSystems was not following security requirements when Visa found out about the breach. CardSystems says that it was audited in late 2003 by an independent auditor and that the Visa payment associations approved its operations in June 2004.

In California, state law now requires companies to notify customers when their personal data have been compromised. The U.S. Congress is considering similar legislation on the federal level. This legal pressure may account for the increase in reports of data security problems in 2004 and 2005. Approximately a week before the MasterCard announcement, Citigroup announced that United Parcel Service had lost a shipment of tapes containing unencrypted data for 3.9 million customers of its CitiFinancial subsidiary. Citigroup suffered a similar setback in early 2004 when data tapes from its Citibank division were lost during transit from a data management center in Singapore. In that case, the names, addresses, account numbers, and balances of 120,000 Japanese customers were lost. Bank of America, Wachovia, the data brokers ChoicePoint and LexisNexis, as well as the University of California at Berkeley and Stanford University all reported data leaks during a similar period. Legislation of data theft reporting does not change the fact that financial institutions, and particularly data processing companies, remain popular and ripe targets for account and identity thieves.

Stolen credit card account numbers, especially those that include security codes, are so valuable to cybercriminals because they are elastic commodities. Thieves can use individual accounts to purchase goods fraudulently or receive cash advances. They can also sell the stolen accounts in bulk to individuals or organizations that deal on the black market. The FBI has shut down some of these organizations, which often have ominous names,

such as ShadowCrew and DarkProfits. However, the black market thrives, especially online where it is highly structured and organizations are brazen; one Web site that sells stolen card data is iaaca.com, which stands for International Association for the Advancement of Criminal Activity. The criminals are spread throughout the world, but a large percentage of their activity is hosted on servers in the former Soviet republics, where law enforcement officials have difficulty finding them. The black market even has its own lingo for products and services. Opinions vary on whether law enforcement can win the battle with cybercriminals, given the weaknesses in data security and the ever-advancing technological expertise of the foe. Credit card processing companies remain very attractive targets for cybercriminals because they store such large numbers of payment records.

Within a very short time after the revelation of the CardSystems breach, opportunistic phishing scams targeted at MasterCard customers began circulating. The e-mails provided a link that the users were instructed to click on in order to enter their user names and passwords so that they could verify or update their account data.

Mike Gibbons, a security consultant for Unisys, says that fighting cybercriminals requires a holistic approach that includes securing online access methods, stronger methods of customer authentication, hiring dedicated security staff, and improving methods for moving large amounts of customer data. In addition to protecting data resources from outside intruders, companies must also strengthen internal controls so that employees cannot access files, applications, and areas of the network that are not relevant to their jobs. Companies can establish these controls by fortifying password protection with complex passwords, tokens, smart cards, and biometric devices. However, most companies would require a motivation for taking such costly measures other than that they are for the good of the people.

One potential motivator is further pressure from legislation. When the Sarbanes–Oxley Act went into effect in 2002, public companies were forced to have the accuracy of their financial records validated by auditors. Compliance with Sarbanes–Oxley includes proving that the networks on which financial data reside are safeguarded against tampering. Failure to comply can result in penalties for the companies and for the individual officers responsible for financial reporting. Data security expert Bruce Schneier believes that the government should apply this model to personal data security and impose fines for every account that a company loses ($1,000 per name). Democratic Senator Charles Schumer of New York has proposed an Office of Identity Theft to operate under the Federal Trade Commission. The office would set minimum security standards for any organization that handles sensitive personal data, as well as fine organizations that fail to uphold the standards. Republican Representative Clif Stearns of Florida has proposed a similar bill that would require companies to develop written data security policies.

Some of the recent personal data security breaches have been categorized as simple mishaps rather than as attacks or crimes, particularly those in which shipping companies lost data tapes. However, even these incidents point out the critical need to improve the security of sensitive data. Replacing the shipment of data on physical tapes with transmission over secure, high-speed networks, which is a significant financial commitment, is another decision confronting companies such as MasterCard.

In the wake of the CardSystems breach, California consumers and retailers filed a class action lawsuit against CardSystems, MasterCard, and Visa for violating state law by failing to properly secure their networks and by failing to quickly notify consumers after the breach occurred. Visa and American Express terminated their relationship with CardSystems. Without these large clients, CardSystems was no longer a viable business. In September 2005 CyberSource Corporation announced plans to purchase all of CardSystems' assets.

*Sources:* Eric Dash and Tom Zeller, Jr., "MasterCard Says 40 Million Files Put at Risk," *The New York Times,* www.nytimes.com, accessed June 18, 2005; Eric Dash, "Lost Credit Data Improperly Kept, Company Admits," *The New York Times,* www.nytimes.com, accessed June 20, 2005; The Associate Press, "Security Leak Reveals Weaknesses," *The New York Times,* www.nytimes.com, accessed June 20, 2005; Tom Zeller, Jr., "Black Market in Stolen Credit Card Data Thrives on Internet," *The New York Times,* www.nytimes.com, accessed June 21, 2005; "Responding to Data-Security Needs," *Top Tech News,* October 20, 2005; Joris Evers, "MasterCard Scandal: Worst Data Theft Ever?," www.silicon.com, accessed June 20, 2005; Julie Creswell and Eric Dash, "Banks Unsure Which Cards Were Exposed in Breach," *The New York Times,* www.nytimes.com, accessed June 21, 2005; Tom Zeller, Jr., "The Scramble to Protect Personal Data," *The New York Times,* June 9, 2005; Riva Richmond, "Who Goes There?" *The Wall Street Journal,* March 21, 2005; Jeanne Sahadi, "ID Data Breaches: As Rampant as It Seems," *CNNMoney,* www.cnnmoney.com, accessed June 21, 2005; John Leyden, "MasterCard Hack Spawns Phishing Attack," *The Register,* www.theregister.co.uk, accessed June 20, 2005; Robert Lemos, "Phishers Look to Net Small Fry," *The Register,* www.theregister.co.uk, accessed June 20, 2005; and Eric Dash, "Regulators Start Inquiry in Data Loss," *The New York Times,* www.nytimes.com, accessed June 22, 2005.

## Case Study Questions

1. What is the problem faced by MasterCard and the other credit card companies and banks in this case? What caused the problem? What is its impact?

2. Has MasterCard correctly identified the problem? What are the people, organization, and technology issues associated with the problem? Has MasterCard identified these issues? What other evidence or information do you recommend that the credit card companies and banks obtain about this problem?

3. What solutions were considered by MasterCard and the other companies that are dealing with this problem? Were the solutions appropriate? Are there other solutions that should have been considered?

4. What is the best solution to this problem for the parties involved? Why? Do you think that MasterCard will be successful in solving this problem? Explain your answer.

5. Explain the differences in approach to this problem taken by MasterCard, CardSystems, security experts, and the government.

# Key System Applications for the Digital Age

## PART III

Part III examines the core information system applications businesses are using today to improve operational excellence and decision making. These applications include enterprise systems; systems for supply chain management, customer relationship management, and knowledge management; e-commerce applications; decision-support systems; and executive support systems. This part answers questions such as these: How can enterprise applications improve business performance? How do firms use e-commerce to extend the reach of their businesses? How can systems improve decision making and help companies make better use of their knowledge assets?

# Achieving Operational Excellence and Customer Intimacy: Enterprise Applications

CHAPTER **8**

## STUDENT OBJECTIVES

After completing this chapter, you will be able to:

1. Demonstrate how enterprise systems achieve operational excellence by integrating and coordinating diverse functions and business processes in the firm.

2. Demonstrate how supply chain management systems coordinate planning, production, and logistics with suppliers.

3. Demonstrate how customer relationship management systems achieve customer intimacy by integrating all customer information and making it available throughout the firm.

4. Assess the challenges and new opportunities raised by enterprise applications.

## Chapter Outline

## WHIRLPOOL FIXES ITS SUPPLY CHAIN

**Whirlpool, based in Benton Harbor,** Michigan, is the number one U.S. home appliance maker, producing washers, dryers, refrigerators, ovens, and more under brand names such as Whirlpool, Kitchen Aid, Roper, and Speed Queen. Whirlpool has nearly 50 manufacturing and research centers all over the world and 68,000 employees. The company had grown so much by acquisition and geographic expansion that it strained its old systems for supply chain management.

By 2000, Whirlpool's supply chain "system" had become what salespeople called a "sales disabler." Whirlpool's inventory of finished goods was very high, yet the percentage of time that Whirlpool's products were available when customers needed them was an unacceptably low 87 percent. Staff grimly joked that among the four major U.S. appliance makers, Whirlpool ranked fifth in delivery performance.

The systems Whirlpool used at that time to manage its North American supply chain consisted of aging custom-developed systems for production scheduling and distribution planning; demand forecasting software from i2 Technologies that had been installed in 1997; and SAP's R/3 enterprise resource planning (ERP) software for accounting and order processing. The homegrown systems were very outdated and not well integrated with the ERP system or each other. They also weren't integrated with the systems of major suppliers of parts and materials and of wholesale customers. As a result, Whirlpool's supply chain management systems lacked precision and could only balance priorities and constraints through slow and cumbersome manual procedures.

In 2001, Whirlpool began a global overhaul of its supply chain systems. Manufacturing companies typically think about their supply chains as something that originates with suppliers. Whirlpool's management decided its supply chain solution should focus on serving the customer. A world-class solution that would surpass the performance of Whirlpool's best competitors on every front would cost $85 million, which was much too expensive. So managers settled on alternative solutions where the company could meet—and sometimes beat—the competition at a minimum cost. Whirlpool implemented an advanced planning and scheduling (APS) system that included a suite of supply chain integration and optimization software from i2 Technologies. These tools consisted of Supply Chain Planner for Master Scheduling, Deployment Planning, and Inventory Planning. These three modules were implemented in three phases in 2001 and 2002.

In 2002, Whirlpool installed i2 TradeMatrix Collaborative Planning, Forecasting, and Replenishment (CPFR), a Web-based tool for sharing and combining the sales forecasts of Whirlpool and its major sales partners—Sears, Roebuck and Co., Lowe's, and Best Buy.

Even before Whirlpool's supply chain project was completed, it had already produced huge improvements in customer service and reduced supply chain costs. APS boosted availability in North America to 97 percent while reducing finished-goods inventories by more than 20 percent, and freight and warehouse costs by 5 percent. CPFR cut the number of forecasting errors in half. ■

*Sources:* Gary H. Anthes, "Supply Chain Whirl," *Computerworld,* June 6, 2005, www.whirlpool.com, accessed June 8, 2005; and Reuben E. Slone, "Leading a Supply Chain Turnaround," *Harvard Business Review,* October 2004.


Like all large firms, Whirlpool has several hundred main suppliers of parts (the first tier of Whirlpool's supply chain), and these suppliers in turn have several hundred suppliers of basic raw materials (the second tier of Whirlpool's supply chain). Altogether, Whirlpool has several thousand firms that sell everything from steel and plastic assemblies, to computer chips and controls that end up in Whirlpool appliances. Coordinating all these firms so the right parts show up at the Whirlpool factories just at the right time and the right amount of finished appliances actually ordered by customers are in the warehouses is a major problem for Whirlpool. All firms—big and small—face the same kind of problem: how to coordinate the activities of their suppliers and distribution channels.

Whirlpool's problems with its supply chain illustrate the critical role of supply chain management in business. Whirlpool lost sales because it couldn't balance supply with demand across multiple distribution sites and locations to make sure the right amount of products required by customers were in the right stores and warehouses at the right time. The company needed better control over its supply chain.

One solution tried by Whirlpool was to overstock its warehouses to ensure items were in plentiful supply, even if there were more than enough for customer orders. However, this raised inventory carrying costs, further eroding profits. Moreover, the company continued to lose sales because its systems still made the wrong decisions about which specific items to stock in warehouses. Retail sellers still did not have the appliances customers wanted at the time of purchase. An $85 million design that would give Whirlpool superior performance over competitors was rejected as too expensive.

Whirlpool had to choose among several alternative system designs. The most promising solution for Whirlpool was to develop new supply chain management systems that did a bet-

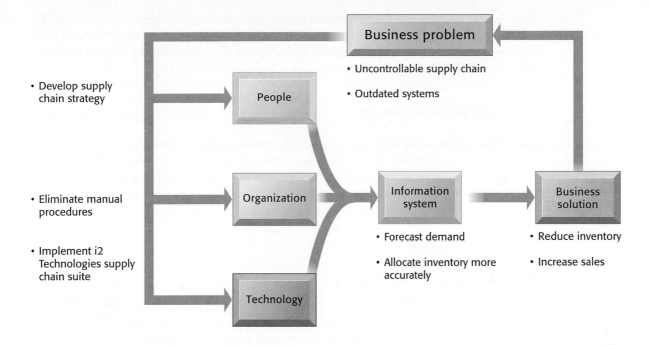

ter job at balancing supply with demand and that focused on availability of goods for the customer. Management believed the most appropriate solution was a series of systems that gave Whirlpool enough supply chain management capability to at least match—and sometimes beat—the competition at a minimum cost. The opening case provides evidence that Whirlpool's new supply chain management systems have already improved operational efficiency and customer service.

---

**HEADS UP**

This chapter focuses on how firms use enterprise-wide systems to achieve the business objectives of operational excellence, customer intimacy, and improved decision making. Electronic commerce and global competition require firms to increase their speed to market, improve customer service, and become more efficient. These changes call for powerful new systems that integrate information from many different parts of the business, forge closer ties with customers, and coordinate firm activities with those of suppliers and other business partners.

• If your career is in finance and accounting, you will be working with enterprise resource planning systems with comprehensive financial modules that integrate financial information from manufacturing, marketing, and sales.

• If your career is in human resources, you will be helping your firm deal with the "people" issues that are critical to the successful implementation of enterprise applications, such as changing job responsibilities, new training, and overcoming resistance to the change.

• If your career is in manufacturing, production, or operations management, you will be using enterprise systems and supply chain management systems to plan, make, and deliver products and services to customers more rapidly and accurately at lower cost.

• If your career is in sales and marketing, you will be using customer relationship management systems to plan marketing campaigns, implement cross-selling activities, identify profitable customers, advance new products and services, generate sales leads, manage customer orders, and fine-tune customer service.

This chapter describes three major enterprise applications—enterprise systems and systems for supply chain management and customer relationship management. You'll learn how they work, their business benefits, and some of their challenges and opportunities. We discuss knowledge management systems in the following chapter.

## 8.1 Enterprise Systems

Around the globe, companies are increasingly becoming more connected, both internally and with other companies. If you run a business, you'll want to be able to react instantaneously when a customer places a large order or when a shipment from a supplier is delayed. You may also want to know the impact of these events on every part of the business and how the business is performing at any point in time, especially if you're running a large company. Enterprise systems provide the integration to make this possible. Let's look at how they work and what they can do for the firm.

### What Are Enterprise Systems?

Imagine that you had to run a business based on information from tens or even hundreds of different databases and systems, none of which could speak to one another. Imagine your company had 10 different major product lines, each produced in separate factories, and each with separate and incompatible sets of systems controlling production, warehousing, and distribution. At the very least, your decision making would often be based on manual hard copy reports, often out of date, and it would be difficult to really understand what is happening in the business as whole. You now have a good idea of why firms need a special enterprise system to integrate information.

Chapter 2 introduced enterprise systems, also known as enterprise resource planning (ERP) systems, which are based on a suite of integrated software modules and a common central database. The database collects data from many different divisions and departments in a firm, and from a large number of key business processes in manufacturing and production, finance and accounting, sales and marketing, and human resources, making the data available for applications that support nearly all of an organization's internal business activities. When new information is entered by one process, the information is made immediately available to other business processes (see Figure 8-1).

**Figure 8-1**
How Enterprise
Systems Work
*Enterprise systems feature a set of integrated software modules and a central database that enables data to be shared by many different business processes and functional areas throughout the enterprise.*

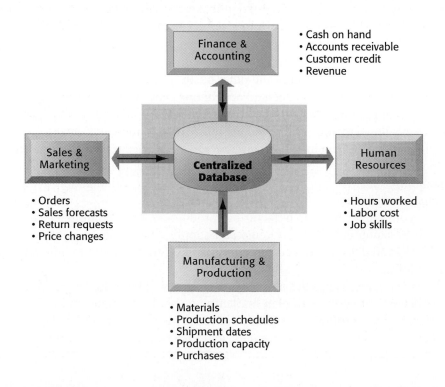

• Cash on hand
• Accounts receivable
• Customer credit
• Revenue

Finance & Accounting

Sales & Marketing

Centralized Database

Human Resources

• Orders
• Sales forecasts
• Return requests
• Price changes

• Hours worked
• Labor cost
• Job skills

Manufacturing & Production

• Materials
• Production schedules
• Shipment dates
• Production capacity
• Purchases

If a sales representative places an order for tire rims, for example, the system verifies the customer's credit limit, schedules the shipment, identifies the best shipping route, and reserves the necessary items from inventory. If inventory stock were insufficient to fill the order, the system schedules the manufacture of more rims, ordering the needed materials and components from suppliers. Sales and production forecasts are immediately updated. General ledger and corporate cash levels are automatically updated with the revenue and cost information from the order. Users could tap into the system and find out where that particular order was at any minute. Management could obtain information at any point in time about how the business was operating. The system could also generate enterprise-wide data for management analyses of product cost and profitability.

## How Enterprise Systems Work

**Enterprise software** is built around thousands of predefined business processes that reflect best practices. **Best practices** are the most successful solutions or problem-solving methods for consistently and effectively achieving a business objective. Table 8.1 describes some of the major business processes supported by enterprise software.

Companies implementing this software would have to first select the functions of the system they wished to use and then map their business processes to the predefined business processes in the software. A particular firm would use configuration tables provided by the software to tailor a particular aspect of the system to the way it does business. For example, the firm could use these tables to select whether it wants to track revenue by product line, geographical unit, or distribution channel.

If the enterprise software does not support the way the organization does business, companies can rewrite some of the software to support the way their business processes work. However, enterprise software is unusually complex, and extensive customization may degrade system performance, compromising the information and process integration that are the main benefits of the system. If companies want to reap the maximum benefits from enterprise software, they must change the way they work to conform to the business processes in the software.

Major enterprise software vendors include SAP, Oracle-PeopleSoft, and SSA Global. There are versions of enterprise software packages designed for small businesses and versions obtained through application service providers over the Web. Although initially designed to automate the firm's internal "back-office" business processes, enterprise systems have become more externally oriented and capable of communicating with customers, suppliers, and other organizations.

**TABLE 8.1**

**Business Processes Supported by Enterprise Systems**

*Financial and accounting processes,* including general ledger, accounts payable, accounts receivable, fixed assets, cash management and forecasting, product–cost accounting, cost-center accounting, asset accounting, tax accounting, credit management, and financial reporting

*Human resources processes,* including personnel administration, time accounting, payroll, personnel planning and development, benefits accounting, applicant tracking, time management, compensation, workforce planning, performance management, and travel expense reporting

*Manufacturing and production processes,* including procurement, inventory management, purchasing, shipping, production planning, production scheduling, material requirements planning, quality control, distribution, transportation execution, and plant and equipment maintenance

*Sales and marketing processes,* including order processing, quotations, contracts, product configuration, pricing, billing, credit checking, incentive and commission management, and sales planning

## Business Value of Enterprise Systems

Enterprise systems provide value both by increasing operational efficiency and by providing firmwide information to help managers make better decisions. Large companies with many operating units in different locations have used enterprise systems to enforce standard practices and data so that everyone does business the same way worldwide. Nestlé SA, for instance, installed an SAP R/3 enterprise system as a way of standardizing and coordinating its business processes in 500 facilities in 80 countries. Its management had found that decentralized management and lack of standard business processes prevented the company from leveraging its worldwide buying power to obtain lower prices for raw materials and from measuring the effectiveness of its promotional activities.

Enterprise systems help firms respond rapidly to customer requests for information or products. Because the system integrates order, manufacturing, and delivery data, manufacturing is better informed about producing only what customers have ordered, procuring exactly the right amount of components or raw materials to fill actual orders, staging production, and minimizing the time that components or finished products are in inventory.

Enterprise software includes analytical tools for using data captured by the system to evaluate overall organizational performance. Enterprise system data have common standardized definitions and formats that are accepted by the entire organization. Performance figures mean the same thing across the company. Enterprise systems allow senior management to easily find out at any moment how a particular organizational unit is performing or to determine which products are most or least profitable.

The Focus on Technology describes how China Telecom achieved some of these benefits from its enterprise system. This company had been transformed from a local state-run telecommunications company into an international powerhouse. It decided to implement mySAP ERP software to tie its operations together and integrate them so it could meet international accounting and business standards and operate as a much larger global company. As you read this case, try to identify the problem this company was facing; what alternative solutions were available to management; how well the chosen solution worked; and the people, organization, and technology issues that had to be addressed when developing the solution.

## 8.2 Supply Chain Management Systems

If you manage a small firm that makes a few products or sells a few services, chances are you will have a small number of suppliers. You could coordinate your supplier orders and deliveries using a telephone and fax machine, which are the typical tools used in very small businesses for managing suppliers. But if you manage a firm that produces more complex products and services, or a firm that operates on a regional, national, or global basis, then you will have hundreds of suppliers, and your suppliers will each have their own set of suppliers. Suddenly, you are in a situation where you will need to coordinate the activities of hundreds or even thousands of other firms in order to produce your products and services. Supply chain management systems, which we introduced in Chapter 2, are an answer to these problems of supply chain complexity and scale.

Firms use supply chain management systems to exchange information with their suppliers about availability of materials and components, delivery dates for shipments of supplies, and production requirements. Firms also use these systems to exchange information with their distributors and shippers about inventory levels, the status of orders being fulfilled, and delivery dates for shipments of finished goods.

### The Supply Chain

A firm's **supply chain** is a network of organizations and business processes for procuring raw materials, transforming these materials into intermediate and finished products, and distributing the finished products to customers. It links suppliers, manufacturing plants, distribution centers, retail outlets, and customers to supply goods and services from source

# FOCUS ON TECHNOLOGY    China Telecom Turns to Enterprise Resource Planning

China Telecom Corporation, the world's largest operator of fixed-line communications, was formed when the state-owned China Telecommunications Corporation reorganized. China Telecom employs 350,000 workers throughout China, who attend to the company's operations in domestic and international fixed-line networks; fixed-line voice, data, and information services; and the settlement of international telecommunications accounts. The company has maintained steady growth despite heavy competition from mobile phone services.

In 2002, the company became a public company listed on the New York Stock Exchange. That same year, the United States granted China Telecom a license to provide international telephone and Internet service between the countries.

These steps were part of a transition from a traditional state-run enterprise to a modern enterprise based on larger profits and a wider customer base. However, to succeed as an international telecommunications powerhouse, China Telecom had to solve several problems. First, the company required a state-of-the-art IT infrastructure. Second, it needed to comply with international reporting regulations for publicly traded companies. Third, it needed to integrate all of its business functions and enable real-time management. Together, these initiatives would increase organizational efficiency, tighten control over internal operations, and promote better collaboration among different departments.

For a solution, China Telecom decided to invest in enterprise resource planning (ERP) software. The company could have written its own software to link its different business functions and organizational units, but this would have been very costly and time-consuming. It was much easier to use an ERP software package from a recognized vendor. The software is based on best-practice business processes, which would help the company meet international reporting requirements.

According to Shiping Liang, director of the application division at China Telecom, the company chose mySAP ERP from SAP as the backbone system because of its powerful functionality and integration capabilities. Among the core business processes that mySAP ERP supports for China Telecom are engineering project management, finance, controlling, procurement, and human capital management. SAP's ERP financials module supports local currencies, markets, and languages, including Chinese. The SAP human capital management module automates human resources processes and integrates them across global operations. The software meets regulatory requirements for more than 50 countries.

To promote data integration, China Telecom also adopted two components of SAP Netweaver: SAP Business Intelligence (SAP BI) and SAP Enterprise Portal (SAP EP). SAP Netweaver uses XML and Web services to link the enterprise system with a company's existing systems to create new cross-functional applications. SAP Enterprise Portal provides a single point of access to data from multiple systems, integrating the data in a single view for the user. SAP Business Intelligence provides data warehousing capabilities to integrate business data from multiple sources for company-wide reporting.

After considering a number of vendors, China Telecom selected Hewlett-Packard (HP) hardware to run its ERP software because of its scalability, flexibility, low total cost of ownership, and ability to support SAP. Specifically, China Telecom chose the HP 9000 server family to run its SAP applications and HP StorageWorks XP128 Disk Array for its network storage infrastructure.

Eventually, more than 30,000 employees will use the SAP and HP solution at more than 20 China Telecom subsidiaries. The deployment of the SAP software reflects the needs of each subsidiary. For example, most of China Telecom's business comes through Guangzhou and Shanghai, so those offices will use the financial, operations, human capital management, and analytics capabilities of mySAP ERP. The headquarters in Beijing will use mySAP ERP to run human capital management functions to centralize human resources management and consolidate enterprise-wide information.

The integration of data from mySAP ERP has accelerated the flow of information among accounting, procurement, and engineering management functions and encouraged collaboration among departments. Integration of data between the human resources and accounting functions facilitates analysis of personnel costs and performance-based compensation plans, which were previously very time-consuming. The software provides users with quick and easy access to unified data and applications through a Web browser. The hardware platform has stood up to the test of making large volumes of critical data available 24/7.

Going forward, China Telecom will focus on using mySAP ERP to further integrate with other systems so the company has a complete view of all its processes with customers, employees, and supply chain partners.

*Sources:* "SAP Customer Success Story: China Telecom Corporation," www.mysap.com, accessed June 14, 2005; Le Min Lim, "China Telecom Seeks Partner for Expertise," *Bloomberg News,* May 26, 2005, www.iht.com, accessed June 16, 2005; Hou Mingjuan, "China Telecom Gets US License," *China Daily,* June 9, 2002, www.chinatelecom.com.cn, accessed June 15, 2005; and "China's Telecom Industry Faces an Engagement with All Rivals," *People's Daily Online,* english.people.com.cn, May 17, 2005, accessed June 16, 2005.

**To Think About:**

What problems did China Telecom face? How did these problems affect China Telecom's business? How has the company chosen to solve these problems? What other solutions might the company have tried? Analyze the solution that China Telecom chose from the people, technology, and organization perspectives. Did China Telecom choose the best solution? Explain your answer.

through consumption. Materials, information, and payments flow through the supply chain in both directions.

Goods start out as raw materials and, as they move through the supply chain, are transformed into intermediate products (also referred to as components or parts), and finally, into finished products. The finished products are shipped to distribution centers and from there to retailers and customers. Returned items flow in the reverse direction from the buyer back to the seller.

Let's look at the supply chain for Nike sneakers as an example. Nike designs, markets, and sells sneakers, socks, athletic clothing, and accessories throughout the world. Its primary suppliers are contract manufacturers with factories in China, Thailand, Indonesia, Brazil, and other countries. These companies fashion Nike's finished products.

Nike's contract suppliers do not manufacture sneakers from scratch. They obtain components for the sneakers—the laces, eyelets, uppers, and soles—from other suppliers and then assemble them into finished sneakers. These suppliers in turn have their own suppliers. For example, the suppliers of soles have suppliers for synthetic rubber, suppliers for chemicals used to melt the rubber for molding, and suppliers for the molds into which to pour the rubber. Suppliers of laces would have suppliers for their thread, for dyes, and for the plastic lace tips.

Figure 8-2 provides a simplified illustration of Nike's supply chain for sneakers; it shows the flow of information and materials among suppliers, Nike, and Nike's distributors, retailers, and customers. Nike's contract manufacturers are its primary suppliers. The suppliers of soles, eyelets, uppers, and laces are the secondary (Tier 2) suppliers. Suppliers to these suppliers are the tertiary (Tier 3) suppliers.

The *upstream* portion of the supply chain includes the company's suppliers, the suppliers' suppliers, and the processes for managing relationships with them. The *downstream*

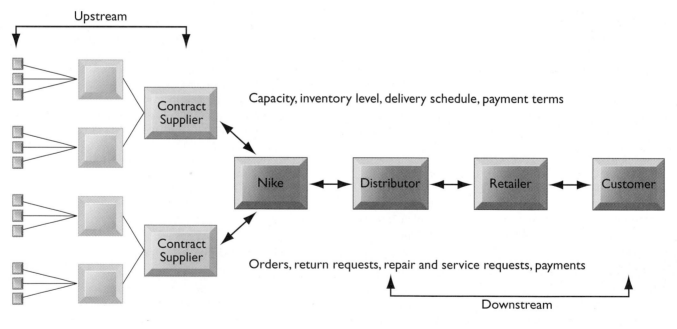

**Figure 8-2**
Nike's Supply Chain
*This figure illustrates the major entities in Nike's supply chain and the flow of information upstream and downstream to coordinate the activities involved in buying, making, and moving a product. Shown here is a simplified supply chain, with the upstream portion focusing only on the suppliers for sneakers and sneaker soles.*

portion consists of the organizations and processes for distributing and delivering products to the final customers. Companies doing manufacturing, such as the Nike's contract suppliers of sneakers, also manage their own *internal supply chain* processes for transforming materials, components, and services furnished by their suppliers into finished products or intermediate products (components or parts) for their customers and for managing materials and inventory.

The supply chain illustrated in Figure 8-2 has been simplified. It only shows two contract manufacturers for sneakers and only the upstream supply chain for sneaker soles. Nike has hundreds of contract manufacturers turning out finished sneakers, socks, and athletic clothing, each with its own set of suppliers. The upstream portion of Nike's supply chain would actually comprise thousands of entities. Nike also has numerous distributors and many thousands of retail stores where its shoes are sold, so the downstream portion of its supply chain is also large and complex.

## Information and Supply Chain Management

Inefficiencies in the supply chain, such as parts shortages, underutilized plant capacity, excessive finished goods inventory, or high transportation costs, are caused by inaccurate or untimely information. For example, manufacturers may keep too many parts in inventory because they do not know exactly when they will receive their next shipments from their suppliers. Suppliers may order too few raw materials because they do not have precise information on demand. These supply chain inefficiencies waste as much as 25 percent of a company's operating costs.

If a manufacturer had perfect information about exactly how many units of product customers wanted, when they wanted them, and when they could be produced, it would be possible to implement a highly efficient **just-in-time** strategy. Components would arrive exactly at the moment they were needed and finished goods would be shipped as they left the assembly line.

In a supply chain, however, uncertainties arise because many events cannot be foreseen—uncertain product demand, late shipments from suppliers, defective parts or raw materials, or production process breakdowns. To satisfy customers, manufacturers often deal with such uncertainties and unforeseen events by keeping more material or products in inventory than what they think they may actually need. The *safety stock* acts as a buffer for the lack of flexibility in the supply chain. Although excess inventory is expensive, low fill rates are also costly because business may be lost from canceled orders.

One recurring problem in supply chain management is the **bullwhip effect**, in which information about the demand for a product gets distorted as it passes from one entity to the next across the supply chain. A slight rise in demand for an item might cause different members in the supply chain—distributors, manufacturers, suppliers, secondary suppliers (suppliers' suppliers), and tertiary suppliers (suppliers' suppliers' suppliers)—to stockpile inventory so each has enough "just in case." These changes ripple throughout the supply chain, magnifying what started out as a small change from planned orders, creating excess inventory, production, warehousing, and shipping costs (see Figure 8-3).

For example, Procter & Gamble (P&G) found it had excessively high inventories of its Pampers disposable diapers at various points along its supply chain because of such distorted information. Although customer purchases in stores were fairly stable, orders from distributors would spike when P&G offered aggressive price promotions. Pampers and Pampers' components accumulated in warehouses along the supply chain to meet demand that did not actually exist. To eliminate this problem, P&G revised its marketing, sales, and supply chain processes and used more accurate demand forecasting (Lee, Padmanabhan, and Wang, 1997).

The bullwhip is tamed by reducing uncertainties about demand and supply when all members of the supply chain have accurate and up-to-date information. If all members of the

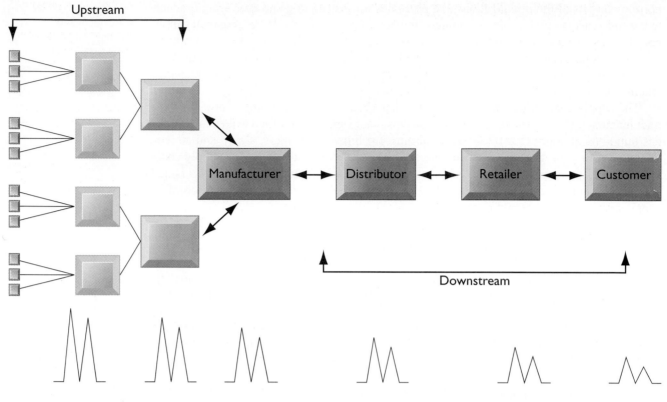

**Figure 8-3**
The Bullwhip Effect
*Inaccurate information can cause minor fluctuations in demand for a product to be amplified as one moves further back in the supply chain. Minor fluctuations in retail sales for a product can create excess inventory for distributors, manufacturers, and suppliers.*

supply chain could share dynamic information about inventory levels, schedules, forecasts, and shipments, they would have a more precise idea of how to adjust their sourcing, manufacturing, and distribution plans. Supply chain management systems provide the kind of information that can help members of the supply chain make better purchasing and scheduling decisions.

## Supply Chain Management Applications

The central objective of supply chain management systems is information visibility—open and rapid communication and information sharing among members of the supply chain. Correct movement of accurate information makes it possible to time orders, shipments, and production properly in order to minimize stocking levels and expedite deliveries to customers. Supply chain management systems automate the flow of information between a company and its supply chain partners so they can make better decisions to optimize their performance.

Supply chain software is classified as either software to help businesses plan their supply chains (supply chain planning) or software to help them execute the supply chain steps (supply chain execution). **Supply chain planning systems** enable the firm to generate demand forecasts for a product and to develop sourcing and manufacturing plans for that product. Such systems help companies make better operating decisions, such as

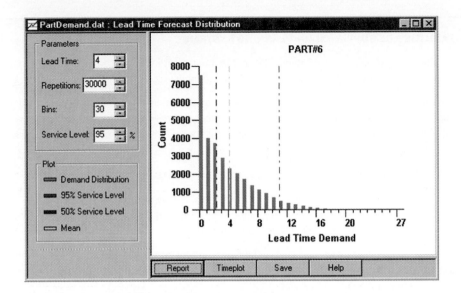

An important use of SmartForecasts demand planning software from Smart Software is to forecast future demand for products where demand is intermittent or irregular. Shown here is a forecast graph for the distribution of total, cumulative demand for a spare part over a four-month lead time.

Reprinted with permission of Smart Software, Inc.

determining how much of a specific product to manufacture in a given time period; establishing inventory levels for raw materials, intermediate products, and finished goods; determining where to store finished goods; and identifying the transportation mode to use for product delivery.

For example, if a large customer places a larger order than usual or changes that order on short notice, it can have a widespread impact throughout the supply chain. Additional raw materials or a different mix of raw materials may need to be ordered from suppliers. Manufacturing may have to change job scheduling. A transportation carrier may have to reschedule deliveries. Supply chain planning software makes the necessary adjustments to production and distribution plans. Information about changes is shared among the relevant supply chain members so that their work can be coordinated. One of the most important—and complex—supply chain planning functions is **demand planning**, which determines how much product a business needs to make to satisfy all of its customers' demands.

**Supply chain execution systems** manage the flow of products through distribution centers and warehouses to ensure that products are delivered to the right locations in the most efficient manner. They track the physical status of goods, the management of materials, warehouse and transportation operations, and financial information involving all parties. Manugistics and i2 Technologies are major supply chain management software vendors, and enterprise software vendors SAP and Oracle-PeopleSoft offer supply chain management modules. Table 8.2 provides more details on supply chain planning and execution systems.

## Supply Chain Management and the Internet

Before the Internet, supply chain coordination was hampered by the difficulties of making information flow smoothly among disparate internal supply chain systems for purchasing, materials management, manufacturing, and distribution. It was also difficult to share information with external supply chain partners because the systems of suppliers, distributors, or logistics providers were based on incompatible technology platforms and standards. Enterprise systems could supply some integration of internal supply chain processes but they were not designed to deal with external supply chain processes.

Some supply chain integration is supplied inexpensively using Internet technology. Firms use *intranets* to improve coordination among their internal supply chain processes,

**TABLE 8.2**

**Supply Chain Planning and Execution Systems**

**CAPABILITIES OF SUPPLY CHAIN PLANNING SYSTEMS**

*Order planning.* Select an order fulfillment plan that best meets the desired level of service to the customer given existing transportation and manufacturing constraints.

*Advanced scheduling and manufacturing planning.* Provide detailed coordination of scheduling based on an analysis of changing factors, such as customer orders, equipment outages, or supply interruptions. Scheduling modules create job schedules for the manufacturing process and supplier logistics.

*Demand planning.* Generate demand forecasts from all business units using statistical tools and business forecasting techniques.

*Distribution planning.* Create operating plans for logistics managers for order fulfillment based on input from demand and manufacturing planning modules.

*Transportation planning.* Track and analyze inbound, outbound, and intracompany movement of materials and products to ensure that materials and finished goods are delivered at the right time and place at the minimum cost.

**CAPABILITIES OF SUPPLY CHAIN EXECUTION SYSTEMS**

*Order commitments.* Enable vendors to quote accurate delivery dates to customers by providing more real-time detailed information on the status of orders from availability of raw materials and inventory to production and shipment status.

*Final production.* Organize and schedule final subassemblies required to make each final product.

*Replenishment.* Coordinate component replenishment work so that warehouses remain stocked with the minimum amount of inventory in the pipeline.

*Distribution management.* Coordinate the process of transporting goods from the manufacturer to distribution centers to the final customer. Provide online customer access to shipment and delivery data.

*Reverse distribution.* Track the shipment and accounting for returned goods or remanufactured products.

and they use *extranets* to coordinate supply chain processes shared with their business partners (see Figure 8-4).

Using intranets and extranets, all members of the supply chain are instantly able to communicate with each other, using up-to-date information to adjust purchasing, logistics, manufacturing, packaging, and schedules. A manager will use a Web interface to tap into suppliers' systems to determine whether inventory and production capabilities match demand for the firm's products. Business partners will use Web-based supply chain management tools to collaborate online on forecasts. Sales representatives will access suppliers' production schedules and logistics information to monitor customers' order status. Many companies now use suppliers from many different countries, and the Internet helps them coordinate overseas sourcing, transportation, communications, financing, and compliance with customs regulations.

### Demand-Driven Supply Chains: From Push to Pull Manufacturing and Efficient Customer Response

In addition to reducing costs, supply chain management systems facilitate efficient customer response, enabling the workings of the business to be driven more by customer demand. (We introduced efficient customer response systems in Chapter 3.)

Earlier supply chain management systems were driven by a push-based model (also known as *build-to-stock*). In a **push-based model**, production master schedules are based

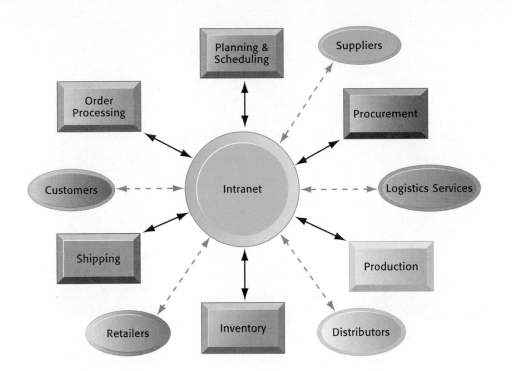

**Figure 8-4**
Intranets and Extranets for Supply Chain Management
*Intranets integrate information from isolated business processes within the firm to help manage its internal supply chain. Access to these private intranets can also be extended to authorized suppliers, distributors, logistics services, and, sometimes, to retail customers to improve coordination of external supply chain processes.*

on forecasts or best guesses of demand for products, and products are "pushed" to customers. With new flows of information made possible by Web-based tools, supply chain management more easily follows a **pull-based model**. In a pull-based model, also known as a *demand-driven model* or *build-to-order,* actual customer orders or purchases trigger events in the supply chain. Transactions to produce and deliver only what customers have ordered move up the supply chain from retailers to distributors to manufacturers and eventually to suppliers. Only products to fulfill these orders move back down the supply chain to the retailer. Manufacturers would use only actual order demand information to drive their production schedules and the procurement of components or raw materials, as illustrated in Figure 8-5. Wal-Mart's continuous replenishment system and Dell Inc.'s build-to-order system, both described in Chapter 3, are examples of the pull-based model.

The Internet and Internet technology make it possible to move from sequential supply chains, where information and materials flow sequentially from company to company, to concurrent supply chains, where information flows in many directions simultaneously

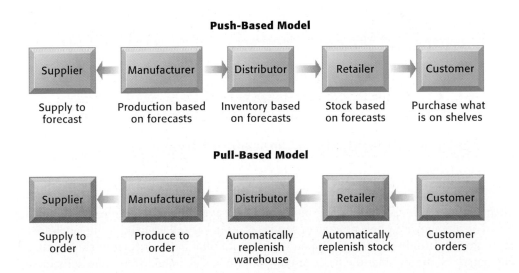

**Figure 8-5**
Push- Versus Pull-Based Supply Chain Models
*The difference between push- and pull-based models is summarized by the slogan "Make what we sell, not sell what we make."*

**Figure 8-6**
The Future Internet-
Driven Supply Chain
*The future Internet-
driven supply chain
operates like a digital
logistics nervous sys-
tem. It provides multidi-
rectional communica-
tion among firms,
networks of firms, and
e-marketplaces so that
entire networks of sup-
ply chain partners can
immediately adjust
inventories, orders, and
capacities.*

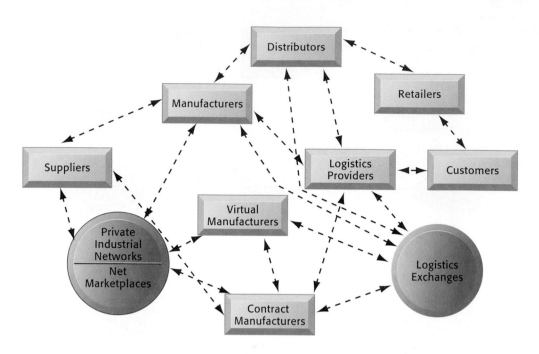

among members of a supply chain network. Members of the network immediately adjust to
changes in schedules or orders. Ultimately, the Internet could create a "digital logistics nervous system" throughout the supply chain. This system permits simultaneous, multidirec-
tional communication of information about participants' inventories, orders, and capacities,
optimizing the activities of individual firms and groups of firms interacting in e-commerce
marketplaces (see Figure 8-6).

## Business Value of Supply Chain Management Systems

You've just seen how supply chain management systems enable firms to streamline both
their internal and external supply chain processes and provide management with more accurate information about what to produce, store, and move. By implementing a networked and
integrated supply chain management system, companies match supply to demand, reduce
inventory levels, improve delivery service, speed product time to market, and use assets
more effectively.

Total supply chain costs represent the majority of operating expenses for many businesses and in some industries approach 75 percent of the total operating budget (Handfield,
1999). Reducing supply chain costs may have a major impact on firm profitability.

In addition to reducing costs, supply chain management systems help increase sales. If a
product is not available when a customer wants it, customers often try to purchase it from
someone else. More precise control of the supply chain enhances the firm's ability to have
the right product available for customer purchases at the right time, as illustrated by the
chapter-opening case on Whirlpool.

## 8.3 Customer Relationship Management Systems

You've probably heard phrases such as "the customer is always right" or "the customer
comes first" or "the customer is king." Obviously, without customers, there would be no
business. Today, these words ring more true than ever. Because competitive advantage
based on an innovative new product or service is often very short-lived, companies are realizing that their only enduring competitive strength may be their relationships with their
customers. Some say that the basis of competition has switched from who sells the most

products and services to who "owns" the customer, and that customer relationships represent a firm's most valuable asset.

## What Is Customer Relationship Management?

What kinds of information would you need to build and nurture strong, long-lasting relationships with customers? You'd want to know exactly who your customers are, how to contact them, whether they are costly to service and sell to, what kinds of products and services they are interested in, and how much money they spend on your company. If you could, you'd want to make sure you knew each of your customers well, as if you were running a small-town store. And you'd want to make your good customers feel special.

In a small business operating in a neighborhood, it is possible for business owners and managers to really know their customers on a personal, face-to-face basis. A good local store manager will remember the faces, and typical purchases of hundreds of customers, as well as family circumstances, such as marriages, births, health, and illnesses. But in a large business operating on a metropolitan, regional, national, or even global basis, it is impossible to "know your customer" in this intimate way. In these kinds of businesses there are too many customers and too many different ways that customers interact with the firm (over the Web, the phone, fax, and face to face). It becomes especially difficult to integrate information from all these sources and to deal with the large numbers of customers.

This is where customer relationship management systems help. Customer relationship management (CRM) systems, which we introduced in Chapter 2, capture and integrate customer data from all over the organization, consolidate the data, analyze the data, and then distribute the results to various systems and customer touch points across the enterprise. A **touch point** (also known as a *contact point*) is a method of interaction with the customer, such as telephone, e-mail, customer service desk, conventional mail, Web site, wireless device, or retail store.

Well-designed CRM systems provide a single enterprise view of customers that is useful for improving both sales and customer service. Such systems likewise provide customers with a single view of the company regardless of what touch point the customer uses (see Figure 8-7).

Good CRM systems provide data and analytical tools for answering questions such as these: "What is the value of a particular customer to the firm over his or her lifetime?" "Who are our most loyal customers?" (It can cost six times more to sell to a new customer than to an existing customer.) "Who are our most profitable customers?" and "What do

**Figure 8-7**
Customer Relationship Management (CRM)
*CRM systems examine customers from a multi-faceted perspective. These systems use a set of integrated applications to address all aspects of the customer relationship, including customer service, sales, and marketing.*

these profitable customers want to buy?" Firms use the answers to these questions to acquire new customers, provide better service and support to existing customers, customize their offerings more precisely to customer preferences, and provide ongoing value to retain profitable customers.

The Focus on Organizations describes how the International House of Pancakes (IHOP) benefited from customer relationship management systems. To learn more about its customers and improve customer communication, IHOP installed Oracle Corporation's Customer Data Hub and Oracle Teleservice software. As you read this case, try to identify the problem this company was facing; what alternative solutions were available to management; how well the chosen solution worked; and the people, organization, and technology issues that had to be addressed when developing the solution.

## CRM Software

Commercial CRM software packages range from niche tools that perform limited functions, such as personalizing Web sites for specific customers, to large-scale enterprise applications that capture myriad interactions with customers, analyze them with sophisticated reporting tools, and link to other major enterprise applications, such as supply chain management and enterprise systems. The more comprehensive CRM packages contain modules for **partner relationship management (PRM)** and **employee relationship management (ERM)**.

PRM uses many of the same data, tools, and systems as customer relationship management to enhance collaboration between a company and its selling partners. If a company does not sell directly to customers but rather works through distributors or retailers, PRM helps these channels sell to customers directly. It provides a company and its selling partners with the ability to trade information and distribute leads and data about customers, integrating lead generation, pricing, promotions, order configurations, and availability. It also provides a firm with tools to assess its partners' performances so it can make sure its best partners receive the support they need to close more business.

ERM software deals with employee issues that are closely related to CRM, such as setting objectives, employee performance management, performance-based compensation, and employee training. Major CRM application software vendors include Siebel Systems, (acquired by Oracle Corp). Clarify, and salesforce.com. Enterprise software vendors, such as SAP and Oracle-PeopleSoft, are also active in customer relationship management and feature tools for integrating their enterprise system modules with their customer relationship management modules.

Customer relationship management systems typically provide software and online tools for sales, customer service, and marketing. Their capabilities include the following.

### Sales Force Automation (SFA)

Sales force automation modules in CRM systems help sales staff increase their productivity by focusing sales efforts on the most profitable customers, those who are good candidates for sales and services. CRM systems provide sales prospect and contact information, product information, product configuration capabilities, and sales quote generation capabilities. Such software can assemble information about a particular customer's past purchases to help the salesperson make personalized recommendations. CRM software enables sales, marketing, and delivery departments to easily share customer and prospect information. It increases each salesperson's efficiency in reducing the cost per sale as well as the cost of acquiring new customers and retaining old ones. CRM software also has capabilities for sales forecasting, territory management, and team selling.

### Customer Service

Customer service modules in CRM systems provide information and tools to increase the efficiency of call centers, help desks, and customer support staff. They have capabilities for assigning and managing customer service requests.

# FOCUS ON ORGANIZATIONS    IHOP Cooks Customer Data to Order

The International House of Pancakes (IHOP) is known best for serving an estimated three-quarter billion pancakes annually to diners across the United States and Canada. The chain, which is based in Glendale, California, has expanded its menu over the years to include a growing number of traditional lunch and dinner items as well. The promise of a simple, economical, and taste-bud-satisfying dining experience has enabled IHOP to maintain its position as one of the top family restaurant chains in the United States. More than 90 percent of Americans are familiar with the IHOP brand name. The chain includes approximately 1,200 restaurants, more than 90 percent of which are owned by independent franchisees.

IHOP's slogan is "Come Hungry, Leave Happy." But IHOP didn't know as much as it wanted about its customers and how to make them happier. IHOP had been conducting extensive research into demographic trends, spending patterns, and customer preferences. However, according to Patrick Piccininno, IHOP's vice president of information technology, the information in its systems "wasn't available in a useful, easy to access way." Each IHOP division worked with a different slice of customer data. In fact, the company employed five different systems for processing sales data, and there was no method for synchronizing or cleansing the data. Piccininno had no idea if separate franchises were finding the same problems or trends. What IHOP needed is what Piccininno describes as "a single source of truth. One record, one database, one central repository of all [our] customer information" is vital to establishing "consistency across all groups with the corporation."

IHOP could have built an entirely new system based on a centralized company-wide database that was a single source of customer information. This approach would have been prohibitively costly and complicated. Instead, it chose to use Oracle Customer Data Hub middleware to create a single view of the customers by integrating data from its various legacy systems. Oracle Customer Data Hub creates a single company-wide view of the customer so that every single customer touch point displays current and consistent information without disrupting existing systems.

IHOP's Oracle Customer Data Hub collects and integrates customer data from six point-of-sales systems, human resources, and financial systems based on Lawson software and an Oracle data warehouse. The hub creates a comprehensive view of each IHOP customer. The Customer Data Hub also cleans and enriches the customer data as they are collected from source applications.

In the past, the company required separate data cleansing, support, and processing work for each of its systems, which was quite costly. Duplicate and inconsistent data have been eliminated.

IHOP adopted Oracle TeleService to improve communication with its customers through a call center. Previously, diners communicated with IHOP via e-mail. However, the company lacked a central process for tracking the email. Consequently, some e-mail was not addressed in a timely manner. There was no mechanism for knowing how long it would take to solve a problem or if specific problems that had been reported were ever solved at all. With Oracle TeleService, IHOP receives comments and feedback from restaurant guests on a toll-free number. Its information systems department is able to log the calls, route the collected data to the appropriate resource, and track the progress of resolutions to customers' questions and problems. Now, restaurant guests who report problems receive a resolution in three days on average. The centralized and encompassing nature of TeleService also enables IHOP to notice trends among its clientele, based on its messages, and take the appropriate action to address the trends.

Individual franchisees have access to the CRM system through portals created with Oracle AS Portal 10g software. Users connect to the portal through a Web browser. IHOP restaurant franchisees are able to see daily sales data, the average check for each day, how promotions are performing, and figures on how well they manage their operations. The portal is customizable to help restaurant owners access the specific types of information they need, while giving IHOP an improved ability to measure customer service.

*Sources:* Colin Beasty, "CRM Where You Least Expect It," *Customer Relationship Management,* March 2005, www.destinationCRM.com, accessed June 7, 2005; "Fresh Guest Data Helps IHOP Franchises Thrive," www.oracle.com/pls/cis/Profiles.print_html?p_profile_id=100021, accessed June 7, 2005; Robert Westervelt, "Customer Data Hub Keeps IHOP Stats Hot," http://searchoracle.techtarget.com/originalContent/0,289142,sid41_gci947193,00.html, accessed June 7, 2005; Charles Babcock, "Customer-Data Hubs Inch Ahead," *InformationWeek,* April 25, 2005, accessed June 7, 2005; and www.ihop.com, accessed June 8, 2005.

**To Think About:**

What problems did IHOP face? How did they affect IHOP's business performance? How has the company chosen to solve those problems? What alternatives were available? Analyze the people, organization, and technology dimensions of the solution. Did IHOP choose the best alternative? Explain your answer.

One such capability is an appointment or advice telephone line: When a customer calls a standard phone number, the system routes the call to the correct service person, who inputs information about that customer into the system only once. Once the customer's data are in the system, any service representative can handle the customer relationship. Improved access to consistent and accurate customer information helps call centers handle more calls per day and decreases the duration of each call. Thus, call centers and customer service groups achieve greater productivity, reduced transaction time, and higher quality of service at lower cost. The customer is happier because he or she spends less time on the phone restating his or her problem to customer service representatives.

CRM systems may also include Web-based self-service capabilities: The company Web site can be set up to provide inquiring customers personalized support information as well as the option to contact customer service staff by phone for additional assistance.

### Marketing

CRM systems support direct-marketing campaigns by providing capabilities for capturing prospect and customer data, for providing product and service information, for qualifying leads for targeted marketing, and for scheduling and tracking direct-marketing mailings or e-mail (see Figure 8-8). Marketing modules also include tools for analyzing marketing and customer data—identifying profitable and unprofitable customers, designing products and services to satisfy specific customer needs and interests, and identifying opportunities for cross-selling, up-selling, and bundling.

**Cross-selling** is the marketing of complementary products to customers. (For example, in financial services, a customer with a checking account might be sold a money market account or a home improvement loan.) **Up-selling** is the marketing of higher-value products or services to new or existing customers. (An example might be a credit card company persuading a good customer to upgrade from a conventional credit card to a "platinum" card with a larger credit line, additional services, and a higher annual fee.)

**Bundling** is one kind of cross-selling in which a combination of products is sold as a bundle at a price lower than the total cost of the individual products. For example, Verizon sells bundled telephone services that include local and long-distance service, voice mail service, caller identification, and digital subscriber line (DSL) access to the Internet. CRM tools also help firms manage and execute marketing campaigns at all stages, from planning to determining the rate of success for each campaign.

**Figure 8-8**
How CRM Systems Support Marketing
*Customer relationship management software provides a single point for users to manage and evaluate marketing campaigns across multiple channels, including e-mail, direct mail, telephone, the Web, and wireless messages.*

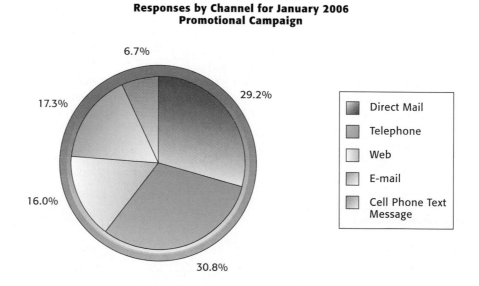

**Responses by Channel for January 2006 Promotional Campaign**

6.7%

29.2%

17.3%

16.0%

30.8%

- Direct Mail
- Telephone
- Web
- E-mail
- Cell Phone Text Message

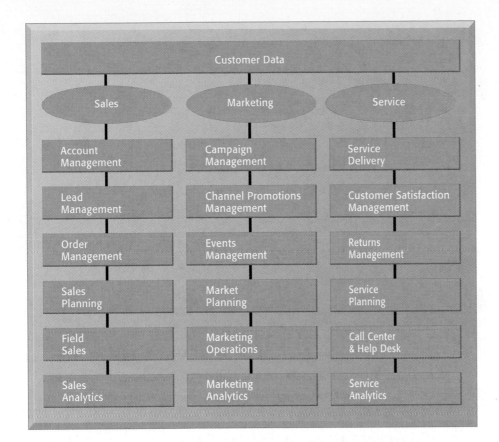

**Figure 8-9**
CRM Software
Capabilities
*The major CRM software products support business processes in sales, service, and marketing, integrating customer information from many different sources. Included are support for both the operational and analytical aspects of CRM.*

Figure 8-9 illustrates the most important capabilities for sales, service, and marketing processes that would be found in major CRM software products. Like enterprise software, this software is business-process driven, incorporating hundreds of business processes thought to represent best practices in each of these areas.

Siebel Systems, a leading vendor of CRM software that was recently acquired by Oracle Corp., provides both generic and industry-specific best practices for its software. To achieve maximum benefit from implementing Siebel software, companies would revise and model their business processes to correspond to the best-practice business processes for CRM in the Siebel system.

Figure 8-10 illustrates how a best practice for increasing customer loyalty through customer service might be modeled by CRM software. Directly servicing customers provides firms with opportunities to increase customer retention by singling out profitable long-term customers for preferential treatment. CRM software can assign each customer a score based on that person's value and loyalty to the company and provide that information to help call centers route each customer's service request to agents who can best handle that customer's needs. The system would automatically provide the service agent with a detailed profile of that customer that included his or her score for value and loyalty. The service agent would use this information to present special offers or additional service to the customer to encourage the customer to keep transacting business with the company. You will find more information on other best-practice business processes in the Siebel CRM system in the Learning Tracks at the Laudon Web site for this chapter.

## Operational and Analytical CRM

All of the applications we have just described support either the operational or analytical aspects of customer relationship management. **Operational CRM** includes customer-facing

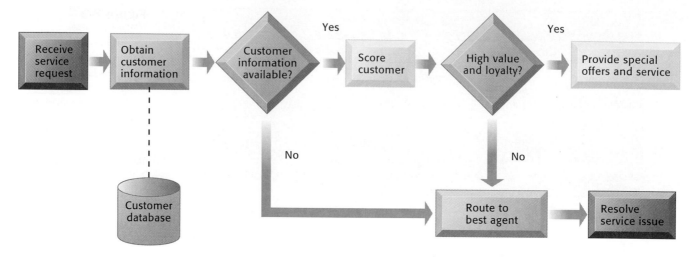

**Figure 8-10**

Customer Loyalty Management Process Map

*This process map shows how a best practice for promoting customer loyalty through customer service would be modeled by customer relationship management software. The CRM software helps firms identify high-value customers for preferential treatment.*

applications, such as tools for sales force automation, call center and customer service support, and marketing automation. **Analytical CRM** includes applications that analyze customer data generated by operational CRM applications to provide information for improving business performance management. Table 8.3 provides more specific examples of operational and analytical CRM functions.

Analytical CRM applications are based on data warehouses that consolidate the data from operational CRM systems and customer touch points for use with online analytical processing (OLAP), data mining, and other data analysis techniques (see Chapter 5). Customer data collected by the organization might be combined with data from other

*Salesforce.com presents key sales metrics in interactive charts, graphs, and dashboards. These powerful analytical tools help firms identify their most important customers, predict future buying patterns, and position the correct resources to close more deals.*

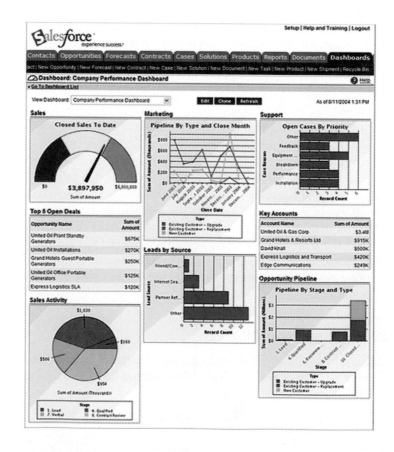

| Operational CRM | Analytical CRM |
|---|---|
| Campaign management | Develop customer segmentation strategies |
| E-marketing | Develop customer profiles |
| Account and contact management | Analyze customer profitability |
| Lead management | Analyze product profitability |
| Telemarketing | Identify cross-selling and up-selling opportunities |
| Teleselling | Select the best marketing, service, and sales channels for each customer group |
| E-selling | Identify trends in sales cycle length, win rate, and average deal size |
| Field sales | Analyze service resolution times, service levels based on communication channels, and service activity by product line and account |
| Field service dispatch | Analyze leads generated and conversion rates |
| Customer care and help desk | Analyze sales representative and customer service representative productivity |

**TABLE 8.3**

**Examples of Operational Versus Analytical CRM**

sources, such as customer lists for direct-marketing campaigns purchased from other companies or demographic data. Such data are analyzed to identify buying patterns, to create segments for targeted marketing, and to pinpoint profitable and unprofitable customers (see Figure 8-11).

Another important output of analytical CRM is the customer's lifetime value to the firm (see Figure 8-12). **Customer lifetime value (CLTV)** is based on the relationship between the revenue produced by a specific customer, the expenses incurred in acquiring and servicing that customer, and the expected life of the relationship between the customer and the company.

## Business Value of Customer Relationship Management Systems

Companies with effective customer relationship management systems realize many benefits, including increased customer satisfaction, reduced direct-marketing costs, more effective

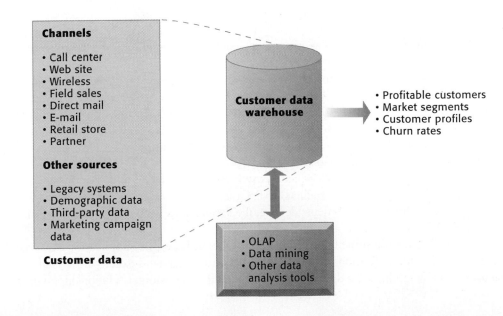

**Figure 8-11**
Analytical CRM Data Warehouse
*Analytical CRM uses a customer data warehouse and tools to analyze customer data collected from the firm's customer touch points and from other sources.*

**Figure 8-12**
Customer Lifetime
Value (CLTV)
*Customer relationship
management software
provides analytical tools
to help firms identify
their most important
customers, with the
ability to calculate an
individual customer's
lifetime value to the
company.*

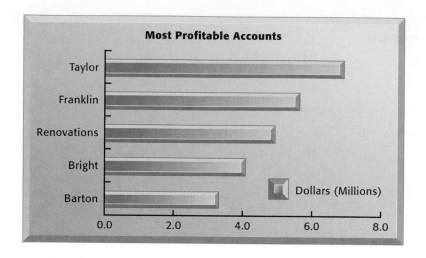

marketing, and lower costs for customer acquisition and retention. Information from CRM systems increases sales revenue by identifying the most profitable customers and segments for focused marketing, cross-selling, and up-selling.

Customer churn is reduced as sales, service, and marketing better respond to customer needs. The **churn rate** measures the number of customers who stop using or purchasing products or services from a company. It is an important indicator of the growth or decline of a firm's customer base.

## 8.4 Enterprise Applications: New Opportunities and Challenges

Many firms have implemented enterprise systems and systems for supply chain management and customer relationship management because they are such powerful instruments for achieving operational excellence and enhancing decision making. But precisely because they are so powerful in changing the way the organization works, they are challenging to implement. Let's briefly examine some of these challenges, as well as new ways of wringing even more value out of these systems.

## Challenges and Opportunities

Promises of dramatic reductions in inventory costs, order-to-delivery time, as well as more efficient customer response and higher product and customer profitability make enterprise systems and systems for supply chain management and customer relationship management very alluring. But to obtain this value, you must clearly understand how your business has to change to use these systems effectively.

Enterprise applications require not only deep-seated technological changes but also fundamental changes in the way the business operates. Business processes change dramatically, as do organizational structure and culture. Employees must accept new job functions and responsibilities. They will have to learn how to perform a new set of work activities and understand how the information they enter into the system can affect other parts of the company. This requires new organizational learning.

Enterprise applications also introduce "switching costs." Once you adopt an enterprise application from a single vendor, such as SAP, Oracle, or others, it is very costly to switch vendors, and your firm becomes dependent on the vendor to upgrade its product and maintain your installation.

You'll need to devote some time to data management. Enterprise applications are based on organization-wide definitions of data. You'll need to understand exactly how your business uses its data and how the data would be organized in a customer relationship management, supply chain management, or enterprise system. CRM systems typically require some data cleansing work.

In a nutshell, it takes a lot of work to get enterprise applications to work properly. Everyone in the organization must be involved. Of course, for those companies with successful CRM, SCM, and enterprise systems, the results are clearly worth the effort.

## Extending Enterprise Software

Today, many experienced business firms are looking for ways to wring even more value from their enterprise applications. One way is to make them more flexible and capable of integration with other systems. The major enterprise software vendors have created what they call *enterprise solutions, enterprise suites,* or *e-business suites* to make their customer relationship management, supply chain management, and enterprise systems work closely together with each other, and link to systems of customers and suppliers. SAP's mySAP and Oracle's e-Business Suite are examples. The enterprise vendors also provide middleware and tools that use XML and Web services for integrating enterprise applications with older legacy applications and systems from other vendors (see Chapter 4).

---

### LEARNING TRACKS

1. If you want to learn more about how SAP enterprise software works, you will find a Learning Track on SAP's Business Process Map at the Laudon Web site for this chapter.
2. If you want to learn more about the major business processes in supply chain management and metrics for measuring supply chain performance, you will find a Learning Track on the Supply Chain Operations Reference Model and supply chain metrics at the Laudon Web site for this chapter.
3. If you want to learn more about customer related business processes supported by CRM software, you will find a Learning Track on Siebel Systems' best-practice business processes at the Laudon Web site for this chapter.

---

## Summary

**1** **Demonstrate how enterprise systems achieve operational excellence by integrating and coordinating diverse functions and business processes in the firm.** Enterprise systems integrate the key business processes of a firm into a single software system so that information can flow seamlessly throughout the organization, improving coordination, efficiency, and decision making. Enterprise software is based on a suite of integrated software modules and a common central database. The database collects data from and feeds the data into numerous applications that can support nearly all of an organization's internal business activities. When new information is entered by one process, the information is made available immediately to other business processes. Organizations implementing enterprise software would have to adopt the business processes embedded in the software and, if necessary, change their business processes to conform to those in the software.

Enterprise systems support organizational centralization by enforcing uniform data standards and business processes throughout the company and a single unified technology platform. The firmwide data generated by enterprise systems helps managers evaluate organizational performance. By integrating business processes in sales, production, finance, and logistics, the entire organization will more efficiently respond to customer requests for products or information, forecast new products, and build and deliver them as demand requires.

**2** **Demonstrate how supply chain management systems coordinate planning, production, and logistics with suppliers.** Supply chain management systems automate the flow of information among members of the supply chain so they can use it to make better decisions about when and how much to purchase, produce, or ship. More accurate information from supply chain management systems reduces uncertainty and the impact of the bullwhip effect. The correct movement of information makes it possible to time orders, shipments, and production properly to minimize inventory levels and expedite deliveries to customers.

Supply chain management software includes software for supply chain planning and for supply chain execution. Supply chain planning systems enable the firm to generate demand forecasts for a product and to develop sourcing, manufacturing, and distribution plans. Supply chain execution systems manage the flow of products through the final stages of production, distribution, and delivery. Firms can use intranets to improve coordination among their internal supply chain processes, and they can use extranets to coordinate supply chain processes shared with their business partners. Internet technology facilitates the management of global supply chains by providing the connectivity for organizations in different countries to share supply chain information. Improved communication among supply chain members also facilitates efficient customer response and movement toward a demand-driven model.

**3** **Demonstrate how customer relationship management systems achieve customer intimacy by integrating all customer information and making it available throughout the firm.**
Customer relationship management (CRM) systems integrate and automate many customer-facing processes in sales, marketing, and customer service, providing an enterprise-wide view of customers. These systems track all of the ways in which a company interacts with its customers and analyze these interactions to maximize customer lifetime value for the firm. CRM systems capture and integrate customer data from all over the organization, analyzing the data and distributing the results to customer-related systems and customer touch points across the enterprise. Companies can use this customer knowledge when they interact with customers to provide them with better service or to sell new products and services. These systems also identify profitable or nonprofitable customers or opportunities to reduce the churn rate.

The major customer relationship management software packages integrate customer-related processes in sales, marketing, and customer service and provide capabilities for both operational CRM and analytical CRM. They often include modules for managing relationships with selling partners (partner relationship management) and for employee relationship management.

If they are properly implemented, CRM systems help firms increase customer satisfaction, reduce direct-marketing costs, and lower costs for customer acquisition and retention. Information from CRM systems increases sales revenue by identifying the most profitable customers and segments for focused marketing, cross-selling, and up-selling. Customer churn will be reduced as sales, service, and marketing better respond to customer needs.

**4** **Assess the challenges and new opportunities raised by enterprise applications.**
Enterprise applications require extensive organizational change, large new software investments, and careful assessment of how these systems will enhance organizational performance. Enterprise applications create new interconnections among myriad business processes and data flows inside the firm (and in the case of supply chain management systems, between the firm and its external supply chain partners). Employees require training to prepare for new procedures and roles. Attention to data management is essential.

Businesses are extending their enterprise applications by using middleware tools that integrate these systems with each other, with older legacy systems, and with the systems of customers and suppliers.

## Key Terms

| | | |
|---|---|---|
| Analytical CRM, 280 | Customer lifetime value | Just-in-time, 269 |
| Best practices, 265 | (CLTV), 281 | Operational CRM, 279 |
| Bullwhip effect, 269 | Demand planning, 271 | Partner relationship |
| Bundling, 278 | Employee relationship | management (PRM), 276 |
| Churn rate, 282 | management (ERM), 276 | Pull-based model, 273 |
| Cross-selling, 278 | Enterprise software, 265 | Push-based model, 272 |

## Review Questions

**8.1** What is an enterprise system? How does enterprise software work?

**8.2** How do enterprise systems provide value for a business?

**8.3** What is a supply chain? What entities does it comprise?

**8.4** What is the bullwhip effect? How can supply chain management systems deal with it?

**8.5** What are supply chain planning systems and supply chain execution systems? What functions do they perform?

**8.6** How can the Internet and Internet technology facilitate supply chain management?

**8.7** Distinguish between a push-based and pull-based model of supply chain management. How can contemporary supply chain management systems facilitate a pull-based model?

**8.8** How do supply chain management systems provide value for a business?

**8.9** What is customer relationship management? Why are customer relationships so important today?

**8.10** How are partner relationship management (PRM) and employee relationship management (ERM) related to customer relationship management (CRM)?

**8.11** Describe the tools and capabilities of customer relationship management software for sales, marketing, and customer service.

**8.12** Distinguish between operational and analytical CRM.

**8.13** Define the following terms and explain why they are important for customer relationship management: churn rate, customer lifetime value (CLTV), and best practices.

**8.14** How can enterprise applications be extended to provide more value?

**8.15** What are the challenges posed by enterprise applications? How can these challenges be addressed?

## Discussion Questions

**8.1** Supply chain management is less about managing the physical movement of goods and more about managing information. Discuss the implications of this statement.

**8.2** If a company wants to implement an enterprise application, it had better do its homework. Discuss the implications of this statement.

## Application Software Exercise

### Database Exercise: Managing Customer Service Requests

Software skills: Database design; querying and reporting

Business skills: Customer service analysis

Prime Service is a large service company that provides maintenance and repair services for close to 1,200 commercial businesses in New York, New Jersey, and Connecticut. Its customers include businesses of all sizes. Customers with service needs call into its customer service department with requests for repairing heating ducts, broken windows, leaky roofs, broken water pipes, and other problems. The company assigns each request a number and writes down the service request number, identification number of the customer account, the date of the request, the type of equipment requiring repair, and a brief description of the problem. The service requests are handled on a first-come, first-served basis. After the service work has been completed, Prime calculates the cost of the work, enters the price on the service request form, and bills the client.

Management is not happy with this arrangement because the most important and profitable clients—those with accounts of more than $70,000—are treated no differently from its clients with small accounts. It would like to find a way to provide its best customers with better service. Management would also like to know which types of service problems occur the most frequently so that it can make sure it has adequate resources to address them.

Prime Service has a small database with client account information, which can be found on the Laudon Web site for Chapter 8. It includes fields for the account ID, company (account) name, street address, city, state, ZIP code, account size (in dollars), contact last name, contact first name, and contact telephone number. The contact is the name of the person in each company who is responsible for contacting Prime about maintenance and repair work. Use your database software to design a solution that would enable Prime's customer service representatives to identify the most important customers so that they could receive priority service. Your solution will require more than one table. Populate your database with at least 15 service requests. Create several reports that would be of interest to management, such as a list of the highest- and lowest-priority accounts or a report showing the most frequently occurring service problems. Create a report showing customer service representatives which service calls they should respond to first on a specific date.

## Identifying Supply Chain Management Solutions

Business skills: Locating and evaluating suppliers

A growing number of Dirt Bikes's orders cannot be fulfilled on time because of delays in obtaining some important components and parts for its motorcycles, especially their fuel tanks. Complaints are mounting from distributors who fear losing sales if the dirt bikes they have ordered are delayed too long. Dirt Bikes's management has asked you to help it address some of its supply chain issues.

1. Use the Internet to locate alternative suppliers for motorcycle fuel tanks. Identify two or three suppliers. Find out the amount of time and cost to ship a fuel tank (weighing about five pounds) by ground (surface delivery) from each supplier to Dirt Bikes in Carbondale, Colorado. Which supplier is most likely to take the shortest amount of time and cost the least to ship the fuel tanks?
2. Dirt Bikes's management would like to know if there is any supply chain management software for a small business that would be appropriate for Dirt Bikes. Use the Internet to locate two supply chain management software providers for companies such as Dirt Bikes. Briefly describe the capabilities of the two software applications and indicate how they could help Dirt Bikes. Which supply chain management software product would be more appropriate for Dirt Bikes? Why?
3. (Optional) Use electronic presentation software to summarize your findings for management.

## Building Internet Skills

## Evaluating Supply Chain Management Services

This project will help develop your Internet skills in using the Web to research and evaluate business services.

Trucking companies no longer merely carry goods from one place to another. Some also provide supply chain management services to their customers and help them manage their information. Investigate the Web sites of two companies, J.B. Hunt and Schneider Logistics, to see how these companies' services can be used for supply chain management. Then, respond to the following questions:

1. What supply chain processes can each of these companies support for their clients?
2. How can customers use the Web sites of each company to help them with supply chain management?
3. Compare the supply chain management services provided by these companies. Which company would you select to help your firm manage its supply chain? Why?

## Video Case

You will find a video case illustrating some of the concepts in this chapter on the Laudon Web site at **www.prenhall.com/laudon** along with questions to help you analyze the case.

## Teamwork

### Analyzing Enterprise Application Vendors

With a group of three or four students, use the Web to research and evaluate the products of two vendors of enterprise application software. You could compare, for example, the SAP and Oracle enterprise systems, the supply chain management systems from i2 and Manugistics, or the customer relationship management systems of Siebel Systems and salesforce.com. Use what you have learned from these companies' Web sites to compare the software packages you have selected in terms of business functions supported, technology platforms, cost, and ease of use. Which vendor would you select? Why? Would you select the same vendor for a small business as well as a large one? If possible, use electronic presentation software to present your findings to the class.

## BUSINESS PROBLEM-SOLVING CASE

### Philip Morris International's Supply Chain Dilemma

Intense pressure from the European Union (EU) has forced Philip Morris International (PMI) to address lapses in its supply chain management. The European Commission (EC) believes that these lapses create an environment in which cigarette smuggling and counterfeiting prosper.

One particular event in the fall of 2004 exposed the extent to which contraband and counterfeiting have become problematic. On November 16, 2004, agents from the U.S. Department of Justice's Bureau of Alcohol, Tobacco, Firearms, and Explosives detained a DHL express freight plane on the runway at John F. Kennedy International Airport (JFK) in New York. Inside the plane were 82,000 cartons of illicit cigarettes worth more than $1.1 million. An online Swiss tobacco company named Otamedia shipped the cargo to the United States to fulfill orders placed by American customers. Such transactions are illegal in the United States, but the appeal of cheaper cigarettes that aren't subject to taxes and import duties is too great for many smokers.

Philip Morris International came under fire for this incident because the detained shipment included large quantities of its Marlboro and Marlboro Lights cigarettes. Reports indicate that PMI, which is based in Lausanne, Switzerland, manufactured the cigarettes in Europe where Otamedia purchased them. By circumventing taxes and import duties, Otamedia was able to save American customers upward of 40 percent on cigarettes. Philip Morris characterizes Otamedia as an unauthorized distributor and has taken legal action to stop the Swiss company from continuing these illicit sales. However, government regulators in the European Union have taken a hard-line stance on the issue, insisting that tobacco companies are responsible for the full length of their supply chains.

The incident in New York illustrates just how difficult it is to control the cigarette supply chain. The seizure at JFK occurred four years after the European Union and 10 member states filed a civil suit in U.S. federal courts against three tobacco companies, including PMI, alleging smuggling, money laundering, and other illicit activity. On July 9, 2004, PMI agreed to a landmark, multifaceted settlement in the case. As part of the deal, PMI must strengthen its procedures for selecting and monitoring customers. And, PMI is responsible for paying taxes and customs duties on any Philip Morris products that have been seized in the European Union as smuggled goods.

Then there is the financial portion of the settlement. PMI's parent company, Altria Group, has agreed to pay $1.25 billion to the European Union over 12 years. The first payment amounts to $250 million. For Altria, a company that most recently enjoyed revenue of $67 billion and net income of $9.8 billion, the financial commitment is far from being the most difficult part of the settlement. Jack Holleran, senior vice president for Compliance and Brand Integrity for Philip Morris USA (PM USA), admits that the company needs to implement technology to track and trace its products more completely and precisely. However, he also says that the company "can't keep track of every single pack of cigarettes as it makes its way through distributors and retailers." That is, in effect, what the deal with the European Union insists Philip Morris do.

So how is PMI going to implement such tight control over its supply chain that it can trace every cigarette carton from factory to retail shelf? Experts from the company's packaging, research and development, information technology, and brand integrity departments have been meeting monthly to explore new technologies. PMI has earmarked between $10 million and $20 million for new information systems to support the new tracking systems that the company will require.

One of the most talked about solution available to PMI is Radio Frequency Identification (RFID). RFID technology involves placing tags with tiny antennas and computer chips on products. The tags store information and emit radio signals that are scanned by readers and transmitted to a computer for tracking and analysis. Experts say that RFID may be too expensive for PMI's purposes. AMR research analyst Kara Romanov says that Altria would need to spend between $1 million and $3 million for an RFID pilot program. A full rollout of the technology, including tags, readers, and software, would cost anywhere from $13 million to $23 million, which is near the amount that PMI intends to spend.

However, those costs relate to the typical scenario in which RFID tags are placed on pallets of goods. For PMI to meet the demands of its agreement, the company would have to place tags on individual cartons of cigarettes, dramatically increasing the number of tags that would be required. At 50 cents each, Altria would be looking at a price tag of more than $2 billion for RFID tags, without even factoring in the cost of readers, software, and other hardware. One way to absorb such a cost would be to raise the price of a carton of cigarettes, which both PMI and PM USA did in December 2004.

Currently, bar codes inform Phillip Morris when a legitimate retailer sells a carton or pack of cigarettes. Bar codes carry very limited information about a product. They indicate that a product has been sold and the price, but carry no information that uniquely identifies each cigarette carton or pack or that shows the route that the product followed to its destination. And, certainly, unauthorized dealers would not be scanning bar codes. Some factories producing cigarettes for Phillip Morris do use an ink-based code that marks cartons with the location and date of manufacture. However, the company uses this information only to respond to customer complaints about product inferiority.

To comply with the EU, PMI must provide much more information. In addition to the date and place of manufacture, PMI must emboss every carton and pack of cigarettes with the identity of the manufacturing facility, the specific machine used, and the shift during which the product was manufactured. PMI must also mark each pack with the country of destination.

On top of these requirements, PMI is required to build a database to keep track of its supply chain data and provide the database to OLAF, the European body that investigates matters of fraud. The database would allow investigators to identify exactly which distributors have received Philip Morris shipments. In the event of a seizure, OLAF must be able to identify the last known purchaser using the database, which is to be accessible online at all times. Finally, the settlement agreement obligates PMI to create databases of contact information for its first level and second level of distributors. (Second-level distributors are those that purchase from the first level.) The database of first-purchaser distributors was due in October 2004 but had not been turned over to OLAF as of June 2005.

With so much information required for each unit of product, it is difficult to ignore the potential of RFID technology. The 28-digit electronic product code (EPC) that RFID would use can store significantly more data than the 12-digit universal product code (UPC) of the standard bar code. However, Philip Morris has concerns beyond the cost of RFID. While not divulging many details for security reasons, one cause for concern seems to be the speed with which RFID tags could be attached to so many packages. Philip Morris production lines produce more than 14,000 cartons of cigarettes per minute. Both branches of the company have tested RFID implementation, and all of their tracking and tracing tests have resulted in slower production. A loss in production combined with the expense of implementing RFID, including $500 to $1,000 for each reader at each distribution location for first- and second-tier distributors and 40 cents to 50 cents per RFID tag, would give any business pause. PMI and PM USA each has 1,000 distributors worldwide.

Philip Morris may receive some assistance in getting through the rough stages of RFID testing and development from Altria's main business software provider, SAP. PMI and PM USA use the mySAP suite for enterprise resource planning and supply chain management. SAP is working with hardware manufacturers and Altria's customers to determine how best to serve them in an RFID environment. SAP is also updating its software to include for tracking RFID data. Amar Singh, SAP's vice president of global RFID and business development, cautions that bar codes appear to be the better solution for the foreseeable future because of the cost differences. If not for the size of the investment, RFID clearly would be the better choice. Most companies that are using RFID are using tags to track pallets of goods rather than individual items.

Another alternative worth exploring is an ink-based product. The Swiss security firm SICPA produces anti-counterfeiting inks for currencies, including the U.S. dollar. SICPA offers a product, called SICPATrace that encodes packages with a special form of bar code using ink that the naked eye cannot detect. The bar code, which is formed by a sequence of light and dark squares similar to a crossword puzzle, has larger storage capacity than a standard bar code. It differs from an RFID tag in that there is no computer chip. A scanner can read thousands of the ink codes at a time and store their data in a database. A serial number encoded on each item could be recorded in a database, along with sales and tax history data, providing enough information to track the item throughout the supply chain. The range is much shorter than that of RFID (the scanner must be within six inches of each item to read its code).

Still, John Thorpe, the former managing director of SICPA's product security division, believes that the technology provides PMI with almost everything it needs: low cost, detailed product marking, and the ability to spot-check products at various points along the supply chain. Even the simple absence of a code could reveal counterfeit merchandise. Philip Morris has tested SICPA's technology and claims that its marking system falls short of PMI's and PM USA's speed requirements of 450 to 700 packs per minute on the production line. Thorpe insists that the technology achieves all of the goals that Philip

Morris has set and that the tobacco company is really ambivalent toward the smuggling issue.

According to Ian Walton-George, head of the customs unit for the European Anti-Fraud Office, there has been little progress in the months since the settlement between PMI and the European Union. He notes, "We're still seizing thousands of cigarettes every day somewhere in Europe." Walton-George characterizes the agreement as "all talk and no action" and laments the fact that PMI has not yet provided a first-purchaser database or been forthcoming about the improvements the company has made in tracking and tracing cigarettes.

*Sources:* Larry Barrett and David F. Carr, "Philip Morris International: Smoke Screen," *Baseline,* February 1, 2005; Sean Nolan, "Planner: Calculating Costs of Tracking Individual Items with RFID," *Baseline,* February 1, 2005; David F. Carr, "Gotcha!: Frequent Radio Frequency Obstacles," *Baseline,* February 1, 2005; Siim Kallas, "The Fight Against Cigarette Smuggling Across the EU," speech to the European Parliament, May 25, 2005, europa.eu.int/rapid, accessed June 13, 2005; Barnaby J. Feder, "I.B.M. Expands Efforts to Promote Radio Tags to Track Goods," *The New York Times,* June 14, 2005, www.philipmorrisinternational.com, accessed June 13, 2005; and Form 10-K, Altria Group, Inc., www.sec.gov, EDGAR database, accessed June 13, 2005.

**Case Study Questions**

1. What is the problem faced by the organizations in this case? What is the cause of the problem? What is its impact?

2. Has PMI correctly identified the problem it faces? Has PMI identified the people, organization, and technology issues associated with the problem? What are these issues? What additional evidence or data do you recommend that they obtain?

3. What solutions were considered by PMI? Were these solutions appropriate to the problem? Were there other solutions that PMI or the EU should have considered but did not?

4. What is the best solution for PMI? Why? Do you think PMI will be successful in solving the problem? Explain your answer.

5. Who has more at stake in solving this problem, Philip Morris or the European Union? Why?

# E-Commerce: Digital Markets, Digital Goods

CHAPTER 9

## STUDENT OBJECTIVES

**After completing this chapter, you will be able to:**

1. Describe the unique features of e-commerce, digital markets, and digital goods.

2. Analyze how Internet technology has changed value propositions and business models.

3. Describe the various types of e-commerce and how e-commerce has changed consumer retailing and business-to-business transactions.

4. Evaluate the role of m-commerce in business and describe the most important m-commerce applications.

5. Compare the principal payment systems for electronic commerce.

## CHAPTER OUTLINE

## GAP REMODELS ITS WEB SITES

**Gap Inc. had to do** something about its Web sites and it did. On August 24, 2005, visitors to Gap.com found that this Web site was not up and running. A message on Gap.com explained, "We're updating our site to bring you a better shopping experience. Gap.com is temporarily closed for scheduled site improvements." Also shut down around the same time were the Web sites of Gap affiliates—OldNavy.com, BananaRepublic.com, GapKids.com, BabyGap.com, GapMaternity.com, GapBody.com, and OldNavyKids.com.

Gap had waited until families had finished most of their back-to-school shopping, and picked late summer for refurbishing its Web sites so that the work could be done before the busy holiday shopping period. Management wanted to make sure the new site was reliable and stable so it could handle the holiday spike in traffic. Gap had been experiencing a slowdown in revenue, and it wanted a bigger share of the online apparel market, predicted to double from $12.5 billion to $25 billion by 2010.

It took several weeks for the new Web sites to come back online. During that time, the shuttered Web sites turned away thousands of customers and millions of dollars in business. Why was Gap willing to bear these costs?

The reason was the "too many clicks problem." Visitors to Gap Web sites had to click dozens of times to wade through pull-down menus for the size, color, and style of its clothing items. Each time a shopper needed information, all of these clicks bounced him or her off the browsing path. The online shopping experience was much more troublesome than going into a retail store, where shoppers can quickly scan the racks for sizes and colors, select items, and keep going.

The new Web sites try to replicate the ease of an in-store shopping experience. When a woman browses the Gap T-shirt section, she does not have to click to a new page to see details about any of the 16 T-shirts displayed on each page. Instead, positioning the cursor over an item (called "mousing over") launches a pop-up window showing a model wearing the shirt along with swatches of colors for the shirt. "Mousing over" each color swatch turns the shirt on the model into the hue of that swatch. The same window also tells the sizes that are in stock.

If the shopper clicks "add to bag" from within that window, the site does not transport her to a checkout page, as do the sites of other Web retailers. Instead, a small window displaying the shopping bag replaces the previous window. The shopping bag window displays images of the items inside the bag. The shopper can ignore the window or click on the "Close" button to make the window disappear, and she can continue looking at the T-shirts from the original page. This use of mouse overs and pop-up windows prevents shoppers from being bounced off their browsing paths each time they need information. In other words, Gap Web sites allow shoppers to put together an outfit and buy it off a single Web page. A Quick Checkout capability takes shoppers to an "express line."

According to Carrie Johnson, a retail analyst at Forrester Research, "Gap's new sites leapfrog every other retail site out there today." And Gap Inc. may be able to sustain this competitive advantage for a while. The company wrote its own software for the systems that drive its new Web sites. Most Web retailers use commercial e-commerce software from vendors such as IBM, Microsoft, BroadVision, or Blue Martini, or give their electronic retailing business to specialists, such as Amazon.com. That may slow down their ability to change their Web sites to perform like Gap's. ■

*Sources:* Bob Tedeschi, "New Approach from Gap to Cut Down on Clicks," *The New York Times,* September 12, 2005; Jason Boog, "Gap Can't Afford Online Retail Holes," *CIO Insight,* September 21, 2005; and "Gap Closed for Remodeling," *Red Herring,* September 1, 2005.

Gap's Web site redesign effort shows how much importance many businesses today attach to electronic commerce. Gap companies have been challenged to sustain earnings and must compete with other apparel retailers such as J. Crew, Abercrombie & Fitch, Target, and Wal-Mart. Gap management believed its Web sites were dampening sales because they did not provide visitors with a seamless shopping experience. Shoppers needed to take too many actions with their mouse buttons in order to view merchandise, make selections, and make purchases. The Web sites of Gap's competitors were no better.

Gap could have fine-tuned its existing Web sites or spent more on special promotions and online campaigns to attract more shoppers. These alternatives would not have provided much advantage because competitors could quickly imitate such changes. Gap's management realized that the company had an opportunity to provide a superior shopping experience on the Web if it wrote its own software, streamlining its Web site. Gap Inc. was willing to go to great expense to make the required changes in its Web sites, and even forgo sales for more than two weeks in order to implement this solution.

Initial responses to the new Gap Web sites have been highly enthusiastic. But it will take some time to determine whether management made the right choice for a solution. The Web sites have to be proven capable of handling very large numbers of visitors and online shoppers during the pre-Christmas selling period. If competitors can quickly enhance their Web sites to match the functionality of Gap's, much of Gap's competitive advantage will be lost.

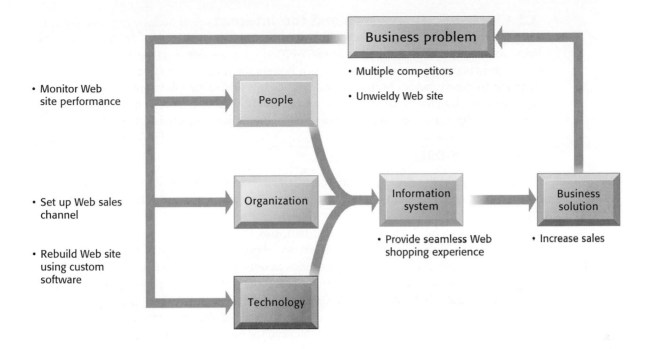

Gap's management was willing to take the chance because the potential returns to the company are so high.

---

**HEADS UP**

This chapter focuses on e-commerce and how businesses use e-commerce to achieve operational excellence and customer intimacy. E-commerce is also transforming business and industries. Retail e-commerce is the fastest-growing form of retail, and interbusiness uses of e-commerce channels now top $1 trillion. E-commerce advertising revenues are growing faster than any other forms of advertising. Every large company, and most medium and small companies, have Web sites that speak directly to customers. If you work in business today, you need to know about e-commerce.

•   If your career is in finance and accounting, you will be working with systems for receiving payments electronically over the Internet and for delivering new online financial services based on the Web.

•   If your career is in human resources, you will be using online job-hunting sites to attract new employees.

•   If your career is in manufacturing, production or operations management, you will be using the Internet for sourcing, and using public B2B commerce systems and private industrial networks for procurement and management of your supply chain.

•   If your career is in sales and marketing, you will be using the Web to provide digital products and services, and to sell and promote products by using personalization, customization, and community marketing techniques.

---

In this chapter, we examine e-commerce and its impact on the business world. We start by describing the unique features of e-commerce and e-commerce business models. Next, we learn how businesses use e-commerce in consumer retailing and in transactions with other businesses. We'll look at the various types of e-commerce, including m-commerce based on wireless devices. Finally, we examine the principal e-commerce payment systems.

## 9.1 Electronic Commerce and the Internet

Have you ever purchased music over the Web? Have you ever used the Web to search for information about your sneakers before you bought them in a retail store? If so, you've participated in e-commerce. So have hundreds of millions of people around the globe. And although most purchases still take place through traditional channels, e-commerce continues to grow rapidly and to transform the way many companies do business.

### E-Commerce Today

E-commerce refers to the use of the Internet and the Web to transact business. More formally, e-commerce is about digitally enabled commercial transactions between and among organizations and individuals. Digitally enabled transactions include all transactions mediated by digital technology. For the most part, this means transactions that occur over the Internet and the Web. Commercial transactions involve the exchange of value (e.g., money) across organizational or individual boundaries in return for products and services.

E-commerce began in 1995 when one of the first Internet portals, Netscape.com, accepted the first ads from major corporations and popularized the idea that the Web could be used as a new medium for advertising and sales. No one envisioned at the time what would turn out to be an exponential growth curve for e-commerce retail sales, which tripled and doubled in the early years. Only since 2006 has consumer e-commerce "slowed" to a 25 percent annual growth rate (Figure 9-1).

Mirroring the history of commercial innovations, such as the telephone, radio, and television, the very rapid growth in e-commerce in the early years created a stock market bubble in e-commerce stocks. Like all bubbles, the "dot-com" bubble burst in March 2001. When the stock market value of e-commerce, telecommunications, and other technology stocks plummeted by more than 90 percent, many people thought e-commerce growth would stagnate, customer growth would fall off, and the Internet audience itself would plateau.

A large number of e-commerce companies failed during this process. Yet for many others, such as Amazon, eBay, Expedia, and Google, the results have been more positive: soaring revenues, fine-tuned business models that produce profits, and rising stock prices. By 2006, e-commerce revenues returned to solid growth again.

- Online consumer sales expanded by more than 23 percent in 2005 to an estimated $141 billion to $172 billion (eMarketer, 2005a).
- The number of individuals online in the United States expanded to 175 million in 2005, up from 170 million in 2004 (eMarketer, 2005). In the world, nearly one billion people are now connected to the Internet. Growth in the overall Internet population has spurred growth in e-commerce.
- On the average day, 70 million people go online, 140 million send e-mail, 5 million write on their blogs, 4 million share music on peer-to-peer networks, and 3 million use the Internet to rate a person, product, or service.

**Figure 9-1**
The Growth of E-Commerce
*Retail e-commerce revenues have grown exponentially since 1995 and have only recently "slowed" to a very rapid 25 percent annual increase, which is projected to remain the same until 2008.*

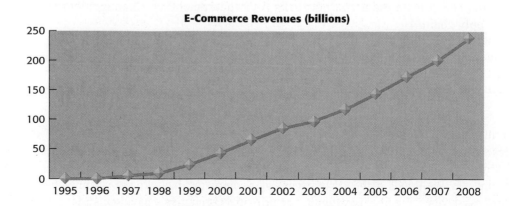

**TABLE 9.1**

**New Developments in E-Commerce**

**BUSINESS TRANSFORMATION**

- The first wave of e-commerce transformed the business world of books, music, and air travel. In the second wave, eight new industries are facing a similar transformation scenario: telephones, movies, television, jewelry, real estate, hotels, bill payments, and software.

- The breadth of e-commerce offerings grows, especially in travel, information clearinghouses, entertainment, retail apparel, appliances, and home furnishings.

- Retail consumer e-commerce continues to grow at double-digit rates.

- The online demographics of shoppers continues to broaden to match that of ordinary shoppers.

- Pure e-commerce business models will be refined further to achieve higher levels of profitability, whereas traditional retail brands, such as Sears, JC Penney, and Wal-Mart, will use e-commerce to retain their dominant retail positions.

- Small businesses and entrepreneurs continue to flood the e-commerce marketplace, often riding on the infrastructures created by industry giants, such as Amazon, eBay, and Overture.

**TECHNOLOGY FOUNDATIONS**

- Wireless Internet connections (Wi-Fi, Wi-Max, and 3G mobile phone) grow rapidly.

- Podcasting takes off as a new medium for distribution of radio and user-generated commentary.

- The Internet broadband foundation becomes stronger in households and businesses as transmission prices fall. More than 42 million households had broadband cable or DSL access to the Internet in 2005—about 38 percent of all households (eMarketer, 2005b).

- RSS (really simple syndication) grows to become a major new form of user-controlled information distribution that rivals e-mail in some applications.

- Computing and networking component prices continue to fall dramatically.

- New Internet-based models of computing, such as .NET and Web services, expand B2B opportunities.

**NEW MODELS EMERGE**

- User-generated content and syndication in the form of blogs and social networks grow to form an entirely new self-publishing forum.

- Newspapers and other traditional media adopt online, interactive models.

- Social networking sites: More than half the Internet user population (about 80 million adults) join a social group on the Internet.

- Advertisers begin taking advantage of blogs as a new commercial medium.

---

- The number of people who have purchased something online expanded to about 110 million, with additional millions shopping (gathering information) but not purchasing.
- B2B e-commerce—use of the Internet for business-to-business commerce—expanded about 30 percent in 2005 to more than $1.5 trillion and continues to strengthen (U.S. Department of Commerce, 2005).

The e-commerce revolution is still just beginning. Individuals and businesses will increasingly use the Internet to conduct commerce as more products and services come online and households switch to broadband telecommunications. More industries will be transformed by e-commerce, including travel reservations, music and entertainment, news, software, education, and finance. Table 9.1 highlights these new e-commerce developments.

**TABLE 9.2**

**Seven Unique Features of E-Commerce Technology**

| E-Commerce Technology Dimension | Business Significance |
|---|---|
| *Ubiquity.* Internet/Web technology is available everywhere: at work, at home, and elsewhere via mobile devices, anytime. | The marketplace is extended beyond traditional boundaries and is removed from a temporal and geographic location. "Marketspace" is created; shopping can take place anywhere. Customer convenience is enhanced, and shopping costs are reduced. |
| *Global Reach.* The technology reaches across national boundaries, around the earth. | Commerce is enabled across cultural and national boundaries seamlessly and without modification. The marketspace includes, potentially, billions of consumers and millions of businesses worldwide. |
| *Universal Standards.* There is one set of technology standards, namely Internet standards. | There is one set of technical standards across the globe so that disparate computer systems can easily communicate with each other. |
| *Richness.* Video, audio, and text messages are possible. | Video, audio, and text marketing messages are integrated into a single marketing message and consumer experience. |
| *Interactivity.* The technology works through interaction with the user. | Consumers are engaged in a dialog that dynamically adjusts the experience to the individual, and makes the consumer a co-participant in the process of delivering goods to the market. |
| *Information Density.* The technology reduces information costs and raises quality. | Information processing, storage, and communication costs drop dramatically, whereas currency, accuracy, and timeliness improve greatly. Information becomes plentiful, cheap, and more accurate. |
| *Personalization/Customization.* The technology allows personalized messages to be delivered to individuals as well as groups. | Personalization of marketing messages and customization of products and services are based on individual characteristics. |

## Why E-commerce Is Different

Why has e-commerce grown so rapidly? Why are there college courses on e-commerce? The answer lies in the unique nature of the Internet and the Web. Simply put, the Internet and e-commerce technologies are much more rich and powerful than previous technology revolutions. Table 9.2 describes the unique features of the Internet and Web as a commercial medium. Let's explore each of these unique features in more detail.

### Ubiquity

In traditional commerce, a marketplace is a physical place, such as a retail store, you visit in order to transact business. E-commerce is ubiquitous, meaning that is it available just about everywhere, at all times. It makes it possible to shop from your desktop, at home, at work, or even from your car, using mobile commerce. The result is called a **marketspace**—a marketplace extended beyond traditional boundaries and removed from a temporal and geographic location.

From a consumer point of view, ubiquity reduces **transaction costs**—the costs of participating in a market. To transact business, it is no longer necessary that you spend time or money traveling to a market, and much less mental effort is required to make a purchase.

## Global Reach

E-commerce technology permits commercial transactions to cross cultural and national boundaries far more conveniently and cost-effectively than is true in traditional commerce. As a result, the potential market size for e-commerce merchants is roughly equal to the size of the world's online population (more than 900 million in 2005, and growing rapidly).

In contrast, most traditional commerce is local or regional—it involves local merchants or national merchants with local outlets. Television and radio stations and newspapers, for instance, are primarily local and regional institutions with limited, but powerful, national networks that can attract a national audience but not easily cross national boundaries to a global audience.

## Universal Standards

One strikingly unusual feature of e-commerce technologies is that the technical standards of the Internet and, therefore, the technical standards for conducting e-commerce are universal standards. They are shared by all nations around the world and enable any computer to link with any other computer regardless of the technology platform each is using. In contrast, most traditional commerce technologies differ from one nation to the next. For instance, television and radio standards differ around the world, as does cell telephone technology.

The universal technical standards of the Internet and e-commerce greatly lower **market entry costs**—the cost merchants must pay simply to bring their goods to market. At the same time, for consumers, universal standards reduce **search costs**—the effort required to find suitable products.

## Richness

Information **richness** refers to the complexity and content of a message. Traditional markets, national sales forces, and small retail stores have great richness: They are able to provide personal, face-to-face service using aural and visual cues when making a sale. The richness of traditional markets makes them powerful selling or commercial environments. Prior to the development of the Web, there was a trade-off between richness and reach: The larger the audience reached, the less rich the message.

## Interactivity

Unlike any of the commercial technologies of the twentieth century, with the possible exception of the telephone, e-commerce technologies are interactive, meaning they allow for two-way communication between merchant and consumer. Television, for instance, cannot easily ask viewers questions or enter into conversations with them, and it cannot request that customer information be entered into a form. In contrast, all of these activities are possible on an e-commerce Web site. Interactivity allows an online merchant to engage a consumer in ways similar to a face-to-face experience but on a massive, global scale.

## Information Density

The Internet and the Web vastly increase **information density**—the total amount and quality of information available to all market participants, consumers, and merchants alike. E-commerce technologies reduce information collection, storage, processing, and communication costs while greatly increasing the currency, accuracy, and timeliness of information.

Information density in e-commerce markets make prices and costs more transparent. **Price transparency** refers to the ease with which consumers can find out the variety of prices in a market; **cost transparency** refers to the ability of consumers to discover the actual costs merchants pay for products.

There are advantages for merchants as well. Online merchants can discover much more about consumers than in the past. This allows merchants to segment the market into groups who are willing to pay different prices and permits the merchants to engage in **price discrimination**—selling the same goods, or nearly the same goods, to different targeted groups at different prices. For instance, an online merchant can discover a consumer's avid interest in expensive, exotic vacations and then pitch expensive, exotic vacation plans to that consumer at a premium price, knowing this person is willing to pay extra for such a vacation. At the same time, the online merchant can pitch the same vacation plan at a lower price to a more price-sensitive consumer. Information density also helps merchants differentiate their products in terms of cost, brand, and quality.

### Personalization/Customization

E-commerce technologies permit **personalization**: Merchants can target their marketing messages to specific individuals by adjusting the message to a person's name, interests, and past purchases. The technology also permits **customization**—changing the delivered product or service based on a user's preferences or prior behavior. Given the interactive nature of e-commerce technology, much information about the consumer can be gathered in the marketplace at the moment of purchase. With the increase in information density, a great deal of information about the consumer's past purchases and behavior can be stored and used by online merchants. The result is a level of personalization and customization unthinkable with existing commerce technologies. For instance, you may be able to shape what you see on television by selecting a channel, but you cannot change the content of the channel you have chosen. In contrast, the *Wall Street Journal Online* allows you to select the type of news stories you want to see first and gives you the opportunity to be alerted when certain events happen.

## Key Concepts in E-commerce: Digital Markets and Digital Goods

There is a connection between information and business: The location, timing, and revenue models of business are based in some part on the cost and distribution of information. The Internet has created a digital marketplace where millions of people are able to exchange massive amounts of information directly, instantly, and for free. As a result, the Internet has changed the way companies conduct business.

The Internet shrinks information asymmetry. An **information asymmetry** exists when one party in a transaction has more information that is important for the transaction than the other party. That information helps determine their relative bargaining power. In digital markets, consumers and suppliers can "see" the prices being charged for goods, and in that sense digital markets are said to be more "transparent" than traditional markets.

For example, until auto retailing sites appeared on the Web, there was a pronounced information asymmetry between auto dealers and customers. Only the auto dealers knew the manufacturers' prices, and it was difficult for consumers to shop around for the best price. Auto dealers' profit margins depended on this asymmetry of information. Today's consumers have access to a legion of Web sites providing competitive pricing information, and three-fourths of U.S. auto buyers use the Internet to shop around for the best deal. Thus, the Web has reduced the information asymmetry surrounding an auto purchase. The Internet has also helped businesses seeking to purchase from other businesses reduce information asymmetries and locate better prices and terms.

Digital markets are very flexible and efficient because they operate with reduced search and transaction costs, lower **menu costs** (merchants' costs of changing prices), price discrimination, and the ability to change prices dynamically based on market conditions. In **dynamic pricing**, the price of a product varies depending on the demand characteristics of the customer or the supply situation of the seller. These markets may either reduce or increase switching costs, depending on the nature of the product or service being sold, and they may cause some extra delay in gratification. Unlike a physical market, you can't immediately consume a product such as clothing purchased over the Web (although immediate consumption is possible with digital music downloads and other digital products).

Digital markets provide many opportunities to sell directly to the consumer, bypassing intermediaries, such as distributors or retail outlets. Eliminating intermediaries in the distribution channel can significantly lower purchase transaction costs. To pay for all the steps in a traditional distribution channel, a product may have to be priced as high as 135 percent of its original cost to manufacture. Figure 9-2 illustrates how much savings result from eliminating each of these layers in the distribution process. By selling directly to consumers or reducing the number of intermediaries, companies are able to raise profits while charging

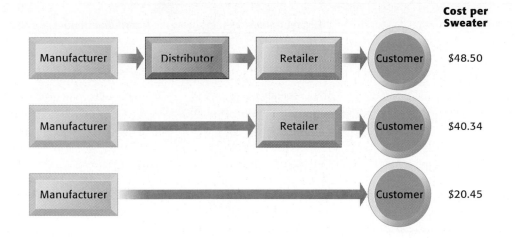

Cost per Sweater

Manufacturer → Distributor → Retailer → Customer    $48.50

Manufacturer → Retailer → Customer    $40.34

Manufacturer → Customer    $20.45

**Figure 9-2**
The Benefits of Disintermediation to the Consumer
*The typical distribution channel has several intermediary layers, each of which adds to the final cost of a product, such as a sweater. Removing layers lowers the final cost to the consumer.*

lower prices. The removal of organizations or business process layers responsible for intermediary steps in a value chain is called **disintermediation**.

Disintermediation is also taking place in the market for services. Airlines and hotels operating their own reservation sites online earn more per ticket because they have eliminated travel agents as intermediaries. Table 9.3 summarizes the differences between digital markets and traditional markets.

## Digital Goods

The Internet digital marketplace has greatly expanded sales of digital goods. **Digital goods** are goods that can be delivered over a digital network. Music tracks, video, software, newspapers, magazines, and books can all be expressed, stored, delivered, and sold as purely digital products. Currently, most of these products are sold as physical goods, for example, CDs, DVDs, and hard copy books. But the Internet offers the possibility of delivering all these products on demand as digital products.

In general, for digital goods, the marginal cost of producing another unit is about zero (it costs nothing to make a copy of a music file). However, the cost of producing the original first unit is relatively high—in fact it is nearly the total cost of the product because there are few other costs of inventory and distribution. Costs of delivery over the Internet are very

| | Digital Markets | Traditional Markets |
|---|---|---|
| Information asymmetry | Asymmetry reduced | Asymmetry high |
| Search costs | Low | High |
| Transaction costs | Low (sometimes virtually nothing) | High (time, travel) |
| Delayed gratification | High (or lower in the case of a digital good) | Lower: purchase now |
| Menu costs | Low | High |
| Dynamic Pricing | Low cost, instant | High cost, delayed |
| Price discrimination | Low cost, instant | High cost, delayed |
| Market segmentation | Low cost, moderate precision | High cost, less precision |
| Switching costs | Higher/lower (depending on product characteristics) | High |
| Network effects | Strong | Weaker |
| Disintermediation | More possible/likely | Less possible/unlikely |

**TABLE 9.3**

**Digital Markets Compared to Traditional Markets**

**TABLE 9.4**

**How the Internet Changes the Markets for Digital Goods**

|  | Digital Goods | Traditional Goods |
|---|---|---|
| Marginal cost/unit | Zero | Greater than zero, high |
| Cost of production | High (most of the cost) | Variable |
| Copying cost | Approximately zero | Greater than zero, high |
| Distributed delivery cost | Low | High |
| Inventory cost | Low | High |
| Marketing cost | Variable | Variable |
| Pricing | More variable (bundling, random pricing games) | Fixed, based on unit costs |

low; marketing costs remain the same; and pricing can be highly variable. (On the Internet the merchant can change prices as often as desired because of low menu costs.)

The impact of the Internet on the market for these kinds of digital goods is nothing short of revolutionary, and we see the results around us every day. Businesses dependent on physical products for sales—such as bookstores, book publishers, music labels, and film studios—face the possibility of declining sales and even destruction of their businesses. Newspapers and magazines are losing readers to the Internet, and losing advertisers. Record label companies are losing sales to Internet piracy and record stores are going out of business. Video rental firms, such as Blockbuster, based on a physical DVD market and physical stores are losing sales to NetFlix using an Internet model (see the Chapter 3 ending case). Hollywood studios as well, face the prospect that Internet pirates will distribute their product as digital streams, bypassing Hollywood's monopoly on DVD rentals and sales, which now accounts for more than half of industry film revenues. Table 9.4 describes digital goods and how they differ from traditional physical goods.

### Internet Business Models

The bottom line result of these changes in the economics of information is nearly a revolution in commerce, with many new business models appearing and many old business models no longer tenable. Table 9.5 describes some of the most important Internet business models that have emerged. All, in one way or another, use the Internet to add extra value to existing products and services or to provide the foundation for new products and services.

### Communication and Community

Some of these new business models take advantage of the Internet's rich communication capabilities. eBay is an online auction forum that uses e-mail and other interactive features of the Web. The system accepts bids entered on the Internet, evaluates the bids, and notifies the highest bidder. eBay collects a small commission on each listing and sale. eBay has become so popular that its site serves as a huge trading platform for other companies, hosting hundreds of thousands of "virtual storefronts." The case study concluding this chapter discusses eBay and its business model in greater detail.

Business-to-business auctions have also emerged. GoIndustry, for instance, features Web-based auction services for business-to-business sales of industrial equipment and machinery.

The Internet has created online communities, where people with similar interests exchange ideas from many different locations. Some of these virtual communities are providing the foundation for new businesses. iVillage.com provides an online community for women sharing similar interests, such as diet and fitness, pregnancy, parenting, home and garden, and food. Members post their own personal Web pages, participate in online discussion groups, and join online "clubs" with other like-minded people.

A major source of revenue for these communities involves providing ways for corporate clients to target customers, including the placement of banner ads and pop-up ads on their Web sites. A **banner ad** is a graphic display on a Web page used for advertising. The banner

**TABLE 9.5**

**Internet Business Models**

| Category | Description | Examples |
|---|---|---|
| Virtual storefront | Sells physical products directly to consumers or to individual businesses. | Amazon.com RedEnvelope.com |
| Information broker | Provides product, pricing, and availability information to individuals and businesses. Generates revenue from advertising or from directing buyers to sellers. | Edmunds.com Kbb.com Insweb.com Realtor.com |
| Transaction broker | Saves users money and time by processing online sales transactions and generating a fee each time a transaction occurs. Also provides information on rates and terms. | E*TRADE.com Expedia.com |
| Online marketplace | Provides a digital environment where buyers and sellers can meet, search for products, display products, and establish prices for those products. Can provide online auctions or reverse auctions in which buyers submit bids to multiple sellers to purchase at a buyer-specified price as well as negotiated or fixed pricing. Can serve consumers or B2B e-commerce, generating revenue from transaction fees. | eBay.com Priceline.com ChemConnect.com |
| Content provider | Creates revenue by providing digital content, such as digital news, music, photos, or video, over the Web. The customer may pay to access the content, or revenue may be generated by selling advertising space. | WSJ.com GettyImages.com iTunes.com Turner Sports Interactive |
| Online service provider | Provides online service for individuals and businesses. Generates revenue from subscription or transaction fees, from advertising, or from collecting marketing information from users. | Streamload.com Xdrive.com KodakGallery.com Salesforce.com |
| Virtual community | Provides an online meeting place where people with similar interests can communicate and find useful information. | Motocross.com MySpace.com iVillage.com |
| Portal | Provides initial point of entry to the Web along with specialized content and other services. | Yahoo.com MSN.com StarMedia.com |

is linked to the advertiser's Web site so that a person clicking the banner is transported to a Web page with more information about the advertiser. **Pop-up ads** work in the opposite manner. They automatically open up when a user accesses a specific Web site, and the user must click the ad to make it disappear.

**Social networking sites** are a type of online community that has become increasingly popular. Social networking is the practice of expanding the number of one's business or social contacts by making connections through individuals. Social networking sites link people through their mutual business or personal connections, enabling them to mine their friends (and their friends' friends) for sales leads, job-hunting tips, or new friends. Friendster.com, Tribe.net, and MySpace.com appeal to people who are primarily interested in extending their friendships. LinkedIn.com, Ryze.com, and Spoke.com focus on job networking.

### Digital Content, Entertainment, and Services

The ability to deliver digital goods and digital content over the Web has created new alternatives to traditional print and broadcast media. There are Web sites for digital versions of print publications, such as the *New York Times* or the *Wall Street Journal,* and for new online journals such as Salon.com. Some of the most popular Web sites deliver entertainment in digital form. Online games, including Web versions of board games, card games, and video games, attract huge numbers of players.

Television broadcasters provide streaming video over the Internet consisting of news clips and excerpts from other shows, including previews of future shows and interviews with actors. News sites, such as CNN.com, and sports sites, such as Turner Sports Interactive and NFL.com, feature video clips, audio clips, and replays from television shows. Visitors to ABC.com can watch video clips on the latest developments in the network's most popular soap operas. Some sites charge for their entertainment content. Broadband connections are making it possible for Web sites to display full-length films and television shows in the future.

You can listen to some of your favorite radio channels, such as Classic Rock or the BBC, on the Web as well as many independent channels. Because the radio signal is relayed over the Internet, it is possible to access stations from anywhere in the world. Services such as Yahoo!'s Launchcast and RealNetworks' Rhapsody even put together individualized radio channels for listeners.

Many of you use the Web to preview and download music. Although some of this Internet music is free of charge, Apple's iTunes and other sites are generating revenue by charging for each song or album downloaded from their Web sites. The phenomenal popularity of Apple's iTunes music service and Apple's iPod portable music player has inspired a new form of digital content delivery called *podcasting.* **Podcasting** is a method of publishing audio broadcasts via the Internet, allowing subscribing users to download audio files onto their personal computers or portable music players. Podcasting enables independent producers to self-publish their own audio content and gives broadcast radio programs a new distribution method.

The Web's information resources are so vast and rich that *portals* have emerged as an Internet business model to help individuals and organizations locate information more efficiently. In Chapter 2, we defined a portal as a Web interface for presenting integrated, personalized information from a variety of sources. As an e-commerce business model, a *portal* is a "supersite" that provides a comprehensive entry point for a huge array of resources and services on the Internet.

Yahoo! is an example. It provides capabilities for locating information on the Internet along with news, sports, weather, telephone directories, maps, games, shopping, e-mail, chat, discussion boards, and links to other sites. Also, specialized portals help users with specific interests. For example, StarMedia is a portal customized for Latin American Internet users, and the portal Sina.com is customized for Chinese users.

Yahoo! and other portals and Web content sites often combine content and applications from many different sources and service providers. Other Internet business models use syndication as well to provide additional value. For example, E*TRADE, the discount Web trading site, purchases most of its content from outside sources such as Reuters (news) and BigCharts.com (charts). Online **syndicators**, who aggregate content or applications from multiple sources, package them for distribution, and resell them to third-party Web sites, have emerged as another variant of the online content provider business model. The Web makes it much easier for companies to aggregate, repackage, and distribute information and information-based services.

Chapter 4 describes application service providers, such as Employease.com or Salesforce.com, that feature software that runs over the Web. They provide online services to subscribing businesses. Other online service providers offer services to individual consumers, such as remote storage of data at Xdrive.com or online photo storage and digital photo printouts at KodakGallery.com. Service providers generate revenue through subscription fees or from advertising.

Most of the business models described in Table 9.5 are called **pure-play** business models because they are based purely on the Internet. These firms did not have an existing bricks-and-mortar business when they designed their Internet business. However, many existing retail firms, such as L.L. Bean, Office Depot, R.E.I., and the *Wall Street Journal,* have developed Web sites as extensions of their traditional bricks-and-mortar businesses. Such businesses represent a hybrid **clicks-and-mortar** business model.

## 9.2 Electronic Commerce

Although most commercial transactions still take place through traditional retail channels, rising numbers of consumers and businesses are using the Internet for electronic commerce. Today, e-commerce revenue represents about 2 percent of all retail sales in the United States, and there is tremendous upside potential for growth.

### Categories of Electronic Commerce

There are many ways to classify electronic commerce transactions. One is by looking at the nature of the participants in the electronic commerce transaction. The three major electronic commerce categories are business-to-consumer (B2C) e-commerce, business-to-business (B2B) e-commerce, and consumer-to-consumer (C2C) e-commerce.

- **Business-to-consumer (B2C) electronic commerce** involves retailing products and services to individual shoppers. BarnesandNoble.com, which sells books, software, and music to individual consumers, is an example of B2C e-commerce.
- **Business-to-business (B2B) electronic commerce** involves sales of goods and services among businesses. Milacron's Web site for selling machinery; mold bases; and related tooling, supplies, and services to companies engaged in plastics processing is an example of B2B e-commerce.
- **Consumer-to-consumer (C2C) electronic commerce** involves consumers selling directly to consumers. For example, eBay, the giant Web auction site, enables people to sell their goods to other consumers by auctioning the merchandise off to the highest bidder.

Another way of classifying electronic commerce transactions is in terms of the participants' physical connection to the Web. Until recently, almost all e-commerce transactions took place over wired networks. Now mobile phones and other wireless handheld digital appliances are Internet enabled to send text messages and e-mail, access Web sites, and make purchases. Companies are offering new types of Web-based products and services that can be accessed by these wireless devices. The use of handheld wireless devices for purchasing goods and services from any location has been termed **mobile commerce** or **m-commerce**. Both business-to-business and business-to-consumer e-commerce transactions can take place using m-commerce technology, which we discuss in detail in Section 9.3.

### Achieving Customer Intimacy: Interactive Marketing, Personalization, and Self-Service

The unique dimensions of e-commerce technologies that we have just described offer many new possibilities for marketing and selling. The Internet provides companies with additional channels of communication and interaction for closer yet more cost-effective relationships with customers in sales, marketing, and customer support.

## Interactive Marketing and Personalization

The Internet and e-commerce have helped some merchants achieve the holy grail of marketing: making products for millions of consumers that are personal, an impossible task in traditional markets. Web sites, such as that for Lands' End (shirts and pants) and VistaPrint (business cards, note cards, and labels), feature online tools that allow consumers to purchase products tailored to their individual specifications.

Web sites have become a bountiful source of detailed information about customer behavior, preferences, needs, and buying patterns that companies can use to tailor promotions, products, services, and pricing. Some customer information may be obtained by asking visitors to "register" online and provide information about themselves, but many companies also collect customer information using software tools that track the activities of Web site visitors.

**Clickstream tracking** tools collect data on customer activities at Web sites and store them in a log. The tools record the site that users visited prior to coming to a particular Web site and where these users go when they leave that site. They also record the specific pages visited on the particular site, the time spent on each page of the site, the types of pages visited, and what the visitors purchased (see Figure 9-3). Firms analyze this information about customer interests and behavior to develop precise profiles of existing and potential customers.

Such information enables firms to create unique personalized Web pages that display content or ads for products or services of special interest to each user, improving the customer's experience and creating additional value (see Figure 9-4). By using personalization technology to modify the Web pages presented to each customer, marketers achieve the benefits of using individual salespeople at dramatically lower costs. Personalization can also help firms form lasting relationships with customers by providing individualized content, information, and services.

One technique for Web personalization is **collaborative filtering**, which compares information gathered about a specific user's behavior at a Web site to data about other customers with similar interests to predict what the user would like to see next. The software then makes recommendations to users based on their assumed interests. For example, Amazon.com and BarnesandNoble.com use collaborative filtering software to prepare personalized book recommendations: "Customers who bought this book also bought . . . ."

**Figure 9-3**

Web Site Visitor Tracking

*E-commerce Web sites have tools to track a shopper's every step through an online store. Close examination of customer behavior at a Web site selling women's clothing shows what the store might learn at each step and what actions it could take to increase sales.*

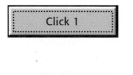

The shopper clicks on the home page. The store can tell that the shopper arrived from the Yahoo! portal at 2:30 PM (which might help determine staffing for customer service centers) and how long she lingered on the home page (which might indicate trouble navigating the site).

The shopper clicks on blouses, clicks to select a woman's white blouse, then clicks to view the same item in pink. The shopper clicks to select this item in a size 10 in pink and clicks to place it in her shopping cart. This information can help the store determine which sizes and colors are most popular.

From the shopping cart page, the shopper clicks to close the browser to leave the Web site without purchasing the blouse. This action could indicate the shopper changed her mind or that she had a problem with the Web site's checkout and payment process. Such behavior might signal that the Web site was not well designed.

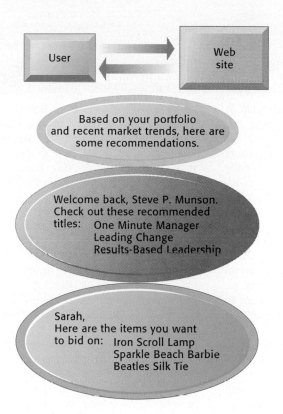

**Figure 9-4**
Web Site
Personalization
*Firms can create unique personalized Web pages that display content or ads for products or services of special interest to individual users, improving the customer experience and creating additional value.*

These recommendations are made just at the point of purchase, an ideal time to prompt a consumer into purchasing a related product.

### Blogs

Blogs have emerged as another promising Web-based tool for marketing. A **blog**, the popular term for a Weblog, is an informal yet structured Web site where subscribing individuals can publish stories, opinions, and links to other Web sites of interest. Specialized *moblogs* post photos with captions from mobile phones and allow users to comment on other people's shots, whereas *vlogs* post video diaries online. Companies also use blogs internally to communicate and exchange ideas about projects and company news.

Companies are posting ads on some of the most popular blogs published by individuals or by other organizations. Some firms have developed their own blogs as a new channel for reaching customers. These corporate blogs provide a personal and conversational way for businesses to present information to the public and prospective customers about new products and services. Readers are often invited to post comments.

The Focus on People describes how organic yogurt company Stonyfield Farm Inc. is taking advantage of these capabilities to create tighter relationships with its customers. As you read this case, try to identify the problem this company was facing; what alternative solutions were available to management; how well the chosen solution worked; and the people, organization, and technology issues that had to be addressed when developing the solution.

Marketers are starting to analyze blogs as well as chat groups and message boards to see what is being said online about new products, old brands, and ad campaigns. Blog-watching services that monitor popular blogs claim that "blog watching" can be cheaper and faster for analyzing consumer interests and sentiment than traditional focus groups and surveys. For example, blog watching helped U.S. Cellular learn that many teenagers were anxious about exceeding their cellular minute allotments with charges for incoming calls because parents would make them pay if they talked too much. The company then started offering unlimited "call me" minutes to attract this group. Polaroid learned from blogs that consumers online frequently discuss photo longevity and archiving, prompting it to pay more attention to long-lasting photos in its product development.

# FOCUS ON PEOPLE    Stonyfield Farm Blogs for Organic Communication

The story of Stonyfield Farm is something of a legend. In 1983, friends and social activists Gary Hirschberg and Samuel Kaymen started out with a great yogurt recipe, seven cows, and a dream. They set up an organic yogurt company in Wilton, New Hampshire, to capitalize on baby boomers' growing concerns with pure foods and health, and to revitalize the New England dairy industry. Stonyfield Farm has grown to become the third largest organic company in the world, with more than $50 million in annual sales in 50 states. It produces more than 18 million cups of yogurt each month.

Stonyfield Farm's phenomenal growth is in part attributable to its ability to provide a product for a special niche market—people who treasure healthy foods and want to protect the environment. These values have become embedded in the company's "personality." Stonyfield pledges to use in its products only natural ingredients and milk that have not been produced with antibiotics, synthetic growth hormones, and toxic pesticides and fertilizers. The company donates 10 percent of its profits each year to efforts that help protect or restore the Earth.

As the company expanded, management feared it would lose touch with its loyal and committed customer base. Traditional media-based advertising was expensive and wouldn't really help the company "connect" with the kinds of people it was trying to reach. This company prefers "word-of-mouth" approaches that get its message to customers in ways that are more compatible with its grassroots, organic, activist "people-friendly" image. Stonyfield has several active e-mail newsletters with more than 500,000 subscribers, and it regularly places messages promoting causes it supports on the lids of its yogurt cups. Now, it is turning to blogs to further personalize its relationship with customers and reach even more people.

Inspired by Howard Dean's presidential campaign and tutorials from Dean's bloggers, CEO Hirschberg became convinced that Stonyfield could use blogs to create a more personal relationship with consumers that is different from the traditional selling relationship. "The blogs give us what we call a handshake with consumers" and "a little more access to us as a people with a mission," he says.

Stonyfield actually publishes four different blogs on its Web site. Creating Healthy Kids features information about the company's Menu for Change program, which seeks to change the way children eat and to encourage healthy food consumption in public schools. Strong Women Daily features fitness and health tips, stress-coping strategies, and information on the company's Strong Women events. Baby Babble provides a forum for Stonyfield employees and other parents of young children to meet and talk about child development and balancing work with family. The Bovine Bugle provides reports from Jonathan Gates' organic dairy farm in Franklin, Vermont, a member of the organic cooperative that supplies the milk for Stonyfield products. This blog elicits a large number of nostalgic comments from readers remembering their childhood on a farm. As organic foods go mainstream, the blogs help the company show how its brand differs from others and invite customers to help them in that effort.

Stonyfield posts new content to each of the blogs daily, five days a week. Readers can subscribe to any of these blogs and automatically receive updates when they become available. And of course, they can respond to the postings.

Stonyfield hired Christine Halverson, a former journalist and almanac writer, to produce all of the blogs in-house. Her job includes researching and writing new entries and providing personal insight. Google news alerts send her news stories on the topics she covers and she does some original reporting.

At this point, the benefits of Stonyfield's blogs have not yet been quantified, but management has faith that there are real benefits. The blogs have created a positive response to the Stonyfield brand by providing readers with something that inspires them or piques their interest. If the blogs give readers new information, inspire them to take environmental actions, or ask for opinions, management believes they will remember the brand when they stand in front of the yogurt case at the supermarket or grocery store and that they will reach for Stonyfield rather than a competing product when given the choice.

Stonyfield has a very large Web site. The blogs provide a way to highlight some of the Web content that might otherwise get lost. This, too, helps steer some blog readers to buy Stonyfield products.

*Sources:* "Online Extra: Stonyfield Farm's Blog Culture, "*BusinessWeek*, May 2, 2005; Sarah Needleman, "Blogging Becomes a Corporate Job: Digital 'Handshake'?" *The Wall Street Journal*, May 31, 2005; and Jason Imber, "Organic Communication," *Portals Magazine*, August/September 2004; and www.stonyfieldfarms.com, accessed September 12, 2005.

**To Think About:**

What are Stonyfield Farm's business model and business strategy? What challenges and problems does the company face? How do blogs help the company solve these problems and compete in the industry? How successful is this solution? Explain your answer.

## Customer Self-Service

Many companies are using their Web sites and e-mail to answer customer questions or to provide customers with helpful information. The Web provides a medium for customers to interact with the company, at the customers' convenience, and find information that previously required a human customer-support expert.

For instance, American, Northwest, and other major airlines have created Web sites where customers can review flight departure and arrival times, seating charts, and airport logistics; check frequent-flyer miles; and purchase tickets online. Chapter 1 describes how customers of UPS can use its Web site to track shipments, calculate shipping costs, determine time in transit, and arrange for a package pickup. FedEx and other package delivery firms provide similar Web-based services. Automated self-service or other Web-based responses to customer questions cost only a fraction of what a live customer service representative on the telephone would cost.

New software products are even integrating the Web with customer call centers, where customer service problems have been traditionally handled over the telephone. A **call center** is an organizational department responsible for handling customer service issues by telephone and other channels. For example, a visitor to the Lands' End Web site can request a phone call from customer service by entering his or her telephone number. A call-center system directs a customer service representative to place a voice telephone call to the user's phone. Some systems let the customer interact with a service representative on the Web while talking on the phone at the same time.

## Business-to-Business Electronic Commerce: New Efficiencies and Relationships

About 80 percent of B2B e commerce is still based on proprietary systems for electronic data interchange (EDI). **Electronic data interchange (EDI)** enables the computer-to-computer exchange between two organizations of standard transactions such as invoices, bills of lading, shipment schedules, or purchase orders. Transactions are automatically transmitted from one information system to another through a network, eliminating the printing and handling of paper at one end and the inputting of data at the other. Each major industry in the United States and much of the rest of the world has EDI standards that define the structure and information fields of electronic transactions for that industry.

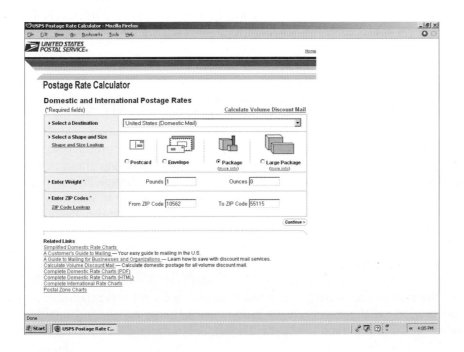

Visitors to the United States Postal Service Web site can calculate postage, print shipping labels, schedule package pickups, and track shipments. Web sites for customer self-service are convenient for customers and help organizations lower their customer service and support costs.

**Figure 9-5**
Electronic Data
Interchange (EDI)
*Companies use EDI to
automate transactions
for B2B e-commerce
and continuous inven-
tory replenishment.
Suppliers can automati-
cally send data about
shipments to purchas-
ing firms. The purchas-
ing firms can use EDI to
provide production and
inventory requirements
and payment data to
suppliers.*

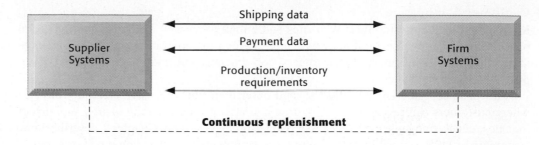

EDI originally automated the exchange of documents for purchase orders, invoices, and shipping notices. Although some companies still use EDI for document automation, firms engaged in just-in-time inventory replenishment and continuous production use EDI as a system for continuous replenishment. Suppliers have online access to selected parts of the purchasing firm's production and delivery schedules and automatically ship materials and goods to meet prespecified targets without intervention by firm purchasing agents (see Figure 9-5).

Although many organizations still use private networks for EDI, companies are increasingly turning to the Internet for this purpose because it provides a much more flexible and low-cost platform for linking to other firms. Using the Internet, businesses are able to extend digital technology to a wider range of activities and broaden their circle of trading partners.

Take procurement, for example. **Procurement** involves not only purchasing goods and materials but also sourcing, negotiating with suppliers, paying for goods, and making delivery arrangements. Businesses can now use the Internet to locate the most low-cost supplier, search online catalogs of supplier products, negotiate with suppliers, place orders, make payments, and arrange transportation. They are not limited to partners linked by traditional EDI networks but use the Web to work with any other business that is linked to the Internet. *E-procurement* over the Internet provides new opportunities for lowering costs and improving service because Internet technology enables businesses to cast their nets more widely.

The Internet and Web technology enable businesses to create new electronic storefronts for selling to other businesses with multimedia graphic displays and interactive features similar to those for B2C commerce. Alternatively, businesses can use Internet technology to create extranets or electronic marketplaces for linking to other businesses for purchase and sale transactions.

**Private industrial networks** are B2B extranets that focus on continuous business process coordination between companies for collaboration and supply chain management. A private industrial network typically consists of a large firm using an extranet to link to its suppliers and other key business partners (see Figure 9-6). The network is owned by the buyer, and it permits the firm and designated suppliers, distributors, and other business partners to share product design and development, marketing, production scheduling, inventory management, and unstructured communication, including graphics and e-mail.

Another term for a private industrial network is a **private exchange**. Private exchanges are currently the fastest-growing type of B2B commerce. An example is VWGroupSupply.com, which links the Volkswagen Group and its suppliers. VWGroupSupply.com handles 90 percent of all global purchasing for Volkswagen, including all automotive and parts components.

**Net marketplaces**, which are sometimes called *e-hubs,* provide a single, digital marketplace based on Internet technology for many different buyers and sellers (see Figure 9-7). They are industry owned or operate as independent intermediaries between buyers and sellers. Net marketplaces are more transaction oriented (and less relationship oriented) than private industrial networks, generating revenue from purchase and sale transactions and other services provided to clients. Participants in Net marketplaces can establish

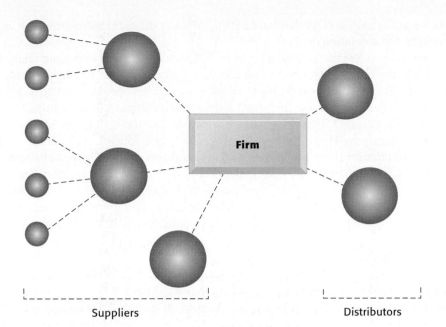

**Figure 9-6**
A Private Industrial Network
*A private industrial network, also known as a private exchange, links a firm to its suppliers, distributors, and other key business partners for efficient supply chain management and other collaborative commerce activities.*

Suppliers                                        Distributors

prices through online negotiations, auctions, or requests for quotations, or they can use fixed prices. Customers benefit from lower search costs, lower transaction costs, and wider selection.

There are many different types of Net marketplaces and ways of classifying them. Some Net marketplaces sell direct goods and some sell indirect goods. *Direct goods* are goods used in a production process, such as sheet steel for auto body production. *Indirect goods* are all other goods not directly involved in the production process, such as office supplies or products for maintenance and repair. Some Net marketplaces support contractual purchasing based on long-term relationships with designated suppliers, and others support short-term spot purchasing, where goods are purchased based on immediate needs, often from many different suppliers. Some Net marketplaces serve vertical markets for specific industries, such as automobiles, telecommunications, or machine tools, whereas others serve horizontal

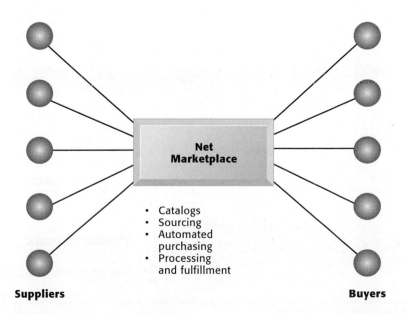

**Figure 9-7**
A Net Marketplace
*Net marketplaces are online marketplaces where multiple buyers can purchase from multiple sellers.*

Net Marketplace

- Catalogs
- Sourcing
- Automated purchasing
- Processing and fulfillment

Suppliers                                        Buyers

markets for goods and services that can be found in many different industries, such as office equipment or transportation.

Industry-owned Net marketplaces focus on long-term contract purchasing relationships and on providing common networks and computing platforms for reducing supply chain inefficiencies. Buyer firms benefit from competitive pricing among alternative suppliers, and suppliers benefit from stable long-term selling relationships with large firms.

Exostar is an example. This aerospace and defense industry–sponsored Net marketplace was founded jointly by BAE Systems, Boeing, Lockheed Martin, Raytheon, and Rolls-Royce PLC to connect these companies to their suppliers and facilitate collaboration on major projects. More than 16,000 trading partners in the commercial, military, and government sectors use Exostar's sourcing, e-procurement, and collaboration tools for both direct and indirect goods. Exostar includes capabilities for auctioning, purchase forecasting, issuing electronic payments and receipts, and linking to participants' internal corporate systems. Also featured are capabilities for collaboration on joint development projects and sharing engineering product data.

**Exchanges** are independently owned third-party Net marketplaces that can connect thousands of suppliers and buyers for spot purchasing. Many exchanges provide vertical markets for a single industry, such as food, electronics, or industrial equipment, and they primarily deal with direct inputs. For example, FoodTrader.com automates spot purchases among buyers and sellers from more than 170 countries in the food and agriculture industry.

Exchanges proliferated during the early years of e-commerce, but many have failed. Suppliers were reluctant to participate because the exchanges encouraged competitive bidding that drove prices down and did not offer any long-term relationships with buyers or services to make lowering prices worthwhile. Many essential direct purchases are not conducted on a spot basis because they require contracts and consideration of issues such as delivery timing, customization, and quality of products.

## 9.3 M-Commerce

Wireless mobile devices are starting to be used for purchasing goods and services as well as for transmitting messages. Although m-commerce represents a small fraction of total e-commerce transactions, revenue has been steadily growing (see Figure 9-8). In 2005 there were an estimated 175 million cell phone users in the United States and over 1.6 billion wireless and mobile devices worldwide.

FoodTrader.com is a Net marketplace serving the food and agricultural industries. Over 100,000 growers, packers, processors, and retail chains in 170 countries use the site as a one-stop source to buy and sell food products directly.

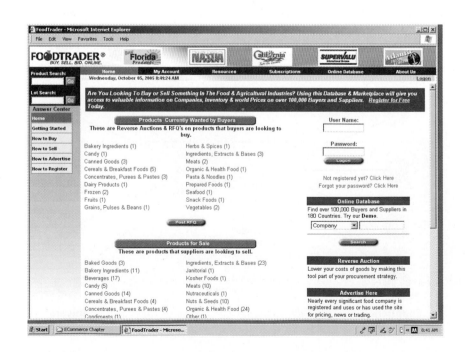

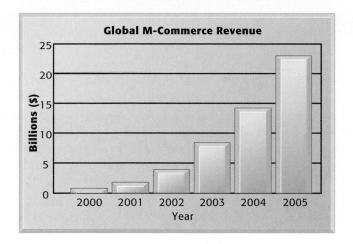

**Figure 9-8**
Global M-Commerce
Revenue,
2000–2005
*M-commerce sales rep-resent a small fraction
of total e-commerce
sales, but that percent-age is steadily growing.*

*Source:* Jupiter Research
and authors.

## M-Commerce Services and Applications

Table 9.6 describes the most popular categories of m-commerce services and applications for mobile computing. Location-based applications are of special interest because they take advantage of the unique capabilities of mobile technology. Whenever a user is connected to the Internet by a wireless device (cell phone, PDA, or handheld), the transmission technology can be leveraged to determine that person's location and beam location-specific services or product information. For example, drivers could use this capability to obtain local weather data and traffic information along with alternate route suggestions and descriptions of nearby restaurants.

Instead of focusing on how to bring a customer to a Web site, wireless marketing strategies focus on finding ways to bring the message directly to the customer at the point of need. Figure 9-9 illustrates how the ubiquitous Internet and m-commerce can extend personalization.

M-commerce applications have taken off for services that are time-critical, that appeal to people on the move, or that accomplish a task more efficiently than other methods. They are especially popular in Europe, Japan, South Korea, and other countries where fees for conventional Internet usage are very expensive. Following are some examples.

### Mobile Bill Payment

SmartPay Jieyin, working with mobile providers, banks, and utility companies, provides a service for people in Shanghai and Beijing, China, to pay their utility bills by cell phone. Most people in China do not have checking accounts and very few have credit cards, so bills must be paid by standing in a long line at a bank. The system flashes a message on a subscriber's cell phone when a payment is due. The user then types in a secret number to authorize the payment from his or her bank account.

| M-Commerce Service | Applications |
| --- | --- |
| Information-based services | Instant messaging, e-mail, searching for a movie or restaurant using a cell phone or handheld PDA |
| Transaction-based services | Purchasing stocks, concert tickets, music, or games; searching for the best price on an item using a cell phone and buying it in a physical store or on the Web |
| Personalized services | Services that anticipate what a customer wants based on that person's location or data profile, such as updated airline flight information or beaming coupons for nearby restaurants |

**TABLE 9.6**

**M-Commerce
Services and
Applications for
Mobile Computing**

**Figure 9-9**
Customer
Personalization with
the Ubiquitous
Internet
*Companies can use
mobile wireless devices
to deliver new value-
added services directly
to customers at any
time and in any place,
extending personaliza-
tion and deepening their
relationships.*

| Target | Platform | When | Content and Service |
|---|---|---|---|
| Traveler | Computer-equipped car  | Whenever car is moving | Provide maps, driving directions, weather reports, ads for nearby restaurants and hotels. |
| Parent | Cell phone 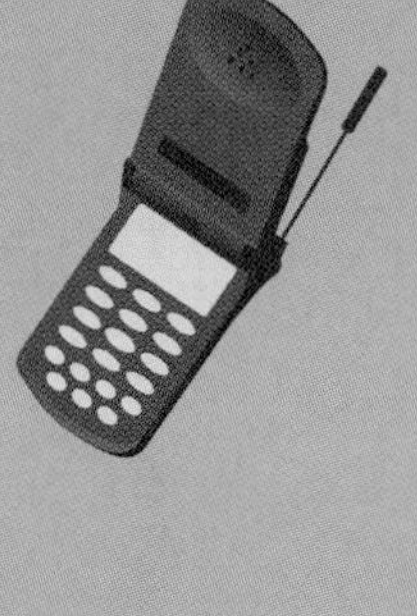 | During school days | Notify about school-related closings: Hello, Caroline. Your children's school is closing early. Press 1 for closure reason Press 2 for weather reports Press 3 for traffic reports |
| Stockbroker | Pager  | During trading days. Notify if unusually high trading volume. | Summary portfolio analysis showing changes in positions for each holding. |

### Content and Products

Vindigo offers city guides for mobile devices for a subscription price of several dollars per month. Vindigo worked with MapQuest to develop MapQuest Mobile, which provides driving directions and is available to customers of major wireless carriers for about $4 per month.

Subscribers to NTT DoCoMo wireless services in Japan can access wireless Web sites to check train schedules, obtain movie listings, browse restaurant guides, purchase tickets on Japan Airlines, trade stocks, view new cartoons, and read Japan's largest daily newspaper.

### Banking and Financial Services

Citibank offers wireless alerts about changes in account information on digital cell phones that support text messaging. Thailand's Bank of Asia offers a mobile service called ASIA M-Banking. Enrolled customers can check account balances, transfer funds between savings and other accounts, and pay their mobile phone and Internet usage charges using a Web-enabled mobile phone. They can complete these banking transactions anywhere at any time without having to visit a bank branch. Seoul-based Infobank offers a secure wireless platform for mobile phone users interested in securities trading.

### Wireless Advertising

The online travel company Expedia worked with Enpocket, a mobile marketing technology provider, to launch a demographically-targeted marketing campaign. Frequent travelers between the ages of 18 and 50 received mobile phone text messages aimed at driving recipients to the Expedia Web site. Once on the Web site, these mobile phone users were given the choice of receiving future travel offers, itineraries, flight information, and other services on their mobile phones. Ninety percent of the recipients read the message, 40 percent visited the Web site, and 4 percent made a purchase.

### Location-Based Services

Vodafone Italy, which has offered mobile services since 1995 to 19 million customers, started offering location-based services in mid-2002. Vodafone customers can access relevant traffic information; calculate itineraries; and search for nearby gas stations, hotels, restaurants, and healthcare centers. In London, Zingo offers a service for using a mobile phone to hail nearby taxicabs. A mobile phone call to a specified telephone number connects to the closest available taxi driver. The caller speaks directly to the driver to confirm the details of the trip.

### Games and Entertainment

Cell phones are quickly turning into portable entertainment platforms. Mobile phone services offer downloadable digital games and **ringtones** (digitized snippets of music that play on mobile phones when a user receives or places a call). New handset models combine the features of a cell phone and a portable music player. Users of broadband services from the major wireless vendors can download on demand movie trailers, music videos, sports clips, news clips, and weather reports. MobiTV, offered by Sprint and Cingular Wireless, features 25 live TV programs, including MSNBC and Fox Sports. South Korea's SK Telecom Co. also provides live television cellular-TV service. Film companies are starting to produce short films explicitly designed to play on mobile phones.

## Accessing Information from the Wireless Web

Although cell phones, PDAs, and other handheld mobile devices can access the Web at any time and from any place, the amount of information that they can actually handle at one time is very limited. Until 3G broadband service comes into widespread use, these devices will not be able to transmit or receive large amounts of data. The information must fit onto small display screens.

Some Web sites have been specifically designed for m-commerce. They feature Web pages with very few graphics and just enough information to fit on a small mobile handheld screen. Special **wireless portals** (also known as *mobile portals*) feature content and services optimized for mobile devices to steer users to the information they are most likely to need. They typically offer a variety of features, links to other wireless sites, the ability to select content to be pushed to the user's device, as well as providing a point of entry for anyone to send the user a message. For example, Microsoft's wireless portal provides access to news from MSNBC, sports from ESPN, movie times, local traffic reports, restaurant listings, Yellow Pages, and stock market reports, as well as capabilities for managing e-mail messages and instant messaging.

## M-Commerce Challenges

The number of Wi-Fi hotspots for wireless Internet access has been mushrooming in many countries because the technology combines high-speed Internet access with a measure of flexibility and mobility. Rollout of mobile m-commerce services, however, has proved more

The ROKR mobile handset developed by Motorola and Apple combines the features of a cell phone and a portable music player.

Yahoo! provides a mobile version of its popular portal service to help cell phone users access Web content.

problematic. Keyboards and screens on cell phones are still tiny and awkward to use. The data transfer speeds on second-generation cellular networks are very slow compared to dial-up and high-speed Internet connections for PCs. Each second waiting for data to download costs the customer money. Most Internet-enabled phones have limited memory and power supplies.

Web content for wireless devices is primarily in the form of text with very little graphics. For mobile commerce to become popular and successful, more Web sites need to be designed specifically for small wireless devices, and these wireless devices need to be more Web friendly. M-commerce will benefit from 3G networks and other cellular broadband services and from interoperable payment systems.

## 9.4 Electronic Commerce Payment Systems

Special electronic payment systems have been developed to pay for goods electronically on the Internet. Electronic payment systems for the Internet include systems for digital credit card payments, digital wallets, accumulated balance digital payment systems, stored value payment systems, digital cash, peer-to-peer payment systems, digital checking, and electronic billing presentment and payment systems.

### Types of Electronic Payment Systems

Credit cards account for 80 percent of online payments in the United States and about 50 percent of online purchases outside the United States. The more sophisticated electronic commerce software has capabilities for processing credit card purchases on the Web. Businesses can also contract with services that extend the functionality of existing credit card payment systems. **Digital credit card payment systems** extend the functionality of credit cards so they can be used for online shopping payments. They make credit cards safer and more convenient for online merchants and consumers by providing mechanisms for authenticating the purchaser's credit card to make sure it is valid and arranging for the bank that issued the credit card to deposit money for the amount of the purchase in the seller's bank account.

Digital wallets make paying for purchases over the Web more efficient by eliminating the need for shoppers to enter their address and credit card information repeatedly each time they buy something. A **digital wallet** securely stores credit card and owner identification information, and provides that information at an electronic commerce site's "checkout counter." The digital wallet enters the shopper's name, credit card number, and shipping information automatically when invoked to complete the purchase. Q*Wallet, Gator eWallet, and Google Toolbar AutoFill are examples of digital wallets.

**Micropayment** systems have been developed for purchases of less than $10, such as downloads of individual articles or music clips, which would be too small for conventional credit card payments. Accumulated balance digital payment systems or stored value payment systems are useful for such purposes.

**Accumulated balance digital payment systems** enable users to make micropayments and purchases on the Web, accumulating a debit balance that they must pay periodically on their credit card or telephone bills. QPass enables wireless customers to charge ringtones, games, and other digital products and services to their monthly phone bills.

**Stored value payment systems** such as eCount and eCharge enable consumers to make instant online payments to merchants and other individuals based on value stored in a digital account. Online value systems rely on the value stored in a consumer's bank, checking, or credit card account, and some of these systems require the use of a digital wallet.

Smart cards are another type of stored value system used for micropayments. A smart card, which we introduced in Chapter 7, can store health records, identification data, or telephone numbers, or it can serve as an "electronic purse" in place of cash. The Mondex smart card contains electronic cash and can be used to transfer funds to merchants in physical storefronts and to merchants on the Internet. It requires use of a special card-reading device whenever the card needs to transfer cash to either an online or offline merchant.

Digital cash (also known as *electronic cash* or *e-cash*) can also be used for micropayments or larger purchases. **Digital cash** is currency represented in electronic form that moves outside the normal network of money (paper currency, coins, checks, and credit cards). Users are supplied with client software and can exchange money with another e-cash user over the Internet or with a retailer accepting e-cash. eCoin.net is an example of a digital cash service. In addition to facilitating micropayments, digital cash can be useful for people who do not have credit cards and wish to make Web purchases.

New Web-based **peer-to-peer payment systems**, such as PayPal, serve people who want to send money to vendors or individuals who are not set up to accept credit card payments. The party sending money uses his or her credit card to create an account with the designated payment at a Web site dedicated to peer-to-peer payments. The recipient "picks up" the payment by visiting the Web site and supplying information about where to send the payment (a bank account or a physical address).

**Digital checking** payment systems, such as Western Union MoneyZap and eCheck, extend the functionality of existing checking accounts so they can be used for online shopping payments. Digital checks are less expensive than credit cards and much faster than traditional paper-based checking. These checks are encrypted with a digital signature that can

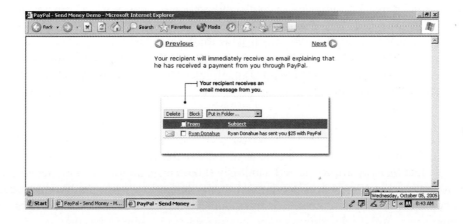

PayPal is a peer-to-peer payment system which enables users to pay anyone with an e-mail address or send a personal or group bill online.

**TABLE 9.7**

**Examples of Electronic Payment Systems for E-Commerce**

| Payment System | Description | Commercial Example |
| --- | --- | --- |
| Digital credit card payment systems | Secure services for credit card payments on the Internet protect information transmitted among users, merchant sites, and processing banks | eCharge<br>MBNA SafeShop |
| Digital wallet | Software that stores credit card and other information to facilitate form completion and payment for goods on the Web | Q*Wallet, Gator eWallet, Google Toolbar AutoFill |
| Accumulated balance digital payment systems | Accumulates micropayment purchases as a debit balance that must be paid periodically on credit card or telephone bills | QPass, Valista, Peppercoin |
| Stored value payment systems | Enables consumers to make instant payments to merchants based on value stored in a digital account | eCount, eCharge, Mondex card |
| Digital cash | Digital currency that can be used for micropayments or larger purchases | eCoin.net ClearBit |
| Peer-to-peer payment systems | Sends money using the Web to individuals or vendors who are not set up to accept credit card payments | PayPal |
| Digital checking | Electronic check with a secure digital signature | Western Union MoneyZap, eCheck |
| Electronic billing presentment and payment systems | Supports electronic payment for online and physical store purchases of goods or services after the purchase has taken place | CheckFree, Yahoo! Bill Pay |

be verified and used for payments in electronic commerce. Electronic check systems are useful in business-to-business electronic commerce.

**Electronic billing presentment and payment systems** are used for paying routine monthly bills. They enable users to view their bills electronically and pay them through electronic fund transfers from bank or credit card accounts. These services support payment for online and physical store purchases of goods or services after the purchase has taken place. They notify purchasers about bills that are due, present the bills, and process the payments. Some of these services, such as CheckFree, consolidate subscribers' bills from various sources so that they can all be paid at one time. Table 9.7 summarizes the features of some of these payment systems.

## Digital Payment Systems for M-Commerce

With a Wi-Fi connection, you can take advantage of all existing forms of Internet payment—the fact that you are connected wirelessly should have no impact. Cell phones, handhelds, and other wireless devices equipped with attachments to swipe credit cards are gaining in popularity. Many m-commerce transactions, however, are small, frequent purchases for items such as soft drinks, sports scores, newspapers, or mobile games that require special micropayment systems.

# FOCUS ON ORGANIZATIONS  Can NTT DoCoMo Turn a Cell Phone into a Credit Card?

NTT DoCoMo is Japan's leading cell phone company, with 49 million customers. Since its creation in 1992, DoCoMo has established a track record of success and innovation.

Now the company is in unfamiliar territory. For the first time ever, DoCoMo's revenue decreased from March 31, 2004, through March 31, 2005. DoCoMo must confront increasing competition in the market from KDDI Corp. and Vodafone's Japan unit, which are pushing down fees for both regular calls and data services.

DoCoMo blazed the trail for cell phone e-mail and Web browsing services, as well as downloadable ringtones. Then came a service that delivered information to customers on their small cell phone screens, including the ability to access their bank accounts. DoCoMo enlisted other companies to provide content for the service, with usage charged to users' DoCoMo phone bills. DoCoMo would then take a 9 percent cut of all transactions.

The service, named i-mode, was launched in 1999 to great success. (Chapter 6 provides details on how this technology works.) DoCoMo became a leader in what was dubbed "third-generation" phone service.

Akio Shiibashi, an engineer at East Japan Railway, had developed a system that would enable train passengers to pass through station turnstiles by waving a card near a sensor. His ultimate goal was to install a card containing a Sony FeliCa radio frequency identification (RFID) chip in cell phones. The product soon became a priority for DoCoMo as a way to raise customer loyalty.

DoCoMo's i-mode mobile wallet phones featuring the FeliCa chip reached the market in July 2004. Each phone stores up to the equivalent of U.S. $450 in cash and credit card numbers for some credit cards widely used in Japan so people can use the phone to charge purchases. The train ticket use for which the phone was initially intended was not available right away, but subscribers immediately started using the phones to carry electronic cash, open the doors to their homes, sign in at karaoke bars, and accumulate frequent-shopper points from retailers. Today, users can make purchases with their phones from 20,000 merchants, including restaurants and supermarkets. DoCoMo is trying to sign up as many payment services as possible to make use of the ubiquitous i-mode FeliCa.

The technology faces some obstacles. Japanese consumers prefer to use cash in general. They also have security concerns. And some merchants are unwilling to pay the commissions, usually 2 to 5 percent, that accompany this form of payment. DoCoMo addressed security concerns by adding remote locking mechanisms to the FeliCa chip so that lost or stolen phones could not be used for illegal purchases. The company also tried to entice merchants to accept FeliCa payments by paying for the installation of the FeliCa readers that connect to cash registers.

With five million wallet phones sold, DoCoMo is far ahead of most telecommunications companies in the world when it comes to m-commerce. It is difficult to call the product a success, though, because many subscribers are not using the wallet features. Soon, DoCoMo's rivals KDDI and Vodafone will release their own phones equipped with FeliCa chips.

Now senior Vice President Takeshi Natsuno wants to turn NTT DoCoMo cell phones into credit cards. The next generation of DoCoMo phones will come with an embedded credit card—one that bares the DoCoMo logo. Natsuno hopes that the i-mode FeliCa phones will enable DoCoMo to tap into Japan's $256 billion micropayment market (purchases of $30 and under). Once consumers become comfortable with making these types of purchases with their phones, Natsuno believes that they will make larger purchases on credit.

For the credit card phone to take off, DoCoMo must divorce customers of their cash-spending preference and overcome their lack of experience in finance. It also must train staff to field credit card-related issues and maintain good relationships with banks. Finally, merchants and banks must equip their stores and ATMs with credit card chip readers. This latest initiative is a great risk, but one that DoCoMo managers believe it must take to counter dwindling sales and create a new revenue stream.

*Sources:* Ginny Parker Woods, "Japan's Cellphone Giant Tries Expansion into Credit Cards," *The Wall Street Journal*, August 16, 2005; Dan Balaban, "DoCoMo Keeps Plugging the e-Wallet," The Deal.com, June 21, 2005, accessed through cnet news.com, August 26, 2005; Sinead Carew (Reuters), "Wireless Wallets Come Closer to Reality," *Computerworld*, August 1, 2005; Kevin Maney, "Melding of Cell Phones and Wi-Fi Will Be Cosmic, Man," *USA Today*, August 23, 2005; and "DoCoMo Quarterly Net Rises on Subscribers, Sale Gain," *Bloomberg*, July 29, 2005.

**To Think About:**

What problem is DoCoMo facing? What strategy has the company chosen to address this problem? Is this a good strategy? Why or why not? Are there any other strategies that DoCoMo might have considered? What outside forces have contributed to the challenges DoCoMo faces?

Micropayment systems are working well in Europe and Asia, where mobile operators and Internet service providers handle small payments by adding them up and presenting them on a single bill, such as the mobile telephone bill. In London, you can buy Virgin Cola using a Virgin Mobile phone by simply dialing a number on the vending machine (the cost of the drink is simply charged to your cell phone account). A mobile micropayment system from Finland's Sonera enables users in Helsinki to pay for parking using their mobile phones and have the payment amount invoiced on their mobile phone bills.

In Japan, NTT DoCoMo, the wireless arm of Nippon Telegraph and Telephone Company, has been a leader in cell phone payment systems. The Focus on Organizations shows how this company developed cell phones with a stored payment system for purchases in designated stores, restaurants, and vending machines to grow its business. DoCoMo now faces stiff competition and is pinning its hopes on a new phone that functions as a credit card and does not require a swipe attachment. As you read this case, try to identify the problem this company was facing; what alternative solutions were available to management; how well the chosen solution worked; and the people, organization, and technology issues that had to be addressed when developing the solution.

In both the United States and Europe, the micropayment services just described are based on a "walled garden" model in which individual service providers run their own separate payment systems. What is needed to help m-commerce take off is more interoperability achieved by having all the players agree on a common, secure platform for wireless m-commerce payments. To become widely adopted, a universal m-commerce payment system requires the backing of most of the major stakeholders in payment systems—consumers, vendors, phone equipment manufacturers, wireless service providers, and financial industry participants.

---

**LEARNING TRACKS**

1. If you want to learn more about the challenges of electronic commerce, you will find a Learning Track on this topic at the Laudon Web site for this chapter.

---

## Summary

1 **Describe the unique features of e-commerce, digital markets, and digital goods.** E-commerce involves digitally enabled commercial transactions between and among organizations and individuals. There are seven unique features of e-commerce technology: E-commerce technology is ubiquitous, meaning that is it available just about everywhere a computer can connect to the Internet. It has global reach, permitting commercial transactions to cross-cultural and national boundaries far more conveniently and cost-effectively than is true in traditional commerce. It operates according to universal standards shared by all nations around the world, whereas most traditional commerce technologies differ from one nation to the next. It provides information richness, enabling an online merchant to deliver to an audience of millions complex and rich marketing messages with text, video, and audio in a way not possible with traditional commerce technologies, such as radio, television, or magazines. It is interactive, meaning it allows for two-way communication between merchant and consumer and enables the merchant to engage a consumer in ways similar to a face-to-face experience but on a much more massive, global scale. It increases information density (the total amount and quality of information available to all market participants). It permits personalization and customization: Merchants can target their marketing messages to specific individuals by adjusting the message to a person's name, interests, and past purchases.

The Internet has created a digital marketplace where millions of people are able to exchange massive amounts of information directly, instantly, and for free. Digital markets are said to be more "transparent" than traditional markets. Information asymmetry is reduced. Digital markets are very flexible and efficient, with reduced search and transaction costs, lower menu costs, and the ability to change prices dynamically based on market conditions. Digital markets provide many opportunities to sell directly to the consumer, bypassing intermediaries, such as distributors or retail outlets.

Digital goods are goods, such as music, video, software, newspapers, magazines, and books, that can be delivered over a digital network. Once a digital product has been produced, the cost of delivering that product digitally is extremely low. New business models based on delivering digital goods are challenging bookstores, publishers, music labels, and film studios that depend on delivery of physical goods.

**2** **Analyze how Internet technology has changed value propositions and business models.** The Internet radically reduces the cost of creating, sending, and storing information while making that information more widely available. Information is not limited to traditional physical methods of delivery. This unbundling of information from traditional value chain channels is having a disruptive effect on old business models, and it is creating new business models. Some of the traditional channels for exchanging product information have become unnecessary or uneconomical, and business models based on the coupling of information with products and services may no longer be necessary.

The Internet can help companies create and capture profits in new ways by adding extra value to existing products and services or by providing the foundation for new products and services. Many different business models for electronic commerce on the Internet have emerged, including virtual storefronts, information brokers, transaction brokers, Net marketplaces, content providers, online service providers, virtual communities, and portals. Business models that take advantage of the Internet's capabilities for communication, community-building capabilities, and digital goods distribution have become especially prominent.

**3** **Describe the various types of e-commerce and how e-commerce has changed consumer retailing and business-to-business transactions.** The three major types of electronic commerce are business-to-consumer (B2C), business-to-business (B2B), and consumer-to-consumer (C2C). Another way of classifying electronic commerce transactions is in terms of the participants' physical connections to the Web. Conventional e-commerce transactions, which take place over wired networks, can be distinguished from mobile commerce, or m-commerce, which is the purchase of goods and services using handheld wireless devices.

The Internet provides a universally available set of technologies for electronic commerce that can be used to create new channels for marketing, sales, and customer support and to eliminate intermediaries in buy-and-sell transactions. Interactive capabilities on the Web can be used to build closer relationships with customers in marketing and customer support. Firms can use various Web personalization technologies to deliver Web pages with content geared to the specific interests of each user, including technologies that deliver personalized information and ads through m-commerce channels. Companies can also reduce costs and improve customer service by using Web sites, as well as e-mail and even telephone access to customer service representatives, to provide helpful information.

B2B e-commerce generates efficiencies by enabling companies to locate suppliers, solicit bids, place orders, and track shipments in transit electronically. Businesses can use their own Web sites to sell to other businesses or use Net marketplaces or private industrial networks. Net marketplaces provide a single, digital marketplace based on Internet technology for many buyers and sellers. Net marketplaces can be differentiated by whether they sell direct or indirect goods, support spot or long-term purchasing, or serve vertical or horizontal markets. Private industrial networks link a firm with its suppliers and other strategic business partners to develop highly efficient supply chains and to respond quickly to customer demands.

**4** **Evaluate the role of m-commerce in business and describe the most important m-commerce applications.** M-commerce uses the Internet for purchasing goods and services as well as for transmitting messages using wireless mobile devices. It is especially well-suited for location-based applications, such as finding local hotels and restaurants, monitoring local traffic and weather, and providing personalized location-based marketing. Mobile phones and handhelds are being used for mobile bill payment; banking; securities trading; transportation schedule updates; and downloads of digital content, such as music, games, and video clips.

Wireless portals (mobile portals) feature content and services optimized for mobile devices to steer users to the information they are most likely to need. M-commerce requires special digital payment systems that can handle micropayments because most m-commerce purchases today are for very small amounts.

M-commerce represents a tiny fraction of all online purchases because wireless mobile devices can't display merchandise very well. Mobile phones have tiny keyboards, small screens, and slow data transfer speeds (9.6 to 14.4 Kbps). M-commerce will benefit from interoperable payment systems for wireless devices and faster wireless networks to support more data-rich communication.

**5** **Compare the principal payment systems for electronic commerce.**   The principal electronic payment systems for electronic commerce are digital credit card payment systems, digital wallets, accumulated balance digital payment systems, stored value payment systems, digital cash, peer-to-peer payment systems, digital checking, and electronic billing presentment and payment systems. Accumulated balance systems, stored value systems (including smart cards), and digital cash are useful for small micropayments.

## Key Terms

Accumulated balance digital payment systems, 315
Banner ad, 300
Blog, 305
Business-to-business (B2B) electronic commerce, 303
Business-to-consumer (B2C) electronic commerce, 303
Call center, 307
Clicks-and-mortar, 303
Clickstream tracking, 304
Collaborative filtering, 304
Consumer-to-consumer (C2C) electronic commerce, 303
Cost transparency, 297
Customization, 298
Digital cash, 315
Digital checking, 315
Digital credit card payment systems, 314

Digital goods, 299
Digital wallet, 314
Disintermediation, 299
Dynamic pricing, 298
Electronic billing presentment and payment systems, 316
Electronic data interchange (EDI), 307
Exchanges, 310
Information asymmetry, 298
Information density, 297
Market entry costs, 297
Marketspace, 296
Menu costs, 298
Micropayment, 315
Mobile commerce (m-commerce), 303
Net marketplaces, 308
Peer-to-peer payment systems, 315

Personalization, 298
Podcasting, 302
Pop-up ads, 301
Price discrimination, 297
Price transparency, 297
Private exchange, 308
Private industrial networks, 308
Procurement, 308
Pure-play, 303
Richness, 297
Ringtones, 313
Search costs, 297
Social networking sites, 301
Stored value payment systems, 315
Syndicators, 302
Transaction costs, 296
Wireless portals, 313

## Review Questions

**9.1** Name and describe four business trends and three technology trends shaping e-commerce today.

**9.2** List and describe the seven unique features of e-commerce.

**9.3** Define a digital market and describe its distinguishing features.

**9.4** Define digital goods and describe their distinguishing features.

**9.5** How is the Internet changing the economics of information and business models?

**9.6** Name and describe six Internet business models for electronic commerce. Distinguish between a pure-play Internet business model and a clicks-and-mortar business model.

**9.7** Name and describe the various categories of electronic commerce.

**9.8** How can the Internet facilitate sales and marketing for individual customers? Describe the role played by Web personalization.

**9.9** How can the Internet help provide customer service?

**9.10** How can Internet technology support business-to-business electronic commerce?

**9.11** What are Net marketplaces? Why do they represent an important business model for B2B

e-commerce? How do they differ from private industrial networks?

**9.12** List and describe the most important types of m-commerce services and applications.

**9.13** How do wireless portals help users access information on the Web?

**9.14** What are some of the barriers to m-commerce?

**9.15** Name and describe the principal electronic payment systems used on the Internet. What types of payment systems are used in m-commerce?

## Discussion Questions

**9.1** How does the Internet change consumer and supplier relationships?

**9.2** The Internet may not make corporations obsolete, but the corporations will have to change their business models. Do you agree? Why or why not?

## Application Software Exercise

### Spreadsheet Exercise: Analyzing a Dot-Com Business

Software skills: Spreadsheet downloading, formatting, and formulas

Business skills: Financial statement analysis

Pick one e-commerce company on the Internet, for example, Ashford.com, Buy.com, Yahoo.com, or Priceline.com. Study the Web pages that describe the company and explain its purpose and structure. Look for articles at Web sites such as BigCharts.com or Hoovers.com that comment on the company. Then visit the Securities and Exchange Commission's Web site at www.sec.gov and access the company's 10-K (annual report) forms showing income statements and balance sheets. Select only the sections of the 10-K form containing the desired portions of financial statements that you need to examine, and download them into your spreadsheet. (*Hint:* When you find the page that lists specific forms, select the text version. Do not select the HTML version. The Laudon Web site for Chapter 9 provides more detailed instructions on how to download this 10-K data into a spreadsheet.) Create simplified spreadsheets of the company's balance sheets and income statements for the past three years.

Is the company a dot-com success, borderline business, or failure? What information dictates the basis of your decision? Why? When answering these questions, pay special attention to the company's three-year trends in revenues, costs of sales, gross margins, operating expenses, and net margins. See the Laudon Web site for Chapter 9 for definitions of these terms and how they are calculated. Prepare an overhead presentation (with a minimum of five slides), including appropriate spreadsheets or charts, and present your work to your professor and classmates. If the company is successful, which additional business strategies could it pursue to become even more successful? If the company is a borderline or failing business, which specific business strategies (if any) could make it more successful?

## Developing an E-Commerce Strategy

Business skills: Strategic analysis

Dirt Bikes's management believes that the company could benefit from e-commerce. The company has sold motorcycles and parts primarily through authorized dealers. Dirt Bikes advertises in various magazines catering to dirt bike enthusiasts and maintains booths at important off-road motorcycle racing events. You have been asked to explore how Dirt Bikes could benefit from e-commerce and a Dirt Bikes Web site. Prepare a report for management that answers the following questions:

1. How could Dirt Bikes benefit from e-commerce? Should it sell motorcycles or parts over the Web? Should it use its Web site primarily to advertise its products and services? Should it use the Web for customer service?
2. How would a Web site provide value to Dirt Bikes? Use the Web to research the cost of an e-commerce site for a small to medium-sized company. How much revenue or cost savings would the Web site have to produce to make it a worthwhile investment for Dirt Bikes?
3. Prepare specifications describing the functions that should be performed by Dirt Bikes's Web site. Include links to other Web sites or other systems in your specifications.
4. (Optional) Design the home page and an important secondary page linked to the home page using the capabilities of word processing software or a Web page development tool of your choice.

## Building Internet Skills

### Comparing Online Storefront Hosting Services

This project will help develop your Internet skills in evaluating e-commerce hosting services.

You would like to set up a Web site to sell towels, linens, pottery, and tableware from Portugal and are examining services for hosting small-business Internet storefronts. Your Web site should be able to take secure credit card payments and to calculate shipping costs and taxes. Initially, you would like to display photos and descriptions of 40 different products. Visit Yahoo! Store and Freemerchant.com and compare the range of e-commerce hosting services they offer to small businesses, their capabilities and costs. Also examine the tools they provide for creating an e-commerce site. Compare both of these services and decide which of the two you would use if you were actually establishing a Web store. Write a brief report indicating your choice and explaining the strengths and weaknesses of both.

## Video Case

You will find a video case illustrating some of the concepts in this chapter on the Laudon Web site at **www.prenhall.com/laudon** along with questions to help you analyze the case.

## Teamwork

### Performing a Competitive Analysis of E-Commerce Sites

Form a group with three or four of your classmates. Select two businesses that are competitors in the same industry and that use their Web sites for electronic commerce. Visit these Web sites. You might compare, for example, the Web sites for iTunes and Napster, Amazon.com and BarnesandNoble.com, or E*TRADE and Scottrade. Prepare an evaluation of each business's Web site in terms of its functions, user-friendliness, and ability to support the company's business strategy. Which Web site does a better job? Why? Can you make some recommendations to improve these Web sites?

## BUSINESS PROBLEM-SOLVING CASE

### Can eBay Keep It Up?

Since Pierre Omidyar and Jeff Skoll founded eBay in 1995, this company has been an unmitigated e-commerce success story. eBay.com is an online auction service whose business model is ideally suited to the Web. eBay stores no inventory and ships no products. Instead, it derives its revenue from the movement of information, an ideal task for the Internet. In 2004, nearly a quarter of all transactions completed on the Internet in the United States were hosted by eBay.

The company has been profitable since day one and has grown consistently. In 1998 eBay had two million confirmed registered users. By 2003, the number of registered users had jumped to 94 million and by 2005, to more than 147 million. eBay now employs more than 8,000 full-time workers and has operations in 32 countries, including an equity investment in MercadoLibre, which services Mexico and eight South American countries. In 2005, eBay users listed 1.8 billion items for auction, resulting in $40 billion worth of goods changing hands.

eBay has mass appeal because its fully automated auction service helps buyers and sellers trade high-end articles, such as fine art, automobiles, and jewelry, as well as more mundane and practical items, such as clothing, consumer electronics, and housewares. Users can list their goods under more than 30 main categories and tens of thousands of subcategories.

The success of eBay relies on a unique formula. eBay derives the bulk of its revenue from fees and commissions associated with its trading services. This revenue, however, is only made possible by the hundreds of thousands of people who put time and effort into selling goods on eBay but do not work for the company. Nearly half a million people rely on eBay auctions as their main source of income. The seller pays an insertion fee for listing goods that operates on a sliding scale. For example, if the opening bid price starts between 1 cent and 99 cents, eBay charges the seller a 25-cent insertion fee. The fee increases as the opening price increases all the way up to $4.80 for goods starting at $500 or more. eBay also collects a fee from the seller when an auction is successful. These final fees begin at 5.25 percent of the closing price.

A portion of eBay's revenue also comes from direct advertising on the site, as well as end-to-end service providers whose services increase the ease and speed of eBay transactions. The acquisition of PayPal, whose service enables the exchange of money between individuals over the Internet, brings additional transaction-based fee revenue. PayPal charges the recipients of payments a flat fee plus a percentage of the total transaction size and has more than 70 million user accounts.

eBay's growth strategy is based on expansion in geography and scope and on continuing innovation to enhance the variety and appeal of products on its sites. eBay has taken its model to numerous foreign markets and been successful, particularly in England, France, and Germany. It is also working hard to gain a foothold in the Chinese online auction market. Growth rates have been hindered somewhat in the United States and Germany by an increase in seller fees, but these losses have been covered by rapid growth in places such as France and Italy. Although eBay's domestic growth has slowed to about 20 to 30 percent annually, the company's international business is growing at 50 percent per year. The first quarter of 2005 marked the first time

that international users outnumbered those in the United States. Transactions completed on international Web sites accounted for approximately half of eBay's business that year.

In 2000, eBay introduced eBay Motors as part of an effort to encourage the sale of bulky items that are too expensive to ship. Critics believed that consumers would find purchasing a used car over the Web too risky. However, eBay added extra measures of protection in the form of used-vehicle warranties and purchase protection up to $20,000. These measures combined with the standard eBay seller feedback ratings to give users enough security to buy one million cars within four years. eBay Motors now includes subcategories for boats, motorcycles, parts and accessories, and more.

Also in 2000, eBay implemented the "Buy It Now" feature, which enables sellers to name a price at which they would be willing to sell an item to any buyer. Buyers have the option to purchase the item instantly without waiting for an auction to end. Additionally, eBay acquired Half.com, which offers person-to-person selling of goods such as books, CDs, videos, and games without the auction process. On Half.com, listings are free but eBay collects a commission for completed sales, as low as 5 percent for items that sell for more than $500 all the way up to 15 percent for items that sell for under $50. In another attempt to reinvigorate its growth, eBay agreed to buy Shopping.com, an online shopping comparison site, for $620 million in mid-2005.

In 2001, the company launched eBay Stores. eBay Stores enable sellers with a proven track record (feedback rating score of at least 20), a verified ID, or a PayPal account to set up an online storefront and offer fixed-price merchandise. eBay Store owners pay subscription fees (from $15.95 to $499.95 per month), insertion fees, and final value fees on a sliding scale. Optional services, such as upgraded listings and pictures, are available for additional fees.

In September 2005, eBay acquired VoIP service provider Skype Technologies for $2.6 billion. Skype provides a service for free or low-cost voice calls over the Internet. eBay is betting heavily that Internet telephony will become an integral part of the e-commerce experience and accelerate trade on its Web site. The service could potentially generate $3.5 billion in revenue from markets that eBay traditionally had trouble penetrating, such as real estate, travel, new-car sales, and expensive collectibles. Those markets require more communication among buyers and sellers than eBay currently offers, and Skype will provide voice communication services to help. Internet companies such as Google and Microsoft are now offering VoIP services, and VoIP may become a required capability for all major companies that do business online.

However, some analysts report that many of eBay's top sellers aren't interested in adding voice calls to their sales models. They can barely keep up with the e-mail they receive on eBay and may like the simplicity and anonymity that eBay provided pre-Skype. VoIP could also stimulate eBay's "gray market," consisting of items sold outside the eBay structure to avoid seller fees.

eBay faces other challenges. Its expansion into Asia was dealt a major blow in 2002 when Yahoo! teamed up with Softbank to auction eBay right out of the Japanese market. eBay faces a similar fate in China, the biggest, untapped, potentially lucrative market in the world. China has 103 million Internet users, second only to the United States. In August 2005, Yahoo! announced that it had invested $1 billion in cash in the Chinese e-commerce company Alibaba.com. Yahoo! received 40 percent ownership of Alibaba and folded all of its China-based operations into the Alibaba domain. The deal has set up Alibaba's online auction site, named Taobao, as a serious threat to eBay's prosperity in China.

Both companies are still trying to figure out the market for their services in China, where only 6 percent of the people have computers in their homes and only 8 percent of the country's 1.3 billion people actually use the Internet. eBay and Taobao have roughly 20 million registered users combined, an almost insignificant percentage of the population. Working against their success is a per capita income of only $1,200. However, the potential reward is great enough that eBay has earmarked $100 million to promote and enhance its Chinese operations.

eBay's growing international presence may make it difficult to monitor compliance with the variety of laws and regulations that apply in different jurisdictions. The law related to the liability of providers of online services for the activities of their users is unsettled. Even though eBay has taken steps to prohibit the listing of certain items, it may be liable if its members nonetheless manage to use it to sell unlawful goods, such as weapons, drugs, alcohol, adult material, and cigarettes, or if its members defame or libel one another in eBay's Feedback Forum.

Clearly, the largest threat to eBay is the honesty and integrity of its auctions, over which it has some—but not total—control. As eBay ventured into the realm of higher-priced antiques and collectibles, it opened itself up to lawsuits from buyers claiming to have been defrauded by online sellers; some buyers have alleged that eBay does not do enough to prevent unscrupulous sellers from collecting inflated fees for goods that are not legitimate, or worse, do not exist. eBay users have also been the victims of identity theft scams that resulted in the unauthorized use of their accounts—and hundreds of thousands of dollars worth of fraudulent sales.

With online crime becoming more and more sophisticated, the onus is on eBay to provide its users with a secure trade environment. Some users, and former users, believe that the company has not adequately addressed the issue of fraud. Part of the problem may be that the growing scale of eBay makes fraud protection prohibitive. Smaller sites, such as StubHub.com, a trading post for tickets to sporting and entertain-

ment events, guarantee the authenticity and quality of transactions and vendors. eBay insists that the percentage of listings on its site that are fraudulent is tiny and that the success of the marketplace bares that out.

Another area in which the sheer size of eBay may be a hindrance is customer service. The company understandably struggles with the task of satisfying two types of "customers": online buyers and online sellers. What's good for one isn't always good for the other. Fraud complaints often result in an automated response from eBay that encourages buyers and sellers to resolve disputes on their own. As eBay has seen, one unilateral policy decision can set off a negative chain reaction. When eBay Store fees were raised, some 7,000 storeowners shut down their stores and looked for other means to conduct their businesses. An exodus of dissatisfied customers scares Wall Street investors. But eBay is in a bind because addressing customer service issues costs money. The more money eBay spends, the more it cuts into its profits, which also makes Wall Street nervous.

eBay does make an effort to remain in touch with its community of users. A program called Voices brings buyers and sellers together 10 times a year at corporate headquarters. The users engage in two full days of give-and-take with company officials about the best and worst aspects of eBay's services. eBay also monitors every transaction and usage statistics in real time, enabling timely troubleshooting. A Rules, Trust, and Safety committee judges whether questionable listings should be permitted on the site (human organs have been banned, for example).

eBay's track record of growth and profitability suggests that its operations are less risky than other e-commerce ventures, but management must continue to strengthen the brand, build the user base, and continue to foster the growth of trading to maintain the past success. Penetration of the U.S. market is quite high, and many other established retailers, such as Yahoo! and Amazon have built viable e-commerce alternatives.

*Sources:* Nicholas Hoover, "eBay Bets on VoIP, but Do Sellers Want to Chat?" *InformationWeek,* September 19, 2005; CNBC, "Ten Things You Didn't Know About eBay," msnbc.com, accessed June 29, 2005; Michael S. Malone, "eBay: The Ultimate Success Story," http://members.cox.net/mrswebauthor/success/elixer.html; Robert D. Hof, "eBay Loses Some Mojo," *Business Week,* January 20, 2005; Gary Rivlin, "eBay's Profit Increases 28%, but Fails to Impress Wall St.," *The New York Times,* April 21, 2005; Patricia O'Connell, "A Speed Demon Called eBay Motors," *Business Week,* July 20, 2004; Ian Austen, "On eBay, E-Mail Phishers Find a Well-Stocked Pond," *The New York Times,* March 7, 2005; Wired News, "Yahoo Buys Stake in Alibaba," *Wired,* August 11, 2005; Mylene Mangalindan, "In a Challenging China Market, eBay Confronts a Big New Rival," *The Wall Street Journal,* August 12, 2005; David Kesmodel, "Beyond eBay," *The Wall Street Journal,* July 18, 2005; Nick Wingfield, "Problem for Cops on eBay Beat: Crooks Keep Getting Smarter," *The Wall Street Journal,* August 3, 2004; and Mylene Mangalindan and Dennis K. Berman, "eBay agrees to Acquire Shopping.com," *The Wall Street Journal,* June 2, 2005.

**Case Study Questions**

1. What is eBay's business model and business strategy? How successful has it been?
2. What are the problems that eBay is currently facing?
3. How is eBay trying to solve these problems? Are these good solutions? Are there any other solutions that eBay should consider?
4. What people, technology, and organization factors play a role in eBay's response to its problems?
5. Will eBay be successful in the long run? Why or why not?

# Improving Decision Making and Managing Knowledge

**CHAPTER 10**

## STUDENT OBJECTIVES

After completing this chapter, you will be able to:

1. Compare different types of decisions and describe the decision-making process.

2. Evaluate the role of information systems in helping people working individually and in groups make decisions more effectively.

3. Evaluate the business benefits of using intelligent techniques in decision making and knowledge management.

4. Define and describe the types of systems used for enterprise-wide knowledge management and demonstrate how they provide value for businesses.

5. Define and describe the major types of knowledge work systems and demonstrate how they provide value for firms.

## Chapter Outline

## PROCTER & GAMBLE RESTRUCTURES ITS SUPPLY CHAIN

**Procter & Gamble (P&G)** is one of the world's largest consumer goods companies, with annual revenue of $51 billion and 80,000 employees in 140 countries. The company sells more than 300 brands worldwide, including Crest, Charmin, Tide, Pringles, and Pampers. Although P&G is known for innovation and marketing muscle, it is always looking for ways to lower its costs, in response both to competitors and to pressure from large customers, such as Wal-Mart.

In the early 1990s, P&G started looking at ways to reduce supply chain costs and improve efficiency throughout its entire North American manufacturing and distribution network. Management wanted answers to questions such as, "How many plants should there be for a new product?" "Where should they be located?" "Where should distribution centers be located?" and "How can we deliver these products faster and better to our major customers?"

Answers were not easy to obtain because P&G's supply chains are incredibly complex, with more than 100,000 suppliers. P&G's Global Beauty Care division alone has hundreds of combinations of suppliers, manufacturing facilities, and markets to deal with, compounded by 10 to 15 new product launches per year. Each of the company's dozens of beauty care products has multiple sizes and package designs. A tiny change—and changes are constant—ripples through the supply chain, impacting inventory levels, service levels, and costs.

Jean Kinney, a P&G purchasing manager, recalls the launch of a new global healthcare product whose success depended on the choice of plant locations and sources of raw materials. The problem was very complicated and there were millions of possible solutions. If you asked the managers in the countries that would be marketing this product, they would all say the plants should be located in their countries. Corporate experts, however, would say that scale is important and P&G should build a single megaplant instead of distributing production. In between were millions of other options. What was the best approach?

P&G turned to its IT Global Analytics group for a solution. IT Global Analytics constructed some models using Microsoft Excel spreadsheet software enhanced by Lindo System's What'sBest for more powerful optimization and Palisade's @RISK software for Monte Carlo simulation, which randomly generates values for uncertain variables. The models tried to maximize the value of the investment, considering manufacturing costs, freight costs, import/export duties, local wage rates, foreign exchange rates, taxes, and the cost of capital.

This model was one of a series of models developed by IT Global Analytics for restructuring P&G's supply chain. P&G used optimization models to determine how best to allocate supply chain resources and simulation models to mathematically try out various options to see how they reacted to changes in important variables. In addition, the company used techniques, such as decision trees, that combined the possibilities of various outcomes with their financial results. Using these decision-support tools, IT Global Analytics found that the success of a supply chain is not necessarily based on the most optimal solution but rather a robust solution that would stand up under real-world conditions.

P&G uses a number of different software tools for implementing its models. In addition to Excel and add-on products, P&G also uses stand-alone software packages. These packages include Xpress-MP from Dash Optimization Inc. and Cplex from Ilog Inc. for building optimization models, and Extend from Imagine That Inc. for building simulation models. Most of the data for these decision-support systems come from a massive Oracle data warehouse with 36 months of data on supplier, manufacturing, customer, and consumer histories by region.

P&G's use of decision-support systems for restructuring its supply chain has paid off. The company consolidated North American plants by 20 percent and lowered supply chain costs by $200 million each year. ■

*Sources:* Gary H. Anthes, "Modeling Magic," *Computerworld*, February 7, 2005; "Procter & Gamble Uses @RISK and PrecisionTree World-Wide," www.palisade.com, accessed August 6, 2005; and www.pg.com, accessed August 6, 2005.

**P**rocter & Gamble's use of information systems to restructure its supply chain illustrates how information systems improve decision making. Management was unable to make good decisions about where to locate plants and distribution centers for new products because P&G's supply chain was extremely large, complex, and affected by many different variables. Bad decisions about where to locate plants and distribution centers increased costs to procure, manufacture, warehouse, and ship P&G products because plants and distribution centers did not operate efficiently.

P&G initially polled managers in different parts of the business for ideas on where to allocate supply chain resources. This alternative did not work because it only returned a few alternative designs that reflected local and corporate management biases and ruled out many other possible design options.

The solution that worked best was to build new, model-based, decision-support systems that could evaluate large quantities of data and thousands of variables, and determine an optimal allocation of supply chain resources from both operational and financial standpoints. By improving decisions about how to restructure P&G's supply chain, these systems

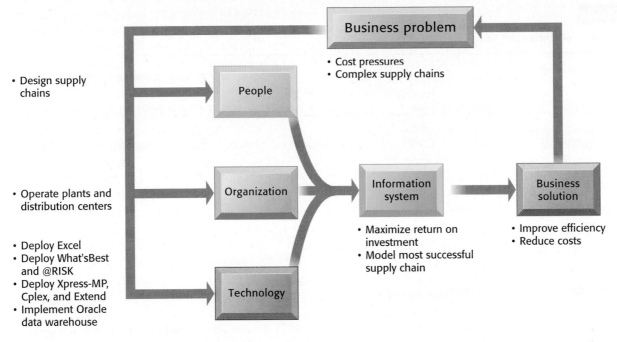

- Design supply chains

- Operate plants and distribution centers

- Deploy Excel
- Deploy What'sBest and @RISK
- Deploy Xpress-MP, Cplex, and Extend
- Implement Oracle data warehouse

**Business problem**
- Cost pressures
- Complex supply chains

People

Organization

Technology

**Information system**
- Maximize return on investment
- Model most successful supply chain

**Business solution**
- Improve efficiency
- Reduce costs

helped the company operate more efficiently, reduce its costs, and increase responsiveness to customers and to the marketplace.

---

**HEADS UP**

This chapter focuses on how business firms use information systems to improve decision making. Until the past decade, most businesses and their managers and employees operated in an information and knowledge fog, making decisions based on best guesses about the past and present, and making expensive errors in the process. This is less true. Today, firms use a wide variety of information systems to directly improve decision making throughout the firm from the executive suite to the call center customer service representative, and from the financial advisor's desk to the factory floor. Even customers are provided with systems to help them make better decisions. It would not be an overstatement to say that a primary contribution of information systems to business firms has been to improve decision making at all levels.

•   If your career is in finance and accounting, you will be working with decision-support systems that use financial models for break-even analysis, profitability analysis, capital budgeting, and financial forecasting, and with executive support systems (ESS) providing overviews of firmwide financial performance.

•   If your career is in human resources, you will use decision-support systems for analyzing the impact of employee compensation plans and for projecting the firm's long-term labor force requirements.

•   If your career is in manufacturing, production, or operations management, you will be using decision-support systems to guide decisions about the optimization of sourcing, production, logistics, and maintenance that must evaluate many interrelated variables.

•   If your career is in sales and marketing, you will be working with decision-support systems to guide decisions about product pricing, sales forecasting, advertising and promotional campaigns, and location of retail outlets.

---

In this chapter, we examine the systems firms use to achieve better decision making. First, we describe the decision-making process. Next we examine management information systems (MIS), decision-support systems (DSS), group decision-support systems (GDSS), and

**TABLE 10.1**

**Business Value of Enhanced Decision Making**

| Example Decision | Decision Maker | Number of Annual Decisions | Estimated Value to Firm of a Single Improved Decision | Annual Vaue |
|---|---|---|---|---|
| Allocate support to most valuable customers | Accounts manager | 12 | $ 100,000 | $1,200,000 |
| Predict call center daily demand | Call Center management | 4 | 150,000 | 600,000 |
| Decide parts inventory levels daily | Inventory manager | 365 | 5,000 | 1,825,000 |
| Identify competitive bids from major suppliers | Senior management | 1 | 2,000,000 | 2,000,000 |
| Schedule production to fill orders | Manufacturing manager | 150 | 10,000 | 1,500,000 |
| Allocate labor to complete a job | Production floor manager | 100 | 4,000 | 400,000 |

executive support systems (ESS). Finally, we discuss systems for knowledge management that improve the quality of the knowledge used in decision making and the execution of business processes. You'll learn how these systems work and exactly how they provide value for the business.

## 10.1 Decision Making and Information Systems

One of the main contributions of information systems has been to improve decision making, both for individuals and groups. Decision making in businesses used to be limited to management. Today, lower-level employees are responsible for some of these decisions, as information systems make information available to lower levels of the business. But what do we mean by better decision making? How does decision making take place in businesses and other organizations? Let's take a closer look.

### Business Value of Improved Decision Making

What does it mean to the business to be able to make a better decision? What is the monetary value to the business of better, improved decision making? Table 10.1 attempts to measure the monetary value of improved decision making for a small U.S. manufacturing firm with $280 million in annual revenue and 140 employees. The firm has identified a number of key decisions where new system investments might improve the quality of decision making. The table provides selected estimates of annual value (in the form of cost savings or increased revenue) from improved decision making in selected areas of the business.

We can see from Table 10.1 that decisions are made at all levels of the firm and that some of these decisions are common, routine, and numerous. Although the value of improving any single decision may be small, improving hundreds of thousands of "small" decisions adds up to a large annual value for the business.

### Types of Decisions

Chapter 2 showed that there are different levels in an organization. Each of these levels has different information requirements for decision support and responsibility for different types of decisions (see Figure 10-1). Decisions are classified as structured, semistructured, and unstructured.

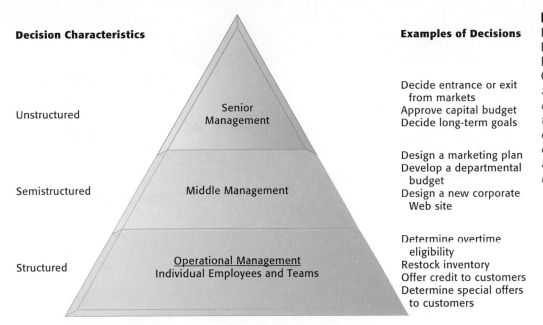

**Figure 10-1**
Information
Requirements of Key
Decision-Making
Groups in a Firm
*Senior managers, middle managers, operational managers, and employees have different types of decisions and information requirements.*

**Unstructured decisions** are those in which the decision maker must provide judgment, evaluation, and insight to solve the problem. Each of these decisions is novel, important, and nonroutine, and there is no well-understood or agreed-on procedure for making them.

**Structured decisions**, by contrast, are repetitive and routine, and they involve a definite procedure for handling them so that they do not have to be treated each time as if they were new. Many decisions have elements of both types of decisions and are **semistructured**, where only part of the problem has a clear-cut answer provided by an accepted procedure. In general, structured decisions are more prevalent at lower organizational levels, whereas unstructured problems are more common at higher levels of the firm.

Senior executives face many unstructured decision situations, such as establishing the firm's five- or ten-year goals or deciding which new markets to enter. Answering the question "Should we enter a new market?" would require access to news, government reports, and industry views as well as high-level summaries of firm performance. However, the answer would also require senior managers to use their own best judgment and poll other managers for their opinions.

Middle management faces more structured decision scenarios but their decisions may include unstructured components. A typical middle-level management decision problem might be "Why is the reported order fulfillment report showing a decline over the past six months at a distribution center in Minneapolis?" This middle manager could obtain a report from the firm's enterprise system or distribution management system on order activity and operational efficiency at the Minneapolis distribution center. This is the structured part of the decision. But before arriving at an answer, this middle manager will have to interview employees and gather more unstructured information from external sources about local economic conditions or sales trends.

Operational management and rank-and-file employees tend to make more structured decisions. For example, a supervisor on an assembly line has to decide whether an hourly paid worker is entitled to overtime pay. If the employee worked more than eight hours on a particular day, the supervisor would routinely grant overtime pay for any time beyond eight hours that was clocked on that day.

A sales account representative often has to make decisions about extending credit to customers by consulting the firm's customer database that contains credit information. If the customer met the firm's prespecified criteria for granting credit, the account representative would grant that customer credit to make a purchase. In both instances, the decisions are highly structured and are routinely made thousands of times each day in most large firms. The answer has been preprogrammed into the firm's payroll and accounts receivable systems.

**Figure 10-2**
Stages in Decision
Making
*The decision-making
process can be broken
down into four stages.*

Problem discovery:
What is the problem?

Solution discovery:
What are the possible solutions?

Choosing solutions:
What is the best solution?

Solution testing:
Is the solution working?
Can we make it work better?

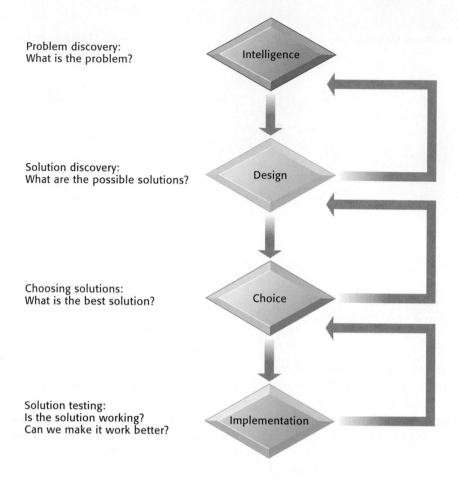

## The Decision-Making Process

Making a decision is a multistep process. Simon (1960) described four different stages in decision making: intelligence, design, choice, and implementation (see Figure 10-2). These stages correspond to the four steps in problem-solving used throughout this book.

**Intelligence** consists of discovering, identifying, and understanding the problems occurring in the organization—why is there a problem, where, and what effects it is having on the firm.

**Design** involves identifying and exploring various solutions to the problem.

**Choice** consists of choosing among solution alternatives.

**Implementation** involves making the chosen alternative work and continuing to monitor how well the solution is working.

What happens if the solution you have chosen doesn't work? Figure 10-2 shows that you can return to an earlier stage in the decision-making process and repeat it if necessary. For instance, in the face of declining sales, a sales management team may decide to pay the sales force a higher commission for making more sales to spur on the sales effort. If this does not produce sales increases, managers would need to investigate whether the problem stems from poor product design, inadequate customer support, or a host of other causes that call for a different solution.

## Quality of Decisions and Decision Making

How can you tell if a decision has become "better" or the decision-making process "improved"? Accuracy is one important dimension of quality: In general, we think decisions are "better" if they accurately reflect the real-world data. Speed is another dimension: We tend to think that the decision-making process should be efficient, even speedy. For instance, when you apply for car insurance, you want the decision making by the insurance firm to be fast and accurate. But there are many other dimensions of quality in decisions and the decision-making process to consider. Which is important for you will depend on the business firm where you work, the various parties involved in the decision, and your own

| Quality Dimension | Description |
| --- | --- |
| Accuracy | Decision reflects reality |
| Comprehensiveness | Decision reflects a full consideration of the facts and circumstances |
| Fairness | Decision faithfully reflects the concerns and interests of affected parties |
| Speed (efficiency) | Decision making is efficient with respect to time and other resources, including the time and resources of affected parties, such as customers |
| Coherence | Decision reflects a rational process that can be explained to others and made understandable |
| Due process | Decision is the result of a known process and can be appealed to a higher authority |

**TABLE 10.2**

**Qualities of Decisions and the Decision-Making Process**

personal values. Table 10.2 describes some quality dimensions for decision making. When we describe how systems "improve decisions and the decision-making process" in this chapter, we are referencing the dimensions in this table.

## Systems and Technologies for Supporting Decisions

There are four kinds of systems for supporting the different levels and types of decisions we have just described. We introduced these systems in Chapter 2. *Management information systems (MIS)* provide routine reports and summaries of transaction-level data to middle and operational level managers to provide answers to structured and semistructured decision problems. *Decision-support systems (DSS)* provide analytical models or tools for analyzing large quantities of data and supportive interactive queries for middle managers who face semistructured decision situations. *Executive support systems (ESS)* are systems that provide senior management, making primarily unstructured decisions, with external information (news, stock analyses, and industry trends) and high-level summaries of firm performance. *Group decision-support systems (GDSS)* are specialized systems that provide a group electronic environment in which managers and teams can collectively make decisions and design solutions for unstructured and semistructured problems.

Decision making is also enhanced by intelligent techniques and knowledge management systems. **Intelligent techniques** consist of expert systems, case-based reasoning, genetic algorithms, neural networks, fuzzy logic, and intelligent agents. These technologies aid decision makers by capturing individual and collective knowledge, discovering patterns and behaviors in very large quantities of data, and generating solutions to problems that are too large and complex for human beings to solve on their own.

Knowledge management systems, which we introduced in Chapter 2, and knowledge work systems provide tools for knowledge discovery, communication, and collaboration that make knowledge more easily available to decision makers and integrate it into the business processes of the firm.

## 10.2 Systems for Decision Support

Exactly how do these different types of systems for supporting decisions affect a business? What can today's decision-support systems do for a business? Let's look more closely at how each major type of decision-support system works and provides value.

### Management Information Systems (MIS)

Management information systems (MIS), which we introduced in Chapter 2, help managers monitor and control the business by providing information on the firm's performance. They

**TABLE 10.3**

**Examples of MIS Applications**

| Company | MIS Application |
| --- | --- |
| California Pizza Kitchen | Inventory Express application "remembers" each restaurant's ordering patterns and compares the amount of ingredients used per menu item to predefined portion measurements established by management. The system identifies restaurants with out-of-line portions and notifies their managers so that corrective actions can be taken. |
| PharMark | Extranet MIS identifies patients with drug-use patterns that place them at risk for adverse outcomes. |
| Black & Veatch | Intranet MIS tracks construction costs for various projects across the United States. |
| Taco Bell | Total Automation of Company Operations (TACO) system provides information on food, labor, and period-to-date costs for each restaurant. |

typically produce fixed, regularly scheduled reports based on data extracted and summarized from the firm's underlying transaction processing systems (TPS). The formats for these reports are often specified in advance. A typical MIS report might show a summary of monthly or annual sales for each of the major sales territories of a company. Sometimes, MIS reports are exception reports, highlighting only exceptional conditions, such as when the sales quotas for a specific territory fall below an anticipated level or employees have exceeded their spending limits in a dental care plan.

Traditional MIS produced primarily hard-copy reports. Today, many of these reports are available online through an intranet, and more MIS reports can be generated on demand. Table 10.3 provides some examples of MIS applications.

## Decision-Support Systems (DSS)

Whereas MIS primarily address structured problems, DSS support semistructured and unstructured problem analysis. The earliest DSS were heavily model driven, using some type of model to perform "what if" and other kinds of analyses. In a "what-if" analysis, a model is developed and various input factors are changed and the resulting output changes measured (see the following section). The DSS analysis capabilities were based on a strong theory or model combined with a good user interface that made the system easy to use. Procter & Gamble's systems for supply chain restructuring in the chapter-opening case are examples of model-driven DSS.

Some contemporary DSS are data driven, using online analytical processing (OLAP) and data mining to analyze large pools of data in major corporate systems. The business intelligence applications described in Chapter 5 are examples of these data-driven DSS. They support decision making by enabling users to extract useful information that was previously buried in large quantities of data.

### Components of DSS
Figure 10-3 illustrates the components of a DSS. They include a database of data used for query and analysis; a software system with models, data mining, and other analytical tools; and a user interface.

The **DSS database** is a collection of current or historical data from a number of applications or groups. It may be a small database residing on a PC that contains a subset of corporate data that has been downloaded and possibly combined with external data. Alternatively, the DSS database may be a massive data warehouse that is continuously updated by major corporate TPS (including enterprise systems and data generated by Web site transactions). The data in DSS databases are generally extracts or copies of production databases so that using the DSS does not interfere with critical operational systems.

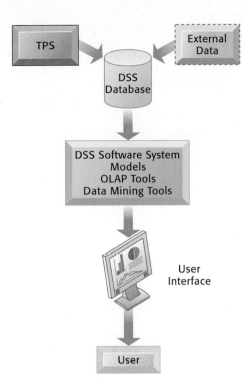

**Figure 10-3**
Overview of a
Decision-Support
System
*The main components
of the DSS are the DSS
database, the DSS soft-
ware system, and the
user interface. The DSS
database may be a
small database residing
on a PC or a large data
warehouse.*

The **DSS software system** contains the software tools that are used for data analysis. It may contain various OLAP tools, data mining tools, or a collection of mathematical and analytical models that easily can be made accessible to the DSS user. A **model** is an abstract representation that illustrates the components or relationships of a phenomenon. A model can be a physical model (such as a model airplane), a mathematical model (such as an equation), or a verbal model (such as a description of a procedure for writing an order).

Statistical modeling helps establish relationships, such as relating product sales to differences in age, income, or other factors between communities. Optimization models determine optimal resource allocation to maximize or minimize specified variables, such as cost or time. A classic use of optimization models is to determine the proper mix of products within a given market to maximize profits. P&G uses optimization models to determine how to maximize its return on investment from the organization of its supply chain.

Forecasting models often are used to forecast sales. The user of this type of model might supply a range of historical data to project future conditions and the sales that might result from those conditions. The decision maker could vary those future conditions (entering, for example, a rise in raw materials costs or the entry of a new, low-priced competitor in the market) to determine how new conditions might affect sales.

**Sensitivity analysis** models ask "what-if" questions repeatedly to determine the impact on outcomes of changes in one or more factors. *What-if analysis*—working forward from known or assumed conditions—allows the user to vary certain values to test results to better predict outcomes if changes occur in those values. What happens if we raise product price by 5 percent or increase the advertising budget by $100,000? What happens if we keep the price and advertising budgets the same? Desktop spreadsheet software, such as Microsoft Excel, is often used for this purpose (see Figure 10-4). Backward sensitivity analysis software helps decision makers with goal seeking: If I want to sell one million product units next year, how much must I reduce the price of the product?

The DSS user interface permits easy interaction between users of the system and the DSS software tools. Many DSS today have Web interfaces to take advantage of graphic displays, interactivity, and ease of use.

### Examples of DSS

DSS have become very powerful and sophisticated, providing fine-grained information for decisions that enable the firm to coordinate both internal and external business processes precisely. Some of these DSS are helping companies with decisions in supply chain management

| Total fixed costs | 19000 | | | | | |
| Variable cost per unit | 3 | | | | | |
| Average sales price | 17 | | | | | |
| Contribution margin | 14 | | | | | |
| Break-even point | 1357 | | | | | |
| | | | **Variable Cost per Unit** | | | |
| Sales | 1357 | 2 | 3 | 4 | 5 | 6 |
| Price | 14 | 1583 | 1727 | 1900 | 2111 | 2375 |
| | 15 | 1462 | 1583 | 1727 | 1900 | 2111 |
| | 16 | 1357 | 1462 | 1583 | 1727 | 1900 |
| | 17 | 1267 | 1357 | 1462 | 1583 | 1727 |
| | 18 | 1188 | 1267 | 1357 | 1462 | 1583 |

**Figure 10-4**
Sensitivity Analysis
*This table displays the results of a sensitivity analysis of the effect of changing the sales price of a necktie and the cost per unit on the product's break-even point. It answers the question, "What happens to the break-even point if the sales price and the cost to make each unit increase or decrease?"*

(such as P&G's supply chain restructuring applications described in the chapter-opening case) or customer relationship management. Some take advantage of the company-wide data provided by enterprise systems. DSS today can also harness the interactive capabilities of the Web to provide decision-support tools to both employees and customers. Here are some examples that illustrate the range of DSS capabilities.

**Burlington Coat Factory: DSS for Pricing Decisions**  Many large retailers lose millions of dollars because their prices are "best guesses." If they wait too long to discount an item that isn't selling well, they will be stuck with excess. If they discount too early, or discount too heavily, they lose profits because people buy goods they might have bought at a higher price. Burlington Coat Factory Warehouse and Children's Place have solved this problem by implementing price optimization software.

Burlington Coat Factory uses ProfitLogic's Markdown Optimization Solution to manage pricing and inventory at all of its stores nationwide. ProfitLogic considers complex interdependencies between initial prices set for merchandise, prices for promotions, and prices for markdowns, including cross-item pricing effects and item seasonality. It enables Burlington to gain earlier visibility into the performance of merchandise in order to clear out underperforming items and free up inventory to stock fresher merchandise that is more in demand (Murphy, 2005; ProfitLogic, 2005).

**Parkway Corporation: DSS for Asset Utilization**  Parkway Corporation, headquartered in Philadelphia, owns and manages 30,000 parking spaces and 100 garages in East Coast cities stretching from Toronto, Canada, to Jacksonville, Florida. Its revenues surged during the late 1990s, but so did its costs, to the point where they were seriously eroding gains. Parkway was saddled by paper-based reporting systems that could not provide the information it needed to better manage its costs and revenues. For example, Parkway could measure the performance of individual lots but could not quickly obtain a unified company-wide view of how all its lots were performing in total or in relation to each other. Nor could management determine which lots, type of garage (automated, self-service, or valet parking), and customers were the most profitable or which employees were responsible for the most overtime claims or damage costs.

In 2001, Parkway implemented a data warehouse and analytics software to answer these questions. The new system enables Parkway to analyze revenue by type of garage, length of stay, rate structure, overtime costs, and utilization rates so that managers can make better decisions on prices and garage space allocation. Parkway can also use this system to determine the best mix of monthly, daily, and weekly parking in a particular city and to identify its most profitable customers. The system has helped Parkway management reduce overtime costs by 65 percent, increase the percentage of filled spaces per lot, and increase revenues between 5 and 10 percent. Car damage claims can be tracked by garage, employee, and time of day (Lindorff, 2003).

**Compass Bank: DSS for Customer Relationship Management** Some of the analytical CRM applications described in Chapter 8 are DSS for customer relationship management, using data mining to guide decisions about pricing, customer retention, market share, and new revenue streams. These systems typically consolidate customer data from a variety of systems, including data captured from Web site transactions, into massive data warehouses and use various analytical tools to slice it into tiny segments for one-to-one marketing and predictive analysis.

Compass Bank, a leading financial holding company with 376 banking centers and more than $28 billion in assets, uses a DSS to help it minimize default risk in its credit card business. Although credit cards generate considerable revenue and help the bank cross-sell its other financial products, credit card debt also represents a significant risk. (Compass had written off $34 million in bad credit card debt in 2003.) About 80 percent of Compass credit card accounts are opened by customers who already have checking and savings accounts. Compass uses Siebel Business Analytics to analyze the relationship between checking and savings account activity and default risk. The system is able to pull together and analyze 13 months of detailed data from multiple databases to flag customer accounts in danger of defaulting. Operational since the spring of 2004, the system helped Compass reduce credit card losses by 7 percent during its first year of operation (Siebel, 2005).

### Data Visualization and Geographic Information Systems (GIS)

Data from information systems can be made easier for users to digest and act on by using graphics, charts, tables, maps, digital images, three-dimensional presentations, animations, and other data visualization technologies. By presenting data in graphical form, **data visualization** tools help users see patterns and relationships in large amounts of data that would be difficult to discern if the data were presented as traditional lists of text. Some data visualization tools are interactive, enabling users to manipulate data and see the graphical displays change in response to the changes they make.

**Geographic information systems (GIS)** are a special category of DSS that use data visualization technology to analyze and display data for planning and decision making in the form of digitized maps. The software assembles, stores, manipulates, and displays geographically referenced information, tying data to points, lines, and areas on a map. GIS have modeling capabilities, enabling managers to change data and automatically revise business scenarios to find better solutions.

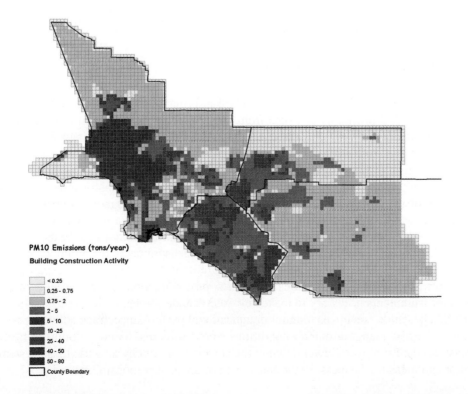

California's South Coast Air Quality Management District (AQMD) is responsible for monitoring and controlling emissions in all of Orange County and the urban portions of Los Angeles, Riverside, and San Bernardino counties. Displayed is a map produced with ESRI geographic information system (GIS) software tracking particulate matter emissions from building construction activity in a two-by-two kilometer gridded format.

GIS support decisions that require knowledge about the geographic distribution of people or other resources. For example, GIS might be used to help state and local governments calculate emergency response times to natural disasters, to help retail chains identify profitable new store locations, or to help banks identify the best locations for installing new branches or automatic teller machine (ATM) terminals. Carvel Ice Cream used a GIS from MapInfo to determine where to open more Carvel outlets without cannibalizing the sales of existing franchises (Chittum, 2005).

The Focus on Technology describes a geographic information system used by the Bermuda Department of Health to control its rat population and to coordinate work with the planning department. As you read this case, try to identify the problem this organization was facing; what alternative solutions were available to management; how well the chosen solution worked; and the people, organization, and technology issues that had to be addressed when developing the solution.

### Web-Based Customer Decision-Support Systems (CDSS)

The growth of electronic commerce has encouraged many companies to develop DSS for customers that use Internet information resources and Web capabilities for interactivity and personalization to help users select products and services. DSS based on the Web and the Internet support decision making by providing online access to various databases and information pools along with software for data analysis. Companies are finding that deciding which products and services to purchase has become increasingly information intensive. People are now using more information from multiple sources to make purchasing decisions (such as purchasing a car or computer) before they interact with the product or sales staff. For instance, nearly all automobile companies use customer decision-support systems that allow Web site visitors to configure their desired car. **Customer decision-support systems (CDSS)** support the decision-making process of an existing or potential customer.

People interested in purchasing a product or service can use Internet search engines, intelligent agents, online catalogs, Web directories, newsgroup discussions, e-mail, and other tools to help them locate the information they need to help with their decision. Companies have developed specific customer Web sites where all the information, models, or other analytical tools for evaluating alternatives are concentrated in one location. Web-based DSS have become especially popular in the financial services area because so many people are trying to manage their own assets and retirement savings.

## Executive Support Systems (ESS)

If you were a senior executive and you wanted a picture of the overall performance of your firm, where would you find that information? You would turn to an executive support system. Executive support systems (ESS), which we introduced in Chapter 2, help solve unstructured and semistructured problems by focusing on the information needs of senior management. Contemporary ESS bring together data from many different internal and external sources, including data from the Web, often through a portal. These systems provide easy-to-use analytical tools and online displays to help users select, access, and tailor the data as needed.

You can think of ESS as generalized computing, communications, and graphic systems that, similar to a zoom lens, can focus quickly on detailed problems or retract back for a broad view of the company. ESS have a capability to **drill down**, moving from a piece of summary data to lower and lower levels of detail. Some display a high-level view of firm performance in the form of a digital dashboard. A **digital dashboard**, or "executive dashboard," displays on a single screen all of the critical measurements for piloting a company, similar to the cockpit of an airplane or an automobile dashboard. The dashboard presents key performance indicators as graphs and charts, providing a one-page overview of all the critical measurements necessary to make key executive decisions.

ESS help senior executives monitor organizational performance, track activities of competitors, identify changing market conditions, spot problems, identify opportunities, and forecast trends. Employees lower down in the corporate hierarchy also use these systems to monitor and measure business performance in their areas of responsibility.

# FOCUS ON TECHNOLOGY  Bermuda's High-Tech Rat Trap

Bermuda is a well-known island vacation destination located 550 miles east of the Carolinas in the Atlantic Ocean, attracting 500,000 tourists each year. The island has 65,000 full-time residents—not including its rats. Yes, Bermuda has a problematic rat population. If the rat population spun out of control, it could discourage tourists, which would be very harmful to the island's economic health. Tourist dollars account for 30 percent of Bermuda's economy.

With so much at stake, Bermuda has taken a unique approach to controlling its rat population. Several years ago, the Department of Health turned to geographic information system (GIS) software from the Environmental Systems Research Institute (ESRI).

The health department hired Scientific Technologies Corp. from Tucson, Arizona, to help it develop a series of GIS. Together they built the Bermuda Environmental Health Database System (BEHDS). The system is Web based and users access it through a Web site written in HTML and Java. An Oracle 8 database stores the public health records, and ArcIMS GIS put together by ESRI builds the maps. The health department paid $500,000 for the system, which required two years to deploy. Two of the greatest challenges of the rollout were training employees who were not computer literate and designing a system that could communicate with other systems in use by the government.

The mapping system covers topographical details, including elevations and coastlines, as well as buildings, utility structures, and the transportation systems. Using these maps, BEHDS can track the movement of rats throughout the island; monitor high-traffic areas, such as garbage dumps and sewers; dispatch pest control officers to distribute poison; and monitor families of rats until they are exterminated.

The people of Bermuda prompt BEHDS into action by contacting the health department by phone with a rat sighting. The system displays call history for repeat callers. The call center is linked to the Works and Engineering master address database so the system can verify the names and addresses of new callers before their complaints enter the system. The department saves time and money by not having to cleanse inaccurate data later.

A typical day's business involves sorting the previous day's calls according to the 80 postal codes used in Bermuda. The department divides these zones among five inspectors, each of whom is responsible for approximately 15 zones. The inspectors head out to their territories with work orders and two map sets. One set has directions to the inspector's assigned zones. The other set displays the exact buildings, structures, or other areas that require inspection. During the course of the day, the inspectors make note of rodent trails, burrows, garbage piles, and trap placements. At the end of the day, the inspectors return to the office to enter their activities and findings into the mapping system. Entries include the complaint, the service call, and bait placement. A dot marks each entry on a map. Supervisors can click the dots to access details about each call.

The GIS clearly reveals clusters of rats and their migration patterns. When BEHDS reveals a cluster, the health department can determine what is drawing the rats to a particular area. Generally, it is the presence of a garbage dump or sewer. Patterns also enable the department to predict where a cluster of rats will move next in search of food. Pest control officers can then try to thwart the prosperity of the rats by placing baited traps or poison before the cluster arrives at its next location.

The health department is trying to integrate BEHDS with a planning department system to help it distribute and track building assignments to its inspectors, as well as facilitate inspectors' reports. Scientific Technologies worked with the various government agencies to standardize the data their systems must exchange.

BEHDS has enabled the Bermuda Department of Health to address its rat problem more efficiently. Workers are able to accomplish more in a day than they could without the system. The department measures its success by the number of rodent complaints that it receives. Since launching the system in 2001, the island has seen its number of rat complaints drop by more than one-third. In the fourth quarter of 2004 alone, the number of complaints dropped by 20 percent as compared with the same period the previous year. The health department used 18 percent fewer pounds of poison during that time as well.

*Sources:* John McCormick, "Bermuda Department of Health: Rat Man Begins," *Baseline,* July 8, 2005; David Kendell and Stephanie Fiedler, "Internet GIS for Bermuda's Environmental Health Department," www.gita.org/members_only/downloads/kendell.pdf, accessed August 16, 2005; and www.esri.com, accessed August 15, 2005.

**To Think About:**
What was the problem facing the island of Bermuda? What was the business impact of the problem? How did the GIS solve the problem? Was it a good solution? Describe the technology involved in the solution. Do you think there was room for improvement on any aspect of the solution? What else might have been done?

The TRUEreq Executive Dashboard™ provides a graphical snapshot of requirement and issue status for product development. The digital dashboard helps transform data into immediate, accurate, and understandable information.

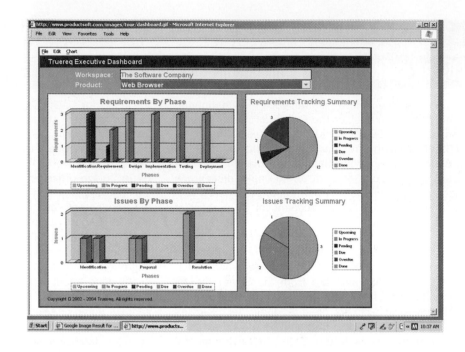

In the short cases that follow, we describe several examples of ESS applications for gathering business intelligence and monitoring corporate performance, including ESS based on enterprise systems.

### National Life: ESS for Business Intelligence

Headquartered in Toronto, Canada, National Life markets individual life insurance, health insurance, and retirement/investment products to individuals and groups. The company has more than 370 employees in Toronto and its regional offices. The company uses an executive information system based on Information Builders' WebFOCUS, which allows senior managers to access information from corporate databases through a Web interface. The system provides statistical reporting and the ability to drill down into current sales information, which is organized to show premium dollars by salesperson. Authorized users can drill down into these data to see the product, agent, and client for each sale. They can examine the data many different ways—by region, by product, and by broker, accessing data for monthly, quarterly, and annual time periods (Information Builders, 2005).

### Digital Dashboards: Bonita Bay Properties and Verizon Communications

Bonita Bay Properties Inc. develops planned communities centered around golf courses and fitness centers in southwest Florida. The company purchases large tracts of land, develops the master plans, and builds the core recreational facilities, allowing housing developers to build the homes in these communities. Bonita Bay's managers are responsible for running the golf courses, clubhouses, restaurants, and fitness centers, as well as security approval for their development projects from municipal and regional governments. Analytical tools from QlikTech International pull data from many different systems to populate dashboards with key performance indicators for senior executives and high-level operational managers. The dashboards display summaries from point-of-sale systems and general-ledger accounts to show how the business is performing on a daily basis and whether staffing levels are appropriate for the areas where the company is making its profits. Senior managers can also drill down to compare the performance of fitness centers or to see whether activity on a golf course experiencing a slowdown has been picking up (Babcock, 2005).

Paul Lacouture, president of network services for Verizon Communications, uses a digital dashboard displaying up-to-the-minute key performance statistics, such as the number of customer complaints or the number or repairs needed. When he spots an unusually high number of line outages in a particular location, he can immediately contact the area manger to discuss the quickest way to solve the problem. Before this dashboard system was in place, Lacouture could obtain information about problems only by going through several layers of managers, and the managers would rely on months-old data stored in thick binders (Latour, 2004).

### Caesar's Entertainment: Enterprise-Wide Performance Analysis

Caesar's Entertainment, one the world's leading gaming companies recently acquired by Harrah's Entertainment Inc. has an integrated reporting structure to help management determine how well it is performing against forecasts on a daily basis. The system uses software from Cognos and SSA Global to integrate data from internal transaction processing systems with data from other internal and external sources. It gathers financial data from the general-ledger system, personnel data, and weather pattern and real estate data to deliver daily cost, effect, impact analysis, and profit-and-loss reports to Caesar's executives. These reports predict the combined effect of all of these factors on the company's business performance. The system lets Caesar's executives adjust plans as required online (Cognos, 2005).

## Group Decision-Support Systems (GDSS)

The systems we have just described focus primarily on helping you make a decision acting alone. But what if you are part of a team and need to make a decision as a group? You would use a special category of systems called group decision-support systems (GDSS) for this purpose.

A **group decision-support system (GDSS)** is an interactive computer-based system for facilitating the solution of unstructured problems by a set of decision makers working together as a group in the same location or in different locations. Groupware and Web-based tools for videoconferencing and electronic meetings described earlier in this text support some group decision processes, but their focus is primarily on communication. GDSS, however, provide tools and technologies geared explicitly toward group decision making.

GDSS-guided meetings take place in conference rooms with special hardware and software tools to facilitate group decision making. The hardware includes computer and networking equipment, overhead projectors, and display screens. Special electronic meeting software collects, documents, ranks, edits, and stores the ideas offered in a decision-making meeting. The more elaborate GDSS use a professional facilitator and support staff. The facilitator selects the software tools and helps organize and run the meeting.

A sophisticated GDSS provides each attendee with a dedicated desktop computer under that person's individual control. No one will be able to see what individuals do on their computers until those participants are ready to share information. Their input is transmitted over a network to a central server that stores information generated by the meeting and makes it available to all on the meeting network. Data can also be projected on a large screen in the meeting room. Figure 10-5 illustrates the sequence of activities at a typical GDSS meeting along with the types of tools used and the output of those tools.

GDSS make it possible to increase meeting size while at the same time increasing productivity because individuals contribute simultaneously rather than one at a time. A GDSS promotes a collaborative atmosphere by guaranteeing contributors' anonymity so that attendees can focus on evaluating the ideas themselves without fear of personally being criticized or of having their ideas rejected based on the contributor. GDSS software tools follow structured methods for organizing and evaluating ideas and for preserving the results of meetings, enabling nonattendees to locate needed information after the meeting. GDSS effectiveness depends on the nature of the problem and the group and on how well a meeting is planned and conducted.

## 10.4 Intelligent Systems for Decision Support

A number of intelligent techniques for enhancing decision making are based on **artificial intelligence (AI)** technology, which consists of computer-based systems (both hardware and software) that attempt to emulate human behavior and thought patterns. These techniques include expert systems, case-based reasoning, fuzzy logic, neural networks, genetic algorithms, and intelligent agents.

**Figure 10-5**
Group System Tools
*The sequence of activities and collaborative support tools used in an electronic meeting system facilitate communication among attendees and generate a full record of the meeting.*

*Source:* Nunamaker et al., "Electronic Meeting Systems to Support Group Work," *Communications of the ACM,* July 1991. Reprinted by permission.

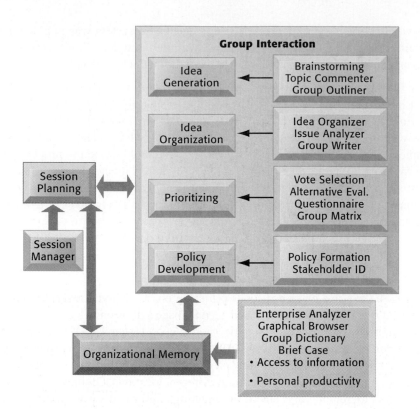

## Expert Systems

What if employees in your firm had to make decisions that required some special knowledge, such as how to formulate a fast-drying sealing compound or how to diagnose and repair a malfunctioning diesel engine, but all the people with that expertise had left the firm? Expert systems are one type of decision-making aid that could help you out. An **expert system** captures human expertise in a limited domain of knowledge as a set of rules in a software system that can be used by others in the organization. These systems typically perform a limited number of tasks that can be performed by professionals in a few minutes or hours, such as diagnosing a malfunctioning machine or determining whether to grant credit for a loan. They are useful in decision-making situations where expertise is expensive or in short supply.

### How Expert Systems Work

Human knowledge must be modeled or represented in a form that a computer can process. Expert systems model human knowledge as a set of rules that collectively are called the **knowledge base**. Expert systems can have from 200 to many thousands of these rules, depending on the complexity of the decision-making problem. These rules are much more interconnected and nested than in a traditional software program (see Figure 10-6).

The strategy used to search through the collection of rules and formulate conclusions is called the **inference engine**. The inference engine works by searching through the rules and "firing" those rules that are triggered by facts gathered and entered by the user.

Developing an expert system requires input from one or more experts who have a thorough command of the knowledge base and one or more knowledge engineers who translate the knowledge (as described by the expert) into a set of rules. A **knowledge engineer** is an information systems specialist with expertise in eliciting information and expertise from other professionals.

### Examples of Expert Systems

Expert systems provide businesses with an array of benefits, including improved decisions, reduced errors, reduced costs, reduced training time, and improved quality and service. Here are several examples:

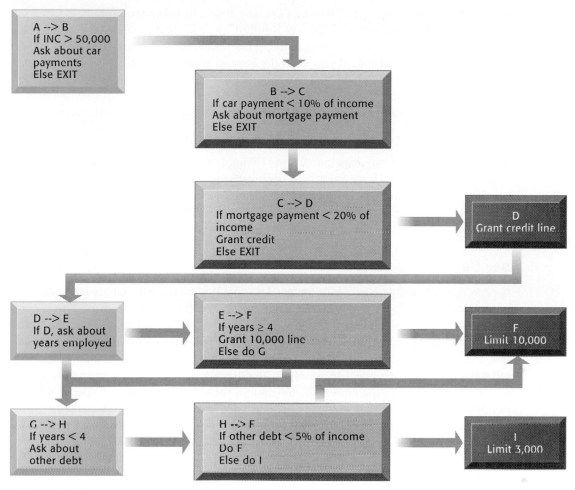

**Figure 10-6**

Rules in an Expert System

*An expert system contains a set of rules to be followed. The rules are interconnected; the number of outcomes is known in advance and is limited; there are multiple paths to the same outcome; and the system can consider multiple rules at a single time. The rules illustrated are for a simple credit-granting expert system.*

Countrywide Funding Corporation in Pasadena, California, uses an expert system to improve decisions about granting loans. This loan-underwriting firm employs about 400 underwriters in 150 offices around the country. The company developed a PC-based expert system to make preliminary creditworthiness decisions on loan requests. The company had experienced rapid, continuing growth and wanted the system to help ensure consistent, high-quality loan decisions. Countrywide's Loan Underwriting Expert System (CLUES) has about 400 rules. Countrywide tested the system by sending every loan application handled by a human underwriter to CLUES as well. The system was refined until it agreed with the underwriters in 95 percent of the cases.

Countrywide does not rely on CLUES to reject loans because the expert system cannot be programmed to handle exceptional situations, such as those involving a self-employed person or complex financial schemes. An underwriter must review all rejected loans and makes the final decision. CLUES has other benefits. Traditionally, an underwriter could handle six or seven applications a day. Using CLUES, the same underwriter can evaluate at least 16 per day. Countrywide now is using the rules in its expert system to answer inquiries from visitors to its Web site who want to know if they qualify for a loan.

Galeria Kaufhof, a German superstore chain, uses a rule-based system to help it inspect the quality of goods that it receives each day, ranging from clothing to complex electronics and fine china. The company receives 120,000 deliveries daily. Inspecting each delivery is time-consuming and expensive, but the company wants to make sure that it is receiving goods that are not damaged or defective. Kaufhof implemented a rule-based system that identifies high-risk deliveries and passes along lower-risk ones automatically. The system scans delivery labels and identifies each delivery in terms of its size, type of product, whether the product is new, and the supplier's past history of deliveries to Kaufhof. Deliveries of large numbers of complex products that are new or that have suppliers with unfavorable delivery histories are carefully inspected, whereas other deliveries are passed on without inspection (Booth and Buluswar, 2002).

Although expert systems lack the robust and general intelligence of human beings, they can provide benefits to organizations if their limitations are well understood. Only certain classes of problems can be solved using expert systems. Virtually all successful expert systems deal with problems of classification in which there are relatively few alternative outcomes and in which these possible outcomes are all known in advance. Expert systems are much less useful for dealing with unstructured problems typically encountered by managers.

## Case-Based Reasoning

Expert systems primarily capture the knowledge of individual experts, but organizations also have collective knowledge and expertise that they have built up over the years. This organizational knowledge can be captured and stored using case-based reasoning. In **case-based reasoning (CBR)**, descriptions of past experiences of human specialists, represented as cases, are stored in a database for later retrieval when the user encounters a new case with similar parameters. The system searches for stored cases with problem characteristics similar to the new one, finds the closest fit, and applies the solutions of the old case to the new case. Successful solutions are tagged to the new case and both are stored together with the other cases in the knowledge base. Unsuccessful solutions also are appended to the case database along with explanations as to why the solutions did not work (see Figure 10-7).

Expert systems work by applying a set of IF–THEN–ELSE rules against a knowledge base, both of which are extracted from human experts. Case-based reasoning, in contrast, represents knowledge as a series of cases, and this knowledge base is continuously expanded and refined by users. You'll find case-based reasoning in diagnostic systems in medicine or customer support where users can retrieve past cases whose characteristics are similar to the new case. The system suggests a solution or diagnosis based on the best-matching retrieved case.

## Fuzzy Logic Systems

Most people do not think in terms of traditional IF–THEN rules or precise numbers. Humans tend to categorize things imprecisely, using rules for making decisions that may have many shades of meaning. For example, a man or a woman may be *strong* or *intelligent.* A company may be *large, medium,* or *small* in size. Temperature may be *hot, cold, cool,* or *warm.* These categories represent a range of values.

**Fuzzy logic** is a rule-based technology that represents such imprecision by creating rules that use approximate or subjective values. It describes a particular phenomenon or process linguistically and then represents that description in a small number of flexible rules.

Let's look at the way fuzzy logic would represent various temperatures in a computer application to control room temperature automatically. The terms (known as *membership functions*) are imprecisely defined so that, for example, in Figure 10-8, cool is between 50 degrees and 70 degrees, although the temperature is most clearly cool between about 60 degrees and 67 degrees. Note that *cool* is overlapped by *cold* or *norm.* To control the room environment using this logic, the programmer would develop similarly imprecise definitions for humidity and other factors, such as outdoor wind and temperature. The rules might include one that says, "If the temperature is *cool* or *cold* and the humidity is low while the outdoor wind is high and the outdoor temperature is low, raise the heat and humidity in the room." The computer would combine the membership function readings in a weighted manner and, using all the rules, raise and lower the temperature and humidity.

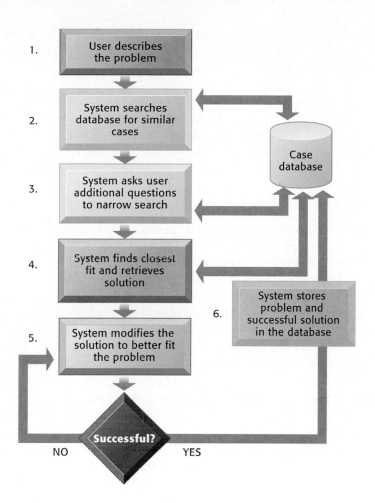

**Figure 10-7**
How Case-Based
Reasoning Works
*Case-based reasoning
represents knowledge
as a database of past
cases and their solu-
tions. The system uses
a six-step process to
generate solutions to
new problems encoun-
tered by the user.*

Fuzzy logic provides solutions to problems requiring expertise that is difficult to represent in the form of crisp IF–THEN rules. In Japan, Sendai's subway system uses fuzzy logic
controls to accelerate so smoothly that standing passengers need not hold on. Mitsubishi
Heavy Industries in Tokyo has been able to reduce the power consumption of its air condi-

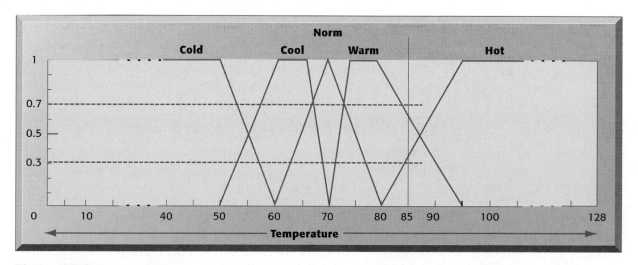

**Figure 10-8**
Implementing Fuzzy Logic Rules in Hardware
*The membership functions for the input called "temperature" are in the logic of the thermostat to
control the room temperature. Membership functions help translate linguistic expressions, such
as* warm, *into numbers that the computer can manipulate.*

*Source:* James M. Sibigtroth, "Implementing Fuzzy Expert Rules in Hardware," *AI Expert,* April 1992. © 1992
Miller Freeman, Inc. Reprinted with permission.

tioners by 20 percent by implementing control programs in fuzzy logic. In these instances, fuzzy logic allows incremental changes in inputs to produce smooth changes in outputs instead of discontinuous ones, making it useful for consumer electronics and engineering applications.

Management has found fuzzy logic useful for decision making and organizational control. A Wall Street firm created a system that selects companies for potential acquisition, using the language stock traders understand. A fuzzy logic system has been developed to detect possible fraud in medical claims submitted by healthcare providers anywhere in the United States.

## Neural Networks

**Neural networks** are used for solving complex, poorly understood problems for which large amounts of data have been collected. They find patterns and relationships in massive amounts of data that would be too complicated and difficult for a human being to analyze. Neural networks discover this knowledge by using hardware and software that parallel the processing patterns of the biological or human brain. Neural networks "learn" patterns from large quantities of data by sifting through data, searching for relationships, building models, and correcting over and over again the model's own mistakes.

A neural network has a large number of sensing and processing nodes that continuously interact with each other. Figure 10-9 represents one type of neural network comprising an input layer, an output layer, and a hidden processing layer. Humans "train" the network by feeding it a set of training data for which the inputs produce a known set of outputs or conclusions. This helps the computer learn the correct solution by example. As the computer is fed more data, each case is compared with the known outcome. If it differs, a correction is calculated and applied to the nodes in the hidden processing layer. These steps are repeated until a condition, such as corrections being less than a certain amount, is reached. The neural network in Figure 10-9 has learned how to identify a fraudulent credit card purchase. Also, self-organizing neural networks can be trained by exposing them to large amounts of data and allowing them to discover the patterns and relationships in the data.

Whereas expert systems seek to emulate or model a human expert's way of solving problems, neural network builders claim that they do not program solutions and do not aim to solve specific problems. Instead, neural network designers seek to put intelligence into the hardware in the form of a generalized capability to learn. In contrast, the expert system is highly specific to a given problem and cannot be retrained easily.

Neural network applications in medicine, science, and business address problems in pattern classification, prediction, financial analysis, and control and optimization. In medicine, neural network applications are used for screening patients for coronary artery disease, for diagnosing patients with epilepsy and Alzheimer's disease, and for performing pattern

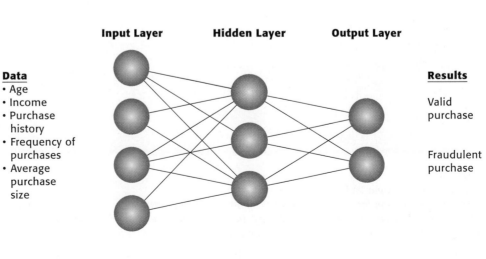

**Figure 10-9**
How a Neural
Network Works
*A neural network uses rules it "learns" from patterns in data to construct a hidden layer of logic. The hidden layer then processes inputs, classifying them based on the experience of the model. In this example, the neural network has been trained to distinguish between valid and fraudulent credit card purchases.*

**Input Layer**   **Hidden Layer**   **Output Layer**

**Data**
• Age
• Income
• Purchase history
• Frequency of purchases
• Average purchase size

**Results**

Valid purchase

Fraudulent purchase

recognition of pathology images. The financial industry uses neural networks to discern patterns in vast pools of data that might help investment firms predict the performance of equities, corporate bond ratings, or corporate bankruptcies. Visa International uses a neural network to help detect credit card fraud by monitoring all Visa transactions for sudden changes in the buying patterns of cardholders.

There are many puzzling aspects of neural networks. Unlike expert systems, which typically provide explanations for their solutions, neural networks cannot always explain why they arrived at a particular solution. Moreover, they cannot always guarantee a completely certain solution, arrive at the same solution again with the same input data, or always guarantee the best solution. They are very sensitive and may not perform well if their training covers too little or too much data. In most current applications, neural networks are best used as aids to human decision makers instead of substitutes for them.

## Genetic Algorithms

**Genetic algorithms** are useful for finding the optimal solution for a specific problem by examining a very large number of alternative solutions for that problem. Their problem-solving techniques are conceptually based on the method that living organisms use to adapt to their environments—the process of evolution. They are programmed to work the way populations solve problems—by changing and reorganizing their component parts using processes, such as reproduction, mutation, and natural selection.

Thus, genetic algorithms promote the evolution of solutions to particular problems, controlling the generation, variation, adaptation, and selection of possible solutions using genetically based processes. As solutions alter and combine, the worst ones are discarded and the better ones survive to go on to produce even better solutions.

A genetic algorithm works by representing information as a string of 0s and 1s. A possible solution can be represented by a long string of these digits. The genetic algorithm provides methods of searching all possible combinations of digits to identify the right string representing the best possible structure for the problem.

In one method, the programmer first randomly generates a population of strings consisting of combinations of binary digits (see Figure 10-10). Each string corresponds to one

| | | Color | Speed | Intelligence | Fitness |
|---|---|---|---|---|---|
| | 1 | White | Medium | Dumb | 40 |
| | 2 | Black | Slow | Dumb | 43 |
| | 3 | White | Slow | Very dumb | 22 |
| | 4 | Black | Fast | Dumb | 71 |
| | 5 | White | Medium | Very smart | 53 |
| **A population of chromosomes** | | | **Decoding of chromosomes** | | **Evaluation of chromosomes** |

## Figure 10-10
The Components of a Genetic Algorithm
*This example illustrates an initial population of "chromosomes," each representing a different solution. The genetic algorithm uses an iterative process to refine the initial solutions so that the better ones, those with the higher fitness, are more likely to emerge as the best solution.*

*Source:* Vasant Dhar and Roger Stein, *Seven Methods for Transforming Corporate Data into Business Intelligence*, p. 65, © 1997. Reprinted by permission of Prentice Hall, Upper Saddle River, New Jersey.

of the variables in the problem. One applies a test for fitness, ranking the strings in the population according to their level of desirability as possible solutions. After the initial population is evaluated for fitness, the algorithm then produces the next generation of strings, consisting of strings that survived the fitness test plus offspring strings produced from mating pairs of strings, and tests their fitness. The process continues until a solution is reached.

Many business problems require optimization because they deal with decisions about minimization of costs, maximization of profits, efficient scheduling, and use of resources. If these problems are very dynamic and complex, involving hundreds or thousands of variables or formulas, genetic algorithms expedite the solution because they can evaluate many different solution alternatives quickly to find the best one.

For example, General Electric engineers used genetic algorithms to help optimize the design for jet turbine aircraft engines, where each design change required changes in up to 100 variables. The supply chain management software from i2 Technologies uses genetic algorithms to optimize production-scheduling models, incorporating hundreds of thousands of details about customer orders, material and resource availability, manufacturing and distribution capability, and delivery dates. International Truck and Engine used this software to iron out snags in production, reducing costly schedule disruptions by 90 percent in five of its plants. Genetic algorithms have helped market researchers performing market segmentation analysis. (Burtka, 1993; Kuo, Chang, and Chien, 2004; Wakefield, 2001).

## Intelligent Agents

Intelligent agent technology helps businesses and decision makers navigate through large amounts of data to locate and act on information that is considered important. **Intelligent agents** are software programs that work in the background without direct human intervention to carry out specific, repetitive, and predictable tasks for an individual user, business process, or software application. The agent uses a limited built-in or learned knowledge base to accomplish tasks or make decisions on the user's behalf, such as deleting junk e-mail, scheduling appointments, or traveling over interconnected networks to find the cheapest airfare to California.

There are many intelligent agent applications today in operating systems, application software, e-mail systems, mobile computing software, and network tools. Of special interest to business are intelligent agents that search for information on the Internet. Chapter 6 describes how shopping bots help consumers find products they want and assist them in comparing prices and other features.

Agent technology is finding applications in supply chain management for improving coordination among different members of the supply chain in response to changing business conditions. In addition to the optimization and simulation modeling described in the chapter-opening case, Procter & Gamble used intelligent agent technology to make its supply chain more efficient. Figure 10-11 illustrates the use of intelligent agents in Procter & Gamble's supply chain network. The network models a complex supply chain as a group of semiautonomous "agents" representing individual supply chain components, such as trucks, production facilities, distributors, and retail stores. The behavior of each agent is programmed to follow rules that mimic actual behavior, such as "order an item when it is out of stock." Simulations using the agents enable the company to perform what-if analyses on inventory levels, in-store stockouts, and transportation costs.

Using intelligent agent models, P&G discovered that trucks should often be dispatched before being fully loaded. Although transportation costs would be higher using partially loaded trucks because of both driver time and fuel to deliver fewer goods, the simulation showed that retail store stockouts would occur less often, thus reducing the amount of lost sales, which would more than make up for the higher distribution costs. Agent-based modeling has saved P&G $300 million annually on an investment of less than 1 percent of that amount (Anthes, 2003).

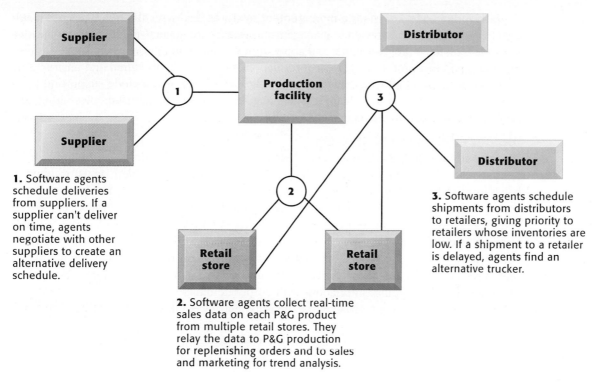

**Figure 10-11**
Intelligent Agents in P&G's Supply Chain Network
*Intelligent agents are helping Procter & Gamble shorten the replenishment cycles for products, such as a box of Tide.*

## 10.4 Systems for Managing Knowledge

Systems for knowledge management improve the quality and utilization of knowledge used in the decision-making process. **Knowledge management** refers to the set of business processes developed in an organization to create, store, transfer, and apply knowledge. Knowledge management increases the ability of the organization to learn from its environment and to incorporate knowledge into its business processes and decision making.

Knowledge that is not shared and applied to the problems facing firms and managers does not add any value to the business. Knowing how to do things effectively and efficiently in ways that other organizations cannot duplicate is a major source of profit and competitive advantage. Why? Because the knowledge you generate about your own production processes, and about your customers, usually stays within your firm and cannot be sold or purchased on the open market. In this sense, self-generated business knowledge is a strategic resource and can provide strategic advantage. Businesses will operate less effectively and efficiently if this unique knowledge is not available for decision making and ongoing operations. There are two major types of knowledge management systems: enterprise-wide knowledge management systems and knowledge work systems.

### Enterprise-Wide Knowledge Management Systems

Firms must deal with at least three kinds of knowledge. Some knowledge exists within the firm in the form of structured text documents (reports and presentations). Decision makers also need knowledge that is semistructured, such as e-mail, voice mail, chat room exchanges, videos, digital pictures, brochures, or bulletin board postings. In still other cases, there is no formal or digital information of any kind; the knowledge resides in the heads of experienced employees somewhere in the company. Much of this knowledge is **tacit knowledge** and is rarely written down.

**Enterprise-wide knowledge management systems** deal with all three types of knowledge. Enterprise-wide knowledge management systems are general-purpose, firmwide systems that collect, store, distribute, and apply digital content and knowledge. These systems include capabilities for searching for information, storing both structured and unstructured data, and locating employee expertise within the firm. They also include supporting technologies such as portals, search engines, collaboration tools (e-mail, instant messaging, and groupware) and learning management systems.

### Structured Knowledge Systems

**Structured knowledge** is explicit knowledge that exists in formal documents, as well as in formal rules that organizations derive by observing experts and their decision-making behaviors. The essential problem in managing structured knowledge is the creation of an appropriate classification scheme to organize the information into meaningful categories and the creation of a database that can be easily accessed by employees in a variety of situations. Once the categories for classifying knowledge have been created, each document needs to be "tagged," or coded, so that search engines can retrieve it and the quality of search results can be improved. **Structured knowledge systems** perform the functions of implementing the tagging, interfacing with corporate databases where the documents are stored, and creating an enterprise portal environment for employees to use when searching for corporate knowledge.

One of the world's largest structured knowledge systems is KPMG's KWorld. KPMG International is an international tax and accounting firm with 95,000 professionals serving clients through 1,100 offices in 820 cities and 150 countries. With such a large global base of employees and clients, KPMG faced a number of problems in sharing knowledge, preventing the loss of knowledge as consultants retired or left the firm, disseminating best practices, and coping with information overload of individual consultants.

KWorld addresses these problems by providing an integrated set of knowledge content and collaboration tools for use worldwide. Although it is primarily a document repository, KWorld also provides online collaboration capabilities for the firm's consultants and an internal reporting system. KWorld stores white papers, presentations, best-practice proposals, articles, presentations, internal discussions, marketing materials, engagement histories, news feeds, external industry research, and other intellectual capital.

The content is organized into nine levels by KPMG products and market segments (see Figure 10-12). Within each of these levels are many subcategories of knowledge. For

**Figure 10-12**
KWorld's Knowledge
Domains
*KPMG's KWorld is organized into levels of content that are further classified by product, market segment, and geographic area.*

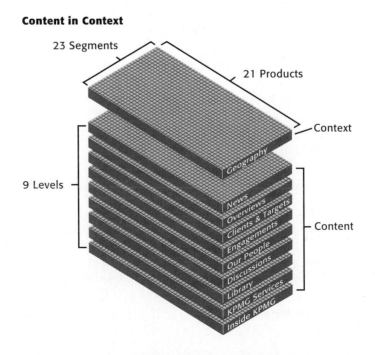

**Content in Context**

23 Segments

21 Products

Context

9 Levels

Geography

News
Overviews
Clients & Targets
Engagements
Our People
Discussions
Library
KPMG Services
Inside KPMG

Content

instance, the client knowledge domain includes entries on financials, industry dynamics, change dynamics, client organizations, client products and customers, and KPMG's history of engagements. Consultants use KWorld to coordinate their work as a team with a client, and the client is allowed access to the collaboration environment as well.

## Semistructured Knowledge Systems

Semistructured information is all the digital information in a firm that does not exist in a formal document or a formal report. It has been estimated that at least 80 percent of an organization's business content is unstructured—information in folders, messages, memos, proposals, e-mails, graphics, electronic slide presentations, and even videos created in different formats and stored in many locations.

Increasingly firms are required to track and manage this semistructured content in order to comply with the Sarbanes–Oxley Act of 2002 and other government legislation, and to manage their information assets more efficiently. Firms subject to Sarbanes–Oxley, for instance, must retain digital records of employee e-mail and phone conversations for a minimum of five years. Firms such as Coca-Cola, for instance, need to keep track of all the images of the Coca-Cola brand that have been created in the past at all their worldwide offices, both to avoid duplicating efforts and to avoid variation from a standard brand image.

A number of vendors have responded to this need with **semistructured knowledge systems** that track, store, and organize semistructured documents, as well as more structured traditional documents. For example, Hummingbird, a Canadian software company, specializes in "integrated knowledge management systems" (see Figure 10-13). In addition to providing

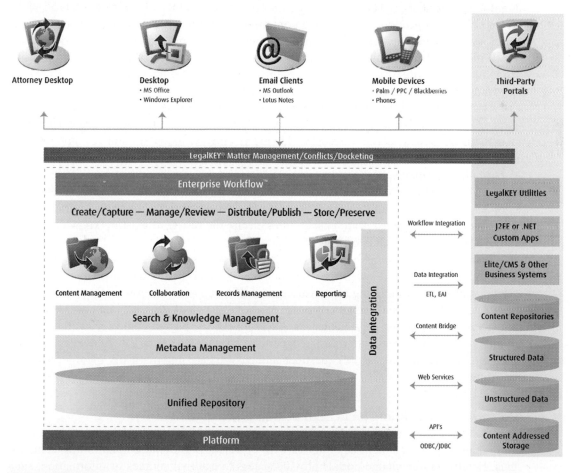

## Figure 10-13

Hummingbird's Integrated Knowledge Management System
*Hummingbird's enterprise solution combines document management, knowledge management, business intelligence, and portal technologies and can be used for managing semistructured as well as structured knowledge.*

centralized repositories for document management, Hummingbird provides a rules-based e-mail management program that automatically profiles incoming and outgoing mail messages using rules developed by line managers.

For example, Los Angeles law firm Hennigan, Bennett, and Dorman LLP uses Hummingbird to help it search e-mail for potential evidence. Instead of sifting through piles of printed copies of e-mails, attorneys run powerful electronic searches, locating only the e-mails they need for a case and marking them up electronically. The system also re-creates all of the threads of an entire e-mail discussion for attorneys to follow. Using this system has cut the time to process e-mail in half (Hummingbird, 2004).

Another Hummingbird user is the Canadian law firm Stikeman Elliott, which is described in the Focus on Organizations. Like other law firms, Stikeman Elliott is a knowledge-intensive company, but its employees, offices, and knowledge resources are distributed in many different locations. It implemented Hummingbird tools to help it leverage this knowledge and use it more efficiently. As you read this case, try to identify the problem this company was facing; what alternative solutions were available to management; how well the chosen solution worked; and the people, organization, and technology issues that had to be addressed when developing the solution.

### Knowledge Network Systems

**Knowledge network systems**, also known as *expertise location and management systems,* address the problem that arises when the appropriate knowledge is not in the form of a digital document but instead resides in the memory of expert individuals in the firm. Knowledge network systems provide an online directory of corporate experts in well-defined knowledge domains and use communication technologies to make it easy for employees to find the appropriate expert in a company. Some knowledge network systems go further by systematizing the solutions developed by experts and then storing the solutions in a knowledge database as a best-practices or frequently asked questions (FAQ) repository.

AskMe, Inc. offers a widely adopted enterprise knowledge network system. Its users include Procter & Gamble and Intec Engineering Partnership, a project management company with more than 500 employees worldwide serving the global oil and gas industry. The software, AskMe Enterprise, enables firms to develop a database of employee expertise and know-how, documents, best practices, and FAQs, and then to share that information across the firm using whichever portal technology the firm has adopted. Content can be further categorized through community spaces that organize expertise and knowledge around a common discipline. Federated search capabilities ensure the re-use of existing knowledge from internal repositories, Web sites, and other data sources.

Figure 10-14 illustrates how AskMe Enterprise works. An Intec engineer with a question, for instance, could access relevant documents, Web links, and answers to previous related questions by initiating a keyword search. If no answer was found, that person could post a general question on a Web page for categories, such as Pipeline or Subsea, for other engineers accessing that page to answer. Alternatively, the person could review the profiles of all company engineers with relevant expertise and send a detailed e-mail query to experts who might have the answer. All questions and answers are automatically incorporated into the knowledge database.

### Portals, Collaboration Tools, and Learning Management Systems

The major commercial knowledge management system vendors are integrating their content and document management capabilities with powerful portal and collaboration technologies. Enterprise knowledge portals provide access to external sources of information, such as news feeds and research, as well as to internal knowledge resources along with capabilities for e-mail, chat/instant messaging, discussion groups, and videoconferencing. Users can, for example, easily add a collection of documents obtained through a portal to a collaborative workspace.

# FOCUS ON ORGANIZATIONS  Stikeman Elliot Computerizes Its Brainpower

Stikeman Elliott is an international business law firm based in Toronto, Ontario, Canada, noted for its work in mergers and acquisitions, antitrust, banking and finance, insolvency, intellectual property, and technology. The firm started with two lawyers in 1952 and today operates with more than 400 lawyers in nine offices in Canada, New York, London, and Sydney. It is one of the top business law firms in Canada.

Stikeman Elliott tries to promote a culture of initiative and high-performance standards. The key to creating and maintaining such a culture is in finding the best way to share the vast repositories of knowledge that reside in the brains of the lawyers and in the documents and files that the lawyers have been collecting throughout their careers. Foremost among the forms of knowledge critical to lawyers are precedents, which can include documents, forms, guidelines, and best practices.

Stikeman Elliott realized that an effective knowledge management (KM) system would enable the firm's lawyers to be more productive and contribute to sustaining the growth of the firm over the long term. In 2001, Stikeman Elliott selected Hummingbird Enterprise Webtop from Hummingbird Ltd. to build a portal for the firm's corporate intranet. The portal officially launched in 2002 under the name STELLA, which is a play on the name of the firm.

With STELLA in place, all of the firm's lawyers have easy access to the firm's knowledge assets, including important precedents, through a single access point using a Web browser. STELLA includes an expertise database, identifying lawyers with proficiency in specific areas. The portal also codifies the generation and organization of new precedents. Margaret Grottenthaler, the co-chair of Stikeman Elliott's national knowledge management committee, points out the importance of STELLA to the firm's junior employees: "It's the way to access all our research, all the legal how-tos. It's absolutely critical they use it. The more junior they are, the more likely they are to use it for those purposes."

An additional benefit of STELLA has been its ability to encourage the sense of community that Stikeman Elliott wishes to foster in its firm by growing organically rather than through mergers or acquisitions. Everyone in the firm, regardless of which office they work in, has access to the same resources. With everyone on equal footing, the multiple-office structure maintains the feel of a single organization. Stikeman Elliott believes that this working atmosphere positions the firm well among its competitors. The increased level of communication among the offices also prevents lawyers from duplicating work that has already been done. Lawyers can customize the portal's home page so that they have quick access to the information they need most, whether it is their case files, news about their clients, or news about their clients' industries.

Stikeman Elliott integrated its portal closely with its document management (DM) system, which was also based on Hummingbird DOCS Open software. Stikeman employees use the Hummingbird SearchServer search engine to search through the firm's document repository and internal legal and business content, including e-mail, and some external resources, such as LexisNexis.

Of course, a KM system is only useful if it is populated with the knowledge of its users. Some firms have difficulty with partners who hoard their knowledge, it being a valuable commodity. At Stikeman Elliott, the greater obstacle has been time. Partners are often too busy to contribute their work to the system. To combat this problem, the firm is building tools to automate the population of the knowledge database. With these tools, lawyers can easily create Web sites for their cases, clients, and industry research. STELLA has extranet capabilities that enable Stikeman Elliott to create sites on which clients can review and work with documents pertaining to their cases in a collaborative manner. Grottenthaler points out that the firm's KM system is actually geared toward the client, not the lawyer, because the ultimate goal is to serve the client better.

The KM team at Stikeman Elliott includes library staff and law clerks in addition to lawyers. All three groups can add precedents, memos, and even meeting notes to the system. The team emphasizes the importance of the human presence in KM and keeps in close contact with the firm's lawyers to make sure they have access to the knowledge they need. A human subject matter expert also reviews content that has been added and categorized by automated procedures, which ensures the quality of the information.

*Sources:* Judith Lamont, "Smart by Any Name—Enterprise Suites Offer Broad Benefits," *KMWorld Magazine,* April 2005; "Stikeman Elliott Collaborates with Hummingbird and ii3," www.hummingbird.com, accessed February 8, 2005; www.stikeman.com, accessed August 15, 2005; and Gerry Blackwell, "Computer and Technology Law," *Canadian Lawyer,* August 2003.

**To Think About:**

What are the problems and challenges that a law firm such as Stikeman Elliott faces? What solutions are available to solve these problems? How did implementing Hummingbird address these problems? How successful was the solution? Did Stikeman Elliott choose the best alternative?

**Figure 10-14**
AskMe Enterprise
Knowledge Network
System
*A knowledge network maintains a database of firm experts, as well as accepted solutions to known problems. The system facilitates the communication between employees looking for knowledge and internal solution providers, either through the Web-based system, standard e-mail such as Outlook, and instant messaging solutions or handheld devices. Solutions created in this communication are then added to a database of solutions in the form of frequently asked questions (FAQs), best practices, or other documents.*

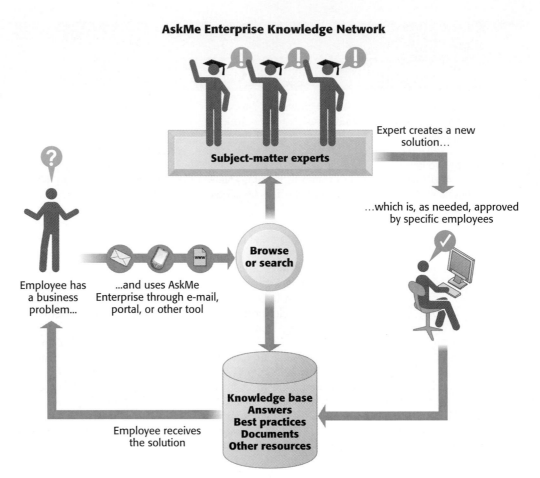

Companies need ways to keep track of and manage employee learning and to integrate it more fully into their knowledge management and other corporate systems. A **learning management system (LMS)** provides tools for the management, delivery, tracking, and assessment of various types of employee learning and training.

For example, the Naval Education Training Command (NETC) uses the THINQ Training Server Learning Management System to manage training for 47,000 officers and enlisted people enrolled in 3,600 different courses. The THINQ Learning Management System launches and tracks e-learning courseware and supports instructor-led training. It provides tools for training administrators to assess individual skills and competencies, manage personalized learning plans, and track required certifications. Each learner can use the system to find out exactly what training he or she should receive for specific career paths and assignments. The system saves the Navy about $40 million in travel costs per year and has also reduced the amount of time required for training, (Hollis, 2004).

## Knowledge Work Systems (KWS)

The enterprise-wide knowledge systems we have just described provide a wide range of capabilities used by many, if not all, the workers and groups in an organization. Firms also have specialized systems for knowledge workers to help them create new knowledge for improving the firm's business processes and decision making. **Knowledge work systems (KWS)** are specialized systems for engineers, scientists, and other knowledge workers that are designed to promote the creation of knowledge and to ensure that new knowledge and technical expertise are properly integrated into the business.

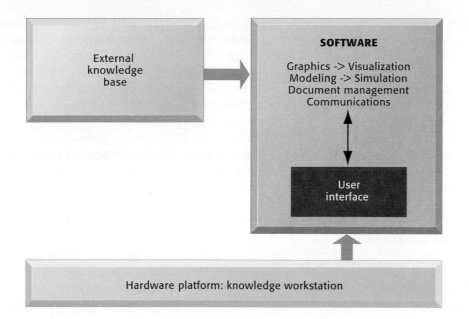

**Figure 10-15**
Requirements of
Knowledge Work
Systems
*Knowledge work systems require strong links to external knowledge bases in addition to specialized hardware and software.*

### Requirements of Knowledge Work Systems

Knowledge work systems give knowledge workers the specialized tools they need, such as powerful graphics, analytical tools, and communications and document management. These systems require great computing power to handle the sophisticated graphics or complex calculations necessary for such knowledge workers as scientific researchers, product designers, and financial analysts. Because knowledge workers are so focused on knowledge in the external world, these systems also must give the worker quick and easy access to external databases. They typically feature user-friendly interfaces that enable users to perform needed tasks without having to spend a lot of time learning how to use the computer. Figure 10-15 summarizes the requirements of knowledge work systems.

Knowledge workstations often are designed and optimized for the specific tasks to be performed. A design engineer requires a different workstation setup than a financial analyst. Design engineers need graphics with enough power to handle three-dimensional, computer-aided design (CAD) systems. However, financial analysts are more interested in access to a myriad of external databases and technology for efficiently storing and accessing massive amounts of financial data.

### Examples of Knowledge Work Systems

Major knowledge work applications include computer-aided design (CAD) systems (which we introduced in Chapter 3), virtual reality systems for simulation and modeling, and financial workstations.

Contemporary CAD systems are capable of generating realistic-looking three-dimensional graphic designs that can be rotated and viewed from all sides. Architects from Skidmore, Owings, & Merrill LLP used a three-dimensional CAD program called Revit to work out the creative and technical details of the design for the Freedom Tower at the site of the former World Trade Center. The software enabled the architects to strip away the outer layer to manipulate the shape of the floors. Changes appeared immediately in the entire model, and the software automatically recalculated the technical details in the blueprints (Frangos, 2004).

**Virtual reality systems** use interactive graphics software to create computer-generated simulations that are so close to reality that users almost believe they are participating in a real-world situation. In many virtual reality systems, the user dons special clothing, headgear, and equipment, depending on the application. The clothing contains sensors that record the user's movements and immediately transmit that information back to the computer. For instance, to walk through a virtual reality simulation of a house, you would need garb that monitors the movement of your feet, hands, and head. You also would need goggles containing video screens and sometimes audio attachments and feeling gloves so that you are immersed in the computer feedback.

Virtual reality is just starting to provide benefits in educational, scientific, and business work. For example, neuroradiologists at New York's Beth Israel Medical Center use the Siemens Medical Systems 3D Virtuoso System to peek at the interplay of tiny blood vessels or take a fly-through of the aorta. Surgeons at New York University School of Medicine use three-dimensional modeling to target brain tumors more precisely, thereby reducing bleeding and trauma during surgery.

Virtual reality applications developed for the Web use a standard called **Virtual Reality Modeling Language (VRML)**. VRML is a set of specifications for interactive, three-dimensional modeling on the World Wide Web that organize multiple media types, including animation, images, and audio to put users in a simulated real-world environment. VRML is platform independent, operates over a desktop computer, and requires little bandwidth.

DuPont, the Wilmington, Delaware, chemical company, created a VRML application called HyperPlant, which enables users to access three-dimensional data over the Internet using Web browser software. Engineers can go through three-dimensional models as if they were physically walking through a plant, viewing objects at eye level. This level of detail reduces the number of mistakes they make during construction of oil rigs, oil plants, and other structures.

The financial industry is using specialized **Investment workstations** to leverage the knowledge and time of its brokers, traders, and portfolio managers. Firms such as Merrill Lynch and UBS Financial Services have installed investment workstations that integrate a wide range of data from both internal and external sources, including contact management data, real-time and historical market data, and research reports. Previously, financial professionals had to spend considerable time accessing data from separate systems and piecing together the information they needed. By providing one-stop information faster and with fewer errors, the workstations streamline the entire investment process from stock selection to updating client records.

---

**LEARNING TRACKS**

1. If you want to learn more about how an expert system inference engine works, you will find a Learning Track on this topic at the Laudon Web site for this chapter.
2. If you want to learn more about the challenges of implementing and using knowledge management systems, you will find a Learning Track on this topic at the Laudon Web site for this chapter.

## Summary

1  **Compare different types of decisions and describe the decision-making process.** The different levels in an organization (strategic, management, and operational) have different decision-making requirements. Decisions may be structured, semistructured, or unstructured, with structured decisions clustering at the operational level of the organization and unstructured decisions at the strategic level. Decision making can be performed by individuals or groups and includes employees as well as operational, middle, and senior managers. There are four stages in decision making: intelligence, design, choice, and implementation.

2 **Evaluate the role of information systems in helping people working individually and in groups make decisions more effectively.** Specialized systems specifically designed to help managers and employees make better decisions include management information systems (MIS), decision-support systems (DSS), group decision-support systems (GDSS), and executive support systems (ESS).

Management information systems provide information on firm performance to help managers monitor and control the business, often in the form of fixed regularly scheduled reports based on data summarized from the firm's transaction processing systems. MIS support structured decisions and some semistructured decisions.

Decision-support systems combine data, sophisticated analytical models and tools, and user-friendly software into a single powerful system that can support semistructured or unstructured decision making. The components of a DSS are the DSS database, the DSS software system, and the user interface. DSS support decisions for pricing, asset utilization, supply chain management, and customer relationship management, as well as model alternative business scenarios. DSS targeted toward customers as well as managers are becoming available on the Web. A special category of DSS called geographic information systems (GIS) uses data visualization technology to analyze and display data for planning and decision making with digitized maps.

People working together in a group can use group decision-support systems to help them in the process of arriving at a decision. Group decision-support systems use special conference room facilities where participants contribute their ideas using networked computers and software tools for organizing ideas, gathering information, ranking and setting priorities, and documenting meeting sessions. A GDSS helps decision makers meeting together arrive at a decision more efficiently and is especially useful for increasing the productivity of meetings of more than four or five people.

Executive support systems help senior managers with unstructured problems that occur at the strategic level of the firm. ESS provide data from both internal and external sources and provide a generalized computing and communications environment that can be focused and applied to a changing array of problems. ESS help senior executives monitor firm performance, spot problems, identify opportunities, and forecast trends. These systems can filter out extraneous details for high-level overviews or drill down to provide senior managers with detailed transaction data if required.

3 **Evaluate the business benefits of using intelligent techniques in decision making and knowledge management.** Intelligent techniques aid decision makers by capturing individual and collective knowledge, discovering patterns and behaviors in vast quantities of data, and generating solutions to problems that are too large and complex for human beings to solve on their own.

Expert systems capture tacit knowledge from a limited domain of human expertise and express that knowledge in the form of rules. The strategy to search through the knowledge base is called the *inference engine*. Expert systems are most useful for problems of classification or diagnosis. Case-based reasoning represents organizational knowledge as a database of cases that can be continually expanded and refined. When the user encounters a new case, the system searches for similar cases, finds the closest fit, and applies the solutions of the old case to the new case. The new case is stored with successful solutions in the case database.

Fuzzy logic is a software technology for expressing knowledge in the form of rules that uses approximate or subjective values. Fuzzy logic has been used for controlling physical devices and is starting to be used for limited decision-making applications.

Neural networks consist of hardware and software that attempt to mimic the thought processes of the human brain. Neural networks are notable for their ability to learn without programming and to recognize patterns that cannot be described easily by humans. They are being used in science, medicine, and business primarily to discriminate patterns in massive amounts of data.

Genetic algorithms develop solutions to particular problems using genetically based processes, such as fitness, crossover, and mutation. Genetic algorithms are beginning to be applied to problems involving optimization and product design, and to monitor industrial systems where many alternatives or variables must be evaluated to generate an optimal solution.

Intelligent agents are software programs with built-in or learned knowledge bases that carry out specific, repetitive, and predictable tasks for an individual user, business process, or software application. Intelligent agents can be programmed to navigate through large amounts of data to locate useful information and in some cases act on that information on behalf of the user.

**4** **Define and describe the types of systems used for enterprise-wide knowledge management and demonstrate how they provide value for businesses.** Enterprise-wide knowledge management systems are firmwide efforts to collect, store, distribute, and apply digital content and knowledge. Structured knowledge systems provide databases and tools for organizing and storing structured documents, whereas semistructured knowledge systems provide databases and tools for organizing and storing semistructured knowledge, such as e-mail or rich media. Knowledge network systems provide directories and tools for locating firm employees with special expertise who are important sources of tacit knowledge. Often these systems include group collaboration tools, portals to simplify information access, search tools, and tools for classifying information based on a taxonomy that is appropriate for the organization. Learning management systems support enterprise-wide knowledge management with tools for the management, delivery, tracking, and assessment of various types of employee learning and training. These systems provide value to the business by reducing the time and cost to acquire and utilize knowledge and by providing knowledge for higher-quality decisions.

**5** **Define and describe the major types of knowledge work systems and demonstrate how they provide value for firms.** Knowledge work systems (KWS) support the creation of new knowledge and its integration into the organization. KWS require easy access to an external knowledge base; powerful computer hardware that can support software with intensive graphics, analysis, document management, and communications capabilities; and a user-friendly interface. These capabilities can increase the productivity of highly paid knowledge workers. KWS often run on workstations that are customized for the work they must perform. Computer-aided design (CAD) systems and virtual reality systems, which create interactive simulations that behave like the real world, require graphics and powerful modeling capabilities. KWS for financial professionals provide access to external databases and the ability to analyze massive amounts of financial data very quickly.

## Key Terms

Artificial intelligence (AI), 341
Case-based reasoning (CBR), 344
Choice, 332
Customer decision-support systems (CDSS), 338
Data visualization, 337
Design, 332
Digital dashboard, 338
Drill down, 338
DSS database, 334
DSS software system, 335
Enterprise-wide knowledge management systems, 350
Expert system, 342
Fuzzy logic, 344
Genetic algorithms, 347

Geographic information systems (GIS), 337
Group decision-support systems (GDSS), 341
Implementation, 332
Intelligence, 332
Inference engine, 342
Intelligent agents, 348
Intelligent techniques, 333
Investment workstations, 356
Knowledge base, 342
Knowledge engineer, 342
Knowledge management, 349
Knowledge network systems, 352
Knowledge work systems (KWS), 354

Learning management system (LMS), 354
Model, 335
Neural networks, 346
Semistructured decisions, 331
Semistructured knowledge systems, 351
Sensitivity analysis, 335
Structured decisions, 331
Structured knowledge, 350
Structured knowledge systems, 350
Tacit knowledge, 349
Unstructured decisions, 331
Virtual reality systems, 355
Virtual Reality Modeling Language (VRML), 356

## Review Questions

**10.1** What are the different decision-making levels and decision-making groups in organizations? How do their decision-making requirements differ?

**10.2** What is the difference between an unstructured, semistructured, and structured decision?

**10.3** List and describe the stages in decision making.

**10.4** What is the difference between a decision-support system (DSS) and a management information system (MIS)?

**10.5** What are the three basic components of a DSS? Briefly describe each.

**10.6** What is a geographic information system (GIS)? How does it use data visualization technology? How can it support decision making?

**10.7** What is a customer decision-support system? How can the Internet be used for this purpose?

**10.8** Define and describe the capabilities of an executive support system (ESS). How do ESS enhance managerial decision making? How do they provide value for a business?

**10.9** What is a group decision-support system (GDSS)? How does it work? What problems does it solve?

**10.10** Define an expert system, describe how it works, and explain its value to business.

**10.11** What is case-based reasoning? How does it differ from an expert system?

**10.12** What is a neural network? How does it work? How can neural networks benefit business?

**10.13** Define and describe fuzzy logic, genetic algorithms, and intelligent agents. How do they work? For what kinds of problems are they suited?

**10.14** What is knowledge management? How does it promote organizational learning? Why is it of great interest to business?

**10.15** Define and describe the various types of enterprise-wide knowledge systems. How do they provide value for businesses?

**10.16** Describe the role of the following in facilitating knowledge management: portals, collaboration tools, and learning management systems.

**10.17** What are knowledge work systems? What role do they play in knowledge management? What are the generic requirements of knowledge work systems?

**10.18** Describe how the following systems support knowledge work: computer-aided design (CAD), virtual reality, and investment workstations.

## Discussion Questions

**10.1** If businesses used DSS, GDSS, and ESS more widely, would they make better decisions? Do you agree? Why or why not?

**10.2** Describe various ways that knowledge management systems could help firms with sales and marketing or with manufacturing and production.

## Application Software Exercise

### Spreadsheet Exercise: Performing Break-Even Analysis and Sensitivity Analysis

Software skills: Spreadsheet formulas, creating a two-variable data table
Business skills: Break-even analysis

Selmore Collectible Toy Company (SCTC) makes toy sets consisting of collectible trucks, vans, and cars for the retail market. The firm is developing a new toy set that includes a battery-powered tractor trailer, complete with cab and trailer; a sports car; and a motorcycle. Each set sells for $100. Table 1 shows the major components of SCTC's annual fixed costs for the toy set. Each component includes the cost of purchases, depreciation, and operating expenses. Table 2 shows the major components of SCTC's variable costs.

**TABLE 1**

**SCTC's Fixed Costs**

| Category | Amount |
|---|---|
| Land | $44,500 |
| Buildings | 392,500 |
| Manufacturing machinery | 572,000 |
| Office equipment | 212,800 |
| Utilities | 30,500 |
| Insurance | 80,700 |
| Total | 1,333,000 |

**TABLE 2**

**SCTC's Variable Costs**

| Category | Amount |
|---|---|
| Labor | $15.00 |
| Advertising | 1.00 |
| Shipping and receiving | 5.00 |
| Total | 21.00 |

Prepare a spreadsheet to support the decision-making needs of SCTC's managers. The spreadsheet should show the fixed costs, variable costs per unit, the contribution margin, and the break-even point for this product. How many sets does SCTC have to sell before it can start turning a profit? Include a data table to show alternative break-even points, assuming variations in insurance costs and labor costs. How would increasing the sale price to $125 affect the break-even point? The Laudon Web site for Chapter 10 provides more detail on the range of costs to include in your sensitivity analysis and on the calculations required for a simple break-even analysis.

## Analyzing the Impact of Component Price Changes

Software skills: Spreadsheet formulas, creating a two-variable data table
Business skills: Manufacturing bill of materials sensitivity analysis

Dirt Bikes's management has asked you to explore the impact of changes in some of its parts components on production costs. Review the following bill of materials information for the brake system for Dirt Bikes's Moto 300 model. A bill of materials is used in manufacturing and production to show all of the parts and materials required to manufacture a specific item or for the subassembly of a finished product, such as a motorcycle. The information in the bill of materials is useful for determining product costs, coordinating orders, and managing inventory. It can also tell how product costs will be affected by price changes in components or raw materials. The bill of materials for this case has been simplified for instructional purposes.

**Bill of Materials: Moto 300 Brake System**

| Component | Component No. | Source | Unit Cost | Quantity | Extended Cost |
|---|---|---|---|---|---|
| Brake cable | M0593 | Nissin | $27.81 | 1 | |
| Brake pedal | M0546 | Harrison Billet | 6.03 | 2 | |
| Brake pad | M3203 | Russell | 27.05 | 2 | |
| Front brake pump | M0959 | Brembo | 66.05 | 1 | |
| Rear brake pump | M4739 | Brembo | 54.00 | 1 | |
| Front brake caliper | M5930 | Nissin | 105.20 | 1 | |
| Rear brake caliper | M7942 | Nissin | 106.78 | 1 | |
| Front brake disc | M3920 | Russell | 143.80 | 1 | |
| Rear brake disc | M0588 | Russell | 56.42 | 1 | |
| Brake pipe | M0943 | Harrison Billet | 28.52 | 1 | |
| Brake lever cover | M1059 | Brembo | 2.62 | 1 | |

The bill of materials for this assignment should contain the description of the component, the identification number of each component, the source of the component, the unit cost of each component, the quantity of each component needed to make each finished brake system, the extended cost of each component, and the total materials cost. The extended cost is calculated by multiplying the quantity of each component needed to produce the finished brake system by the unit cost. The prices of components are constantly changing, and you will need to develop a spreadsheet application that can show management the impact of such price changes on the cost to produce each brake system and on total production costs for the Moto 300 model.

1. Complete the bill of materials by calculating the extended cost of each component and the total materials cost for each brake system.
2. Develop a sensitivity analysis to show the impact on total brake system materials costs if the front brake calipers unit cost ranges from $103 to $107 and if the brake pipe unit cost ranges from $27 to $30.
3. The brake system represents 30 percent of the total materials cost for one Moto 300 motorcycle. Use sensitivity analysis again to show the impact of the changes in front brake caliper unit costs and brake pipe unit costs described previously on total materials costs for this motorcycle model.

## Building Internet Skills

## Using Intelligent Agents for Comparison Shopping

This project will help develop your Internet skills in using shopping bots to compare product pricing, features, and availability.

You have decided it is time to supplement your old film camera with a new digital camera. Select a digital camera you might want to purchase, such as the Kodak EasyShare V550 or the Canon PowerShot S500. You would like to purchase the camera as inexpensively as possible. Try several of the shopping bot sites, which do the price comparisons for you. Visit MySimon.com, Froogle.com, PriceGrabber.com, BizRate.com, or Shopping.com. Compare these sites in terms of their ease of use, number of offerings, speed in obtaining information, thoroughness of information offered about the product and seller, and price selection. Which site or sites would you use and why?

## Video Case

You will find a video case illustrating some of the concepts in this chapter on the Laudon Web site at **www.prenhall.com/laudon** along with questions to help you analyze the case.

## Teamwork

### Rating Knowledge Network Systems

With a group of classmates, select two knowledge network system products, such as AskMe, Tacit ActiveNet, or DOC Insider. Compare their features and capabilities. To prepare your analysis, use articles from computer magazines and the Web sites for the knowledge network software vendors. If possible, use electronic presentation software to present your findings to the class.

## BUSINESS PROBLEM-SOLVING CASE

### Can Information Systems Make Your Doctor Better?

Imagine that you have just been admitted to the hospital with a blood clot in your leg. You are already taking Tagament for treating ulcers. The hospital prescribes Coumadin to dissolve the clot. You refuse to take the medicine until someone double-checks the prescription to make sure there will be no adverse interaction with your other medication. In the end, you learn that you were correct. The Tagament interacts adversely with the Coumadin, leading to excess blood thinning and bleeding, and you must stop taking the Tagament until your blood clot has dissolved.

In the preceding scenario, the mistake probably would not have produced negative consequences because the error was caught in time. However, such errors do occur in hospitals and they are not always so innocuous. More than 7,000 Americans are killed each year because of inappropriate prescriptions taken by patients, ignoring drug interaction problems. Adverse drug events account for 41 percent of hospital admissions and more than $2 billion in annual inpatient costs.

Many of these errors are the results of human factors: poor handwriting, memory lapses, fatigue, and distractions. To prevent these factors from negatively impacting patients, some healthcare facilities are using information systems to help doctors and nurses make better prescription decisions. A computerized physician order entry, or CPOE, system tries to reduce prescription and dosage errors for medications, keep physicians updated on treatment guidelines, and prevent physicians from ordering superfluous tests or drugs that are not part of the standard formularies.

Physicians must be willing to incorporate the use of these systems into their workflow. Many doctors resist changing their ways because a system is complex or takes more time to use than the procedures to which they are accustomed. Therefore, any organization that plans to implement a CPOE must do so carefully. According to Asif Ahmad, vice president and chief information officer (CIO) of Duke University Health System, "CPOE is one system that no hospital can just deploy. What you buy from a vendor is just a shell." He likens the system to a blank notebook in which you have to fill the pages.

A study of errors at the Veterans Administration (VA) Medical Center in Salt Lake City, Utah, published in the

American Medical Association's *Archives of Internal Medicine,* found that the use of simple systems that eliminate handwriting mistakes and offer only basic decision support, such as drug allergy and interaction alerts, do not significantly reduce high rates of adverse drug events. A similar study at the hospital of the University of Pennsylvania found numerous potential glitches in its hospital system. That system actually created new ways of making errors because of its design. It scattered patient data and drug-ordering forms over many different computer windows, increasing the likelihood that physicians would order the wrong medications. To impact the rate of adverse drug events, CPOE sytems must support sophisticated decisions, such as drug choice, dosages, and patient-monitoring strategies, and they must be well designed.

Carolyn Clancy, director of the federal Agency for Healthcare Research and Quality, believes that the discovery of weaknesses in decision-support systems does not negate their worth; they simply need to be improved. Dr. Clancy states, "We can't improve safety until we see what the problems are, and these studies are showing us that we still have a lot to learn." However, hospitals may use the studies as justification for not investing the $8 million to $12 million that a CPOE system costs. The initial cost overshadows the return on investment, which they would likely see in a few years. Only 5 to 10 percent of all hospitals have CPOE systems.

Supporters of CPOE systems, such as Dr. Jonathan Teich of Harvard University and the medical IT company Healthvision, do not expect computers to replace the human expertise behind a doctor's diagnosis or course of treatment. Teich says that the value of decision support lies in its ability to remember thousands of details and bring the right ones to the attention of doctors at the right times. These are details that doctors know very well, but they may lose sight of small facts or rules amongst the myriad of tasks they need to perform. One pertinent example from the VA study involved doctors forgetting to prescribe laxatives or stool softeners for patients being treated for pain with narcotics. The secondary prescription would have prevented constipation caused by the narcotics. Instead, patients suffered from bowel impaction and some required emergency surgery.

Sophisticated CPOE systems, such as the one at the University of Pittsburgh Medical Center Children's Hospital, aim to reduce such mistakes. Here, the system calculates drug doses based on a patient's age and weight in addition to raising allergy and drug interaction issues. Even though a physician may be aware of these factors, the system acts as insurance. The extra check is particularly important for patients whose health is already compromised, such as those who have suffered kidney failure. Doctors must adjust drug dosages for these patients based on their precise conditions.

Assistant Duke University CIO Michael Russell says that mapping workflow "is a tedious process and requires the ability to translate physician-speak into computerese." To ensure that all critical processes are covered, his department makes rounds with physicians, sifts through stacks of orders, and holds committee meetings with members of the various hospital teams. One of the pitfalls to avoid is gearing the system too much toward physicians and not enough toward nurses, who may feel the greater impact on their daily tasks when a CPOE system is installed.

One side effect of a CPOE system is that it can be more rigid than traditional paperwork. For instance, under a paper system, a doctor might be able to write orders for a patient before that patient is formally admitted to the hospital. A stringent CPOE system might flag an attempt to enter orders for a patient who has not been admitted yet. To solve this problem, Duke added a new unit to its CPOE system that permits virtual admissions of cardiac patients. Hospital administrators determined that the practice would not violate regulations.

However, this same rigidity can provide benefits. It enables the Duke University hospital to identify sets of related activities that the CPOE system can automate. Then, when a physician enters a cardiac admission into the system, the system pulls out all of the necessary procedures, which serve as prompts for the course of treatment.

With a uniform architecture in place, communications between doctors and nurses run much more smoothly. The hospital staff members can avoid literally running back and forth to consult each other because the system contains all of the pertinent information. Doctors save time on their rounds by visiting patients with laptops in tow. They can enter orders for drugs and labs, as well as view lab results, without having to return to their offices midround. The orders are less likely to contain errors or be misread by labs or pharmacies because they are not handwritten. Some studies have shown that CPOE systems can prevent one-fourth of all adverse drug effects.

Doctors and nurses still must communicate effectively and they must trust the system. If they do not trust the system, they are more likely to ignore the automated prompts. Using decision-support software can be a difficult sell for doctors because they prefer to trust their experience and training. Some doctors resist the idea that they need help remembering procedures and treatments.

Jason Maude is a father who believes that the usefulness of decision-support software extends to diagnos-tics. In 1999, Maude's three-year-old daughter nearly died when doctors struggled to identify her malady over a period of months. The experience prompted Maude to leave his job as an investment manager to co-found an enterprise that makes diagnostic-decision-support (DDS) software. The software tries to reduce misdiagnoses by presenting doctors with a comprehensive list of possible conditions. DDS systems also direct doctors to helpful information, such as medical journal articles with the latest research. Proponents of DSS systems point out that the doctors are already becoming more accustomed to using information systems in their practices, whether for keeping medical records, managing referrals, or ordering drugs and tests.

Dr. Charles Burger of Bangor, Maine, says that according to statistics, doctors are doing a poor job of making correct diagnoses quickly. DDS will make healthcare more efficient and save money for patients and insurance companies. Maude's software, named after his daughter, Isabel, was tested in a study published by the United Kingdom's Medical Protection Society. In the study, Isabel Healthcare considered 88 cases of doctors' misdiagnoses or delayed diagnoses. The software made correct diagnoses in 69 percent of the cases using its pattern matching technique, as opposed to keyword searches.

However, many physicians argue that diagnosing medical conditions is as much an art as it is a science and DDS systems have not proved to be more successful than human diagnostics. As a result, estimates place the percentage of doctors in the United States who use such systems at no higher than 2 percent. Doctors balk at the cost of systems such as Isabel ($750 per year), as well as the time it would take to enter the necessary patient data into the systems. "If your HMO allows you 10.5 minutes to see a patient, how are you going to do this?" notes Dr. David Goldmann, vice president and editor-in-chief of the Physicians' Information and Education Resource.

Isabel Healthcare's Web site offers a return on investment (ROI) calculator and notes that the system can help prevent costly malpractice cases. The company reminds users that its software is a "diagnosis reminder" and that the final decision is up to the doctor. As the technology improves and doctors become more involved in the development of DDS systems, the systems may become more desirable. Isabel is available for personal digital assistants, which many doctors are now using.

Both types of DSS systems will benefit from hospitals and physicians adopting digital patient record systems. For example, Hackensack University Medical Center in Hackensack, New Jersey, uses networked software that forms a central nervous system for the hospital. Using laptops, doctors and nurses can record symptoms; order prescriptions, X-rays, and labs; and keep track of patients' schedules. Because the system contains all of the patient and treatment data, the staff does not need to engage in frequent communications that take time and could lead to errors. Doctors can even visit patients remotely using a robot equipped with two-way video named Mr. Rounder. In the past four years, overall patient mortality at the hospital is down

16 percent. Hackensack uses a CPOE system, and it spent many hours refining the software to eliminate many of the problems described in the University of Pennsylvania study. However, only one-tenth of tests and orders at that hospital are currently placed electronically.

*Sources:* Laura Landro, "Drug Errors Show Need for Tech Aid," *The Wall Street Journal,* June 1, 2005; Jeannette Borzo, "Software for Symptoms," *The Wall Street Journal,* May 23, 2005; M. L. Baker, "Duke Health Uses IT to Get Beyond Doctors' Handwriting," *CIO Insight,* March 23, 2005; and Timothy J. Mullaney and Arlene Weintraub, "The Digital Hospital," *BusinessWeek,* March 28, 2005.

## Case Study Questions

1. What problems are hospitals and physicians encountering in diagnosing diseases and prescribing medications?
2. Has the medical industry correctly identified the problems it faces? What alternative solutions are available?
3. Are CPOE and DDS systems successful solutions? Why or why not? What people, technology, and organization issues are involved in the use of these systems?
4. What obstacles prevent computer systems from improving the medical industry? How can these obstacles be removed?

# Building and Managing Systems

**PART IV**

**P**art IV shows how to use the knowledge acquired in earlier chapters to analyze and design information system solutions to business problems. This part answers questions such as these: How can I develop a solution to an information system problem that provides genuine business benefits? How can the firm adjust to the changes introduced by the new system solution? What alternative approaches are available for building system solutions? What broader ethical and social issues should be addressed when building and using information systems?

# Building Information Systems

## STUDENT OBJECTIVES

After completing this chapter, you will be able to:

1. Identify and describe the core problem-solving steps for developing new information systems.

2. Evaluate models for assessing the business value of information systems.

3. Assess the requirements for successfully managing change created by new systems.

4. Evaluate alternative methods for building information systems.

5. Compare alternative methodologies for modeling and designing systems.

## CHAPTER OUTLINE

## A NEW ORDERING SYSTEM FOR GIRL SCOUT COOKIES

### Peanut Butter Petites, Caramel DeLites, Thin Mints—

Girl Scout Cookies have been American favorites since the organization's first cookie drive in 1917. The Girl Scouts have been so successful selling cookies that cookie sales are a major source of funding for this organization. The Girl Scouts sell so many cookies that collecting, counting, and organizing the annual avalanche of orders has become a tremendous challenge.

The Girl Scouts' traditional cookie-ordering process depended on mountains of paperwork. During the peak sales period in January, each Girl Scout marked her sales on an individual order card and turned the card into the troop leader when she was finished. The troop leader would transfer the information onto a five-part form and give this form to a community volunteer who tabulated the orders. From there, the orders passed to a regional council headquarters, where they would be batched into final orders for the manufacturer, ABC Cookies. In addition to ordering, Girl Scout volunteers and

troop members had to coordinate cookie deliveries, from the manufacturer to regional ware-houses, to local drop-off sites, to each scout, and to the customers themselves.

The Patriots' Trail Girl Scout Council, representing 65 communities and 18,000 Girl Scouts in the greater Boston area, sold more than 1.6 million boxes of eight different cookie varieties in 2004 alone. According to its associate executive director Deborah Deacetis, the paperwork had become "overwhelming." "It changed hands too many times. There was a lot of opportunity for error, because of all the added columns, multiple prices per box, and cal-culations that had to be made by different people, all on deadline."

The Patriots' Trail Girl Scout Council first looked into building a computerized system using Microsoft Access database management and application development tools. But this alternative would have cost $25,000 to develop and would have taken at least three to four months to get the system up and running. It was too time-consuming, complex, and expen-sive for the Girl Scouts. In addition to Microsoft Access software, the Girl Scouts would have to purchase a server to run the system plus pay for networking and Web site mainte-nance services so the system could be made available on the Web.

After consulting with management consultants Dovetail Associates, the council selected Intuit's QuickBase for Corporate Workgroups. QuickBase is a hosted Web-based software service for small businesses and corporate workgroups. It is especially well suited for build-ing simple database applications very quickly and does not require a great deal of training to use. QuickBase is customizable and designed to collect, organize, and share data among teams in many different locations.

A Dovetail consultant created a working QuickBase prototype with some basic func-tions for the Girl Scouts within a few hours. It only took two months to build, test, and implement the entire system using this software. The cost for developing the entire system was a fraction of the Microsoft Access solution. The Girl Scouts do not have to pay for any hardware, software, or networking services because QuickBase runs everything for them on its servers. QuickBase costs $500 per month for organizations with 100 users and $1,500 per month for organizations with up to 500 users.

The QuickBase solution eliminates paperwork and calculation errors by providing a clear central source of data for the entire council and easy online entry of cookie orders over the Web. Troop leaders collect the Girl Scouts' order cards and enter them directly into the QuickBase system using their home computers linked to the Web. With a few mouse clicks, the council office consolidates the unit totals and transmits the orders electronically to ABC Cookies.

In the past, the council relied on volunteers to handle their paperwork, dropping it off at the council office or mailing it in. "Now we have a way to actually watch the orders coming in," Deacetis notes. As local orders come in, local section leaders can track the data in real time.

The Patriots' Trail Girl Scout Council also uses the QuickBase system to manage the Cookie Cupboard warehouse, where volunteers pick up their cookie orders. Volunteers use the system to make reservations so that the warehouse can prepare the orders in advance, saving time and inventory management costs. The trucking companies that deliver cookie shipments now receive their instructions electronically through QuickBase so that they can create efficient delivery schedules.

Since its implementation, the QuickBase system has cut paperwork by more than 90 per-cent, reduced errors to 1 percent, and reduced the time spent by volunteers by 50 percent. The old system used to take two months to tally the orders and determine which Scouts should be rewarded for selling the most cookies. Now that time has been cut to 48 hours. ■

*Sources:* "Girl Scouts Unite Behind Order Tracking," *Customer Relationship Management,* May 2005; and Intuit Inc., "QuickBase Customer Stories: Patriots' Trail Girl Scouts and Dovetail Associates," www.quickbase.com, accessed July 11, 2005.

The experience of the Patriots' Trail Girl Scout Council illustrates some of the steps required to design and build new information systems. It also illustrates some of the benefits of a new system solution. The Girl Scouts had an outdated manual paper-based system for processing cookie orders that was excessively time-consuming and error-ridden. The Girl Scouts tried several alternative solutions before opting for a new ordering system using

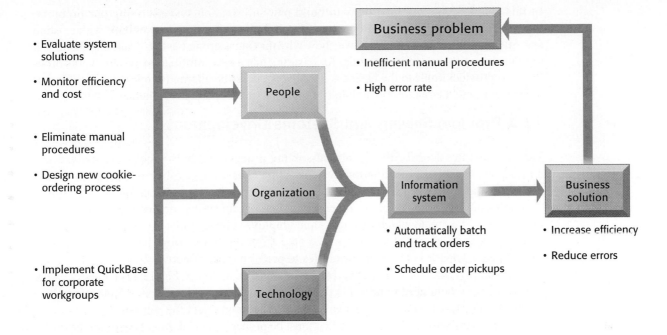

- Evaluate system solutions
- Monitor efficiency and cost

- Eliminate manual procedures
- Design new cookie-ordering process

- Implement QuickBase for corporate workgroups

**Business problem**
- Inefficient manual procedures
- High error rate

People

Organization

Technology

**Information system**
- Automatically batch and track orders
- Schedule order pickups

**Business solution**
- Increase efficiency
- Reduce errors

QuickBase as an application service provider. In this chapter, we will examine the Girl Scouts' search for a system solution as we describe each step of building a new information system using the problem-solving process.

**HEADS UP**

During your career, you will undoubtedly be asked to work on the development of a new system to solve an important challenge for your firm. In the process of building new systems, you will face many choices about hardware and software, and you will have to think about how to redesign business processes and jobs in order to maximize the value derived from the new system. You will also have to decide whether to build your own software solution, or purchase packaged software or online Web services. But the most important decisions you will face involve understanding just exactly what it is you want the software to do and what value it will bring to your firm. This chapter provides you with a methodology to guide you through the problem-solving process of building new information systems and a way to think about the business value of new systems.

•   If your career is in finance and accounting, you will help systems builders analyze the costs and benefits of new information system projects and assess their economic feasibility.

•   If your career is in human resources, you will be analyzing changes in workflows and job responsibilities resulting from the new information systems and arranging for employee training in the new systems.

•   If your career is in manufacturing, production, or operations management, you will work on the development or enhancement of supply chain management systems and enterprise resource planning systems. These can provide significant benefits, but they are among the most difficult systems to implement successfully because they require major changes to the organization as well as new technology.

•   If your career is in sales and marketing, you will be working on new Web-based systems for online sales or a new customer relationship management system because these systems often receive high priority in many firms' information system plans.

In this chapter, you will learn how to build new information systems using our problem-solving model. We start by describing the activities required to analyze problems with existing systems and build new ones. Next, we show why making a strong business case and managing organizational change are so essential for ensuring that a new information system works properly and provides value to the business. Finally, we describe alternative approaches for building systems and alternative methodologies for modeling and designing them.

## 11.1 Problem Solving and Systems Development

We have already described the problem-solving process and how it helps us analyze and understand the role of information systems in business. This problem-solving process is especially valuable when we need to build new systems. A new information system is built as a solution to a problem or set of problems the organization perceives it is facing. The problem may be one in which managers and employees believe that the business is not performing as well as expected, or it may come from the realization that the organization should take advantage of new opportunities to perform more effectively.

Let's apply this problem-solving process to system building. Figure 11-1 illustrates the four steps we would need to take: (1) define and understand the problem, (2) develop alternative solutions, (3) choose the best solution, and (4) implement the solution.

Before a problem can be solved, it first must be properly defined. Members of the organization must agree that a problem actually exists and that it is serious. The problem must be investigated so that it can be better understood. Next comes a period of devising alternative solutions, then one of evaluating each alternative and selecting the best solution. The final stage is one of implementing the solution, in which a detailed design for the solution is specified, translated into a physical system, tested, introduced to the organization, and further refined as it is used over time.

In the information systems world, we have a special name for these activities. Figure 11-1 shows that the first three problem-solving steps, where we identify the problem, gather information, devise alternative solutions, and make a decision about the best solution, are called **systems analysis**.

### Defining and Understanding the Problem

Defining the problem may take some work because various members of the company may have different ideas about the nature of the problem and its severity. What caused the prob-

**Figure 11-1**
Developing an Information System Solution
*Developing an information system solution is based on the problem-solving process.*

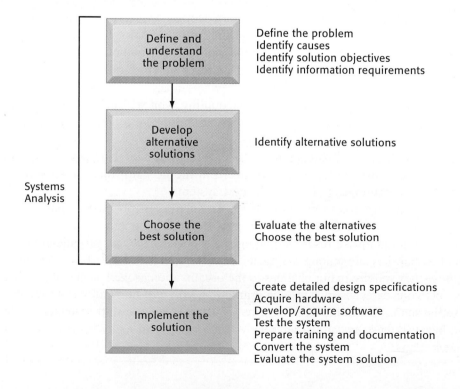

lem? Why is it still around? Why wasn't it solved long ago? Systems analysts typically gather facts about existing systems and problems by examining documents, work papers, procedures, and system operations and by interviewing key users of the system.

Information systems problems in the business world typically result from a combination of people, organization, and technology factors. When identifying a key issue or problem, ask what kind of problem it is: Is it a people problem, an organizational problem, a technology problem, or a combination of these? What people, organizational, and technological factors contributed to the problem?

Once the problem has been defined and analyzed, it is possible to make some decisions about what should and can be done. What are the objectives of a solution to the problem? Is the firm's objective to reduce costs, increase sales, or improve relationships with customers, suppliers, or employees? Do managers have sufficient information for decision making? What information is required to achieve these objectives?

At the most basic level, the **information requirements** of a new system identify who needs what information, where, when, and how. Requirements analysis carefully defines the objectives of the new or modified system and develops a detailed description of the functions that the new system must perform. A system designed around the wrong set of requirements will either have to be discarded because of poor performance or will need to undergo major modifications. Section 11.3 describes alternative approaches to eliciting requirements that help minimize this problem.

Let's return to our opening case about the Girl Scouts. The problem here is that the Girl Scout ordering process is heavily manual and cannot support the large number of volunteers and cookie orders that must be coordinated. As a result, cookie ordering is extremely inefficient, with high error rates and volunteers spending excessive time organizing orders and deliveries.

Organizationally, the Girl Scouts are a voluntary organization distributed across a large area, with cookie sales as the primary source of revenue. The Scouts rely on volunteers with little or no business or computer experience for sales and management of orders and deliveries. They have almost no financial resources and volunteers are strapped for time. The Girl Scout cookie-ordering process requires many steps and coordination of multiple groups and organizations—individual Girl Scouts, volunteers, the council office, the cookie manufacturing factory, trucking companies, and the Cookie Cupboard warehouse.

The objectives of a solution for the Girl Scouts would be to reduce the amount of time, effort, and errors in the cookie-ordering process. Information requirements for the solution include the ability to rapidly total and organize order transactions for transmittal to ABC Cookies; the ability to track orders by type of cookie, troop, and individual Girl Scout; the ability to schedule deliveries to the Cookie Cupboard; and the ability to schedule order pickups from the Cookie Cupboard.

## Developing Alternative Solutions

What alternative solutions are possible for achieving these objectives and meeting these information requirements? The systems analysis lays out the most likely paths to follow given the nature of the problem. Some possible solutions do not require an information system solution but instead call for an adjustment in management, additional training, or refinement of existing organizational procedures. Some, however, do require modifications to the firm's existing information systems or an entirely new information system.

## Evaluating and Choosing Solutions

The systems analysis includes a **feasibility study** to determine whether each proposed solution is feasible, or achievable, from a financial, technical, and organizational standpoint. The feasibility study establishes whether each alternative solution is a good investment, whether the technology needed for the system is available and can be handled by the firm's information systems staff, and whether the organization is capable of accommodating the changes introduced by the system.

A written systems proposal report describes the costs and benefits, and advantages and disadvantages of each alternative solution. Which solution is best in a financial sense? Which works best for the organization? The systems analysis will detail the costs and benefits of each alternative and the changes that the organization will have to make to use the solution effectively. We provide a detailed discussion of how to determine the business value of systems and manage change in the following section. On the basis of this report, management will select what it believes is the best solution for the company.

The Patriots' Trail Girl Scouts had three alternative solutions. One was to streamline existing processes, continuing to rely on manual procedures. However, given the large number of Girl Scouts and cookie orders, as well as relationships with manufacturers and shippers, redesigning and streamlining a manual ordering and delivery process would not have provided many benefits. The Girl Scouts needed an automated solution that accurately tracked thousands of order and delivery transactions, reduced paperwork, and created a central real-time source of sales data that could be accessed by council headquarters and individual volunteers.

A second alternative was to custom-build a cookie-ordering system using Microsoft Access. This alternative was considered too time-consuming, expensive, and technically challenging for the Girl Scouts. It required $25,000 in initial programming costs, plus the purchase of hardware and networking equipment to run the system and link it to the Internet, as well as trained staff to run and maintain the system.

The third alternative was to rapidly create a system using an application service provider. QuickBase provides templates and tools for creating simple database systems in very short periods, provides the hardware for running the application and Web site, and can be accessed by many different users over the Web. This solution does not require the Girl Scouts to purchase any hardware, software, or networking technology or to maintain any information system staff to support the system. This last alternative was the most feasible for the Girl Scouts.

## Implementing the Solution

The first step in implementing a system solution is to create detailed design specifications. **Systems design** shows how the chosen solution should be realized. The system design is the model or blueprint for an information system solution and consists of all the specifications that will deliver the functions identified during systems analysis. These specifications should address all of the technical, organizational, and people components of the system solution. Table 11.1 lists the types of specifications that would be produced during system design.

**TABLE 11.1**

**System Design Specifications**

| | |
|---|---|
| Output | Medium and Content |
| | Timing |
| Input | Flow |
| | Data entry |
| User interface | Feedback and error handling |
| Database | Logical data model |
| | Volume and speed requirements |
| | File and record specifications |
| Processing | Program logic and computations |
| Manual procedures | What activities, who, when, how, and where |
| Security and controls | Access controls |
| | Input, processing and output controls |
| Conversion | Testing method |
| | Conversion strategy |
| Training and documentation | Training modules and platforms |
| | Systems, user and operations documentation |
| Organizational changes | Process design |
| | Organizational structure changes |

A Dovetail Associates consultant elicited information requirements and created a design for the new Girl Scout cookie system. Some of the design specifications for the Girl Scout cookie system would be as follows:

| | |
|---|---|
| Output | Online reports<br>Hard copy reports<br>Online queries<br>Order transactions for ABC Cookies<br>Delivery tickets for the trucking firm |
| Input | Order data entry form<br>Troop data entry form<br>Girl Scout data entry form<br>Shipping/delivery data entry form |
| User interface | Graphical Web interface |
| Database | Database with cookie order file, delivery file, troop contact file |
| Processing | Calculate order totals by type of cookie and number of boxes<br>Track orders by troop and individual Girl Scout<br>Schedule pickups at the Cookie Cupboard<br>Update Girl Scout and troop data for address and member changes |
| Manual procedures | Girl Scouts take orders with paper forms<br>Troop leaders collect order cards from Scouts and enter the order data online |
| Security and controls | Online passwords<br>Control totals |
| Conversion | Input Girl Scout and troop data<br>Transfer factory and delivery data<br>Test system |
| Training and documentation | System guide for users<br>Online practice demonstration<br>Online training sessions<br>Training for ABC Cookies and trucking companies to accept data and instructions automatically from the Girl Scout system |
| Organizational changes | Job design: Volunteers no longer have to tabulate orders<br>Process design: Take orders on manual cards but enter them online into the system<br>Schedule order pickups from the Cookie Cupboard online |

## Completing Implementation

In the final steps of implementing a system solution, the following activities would be performed:

- *Hardware selection and acquisition.* System builders select appropriate hardware for the application. They would either purchase the necessary computers and networking hardware or lease them from a technology provider.

- *Software development and programming.* Software is custom programmed in-house or purchased from an external source, such as an outsourcing vendor, an application software package vendor, or an application service provider.

The Girl Scouts did not have to purchase additional hardware or software. QuickBase offers templates for generating simple database applications. Dovetail consultants used the QuickBase tools to rapidly create the software for the system. The system runs on QuickBase servers.

- *Testing.* The system is thoroughly tested to ensure it produces the right results. The **testing** process requires detailed testing of individual computer programs, called **unit testing**, as well as **system testing**, which tests the performance of the information system as a whole. **Acceptance testing** provides the final certification that the system is ready to be used in a production setting. Information systems tests are evaluated by users and reviewed by management. When all parties are satisfied that the new system meets their standards, the system is formally accepted for installation.

The systems development team works with users to devise a systematic test plan. The **test plan** includes all of the preparations for the series of tests we have just described. Figure 11-2 shows a sample from a test plan that might have been used for the Girl Scout cookie system. The condition being tested is online access of an existing record for a specific Girl Scout troop.

- *Training and documentation.* End users and information system specialists require training so that they will be able to use the new system. Detailed **documentation** showing how the system works from both a technical and end-user standpoint must be prepared.

The Girl Scout cookie system provides an online practice area for users to practice entering data into the system by following step-by-step instructions. Also available on the Web is a step-by-step instruction guide for the system that can be downloaded and printed as a hard copy manual.

- *Conversion.* **Conversion** is the process of changing from the old system to the new system. There are three main conversion strategies: the parallel strategy, the direct cutover strategy, and the phased approach strategy.

**Figure 11-2**
A Sample Test Plan for the Girl Scout Cookie System
*When developing a test plan, it is imperative to include the various conditions to be tested, the requirements for each condition tested, and the expected results. Test plans require input from both end users and information systems specialists.*

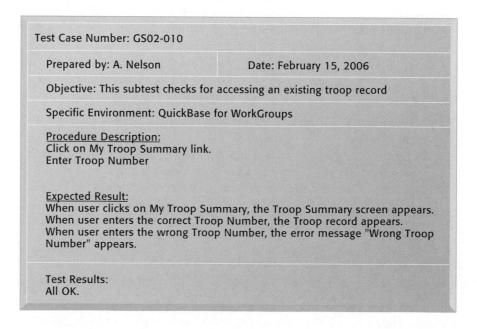

Test Case Number: GS02-010

| Prepared by: A. Nelson | Date: February 15, 2006 |
|---|---|

Objective: This subtest checks for accessing an existing troop record

Specific Environment: QuickBase for WorkGroups

Procedure Description:
Click on My Troop Summary link.
Enter Troop Number

Expected Result:
When user clicks on My Troop Summary, the Troop Summary screen appears.
When user enters the correct Troop Number, the Troop record appears.
When user enters the wrong Troop Number, the error message "Wrong Troop Number" appears.

Test Results:
All OK.

In a **parallel strategy**, both the old system and its potential replacement are run together for a time until everyone is assured that the new one functions correctly. The old system remains available as a backup in case of problems. The **direct cutover** strategy replaces the old system entirely with the new system on an appointed day, carrying the risk that there is no system to fall back on if problems arise. A **phased approach** introduces the system in stages (such as first introducing the modules for ordering Girl Scout cookies and then introducing the modules for transmitting orders and instructions to the cookie factory and shipper).

- *Production and maintenance.* After the new system is installed and conversion is complete, the system is said to be in **production**. During this stage, users and technical specialists review the solution to determine how well it has met its original objectives and to decide whether any revisions or modifications are in order. Changes in hardware, software, documentation, or procedures to a production system to correct errors, meet new requirements, or improve processing efficiency are termed **maintenance**.

The Girl Scouts continued to improve and refine their QuickBase cookie system. In 2005, the system was made more efficient for users with slow Internet connections. Other recent enhancements include capabilities for paying for orders more rapidly, entering troop information and initial orders without waiting for a specified starting date, and receiving online confirmation for reservations to pick up orders from the Cookie Cupboard.

### Managing the Change

Developing a new information system solution is not merely a matter of installing hardware and software. The business must also deal with the organizational changes that the new solution will bring about— new information, new business processes, and perhaps new reporting relationships and decision-making power. A very well-designed solution may not work unless it is introduced to the organization very carefully. The process of planning change in an organization so that it is implemented in an orderly and effective manner is so critical to the success or failure of information system solutions that we devote the next section to a detailed discussion of this topic.

To manage the transition from the old manual cookie-ordering processes to the new system, the Girl Scouts would have to inform troop leaders and volunteers about changes in cookie-ordering procedures, provide training, and provide resources for answering any questions that arose as parents and volunteers started using the system. They would need to work with ABC Cookies and their shippers on new procedures for transmitting and delivering orders.

## 11.2 Understanding the Business Value of Systems and Managing Change

Your company might have developed what appears to be an excellent system solution. Yet when the system is in use, it does not work properly or it doesn't deliver the benefits that were promised. If this occurs, your firm is not alone. There is a very high failure rate among information systems projects because organizations have incorrectly assessed their business value or because firms have failed to manage the organizational change required by the new technology. Let's look more closely at what needs to be done to make sure your information solution is successful.

### Making the Business Case for a New System

As we pointed out earlier, the systems analysis includes an assessment of the economic feasibility of each alternative solution—whether each solution represents a good investment for

**TABLE 11.2**

**Costs and Benefits of Information Systems**

**IMPLEMENTATION COSTS**
Hardware
Telecommunications
Software
Personnel costs

**OPERATIONAL COSTS**
Computer processing time
Maintenance
Operating staff
User time
Ongoing training costs
Facility costs

**TANGIBLE BENEFITS**
Increased productivity
Lower operational costs
Reduced workforce
Lower computer expenses
Lower outside vendor costs
Lower clerical and professional costs
Reduced rate of growth in expenses
Reduced facility costs
Increased sales

**INTANGIBLE BENEFITS**
Improved asset utilization
Improved resource control
Improved organizational planning
Increased organizational flexibility
More timely information
More information
Increased organizational learning
Legal requirements attained
Enhanced employee goodwill
Increased job satisfaction
Improved decision making
Improved operations
Higher client satisfaction
Better corporate image

the company. It would not be good business practice to spend money on an information system unless its benefits outweigh its costs. You need to make a strong business case for the solution alternative you select.

### Financial Issues

Table 11-2 lists some of the more common costs and benefits of systems. **Tangible benefits** can be quantified and assigned a monetary value. **Intangible benefits**, such as more efficient customer service or enhanced decision making, cannot be immediately quantified. Yet systems that produce mainly intangible benefits may still be good investments if they produce quantifiable gains in the long run.

To determine the benefits of a particular solution, you'll need to calculate all of its costs and all of its benefits. Obviously, a solution where costs exceed benefits should be rejected. But even if the benefits outweigh the costs, some additional financial analysis is required to determine whether the investment represents a good return on the firm's invested capital. Capital budgeting methods, such as net present value, internal rate of return (IRR), or accounting rate of return on investment (ROI), would typically be employed to evaluate the proposed information system solution as an investment. You can find out more about how these capital budgeting methods are used to justify information system investments in the Learning Tracks for this chapter.

Some of the tangible benefits obtained by the Girl Scouts were increased productivity and lower operational costs resulting from automating the ordering process and from reducing errors. Intangible benefits include enhanced volunteer job satisfaction and improved operations.

### Nonfinancial Issues

Information systems also create value by strengthening a firm strategically—for example, by differentiating products or services, strengthening ties to customers and suppliers, or providing flexibility to respond rapidly to future changes. The business case for a solution may address these long-term strategic issues.

For example, it would be important to make sure the solution you select fits into your company's overall business plan and strategy. Large companies often create an **information systems plan** for this purpose. Table 11.3 illustrates the major components of such a plan.

1. Purpose of the Plan
   Overview of plan contents
   Current business organization and future organization
   Key business processes
   Management strategy

2. Strategic Business Plan Rationale
   Current situation
   Current business organization
   Changing environments
   Major goals of the business plan
   Firm's strategic plan

3. Current Systems
   Major systems supporting business functions and processes
   Current infrastructure capabilities
       Hardware
       Software
       Database
       Telecommunications and the Internet
   Difficulties meeting business requirements
   Anticipated future demands

4. New Developments
   New system projects
       Project descriptions
       Business rationale
       Applications' role in strategy
   New infrastructure capabilities required
       Hardware
       Software
       Database
       Telecommunications and the Internet

5. Management Strategy
   Acquisition plans
   Milestones and timing
   Organizational realignment
   Internal reorganization
   Management controls
   Major training initiatives
   Personnel strategy

6. Implementation of the Plan
   Anticipated difficulties in implementation
   Progress reports

7. Budget Requirements
   Requirements
   Potential savings
   Financing
   Acquisition cycle

The plan contains a statement of corporate goals and specifies how information technology will help the business attain these goals. The report shows how general goals will be achieved by specific systems projects. It identifies specific target dates and milestones that can be used later to evaluate the plan's progress in terms of how many objectives were actually attained in the time frame specified in the plan. The plan indicates the key management

**Figure 11-3**

*A System Portfolio*
*Companies should examine their portfolio of projects in terms of potential benefits and likely risks. Certain kinds of projects should be avoided altogether and others developed rapidly. There is no ideal mix. Companies in different industries have different information systems needs.*

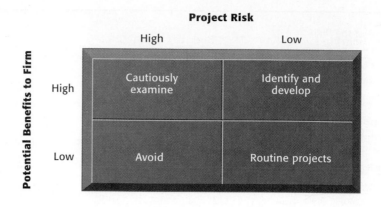

decisions concerning hardware acquisition; telecommunications; centralization/decentralization of authority, data, and hardware; and required organizational change.

The plan should describe organizational changes, including management and employee training requirements; changes in business processes; and changes in authority, structure, or management practice. When you are making the business case for a new information system project, you show how the proposed system fits into that plan.

Once you have determined the overall direction of systems development, **portfolio analysis** will help you evaluate alternative system projects. Portfolio analysis inventories all of the firm's information systems projects and assets, including infrastructure, outsourcing contracts, and licenses. This portfolio of information systems investments can be described as having a certain profile of risk and benefit to the firm (see Figure 11-3), similar to a financial portfolio. Each information systems project carries its own set of risks and benefits. Firms try to improve the return on their information system portfolios by balancing the risk and return from their systems investments.

Obviously, you begin first by focusing on systems of high benefit and low risk. These promise early returns and low risks. Second, high-benefit, high-risk systems should be examined; low-benefit, high-risk systems should be totally avoided; and low-benefit, low-risk systems should be reexamined for the possibility of rebuilding and replacing them with more desirable systems having higher benefits. By using portfolio analysis, management can determine the optimal mix of investment risk and reward for their firms, balancing riskier, high-reward projects with safer, lower-reward ones.

Amsterdam-based ABN Amro Bank NV uses portfolio analysis to evaluate and rank hundreds of information systems projects in the 55 countries where ABN Amro has operations. Portfolio analysis helped the bank establish priorities among the conflicting demands of its business units and justify management's decisions about which systems to build (Hoffman, 2005).

Another method for arriving at a decision on alternative system solutions is a **scoring model**. Scoring models give alternative systems a single score based on the extent to which they meet selected objectives. Table 11.4 shows part of a simple scoring model that could have been used by the Girl Scouts in evaluating their alternative systems. The first column lists the criteria that decision makers use to evaluate the systems. Table 11.4 shows that the Girl Scouts attached the most importance to capabilities for sales order processing, ease of use, ability to support users in many different locations, and low cost. The second column in Table 11.4 lists the weights that decision makers attached to the decision criteria. Columns 3 and 5 show the percentage of requirements for each function that each alternative system meets. Each alternative's score is calculated by multiplying the percentage of requirements met for each function by the weight attached to that function. The QuickBase solution has the highest total score.

## New System Challenges

A very large percentage of information systems fail to deliver benefits or to solve the problems for which they were intended because the process of organizational change surround-

**TABLE 11.4**

**Example of a Scoring Model for the Girl Scouts Cookie System**

| Criteria | Weight | Microsoft Access System (%) | Microsoft Access System Score | QuickBase System (%) | QuickBase System Score |
|---|---|---|---|---|---|
| **1.0 Order processing** | | | | | |
| 1.1 Online order entry | 5 | 67 | 335 | 83 | 415 |
| 1.2 Order tracking by troop | 5 | 81 | 405 | 87 | 435 |
| 1.3 Order tracking by individual Girl Scout | 5 | 72 | 360 | 80 | 400 |
| 1.4 Reserving warehouse pickups | 3 | 66 | 198 | 79 | 237 |
| Total order processing | | | 1,298 | | 1,487 |
| **2.0 Ease of use** | | | | | |
| 2.1 Web access from multiple locations | 5 | 55 | 275 | 92 | 460 |
| 2.2 Short training time | 4 | 79 | 316 | 85 | 340 |
| 2.3 User-friendly screens and data entry forms | 4 | 65 | 260 | 87 | 348 |
| Total ease of use | | | 851 | | 1,148 |
| **3.0 Costs** | | | | | |
| 3.1 Software costs | 3 | 51 | 153 | 65 | 195 |
| 3.2 Hardware (server) costs | 4 | 57 | 228 | 90 | 360 |
| 3.3 Maintenance and support costs | 4 | 42 | 168 | 89 | 356 |
| Total costs | | | 549 | | 911 |
| Grand Total | | | 2,698 | | 3,546 |

ing the system building was not properly addressed. The actual design of the system may fail to capture essential business requirements or improve organizational performance. Information may not be provided quickly enough to be helpful; it may be in a format that is impossible to digest and use; or it may represent the wrong pieces of data.

A system may be designed with a poor user interface. The **user interface** is the part of the system with which end users interact. For example, an input form or an online data entry screen may be so poorly arranged that no one wants to submit data. Web sites discourage visitors from exploring them further if the Web pages are cluttered and poorly arranged, if users cannot easily find the information they are seeking, or if it takes too long to access and display the Web page on the user's computer.

Some systems operate quite smoothly, but their costs to implement or run on a production basis are way over budget. The excessive expenditures cannot be justified by the demonstrated business value of the information they provide.

To manage the organizational change surrounding the introduction of a new information system effectively, you must examine the process of implementation. A broader definition of **implementation** refers to all the organizational activities working toward the adoption and management of an innovation, such as a new information system. In the implementation process, the systems analyst is a **change agent**. The analyst not only develops technical

Building successful information systems requires close cooperation among end users and information systems specialists throughout the systems development process.

solutions but also redefines the interactions, job activities, and power relationships of various organizational groups. The analyst is the catalyst for the entire change process and is responsible for ensuring that all parties involved accept the changes created by a new system.

Whether a new information system succeeds or fails largely depends on the roles of users, the degree of management support, the level of risk and complexity of the implementation project, and how well the implementation process itself is managed.

### User Involvement and Influence

If users are heavily involved in the development of a system, they have more opportunities to mold the system according to their priorities and business requirements, and more opportunities to control the outcome. They also are more likely to react positively to the completed system because they have been active participants in the change process. Incorporating user knowledge and expertise leads to better solutions.

The relationship between end users and information systems specialists has traditionally been a problem area for information systems implementation efforts because of differing backgrounds, interests, and priorities. These differences create a **user–designer communications gap**. Information systems specialists often have a highly technical orientation toward problem solving, focusing on technical solutions in which hardware and software efficiency is optimized at the expense of ease of use or organizational effectiveness. End users prefer systems that are oriented toward solving business problems or facilitating organizational tasks. Often the orientations of both groups are so at odds that they appear to speak in different tongues.

These differences are illustrated in Table 11.5, which depicts the typical concerns of end users and technical specialists (information systems designers) regarding the development of a new information system. Communication problems between end users and designers are a major reason why user requirements are not properly incorporated into information systems and why users are driven out of the implementation process.

### Management Support and Commitment

If an information systems project has the backing and commitment of management at various levels, it is more likely to receive higher priority from both users and the technical information systems staff. Management backing also ensures that a systems project receives sufficient funding and resources to be successful. Furthermore, to be enforced effectively, all the changes in work habits and procedures and any organizational realignments associated with a new system depend on management backing.

**TABLE 11.5**

**The User–Designer Communications Gap**

| User Concerns | Designer Concerns |
| --- | --- |
| Will the system deliver the information I need for my work? | How much disk storage space will the master file consume? |
| How quickly can I access the data? | How many lines of program code will it take to perform this function? |
| How easily can I retrieve the data? | How can we cut down on CPU time when we run the system? |
| How much clerical support will I need to enter data into the system? | What is the most efficient way of storing the data? |
| How will the operation of the system fit into my daily business schedule? | What database management system should we use? |

## Level of Complexity and Risk

Some systems development projects are more likely to fail or suffer delays because they carry a much higher level of risk than others. Large, complex projects—as indicated by the dollars spent, the size of the implementation staff, the time allocated for implementation, and the number of organizational units affected—carry a much higher risk. Very large-scale systems projects, including implementations of large enterprise resource planning and customer relationship management systems, have a failure rate that is 50 to 75 percent higher than that for other projects because such projects are complex and difficult to control (Concours Group, 2000; Xia and Lee, 2004). Risks are also higher for systems where information requirements are not clear and straightforward or the project team must master complex new technology.

## Quality of Project Management

A systems development project must be carefully managed to make sure tasks are completed on time and that all groups involved in the new system work effectively together. Often basic elements of success, such as training to ensure that end users are comfortable with the new system, are forgotten. Without proper management, a systems development project takes longer to complete and often exceeds the allocated budget. The resulting information system most likely is technically inferior and may not be able to demonstrate any benefits to the organization.

## Managing Change Successfully

If these problems sound daunting, don't give up! There are strategies you can follow to increase the chances of a successful system solution. If the new system involves challenging and complex technology, you can recruit project leaders with strong technical and administrative experience. Outsourcing or using external consultants are options if your firm does not have staff with the required technical skills or expertise. **Formal planning and control tools**, such as Program Evaluation and Review Technique (PERT) or Gantt charts (see Figure 11-4), improve project management by listing the specific activities that make up a project, their duration, and the sequence and timing of tasks.

You can overcome user resistance by promoting user participation (to elicit commitment as well as to improve design), by making user education and training easily available, and by providing better incentives for users who cooperate. End users can become active members of the project team, take on leadership roles, and take charge of system installation and training.

You should pay special attention to areas where users interface with the system, with sensitivity to ergonomics issues. **Ergonomics** refers to the interaction of people and machines in the work environment. It considers the design of jobs, health issues, and the end-user interface of information systems.

Users will be more cooperative if organizational problems are solved prior to introducing the new system. In addition to procedural changes, transformations in job functions,

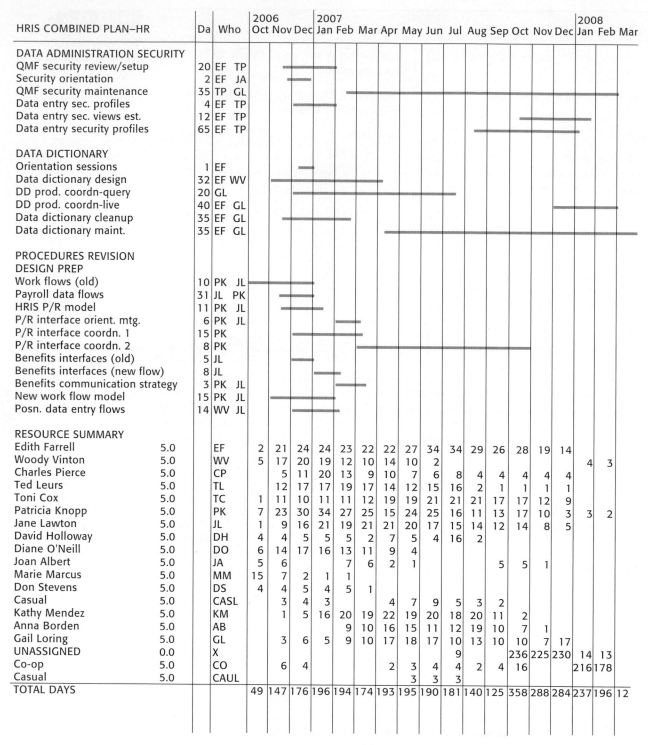

**HRIS COMBINED PLAN–HR** (Gantt chart — task, person-days (Da), responsible initials (Who), and schedule bars)

| Task | Da | Who |
|------|----|-----|
| **DATA ADMINISTRATION SECURITY** | | |
| QMF security review/setup | 20 | EF TP |
| Security orientation | 2 | EF JA |
| QMF security maintenance | 35 | TP GL |
| Data entry sec. profiles | 4 | EF TP |
| Data entry sec. views est. | 12 | EF TP |
| Data entry security profiles | 65 | EF TP |
| **DATA DICTIONARY** | | |
| Orientation sessions | 1 | EF |
| Data dictionary design | 32 | EF WV |
| DD prod. coordn-query | 20 | GL |
| DD prod. coordn-live | 40 | EF GL |
| Data dictionary cleanup | 35 | EF GL |
| Data dictionary maint. | 35 | EF GL |
| **PROCEDURES REVISION DESIGN PREP** | | |
| Work flows (old) | 10 | PK JL |
| Payroll data flows | 31 | JL PK |
| HRIS P/R model | 11 | PK JL |
| P/R interface orient. mtg. | 6 | PK JL |
| P/R interface coordn. 1 | 15 | PK |
| P/R interface coordn. 2 | 8 | PK |
| Benefits interfaces (old) | 5 | JL |
| Benefits interfaces (new flow) | 8 | JL |
| Benefits communication strategy | 3 | PK JL |
| New work flow model | 15 | PK JL |
| Posn. data entry flows | 14 | WV JL |

**RESOURCE SUMMARY**

| | | | 2006 | | | 2007 | | | | | | | | | | | | 2008 | | |
|---|---|---|---|---|---|---|---|---|---|---|---|---|---|---|---|---|---|---|---|---|
| Name | Rate | Who | Oct | Nov | Dec | Jan | Feb | Mar | Apr | May | Jun | Jul | Aug | Sep | Oct | Nov | Dec | Jan | Feb | Mar |
| Edith Farrell | 5.0 | EF | 2 | 21 | 24 | 24 | 23 | 22 | 22 | 27 | 34 | 34 | 29 | 26 | 28 | 19 | 14 | | | |
| Woody Vinton | 5.0 | WV | 5 | 17 | 20 | 19 | 12 | 10 | 14 | 10 | 2 | | | | | | | 4 | 3 | |
| Charles Pierce | 5.0 | CP | | 5 | 11 | 20 | 13 | 9 | 10 | 7 | 6 | 8 | 4 | 4 | 4 | 4 | 4 | | | |
| Ted Leurs | 5.0 | TL | | 12 | 17 | 17 | 19 | 17 | 14 | 12 | 15 | 16 | 2 | 1 | 1 | 1 | 1 | | | |
| Toni Cox | 5.0 | TC | 1 | 11 | 10 | 11 | 11 | 12 | 19 | 19 | 21 | 21 | 21 | 17 | 17 | 12 | 9 | | | |
| Patricia Knopp | 5.0 | PK | 7 | 23 | 30 | 34 | 27 | 25 | 15 | 24 | 25 | 16 | 11 | 13 | 17 | 10 | 3 | 3 | 2 | |
| Jane Lawton | 5.0 | JL | 1 | 9 | 16 | 21 | 19 | 21 | 21 | 20 | 17 | 15 | 14 | 12 | 14 | 8 | 5 | | | |
| David Holloway | 5.0 | DH | 4 | 4 | 5 | 5 | 5 | 2 | 7 | 5 | 4 | 16 | 2 | | | | | | | |
| Diane O'Neill | 5.0 | DO | 6 | 14 | 17 | 16 | 13 | 11 | 9 | 4 | | | | | | | | | | |
| Joan Albert | 5.0 | JA | 5 | 6 | | | 7 | 6 | 2 | 1 | | | | 5 | 5 | 1 | | | | |
| Marie Marcus | 5.0 | MM | 15 | 7 | 2 | 1 | 1 | | | | | | | | | | | | | |
| Don Stevens | 5.0 | DS | 4 | 4 | 5 | 4 | 5 | 1 | | | | | | | | | | | | |
| Casual | 5.0 | CASL | | 3 | 4 | 3 | | | 4 | 7 | 9 | 5 | 3 | 2 | | | | | | |
| Kathy Mendez | 5.0 | KM | | 1 | 5 | 16 | 20 | 19 | 22 | 19 | 20 | 18 | 20 | 11 | 2 | | | | | |
| Anna Borden | 5.0 | AB | | | | 9 | 10 | 16 | 15 | 11 | 12 | 19 | 10 | 7 | 1 | | | | | |
| Gail Loring | 5.0 | GL | | 3 | 6 | 5 | 9 | 10 | 17 | 18 | 17 | 10 | 13 | 10 | 10 | 7 | 17 | | | |
| UNASSIGNED | 0.0 | X | | | | | | | | | | 9 | | | 236 | 225 | 230 | 14 | 13 | |
| Co-op | 5.0 | CO | 6 | 4 | | | | 2 | 3 | 4 | 4 | 2 | 4 | 16 | | | | 216 | 178 | |
| Casual | 5.0 | CAUL | | | | | | | | | 3 | 3 | 3 | | | | | | | |
| **TOTAL DAYS** | | | 49 | 147 | 176 | 196 | 194 | 174 | 193 | 195 | 190 | 181 | 140 | 125 | 358 | 288 | 284 | 237 | 196 | 12 |

**Figure 11-4**

Formal Planning and Control Tools Help Manage Information Systems Projects
*The Gantt chart in this figure shows the task, person-days, and initials of each responsible person, as well as the start and finish dates for each task in a data management project. The resource summary provides a good manager with the total person-days for each month and for each person working on the project.*

organizational structure, power relationships, and behavior should be identified during systems analysis using an **organizational impact analysis**.

The Focus on People illustrates some of these implementation strategies at work. The Australian government built a new system for Centrelink, Australia's massive social welfare agency, to provide efficient online delivery of social services. To build this system successfully,

**FOCUS ON PEOPLE**    **Change Management Delivers for Australian Social Services**

In 1997, the newly elected conservative Australian government moved to overhaul its country's social welfare services. At the time, nearly one-third of Australia's 20 million citizens were receiving payments because they were retired, single parents, unemployed, disabled, students, members of the indigenous population, or fit into other categories of eligibility. Two government organizations served the vast majority of these recipients: the Department of Employment, Education, Training and Youth Affairs (DEETYA) and the Department of Social Services (DSS). DEETYA's main function was to help find jobs for the unemployed through its nearly 300 field offices. DSS provided its services through another 300 regional offices. The two departments employed more than 30,000 workers combined.

Although the DSS benefits system had breadth, it lacked efficiency and was far from customer-friendly. The typical DSS office had a staff of 65 employees. Each office served hundreds of claimants daily covering a variety of benefit types. The process by which a customer filed a claim seemed more intent on weeding out the pool of recipients than providing benefits. DSS put applicants through a series of interviews, assessments, and reviews to ensure the completeness and accuracy of their applications, as well as their eligibility. The officers of the department did not make decisions during a claimant's first appointment, and first-time applicants often had to return anyway because they weren't prepared with all of the information that the application required.

When Prime Minister John Howard's administration took office, one of its first initiatives was to transform the often-aggravating and unfriendly experience of visiting DEETYA and DSS offices into a single, customer-friendly e-business within five years. Among the obstacles were a long-standing rivalry between the departments and a complicated merger of their thousands of employees. The new agency was named Centrelink.

To fill the position of chief information officer (CIO), CEO Sue Vardon looked not for a technical expert but for an exceptional mind. She found one in Jane Treadwell, a former colleague at the South Australia Department of Correctional Services. Vardon valued Treadwell's intelligence and her ability to forecast the future impact of present decisions. She brought a business perspective to a government agency that had an IT problem. To prepare for the challenge, Treadwell studied change management and visited government agencies around the world. Then she set about the task of convincing traditionalists in the government that information systems were not a money pit and that the $312 million price tag of Centrelink would pay dividends.

To achieve its goals, which included self-service telephone and Internet channels for benefits transactions, Centrelink was not able to rely on prepackaged solutions. The organization developed its own customized middleware called the Centrelink Online Framework (COLF). To create viable self-service products, the information systems team had to translate more than 500 pieces of software program code from data dictionary tables in the organization's legacy systems into appropriate conversation prompts for voice recognition software and user-friendly forms for Web pages. Both the telephone and Internet channels were designed to mimic the interaction between a live staff person and a Centrelink customer. Clients can review and update their accounts easily, with the added comfort of anonymity. Centrelink processes information and resolves claims more quickly than its predecessors did.

Customer satisfaction with Centrelink has risen by 23 percentage points since Treadwell's arrival, up to 86 percent. In 2002, Boston Consulting Group measured a 21 percent increase in productivity over the first five years of Centrelink's existence. Much of the credit is given to Treadwell's management and organizational techniques. She changed the perception of IT by incorporating it into upper management and the business realm. Under her leadership, there were no IT projects, only business projects. As a result, Treadwell added the title of Deputy CEO of Business Transformation to CIO.

Treadwell was innovative in other ways as well. Knowing the importance of managing change in a business carefully, she created the Guiding Coalition, which consisted of all 60 Centrelink executives. The Guiding Coalition met every six to eight weeks to see how information technology could promote new opportunities in service. Treadwell also eliminated traditional employment positions in her business transformation group. Employees there are considered part of a talent bank. They are assigned to roles and projects and reassigned when projects end. The goal is to avoid stagnation that can result from permanent positions.

Centrelink now operates the second-largest call center network in Australia. Centrelink's 1,000 offices oversee payments totaling $55 billion (AUS) for 25 government agencies. Having fulfilled her goals, Treadwell left Centrelink in the spring of 2005 to become CIO of the government of Victoria.

*Source:* Lauraine Sayers, "Aussie Whirlwind Sweeps Through Government IT," *CIO Insight,* www.cioinsight.com, accessed May 5, 2005.

**To Think About:**

What problems were Australia's social welfare systems facing? How did Centrelink attempt to solve these problems? What other solutions might have worked? What people, organization, and technology factors impacted this problem and its solution? Describe the role that Jane Treadwell played in the development of Centrelink. What choices and techniques contributed to her success as an executive?

Centrelink's CIO Jane Treadwall had to overcome both technical and organizational challenges. As you read this case, try to identify the problem this organization was facing; what alternative solutions were available to management; how well the chosen solution worked; and the people, organization, and technology issues that had to be addressed when developing the solution.

## 11.3 Alternative Systems-Building Approaches

There are alternative methods for building systems using the basic problem-solving model we have just described. These alternative methods include the traditional systems lifecycle, prototyping, end-user development, application software packages, and outsourcing.

### Traditional Systems Development Lifecycle

The **systems development lifecycle (SDLC)** is the oldest method for building information systems. The lifecycle methodology is a phased approach to building a system, dividing systems development into a series of formal stages, as illustrated in Figure 11-5. Although systems builders can go back and forth among stages in the lifecycle, the systems lifecycle is predominantly a "waterfall" approach in which tasks in one stage are completed before work for the next stage begins.

This approach maintains a very formal division of labor between end users and information systems specialists. Technical specialists, such as systems analysts and programmers, are responsible for much of the systems analysis, design, and implementation work; end users are limited to providing information requirements and reviewing the technical staff's work. The lifecycle also emphasizes formal specifications and paperwork, so many documents are generated during the course of a systems project.

The systems lifecycle is still used for building large, complex systems that require rigorous and formal requirements analysis, predefined specifications, and tight controls over the systems-building process. However, this approach is also time-consuming and expensive to use. Tasks in one stage are supposed to be completed before work for the next stage begins. Activities can be repeated, but volumes of new documents must be generated and steps retraced if requirements and specifications need to be revised. This encourages freezing of specifications relatively early in the development process. The lifecycle approach is also not suitable for many small desktop systems, which tend to be less structured and more individualized.

### Prototyping

**Prototyping** consists of building an experimental system rapidly and inexpensively for end users to evaluate. The prototype is a working version of an information system or part of the

**Figure 11-5**
The Traditional
Systems
Development
Lifecycle
*The systems development lifecycle partitions systems development into formal stages, with each stage requiring completion before the next stage can begin.*

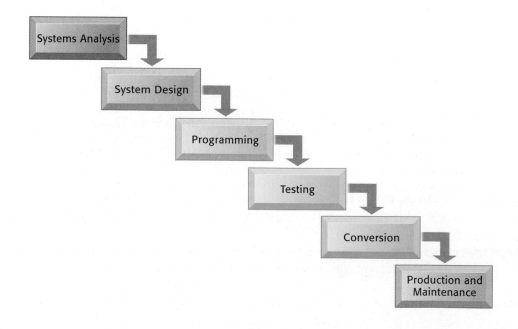

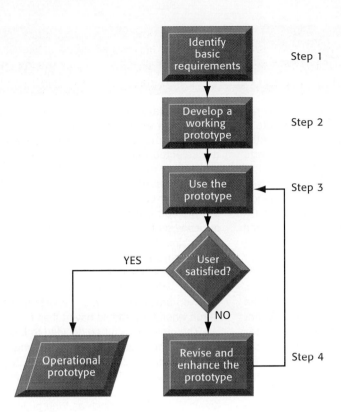

**Figure 11-6**
The Prototyping
Process
*The process of developing a prototype consists of four steps. Because a prototype can be developed quickly and inexpensively, systems builders can go through several iterations, repeating steps 3 and 4, to refine and enhance the prototype before arriving at the final operational one.*

system, but it is intended as only a preliminary model. Users interact with the prototype to get a better idea of their information requirements, refining the prototype multiple times. The chapter-opening case describes how Dovetail Associates used QuickBase to create a prototype that helped the Patriots' Trail Girl Scout Council refine the specifications for their cookie-ordering system. When the design is finalized, the prototype will be converted to a polished production system. Figure 11-6 shows a four-step model of the prototyping process.

**Step 1.** *Identify the user's basic requirements.* The system designer (usually an information systems specialist) works with the user only long enough to capture the user's basic information needs.

**Step 2.** *Develop an initial prototype.* The system designer creates a working prototype quickly, using tools for rapidly generating software.

**Step 3.** *Use the prototype.* The user is encouraged to work with the system to determine how well the prototype meets his or her needs and to make suggestions for improving the prototype.

**Step 4.** *Revise and enhance the prototype.* The system builder notes all changes the user requests and refines the prototype accordingly. After the prototype has been revised, the cycle returns to step 3. Steps 3 and 4 are repeated until the user is satisfied.

Prototyping is especially useful in designing an information system's user interface. Because prototyping encourages intense end-user involvement throughout the systems-development lifecycle, it is more likely to produce systems that fulfill user requirements.

However, rapid prototyping may gloss over essential steps in systems development, such as thorough testing and documentation. If the completed prototype works reasonably well, management may not see the need to build a polished production system. Some hastily constructed systems do not easily accommodate large quantities of data or a large number of users in a production environment.

The Focus on Organizations describes how Marriott Corporation used prototyping when building its One Yield revenue management system. The company needed a new system to determine the optimal price to charge for each room at all of its hotel properties. As you read this case, try to identify the problem this company was facing; what alternative solutions

# FOCUS ON ORGANIZATIONS  Marriott's New Revenue Management System Yields Success

Marriott International, Inc., is a $9 billion company operating 2,600 hotel properties worldwide. Like other hotels, Marriott must keep its rooms filled with guests paying the highest rates that can be charged in order to maximize revenue.

Figuring out how much to charge for each room used to be a major challenge. On high-demand nights. Mariott has to be careful not to sell out early at low rates. On Sundays and slower days, it needs enough rooms offering lower rates to attract customers but not so many that it would be giving away rooms that could command higher prices from someone else.

Marriott had developed two revenue management systems. A demand forecasting system (DFS) served the chain's full-service hotels, and a revenue management system (RMS) backed select-service or extended-stay properties, such as the Courtyard hotels. However, running two separate revenue management systems kept the hotel chain from easily analyzing 62 million reservations annually at all of its properties and it was expensive.

In 2001, Marriott began building a new enterprise-wide revenue management system called One Yield that is now used by 1,700 of the company's 2,600 properties. From the beginning, the leaders of the project linked the business value of One Yield with the company's goals of profitability, preference, and growth. They explained the technical aspects of the system to the business audience in terms that the audience could understand and value.

To obtain information requirements and support for the new system, the development team consulted the future users and the buyers of One Yield (individual Marriott properties pay for their IT installations). The team maintained close communication with the field through Marriott's director of inventory planning, Russell Verb, and was able to exchange valuable feedback with users and general managers (GMs). GMs could ask questions about cost and impact on staff. Users could ask questions about new features or old ones that weren't going to be carried over to the new system. Verb used monthly press releases to provide updates on project status, pilot tests, training tools, and costs.

Users identified two important new features to be incorporated into One Yield: an override button and what the users call the "Monday morning quarterback." The override feature enables the user to reject One Yield's rate recommendations before they are sent to the central reservations system. In cases where the local revenue manager has information that One Yield does not, such as a sudden change in weather that will cause cancellations, this feature is critical to maximizing profit. The Monday morning quarterback is a performance monitor that can analyze four weeks of booking decisions to see how close a revenue manager came to the optimal revenue during the selected period. This feature also provides information about the decisions that a manager should have made to maximize profits.

Another key to One Yield's success was early prototyping. Marriott's information systems department began constructing prototypes of the system's critical modules while the business team was still building its case. The early prototyping ensured that the rollout of the system, which would occur three years in the future, would proceed smoothly. By working with the prototype, the systems-building team resolved problems, such as reports that took five minutes to run when they should have taken five seconds.

The project team had decided to custom build the system as a Web-based application using J2EE architecture and WebSphere development tools. No one at Marriott had ever worked with this technology. Marriott's only Web experience had been with small-scale projects with static displays of content, such as Web pages. Prototyping gave Marriott's team practice with the technology. Although prototyping pushed back the initial launch of One Yield by two months, it probably saved Marriott much time and money that would have been spent on tackling problems that would have arisen if there had been no experience with the system.

One Yield recouped 80 percent of its costs shortly after the rollout. In 2004, Marriott properties using the system enjoyed a 2 percent increase in revenue from leisure travelers, which contributed to an $86 million annual profit increase. The company as a whole has achieved a significant increase in operating revenue since the implementation of One Yield.

*Sources:* Stephanie Overby, "The Price Is Always Right," *CIO Magazine,* www.cio.com, accessed February 15, 2005; "Marriott Named a 'Best Place to Work in Information Technology' by *Computerworld* for Third Consecutive Year," *Hotel News Resource,* www.hotelnewsresource.com, accessed June 29, 2005; and Patrick Thibodeau, "Marriott Links Two Data Streams with Revenue Management System," *Computerworld,* www.computerworld.com, accessed March 14, 2005.

**To Think About:**

What problem did Marriott face? What business goals was the company trying to achieve? What alternatives were available for solving Marriott's problem? Did Marriott select the best solution? How did prototyping help Marriott come up with its solution? What people, organization, and technology factors were involved in the solution that the company chose?

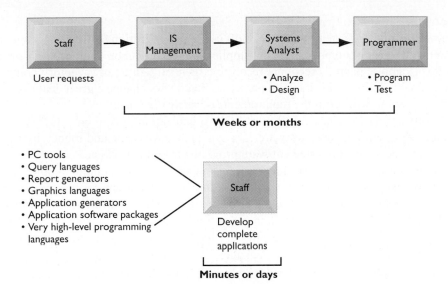

**Figure 11-7**
End-User Development
*Fourth-generation software tools make it possible for end users to develop simple systems and complete them more rapidly than those developed through the traditional systems-development lifecycle.*

were available to management; the role of prototyping in developing the solution; how well the chosen solution worked; and the people, organization, and technology issues that had to be addressed when developing the solution.

## End-User Development

**End-user development** allows end users, with little or no formal assistance from technical specialists, to create simple information systems, reducing the time and steps required to produce a finished application (see Figure 11-7). Using fourth-generation languages, graphics languages, and PC software tools, end users can access data, create reports, and develop entire information systems on their own, with little or no help from professional systems analysts or programmers.

For example, Administaff, which provides human resources services for 5,000 small and midsize businesses around the United States, uses InformationBuilders Inc.'s WebFocus software to give clients access to their employee data. They use WebFocus Studio Developer and other tools to build their own reports and view their data from a central Administaff repository. For example, a manager at one of Administaff's subscribing companies might use these tools to create a report showing how many employees participate in the company savings plan (Babcock, 2005).

On the whole, end-user-developed systems are completed more rapidly than those developed with conventional programming tools. Allowing users to specify their own business needs improves requirements gathering and often leads to a higher level of user involvement and satisfaction with the system. However, fourth-generation tools still cannot replace conventional tools for some business applications because they cannot easily handle the processing of large numbers of transactions or applications with extensive procedural logic and updating requirements.

End-user computing also poses organizational risks because systems are created rapidly, without a formal development methodology, testing, and documentation. To help organizations maximize the benefits of end-user applications development, management should require cost justification of end-user information systems projects and establish hardware, software, and quality standards for user-developed applications.

## Purchasing Solutions: Application Software Packages and Outsourcing

Chapter 4 points out that the software for most systems today is not developed in-house but is purchased from external sources. Firms may choose to purchase a software package from a commercial vendor, rent the software from an application service provider, or outsource the development work to another firm. Selection of the software or software service is often based on a **Request for Proposal (RFP)**, which is a detailed list of questions submitted to external vendors to see how well they meet the requirements for the proposed system.

### Application Software Packages

Most new information systems today are built using an application software package or pre-programmed software components. Many applications are common to all business organizations—for example, payroll, accounts receivable, general ledger, or inventory control. For such universal functions with standard processes that do not change a great deal over time, a generalized system will fulfill the requirements of many organizations.

If a software package can fulfill most of an organization's requirements, the company does not have to write its own software. The company saves time and money by using the prewritten, predesigned, pretested software programs from the package.

Many packages include capabilities for customization to meet unique requirements not addressed by the package software. **Customization** features allow a software package to be modified to meet an organization's unique requirements without destroying the integrity of the packaged software. However, if extensive customization is required, additional programming and customization work may become so expensive and time-consuming that it negates many of the advantages of software packages. If the package cannot be customized, the organization will have to adapt to the package and change its procedures.

### Outsourcing

If a firm does not want to use its internal resources to build or operate information systems, it can outsource the work to an external organization that specializes in providing these services. Application service providers (ASPs), which we describe in Chapter 4, are one form of outsourcing. An example would be the Girl Scouts leasing the software and hardware from QuickBase to run their cookie-ordering system. Subscribing companies use the software and computer hardware provided by the ASP as the technical platform for their systems. In another form of outsourcing, a company would hire an external vendor to design and create the software for its system, but that company would operate the system on its own computers.

The outsourcing vendor might be domestic or in another country. Domestic outsourcing is driven primarily by the fact that outsourcing firms possess skills, resources, and assets which their clients do not have. Installing a new supply chain management system in a very large company might require hiring an additional 30–50 people with specific expertise in supply chain management software licensed, say, from Manugistics or another vendor. Rather than hire permanent new employees, most of whom would need extensive training in the software package, and then release them after the new system is built, it makes more sense, and is often less expensive, to outsource this work for a 12-month period.

In the case of offshore outsourcing, the decision tends to be much more cost-driven. A skilled programmer in India or Russia earns about U.S. $10,000 per year, compared to $70,000 per year for a comparable programmer in the United States. The Internet and low-cost communications technology have drastically reduced the expense and difficulty of coordinating the work of global teams in faraway locations. In addition to cost savings, many offshore outsourcing firms offer world-class technology assets and skills.

For example, the giant European travel firm TUI.AG turned to outsourcing to reduce its costs in the competitive market for travel-booking services. TUI achieved cost savings of 20 percent by contracting with the Indian software and service provider Wipro Ltd. to provide remote support for about 10,000 desktop systems and 300 departmental servers, including help desks and e-mail messaging. TUI is now outsourcing custom systems development and support for new applications to Sonata Software Ltd., another Indian software and services vendor (Ribeiro, 2005).

There is a very strong chance that at some point in your career, you'll be working with offshore outsourcers or global teams. Your firm is most likely to benefit from outsourcing if it takes the time to evaluate all the risks and to make sure outsourcing is appropriate for its particular needs. Any company that outsources its applications must thoroughly understand the project, including its requirements, method of implementation, source of expected benefits, cost components, and metrics for measuring performance.

Many firms underestimate costs for identifying and evaluating vendors of information technology services, for transitioning to a new vendor, for improving internal software development methods to match those of outsourcing vendors, and for monitoring vendors to

**TOTAL COST OF OFFSHORE OUTSOURCING**

| Cost of outsourcing contract | | | | $10,000,000 |
|---|---|---|---|---|
| Hidden Costs | Best Case | Additional Cost ($) | Worst Case | Additional Cost ($) |
| 1. Vendor selection | 0.2% | 20,000 | 2% | 200,000 |
| 2. Transition costs | 2% | 200,000 | 3% | 300,000 |
| 3. Layoffs & retention | 3% | 300,000 | 5% | 500,000 |
| 4. Lost productivity/cultural issues | 3% | 300,000 | 27% | 2,700,000 |
| 5. Improving development processes | 1% | 100,000 | 10% | 1,000,000 |
| 6. Managing the contract | 6% | 600,000 | 10% | 1,000,000 |
| **Total additional costs** | | **1,520,000** | | **5,700,000** |
| | Outstanding Contract ($) | Additional Cost ($) | Total Cost ($) | Additional Cost |
| Total cost of outsourcing (TCO) best case | 10,000,000 | 1,520,000 | 11,520,000 | 15.2% |
| Total cost of outsourcing (TCO) worst case | 10,000,000 | 5,700,000 | 15,700,000 | 57.0% |

**Figure 11-8**
Total Cost of Offshore Outsourcing
*If a firm spends $10 million on offshore outsourcing contracts, that company will actually spend 15.2 percent in extra costs even under the best-case scenario. In the worst-case scenario, where there is a dramatic drop in productivity along with exceptionally high transition and layoff costs, a firm can expect to pay up to 57 percent in extra costs on top of the $10 million outlay for an offshore contract.*

make sure they are fulfilling their contractual obligations. Outsourcing offshore incurs additional costs for coping with cultural differences that drain productivity and dealing with human resources issues, such as terminating or relocating domestic employees. These hidden costs undercut some of the anticipated benefits from outsourcing. Firms should be especially cautious when using an outsourcer to develop or to operate applications that give it some type of competitive advantage.

Figure 11-8 shows best- and worst-case scenarios for the total cost of an offshore outsourcing project. It shows how much hidden costs affect the total project cost. The best case reflects the lowest estimates for additional costs, and the worst case reflects the highest estimates for these costs. As you can see, hidden costs increase the total cost of an offshore outsourcing project by an extra 15 to 57 percent. Even with these extra costs, many firms will benefit from offshore outsourcing if they manage the work well.

## Rapid Application Development for E-Business

Technologies and business conditions are changing so rapidly that agility and scalability have become critical elements of system solutions. Companies are adopting shorter, more informal development processes for many of their e-commerce and e-business applications, processes that provide fast solutions that do not disrupt their core transaction processing systems and organizational databases. In addition to using software packages, application service providers, and other outsourcing services, they are relying more heavily on fast-cycle techniques, such as joint application design (JAD), prototypes, and reusable standardized software components that can be assembled into a complete set of services for e-commerce and e-business.

The term **rapid application development (RAD)** refers to the process of creating workable systems in a very short period of time. RAD includes the use of visual programming and other tools for building graphical user interfaces, iterative prototyping of key systems elements, the automation of program code generation, and close teamwork among end users and information systems specialists. Simple systems often can be assembled from prebuilt components (see Section 11.4). The process does not have to be sequential, and key parts of development can occur simultaneously.

Sometimes a technique called **joint application design (JAD)** will be used to accelerate the generation of information requirements and to develop the initial systems design. JAD brings end users and information systems specialists together in an interactive session to discuss the system's design. Properly prepared and facilitated, JAD sessions can significantly speed up the design phase and involve users at an intense level.

## 11.4 Modeling and Designing Systems: Structured and Object-Oriented Methodologies

We have just described alternative methods for building systems. There are also alternative methodologies for modeling and designing systems. The two most prominent are structured methodologies and object-oriented development.

### Structured Methodologies

Structured methodologies have been used to document, analyze, and design information systems since the 1970s. **Structured** refers to the fact that the techniques are step by step, with each step building on the previous one. Structured methodologies are top-down, progressing from the highest, most abstract level to the lowest level of detail—from the general to the specific.

Structured development methods are process-oriented, focusing primarily on modeling the processes, or actions, that capture, store, manipulate, and distribute data as the data flow through a system. These methods separate data from processes. A separate programming procedure must be written every time someone wants to take an action on a particular piece of data. The procedures act on data that the program passes to them.

The primary tool for representing a system's component processes and the flow of data between them is the **data flow diagram (DFD)**. The data flow diagram offers a logical graphic model of information flow, partitioning a system into modules that show manageable levels of detail. It rigorously specifies the processes or transformations that occur within each module and the interfaces that exist between them.

Figure 11-9 shows a simple data flow diagram for a mail-in university course registration system. The rounded boxes represent processes, which portray the transformation of data. The square box represents an external entity, which is an originator or receiver of information located outside the boundaries of the system being modeled. The open rectangles represent data stores, which are either manual or automated inventories of data. The arrows represent data flows, which show the movement between processes, external entities, and data stores. They always contain packets of data with the name or content of each data flow listed beside the arrow.

**Figure 11-9**
Data Flow Diagram for Mail-in University Registration System
*The system has three processes: Verify availability (1.0), Enroll student (2.0), and Confirm registration (3.0). The name and content of each of the data flows appear adjacent to each arrow. There is one external entity in this system: the student. There are two data stores: the student master file and the course file.*

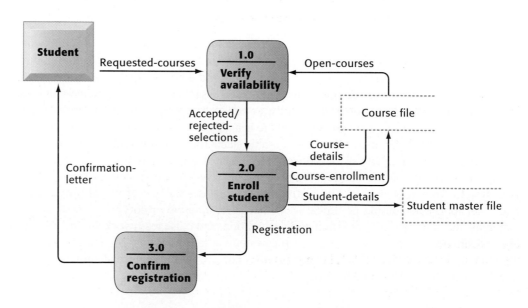

This data flow diagram shows that students submit registration forms with their names, identification numbers, and the numbers of the courses they wish to take. In process 1.0, the system verifies that each course selected is still open by referencing the university's course file. The file distinguishes courses that are open from those that have been canceled or filled. Process 1.0 then determines which of the student's selections can be accepted or rejected. Process 2.0 enrolls the student in the courses for which he or she has been accepted. It updates the university's course file with the student's name and identification number and recalculates the class size. If maximum enrollment has been reached, the course number is flagged as closed. Process 2.0 also updates the university's student master file with information about new students or changes in address. Process 3.0 then sends each student applicant a confirmation-of-registration letter listing the courses for which he or she is registered and noting the course selections that could not be fulfilled.

Through leveled data flow diagrams, a complex process can be broken down into successive levels of detail. An entire system can be divided into subsystems with a high-level data flow diagram. Each subsystem, in turn, can be divided into additional subsystems with lower-level data flow diagrams, and the lower-level subsystems can be broken down again until the lowest level of detail has been reached. **Process specifications** describe the transformation occurring within the lowest level of the data flow diagrams, showing the logic for each process.

In structured methodology, software design is modeled using hierarchical structure charts. The **structure chart** is a top-down chart, showing each level of design, its relationship to other levels, and its place in the overall design structure. The design first considers the main function of a program or system, then breaks this function into subfunctions, and decomposes each subfunction until the lowest level of detail has been reached. Figure 11-10 shows a high-level structure chart for a payroll system. If a design has too many levels to fit onto one structure chart, it can be broken down further on more detailed structure charts. A structure chart may document one program, one system (a set of programs), or part of one program.

## Object-Oriented Development

Structured methods treat data and processes as logically separate entities, whereas in the real world such separation seems unnatural. Different modeling conventions are used for analysis (the data flow diagram) and for design (the structure chart).

**Object-oriented development** addresses these issues. Object-oriented development uses the object, which we introduced in Chapter 4, as the basic unit of systems analysis and design. An object combines data and the specific processes that operate on those data. Data encapsulated in an object can be accessed and modified only by the operations, or methods, associated with that object. Instead of passing data to procedures, programs send a message for an object to perform an operation that is already embedded in it. The system is modeled as a collection of objects and the relationships among them. Because processing logic

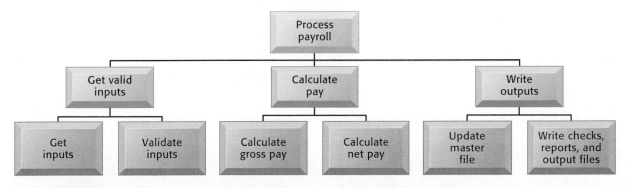

**Figure 11-10**
High-Level Structure Chart for a Payroll System
*This structure chart shows the highest or most abstract level of design for a payroll system, providing an overview of the entire system.*

resides within objects rather that in separate software programs, objects must collaborate with each other to make the system work.

Object-oriented modeling is based on the concepts of *class* and *inheritance*. Objects belonging to a certain class, or general categories of similar objects, have the features of that class. Classes of objects in turn inherit all the structure and behaviors of a more general class and then add variables and behaviors unique to each object. New classes of objects are created by choosing an existing class and specifying how the new class differs from the existing class, instead of starting from scratch each time.

We can see how class and inheritance work in Figure 11-11, which illustrates the relationships among classes concerning employees and how they are paid. Employee is the common ancestor, or superclass, for the other three classes. Salaried, Hourly, and Temporary are subclasses of Employee. The class name is in the top compartment, the attributes for each class are in the middle portion of each box, and the list of operations is in the bottom portion of each box. The features that are shared by all employees (ID, name, address, date hired, position, and pay) are stored in the Employee superclass, whereas each subclass stores features that are specific to that particular type of employee. Specific to Hourly employees, for example, are their hourly rates and overtime rates. A solid line from the subclass to the superclass is a generalization path showing that the subclasses Salaried, Hourly, and Temporary have common features that can be generalized into the superclass Employee.

Object-oriented development is more iterative and incremental than traditional structured development. During systems analysis, systems builders document the functional requirements of the system, specifying its most important properties and what the proposed system must do. Interactions between the system and its users are analyzed to identify objects, which include both data and processes. The object-oriented design phase describes how the objects will behave and how they will interact with one other. Similar objects are grouped together to form a class, and classes are grouped into hierarchies in which a subclass inherits the attributes and methods from its superclass.

The information system is implemented by translating the design into program code, reusing classes that are already available in a library of reusable software objects and adding new ones created during the object-oriented design phase. Implementation may also involve the creation of an object-oriented database. The resulting system must be thoroughly tested and evaluated.

Because objects are reusable, object-oriented development could potentially reduce the time and cost of writing software if organizations reuse software objects that have already been created as building blocks for other applications. New systems can be created by using some existing objects, changing others, and adding a few new objects.

**Figure 11-11**
Class and Inheritance
*This figure illustrates how classes inherit the common features of their superclass.*

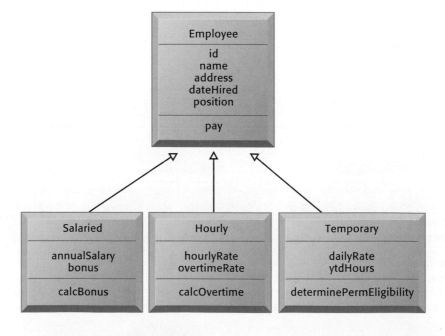

## Component-Based Development and Web Services

To further expedite software creation, groups of objects have been assembled into software components for common functions, such as a graphical user interface or online ordering capability, and these components can be combined to create large-scale business applications. This approach to software development is called **component-based development**. Businesses are using component-based development to create their e-commerce applications by combining commercially available components for shopping carts, user authentication, search engines, and catalogs with pieces of software for their own unique business requirements.

Chapter 4 introduced *Web services* as loosely coupled, reusable software components based on extensible markup language (XML) and other open protocols and standards that enable one application to communicate with another with no custom programming required. In addition to supporting internal and external integration of systems, Web services provide nonproprietary tools for building new information systems applications or enhancing existing systems. Web services perform certain functions on their own, and they can also engage other Web services to complete more complex transactions, such as checking credit, procurement, or ordering products. Because these software services use a universal set of standards, they promise to be less expensive and less difficult to weave together than proprietary components.

## Computer-Aided Software Engineering (CASE)

**Computer-aided software engineering (CASE)**—sometimes called computer-aided systems engineering—provides software tools to automate the methodologies we have just described to reduce the amount of repetitive work in systems development. CASE tools provide automated graphics facilities for producing charts and diagrams, screen and report generators, data dictionaries, extensive reporting facilities, analysis and checking tools, code generators, and documentation generators. CASE tools also contain features for validating design diagrams and specifications.

CASE tools facilitate clear documentation and coordination of team development efforts. Team members can share their work by accessing each other's files to review or modify what has been done. Modest productivity benefits are achieved if the tools are used properly. Many CASE tools are PC-based, with powerful graphical capabilities.

---

**LEARNING TRACKS**

1. If you want to learn more about capital budgeting methods for new information system investments, you will find a Learning Track on this topic at the Laudon Web site for this chapter.
2. If you want to learn more about methodologies for establishing organization-wide information requirements, you will find a Learning Track on Enterprise Analysis (Business Systems Planning) and Critical Success Factors (CSFs) at the Laudon Web site for this chapter.
3. If you want to learn more about standards for representing object-oriented systems, you will find a Learning Track on Unified Modeling Language (UML) at the Laudon Web site for this chapter.

---

# Summary

1 **Identify and describe the core problem-solving steps for developing new information systems.** The core problem-solving steps for developing new information systems are: (1) define and understand the problem, (2) develop alternative solutions, (3) evaluate and choose the solution, and (4) implement the solution. The first step involves defining the problem and identifying its causes, solution objectives, and information requirements. The second step identifies alternative solutions to the problem. The third step entails an assessment of the technical, financial, and organizational feasibility of each alternative and selection of the best solution. The fourth step entails finalizing design specifications, acquiring hardware and software, testing, providing training and documentation, conversion, and evaluating the system solution once it is in production.

2 **Evaluate models for assessing the business value of information systems.** To determine whether an information system is a good investment for the company, one must calculate its costs and benefits. Tangible benefits are quantifiable, and intangible benefits cannot be immediately quantified but may provide quantifiable benefits in the future. Benefits that exceed costs should then be analyzed using capital budgeting methods, such as net present value (NPV), to make sure they represent a good return on the firm's invested capital.

Other models for evaluating information systems investments involve nonfinancial and strategic considerations. Organizations should develop information systems plans that describe how information technology supports the company's overall business plan and strategy. Portfolio analysis and scoring models can be used to evaluate alternative information systems projects.

3 **Assess the requirements for successfully managing change created by new systems.** A very large percentage of information systems fail to deliver benefits or solve the problems for which they were intended because the process of organizational change surrounding systems building was not properly addressed. The principal causes of information systems failure are (1) insufficient or improper user participation in the systems development process, (2) lack of management support, (3) high levels of complexity and risk, and (4) poor project management.

The term *implementation* refers to the entire process of organizational change surrounding the introduction of a new information system. Information systems design and the entire implementation process should be managed as planned organizational change using an organizational impact analysis. Management support and control of the implementation process are essential, as are mechanisms for dealing with the level of risk in each new systems project. Formal planning and control tools track the resource allocations and specific project activities. Users can be encouraged to take active roles in systems development and become involved in installation and training.

4 **Evaluate alternative methods for building information systems.** There are a number of alternative methods for building information systems, each suited to different types of problems. The oldest method for building systems is the systems lifecycle, which requires that information systems be developed in formal stages. The stages must proceed sequentially and have defined outputs; each requires formal approval before the next stage can commence. The systems lifecycle is rigid and costly but nevertheless useful for large projects that need formal specifications and tight management control over each stage of systems building.

Prototyping consists of building an experimental system rapidly and inexpensively for end users to interact with and evaluate. The prototype is refined and enhanced until users are satisfied that it includes all of their requirements and can be used as a template to create the final system. Prototyping encourages end-user involvement in systems development and iteration of design until specifications are captured accurately. The rapid creation of prototypes can result in systems that have not been completely tested or documented or that are technically inadequate for a production environment.

End-user development is the development of information systems by end users, either alone or with minimal assistance from information systems specialists. End-user-developed systems can be created rapidly and informally using fourth-generation software tools. The primary benefits of end-user development are improved requirements determination; reduced application backlog; and increased end-user participation in, and control of, the systems development process. However, end-user development, in conjunction with distributed computing, has introduced new organizational risks by propagating information systems and data resources that do not necessarily meet quality assurance standards and that are not easily controlled.

Firms can also build systems by purchasing software or software services from outside vendors. One alternative is to purchase an application software package, which eliminates the need for writing software programs when developing an information system. Application software packages are helpful if a firm does not have the internal information systems staff or financial resources to custom develop a system.

Another alternative is to outsource systems development work. Outsourcing consists of using an external vendor to build (or operate) a firm's information systems. The work is done by the domestic or offshore vendor rather than by the organization's internal information systems staff. If it is properly managed, outsourcing can save application development costs or enable firms to develop applications without an internal information systems staff. However, firms risk losing control of their information systems and becoming too dependent on external vendors.

Businesses today are often required to build e-commerce and e-business applications very rapidly to remain competitive. Companies are turning to rapid application design, joint application design (JAD), and reusable software components (including Web services) to speed up the systems development process.

5 **Compare alternative methodologies for modeling and designing systems.** The two principal methodologies for modeling and designing information systems are structured methodologies and object-oriented development. Structured methodologies focus on modeling processes and data separately. The data flow diagram is the principal tool for structured analysis and the structure chart is the principal tool for representing structured software design. Object-oriented development models a system as a collection of objects that combine processes and data. Object-oriented development is based on the concepts of class and inheritance.

## Key Terms

Acceptance testing, 374
Change agent, 379
Component-based development, 393
Computer-aided software engineering (CASE), 393
Conversion, 374
Customization, 388
Data flow diagram (DFD), 390
Direct cutover, 375
Documentation, 374
End-user development, 387
Ergonomics, 381
Feasibility study, 371
Formal planning and control tools, 381
Implementation, 379

Information requirements, 371
Information systems plan, 376
Intangible benefits, 376
Joint application design (JAD), 390
Maintenance, 375
Object-oriented development, 391
Organizational impact analysis, 382
Parallel strategy, 375
Phased approach, 375
Portfolio analysis, 378
Process specifications, 391
Production, 375
Prototyping, 384
Rapid application development (RAD), 389

Request for Proposal (RFP), 387
Scoring model, 378
Structure chart, 391
Structured, 390
System testing, 374
Systems analysis, 370
Systems design, 372
Systems development lifecycle (SDLC), 384
Tangible benefits, 376
Test plan, 374
Testing, 374
Unit testing, 374
User interface, 379
User–designer communications gap, 380

## Review Questions

**11.1** List and describe the problem-solving steps for building a new system.

**11.2** What are information requirements? Why are they important for developing a system solution?

**11.3** List the various types of design specifications required for a new information system.

**11.4** Why is the testing stage of systems development so important? Name and describe the three stages of testing for an information system.

**11.5** What role do documentation, conversion, production, and maintenance play in systems development?

**11.6** What is the difference between tangible and intangible benefits? List six tangible benefits and six intangible benefits.

**11.7** What are the major components of an information systems plan?

**11.8** Describe how portfolio analysis and scoring models can be used to establish the worth of systems.

**11.9** Why is it necessary to understand the concept of implementation when managing the organizational change surrounding a new information system? What are the factors determining implementation success or failure?

**11.10** What is the user–designer communications gap? What kinds of implementation problems can it create?

**11.11** What strategies can be used to increase the chances of successful system implementation?

**11.12** What is the traditional systems lifecycle? Describe its advantages and disadvantages for systems building.

**11.13** What do we mean by information systems prototyping? What are its benefits and limitations? List and describe the steps in the prototyping process.

**11.14** What is end-user development? What are its advantages and disadvantages?

**11.15** What are the advantages and disadvantages of developing information systems based on application software packages?

**11.16** What is outsourcing? Under what circumstances should it be used for building information systems? What are the hidden costs of offshore software outsourcing?

**11.17** How can businesses rapidly develop e-business applications?

**11.18** Compare object-oriented and traditional structured approaches for modeling and designing systems.

## Discussion Questions

**11.1** Discuss the role of business end users and information systems professionals in developing a system solution. How do both roles differ when the solution is developed using the systems life-cycle, prototyping or end-user development?

**11.2** It has been said that systems fail when systems builders ignore "people" problems. Why might this be so?

## Application Software Exercise

### Database Exercise: Designing a Customer System for Auto Sales

Software skills: Database design, querying and reporting

Business skills: Lead management and customer analysis

Ace Auto Dealers specializes in selling new vehicles from Subaru. The company advertises in local newspapers and also is listed as an authorized dealer on the Subaru Web site and other major Web sites for auto buyers. The company benefits from a good, local word-of-mouth reputation and name recognition and is a leading source of information for Subaru vehicles in the Portland, Oregon, area.

When a prospective customer enters the showroom, he or she is greeted by an Ace sales representative. The sales representative manually fills out a form with information, such as the prospective customer's name, address, telephone number, date of visit, and model and make of the vehicle in which the customer is interested. The representative also asks where the prospect heard about Ace—whether it was from a newspaper ad, the Web, or word of mouth—and this information is noted on the form also. If the customer decides to purchase an auto, the dealer fills out a bill of sale form.

Ace does not believe it has enough information about its customers. It cannot easily determine which prospects have made auto purchases or the percentage of prospects who have been converted into buyers. Nor can it identify which customer touch points have produced the greatest number of sales leads or actual sales so it can focus advertising and marketing more on the channels that generate the most revenue. Are purchasers discovering Ace from newspaper ads, from word of mouth, or from the Web?

Prepare a systems analysis report detailing Ace's problem and a system solution that can be implemented using PC database management software. Then use database software to develop a simple system solution. Your systems analysis report should include the following:

1. Description of the problem and its organizational and business impact.
2. Proposed solution, solution objectives, and solution feasibility.
3. Costs and benefits of the solution you have selected. The company has a PC with Internet access and the full suite of Microsoft Office desktop productivity tools.
4. Information requirements to be addressed by the solution.
5. People, organization, and technology issues to be addressed by the solution, including changes in business processes.

On the basis of the requirements you have identified, design a simple customer database and populate it with at least 10 records. Then use the system you have created to generate queries and reports that would be of most interest to management. Create several prototype data input forms for the system and review them with your instructor. Then revise the prototypes.

## Designing an Employee Training and Skills Tracking System

Software skills: Database design, querying and reporting

Business skills: Employee training and skills tracking

Dirt Bikes promotes itself as a "learning company"; it pays for employees to take training courses or college courses to help them advance in their careers. Its labor force is quite young and mobile. As employees move on, their job positions become vacant and Dirt Bikes must quickly fill them to maintain its pace of production. Dirt Bikes's human resources staff would like to find a way to quickly identify employees who have the training to fill vacant positions. Once the company knows who these employees are, it has a better chance of filling open positions internally rather than paying to recruit outsiders. Dirt Bikes would like to track each employee's years of education and the title and date of completed training classes that each employee has attended.

Dirt Bikes currently cannot identify such employees. Its existing employee database is limited to basic human resources data, such as employee name, identification number, birth date, address, telephone number, marital status, job position, and salary. You can find some sample records from this database on the Laudon Web site for Chapter 11 and on the Laudon Multimedia Edition CD-ROM. Dirt Bikes's human resources staff keeps skills and training data in paper folders.

Prepare a systems analysis report describing Dirt Bikes's problem and a system solution that can be implemented using PC database software. Then use the database software to develop a simple system solution. Your report should include the following:

1. Description of the problem and its organizational and business impact.
2. Proposed solution and solution objectives.
3. Information requirements to be addressed by the solution.
4. People, organization, and technology issues to be addressed by the solution, including changes in business processes.

On the basis of the requirements you have identified, design the solution using database software and populate it with at least 10 records per table. Consider whether you can use or modify the existing employee database in your design. Print out the design for each table in your new application. Use the system you have developed to create queries and reports that would be of most interest to management (for instance, which employees have training in project management or advanced computer-aided design [CAD] tools).

If possible, use electronic presentation software to summarize your findings for management.

## Building Internet Skills

### Analyzing Web Site Design and Information Requirements

This project will help develop your Internet skills in analyzing Web site design and business functionality.

Visit the Web site of your choice and explore it thoroughly. Prepare a report analyzing the various functions provided by that Web site and its information requirements. Your report should answer these questions: What functions does the Web site perform? What data does it use? What are it inputs, outputs, and processing? What are some of its other design specifications? Does the Web site link to any internal systems or systems of other organizations? What value does this Web site provide the firm?

## Video Case

You will find a video case illustrating some of the concepts in this chapter on the Laudon Web site at **www.prenhall.com/laudon** along with questions to help you analyze the case.

## Teamwork

### Analyzing Web Site Requirements

With three or four of your classmates, visit the Web site of iTunes, MP3.com, the Internet Movie Database, or a company described in this text that uses the Web. Review the Web site for the company you select. Use what you have learned from the Web site and this chapter to prepare a report describing the functions of that Web site and some of its design specifications. If possible, use electronic presentation software to present your findings to the class.

# BUSINESS PROBLEM-SOLVING CASE

## Comair's Crew Scheduling System Breaks Down

Comair is a regional airline carrier based in Cincinnati, Ohio. The airline employs nearly 7,000 aviation professionals, who together oversee and operate more than 1,100 daily flights carrying 30,000 passengers. Comair flies to 113 cities in the United States, Canada, and the Bahamas. At first an independent operator, it is now a wholly owned subsidiary of Delta Airlines. Its routes include major hubs and markets, such as Atlanta, Cincinnati, Orlando, New York, Washington, D.C., and Boston. In 2004, 12.6 million passengers traveled on at least one of Comair's 170 Bombardier CRJ regional jets.

Throughout its history, Comair has been an award-winning leader in the regional carrier industry. The FAA and various trade magazines have recognized Comair multiple times for its profitability; management; and on-time, cancellation, and lost luggage statistics. History, however, could do little to help the airline over the winter holiday season in December 2004 when a critical legacy system failed and Comair suffered a public relations nightmare, not to mention a major financial hit.

On December 25, 2004, a glitch in Comair's flight crew scheduling software forced the airline to cease all operations, grounding its full schedule of 1,100 flights. The action altered or ruined the holiday plans of 30,000 travelers. Comair and Delta lost $20 million. Although the catalyst for the IT disaster was an unfortunate run of bad weather, Comair opened itself up to criticism by making the weather the focus of its explanation of the failure. Terry Tripler, an industry expert from Minneapolis, labeled the performance of Comair "inexcusable" and likened it to Wal-Mart having all of its cash registers crash on the day after Thanksgiving.

The timeline of events that leads up to December 2004 clearly demonstrates that a company can grow steadily even when some of its critical processes are flawed. Comair began its operation with three propeller planes in Cincinnati in 1977. Delta first partnered with the small commuter airline in 1984. As a result of the partnership, Comair became one of the original members of the Delta Connection program.

In 1984, when Comair's fleet consisted of 25 prop planes, the company managed its flight crews using pen and paper. Two years later, union and federal regulations forced Comair to meet higher standards in its management procedures. To comply with the regulations, Comair leased software from SBS International to track its flight crews, which flights the crews were assigned to, and how many hours they were flying. The system performed its duties admirably, and during the next several years, the company continued its march toward the top of its industry. In 1993, Comair became the first of its competitors to purchase a Bombardier CRJ regional jet. However, the

advantage gained from that transaction lasted only a few years. By 1996, other regional airlines had added jets to their rosters of planes. Comair then looked for new ways to gain a competitive edge.

One area that Comair looked to improve was its information systems. The company's systems ran an assortment of applications for crew scheduling, aircraft maintenance, and passenger booking that were not interrelated and were becoming outdated. In 1997, the IT department discussed replacing the SBS legacy system that the company was using for flight crew management. The application was then 11 years old and was written in Fortran, a programming language dating to the 1950s, in which no one in the department was an expert. It was also the only application that still used the company's old IBM AIX version of the UNIX operating system rather than running on HP UNIX. As a result of the discussion, SBS visited Comair to pitch its latest flight crew management software, named Maestro. However, one of the crew supervisors attending the presentation was familiar with the product from a previous job and gave the software an unfavorable review. As a result of this evaluation, Comair passed on Maestro in favor of looking for a better solution. In the meantime, the company's end users worked efficiently enough with the legacy system and would not have to be retrained on a costly system of questionable value.

In 1998, Jim Dublikar, who was then director of risk management and information technology for Comair, organized a consultation with SABRE Airline Solutions. The Southlake, Texas, company provides both airline software and consulting services. The purpose of the consultation was to outline a long-term IT strategy for handling Comair's legacy systems and IT infrastructure. Five months of meetings produced a five-year plan for evaluating the viability of existing systems and retiring, replacing, or adding to them as necessary. One of the key components that was designated for retirement and replacement was the flight crew management system. Dublikar viewed this decision as an easy one to make. Keeping the old system in use was risky and new technologies promised to bring financial benefits through increased productivity and tighter control of expenses. However, the implementation of this part of the plan was hampered by a number of circumstances.

In the years leading up to 2000, Comair's information systems department devoted the lion's share of its time to preparing for the Year 2000 (Y2K) problem, which required programming older legacy systems to recognize century changes in dates. The Y2K issue was part of the five-year plan, as were rolling out an e-ticketing system and a revenue management application, upgrading the corporate network, and changing the maintenance and engineering system. All of these initiatives were in progress or completed by 1999. Replacing the flight crew management system was next in line. Movement in this area was slow because the company had grown so accustomed to the SBS system, and many of Comair's crew management business processes and business rules (such as the definition of a pilot's workday) were related to the 15-year-old software. The selection of a new flight crew management system was finally scheduled for 2000. However, before that time arrived, Comair went through a period of upheaval. First, Dublikar left the organization. Then, Delta acquired Comair, adding new voices to the decision-making process.

Delta viewed Comair as an easy acquisition. Its former partner consistently turned a profit, fared well on the stock market, and was a leader in statistical performance. Based on that view, Delta saw little reason to tinker with Comair's operations. Instead of focusing on IT, Delta focused mainly on marketing. In fact, Delta installed its own marketing department at Comair shortly after taking over.

Dublikar was not replaced until the beginning of 2000, leaving the IT department with a leadership void. According to former Comair IT worker Eric Bardes, members of the IT department tried not to make too many waves in the wake of the Delta takeover and the leadership void. The IT staff was content to wait for the business side of the company to encourage their projects. Meanwhile, the business side was expecting the IT department to be the proactive force. Thus, the remaining projects in the five-year plan, including replacing the flight crew management system, remained incomplete.

In 2001, another event distracted Comair from its IT initiatives. A pilots' strike lasting 89 days crippled both the airline and the Cincinnati/Northern Kentucky International Airport, where Comair runs 90 percent of the flights. With 800 daily flights grounded, Delta lost $200 million for the quarter. When the strike was settled in June, the Comair flight operations group could not simply flip a switch to resume operations. The effort involved in scheduling flights and crews prohibited the airline from entertaining thoughts of replacing the crew scheduling system.

The instability caused by the pilots' strike was dwarfed only a few months later by the impact of the September 11, 2001, terrorist attacks. Delta incurred losses totaling nearly $9 billion in the four years after the attacks. Comair's IT department invited SABRE, SBS, and other vendors to demonstrate crew management systems in late 2002. But the airline did not commit to a new solution at that time because of cost concerns. In June 2004, Delta finally approved the replacement of the legacy crew management system. Comair agreed to terms with SABRE for its AirCrews Operations Manager and scheduled the rollout for 2005. Of course, 2005 did not arrive quickly enough.

In late December 2004, a harsh winter storm descended on the Ohio Valley. The snow and ice took such a toll on planes, runways, and operations that Comair had to cancel or delay more than 90 percent of its flights between December 22nd and December 24th. The weather and the cancellations would be only part of a much larger problem. On the 25th, the nearly two-decade-old flight crew management software crashed. No one at Comair knew that the software logged schedule changes with an antiquated counter that could not handle more than 32,768 changes in a month. The weather of the previous days had necessitated so many schedule changes that the software reached its threshold and then simply shut down. The crash wiped out the entire slate of flights on December 25th and 90 percent of those on the 26th. Comair had no backup system and the software vendor required a full day to reverse the failure. Comair finally returned to full service on December 29th, but the damage was done. Delta lost nearly the entire profit produced by Comair in the previous quarter in a matter of a few days.

Comair maintains that the centerpiece of the problem was the run of bad weather, not the limitations of the aged software. As of March 2005, the airline had not yet implemented the new SABRE software package. Comair was still using the SBS legacy system, now divided into two modules so that pilot schedule changes and flight attendant schedule changes each have a monthly limit of 32,000. Comair is also monitoring the volume of transactions more carefully.

*Sources:* Stephanie Overby, "Bound to Fail," *CIO Magazine,* May 1, 2005; www.comair.com, accessed June 30, 2005; www.saberairlinesolutions.com, accessed June 30, 2005; TechWeb News, "Comair Downed by Computer Counting Limit," *TechWeb,* http://www.techweb.com/wire/56700130, accessed December 29, 2004; Katie Fairbank, "Airlines Holiday Troubles Blasted," *Dallas Morning News,* as posted to www.jsonline.com/bym/news/dec04/287755.asp, accessed December 27, 2004; Jim Wagner, "Comair Back in Air After Computer Outage," *IT Management,* http://itmanagement.earthweb.com/erp/article.php/3451981, accessed December 27, 2004; and Jim Wagner, "Feds to Probe Comair After Computer Outage," *IT Management,* http://itmanagment.earthweb.com/erp/article.php/3452501, accessed December 28, 2004.

## Case Study Questions

1. What problem was Comair having with its systems? What caused the problem? What was the impact of the problem?
2. What solutions were available to management? Did management choose the best solution? Why or why not? Can you think of alternative solutions that Comair did not consider?
3. What people, organization, and technology issues influenced the decision-making processes of the parties involved in this case?
4. What people, organization, and technology issues does Comair have to consider if it chooses to build a new system?

# Ethical and Social Issues in Information Systems

**CHAPTER 12**

## STUDENT OBJECTIVES

After completing this chapter, you will be able to:

1. Analyze the relationships among ethical, social, and political issues that are raised by information systems.

2. Identify the main moral dimensions of an information society and specific principles for conduct that can be used to guide ethical decisions.

3. Evaluate the impact of contemporary information systems and the Internet on the protection of individual privacy and intellectual property.

4. Assess how information systems have affected everyday life.

## Chapter Outline

## DOES LOCATION TRACKING THREATEN PRIVACY?

**For many years, parents** of schoolchildren in the District of Columbia's public schools have complained about buses running late or not showing up. A federal court appointed an independent transportation administrator and enlisted Satellite Security Systems, or S3, to track the movements of the district's buses. S3 is one of a number of private companies providing satellite tracking services to clients such as the District of Columbia, Fairfax County, state and federal government agencies, police departments, and private companies. Individuals use these services as well to keep tabs on Alzheimer's patients, new teenage drivers, and philandering spouses.

These services equip each vehicle or person they are monitoring with a tracking device using global positioning system (GPS) technology. GPS is a navigation system

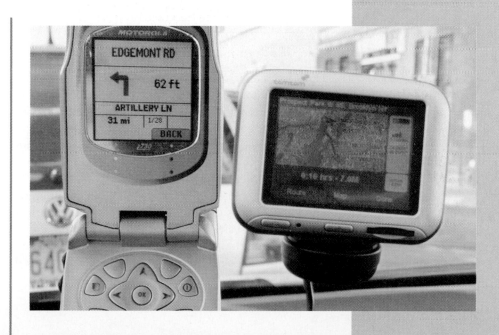

operated by the U.S. Department of Defense based on satellites that continually broadcast their position, time, and date. GPS receivers on the ground, which can be attached to vehicles, cell phones, or other equipment, use information from the satellite signals to calculate their own locations. Cell phones are now equipped with GPS.

The D.C. public school system is spending $6 million on its GPS tracking system. It is equipping buses with GPS locators and special-needs children riding those buses with ID cards that log when they get on and off their buses. Parents receive secret codes that enable them to use the Internet to track their children. S3's monitoring center picks up GPS information from the tracking devices and monitors the locations of the buses on video screens. Most of the monitoring is automated and the S3 staff intervenes primarily in emergencies. S3 maintains each day's tracking data for long periods, and clients can access historical tracking data if they wish.

S3 provides detailed information to the D.C. public schools: each bus's route throughout the day, when the bus stops, when the doors open and close, the speed, and when the ignition is turned on and off. The S3 system includes a database with information on the bus passengers—each child's name, address, disabilities, allergies, contact information, and when their school days begin and end.

David Gilmore, the court-appointed transportation administrator for the D.C. public schools has seen improvement in bus driver performance. Reports of bus drivers making detours to banks or to take long lunches are diminishing.

Parents are also pleased. "I like that the system lets you watch them, because you never know what's going on in the bus," says Deneen Prior, whose three children ride D.C. public school buses. However, she also worries about the location tracking data being misused. "I don't want anybody watching them that's not supposed to be watching them," she notes.

Others feel the same way. Location tracking has benefits, but it also opens the door to invasion of privacy. Many people may not like having their physical movements tracked so closely. Location information might help direct a tow truck to a broken-down car but it could also be used to find out where the driver went during the lunch hour. The Teamsters and other unions have fought to revise their contracts to limit the use of location tracking data in order to discipline workers. Snowplow operators in Boston protested when required to use GPS in their vehicles. ■

*Sources:* Ariana Eunjung Cha, "To Protect and Intrude," *The Washington Post,* January 15, 2005; and Christopher Lindquist, "Watch Carefully," *CIO Magazine,* May 15, 2005.


The use of location tracking systems described in the chapter-opening case shows that technology can be a double-edged sword. It can be the source of many benefits and it can also create new opportunities for breaking the law or taking benefits away from others. The D.C. public school system faced a real problem in trying to make sure its drivers were transporting children safely and promptly to school. Location tracking technology did provide a solution, but it also introduced the possibility that information about the people or vehicles S3 tracked could be used for the wrong purpose.

This solution created what we call an "ethical dilemma," pitting the legitimate need to know what drivers of school buses were doing with the fear that such information could be used to threaten individual privacy. Another ethical dilemma might occur if you were implementing a new information system that reduced labor costs and eliminated employees' jobs. When you design a solution, you need to be aware of the negative impacts of information systems and you need to balance the negative consequences with the positive ones.

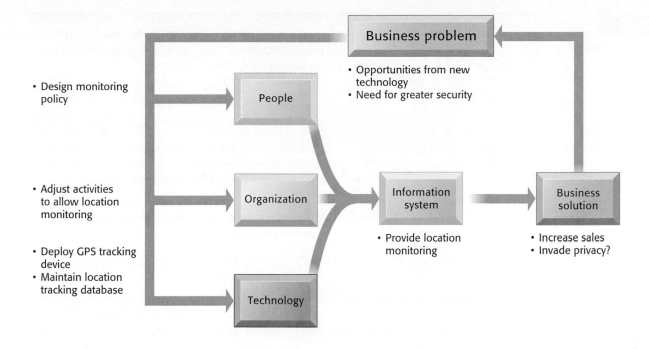

- Design monitoring policy

- Adjust activities to allow location monitoring

- Deploy GPS tracking device
- Maintain location tracking database

**People**

**Organization**

**Technology**

**Business problem**
- Opportunities from new technology
- Need for greater security

**Information system**
- Provide location monitoring

**Business solution**
- Increase sales
- Invade privacy?

---

**HEADS UP**

Information systems raise new and often-perplexing ethical problems. This is more true today than ever before because of the challenges posed by the Internet and electronic commerce to the protection of privacy and intellectual property. Other ethical issues raised by widespread use of information systems include establishing accountability for the consequences of information systems, setting standards to safeguard system quality that protect the safety of individuals and society, and preserving values and institutions considered essential to the quality of life in an information society. Whether you run your own business or work in a large company, you'll be confronting these issues, and you'll need to know how to deal with them.

- If your career is in finance and accounting, you will need to ensure that the information systems you work with are protected from computer fraud and abuse.

- If your career is in human resources, you will be involved in developing and enforcing a corporate ethics policy and in providing special training to sensitize managers and employees to the new ethical issues surrounding information system,

- If your career is in manufacturing, production, or operations management, you will need to deal with data quality and software problems that could interrupt the smooth and accurate flow of information among disparate manufacturing and production systems and among supply chain partners.

- If your career is in sales and marketing, you will need to balance systems that gather and analyze customer data with the need for protecting consumer privacy.

---

This chapter helps you by describing the major ethical and social issues raised by information systems and by providing guidelines for analyzing ethical issues on your own. We first introduce a framework and basic concepts to help you analyze ethical and social issues. Then we discuss each of the major ethical and social issues raised by information systems and use this framework to analyze them.

**TABLE 12.1**

**Recent Examples of Failed Ethical Judgment by Managers**

| | |
|---|---|
| Enron | Top three executives and several middle managers criminally indicted for misstating earnings using illegal accounting schemes. Bankruptcy declared in 2001. |
| WorldCom | Second-largest U.S. telecommunications firm. Chief executive convicted for improperly inflating revenue by billions using illegal accounting methods. Bankruptcy declared in July 2002 with $41 billion in debts. |
| Merrill Lynch | Indicted for assisting Enron in the creation of financial vehicles that had no business purpose, enabling Enron to misstate its earnings. |
| Parmalat | Italy's eighth-largest industrial group indicted for misstating more than $5 billion in revenues, earnings, and assets over several years; senior executives indicted for embezzlement. |
| Bristol-Myers Squibb | Pharmaceutical firm agreed to pay a fine of $150 million for misstating its revenues by $1.5 billion, and inflating its stock value. |

## 12.1 Understanding Ethical and Social Issues Related to Systems

In the past five years we have witnessed, arguably, one of the most ethically challenging periods for U.S. and global business. Table 12.1 provides a small sample of recent cases demonstrating failed ethical judgment by senior and middle managers. These lapses in ethical and business judgment occurred across a broad spectrum of industries.

In today's new legal environment, managers who violate the law and are convicted will most likely spend time in prison. U.S. Federal Sentencing Guidelines adopted in 1987 mandate that federal judges impose stiff sentences on business executives based on the monetary value of the crime, the presence of a conspiracy to prevent discovery of the crime, the use of structured financial transactions to hide the crime, and failure to cooperate with prosecutors (U.S. Sentencing Commission, 2004).

Although in the past business firms would often pay for the legal defense of their employees enmeshed in civil charges and criminal investigations, now firms are encouraged to cooperate with prosecutors to reduce charges against the entire firm for obstructing investigations. These developments mean that, more than ever, as a manager or an employee, you will have to decide for yourself what constitutes proper legal and ethical conduct.

Although these major instances of failed ethical and legal judgment were not masterminded by information systems departments, information systems were instrumental in many of these frauds. In many cases, the perpetrators of these crimes artfully used financial reporting information systems to bury their decisions from public scrutiny in the vain hope they would never be caught. We deal with the issue of control in information systems in Chapter 7. In this chapter we talk about the ethical dimensions of these and other actions based on the use of information systems.

**Ethics** refers to the principles of right and wrong that individuals, acting as free moral agents, use to make choices to guide their behaviors. Information systems raise new ethical questions for both individuals and societies because they create opportunities for intense social change, and thus threaten existing distributions of power, money, rights, and obligations. Like other technologies, such as steam engines, electricity, the telephone, and the radio, information technology can be used to achieve social progress, but it can also be used to commit crimes and threaten cherished social values. The development of information technology will produce benefits for many and costs for others.

Ethical issues in information systems have been given new urgency by the rise of the Internet and electronic commerce. Internet and digital firm technologies make it easier than ever to assemble, integrate, and distribute information, unleashing new concerns about the appropriate use of customer information, the protection of personal privacy, and the protection of intellectual property.

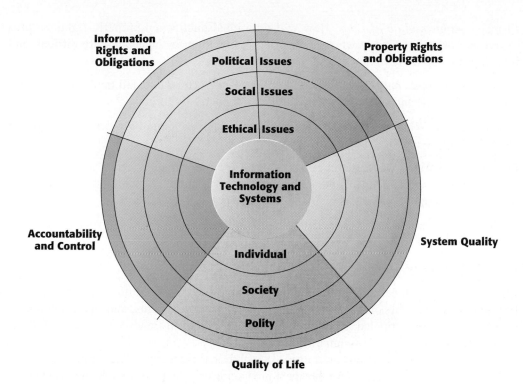

**Figure 12-1**
The Relationship Between Ethical, Social, and Political Issues in an Information Society
*The introduction of new information technology has a ripple effect, raising new ethical, social, and political issues that must be dealt with on the individual, social, and political levels. These issues have five moral dimensions: information rights and obligations, property rights and obligations, system quality, quality of life, and accountability and control.*

Other pressing ethical issues raised by information systems include establishing accountability for the consequences of information systems, setting standards to safeguard system quality that protects the safety of the individual and society, and preserving values and institutions considered essential to the quality of life in an information society. When using information systems, it is essential to ask, "What is the ethical and socially responsible course of action?"

## A Model for Thinking About Ethical, Social, and Political Issues

Ethical, social, and political issues are closely linked. The ethical dilemma you may face when working with information systems typically is reflected in social and political debate. One way to think about these relationships is given in Figure 12.1. Imagine society as a calm pond on a summer day, a delicate ecosystem in partial equilibrium with individuals and with social and political institutions. Individuals know how to act in this pond because social institutions (family, education, organizations) have developed well-honed rules of behavior, and these are supported by laws developed in the political sector that prescribe behavior and promise sanctions for violations. Now toss a rock into the center of the pond. But imagine instead of a rock that the disturbing force is a powerful shock of new information technology and systems hitting a society more or less at rest. What happens? Ripples, of course.

Suddenly, individual actors are confronted with new situations often not covered by the old rules. Social institutions cannot respond overnight to these ripples—it may take years to develop etiquette, expectations, social responsibility, politically correct attitudes, or approved rules. Political institutions also require time before developing new laws and often require the demonstration of real harm before they act. In the meantime, you may have to act. You may be forced to act in a legal gray area.

We can use this model to illustrate the dynamics that connect ethical, social, and political issues. This model is also useful for identifying the main moral dimensions of the information society, which cut across various levels of action—individual, social, and political.

## Five Moral Dimensions of the Information Age

The major ethical, social, and political issues raised by information systems include the following moral dimensions:

*Information rights and obligations.* What **information rights** do individuals and organizations possess with respect to themselves? What can they protect? What obligations do individuals and organizations have concerning this information?

*Property rights and obligations.* How will traditional intellectual property rights be protected in a digital society in which tracing and accounting for ownership are difficult and ignoring such property rights is so easy?

*Accountability and control.* Who can and will be held accountable and liable for the harm done to individual and collective information and property rights?

*System quality.* What standards of data and system quality should we demand to protect individual rights and the safety of society?

*Quality of life.* What values should be preserved in an information- and knowledge-based society? Which institutions should we protect from violation? Which cultural values and practices are supported by the new information technology?

We explore these moral dimensions in detail in Section 12.3.

### Key Technology Trends That Raise Ethical Issues

Ethical issues long preceded information technology. Nevertheless, information technology has heightened ethical concerns, taxed existing social arrangements, and made some laws obsolete or severely crippled. There are four key technological trends responsible for these ethical stresses and they are summarized in Table 12.2.

The doubling of computing power every 18 months has made it possible for most organizations to use information systems for their core production processes. As a result, our dependence on systems and our vulnerability to system errors and poor data quality have increased. Social rules and laws have not yet adjusted to this dependence. Standards for ensuring the accuracy and reliability of information systems (see Chapter 7) are not universally accepted or enforced.

Advances in data storage techniques and rapidly declining storage costs have been responsible for the multiplying databases on individuals—employees, customers, and potential customers—maintained by private and public organizations. These advances in data storage have made the routine violation of individual privacy both cheap and effective. Already massive data storage systems are cheap enough for regional and even local retailing firms to use in identifying customers.

Advances in data analysis techniques for large pools of data are another technological trend that heightens ethical concerns because companies and government agencies are able to find out much detailed personal information about individuals. With contemporary data management tools (see Chapter 5), companies can assemble and combine the myriad pieces of information about you stored on computers much more easily than in the past.

Think of all the ways you generate computer information about yourself—credit card purchases; telephone calls; magazine subscriptions; video rentals; mail-order purchases; banking records; and local, state, and federal government records (including court and police records).

**TABLE 12.2**

**Technology Trends That Raise Ethical Issues**

| Trend | Impact |
|---|---|
| Computing power doubles every 18 months | More organizations depend on computer systems for critical operations |
| Data storage costs rapidly declining | Organizations can easily maintain detailed databases on individuals |
| Data analysis advances | Companies can analyze vast quantities of data gathered on individuals to develop detailed profiles of individual behavior |
| Networking advances and the Internet | Copying data from one location to another and accessing personal data from remote locations are much easier |

Put together and mined properly, this information could reveal not only your credit information but also your driving habits, your tastes, your associations, and your political interests.

Companies with products to sell purchase-relevant information from these sources to help them more finely target their marketing campaigns. Chapters 3 and 5 describe how companies can analyze large pools of data from multiple sources to rapidly identify buying patterns of customers and suggest individual responses. The use of computers to combine data from multiple sources and create electronic dossiers of detailed information on individuals is called **profiling**.

For example, hundreds of Web sites allow DoubleClick (www.doubleclick.net), an Internet advertising broker, to track the activities of their visitors in exchange for revenue from advertisements based on visitor information DoubleClick gathers. DoubleClick uses this information to create a profile of each online visitor, adding more detail to the profile as the visitor accesses an associated DoubleClick site. Over time, DoubleClick can create a detailed dossier of a person's spending and computing habits on the Web that can be sold to companies to help them target their Web ads more precisely.

ChoicePoint, described in the chapter-ending case, gathers data from police, criminal, and motor vehicle records; credit and employment histories; current and previous addresses; professional licenses; and insurance claims to assemble and maintain electronic dossiers on almost every adult in the United Sates. The company sells this personal information to businesses and government agencies.

A new data analysis technology called **nonobvious relationship awareness (NORA)** has given both the government and the private sector even more powerful profiling capabilities. NORA can take information about people from many disparate sources, such as employment applications, telephone records, customer listings, and "wanted" lists, and correlate relationships to find obscure hidden connections that might help identify criminals or terrorists (see Figure 12-2).

NORA technology scans data and extracts information as the data are being generated so that it could, for example, instantly discover a man at an airline ticket counter who shares a phone number with a known terrorist before that person boards an airplane. The technology is considered a valuable tool for homeland security but does have privacy implications because it can provide such a detailed picture of the activities and associations of a single individual.

Finally, advances in networking, including the Internet, promise to reduce greatly the costs of moving and accessing large quantities of data and open the possibility of mining large pools of data remotely using small desktop machines, permitting an invasion of privacy on a scale and with a precision heretofore unimaginable. If computing and networking technologies continue to advance at the same pace as in the past, by 2023 large organizations will be able to

Credit card purchases can make personal information available to market researchers, telemarketers, and direct-mail companies. Advances in information technology facilitate the invasion of privacy.

**Figure 12-2**
Nonobvious
Relationship
Awareness (NORA)
*NORA technology can
take information about
people from disparate
sources and find
obscure, nonobvious
relationships. It might
discover, for example,
that an applicant for a
job at a casino shares a
telephone number with
a known criminal and
issue an alert to the hiring manager.*

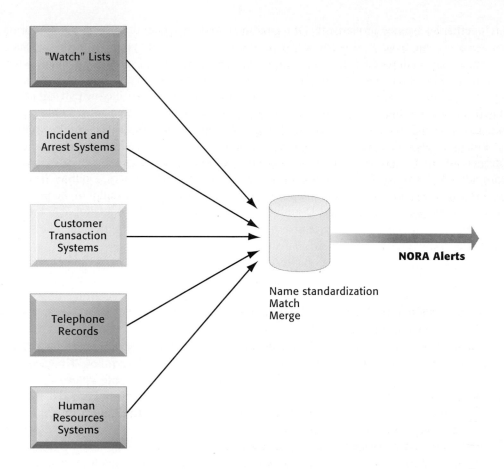

devote the equivalent of a contemporary desktop personal computer to monitoring each of the 350 million individuals who will then be living in the United States (Farmer and Mann, 2003).

The development of global digital superhighway communication networks widely available to individuals and businesses poses many ethical and social concerns. Who will account for the flow of information over these networks? Will you be able to trace information collected about you? What will these networks do to the traditional relationships between family, work, and leisure? How will traditional job designs be altered when millions of "employees" become subcontractors using mobile offices for which they themselves must pay? In the next section we consider some ethical principles and analytical techniques for dealing with these kinds of ethical and social concerns.

## 12.2 Ethics in an Information Society

Ethics is a concern of humans who have freedom of choice. Ethics is about individual choice: When faced with alternative courses of action, what is the correct moral choice? What are the main features of ethical choice?

### Basic Concepts: Responsibility, Accountability, and Liability

Ethical choices are decisions made by individuals who are responsible for the consequences of their actions. **Responsibility** is a key element of ethical action. Responsibility means that you accept the potential costs, duties, and obligations for the decisions you make. **Accountability** is a feature of systems and social institutions: It means that mechanisms are in place to determine who took responsible action, who is responsible. Systems and institutions in which it is impossible to find out who took what action are inherently incapable of ethical analysis or ethical action. Liability extends the concept of responsibility further to the area of laws. **Liability** is a feature of political systems in which a body of laws is in place that permits individuals to recover the damages done to them by other actors, systems, or organizations. **Due process** is a related feature of law-governed societies and is a process in which laws are known and understood and there is an ability to appeal to higher authorities to ensure that the laws are applied correctly.

These basic concepts form the underpinning of an ethical analysis of information systems and those who manage them. First, information technologies are filtered through social institutions, organizations, and individuals. Systems do not have impacts by themselves. Whatever information system impacts exist are products of institutional, organizational, and individual actions and behaviors. Second, responsibility for the consequences of technology falls clearly on the institutions, organizations, and individual managers who choose to use the technology. Using information technology in a socially responsible manner means that you can and will be held accountable for the consequences of your actions. Third, in an ethical, political society, individuals and others can recover damages done to them through a set of laws characterized by due process.

## Ethical Analysis

When confronted with a situation that seems to present ethical issues, how should you analyze it? The following five-step process should help.

1. *Identify and describe clearly the facts.* Find out who did what to whom, and where, when, and how. In many instances, you will be surprised at the errors in the initially reported facts, and often you will find that simply getting the facts straight helps define the solution. It also helps to get the opposing parties involved in an ethical dilemma to agree on the facts.
2. *Define the conflict or dilemma and identify the higher-order values involved.* Ethical, social, and political issues always reference higher values. The parties to a dispute all claim to be pursuing higher values (e.g., freedom, privacy, protection of property, and the free enterprise system). Typically, an ethical issue involves a dilemma: two diametrically opposed courses of action that support worthwhile values. For example, the chapter-ending case study illustrates two competing values: the need to protect citizens from terrorist acts and the need to protect individual privacy.
3. *Identify the stakeholders.* Every ethical, social, and political issue has stakeholders: players in the game who have an interest in the outcome, who have invested in the situation, and have vocal opinions. Find out the identity of these groups and what they want. This will be useful later when designing a solution.
4. *Identify the options that you can reasonably take.* You may find that none of the options satisfy all the interests involved, but that some options do a better job than others. Sometimes arriving at a good or ethical solution may not result in a balancing of consequences to stakeholders.
5. *Identify the potential consequences of your options.* Some options may be ethically correct but disastrous from other points of view. Other options may work in one instance but not in other similar instances. Always ask yourself, "What if I choose this option consistently over time?"

## Candidate Ethical Principles

Once your analysis is complete, what ethical principles or rules should you use to make a decision? What higher-order values should inform your judgment? Although you are the only one who can decide which among many ethical principles you will follow, and how you will prioritize them, it is helpful to consider some ethical principles with deep roots in many cultures that have survived throughout recorded history.

1. Do unto others as you would have them do unto you (the Golden Rule). Putting yourself into the place of others, and thinking of yourself as the object of the decision, can help you think about fairness in decision making.
2. If an action is not right for everyone to take, it is not right for anyone (**Immanuel Kant's Categorical Imperative**). Ask yourself, "If everyone did this, could the organization, or society, survive?"
3. If an action cannot be taken repeatedly, it is not right to take at all (**Descartes' rule of change**). This is the slippery-slope rule: An action may bring about a small change now

that is acceptable, but if it is repeated, it would bring unacceptable changes in the long run. In the vernacular, it might be stated as "once started down a slippery path, you may not be able to stop."

4. Take the action that achieves the higher or greater value (the **Utilitarian Principle**). This rule assumes you can prioritize values in a rank order and understand the consequences of various courses of action.

5. Take the action that produces the least harm or the least potential cost (**Risk Aversion Principle**). Some actions have extremely high failure costs of very low probability (e.g., building a nuclear generating facility in an urban area) or extremely high failure costs of moderate probability (speeding and automobile accidents). Avoid these high-failure-cost actions, paying greater attention obviously to high-failure-cost potential of moderate to high probability.

6. Assume that virtually all tangible and intangible objects are owned by someone else unless there is a specific declaration otherwise. (This is the **ethical "no free lunch" rule**.) If something someone else has created is useful to you, it has value, and you should assume the creator wants compensation for this work.

Although these ethical rules cannot be guides to action, actions that do not easily pass these rules deserve some very close attention and a great deal of caution. The appearance of unethical behavior may do as much harm to you and your company as actual unethical behavior.

## Professional Codes of Conduct

When groups of people claim to be professionals, they take on special rights and obligations because of their special claims to knowledge, wisdom, and respect. Professional codes of conduct are promulgated by associations of professionals, such as the American Medical Association (AMA), the American Bar Association (ABA), the Association of Information Technology Professionals (AITP), and the Association of Computing Machinery (ACM). These professional groups take responsibility for the partial regulation of their professions by determining entrance qualifications and competence. Codes of ethics are promises by professions to regulate themselves in the general interest of society. For example, avoiding harm to others, honoring property rights (including intellectual property), and respecting privacy are among the General Moral Imperatives of the ACM's Code of Ethics and Professional Conduct.

## Some Real-World Ethical Dilemmas

Information systems have created new ethical dilemmas in which one set of interests is pitted against another. For example, many of the large telephone companies in the United States are using information technology to reduce the sizes of their workforces. Voice recognition software reduces the need for human operators by enabling computers to recognize a customer's responses to a series of computerized questions. Many companies monitor what their employees are doing on the Internet to prevent them from wasting company resources on nonbusiness activities (see the Chapter 6 Focus on People).

In each instance, you can find competing values at work, with groups lined up on either side of a debate. A company may argue, for example, that it has a right to use information systems to increase productivity and reduce the size of its workforce to lower costs and stay in business. Employees displaced by information systems may argue that employers have some responsibility for their welfare. Business owners might feel obligated to monitor employee e-mail and Internet use to minimize drains on productivity. Employees might believe they should be able to use the Internet for short personal tasks in place of the telephone. A close analysis of the facts can sometimes produce compromised solutions that give each side "half a loaf." Try to apply some of the principles of ethical analysis described to each of these cases. What is the right thing to do?

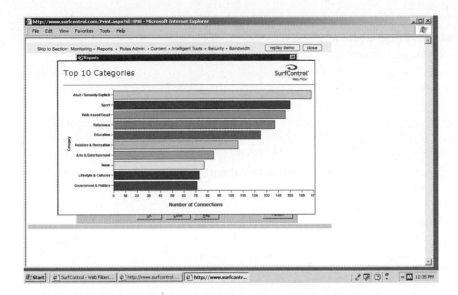

This report from SurfControl.com, accessed on December 1, 2005, shows some of its capabilities for tracking Web and e-mail activity and for filtering unauthorized e-mail and Web site content. The benefits of monitoring employee e-mail and Internet use should be balanced with the need to respect employee privacy.

## 12.3 The Moral Dimensions of Information Systems

In this section, we take a closer look at the five moral dimensions of information systems first described in Figure 12-1. In each dimension we identify the ethical, social, and political levels of analysis and use real-world examples to illustrate the values involved, the stakeholders, and the options chosen.

### Information Rights: Privacy and Freedom in the Internet Age

**Privacy** is the claim of individuals to be left alone, free from surveillance or interference from other individuals or organizations, including the state. Claims to privacy are also involved at the workplace: Millions of employees are subject to electronic and other forms of high-tech surveillance (Ball, 2001). Information technology and systems threaten individual claims to privacy by making the invasion of privacy cheap, profitable, and effective.

The claim to privacy is protected in the U.S., Canadian, and German constitutions in a variety of different ways and in other countries through various statutes. In the United States, the claim to privacy is protected primarily by the First Amendment guarantees of freedom of speech and association, the Fourth Amendment protections against unreasonable search and seizure of one's personal documents or home, and the guarantee of due process.

Table 12.3 describes the major U.S. federal statutes that set forth the conditions for handling information about individuals in such areas as credit reporting, education, financial records, newspaper records, and electronic communications. The Privacy Act of 1974 has been the most important of these laws, regulating the federal government's collection, use, and disclosure of information. At present, most U.S. federal privacy laws apply only to the federal government and regulate very few areas of the private sector.

Most American and European privacy law is based on a regime called Fair Information Practices (FIP) first set forth in a report written in 1973 by a federal government advisory committee (U.S. Department of Health, Education, and Welfare, 1973). **Fair Information Practices (FIP)** is a set of principles governing the collection and use of information about individuals. FIP principles are based on the notion of a mutuality of interest between the record holder and the individual. The individual has an interest in engaging in a transaction, and the record keeper—usually a business or government agency—requires information about the individual to support the transaction. Once information is gathered, the individual maintains an interest in the record, and the record may not be used to support other activities without the individual's consent. In 1998, the Federal Trade Commission (FTC) restated and extended the original FIP to provide guidelines for protecting online privacy. Table 12.4 describes the FTC's Fair Information Practice principles.

**TABLE 12.3**

**Federal Privacy Laws in the United States**

**GENERAL FEDERAL PRIVACY LAWS**

Freedom of Information Act of 1966 as Amended (5 USC 552)
Privacy Act of 1974 as Amended (5 USC 552a)
Electronic Communications Privacy Act of 1986
Computer Matching and Privacy Protection Act of 1988
Computer Security Act of 1987
Federal Managers Financial Integrity Act of 1982
E-Government Act of 2002

**PRIVACY LAWS AFFECTING PRIVATE INSTITUTIONS**

Fair Credit Reporting Act of 1970
Family Educational Rights and Privacy Act of 1974
Right to Financial Privacy Act of 1978
Privacy Protection Act of 1980
Cable Communications Policy Act of 1984
Electronic Communications Privacy Act of 1986
Video Privacy Protection Act of 1988
The Health Insurance Portability and Accountability Act of 1996 (HIPAA)
Children's Online Privacy Protection Act of 1998 (COPPA)
Financial Modernization Act (Gramm–Leach–Bliley Act) of 1999

The FTC's FIP principles are being used as guidelines to drive changes in privacy legislation. In July 1998, the U.S. Congress passed the Children's Online Privacy Protection Act (COPPA), requiring Web sites to obtain parental permission before collecting information on children under the age of 13. Other proposed Internet privacy legislation focuses on protecting against identity theft and phishing, discouraging spyware, and further regulating the sale and use of personally identifiable information.

Privacy protections have also been added to recent laws deregulating financial services and safeguarding the maintenance and transmission of health information about individuals. The Gramm–Leach–Bliley Act of 1999, which repeals earlier restrictions on affiliations among banks, securities firms, and insurance companies, includes some privacy protection for consumers of financial services. All financial institutions are required to disclose their policies and practices for protecting the privacy of nonpublic personal information and to allow customers to opt out of information-sharing arrangements with nonaffiliated third parties.

The Health Insurance Portability and Accountability Act of 1996 (HIPAA), which took effect on April 14, 2003, includes privacy protection for medical records. The law gives patients access to their personal medical records maintained by healthcare providers, hospitals, and health insurers and the right to authorize how protected information about them-

**TABLE 12.4**

**Federal Trade Commission Fair Information Practice Principles**

1. *Notice/awareness (core principle).* Web sites must disclose their information practices before collecting data. Includes identification of collector; uses of data; other recipients of data; nature of collection (active/inactive); voluntary or required status; consequences of refusal; and steps taken to protect confidentiality, integrity, and quality of the data.

2. *Choice/consent (core principle).* There must be a choice regime in place allowing consumers to choose how their information will be used for secondary purposes other than supporting the transaction, including internal use and transfer to third parties.

3. *Access/participation.* Consumers should be able to review and contest the accuracy and completeness of data collected about them in a timely, inexpensive process.

4. *Security.* Data collectors must take responsible steps to assure that consumer information is accurate and secure from unauthorized use.

5. *Enforcement.* There must be in place a mechanism to enforce FIP principles. This can involve self-regulation, legislation giving consumers legal remedies for violations, or federal statutes and regulations.

selves can be used or disclosed. Doctors, hospitals, and other healthcare providers must limit the disclosure of personal information about patients to the minimum amount necessary to achieve a given purpose.

## The European Directive on Data Protection

In Europe, privacy protection is much more stringent than in the United States. Unlike the United States, European countries do not allow businesses to use personally identifiable information without consumers' prior consent. On October 25, 1998, the European Commission's Directive on Data Protection went into effect, broadening privacy protection in the European Union (EU) nations. The directive requires companies to inform people when they collect information about them and disclose how it will be stored and used. Customers must provide their informed consent before any company can legally use data about them, and they have the right to access that information, correct it, and request that no further data be collected. **Informed consent** can be defined as consent given with knowledge of all the facts needed to make a rational decision. EU member nations must translate these principles into their own laws and cannot transfer personal data to countries, such as the United States, that do not have similar privacy protection regulations.

Working with the European Commission, the U.S. Department of Commerce developed a safe harbor framework for U.S. firms. A **safe harbor** is a private, self-regulating policy and enforcement mechanism that meets the objectives of government regulators and legislation but does not involve government regulation or enforcement. U.S. businesses would be allowed to use personal data from EU countries if they develop privacy protection policies that meet EU standards. Enforcement would occur in the United States using self-policing, regulation, and government enforcement of fair trade statutes.

## Internet Challenges to Privacy

Internet technology poses new challenges for the protection of individual privacy. Information sent over this vast network of networks may pass through many different computer systems before it reaches its final destination. Each of these systems is capable of monitoring, capturing, and storing communications that pass through it.

It is possible to record many online activities, including which online newsgroups or files a person has accessed, which Web sites and Web pages he or she has visited, and what items that person has inspected or purchased over the Web. Much of this monitoring and tracking of Web site visitors occurs in the background without the visitor's knowledge. Tools to monitor visits to the World Wide Web have become popular because they help organizations determine who is visiting their Web sites and how to better target their offerings. (Some firms also monitor the Internet usage of their employees to see how they are using company network resources.) Web retailers now have access to software that lets them "watch" the online shopping behavior of individuals and groups while they are visiting a Web site and making purchases. The commercial demand for this personal information is virtually insatiable.

Web sites can learn the identities of their visitors if the visitors voluntarily register at the site to purchase a product or service or to obtain a free service, such as information. Web sites can also capture information about visitors without their knowledge using cookie technology.

**Cookies** are tiny files deposited on a computer hard drive when a user visits certain Web sites. Cookies identify the visitor's Web browser software and track visits to the Web site. When the visitor returns to a site that has stored a cookie, the Web site software will search the visitor's computer, find the cookie, and know what that person has done in the past. It may also update the cookie, depending on the activity during the visit. In this way, the site can customize its contents for each visitor's interests. For example, if you purchase a book on the Amazon.com Web site and return later from the same browser, the site will welcome you by name and recommend other books of interest based on your past purchases. DoubleClick, introduced earlier in this chapter, uses cookies to build its dossiers with details of online purchases and to examine the behavior of Web site visitors. Figure 12-3 illustrates how cookies work.

Web sites using cookie technology cannot directly obtain visitors' names and addresses. However, if a person has registered at a site, that information can be combined with cookie data to identify the visitor. Web site owners can also combine the data they have gathered from cookies and other Web site monitoring tools with personal data from other sources,

**Figure 12-3**

How Cookies Identify
Web Visitors

*Cookies are written by a
Web site on a visitor's
hard drive. When the
visitor returns to that
Web site, the Web
server requests the ID
number from the cookie
and uses it to access
the data stored by that
server on that visitor.
The Web site can then
use these data to dis-
play personalized infor-
mation.*

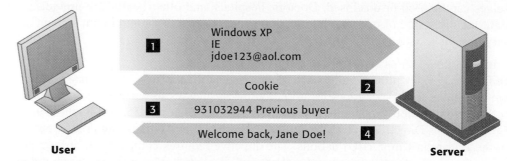

1. The Web server reads the user's Web browser and determines the operating system, browser name, version number, Internet address, and other information.
2. The server transmits a tiny text file with user identification information called a cookie, which the user's browser receives and stores on the user's computer hard drive.
3. When the user returns to the Web site, the server requests the contents of any cookie it deposited previously in the user's computer.
4. The Web server reads the cookie, identifies the visitor, and calls up data on the user.

such as offline data collected from surveys or paper catalog purchases, to develop very detailed profiles of their visitors.

There are now even more subtle and surreptitious tools for surveillance of Internet users. Marketers use Web bugs as another tool to monitor online behavior. **Web bugs** are tiny graphic files embedded in e-mail messages and Web pages that are designed to monitor who is reading the e-mail message or Web page and transmit that information to another computer. Other spyware can secretly install itself on an Internet user's computer by piggyback-ing on larger applications. Once installed, the spyware calls out to Web sites to send banner ads and other unsolicited material to the user, and it can also report the user's movements on the Internet to other computers. More information is available about Web bugs, spyware, and other intrusive software in Chapter 7.

Google has been using tools to scan the contents of messages received by users of its free Web-based e-mail service called Gmail. Ads that users see when they read their e-mail are related to the subjects of these messages. Google's service offers users one gigabyte of storage space—far more than any of its competitors—but privacy advocates find the practice offensive.

The United States has allowed businesses to gather transaction information generated in the marketplace and then use that information for other marketing purposes without obtain-ing the informed consent of the individual whose information is being used. U.S. e-commerce sites are largely content to publish statements on their Web sites informing visitors about how their information will be used. Some have added opt-out selection boxes to these infor-mation policy statements. An **opt-out** model of informed consent permits the collection of personal information until the consumer specifically requests that the data not be collected. Privacy advocates would like to see wider use of an **opt-in** model of informed consent in which a business is prohibited from collecting any personal information unless the con-sumer specifically takes action to approve information collection and use.

The online industry has preferred self-regulation to privacy legislation for protecting consumers. In 1998, the online industry formed the Online Privacy Alliance to encourage self-regulation to develop a set of privacy guidelines for its members. The group promotes the use of online seals, such as that of TRUSTe, certifying Web sites adhering to certain pri-vacy principles. Members of the advertising network industry, including DoubleClick, have created an additional industry association called the Network Advertising Initiative (NAI) to develop its own privacy policies to help consumers opt out of advertising network programs and provide consumers redress from abuses.

In general, however, most Internet businesses do little to protect the privacy of their cus-tomers, and consumers do not do as much as they should to protect themselves. Many com-panies with Web sites do not have privacy policies. Of the companies that do post privacy polices on their Web sites, about half do not monitor their sites to ensure they adhere to these policies. The vast majority of online customers claim they are concerned about online pri-vacy, but less than half read the privacy statements on Web sites (Laudon and Traver, 2006).

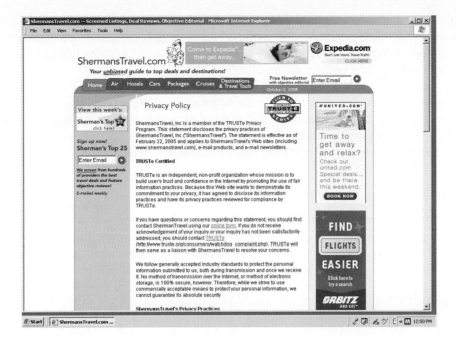

Web sites are starting to post their privacy policies for visitors to review. The TRUSTe seal designates Web sites that have agreed to adhere to TRUSTe's established privacy principles of disclosure, choice, access, and security.

## Technical Solutions

In addition to legislation, new technologies are available to protect user privacy during interactions with Web sites. Many of these tools are used for encrypting e-mail, for making e-mail or surfing activities appear anonymous, for preventing client computers from accepting cookies, or for detecting and eliminating spyware.

There are now tools to help users determine the kind of personal data that can be extracted by Web sites. The Platform for Privacy Preferences, known as P3P, enables automatic communication of privacy policies between an e-commerce site and its visitors. **P3P** provides a standard for communicating a Web site's privacy policy to Internet users and for comparing that policy to the user's preferences or to other standards, such as the FTC's new FIP guidelines or the European Directive on Data Protection. Users can use P3P to select the level of privacy they wish to maintain when interacting with the Web site.

The P3P standard allows Web sites to publish privacy policies in a form that computers can understand. Once it is codified according to P3P rules, the privacy policy becomes part of the software for individual Web pages (see Figure 12-4). Users of recent versions of Microsoft Internet Explorer Web browsing software can access and read the P3P site's privacy policy and a list of all cookies coming from the site. Internet Explorer enables users to

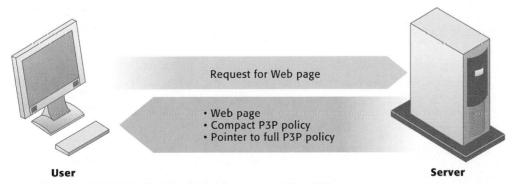

1. The user with P3P Web browsing software requests a Web page.
2. The Web server returns the Web page along with a compact version of the Web site's policy and a pointer to the full P3P policy. If the Web site is not P3P compliant, no P3P data are returned.
3. The user's Web browsing software compares the response from the Web site with the user's privacy preferences. If the Web site does not have a P3P policy or the policy does not match the privacy levels established by the user, it warns the user or rejects the cookies from the Web site. Otherwise, the Web page loads normally.

**Figure 12-4**
The P3P Standard
*P3P enables Web sites to translate their privacy policies into a standard format that can be read by the user's Web browser software. The user's Web browser software evaluates the Web site's privacy policy to determine whether it is compatible with the user's privacy preferences.*

adjust their computers to screen out all cookies or let in selected cookies based on specific levels of privacy. For example, the "medium" level accepts cookies from first-party host sites that have opt-in or opt-out policies but rejects third-party cookies that use personally identifiable information without an opt-in policy.

However, P3P only works with Web sites of members of the World Wide Web Consortium who have translated their Web site privacy policies into P3P format. The technology will display cookies from Web sites that are not part of the consortium, but users will not be able to obtain sender information or privacy statements. Many users may also need to be educated about interpreting company privacy statements and P3P levels of privacy.

## Property Rights: Intellectual Property

Contemporary information systems have severely challenged existing law and social practices that protect private intellectual property. **Intellectual property** is considered to be intangible property created by individuals or corporations. Information technology makes it difficult to protect intellectual property because computerized information can be so easily copied or distributed on networks. Intellectual property is subject to a variety of protections under three different legal traditions: trade secrets, copyright, and patent law.

### Trade Secrets

Any intellectual work product—a formula, device, pattern, or compilation of data—used for a business purpose can be classified as a **trade secret**, provided it is not based on information in the public domain. Protections for trade secrets vary from state to state. In general, trade secret laws grant a monopoly on the ideas behind a work product, but it can be a very tenuous monopoly.

Software that contains novel or unique elements, procedures, or compilations can be included as a trade secret. Trade secret law protects the actual ideas in a work product, not only their manifestation. To make this claim, the creator or owner must take care to bind employees and customers with nondisclosure agreements and to prevent the secret from falling into the public domain.

The limitation of trade secret protection is that, although virtually all software programs of any complexity contain unique elements of some sort, it is difficult to prevent the ideas in the work from falling into the public domain when the software is widely distributed.

### Copyright

**Copyright** is a statutory grant that protects creators of intellectual property from having their work copied by others for any purpose during the life of the author plus an additional 70 years after the author's death. For corporate-owned works, copyright protection lasts for 95 years after their initial creation. Congress has extended copyright protection to books, periodicals, lectures, dramas, musical compositions, maps, drawings, artwork of any kind, and motion pictures. The intent behind copyright laws has been to encourage creativity and authorship by ensuring that creative people receive the financial and other benefits of their work. Most industrial nations have their own copyright laws, and there are several international conventions and bilateral agreements through which nations coordinate and enforce their laws.

In the mid-1960s, the Copyright Office began registering software programs, and in 1980 Congress passed the Computer Software Copyright Act, which clearly provides protection for software program code and for copies of the original sold in commerce, and sets forth the rights of the purchaser to use the software while the creator retains legal title.

Copyright protects against copying entire programs or their parts. Damages and relief are readily obtained for infringement. The drawback to copyright protection is that the underlying ideas behind a work are not protected, only their manifestation in a work. A competitor can use your software, understand how it works, and build new software that follows the same concepts without infringing on a copyright.

"Look and feel" copyright infringement lawsuits are precisely about the distinction between an idea and its expression. For instance, in the early 1990s, Apple Computer sued Microsoft Corporation and Hewlett-Packard for infringement of the expression of Apple's

Macintosh interface, claiming that the defendants copied the expression of overlapping windows. The defendants countered that the idea of overlapping windows can be expressed only in a single way and, therefore, was not protectable under the merger doctrine of copyright law. When ideas and their expression merge, the expression cannot be copyrighted.

In general, courts appear to be following the reasoning of a 1989 case—*Brown Bag Software* vs. *Symantec Corp.*—in which the court dissected the elements of software alleged to be infringing. The court found that similar concept, function, general functional features (e.g., drop-down menus), and colors are not protectable by copyright law (*Brown Bag* vs. *Symantec Corp.*, 1992).

## Patents

A **patent** grants the owner an exclusive monopoly on the ideas behind an invention for 20 years. The congressional intent behind patent law was to ensure that inventors of new machines, devices, or methods receive the full financial and other rewards of their labor and yet still make widespread use of the invention possible by providing detailed diagrams for those wishing to use the idea under license from the patent's owner. The granting of a patent is determined by the Patent Office and relies on court rulings.

The key concepts in patent law are originality, novelty, and invention. The Patent Office did not accept applications for software patents routinely until a 1981 Supreme Court decision that held that computer programs could be a part of a patentable process. Since that time, hundreds of patents have been granted and thousands await consideration.

The strength of patent protection is that it grants a monopoly on the underlying concepts and ideas of software. The difficulty is passing stringent criteria of nonobviousness (e.g., the work must reflect some special understanding and contribution), originality, and novelty, as well as years of waiting to receive protection.

## Challenges to Intellectual Property Rights

Contemporary information technologies, especially software, pose severe challenges to existing intellectual property regimes and, therefore, create significant ethical, social, and political issues. Digital media differ from books, periodicals, and other media in terms of ease of replication; ease of transmission; ease of alteration; difficulty in classifying a software work as a program, book, or even music; compactness—making theft easy; and difficulties in establishing uniqueness.

The proliferation of electronic networks, including the Internet, has made it even more difficult to protect intellectual property. Before widespread use of networks, copies of software, books, magazine articles, or films had to be stored on physical media, such as paper, computer disks, or videotape, creating some hurdles to distribution. Using networks, information can be more widely reproduced and distributed. A study conducted by the International Data Corporation for the Business Software Alliance found that more than one-third of the software worldwide was counterfeit or pirated, and the Business Software Alliance reported $29 billion in yearly losses from software piracy (Geitner, 2004; Lohr, 2004).

The Internet was designed to transmit information freely around the world, including copyrighted information. With the World Wide Web in particular, you can easily copy and distribute virtually anything to thousands and even millions of people around the world, even if they are using different types of computer systems. Information can be illicitly copied from one place and distributed through other systems and networks even though these parties do not willingly participate in the infringement.

Individuals have been illegally copying and distributing digitized MP3 music files on the Internet for a number of years. File sharing services such as Napster, and later Grokster, Kazaa, and Morpheus, sprung up to help users locate and swap digital music files, including those protected by copyright. Illegal file sharing became so widespread that it threatened the viability of the music recording industry. The recording industry won some legal battles for shutting these services down, but has not been able to halt illegal file sharing. (More detail on this topic can be found in the case study concluding Chapter 1.) As more and more homes adopt high-speed Internet access, illegal file sharing of videos will pose similar threats to the motion picture industry.

Mechanisms are being developed to sell and distribute books, articles, and other intellectual property legally on the Internet, and the **Digital Millennium Copyright Act (DMCA)** of 1998 provides some copyright protection. The DMCA implemented a World Intellectual Property Organization Treaty that makes it illegal to circumvent technology-based protections of copyrighted materials. Internet service providers (ISPs) are required to take down sites of copyright infringers that they are hosting once they are notified of the problem.

Microsoft and 1,400 other software and information content firms are represented by the Software and Information Industry Association (SIIA), which lobbies for new laws and enforcement of existing laws to protect intellectual property around the world. (SIIA was formed on January 1, 1999, from the merger of the Software Publishers Association [SPA] and the Information Industry Association [IIA].) The SIIA runs an antipiracy hotline for individuals to report piracy activities and educational programs to help organizations combat software piracy and has published guidelines for employee use of software.

## Accountability, Liability, and Control

Along with privacy and property laws, new information technologies are challenging existing liability law and social practices for holding individuals and institutions accountable. If a person is injured by a machine controlled, in part, by software, who should be held accountable and, therefore, held liable? Should a public bulletin board or an electronic service, such as America Online, permit the transmission of pornographic or offensive material (as broadcasters), or should they be held harmless against any liability for what users transmit (as is true of common carriers, such as the telephone system)? What about the Internet? If you outsource your information processing, can you hold the external vendor liable for injuries done to your customers? Some real-world examples may shed light on these questions.

### Computer-Related Liability Problems
During the weekend of March 15, 2002, tens of thousands of Bank of America customers in California, Arizona, and Nevada were unable to use their paychecks and social security payments that had just been deposited electronically. Checks bounced. Withdrawals were blocked because of insufficient funds. Because of an operating error at the bank's computer center in Nevada, a batch of direct deposit transactions was not processed. The bank lost track of money that should have been credited to customers' accounts, and it took days to rectify the problem (Carr and Gallagher, 2002). Who is liable for any economic harm caused to individuals or businesses that could not access their full account balances in this period?

This case reveals the difficulties faced by information systems executives who ultimately are responsible for any harm done by systems developed by their staffs. In general, insofar as computer software is part of a machine, and the machine injures someone physically or economically, the producer of the software and the operator can be held liable for damages. Insofar as the software acts like a book, storing and displaying information, courts have been reluctant to hold authors, publishers, and booksellers liable for contents (the exception being instances of fraud or defamation), and hence courts have been wary of holding software authors liable for booklike software.

In general, it is very difficult (if not impossible) to hold software producers liable for their software products when those products are considered like books are, regardless of the physical or economic harm that results. Historically, print publishers, books, and periodicals have not been held liable because of fears that liability claims would interfere with First Amendment rights guaranteeing freedom of expression.

What about software as service? ATM machines are a service provided to bank customers. Should this service fail, customers will be inconvenienced and perhaps harmed economically if they cannot access their funds in a timely manner. Should liability protections be extended to software publishers and operators of defective financial, accounting, simulation, or marketing systems?

Software is very different from books. Software users may develop expectations of infallibility about software; software is less easily inspected than a book, and it is more difficult to compare with other software products for quality; software claims actually to perform a task rather than describe a task, as a book does; and people come to depend on services essentially based on software. Given the centrality of software to everyday life, the chances are excellent that liability law will extend its reach to include software even when the software merely provides an information service.

Telephone systems have not been held liable for the messages transmitted because they are regulated common carriers. In return for their right to provide telephone service, they must provide access to all, at reasonable rates, and achieve acceptable reliability. But broadcasters and cable television systems are subject to a wide variety of federal and local constraints on content and facilities. Organizations can be held liable for offensive content on their Web sites; and online services, such as America Online, might be held liable for postings by their users. Although U.S. courts have increasingly exonerated Web sites and ISPs for posting material by third parties, the threat of legal action still has a chilling effect on small companies or individuals who cannot afford to take their cases to trial.

## System Quality: Data Quality and System Errors

The debate over liability and accountability for unintentional consequences of system use raises a related but independent moral dimension: What is an acceptable, technologically feasible level of system quality? At what point should system managers say, "Stop testing, we've done all we can to perfect this software. Ship it!" Individuals and organizations may be held responsible for avoidable and foreseeable consequences, which they have a duty to perceive and correct. The gray area is that some system errors are foreseeable and correctable only at very great expense, an expense so great that pursuing this level of perfection is not feasible economically—no one could afford the product.

For example, although software companies try to debug their products before releasing them to the marketplace, they knowingly ship buggy products because the time and cost of fixing all minor errors would prevent these products from ever being released. What if the product was not offered on the marketplace, would social welfare as a whole not advance and perhaps even decline? Carrying this further, just what is the responsibility of a producer of computer services—should it withdraw the product that can never be perfect, warn the user, or forget about the risk (let the buyer beware)?

Three principal sources of poor system performance are (1) software bugs and errors, (2) hardware or facility failures caused by natural or other causes, and (3) poor input data quality. Computer scientists have found that zero defects in software code of any complexity cannot be achieved and the seriousness of remaining bugs cannot be estimated. Hence, there is a technological barrier to perfect software, and users must be aware of the potential for catastrophic failure. The software industry has not yet arrived at testing standards for producing software of acceptable but not perfect performance.

This topic is explored in the Focus on Technology, which describes how software contributed to the radiation poisoning of 28 patients at Panama's National Cancer Institute. As you read this case, try to determine what factors allowed this terrible tragedy to occur. How much was the software responsible for the problem? How much were "people" factors responsible? Who should be assigned blame? How should problems such as this one be prevented?

Although software bugs and facility catastrophes are likely to be widely reported in the press, by far the most common source of business system failure is data quality. Few companies routinely measure the quality of their data, but studies of individual organizations report data error rates ranging from 0.5 to 30 percent (Redman, 1998).

## Quality of Life: Equity, Access, and Boundaries

The negative social costs of introducing information technologies and systems are beginning to mount along with the power of the technology. Many of these negative social consequences are not violations of individual rights or property crimes. Nevertheless, these negative consequences can be extremely harmful to individuals, societies, and political institutions. Computers and information technologies potentially can destroy valuable elements of our culture and society even while they bring us benefits. If there is a balance of good and

## FOCUS ON TECHNOLOGY    When Software Kills: What Happened at Panama's National Cancer Institute

Victor Garcia feels lucky to be alive. He was one of 28 patients at the National Cancer Institute of Panama who received excessive doses of gamma ray radiation for cancer treatments in November 2000. Since then, 21 of these patients have died, and the International Atomic Energy Agency (IAEA) believes at least five of these deaths were caused by radiation poisoning.

The three Panamanian medical physicists who used the software to figure out the doses of radiation for these patients were charged with second-degree murder. Two of them were convicted and sentenced to four years in prison. Under Panamanian law, they were held responsible because they introduced changes in the software that guided the radiation therapy machine used on these patients. How could this tragedy have happened?

Before administering radiation treatment, a physician devises a treatment plan that determines what dose of radiation can be safely targeted at a cancerous tumor. The plan also specifies where to place metal shields known as "blocks" to protect noncancerous areas. Using this plan, a medical physicist inputs information on the size, shape, and location of the blocks into software for guiding radiation machines. The software creates a three-dimensional picture of how the dose will be distributed and calculates how long the radiation treatment should last.

The Panamanian medical physicists were following a doctor's instructions to be more protective of pelvic organs by adding a fifth block to the four blocks ordinarily used on cancer patients. However, the radiation machine software, which was created by Multidata Systems International of St. Louis, Missouri, was designed for treatments only when four or fewer blocks are prescribed.

Olivia Saldana Gonzalez, one of the Panamanian physicists, tried to make the software work for a fifth block. She entered the dimensions of all five blocks as a single composite shape. Although it looked like the system could work with this composite shape, the software miscalculated appropriate doses. Patients were subjected to 20 to 50 percent more radiation than they should have received.

Multidata insists that it did nothing wrong. Multidata's software manual stated it is "the responsibility of the user" to verify the results of the software's calculations. Had the hospital verified the radiation doses by manually checking the software's calculations or by testing the dosages in water before radiating patients, the staff would have found out about the overdoses before they were administered.

Unfortunately, National Cancer Institute physicists did not always manually verify the results of the software calculations. Three radiation physicists were working overtime to treat more than 100 patients per day because the hospital was understaffed. The IAEA found that the hospi-

tal examined only the functioning of the hardware. It had no quality assurance program for the software or for its results. Consequently, physicists were not required to tell anyone they had changed the way they entered data into the system and no one questioned the software's results.

Independent experts not associated with the case assert that the software that controls medical equipment and other life-critical devices should be designed to pause or shut down if told to execute a task it is not programmed to perform. When the IAEA investigated the National Cancer Institute incident in May 2001, it found other ways to get the software to miscalculate treatment times. Every time investigators treated one, two, or four blocks of varying shapes as a single block, the software miscalculated the treatment times.

The IAEA investigating team and a team from the M.D. Anderson Cancer Center in Houston found Multidata's manual did not describe precisely how to digitize coordinates of shielding blocks. The report also noted that the manual did not provide specific warnings against data entry approaches that are different from the standard procedure described.

Examiners from the U.S. Food and Drug Administration (FDA) who inspected Multidata in May 2001 found that Multidata had received at least six complaints about calculation errors related to the software's inability to handle certain types of blocks correctly. The examiners reported that Multidata had been aware that the errors existed since at least September 1992 but had not taken any corrective action. In 2003, Multidata signed a consent decree with the FDA that it would not make or sell software for radiation therapy devices in the United States, although it can sell its products abroad.

The two medical physicists who were convicted, Saldana Gonzalez and Alexis Concepcion, are appealing their convictions, and the survivors and families of the victims have filed lawsuits against Multidata. Panamanian courts have refused to hear the cases, but the families have filed their cases in St. Louis.

*Sources:* Deborah Gage and Berta Ramona Thayer, "U.S. Bound?" *Baseline,* April 1, 2005; John McCormick and Tom Steinert-Threlkeld, "Panama Technicians Found Guilty," *Baseline,* November 18, 2004; and Deborah Gage and John McCormick, "We Did Nothing Wrong," *Baseline,* March 2004.

**To Think About:**

What management, organization, and technology factors were responsible for the excess radiation doses at Panama's National Cancer Institute? Who was responsible for the malfunctioning of the system? Was an adequate solution developed for this problem? Explain your answer.

bad consequences of using information systems, who do we hold responsible for the bad consequences? Next, we briefly examine some of the negative social consequences of systems, considering individual, social, and political responses.

### Balancing Power: Center Versus Periphery

An early fear of the computer age was that huge, centralized mainframe computers would centralize power at corporate headquarters and in the nation's capital, resulting in a Big Brother society, as was suggested in George Orwell's novel *1984*. The shift toward highly decentralized computing, coupled with an ideology of empowerment of thousands of workers, and the decentralization of decision making to lower organizational levels have reduced the fears of power centralization in institutions. Yet much of the empowerment described in popular business magazines is trivial. Lower-level employees may be empowered to make minor decisions, but the key policy decisions may be as centralized as in the past.

### Rapidity of Change: Reduced Response Time to Competition

Information systems have helped to create much more efficient national and international markets. The now-more-efficient global marketplace has reduced the normal social buffers that permitted businesses many years to adjust to competition. Time-based competition has an ugly side: The business you work for may not have enough time to respond to global competitors and may be wiped out in a year, along with your job. We stand the risk of developing a "just-in-time society" with "just-in-time jobs" and "just-in-time" workplaces, families, and vacations.

### Maintaining Boundaries: Family, Work, and Leisure

Parts of this book were produced on trains and planes, as well as on family vacations and during what otherwise might have been "family" time. The danger of ubiquitous computing, telecommuting, nomad computing, and the "do anything anywhere" computing environment is that it might actually come true. If so, the traditional boundaries that separate work from family and just plain leisure will be weakened. Although authors have traditionally worked just about anywhere (typewriters have been portable for nearly a century), the advent of information systems, coupled with the growth of knowledge-work occupations, means that more and more people will be working when traditionally they would have been playing or communicating with family and friends. The work umbrella now extends far beyond the eight-hour day.

Weakening these institutions poses clear-cut risks. Family and friends historically have provided powerful support mechanisms for individuals, and they act as balance points in a society by preserving private life, providing a place for people to collect their thoughts, and allowing people to think in ways contrary to their employer and to dream.

Although some people enjoy the convenience of working at home, the "do anything anywhere" computing environment can blur the traditional boundaries between work and family time.

## Dependence and Vulnerability

Today, our businesses, governments, schools, and private associations, such as churches, are incredibly dependent on information systems and are, therefore, highly vulnerable if these systems fail. With information systems now as ubiquitous as the telephone system, it is startling to remember that there are no regulatory or standard-setting forces in place that are similar to telephone, electrical, radio, television, or other public-utility technologies. The absence of standards and the criticality of some system applications will probably call forth demands for national standards and perhaps regulatory oversight.

## Computer Crime and Abuse

New technologies, including computers, create new opportunities for committing crime by creating new valuable items to steal, new ways to steal them, and new ways to harm others. *Computer crime,* which we defined in Chapter 7, is the commission of illegal acts through the use of a computer or against a computer system. Computers or computer systems can be the object of the crime (destroying a company's computer center or a company's computer files), as well as the instrument of a crime (stealing computer lists by illegally gaining access to a computer system using a home computer). Simply accessing a computer system without authorization or with intent to do harm, even by accident, is now a federal crime.

*Computer abuse,* which we also introduced in Chapter 7, is the commission of acts involving a computer that may not be illegal but that are considered unethical. The popularity of the Internet and e-mail has turned one form of computer abuse—spamming—into a serious problem for both individuals and businesses. **Spam** is junk e-mail sent by an organization or individual to a mass audience of Internet users who have expressed no interest in the product or service being marketed. Spammers tend to market pornography, fraudulent deals and services, outright scams, and other products not widely approved in most civilized societies. Some countries have passed laws to outlaw spamming or to restrict its use. In the United States, it is still legal if it does not involve fraud and the sender and subject of the e-mail are properly identified.

Spamming has been growing because it only costs a few cents to send thousands of messages advertising wares to Internet users. Hundreds of CDs can be purchased on the Web that offer spammers millions of e-mail addresses harvested by software robots that read message boards, chat rooms, and Web sites. Alternatively, spammers can use their own harvesting tools for this purpose. These minuscule costs make spamming worthwhile if only one recipient in 100,000 e-mail messages sent makes a purchase. Figure 12-5 provides data on the scope of spamming and the types of industries most affected by the practice.

Spam consists of unsolicited e-mail messages, which can be bothersome, offensive, and even a drain on office worker productivity. Spam-filtering software such as McAfee's SpamKiller blocks suspicious e-mail.

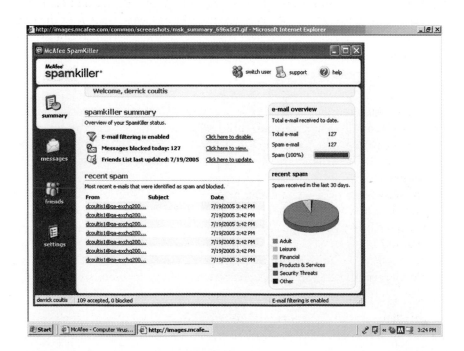

**Spam for Everyone**

Spam e-mail messages hawking many kinds of products and services, including scams, clog in-boxes of employees in many industries.

What is being offered . . .                                    . . .and to whom

*Products and services being sold with*          *Average number of spam e-mail*
*spam e-mail messages*                           *messages received daily per user*

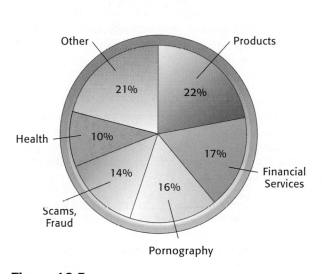

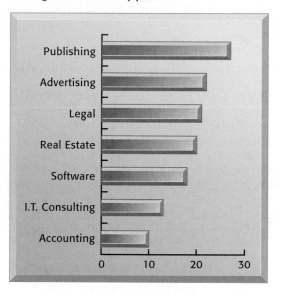

## Figure 12-5
The Spamming Problem
*This figure shows the major types of products and services hawked through spam e-mail messages and the industries that receive the most spam.*

Spamming is more tightly regulated in Europe than in the United States. On May 30, 2002, the European Parliament passed a ban on unsolicited commercial messaging. Electronic marketing can be targeted only to people who have given prior consent.

The spamming problem is a serious one because spam messages clog the Internet, negatively impacting business productivity, and spamming seems to be mushrooming out of control. The Focus on People examines efforts to halt spam through legislation and through technical means. As you read this case, try to identify the causes and scope of the spamming problem, what alternative solutions are available to address it, which solutions have been implemented, and how well the chosen solutions are working.

### Employment: Trickle-Down Technology and Reengineering Job Loss
Reengineering work is typically hailed in the information systems community as a major benefit of new information technology. It is much less frequently noted that redesigning business processes could potentially cause millions of middle-level managers and clerical workers to lose their jobs. One economist has raised the possibility that we will create a society run by a small "high tech elite of corporate professionals . . . in a nation of the permanently unemployed" (Rifkin, 1993).

Other economists are much more sanguine about the potential job losses. They believe relieving bright, educated workers from reengineered jobs will result in these workers moving to better jobs in fast-growth industries. Missing from this equation are unskilled, blue-collar workers and older, less well-educated middle managers. It is not clear that these groups can be retrained easily for high-quality (high-paying) jobs. Careful planning and sensitivity to employee needs can help companies redesign work to minimize job losses.

### Equity and Access: Increasing Racial and Social Class Cleavages
Does everyone have an equal opportunity to participate in the digital age? Information, knowledge, computers, and access to these resources through educational institutions and

E-mail may have made the Internet the most socially interactive medium in history, but spam is turning it into the most cluttered. Spam now accounts for 80 percent of e-mail traffic worldwide. If spam keeps growing at its current rate, the Internet will soon become unusable.

Spam costs for businesses are very high because of the computing and network resources consumed by billions of unwanted e-mail messages and the time consumed in trying to deal with them. Most e-mail messages take only a few seconds for recipients to delete, but some messages use subject headings requiring recipients to read the messages quickly to see if they are worthwhile.

A December 2004 survey from Stanford University found that a typical Internet user spends about 10 working days per year dealing with incoming spam. In a standard 250-day work year, reviewing and processing spam would thus consume 4 percent of each worker's productive time. Industry analysts estimate that the global cost of spam to businesses in terms of lost productivity and network maintenance is about $50 billion per year.

Spam continues to defy most legal and technical efforts to eliminate it. Many spam messages are sent from one country while another country hosts the spam Web site. In the past few years, spammers have teamed up with writers of viruses to steal lists of valid e-mail addresses and to hijack the personal computers of unwitting Internet users (see Chapter 7). Some experts believe that these "zombie networks" have become the major delivery system for spam.

Most corporate networks use spam filters, as do many Internet service providers. Individuals can purchase filtering software from companies such as Symantec, MailFrontier, or Trend Micro or use the filtering capabilities of major e-mail software. These tools block suspicious e-mail before it enters a recipient's e-mail inbox. Another technique for avoiding spam is to block any messages sent from computers or e-mail addresses known to be used by spammers.

However, spam filters can block legitimate messages, and many spammers skirt around filters by continually changing their e-mail accounts, creating false return addresses, or using cryptic phrases that most filters won't catch. Nevertheless, antispam systems appear to be good investments. An International Data Center study found that antispam systems in a typical company with 5,000 e-mail users halved the amount of time employees spent on e-mail, saving the company $783,000.

The U.S. CAN-SPAM Act of 2003, which went into effect on January 1, 2004, does not outlaw spamming but does ban deceptive e-mail practices by requiring commercial e-mail messages to display accurate subject lines, identify the true senders, and offer recipients an easy way to remove their names from e-mail lists. It also prohibits the use of fake return addresses.

This legislation has had little impact. A few people have been prosecuted under the law, and spamming has actually increased since it went into effect. A *Consumer Reports* study surveying more than 2,000 e-mail users found that 47 percent were receiving more spam three months after the law went into effect than before.

Antispam groups have pointed out that the law effectively gives spammers permission to send junk e-mail as long as they follow certain rules. According to Professor David E. Sorkin at the John Marshall School of Law in Chicago, "Before CAN-SPAM, the legal status of spam was ambiguous. Now it's clear: it's regarded as legal." And although CAN-SPAM makes it easier to know who is sending spam, it overrides stronger state statutes, some of which outlaw spam, and it has little impact on spammers based abroad.

CAN-SPAM puts the burden on recipients to choose to be removed from an e-mailer's list, an "opt-out" model of informed consent. Whereas a law-abiding bulk e-mailer would remove a person from its list, spammers tend to take opt-out messages as verification that an e-mail address is valid.

What will it take to stop spamming abuses? It will probably be impossible to outlaw commercial e-mail entirely. There are legitimate business and personal uses for e-mail, and many businesses using direct marketing do not wish to see e-mail heavily regulated. Some experts have suggested making all bulk e-mailers pay for sending mail to everyone's e-mail boxes. That would make legitimate businesses target their e-mail to only their best prospects, as do bulk mailers who use the postal system. If spammers were forced to pay for all the e-mail they spewed out, they might have to stop. Until something is done, the spam scourge is likely to continue—it's just too easy to send.

*Sources:* Tom Zeller, Jr., "Law Barring Junk E-Mail Allows a Flood Instead," *The New York Times,* February 1, 2005; Randall Stross, "How to Stop Junk E-Mail: Charge for the Stamp," *The New York Times,* February 13, 2005; Todd Spangler, "Fighting the Pox on Your Inbox," *Baseline,* March 2005; Saul Hansell, "Junk E-Mail and Fraud Are Focus of Crackdown," *The New York Times,* August 25, 2004; Brent Staples, "The Battle Against Junk Mail and Spyware on the Web," *The New York Times,* January 3, 2004; Thomas Claburn, "Anti-Spam Technologies Prove Their Value," *InformationWeek,* April 26, 2004; and Pui-Wing Tam, "Fruitcake Debutantes Defined by 0, and Other Spam Tricks," *The Wall Street Journal,* May 28, 2004.

**To Think About:**

How big is the spamming problem? What are its causes? What solutions have been proposed to deal with it? How effective are these solutions?

public libraries are inequitably distributed along ethnic and social class lines, as are many other information resources. Several studies have found that certain ethnic and income groups in the United States are less likely to have computers or online Internet access even though computer ownership and Internet access have soared in the past five years. Although the gap is narrowing, higher-income families in each ethnic group are still more likely to have home computers and Internet access than lower-income families in the same group.

A similar **digital divide** exists in U.S. schools, with schools in high-poverty areas less likely to have computers, high-quality educational technology programs, or Internet access availability for their students. Left uncorrected, the digital divide could lead to a society of information haves, computer literate and skilled, versus a large group of information have-nots, computer illiterate and unskilled. Public interest groups want to narrow this digital divide by making digital information services—including the Internet—available to virtually everyone, just as basic telephone service is now.

### Health Risks: RSI, CVS, and Technostress

The most important occupational disease today is **repetitive stress injury (RSI)**. RSI occurs when muscle groups are forced through repetitive actions often with high-impact loads (such as tennis) or tens of thousands of repetitions under low-impact loads (such as working at a computer keyboard).

The single largest source of RSI is computer keyboards. The most common kind of computer-related RSI is **carpal tunnel syndrome (CTS)**, in which pressure on the median nerve through the wrist's bony structure, called a carpal tunnel, produces pain. The pressure is caused by constant repetition of keystrokes: In a single shift, a word processor may perform 23,000 keystrokes. Symptoms of carpal tunnel syndrome include numbness, shooting pain, inability to grasp objects, and tingling. Millions of workers have been diagnosed with carpal tunnel syndrome.

RSI is avoidable. Designing workstations for a neutral wrist position (using a wrist rest to support the wrist), proper monitor stands, and footrests all contribute to proper posture and reduced RSI. New, ergonomically correct keyboards are also an option. These measures should be supported by frequent rest breaks and rotation of employees to different jobs.

RSI is not the only occupational illness computers cause. Back and neck pain, leg stress, and foot pain also result from poor ergonomic designs of workstations. **Computer vision syndrome (CVS)** refers to any eyestrain condition related to computer display screen use. Its symptoms, which are usually temporary, include headaches, blurred vision, and dry and irritated eyes.

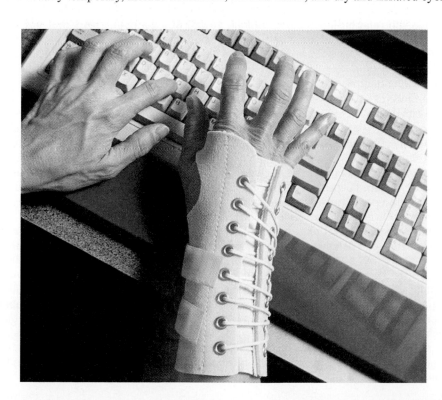

Repetitive stress injury (RSI) is the leading occupational disease today. The single largest cause of RSI is computer keyboard work.

The newest computer-related malady is **technostress**, which is stress induced by computer use. Its symptoms include aggravation, hostility toward humans, impatience, and fatigue. According to experts, humans working continuously with computers come to expect other humans and human institutions to behave like computers, providing instant responses, attentiveness, and an absence of emotion. Technostress is thought to be related to high levels of job turnover in the computer industry, high levels of early retirement from computer-intense occupations, and elevated levels of drug and alcohol abuse.

The incidence of technostress is not known but is thought to be in the millions and growing rapidly in the United States. Computer-related jobs now top the list of stressful occupations based on health statistics in several industrialized countries.

To date, the role of radiation from computer display screens in occupational disease has not been proved. Video display terminals (VDTs) emit nonionizing electric and magnetic fields at low frequencies. These rays enter the body and have unknown effects on enzymes, molecules, chromosomes, and cell membranes. Long-term studies are investigating low-level electromagnetic fields and birth defects, stress, low birth weight, and other diseases. All manufacturers have reduced display screen emissions since the early 1980s, and European countries, such as Sweden, have adopted stiff radiation emission standards.

The computer has become a part of our lives—personally as well as socially, culturally, and politically. It is unlikely that the issues and our choices will become easier as information technology continues to transform our world. The growth of the Internet and the information economy suggests that all the ethical and social issues we have described will be heightened further as we move into the first digital century.

---

**LEARNING TRACKS**

1. If you want to learn more about how to develop a corporate code of ethics for information systems, you will find a Learning Track on this topic at the Laudon Web site for this chapter.

---

## Summary

1. **Analyze the relationships among ethical, social, and political issues that are raised by information systems.** Information technology has raised new possibilities for behavior for which laws and rules of acceptable conduct have not yet been developed. Information technology is introducing changes that create new ethical issues for societies to debate and resolve. Increasing computing power, storage, and networking capabilities—including the Internet—can expand the reach of individual and organizational actions and magnify their impacts. The ease and anonymity with which information can be communicated, copied, and manipulated in online environments are challenging traditional rules of right and wrong behavior. Ethical, social, and political issues are closely related. Ethical issues confront individuals who must choose a course of action, often in a situation in which two or more ethical principles are in conflict (a dilemma). Social issues spring from ethical issues as societies develop expectations in individuals about the correct course of action. Political issues spring from social conflict and are mainly concerned with using laws that prescribe behavior to create situations in which individuals behave correctly.

2. **Identify the main moral dimensions of an information society and specific principles for conduct that can be used to guide ethical decisions.** The moral dimensions of information systems center around information rights and obligations, property rights and obligations, accountability and control, system quality, and quality of life. Six ethical principles are available to judge conduct. These principles are derived independently from several cultural, religious, and intellectual traditions and include the Golden Rule, Immanuel Kant's Categorical Imperative, Descartes' rule of change, the Utilitarian Principle, the Risk Aversion Principle, and the ethical "no free lunch" rule. These principles should be used in conjunction with an ethical analysis to guide decision making. The ethical analysis involves identifying the facts, values, stakeholders, options, and consequences of actions. Once completed, you can consider which ethical principle to apply to a situation to arrive at a judgment.

**3** **Evaluate the impact of contemporary information systems and the Internet on the protection of individual privacy and intellectual property.** Contemporary information systems technology, including Internet technology, challenges traditional regimens for protecting individual privacy and intellectual property. Data storage and data analysis technology enables companies to easily gather personal data about individuals from many different sources and analyze these data to create detailed electronic profiles about individuals and their behaviors. Data flowing over the Internet can be monitored at many points. The activities of Web site visitors can be closely tracked using cookies and other Web monitoring tools. Not all Web sites have strong privacy protection policies, and they do not always allow for informed consent regarding the use of personal information. The online industry prefers self-regulation to the U.S. government tightening privacy protection legislation.

Traditional copyright laws are insufficient to protect against software piracy because digital material can be copied so easily. Internet technology also makes intellectual property even more difficult to protect because digital material can be copied easily and transmitted to many different locations simultaneously over the Net. Web pages can be constructed easily using pieces of content from other Web sites without permission.

**4** **Assess how information systems have affected everyday life.** Although computer systems have been sources of efficiency and wealth, they have some negative impacts. Errors in large computer systems are impossible to eradicate totally. Computer errors can cause serious harm to individuals and organizations, and existing laws and social practices are often unable to establish liability and accountability for these problems. Less serious errors are often attributable to poor data quality, which can cause disruptions and losses for businesses. Jobs can be lost when computers replace workers or tasks become unnecessary in reengineered business processes. The ability to own and use a computer may be exacerbating socioeconomic disparities among different racial groups and social classes. Widespread use of computers increases opportunities for computer crime and computer abuse. Computers can also create health problems, such as repetitive stress injury, computer vision syndrome, and technostress.

## Key Terms

Accountability, 408
Carpal tunnel syndrome (CTS), 425
Computer vision syndrome (CVS), 425
Cookies, 413
Copyright, 416
Descartes' rule of change, 409
Digital divide, 425
Digital Millennium Copyright Act (DMCA), 417
Due process, 408
Ethical "no free lunch" rule, 410

Ethics, 404
Fair Information Practices (FIP), 411
Immanuel Kant's Categorical Imperative, 409
Information rights, 405
Informed consent, 413
Intellectual property, 416
Liability, 408
Nonobvious relationship awareness (NORA), 407
Opt-in, 414
Opt-out, 414
P3P, 415

Patent, 417
Privacy, 411
Profiling, 407
Repetitive stress injury (RSI), 425
Responsibility, 408
Risk Aversion Principle, 410
Safe harbor, 413
Spam, 422
Technostress, 426
Trade secret, 416
Utilitarian Principle, 410
Web bugs, 414

## Review Questions

**12.1** In what ways are ethical, social, and political issues connected? Give some examples.

**12.2** What are the key technological trends that heighten ethical concerns?

**12.3** What are the differences between responsibility, accountability, and liability?

**12.4** What are the five steps in an ethical analysis?

**12.5** Identify and describe six ethical principles.

**12.6** What is a professional code of conduct?

**12.7** What are meant by *privacy* and *fair information practices?*

**12.8** How is the Internet challenging the protection of individual privacy?

**12.9** What role can informed consent, legislation, industry self-regulation, and technology tools play in protecting the individual privacy of Internet users?

**12.10** What are the three different regimes that protect intellectual property rights? What challenges to intellectual property rights does the Internet pose?

**12.11** Why is it so difficult to hold software services liable for failure or injury?

**12.12** What is the most common cause of system quality problems?

**12.13** Name and describe four quality of life impacts of computers and information systems.

**12.14** What is technostress, and how would you identify it?

**12.15** Name three management actions that could reduce RSI injuries.

## Discussion Questions

**12.1** Should producers of software-based services, such as ATMs, be held liable for economic injuries suffered when their systems fail?

**12.2** Should companies be responsible for unemployment caused by their information systems? Why or why not?

## Application Software Exercise

### Word Processing and Web Page Development Tool Exercise: Creating a Simple Web Site

Software skills: Web page creation

Business skills: Web page design

Build a simple Web site of your own design for a business using the Web page creation function of Microsoft Word, Microsoft FrontPage, or a Web page development tool of your choice. Your Web site should include a home page with a description of your business and at least one picture or graphic. From the home page, you must be able to link to a second Web page and, from there, link to a third Web page. Make the home page long enough so that when you arrive at the bottom of the page, you can no longer see the top. At the bottom of your Web page include a link back to the top. Also include a link to one of the secondary Web pages. On the secondary page, include a link to the top of that page and a link back to the top of the home page. Also include a link to the third page, which should contain a link to its own top and a link back to the top of the home page. Finally, on one of the secondary pages, include another picture or graphic, and on the other page include an object that you create using Microsoft Excel or other spreadsheet software. The Laudon Web site for Chapter 5 includes instructions for completing this project. If you have tested every function and all work to your satisfaction, save the pages you have created for submission to your instructor.

### Developing a Web Site Privacy Policy

Business skills: Corporate privacy policy formulation

Dirt Bikes's management wants to make sure it has policies and procedures in place to protect the privacy of visitors to its Web site. You have been asked to develop Dirt Bikes's Web site privacy policy. The TRUSTe Web site at www.truste.org has Model Privacy Disclosures in its Privacy Resources for businesses that you can download and review to help you draft Dirt Bikes's privacy policy. You can also examine specific companies' privacy policies by searching for Web site privacy policies on Yahoo!, Google, or another search engine. Prepare a report for management that addresses the following issues:

1. How much data should Dirt Bikes collect on visitors to its Web site? What information could it discover by tracking visitors' activities at its Web site? What value would this information provide to the company? What are the privacy problems raised by collecting such data?

2. Should Dirt Bikes use cookies? What are the advantages of using cookies for both Dirt Bikes and its Web site visitors? What privacy issues do they create for Dirt Bikes?

3. Should Dirt Bikes join an organization such as TRUSTe to certify that it has adopted approved privacy practices? Why or why not?

4. Should Dirt Bikes design its site so that it conforms to P3P standards? Why or why not?

5. Should Dirt Bikes adopt an opt-in or opt-out model of informed consent?

6. Include in your report a short (two to three pages) privacy statement for the Dirt Bikes Web site. You can use the categories of the TRUSTe Model Privacy Disclosures as a guideline, if you wish.

7. (Optional) Use electronic presentation software to summarize your recommendations for management.

## Building Internet Skills

### Using Internet Newsgroups for Online Market Research

This project will help develop your Internet skills in using newsgroups for marketing.

You are producing hiking boots that you are selling through a few stores at this time. You think your boots are more comfortable than those of your competition. You believe you can undersell many of your competitors if you can significantly increase your production and sales. You would like to use Internet discussion groups interested in hiking, climbing, and camping both to sell your boots and to make them well known. Visit Google's Usenet archives (groups.google.com), which stores discussion postings from many thousands of newsgroups. Through this site you can locate all relevant newsgroups and search them by keyword, author's name, forum, date, and subject. Choose a message and examine it carefully, noting all the information you can obtain, including information about the author.

1. How could you use these newsgroups to market your boots?

2. What ethical principles might you be violating if you use these messages to sell your boots? Do you think there are ethical problems in this type of use of the newsgroups? Explain your answer.

3. Decide whether you want to use the newsgroups to locate Web sites on the hiking boots industry. Examine the various sites to determine whether there are other ways to draw potential buyers to the Web site you may decide to establish.

4. Next, go to Yahoo.com to search for the hiking boots industry and locate sites that will help you develop other new ideas for contacting potential customers.

5. Given what you have learned in this and previous chapters, prepare a plan to use newsgroups and other alternative methods to begin attracting visitors to your site.

## Video Case

You will find a video case illustrating some of the concepts in this chapter on the Laudon Web site at **www.prenhall.com/laudon** along with questions to help you analyze the case.

## Teamwork

### Developing a Corporate Ethics Code

With three or four of your classmates, develop a corporate ethics code on privacy that addresses both employee privacy and the privacy of customers and users of the corporate Web site. Be sure to consider e-mail privacy and employer monitoring of worksites, as well as corporate use of information about employees concerning their off-the-job behavior (e.g., lifestyle, marital arrangements, and so forth). If possible, use electronic presentation software to present your ethics code to the class.

## BUSINESS PROBLEM-SOLVING CASE

### Should We Trust ChoicePoint with Our Personal Data?

Since 1899, Equifax Inc. has been providing information, marketing, and personal services to consumers and businesses from its collection of credit, financial, public record, demographic, and other databases. In 1993, Derek Smith took over a unit at Equifax that collected data for insurers and banks to use in determining whether their customers were creditworthy. Smith saw that the information his unit stored, along with droves of additional information Equifax could acquire, could be used for many more purposes than credit checks and authorizations. He set about acquiring dozens of other data management companies and their thousands of databases filled with criminal records, bankruptcy filings, court judgments, birth and death certificates, divorce records, and lien information.

In 1997, Equifax officially incorporated the unit under the name ChoicePoint, with Smith as the CEO. ChoicePoint's goal was to transition from "the premier source of data to the insurance industry" to "the premier provider of decision-making intelligence to businesses and government." Today, ChoicePoint directs more than 5,000 employees from its headquarters in Alpharetta, Georgia, outside of Atlanta. ChoicePoint describes its operations as the identification, retrieval, storage, analysis, and delivery of data. The company serves businesses of all sizes as well as federal, state, and local governments. In 2004, ChoicePoint performed more than seven million background checks. It processes thousands of credit card transactions every second.

While no one was really paying attention, the company created powerful resources for a huge market in personal data. ChoicePoint builds these resources through an extensive network of contractors who gather bits of information from public filings, financial-services firms, phone directories, and loan application forms. The contractors use police departments, school districts, the department of motor vehicles, and local courts to fill their caches. All of the information is public and legal.

ChoicePoint possesses 19 billion records containing personal information on the vast majority of American adult consumers. According to Daniel J. Solove, associate professor of law at George Washington University, the company has collected information on nearly every adult American and "these are dossiers that J. Edgar Hoover would be envious of."

Unlike banks or companies selling credit reports, companies such as ChoicePoint with massive private databases are largely unregulated. There has been little or no federal or state oversight of how they collect, maintain, and sell their data. But these private data brokers have been allowed to flourish because there is such a huge market for personal information and they provide useful services for insurance companies, banks, employers, and federal, state, and local government agencies. CEO Smith theorizes that society is safer and more secure when its members are able to check each other's backgrounds.

His case is supported by the terrorist attacks of September 11, 2001, the fallout from the attacks, and the Washington, D.C., sniper case. After the terrorist attacks, ChoicePoint experimented with pulling likely terrorists out of its databases. It helped the government screen candidates for the new federally controlled airport security workforce. ChoicePoint also contributed to the very difficult task of identifying victims of the terrorist attacks through its DNA lab. In the sniper case, investigators tracked the suspect's car with ChoicePoint data.

For all the good that ChoicePoint's massive databases have done and can do, the downside is the threat they pose to personal privacy and social well-being. First, they have the potential to do damage because the quality of the data they maintain can be unreliable. Inaccuracies in ChoicePoint data have caused people to lose their jobs and their savings.

In one case, Boston Market received a background check on an employee that included felony convictions. Because the employee had not listed the felonies on his employment application, Boston Market fired him. However, the report had been wrong. The worker had been convicted of misdemeanors but never felonies. He sued Boston Market and his former manager for libel and slander. Boston Market, in turn, sued ChoicePoint for providing faulty data and sought damages to cover those it might owe to the employee. In another case, a retired GE assembly-line worker was charged a higher insurance premium because another person's driving record, with multiple accidents, had been added to his file.

According to ChoicePoint, only .0008 percent of the 7.3 million background checks it turned over to customers in 2004 contained erroneous information. However, ChoicePoint does not check the accuracy of each record it collects and stores. It assumes the data are accurate when they arrive and only counts errors associated with a dispute.

The more visible problem, has been the vulnerability of ChoicePoint's data. ChoicePoint has served customers of all sizes, from the federal government to small storefront businesses. Although not simply anyone can receive an account that grants access to ChoicePoint data, the credentials required to do so are not very stringent. It is this condition that introduces irony into Smith's vision. The very system that he established to reduce crime and promote economic efficiency has created a new door to criminal activity. ChoicePoint's problems with data falling into the wrong hands come at a time when the public is already significantly fearful of identity theft and fraud.

In October 2004, ChoicePoint employees contacted the Los Angeles county sheriff's office. The employees were suspicious of the credentials used by a dozen small-business owners to gain access to the system. Their suspicions were reinforced by contact with a particular customer with an accent who identified himself over the phone as James Garrett of MBS Collections. Shortly after Garrett opened an account, a man whose voice sounded similar to Garrett's opened an account for Gallo Financial under the name John Galloway. When ChoicePoint received faxes of the men's driver's licenses for identification purposes, the photos on the licenses looked identical.

ChoicePoint worked with police to set up a sting operation. They instructed James Garrett to go to a particular store to pick up a fax. Investigators moved in on the man and found him with ChoicePoint forms filled out for both MBS Collections and Gallo Financial. His name was neither James Garrett nor John Galloway. The forms in 41-year-old Nigerian Olatunji Oluwatosin's possession revealed the relative ease with which one could apply for a ChoicePoint account. The most complex piece of information required on the application was a business license number. The rest of the one-page form asked only for basic information and a brief description of how the service would be used for the business. Oluwatosin had filled in this field on both applications with only one simple sentence saying that his company collected debt. The form did include an advisement from ChoicePoint saying that use of its data was limited to appropriate business purposes.

Dan McGinn, a spokesperson for ChoicePoint, admits that the company's vetting procedures during that time included documentation checks but had vulnerabilities that Oluwatosin exploited. The investigation into Oluwatosin's activities reveals that those vulnerabilities had far-reaching consequences. Oluwatosin had multiple cell phones and credit cards issued to different names. The credit cards were obtained fraudulently and used to make thousands of dollars worth of fraudulent charges. Evidence found at Oluwatosin's home pointed investigators to post office boxes that were receiving mail that had been redirected from thousands of different people. In the home, they also discovered printouts from 17,000 searches of ChoicePoint databases.

Further investigation uncovered an identity theft ring, of which Oluwatosin was a part. Detective Duane Decker of the Los Angeles county sheriff's department initially estimated that the thieves may have downloaded the personal profiles of four million people. ChoicePoint acknowledges that 145,000 consumers' profiles were compromised and disputes the authorities' estimate. Overall, the identity theft ring created 50 fraudulent accounts with ChoicePoint using fake business names and paying fees as low as $100. Oluwatosin and the other account operators in the ring changed the mailing addresses of at least 750 people. The criminals then used their victims' identities to open fraudulent credit accounts. Oluwatosin was charged with six felony counts. In February 2005, he pleaded no contest to one count of unlawful use of personal identification and was sentenced to 16 months in prison. He has not cooperated with authorities that want to pin down additional perpetrators.

Authorities did descend on another Nigerian national in Los Angeles, 38-year-old Adedayo Benson. Benson was sentenced to five and a half years in federal prison and ordered to pay more than $150,000 in restitution to 10 different financial institutions. In most cases like this, victims have no responsibility for identity theft. Liability for losses incurred generally falls on the financial institutions, which pass along the expense to merchants.

Not surprisingly, ChoicePoint has come under intense scrutiny for everything from not having adequate security to not disclosing the security breach expeditiously. The company defended the four-month wait saying that law enforcement wanted the incident kept under wraps until the investigation concluded. Lieutenant Ronnie Williams, project director of the Southern California Identity Theft Task Force, says that his agency did ask ChoicePoint to delay disclosure of the security breach for 30 days on November 23, 2004, but the company was free to notify customers by January 1, 2005. ChoicePoint stated that it needed time to determine which records had been stolen. Not disclosing the breach to individual consumers was never an option because approximately 35,000 of them were in California. State law in California compels companies to alert residents whose personal data have been compromised. ChoicePoint notified all of its affected customers throughout the United States.

As a result of the scam, ChoicePoint is changing its approach to selling data. It is curtailing the sale of products that contain sensitive data, such as social security and driver's license ID numbers. In some cases, it is truncating the numbers. The changes will have the greatest impact on small businesses, including private investigators, collection agencies, and nonbank financial institutions, who will find their access to the data much more limited. ChoicePoint is also implementing stronger credentialing processes, in some cases requiring physical site visits to verify the legitimacy of a person or organization. To fortify its efforts, the company named Carol A. DiBattiste, former deputy administrator of the Transportation Security Administration, to the senior management position of Chief Credentialing, Compliance, and Privacy Officer. DiBattiste works out of an independent office in Washington, D.C. From there she oversees the company's screening processes and procedures for reporting security breaches. She will also manage the expansion of the site-visiting program.

On the Privacy section of its Web site, ChoicePoint enumerates the specific measures it has taken to limit access to personal data. The policy states that ChoicePoint only provides personal information under three circumstances: to support consumer-driven transactions, such as insurance and mortgages; to provide authentication or fraud prevention tools to large accredited corporate clients to verify the identities of customers; and to assist federal, state, or local governments, as well as criminal justice agencies. ChoicePoint also outlines the ways in which it is strengthening its customer credentialing procedures: It is expanding its site-visit and audit programs; verifying customer authenticity from multiple sources; monitoring customer account reviews performed by second-level analysts or managers; and enhancing user ID and password protections. In addition to recredentialing much of its customer base, ChoicePoint is also creating a Corporate Credential Center to standardize the credentialing procedure and has appointed a former Secret Service agent to liaison with law enforcement officials.

The breach at ChoicePoint occurred at a time when privacy and data security were already hot-button issues in the nation's capital. Similar incidents at CardSystems Solutions, Citigroup, Bank of America, Time Warner, and LexisNexis have put both consumers and lawmakers on edge. Interest has risen in putting private data brokers' databases under the same regulations that govern credit reports. Senator Dianne Feinstein of California has proposed a federal law that replicates her state's law, which requires companies to inform customers when their personal data files have been compromised. Florida Senator Bill Nelson has explored the idea of empowering the Federal Trade Commission (FTC) to oversee information brokers. The FTC already regulates companies that manage financial and medical records. Marc Rotenberg of the Electronic Privacy Information Center in Washington, D.C., believes that the ChoicePoint case is a clear demonstration that self-regulation does not work in the information business. He has solicited the FTC for an investigation into whether ChoicePoint and other companies are in compliance with the Fair Credit Reporting Act.

Chuck Jones, a spokesperson for ChoicePoint, says that the company might support federal legislation. He states, "ChoicePoint has always been a proponent of responsible use of consumer data and we remain hopeful that there will be a national discussion for improving policies that involves legislators, privacy experts and industry, to help establish better ground rules for this issue moving forward." Ray Everett-Church, a privacy expert who owns the consulting firm PrivacyClue, is skeptical about ChoicePoint's dedication to protecting consumers. Everett-Church charges, "They're taking [consumer data] in the front door with the promise of protection and shoving it out the back door as fast as they can to the highest bidders." He believes that the first priority of companies such as ChoicePoint is to maximize profits for shareholders. ChoicePoint estimates that the changes it has already made will cost the company $15 million to $20 million in annual revenue, which equals approximately 2 percent of its annual sales.

Meanwhile, the company is embroiled in another controversy. The Securities and Exchange Commission (SEC) is investigating whether Smith and chief operating officer (COO) and president Doug Curling illegally sold large quantities of their company stock shortly after the security breach occurred. ChoicePoint claims that these types of sales are approved by the board of directors months ahead of time, specifically to avoid the appearance of impropriety, and the two executives did not even learn of the breach until much later.

Sources: Evan Perez and Rick Brooks, "For Big Vendor of Personal Data, A Theft Lays Bare the Downside," The Wall Street Journal, May 3, 2005; Matt Hines, "ChoicePoint Data Theft Widens to 145,000 People," ZDNet, February 18, 2005; John Schwartz, "Some Sympathy for Paris Hilton," The New York Times, February 27, 2005; Deborah Gage and John McCormick, "Blur," Baseline, June 2005; "ChoicePoint Toughens Data Security," CNN/Money, July 5, 2005; Aleksandr Rozens, "U.S. Probing ChoicePoint over Data Theft," Reuters (accessed through Yahoo! News), March 4, 2005; Evan Perez, "Identity Theft Puts Pressure on Data Sellers," The Wall Street Journal, February 21, 2005; "ChoicePoint Hires to Help Improve Screening," Associated Press (accessed through Yahoo! Finance), March 8, 2005; Tom Zeller, Jr., "Release of Consumers' Data Spurs ChoicePoint Inquiries," The New York Times, March 5, 2005; Christopher Conkey and Emily Nelson, "Senate Spotlight Turns to Data Security," The Wall Street Journal, March 11, 2005; and Tom Zeller, Jr., "Another Data Broker Reports a Breach," The New York Times, March 10, 2005.

## Case Study Questions

1. What are the problems and ethical issues highlighted in this case? What is the source of these problems?
2. Who is responsible for these problems: ChoicePoint, the business community, or state and federal government? Explain your answer.
3. What solutions has ChoicePoint tried to solve the problem? How effective are these solutions?
4. What other solutions should be pursued?

Congratulations! By completing your information systems course and using this book, you've made great strides in preparing for your future business career. Employers are actively seeking people who know how to use information technologies to work more efficiently and effectively, and who can use these tools to help them solve problems.

If you've worked through some or all of these projects, here are some of the skills and competencies you'll be able to demonstrate:

## Business Application Skills

You've acquired software skills and business application knowledge. You know how to use spreadsheet, database, and Web page creation tools in business applications for finance and accounting, human resources, manufacturing and production, and sales and marketing.

## Internet Skills

You know how to use Internet tools to access information, conduct research, or perform online calculations and analysis.

## Analytical, Writing, and Presentation Skills

You know how to research a specific topic, analyze a problem, think creatively, suggest a solution, and prepare a clear written or oral presentation of the solution, working either individually or with others in a group.

The front endpapers of this book contain a complete list of the skills and proficiencies in each of these areas developed by using *Essentials of Business Information Systems,* Seventh Edition. (If you are an instructor, you can use this same list as a learning assessment tool.)

## Making This Book Work for You and Your Career

Keep your work for the Application Software Exercises, running case projects, Building Internet Skills projects, Teamwork projects, and case studies that you have personally completed. You'll definitely be able to use this material when you are job hunting.

We've created a special section of the Laudon student Web site (www.prenhall. com/laudon) devoted to career building. There you'll find instructions and templates to show you how to create a structured digital portfolio demonstrating your mastery of problem-solving and information systems skills for use in job hunting. The Web site includes instructions for the following:

- How to incorporate software, business, and problem-solving skills acquired from this course in resumes and cover letters, both paper-based and electronic. We provide sample resumes and cover letters tailored to jobs in finance, accounting, marketing, human resources, manufacturing/production/operations management, and information systems.
- How and when to highlight your problem-solving and information system skills and business application knowledge in interviews.
- How to organize your work completed for this course into a supplementary digital portfolio and personal Web page for employers requiring more detail about you.
- Tips on career opportunities and job hunting, including links to useful job-hunting sites.

Good luck in developing your career!

**2.5G networks**  Wireless cellular networks that are packet switched and provide higher-speed data transmission rates ranging from 50 to 144 Kbps using the existing cellular network infrastructure.

**3G networks**  Cellular networks based on packet-switched technology with speeds ranging from 144 Kbps for mobile users to more than 2 Mbps for stationary users, enabling users to transmit video, graphics, and other rich media, in addition to voice.

**802.11b**  Wireless LAN standard that can transmit up to 11 Mbps in the unlicensed 2.4-GHz band and has an effective distance of 30 to 50 meters.

**acceptable use policy (AUP)**  Defines acceptable uses of the firm's information resources and computing equipment, including desktop and laptop computers, wireless devices, telephones, and the Internet, and specifies consequences for noncompliance.

**acceptance testing**  Provides the final certification that the system is ready to be used in a production setting.

**access control**  Policies and procedures a company uses to prevent improper access to systems by unauthorized insiders and outsiders.

**access point**  Box in a wireless LAN consisting of a radio receiver/transmitter and antennae that link to a wired network, router, or hub.

**accountability**  The mechanisms for assessing responsibility for decisions made and actions taken.

**accumulated balance digital payment systems**  Systems enabling users to make micropayments and purchases on the Web, accumulating a debit balance on their credit cards or telephone bills.

**analytical CRM**  Customer relationship management applications dealing with the analysis of customer data to provide information for improving business performance.

**antivirus software**  Software designed to detect, and often eliminate, computer viruses from an information system.

**applet**  Miniature program designed to reside on centralized network servers.

**application proxy filtering**  Firewall screening technology that uses a proxy server to inspect and transmit data packets flowing into and out of the organization so that all the organization's internal applications communicate with the outside using a proxy application.

**application server**  Software that handles all application operations between browser-based computers and a company's back-end business applications or databases.

**application service provider (ASP)**  Company providing software that can be rented by other companies over the Web or a private network.

**application software**  Programs written for a specific application to perform functions specified by end users.

**artificial intelligence (AI)**  The effort to develop computer-based systems that can behave like humans, with the ability to learn languages, accomplish physical tasks, use a perceptual apparatus, and emulate human expertise and decision making.

**asynchronous transfer mode (ATM)**  A networking technology that parcels information into 8-byte cells, allowing data to be transmitted between computers from different vendors at any speed.

**attributes**  Pieces of information describing a particular entity.

**audio input**  Voice input devices, such as microphones, that convert spoken words into digital form for processing by the computer.

**audio output**  Voice output devices that convert digital output data back into intelligible speech.

**authentication**  The ability of each party in a transaction to ascertain the identity of the other party.

**authorization management systems**  Systems for allowing each user access only to those portions of a system or the Web that person is permitted to enter, based on information established by a set of access rules.

**authorization policies**  Policies that determine differing levels of access to information assets for different levels of users in an organization.

**autonomic computing**  Effort to develop systems that can manage themselves without user intervention.

**backbone**  Part of a network handling the major traffic and providing the primary path for traffic flowing to or from other networks.

**bandwidth**  The capacity of a communications channel as measured by the difference between the highest and lowest frequencies that can be transmitted by that channel.

**banner ad**  A graphic display on a Web page used for advertising. The banner is linked to the advertiser's Web site so that a person clicking on it will be transported to the advertiser's Web site.

**batch processing**  A method of collecting and processing data in which transactions are accumulated and stored until a specified time when it is convenient or necessary to process them as a group.

**benchmarking**   Setting strict standards for products, services, or activities and measuring organizational performance against those standards.

**best practices**   The most successful solutions or problem-solving methods that have been developed by a specific organization or industry.

**biometric authentication**   Technology for authenticating system users that compares a person's unique characteristics, such as fingerprints, face, or retinal image, against a stored set profile of these characteristics.

**bit**   A binary digit representing the smallest unit of data in a computer system. It can only have one of two states, representing 0 or 1.

**blog**   Popular term for Web log, designating an informal yet structured Web site where individuals can publish stories, opinions, and links to other Web sites of interest.

**Bluetooth**   Standard for wireless personal area networks that can transmit up to 722 Kbps within a 10-meter area.

**botnet**   A group of computers that have been infected with bot malware without users' knowledge, enabling a hacker to use the amassed resources of the computers to launch distributed denial-of-service attacks, phishing campaigns, or spam.

**broadband**   High-speed transmission technology. Also designates a single communications medium that can transmit multiple channels of data simultaneously.

**bullwhip effect**   Distortion of information about the demand for a product as it passes from one entity to the next across the supply chain.

**bundling**   Cross-selling in which a combination of products is sold as a bundle at a price lower than the total cost of the individual products.

**bus networks**   Network topology linking a number of computers by a single circuit with all messages broadcast to the entire network.

**business**   A formal organization whose aim is to produce products or provide services for a profit.

**business continuity planning**   Planning that focuses on how the company can restore business operations after a disaster strikes.

**business intelligence (BI)**   Applications and technologies to help users make better business decisions.

**business model**   An abstraction of what an enterprise is and how the enterprise delivers a product or service, showing how the enterprise creates wealth.

**business process reengineering (BPR)**   The radical redesign of business processes, combining steps to cut waste and eliminating repetitive, paper-intensive tasks in order to improve cost, quality, and service, and to maximize the benefits of information technology.

**business processes**   The unique ways in which organizations coordinate and organize work activities, information, and knowledge to produce a product or service.

**business strategy**   Set of activities and decisions that determine the products and services the firm produces, the industries in which the firm competes, firm competitors, suppliers, and customers, and the firm's long-term goals.

**business-to-business (B2B) electronic commerce**   Electronic sales of goods and services among businesses.

**business-to-consumer (B2C) electronic commerce**   Electronic retailing of products and services directly to individual consumers.

**byte**   A string of bits, usually eight, used to store one number or character in a computer system.

**C**   A powerful programming language with tight control and efficiency of execution; portable across different microprocessors and used primarily with PCs.

**C++**   Object-oriented version of the C programming language.

**cable Internet connections**   Internet connections that use digital cable coaxial lines to deliver high-speed Internet access to homes and businesses.

**call center**   An organizational department responsible for handling customer service issues by telephone and other channels.

**campus area network (CAN)**   An interconnected set of local-area networks in a limited geographical area, such as a college or corporate campus.

**capacity planning**   The process of predicting when a computer hardware system becomes saturated to ensure that adequate computing resources are available for work of different priorities and that the firm has enough computing power for its current and future needs.

**carpal tunnel syndrome (CTS)**   Type of RSI in which pressure on the median nerve through the wrist's bony carpal tunnel structure produces pain.

**case-based reasoning (CBR)**   Artificial intelligence technology that represents knowledge as a database of cases and solutions.

**cathode ray tube (CRT)**   Electronic gun that shoots a beam of electrons illuminating pixels on a display screen.

**CD-ROM (compact disk read-only memory)**   Read-only optical disk storage used for imaging, reference, and database applications with massive amounts of unchanging data and for multimedia.

**CD-RW (CD-ReWritable)**   Optical disk storage that can be rewritten many times by users.

**cellular telephones (cell phones)**   A device that transmits voice or data, using radio waves to communicate with radio antennas placed within adjacent geographic areas called cells.

**central processing unit (CPU)**   Area of the computer system that manipulates symbols, numbers, and letters, and controls the other parts of the computer system.

**centralized processing**   Processing that is accomplished by one large central computer.

**change agent**   In the context of implementation, the individual acting as the catalyst during the change process to ensure successful organizational adaptation to a new system or innovation.

**change management**   Giving proper consideration to the impact of organizational change associated with a new system or alteration of an existing system.

**chat** Live, interactive conversations over a public network.

**chief information officer (CIO)** Senior manager in charge of the information systems function in the firm.

**chief security officer (CSO)** Heads a formal security function for the organization and is responsible for enforcing the firm's security policy.

**choice** Simon's third stage of decision making, when the individual selects among the various solution alternatives.

**churn rate** Measurement of the number of customers who stop using or purchasing products or services from a company. Used as an indicator of the growth or decline of a firm's customer base.

**clicks-and-mortar** Business model where the Web site is an extension of a traditional bricks-and-mortar business.

**clickstream tracking** Tracking data about customer activities at Web sites and storing them in a log.

**client** The user point of entry for the required function in client/server computing; normally a desktop computer, workstation, or laptop computer.

**client/server computing** A model for computing that splits processing between clients and servers on a network, assigning functions to the machine most able to perform the function.

**coaxial cable** A transmission medium consisting of thickly insulated copper wire; can transmit large volumes of data quickly.

**COBOL (COmmon Business Oriented Language)** Major programming language for business applications because it can process large data files with alphanumeric characters.

**Code Division Multiple Access (CDMA)** Major cellular transmission standard in the United States that transmits over several frequencies, occupies the entire spectrum, and randomly assigns users to a range of frequencies over time.

**collaborative filtering** Tracking users' movements on a Web site, comparing the information gleaned about a user's behavior against data about other customers with similar interests to predict what the user would like to see next.

**co-location** Web hosting approach in which the firm actually purchases and owns the server computer housing its Web site but locates the server in the physical facility of the hosting service.

**competitive forces model** Model used to describe the interaction of external influences, specifically threats and opportunities that affect an organization's strategy and ability to compete.

**compiler** Special system software that translates a high-level language into machine language for execution by the computer.

**component-based development** Building large software systems by combining preexisting software components.

**computer** Physical device that takes data as an input, transforms the data by executing stored instructions, and outputs information to a number of devices.

**computer abuse** The commission of acts involving a computer that may not be illegal but are considered unethical.

**computer-aided design (CAD) system** Information system that automates the creation and revision of designs using sophisticated graphics software.

**computer-aided software engineering (CASE)** Automation of step-by-step methodologies for software and systems development to reduce the amounts of repetitive work the developer needs to do.

**computer crime** The commission of illegal acts through the use of a computer or against a computer system.

**computer forensics** The scientific collection, examination, authentication, preservation, and analysis of data held on or retrieved from computer storage media in such a way that the information can be used as evidence in a court of law.

**computer hardware** Physical equipment used for input, processing, and output activities in an information system.

**computer literacy** Knowledge about information technology, focusing on understanding of how computer-based technologies work.

**computer mouse** Handheld device with point-and-click capabilities for selecting commands and controlling a computer display screen.

**computer software** Detailed, preprogrammed instructions that control and coordinate the work of computer hardware components in an information system.

**computer virus** Rogue software program that attaches itself to other software programs or data files in order to be executed, often causing hardware and software malfunctions.

**computer vision syndrome (CVS)** Eyestrain condition related to computer display screen use; symptoms include headaches, blurred vision, and dry and irritated eyes.

**consumer-to-consumer (C2C) electronic commerce** Consumers selling goods and services electronically to other consumers.

**controls** All of the methods, policies, and procedures that ensure protection of the organization's assets, accuracy and reliability of its records, and operational adherence to management standards.

**conversion** The process of changing from the old system to the new system.

**cookies** Tiny files deposited on a computer hard drive when an individual visits certain Web sites; used to identify the visitor and track visits to the Web site.

**copyright** A statutory grant that protects creators of intellectual property against copying by others for any purpose during the life of the author plus an additional 70 years after the author's death.

**core competency** Activity at which a firm excels as a world-class leader.

**cost–benefit ratio** A method for calculating the returns from a capital expenditure by dividing total benefits by total costs.

**cost transparency** The ability of consumers to discover the actual costs merchants pay for products.

**cracker** A hacker with criminal intent.

**critical thinking** Sustained suspension of judgment with an awareness of multiple perspectives and alternatives.

**cross-selling**   Marketing complementary products to customers.

**culture**   Fundamental set of assumptions, values, and ways of doing things that has been accepted by most members of an organization.

**customer decision-support systems (CDSS)**   Systems to support the decision-making process of an existing or potential customer.

**customer lifetime value (CLTV)**   Difference between revenues produced by a specific customer and the expenses for acquiring and servicing that customer over the lifetime of the customer relationship, expressed in today's dollars.

**customer relationship management (CRM) systems**   Information systems that track all the ways in which a company interacts with its customers and analyze these interactions to optimize revenue, profitability, customer satisfaction, and customer retention.

**customization**   The modification of a software package to meet an organization's unique requirements without destroying the package software's integrity.

**cybervandalism**   Intentional disruption, defacement, or even destruction of a Web site or corporate information system.

**cycle time**   The total elapsed time from the beginning of a process to its end.

**data**   Streams of raw facts representing events occurring in organizations or the physical environment before they have been organized and arranged into a form that people can understand and use.

**data administration**   A special organizational function for managing the organization's data resources, concerned with information policy, data planning, maintenance of data dictionaries, and data quality standards.

**data cleansing**   Activities for detecting and correcting data in a database or file that are incorrect, incomplete, improperly formatted, or redundant. Also known as data scrubbing.

**data definition**   Specifies the structure of the content of a database.

**data dictionary**   An automated or manual tool for storing and organizing information about the data maintained in a database.

**data flow diagram (DFD)**   Primary tool for structured analysis that graphically illustrates a system's component processes and the flow of data between them.

**data management software**   Software used for creating and manipulating lists, creating files and databases to store data, and combining information for reports.

**data management technology**   The software that governs the organization of data on physical storage media.

**data manipulation language**   A language associated with a database management system that end users and programmers use to manipulate data in the database.

**data mart**   A small data warehouse containing only a portion of the organization's data for a specified function or population of users.

**data mining**   Analysis of large pools of data to find patterns and rules that can be used to guide decision making and predict future behavior.

**data quality audit**   A survey and/or sample of files to determine accuracy and completeness of data in an information system.

**data visualization**   Technology for helping users see patterns and relationships in large amounts of data by presenting the data in graphical form.

**data warehouse**   A database, with reporting and query tools, that stores current and historical data extracted from various operational systems and consolidated for management reporting and analysis.

**data workers**   People, such as secretaries or bookkeepers, who process the organization's paperwork.

**database**   A group of related files.

**database administration**   Refers to the more technical and operational aspects of managing data, including physical database design and maintenance.

**database management system (DBMS)**   Special software to create and maintain a database and enable individual business applications to extract the data they need without having to create separate files or data definitions in their computer programs.

**database server**   A computer in a client/server environment that is responsible for running a DBMS to process SQL statements and perform database management tasks.

**decision-support systems (DSS)**   Information systems at the organization's management level that combine data and sophisticated analytical models or data analysis tools to support semistructured and unstructured decision making.

**dedicated server computer**   A computer on a network that performs important network functions for client computers, such as serving up Web pages, storing data, and storing the network operating system.

**demand planning**   Determining how much product a business needs to make to satisfy all its customers' demands.

**denial-of-service (DoS) attack**   Flooding a network server or Web server with false communications or requests for services in order to crash the network.

**dense wavelength division multiplexing (DWDM)**   Technology for boosting transmission capacity of optical fiber by using many different wavelengths to carry separate streams of data over the same fiber strand at the same time.

**Descartes' rule of change**   A principle that states that if an action cannot be taken repeatedly, then it is not right to be taken at any time.

**design**   Simon's second stage of decision making, when the individual conceives of possible alternative solutions to a problem.

**desktop publishing**   Technology that produces professional-quality documents combining output from word processors with design, graphics, and special layout features.

**digital cash**   Currency that is represented in electronic form that moves outside the normal network of money.

**digital certificates** Attachments to an electronic message to verify the identity of the sender and to provide the receiver with the means to encode a reply.

**digital checking** Systems that extend the functionality of existing checking accounts so they can be used for online shopping payments.

**digital credit card payment systems** Secure services for credit card payments on the Internet that protect information transmitted among users, merchant sites, and processing banks.

**digital dashboard** Displays all of a firm's key performance indicators as graphs and charts on a single screen to provide a one-page overview of all the critical measurements necessary to make key executive decisions.

**digital divide** Large disparities in access to computers and the Internet among different social groups and different locations.

**digital goods** Goods that can be delivered over a digital network.

**digital market** A marketplace that is created by computer and communication technologies that link many buyers and sellers.

**Digital Millennium Copyright Act (DMCA)** Adjusts copyright laws to the Internet age by making it illegal to make, distribute, or use devices that circumvent technology-based protections of copyrighted materials.

**digital scanner** Device that translates images, such as pictures or documents, into digital form.

**digital signature** A digital code that can be attached to an electronically transmitted message to uniquely identify its contents and the sender.

**digital subscriber line (DSL)** A group of technologies providing high-capacity transmission over existing copper telephone lines.

**digital video disk (DVD)** High-capacity optical storage medium that can store full-length videos and large amounts of data.

**digital wallet** Software that stores credit card, electronic cash, owner identification, and address information, and provides this data automatically during electronic commerce purchase transactions.

**direct cutover** A risky conversion approach, whereby the new system completely replaces the old one on an appointed day.

**disaster recovery planning** Planning for the restoration of computing and communications services after they have been disrupted.

**disintermediation** The removal of organizations or business process layers responsible for certain intermediary steps in a value chain.

**distributed denial-of-service (DDoS) attack** Numerous computers inundate and overwhelm a network from numerous launch points.

**distributed processing** The distribution of computer processing work among multiple computers linked by a communications network.

**documentation** Descriptions of how an information system works from either a technical or end-user standpoint.

**domain name** English-like name that corresponds to the unique 32-bit numeric Internet Protocol (IP) address for each computer connected to the Internet.

**Domain Name System (DNS)** A hierarchical system of servers maintaining a database enabling the conversion of domain names to their numeric IP addresses.

**downsizing** The process of transferring applications from large computers to smaller ones.

**downtime** Period of time in which an information system is not operational.

**drill down** The ability to move from summary data to lower and lower levels of detail.

**DSS database** A collection of current or historical data from a number of applications or groups. Can be a small PC database or a massive data warehouse.

**DSS software system** Collection of software tools that are used for data analysis, such as OLAP tools, data mining tools, or a collection of mathematical and analytical models.

**due process** A process in which laws are well known and understood and there is an ability to appeal to higher authorities to ensure that laws are applied correctly.

**dynamic pricing** Pricing of items based on real-time interactions between buyers and sellers that determine what an item is worth at any particular moment.

**edge computing** Method for distributing the computing load (or work) across many layers of Internet computers in order to minimize response time.

**efficient customer response system** System that directly links consumer behavior back to distribution, production, and supply chains.

**e-government** Use of the Internet and related technologies to digitally enable government and public sector agencies' relationships with citizens, businesses, and other arms of government.

**electronic billing presentment and payment systems** Systems used for paying routine monthly bills that allow users to view their bills electronically and pay them through electronic funds transfers from banks or credit card accounts.

**electronic business (e-business)** The use of the Internet and digital technology to execute all the business processes in the enterprise. Includes e-commerce as well as processes for the internal management of the firm and for coordination with suppliers and other business partners.

**electronic commerce (e-commerce)** The process of buying and selling goods and services electronically involving transactions using the Internet, networks, and other digital technologies.

**electronic data interchange (EDI)** The direct computer-to-computer exchange between two organizations of standard business transactions, such as orders, shipment instructions, or payments.

**electronic records management (ERM)** Policies, procedures, and tools for managing the retention, destruction, and storage of electronic records.

**e-mail** The computer-to-computer exchange of messages.

**e-mail handhelds**   Handheld devices for wireless data transmission that includes a small display screen and a keypad for typing short e-mail messages.

**employee relationship management (ERM)**   Software dealing with employee issues that are closely related to CRM, such as setting objectives, employee performance management, performance-based compensation, and employee training.

**encryption**   The coding and scrambling of messages to prevent their being read or accessed without authorization.

**end-user development**   The development of information systems by end users with little or no formal assistance from technical specialists.

**end-user interface**   The part of an information system through which the end user interacts with the system, such as online screens and commands.

**end users**   Representatives of departments outside the information systems group for whom applications are developed.

**enterprise application integration (EAI) software**   Software that works with specific software platforms to tie together multiple applications to support enterprise integration.

**enterprise applications**   Systems that can coordinate activities, decisions, and knowledge across many different functions, levels, and business units in a firm. Include enterprise systems, supply chain management systems, customer relationship management systems, and knowledge management systems.

**enterprise software**   Set of integrated modules for applications such as sales and distribution, financial accounting, investment management, materials management, production planning, plant maintenance, and human resources that allow data to be used by multiple functions and business processes.

**enterprise systems**   Integrated enterprise-wide information systems that coordinate key internal processes of the firm. Also known as enterprise resource planning (ERP).

**enterprise-wide knowledge management systems**   General-purpose, firmwide systems that collect, store, distribute, and apply digital content and knowledge.

**entity**   A person, place, thing, or event about which information must be kept.

**entity-relationship diagram**   A methodology for documenting databases illustrating the relationship between various entities in the database.

**ergonomics**   The interaction of people and machines in the work environment, including the design of jobs, health issues, and the end-user interface of information systems.

**Ethernet**   The dominant LAN standard at the physical network level, specifying the physical medium to carry signals between computers; access control rules; and a standardized set of bits to carry data over the system.

**ethical "no free lunch" rule**   Assumption that all tangible and intangible objects are owned by someone else, unless there is a specific declaration otherwise, and that the creator wants compensation for this work.

**ethics**   Principles of right and wrong that can be used by individuals acting as free moral agents to make choices to guide their behaviors.

**EV-DO**   Technology used in Verizon's cellular network service for providing anytime, anywhere broadband wireless Internet access for PCs and other devices at average speeds of 300 to 500 Kbps. Stands for evolution data optimized.

**evil twins**   Wireless networks that pretend to be legitimate Wi-Fi networks to entice participants to log on and reveal passwords or credit card numbers.

**exchanges**   Third-party Net marketplaces that are primarily transaction oriented and that connect many buyers and suppliers for spot purchasing.

**executive support systems (ESS)**   Information systems at the organization's strategic level designed to address unstructured decision making through advanced graphics and communications.

**expert systems**   Knowledge-intensive computer programs that capture the expertise of a human in limited domains of knowledge.

**extensible markup language (XML)**   A more powerful and flexible markup language than hypertext markup language (HTML) for Web pages.

**extranets**   Private intranets that are accessible to authorized outsiders.

**Fair Information Practices (FIP)**   A set of principles originally set forth in 1973 that govern the collection and use of information about individuals and forms the basis of most U.S. and European privacy laws.

**fault-tolerant computer systems**   Systems that contain extra hardware, software, and power supply components that can back a system up and keep it running to prevent system failure.

**feasibility study**   As part of the systems analysis process, the way to determine whether the solution is achievable, given the organization's resources and constraints.

**feedback**   Output that is returned to the appropriate members of the organization to help them evaluate or correct input.

**fiber-optic cable**   A fast, light, and durable transmission medium consisting of thin strands of clear glass fiber bound into cables. Data are transmitted as light pulses.

**field**   A grouping of characters into a word, a group of words, or a complete number, such as a person's name or age.

**File Transfer Protocol (FTP)**   Tool for retrieving and transferring files from a remote computer.

**finance and accounting information systems**   Systems that keep track of the firm's financial assets and fund flows.

**firewalls**   Hardware and software placed between an organization's internal network and an external network to prevent outsiders from invading private networks.

**FLOPS**   Stands for floating point operations per second and is a measure of computer processing speed.

**foreign key**   Field in a database table that enables users to find related information in another database table.

**formal planning and control tools**   Tools that improve project management by listing the specific activities that make up a project, their duration, and the sequence and timing of tasks.

**fourth-generation languages**   Programming languages that can be employed directly by end users or less-skilled programmers to develop computer applications more rapidly than conventional programming languages.

**frame relay**   A shared network service technology that packages data into bundles for transmission but does not use error-correction routines. Cheaper and faster than packet switching.

**fuzzy logic**   Rule-based AI that tolerates imprecision by using nonspecific terms called membership functions to solve problems.

**genetic algorithms**   Problem-solving methods that promote the evolution of solutions to specified problems using the model of living organisms adapting to their environments.

**geographic information systems (GIS)**   Systems with software that can analyze and display data using digitized maps to enhance planning and decision making.

**gigabyte**   Approximately one billion bytes.

**Global System for Mobile Communication (GSM)**   Major cellular transmission standard outside the United States, with strong international roaming capability, operating primarily in the 900 MHz and 1.8-GHz frequency bands.

**Gramm-Leach-Bliley Act**   Law that requires financial institutions to ensure the security and confidentiality of customer data.

**graphical user interface (GUI)**   The part of an operating system users interact with that uses graphic icons and the computer mouse to issue commands and make selections.

**grid computing**   Applying the resources of many computers in a network to a single problem.

**group decision-support system (GDSS)**   An interactive computer-based system that facilitates the solutions to unstructured problems by a set of decision makers working together as a group.

**groupware**   Software that provides functions and services that support the collaborative activities of workgroups.

**hacker**   A person who gains unauthorized access to a computer network for profit, criminal mischief, or personal pleasure.

**hard drive**   Magnetic disk resembling a thin steel platter with a metallic coating; used in large computer systems and in most PCs.

**hertz**   Measure of frequency of electrical impulses per second, with one hertz equivalent to one cycle per second.

**high-availability computing**   Tools and technologies, including back-up hardware resources, to enable a system to recover quickly from a crash.

**HIPAA**   Law outlining medical security and privacy rules and procedures for simplifying the administration of healthcare billing and automating the transfer of healthcare data between healthcare providers, payers, and plans.

**home page**   A World Wide Web text and graphical screen display that welcomes the user and explains the organization that has established the page.

**hotspots**   Specific geographic locations in which an access point provides public Wi-Fi network service.

**hubs**   Very simple devices that connect network components, sending a packet of data to all other connected devices.

**human resources information systems**   Systems that maintain employee records; track employee skills, job performance, and training; and support planning for employee compensation and career development.

**hypertext markup language (HTML)**   Page description language for creating Web pages and other hypermedia documents.

**Hypertext Transfer Protocol (HTTP)**   The communications standard used to transfer pages on the Web. Defines how messages are formatted and transmitted.

**identity theft**   Theft of key pieces of personal information, such as credit card or social security numbers, in order to obtain merchandise and services in the name of the victim or to obtain false credentials.

**Immanuel Kant's Categorical Imperative**   A principle that states that if an action is not right for everyone to take it is not right for anyone.

**I-mode**   Standard developed by Japan's NTT DoCoMo mobile phone network for enabling cell phones to received Web-based content and services.

**implementation**   Simon's final stage of decision making, when the individual puts the decision into effect and reports on the progress of the solution. Also refers to all the organizational activities working toward the adoption and management of an innovation.

**inference engine**   The strategy used to search through the rule base in an expert system; can be forward or backward chaining.

**information**   Data that have been shaped into a form that is meaningful and useful to human beings.

**information appliance**   Device that has been customized to perform a few specialized computing tasks well with minimal user effort.

**information asymmetry**   Situation where the relative bargaining power of two parties in a transaction is determined by one party in the transaction possessing more information essential to the transaction than the other party.

**information density**   The total amount and quality of information available to all market participants, consumers, and merchants.

**information policy**   Formal rules governing the maintenance, distribution, and use of information in an organization.

**information requirements**   A detailed statement of the information needs that a new system must satisfy; identifies who needs what information, and when, where, and how the information is needed.

**information rights**   The rights that individuals and organizations have with respect to information that pertains to themselves.

**information system**   Interrelated components working together to collect, process, store, and disseminate information to support decision making, coordination, control, analysis, and visualization in an organization.

**information systems department**   The formal organizational unit that is responsible for the information systems function in the organization.

**information systems literacy**   Broad-based understanding of information systems that includes behavioral knowledge about organizations and individuals using information systems as well as technical knowledge about computers.

**information systems managers**   Leaders of the various specialists in the information systems department.

**information systems plan**   A road map indicating the direction of systems development the rationale, the current situation, the management strategy, the implementation plan, and the budget.

**information technology (IT)**   All the hardware and software technologies that a firm needs to use in order to achieve its business objectives.

**information technology (IT) infrastructure**   Computer hardware, software, data, management technology, and networks providing a portfolio of shared IT resources for the organization.

**informed consent**   Consent given with knowledge of all the facts needed to make a rational decision.

**input**   The capture or collection of raw data from within the organization or from its external environment for processing in an information system.

**input devices**   Devices that gather data and convert them into electronic form for use by the computer.

**instant messaging**   Chat service that allows participants to create their own private chat channels so that a person can be alerted whenever someone on his or her private list is online to initiate a chat session with that particular individual.

**intangible benefits**   Benefits that are not easily quantified; they include more efficient customer service or enhanced decision making.

**Integrated Services Digital Network (ISDN)**   International standard for transmitting voice, video, image, and data to support a wide range of service over public telephone lines.

**integrated software package**   A software package that provides two or more applications, such as word processing and spreadsheets, providing for easy transfer of data between them.

**intellectual property**   Intangible property created by individuals or corporations that are subject to protections under trade secret, copyright, and patent law.

**intelligence**   The first of Simon's four stages of decision making, when the individual collects information to identify problems occurring in the organization.

**intelligent agents**   Software programs that use a built-in or learned knowledge base to carry out specific, repetitive, and predictable tasks for an individual user, business process, or software application.

**intelligent techniques**   Technologies that aid decision makers by capturing individual and collective knowledge, discovering patterns and behaviors in very large quantities of data, and generating solutions to problems that are too large and complex for human beings to solve on their own.

**Internet**   Global network of networks using universal standards to connect millions of different networks.

**Internet Protocol (IP) address**   Four-part numeric address indicating a unique computer location on the Internet.

**Internet service provider (ISP)**   A commercial organization with a permanent connection to the Internet that sells temporary connections to subscribers.

**Internet telephony**   Technologies that use the Internet Protocol's packet-switched connections for voice service.

**Internet2**   Research network with new protocols and transmission speeds that provides an infrastructure for supporting high-bandwidth Internet applications.

**internetworking**   The linking of separate networks, each of which retains its own identity, into an interconnected network.

**interorganizational system**   Information system that automates the flow of information across organizational boundaries and links a company to its customers, distributors, or suppliers.

**intranets**   Internal networks based on Internet and World Wide Web technology and standards.

**intrusion detection systems**   Tools to monitor the most vulnerable points in a network to detect and deter unauthorized intruders.

**investment workstations**   Powerful desktop computers for financial specialists, which are optimized to access and manipulate massive amounts of financial data.

**ISO 17799**   An international set of standards for security and control of information resources.

**Java**   Programming language that can deliver only the software functionality needed for a particular task, such as a small applet downloaded from a network; can run on any computer and operating system.

**joint application design (JAD)**   Process to accelerate the generation of information requirements by having end users and information systems specialists work together in intensive interactive design sessions.

**just-in-time**   Scheduling system for minimizing inventory by having components arrive exactly at the moment they are needed and finished goods shipped as soon as they leave the assembly line.

**key field**   A field in a record that uniquely identifies instances of that record so that it can be retrieved, updated, or sorted.

**key loggers**   Spyware that records every keystroke made on a computer.

**knowledge base**   Model of human knowledge that is used by expert systems.

**knowledge engineer**   A specialist who elicits information and expertise from other professionals and translates it into a set of rules, or frames, for an expert system.

**knowledge management**   The set of processes developed in an organization to create, gather, store, maintain, and disseminate the firm's knowledge.

**knowledge management systems (KMS)**   Systems that support the creation, capture, storage, and dissemination of firm expertise and knowledge.

**knowledge network systems**   Online directory for locating corporate experts in well-defined knowledge domains.

**knowledge work systems**   Information systems that aid knowledge workers in the creation and integration of new knowledge in the organization.

**knowledge workers**   People, such as engineers or architects, who design products or services and create knowledge for the organization.

**learning management system (LMS)**   Tools for the management, delivery, tracking, and assessment of various types of employee learning.

**legacy systems**   Systems that have been in existence for a long time and that continue to be used to avoid the high cost of replacing or redesigning them.

**liability**   The existence of laws that permit individuals to recover the damages done to them by other actors, systems, or organizations.

**Linux**   Reliable and compactly designed operating system that is an offshoot of UNIX and that can run on many different hardware platforms and is available free or at very low cost. Used as alternative to UNIX and Windows NT.

**LISTSERV**   Online discussion groups using e-mail broadcast from mailing list servers.

**local-area network (LAN)**   A telecommunications network that requires its own dedicated channels and that encompasses a limited distance, usually one building or several buildings in close proximity.

**Mac OS X Tiger**   Most recent version of the operating system for the Macintosh computer.

**machine cycle**   Series of operations required to process a single computer machine instruction.

**magnetic disk**   A secondary-storage medium in which data are stored by means of magnetized spots on a hard or floppy disk.

**magnetic ink character recognition (MICR)**   Technology used primarily in check processing for the banking industry to read magnetic ink characters on the bottom of a check.

**magnetic tape**   Inexpensive, older, secondary-storage medium in which large volumes of information are stored sequentially by means of magnetized and nonmagnetized spots on tape.

**mainframe**   Largest category of computers; used for major business processing.

**maintenance**   Changes in hardware, software, documentation, or procedures to a production system to correct errors, meet new requirements, or improve processing efficiency.

**malware**   Malicious software programs, such as computer viruses, worms, and Trojan horses.

**managed security service providers (MSSP)**   Companies that provide security management services for subscribing clients.

**management information systems (MIS)**   The study of information systems focusing on their use in business and management. Also refers to information systems that provide middle management with routine reports on organizational performance.

**manufacturing and production information systems**   Systems that deal with the planning, development, and production of products and services, and with controlling the flow of production.

**market entry costs**   The cost merchants must pay simply to bring their goods to market.

**marketspace**   A marketplace extended beyond traditional boundaries and removed from a temporal and geographic location.

**mashups**   Composite software applications that depend on high-speed networks, universal communication standards, and open-source code and are intended to be greater than the sum of their parts.

**mass customization**   The capacity to offer individually tailored products or services on a large scale.

**megabyte**   Approximately one million bytes.

**megahertz**   A measure of cycle speed, or the pacing of events in a computer; one megahertz equals one million cycles per second.

**menu prices**   Merchants' costs of changing prices.

**metropolitan-area network (MAN)**   Network that spans a metropolitan area, usually a city and its major suburbs. Its geographic scope falls between a WAN and a LAN.

**microbrowser**   Web browser software with a small file size that can work with low-memory constraints, tiny screens of handheld wireless devices, and low bandwidth of wireless networks.

**micropayment**   Payment for a very small sum of money, often less than $10.

**microprocessor**   Very large-scale integrated circuit technology that integrates the computer's memory, logic, and control on a single chip.

**microwave**   A high-volume, long-distance, point-to-point transmission in which high-frequency radio signals are transmitted through the atmosphere from one terrestrial transmission station to another.

**middle management**   People in the middle of the organizational hierarchy who are responsible for carrying out the plans and goals of senior management.

**middleware**   Software that connects two disparate applications, allowing them to communicate with each other and to exchange data.

**midrange computers**   Midsize computers that are capable of supporting the computing needs of smaller organizations or of managing networks of other computers.

**minicomputers**   Midrange computers used in systems for universities, factories, or research laboratories.

**MIS audit**   Identifies all the controls that govern individual information systems and assesses their effectiveness.

**mobile commerce (m-commerce)** The use of wireless devices, such as cell phones or handheld digital information appliances, to conduct both business-to-consumer and business-to-business e-commerce transactions over the Internet.

**moblog** Specialized blog featuring photos with captions posted from mobile phones.

**model** An abstract representation that illustrates the components or relationships of a phenomenon.

**modem** A device for translating a computer's digital signals into analog form for transmission over ordinary telephone lines, or for translating analog signals back into digital form for reception by a computer.

**mouse** Handheld input device with point-and-click capabilities that is usually connected to the computer by a cable.

**MP3 (MPEG3)** Standard for compressing audio files for transfer over the Internet.

**multimedia** Integration of two or more types of media, such as text, graphics, sound, voice, full-motion video, or animation, into a computer-based application.

**multiplexing** Ability of a single communications channel to carry data transmissions from multiple sources simultaneously.

**multitiered (N-tier) client/server architecture** Client/server arrangement that balances the work of the entire network over multiple levels of servers.

**nanosecond** One billionth of a second.

**natural languages** Nonprocedural languages that enable users to communicate with the computer using conversational commands resembling human speech.

**net marketplaces** Digital marketplaces based on Internet technology linking many buyers to many sellers.

**network** The linking of two or more computers to share data or resources, such as a printer.

**network address translation (NAT)** Conceals the IP addresses of the organization's internal host computer(s) to prevent sniffer programs outside the firewall from ascertaining them and using that information to penetrate internal systems.

**network economics** Model of strategic systems at the industry level based on the concept of a network where adding another participant entails zero marginal costs but can create much larger marginal gains.

**network interface card (NIC)** Expansion card inserted into a computer to enable it to connect to a network.

**network operating system (NOS)** Special software that routes and manages communications on the network and coordinates network resources.

**networking and telecommunications technology** Physical devices and software that link various pieces of hardware and transfer data from one physical location to another.

**neural networks** Hardware or software that attempts to emulate the processing patterns of the biological brain.

**nonobvious relationship awareness (NORA)** Technology that can find obscure hidden connections between people or other entities by analyzing information from many different sources to correlate relationships.

**normalization** The process of creating small, stable data structures from complex groups of data when designing a relational database.

**object** Software building block that combines data and the procedures acting on the data.

**object-oriented DBMS** An approach to data management that stores both data and the procedures acting on the data as objects that can be automatically retrieved and shared; the objects can contain multimedia.

**object-oriented development** Approach to systems development that uses the object as the basic unit of systems analysis and design. The system is modeled as a collection of objects and the relationships between them.

**object-relational DBMS** A database management system that combines the capabilities of a relational DBMS for storing traditional information and the capabilities of an object-oriented DBMS for storing graphics and multimedia.

**Office XP and Office 2003** Integrated software suites with capabilities for supporting collaborative work on the Web or incorporating information from the Web into documents.

**offshore software outsourcing** Outsourcing systems development work or maintenance of existing systems to external vendors in another country.

**on-demand computing** Firms off-loading peak demand for computing power to remote, large-scale data processing centers, investing just enough to handle average processing loads and paying for only as much additional computing power as they need. Also called utility computing.

**online analytical processing (OLAP)** Capability for manipulating and analyzing large volumes of data from multiple perspectives.

**online processing** A method of collecting and processing data in which transactions are entered directly into the computer system and processed immediately.

**online transaction processing** Transaction processing mode in which transactions entered online are immediately processed by the computer.

**open-source software** Software that provides free access to its program code, allowing users to modify the program code to make improvements or fix errors.

**operating system** The system software that manages and controls the activities of the computer.

**operational CRM** Customer-facing applications, such as sales force automation, call center and customer service support, and marketing automation.

**operational management** People who monitor the day-to-day activities of the organization.

**opt-in** Model of informed consent permitting the prohibition of an organization from collecting any personal information unless the individual specifically takes action to approve information collection and use.

**opt-out**   Model of informed consent permitting the collection of personal information until the consumer specifically requests that the data not be collected.

**optical character recognition**   Device that can translate specially designed marks, characters, and codes into digital form.

**optical networks**   High-speed networking technologies for transmitting data in the form of light pulses.

**organizational impact analysis**   Study of the way a proposed system will affect organizational structure, attitudes, decision making, and operations.

**output**   The distribution of processed information to the people who will use it or to the activities for which it will be used.

**output devices**   Device that displays data after they have been processed.

**outsourcing**   The practice of contracting computer center operations, telecommunications networks, or applications development to external vendors.

**P3P**   Industry standard designed to give users more control over personal information gathered on Web sites they visit. Stands for Platform for Privacy Preferences Project.

**packet filtering**   Examines selected fields in the headers of data packets flowing back and forth between the trusted network and the Internet.

**packet switching**   Technology that breaks messages into small, fixed bundles of data and routes them in the most economical way through any available communications channel.

**parallel processing**   Type of processing in which more than one instruction can be processed at a time by breaking down a problem into smaller parts and processing them simultaneously with multiple processors.

**parallel strategy**   A safe and conservative conversion approach where both the old system and its potential replacement are run together for a time until everyone is assured that the new one functions correctly.

**partner relationship management (PRM)**   Automation of the firm's relationships with its selling partners using customer data and analytical tools to improve coordination and customer sales.

**patches**   Small pieces of software that repair flaws in programs without disturbing the proper operation of the software.

**patent**   A legal document that grants the owner an exclusive monopoly on the ideas behind an invention for 17 years; designed to ensure that inventors of new machines or methods are rewarded for their labor while making widespread use of their inventions.

**peer-to-peer**   Network architecture that gives equal power to all computers on the network; used primarily in small networks.

**peer-to-peer payment systems**   Electronic payment systems for people who want to send money to vendors or individuals who are not set up to accept credit card payments.

**pen-based input**   Handwriting-recognition devices, such as pen-based tablets, notebooks, and notepads, that convert the motion made by an electronic stylus pressing on a touch-sensitive tablet screen into digital form.

**people perspective**   Consideration of the firm's management, as well as employees as individuals and their interrelationships in workgroups.

**personal computer (PC)**   Small desktop or portable computer.

**personal-area networks (PANs)**   Computer networks used for communication among digital devices (including telephones and PDAs) that are close to one person.

**personal digital assistant (PDA)**   Small, pen-based, handheld computer with built-in wireless telecommunications capable of entirely digital communications transmission.

**personalization**   Ability of merchants to target their marketing messages to specific individuals by adjusting the message for a person's name, interests, and past purchases.

**pharming**   Phishing technique that redirects users to a bogus Web page, even when the individual types the correct Web page address into his or her browser.

**phased approach**   Introduces the new system in stages either by functions or by organizational units.

**phishing**   A form of spoofing involving setting up fake Web sites or sending e-mail messages that look like those of legitimate businesses to ask users for confidential personal data.

**pilot study**   A strategy to introduce the new system to a limited area of the organization until it is proven to be fully functional; only then can the conversion to the new system across the entire organization take place.

**podcasting**   Method of publishing audio broadcasts via the Internet, allowing subscribing users to download audio files onto their personal computers or portable music players.

**pop-up ads**   Ads that open automatically and do not disappear until the user clicks on them.

**portal**   Web interface for presenting integrated personalized content from a variety of sources. Also refers to a Web site service that provides an initial point of entry to the Web.

**portfolio analysis**   An analysis of the portfolio of potential applications within a firm to determine the risks and benefits, and to select among alternatives for information systems.

**predictive analysis**   Use of data mining techniques, historical data, and assumptions about future conditions to predict outcomes of events.

**presentation graphics**   Software to create professional-quality graphics presentations that can incorporate charts, sound, animation, photos, and video clips.

**price discrimination**   Selling the same goods, or nearly the same goods, to different targeted groups at different prices.

**price transparency**   The ease with which consumers can find out the variety of prices in a market.

**primary activities**   Activities most directly related to the production and distribution of a firm's products or services.

**primary key**   Unique identifier for all the information in any row of a database table.

**primary storage**   Part of the computer that temporarily stores program instructions and data being used by the instructions.

**printers**   Devices that produce a printed hard copy of information output.

**privacy**   The claim of individuals to be left alone, free from surveillance or interference from other individuals, organizations, or the state.

**private exchange**   Another term for a private industrial network.

**private industrial networks**   Web-enabled networks linking systems of multiple firms in an industry for the coordination of transorganizational business processes.

**process specifications**   Specifications that describe the logic of the processes occurring within the lowest levels of a data flow diagram.

**processing**   The conversion, manipulation, and analysis of raw input into a form that is meaningful to humans.

**procurement**   Sourcing goods and materials, negotiating with suppliers, paying for goods, and making delivery arrangements.

**product differentiation**   Competitive strategy for creating brand loyalty by developing new and unique products and services that are not easily duplicated by competitors.

**production**   The stage after the new system is installed and the conversion is complete; during this time the system is reviewed by users and technical specialists to determine how well it has met its original goals.

**production or service workers**   People who actually produce the products or services of the organization.

**profiling**   The use of computers to combine data from multiple sources and create electronic dossiers of detailed information on individuals.

**program**   Series of instructions for the computer.

**programmers**   Highly trained technical specialists who write computer software instructions.

**programming**   The process of translating the system specifications prepared during the design stage into program code.

**protocol**   A set of rules and procedures that govern transmissions between the components in a network.

**prototyping**   The process of building an experimental system quickly and inexpensively for demonstration and evaluation so that users can better determine information requirements.

**public key encryption**   Uses two keys one shared (or public) and one private.

**public key infrastructure (PKI)**   System for creating public and private keys using a certificate authority (CA) and digital certificates for authentication.

**pull-based model**   Supply chain driven by actual customer orders or purchases so that members of the supply chain produce and deliver only what customers have ordered.

**pure-play**   Business models based purely on the Internet.

**push-based model**   Supply chain driven by production master schedules based on forecasts or best guesses of demand for products; products are "pushed" to customers.

**quality (customer's perspective)**   Refers to the physical product's standards, the service that accompanies a product, and the psychological aspects of dealing with the product.

**quality (producer's perspective)**   Signifies conformance to specifications or the absence of variation from those specifications.

**query languages**   Software tools that provide immediate online answers to requests for information that are not predefined.

**radio frequency identification (RFID)**   Technology using tiny tags with embedded microchips containing data about an item and its location to transmit short-distance radio signals to special RFID readers that then pass the data on to a computer for processing.

**RAID (redundant array of inexpensive disks)**   Disk storage technology to boost disk performance by packaging more than 100 smaller disk drives, with a controller chip and specialized software, in a single large unit to deliver data over multiple paths simultaneously.

**RAM (random access memory)**   Primary storage of data or program instructions that can directly access any randomly chosen location in the same amount of time.

**rapid application development (RAD)**   Process for developing systems in a very short time period by using prototyping, fourth-generation tools, and close teamwork among users and systems specialists.

**rationalization of procedures**   The streamlining of standard operating procedures, eliminating obvious bottlenecks, so that automation makes operating procedures more efficient.

**reach**   Measurement of how many people a business can connect with and how many products it can offer those people.

**records**   Groups of related fields.

**recovery-oriented computing**   Computer systems designed to recover rapidly when mishaps occur.

**relational database**   A type of logical database model that treats data as if they were stored in two-dimensional tables. It can relate data stored in one table to data in another as long as the two tables share a common data element.

**repetitive stress injury (RSI)**   Occupational disease that occurs when muscle groups are forced through repetitive actions with high-impact loads or thousands of repetitions with low-impact loads.

**Request for Proposal (RFP)**   A detailed list of questions submitted to vendors of software or other services to determine how well the vendor's product can meet the organization's specific requirements.

**responsibility**   Accepting the potential costs, duties, and obligations for the decisions one makes.

**richness**   Measurement of the depth and detail of information that a business can supply to the customer as well as information the business collects about the customer.

**ring networks**   A network topology in which all computers are linked by a closed loop in a manner that passes data in one direction from one computer to another.

**ringtones**   Digitized snippets of music that play on mobile phones when a user receives or places a call.

**risk assessment**   Determining the potential frequency of the occurrence of a problem and the potential damage if the problem were to occur. Used to determine the cost/benefit of a control.

**risk aversion principle**   Principle that one should take the action that produces the least harm or incurs the least cost.

**router**   Specialized communications processor that forwards packets of data from one network to another network.

**RSS**   Technology using aggregator software to pull content from Web sites and feed it automatically to subscribers' computers.

**safe harbor**   Private self-regulating policy and enforcement mechanism that meets the objectives of government regulations but does not involve government regulation or enforcement.

**sales and marketing information systems**   Systems that help the firm identify customers for the firm's products or services, develop products and services to meet their needs, promote these products and services, sell the products and services, and provide ongoing customer support.

**Sarbanes–Oxley Act**   Law passed in 2002 that imposes responsibility on companies and their managements to protect investors by safeguarding the accuracy and integrity of financial information that is used internally and released externally.

**satellites**   The transmission of data using orbiting satellites that serve as relay stations for transmitting microwave signals over very long distances.

**scalability**   The ability of a computer, product, or system to expand to serve a larger number of users without breaking down.

**scoring model**   A quick method for deciding among alternative systems based on a system of ratings for selected objectives.

**search costs**   The time and money spent locating a suitable product and determining the best price for that product.

**search engine marketing**   Use of search engines to deliver sponsored links, for which advertisers have paid, in search engine results.

**search engines**   Tools for locating specific sites or information on the Internet.

**secondary storage**   Relatively long-term, nonvolatile storage of data outside the CPU and primary storage.

**Secure Hypertext Transfer Protocol (S-HTTP)**   Protocol used for encrypting data flowing over the Internet; limited to individual messages.

**secure sockets layer (SSL)**   Enables client and server computers to manage encryption and decryption activities as they communicate with each other during a secure Web session.

**security**   Policies, procedures, and technical measures used to prevent unauthorized access, alteration, theft, or physical damage to information systems.

**security policy**   Statements ranking information risks, identifying acceptable security goals, and identifying the mechanisms for achieving these goals.

**semistructured decisions**   Decisions in which only part of the problem has a clear-cut answer provided by an accepted procedure.

**semistructured knowledge**   Information in the form of less structured objects, such as e-mail, chat room exchanges, videos, graphics, brochures, or bulletin boards.

**semistructured knowledge systems**   Systems for organizing and storing less structured information, such as e-mail, voice mail, videos, graphics, brochures, or bulleting boards. Also known as digital asset management systems.

**senior management**   People occupying the topmost hierarchy in an organization who are responsible for making long-range decisions.

**sensitivity analysis**   Models that ask "what if" questions repeatedly to determine the impact of changes in one or more factors on the outcomes.

**sensors**   Devices that collect data directly from the environment for input into a computer system.

**server**   Computer specifically optimized to provide software and other resources to other computers over a network.

**service-oriented architecture (SOA)**   Software architecture of a firm built on a collection of software programs that communicate with each other to perform assigned tasks to create a working software application.

**shopping bots**   Software with varying levels of built-in intelligence to help electronic commerce shoppers locate and evaluate products or service they might wish to purchase.

**short message service (SMS)**   Text message service used by digital cell phone systems to send and receive short alphanumeric messages less than 160 characters in length.

**Simple Object Access Protocol (SOAP)**   Set of rules that allows Web services applications to pass data and instructions to one another.

**six sigma**   A specific measure of quality, representing 3.4 defects per million opportunities; used to designate a set of methodologies and techniques for improving quality and reducing costs.

**smart card**   A credit-card-size plastic card that stores digital information and that can be used for electronic payments in place of cash.

**smart phones**   Wireless phones with voice, text, and Internet capabilities.

**sniffer** A type of eavesdropping program that monitors information traveling over a network.

**social engineering** Tricking people into revealing their passwords by pretending to be legitimate users or members of a company in need of information.

**social networking sites** Online community for expanding users' business or social contacts by making connections through their mutual business or personal connections.

**software package** A prewritten, precoded, commercially available set of programs that eliminates the need to write software programs for certain functions.

**software suite** Full-featured versions of several different application software tools sold together as a unit, such as Microsoft Office.

**spam** Unsolicited commercial e-mail.

**spamming** A form of abuse in which thousands and even hundreds of thousands of unsolicited e-mail and electronic messages are sent out, creating a nuisance for both businesses and individual users.

**spoofing** Misrepresenting one's identity on the Internet or redirecting a Web link to an address different from the intended one, with the site masquerading as the intended destination.

**spreadsheet** Software displaying data in a grid of columns and rows, with the capability of easily recalculating numerical data.

**spyware** Technology that aids in gathering information about persons or organizations without their knowledge.

**star network** A network topology in which all computers and other devices are connected to a central host computer. All communications between network devices must pass through the host computer.

**stateful inspection** Provides additional security by determining whether packets are part of an ongoing dialogue between a sender and a receiver.

**storage area networks (SAN)** High-speed networks dedicated to storage that connects different kinds of storage devices, such as tape libraries and disk arrays so they can be shared by multiple servers.

**stored value payment systems** Systems enabling consumers to make instant online payments to merchants and other individuals based on value stored in a digital account.

**strategic information system** Computer system at any level of the organization that changes goals, operations, products, services, or environmental relationships to help the organization gain a competitive advantage.

**strategic transitions** A movement from one level of sociotechnical system to another. Often required when adopting strategic systems that demand changes in the social and technical elements of an organization.

**structure chart** System documentation showing each level of design, the relationship among the levels, and the overall place in the design structure; can document one program, one system, or part of one program.

**structured** Refers to the fact that techniques are carefully drawn up, step by step, with each step building on a previous one.

**structured decisions** Decisions that are repetitive, routine, and have a definite procedure for handling them.

**structured knowledge** Knowledge in the form of structured documents and reports.

**structured knowledge systems** Systems for organizing structured knowledge in a repository where it can be accessed throughout the organization. Also known as content management systems.

**Structured Query Language (SQL)** The standard data manipulation language for relational database management systems.

**supercomputer** Highly sophisticated and powerful computer that can perform very complex computations extremely rapidly.

**supply chain** Network of organizations and business processes for procuring materials, transforming raw materials into intermediate and finished products, and distributing the finished products to customers.

**supply chain execution systems** Systems to manage the flow of products through distribution centers and warehouses to ensure that products are delivered to the right locations in the most efficient manner.

**supply chain management (SCM) systems** Information systems that automate the flow of information between a firm and its suppliers in order to optimize the planning, sourcing, manufacturing, and delivery of products and services.

**supply chain planning systems** Systems that enable a firm to generate demand forecasts for a product and to develop sourcing and manufacturing plans for that product.

**support activities** Activities that make the delivery of a firm's primary activities possible. Consist of the organization's infrastructure, human resources, technology, and procurement.

**switch** Device to connect network components that has more intelligence than a hub and can filter and forward data to a specified destination.

**switching costs** The expense a customer or company incurs in lost time and expenditure of resources when changing from one supplier or system to a competing supplier or system.

**syndicators** Business aggregating content or applications from multiple sources, packaging them for distribution, and reselling them to third-party Web sites.

**system software** Generalized programs that manage the computer's resources, such as the central processor, communications links, and peripheral devices.

**system testing** Tests the functioning of the information system as a whole in order to determine whether discrete modules will function together as planned.

**systems analysis** The analysis of a problem that the organization will try to solve with an information system.

**systems analysts** Specialists who translate business problems and requirements into information requirements and systems, acting as liaisons between the information systems department and the rest of the organization.

**systems design**    Details how a system will meet the information requirements as determined by the systems analysis.

**systems development**    The activities that go into producing an information systems solution to an organizational problem or opportunity.

**systems development lifecycle (SDLC)**    A traditional methodology for developing an information system that partitions the systems development process into formal stages that must be completed sequentially with a very formal division of labor between end users and information systems specialists.

**systems integration**    Ensuring that a new infrastructure works with a firm's older, so-called legacy systems and that the new elements of the infrastructure work with one another.

**T lines**    High-speed data lines leased from communications providers, such as T1 lines (with a transmission capacity of 1.544 Mbps).

**tacit knowledge**    Expertise and experience of organizational members that has not been formally documented.

**tangible benefits**    Benefits that can be quantified and assigned a monetary value; they include lower operational costs and increased cash flows.

**taxonomy**    Method of classifying things according to a predetermined system.

**technostress**    Stress induced by computer use; symptoms include aggravation, hostility toward humans, impatience, and enervation.

**Telnet**    Network tool that allows someone to log on to one computer system while doing work on another.

**terabyte**    Approximately one trillion bytes.

**test plan**    Prepared by the development team in conjunction with the users, it includes all of the preparations for the series of tests to be performed on the system.

**testing**    The exhaustive and thorough process that determines whether the system produces the desired results under known conditions.

**token**    Physical device, similar to an identification card, that is designed to prove the identity of a single user.

**topology**    The way in which the components of a network are connected.

**total cost of ownership (TCO)**    Designates the total cost of owning technology resources, including initial purchase costs, the cost of hardware and software upgrades, maintenance, technical support, and training.

**total quality management (TQM)**    A concept that makes quality control a responsibility to be shared by all people in an organization.

**touch point**    Method of firm interaction with a customer, such as telephone, e-mail, customer service desk, conventional mail, or point of purchase.

**touch screen**    Device that allows users to enter limited amounts of data by touching the surface of a sensitized video display monitor with a finger or a pointer.

**trade secret**    Any intellectual work or product used for a business purpose that can be classified as belonging to that business, provided it is not based on information in the public domain.

**transaction costs**    The costs of participating in a market.

**transaction processing systems (TPS)**    Computerized systems that perform and record the daily routine transactions necessary to conduct the business; they serve the organization's operational level.

**Transmission Control Protocol/Internet Protocol (TCP/IP)**    Dominant model for achieving connectivity among different networks. Provides a universally agreed-on method for breaking up digital messages into packets, routing them to the proper addresses, and then reassembling them into coherent messages.

**transnational**    Truly global form of business organization where value-added activities are managed from a global perspective without reference to national borders, optimizing sources of supply and demand and local competitive advantage.

**transport layer security (TLS)**    Successor to SSL, which enables client and server computers to manage encryption and decryption activities as they communicate with each other during a secure Web session.

**Trojan horse**    A software program that appears legitimate but contains a second hidden function that may cause damage.

**tuples**    Rows or records in a relational database.

**twisted wire**    A transmission medium consisting of pairs of twisted copper wires; used to transmit analog phone conversations but can be used for data transmission.

**uniform resource locator (URL)**    The address of a specific resource on the Internet.

**unit testing**    The process of testing each program separately in the system. Sometimes called program testing.

**universal description, discovery, and integration (UDDI)**    Allows a Web service to be listed in a directory of Web services so that it can be easily located by other organizations and systems.

**UNIX**    Operating system for all types of computers, which is machine independent and supports multiuser processing, multitasking, and networking. Used in high-end workstations and servers.

**unstructured decisions**    Nonroutine decisions in which the decision maker must provide judgment, evaluation, and insights into the problem definition; there is no agreed-on procedure for making such decisions.

**up-selling**    Marketing higher-value products or services to new or existing customers.

**USB flash drive**    Provides portable flash memory storage by plugging into a computer's USB port.

**Usenet**    Forums in which people share information and ideas on a defined topic through large electronic bulletin boards where anyone can post messages on the topic for others to see and to which others can respond.

**user-designer communications gap**    The difference in backgrounds, interests, and priorities that impede communication and problem solving among end users and information systems specialists.

**user interface** The part of the information system through which the end user interacts with the system; type of hardware and the series of on-screen commands and responses required for a user to work with the system.

**Utilitarian Principle** Principle that assumes one can put values in rank-order and understand the consequences of various courses of action.

**utility computing** Model of computing in which companies pay only for the information technology resources they actually use during a specified time period. Also called on-demand computing or usage-based pricing.

**value chain model** Model that highlights the primary or support activities that add a margin of value to a firm's products or services where information systems can best be applied to achieve a competitive advantage.

**value web** Customer-driven network of independent firms who use information technology to coordinate their value chains to collectively produce a product or service for a market.

**virtual company** Uses networks to link people, assets, and ideas, enabling it to ally with other companies to create and distribute products and services without being limited by traditional organizational boundaries or physical locations.

**virtual private network (VPN)** A secure connection between two points across the Internet to transmit corporate data. Provides a low-cost alternative to a private network.

**virtual reality modeling language (VRML)** A set of specifications for interactive three-dimensional modeling on the World Wide Web.

**virtual reality systems** Interactive graphics software and hardware that create computer-generated simulations that provide sensations that emulate real-world activities.

**Visual Basic** Widely used visual programming tool and environment for creating applications that run on Microsoft Windows.

**visual programming language** Allows users to manipulate graphic or iconic elements to create programs.

**vlog** Video diary posted online.

**voice over IP (VoIP)** Facilities for managing the delivery of voice information using the Internet Protocol (IP).

**voice portals** Capability for accepting voice commands for accessing Web content, e-mail, and other electronic applications from a cell phone or standard telephone and for translating responses to user requests for information back into speech for the customer.

**war driving** An eavesdropping technique in which eavesdroppers drive by buildings or park outside them trying to intercept wireless network traffic.

**Web browsers** Easy-to-use software tool for accessing the World Wide Web and the Internet.

**Web bugs** Tiny graphic files embedded in e-mail messages and Web pages that are designed to monitor online Internet user behavior.

**Web hosting service** Company with large Web server computers to maintain the Web sites of fee-paying subscribers.

**Web server** Software that manages requests for Web pages on the computer where they are stored and that delivers the page to the user's computer.

**Web services** Set of universal standards using Internet technology for integrating different applications from different sources without time-consuming custom coding. Used for linking systems of different organizations or for linking disparate systems within the same organization.

**Web services description language (WSDL)** A common framework for describing the tasks performed by a Web service and the commands and data it will accept so that it can be used by other applications.

**Web site** All of the World Wide Web pages maintained by an organization or an individual.

**Webmaster** The person in charge of an organization's Web site.

**wide-area network (WAN)** Telecommunications network that spans a large geographical distance. May consist of a variety of cable, satellite, and microwave technologies.

**Wi-Fi** Stands for Wireless Fidelity and refers to the 802.11 family of wireless networking standards.

**WiMax** Popular term for IEEE Standard 802.16 for wireless networking over a range of up to 31 miles with a data transfer rate of up to 75 Mbps. Stands for worldwide interoperability for microwave access.

**Windows 2000** Windows operating system for high-performance PCs and network servers. Supports networking, multitasking, multiprocessing, and Internet services; predecessor to Windows Server 2003.

**Windows CE** Windows platform for devices with minimal storage, such as small handhelds.

**Windows Server 2003** Most recent Windows operating system for servers.

**Windows Vista** Microsoft Windows operating system featuring improved security; diagnostics; parental controls; usability; desktop searching; synchronization with mobile devices, cameras, and Internet services; and better support for video and TV.

**Windows XP** Powerful Windows operating system that provides reliability, robustness, and ease of use for both corporate and home PC users.

**Wireless Application Protocol (WAP)** System of protocols and technologies that lets cell phones and other wireless devices with tiny displays, low-bandwidth connections, and minimal memory access Web-based information and services.

**wireless NIC** Add-in card (network interface card) that has a built-in radio and antenna.

**wireless portals**   Portals with content and services optimized for mobile devices to steer users to the information they are most likely to need.

**wireless sensor networks (WSNs)**   Networks of interconnected wireless devices with built-in processing, storage, and radio frequency sensors, and antennas that are embedded into the physical environment to provide measurements of many points over large spaces.

**word processing software**   Software for electronically creating, editing, formatting, and printing documents.

**workflow management**   The process of streamlining business procedures so that documents can be moved easily and efficiently from one location to another.

**workstation**   Desktop computer with powerful graphics and mathematical capabilities and the ability to perform several complicated tasks at once.

**World Wide Web**   A system with universally accepted standards for storing, retrieving, formatting, and displaying information in a networked environment.

**worms**   Independent software programs that propagate themselves to disrupt the operation of computer networks or destroy data and other programs.

**XML (eXtensible Markup Language)**   General-purpose language that describes the structure of a document and supports links to multiple documents, allowing data to be manipulated by the computer. Used for both Web and non-Web applications.

## Chapter 1

**Bebasat, Izak,** and **Robert W. Zmud.** "The Identity Crisis within the IS Discipline: Defining and Communicating the Discipline's Core Properties." *MIS Quarterly* 27, no. 2 (June 2003).

**Belson, Ken.** "Technology Lets High-End Hotels Anticipate Guests' Whims." *The New York Times* (November 16, 2005).

**Brynjolfsson, Erik.** "VII Pillars of IT Productivity." *Optimize* (May 2005).

**Carr, Nicholas.** "IT Doesn't Matter." *Harvard Business Review* (May 2003).

**Computer Industry Almanac.** "Worldwide Internet Users Will Top 1 Billion in 2005." Press Release, www.c-i-a.com, accessed September 3, 2004.

**Deloitte Research.** "The Power of Synchronization." Deloitte Research (2005).

**Dutta, Amitava,** and **Rahul Roy.** "Offshore Outsourcing: A Dynamic Causal Model of Counteracting Forces." *Journal of Management Information Systems* 22, no. 2 (Fall 2005).

**Greenspan, Alan.** "The Revolution in Information Technology." Boston College Conference on the New Economy (March 6, 2000).

**Gurbaxani, Vijay,** and **Phillippe Jorion.** "The Value of Information Systems Outsourcing Arrangements: An Event Study Analysis." Center for Research on IT and Organizations, University of California, Irvine, Draft (April 2005).

**Internet Systems Consortium.** "ISC Internet Domain Survey." http://www.isc.org/index.pl, accessed July 2005.

**Ives, Blake, Joseph S. Valacich, Richard T. Watson,** and **Robert W. Zmud.** "What Every Business Student Needs to Know about Information Systems." *CAIS* 9, Article 30 (December 2002).

**Pew Research Center.** "Trends 2005; Chapter 4: Internet: Mainstreaming of Online Life." (January 25, 2005).

**Ross, Jeanne W.,** and **Peter Weill.** "Six IT Decisions Your IT People Shouldn't Make." *Harvard Business Review* (November 2002).

**Triplett, Jack E.,** and **Barry P. Bosworth.** "Productivity in Services Industries: Trends and Measurement Issues." Washington DC: The Brookings Institution, (2003).

**Tuomi, Ilkka.** "Data Is More Than Knowledge. *Journal of Management Information Systems* 16, no. 3 (Winter 1999–2000).

**U.S. Bureau of Labor Statistics.** "Tomorrow's Jobs." http://bls.gov/oco/oco2003.htm.

**U.S. Census Bureau.** *Statistical Abstract of the United States 2004/2005* (June 2005).

**Wal-Mart.** "Form 10-K" filed with the Securities and Exchange Commission for the fiscal year ended January 31, 2005." www.sec.gov, accessed November 1, 2005.

**Wolff, Edward N.** "The Growth of Information Workers in the U.S. Economy." *Communications of the ACM* 48, no. 10 (October 2005).

## Chapter 2

**Anthony, R. N.** *Planning and Control Systems: A Framework for Analysis.* Cambridge, MA: Harvard University Press (1965).

**Choi, Soon-Yong,** and **Andrew B. Whinston.** "Communities of Collaboration." *IQ Magazine* (July/August 2001).

**Concours Group.** "ESII: Capitalizing on Enterprise Systems and Infrastructure." (1999).

**Ferdows, Kasra, Michael A. Lewis,** and **Jose A. D. Machuca.** "Rapid-Fire Fulfillment." *Harvard Business Review* (November 2004).

**Gruman, Galen.** "Strategic HR Integration." *CIO Magazine* (August 15, 2005).

**Huber, George P.** "Organizational Information Systems: Determinants of Their Performance and Behavior." *Management Science* 28, no. 2 (1984).

**Johnston, Russell,** and **Michael J. Vitale.** "Creating Competitive Advantage with Interorganizational Information Systems." *MIS Quarterly* 12, no. 2 (June 1988).

**Kalakota, Ravi,** and **Marcia Robinson.** *e-Business2.0: Roadmap for Success.* Reading, MA: Addison-Wesley (2001).

**Keen, Peter G. W.,** and **M. S. Morton.** *Decision Support Systems: An Organizational Perspective.* Reading, MA: Addison-Wesley (1978).

**Malone, Thomas M., Kevin Crowston, Jintae Lee,** and **Brian Pentland.** "Tools for Inventing Organizations: Toward a Handbook of Organizational Processes." *Management Science* 45, no. 3 (March 1999).

**McAfee, Andrew.** "Do You Have Too Much IT?" *MIT Sloan Management Review* (Spring 2004).

**Nolan, Richard,** and **F. Warren McFarland.** "Information Technology and the Board of Directors." *Harvard Business Review* (October 1, 2005).

**O'Leary, Daniel E.** *Enterprise Resource Planning Systems: Systems Life Cycle, Electronic Commerce, and Risk.* New York: Cambridge University Press (2000).

**Oracle Corporation.** "Alcoa Implements Oracle Solution 20% below Projected Cost, Eliminates 43 Legacy Systems." www.oracle.com, accessed August 21, 2005.

**Picarelle, Lisa.** "Planes, Trains, and Automobiles." *Customer Relationship Management* (February 2004).

**SAP.** "Alcan Packaging Implements mySAP SCM to Increase Shareholder Value." http://www.mysap.com, accessed August 20, 2005.

**Siebel Systesms.** "Saab Cars USA Increases Lead Follow-Up from 38 Percent to 50 Percent with Siebel Automotive." www.siebel.com accessed October 15, 2005.

**Sprague, Ralph H., Jr.,** and **Eric D. Carlson.** *Building Effective Decision Support Systems.* Englewood Cliffs, NJ: Prentice Hall (1982).

**Sullivan, Laurie.** "ERPzilla." *Information Week* (July 11, 2005).

**Weill, Peter,** and **Jeanne Ross.** "A Matrixed Approach to Designing IT Governance." *MIT Sloan Management Review* 46, no. 2 (Winter 2005).

## Chapter 3

**Bhatt, Ganesh D.,** and **Varun Grover.** "Types of Information Technology Capabilities and Their Role in Competitive Advantage." *Journal of Management Information Systems* 22, no.2 (Fall 2005).

**Broadbent, Marianne, Peter Weill,** and **Don St. Clair.** "The Implications of Information Technology Infrastructure for Business Process Redesign." *MIS Quarterly* 23, no. 2 (June 1999).

**Cash, J. I.,** and **Benn R. Konsynski.** "IS Redraws Competitive Boundaries." *Harvard Business Review* (March–April 1985).

**Caudron, Shari.** "Safety in Numbers." *Profit Magazine* (February 2004).

**Champy, James A.** *X-Engineering the Corporation: Reinventing Your Business in the Digital Age.* New York: Warner Books (2002).

**Chen, Pei-Yu (Sharon),** and **Lorin M. Hitt.** "Measuring Switching Costs and the Determinants of Customer Retention in Internet-Enabled Businesses: A Study of the Online Brokerage Industry." *Information Systems Research* 13, no.3 (September 2002).

**Christensen, Clayton.** "The Past and Future of Competitive Advantage." *Sloan Management Review* 42, no. 2 (Winter 2001).

**Christensen, Clayton, Jeanne G. Harris,** and **Ajay K. Kohli.** "How Do They Know Their Customers So Well?" *Sloan Management Review* 42, no. 2 (Winter 2001).

**Cohen, Beth, Peter Sorrentino,** and **Walt DuLaney.** "Customization Goes into Overdrive." *Optimize* (March 2005).

**Davenport, Tom.** "Competing on Analytics." *Harvard Business Review* (January 2006).

———. "Rethinking the Mobile Workforce." *Optimize* (August 2005).

**Deans, Candace P.,** and **Michael J. Kane.** *International Dimensions of Information Systems and Technology.* Boston: PWS-Kent (1992).

**Eisenhardt, Kathleen M.** "Has Strategy Changed?" *Sloan Management Review* 43, no.2 (Winter 2002).

**El Sawy, Omar A.** *Redesigning Enterprise Processes for E-Business.* New York: McGraw-Hill (2001).

**Ferguson, Glover, Sanjay Mathur,** and **Baiju Shah.** "Evolving from Information to Insight." *MIT Sloan Management Review* 46, no. 2 (Winter 2005).

**Fine, Charles H., Roger Vardan, Robert Pethick,** and **Jamal E-Hout.** "Rapid-Response Capability in Value-Chain Design." *Sloan Management Review* 43, no. 2 (Winter 2002).

**Hagel, John, III,** and **John Seeley Brown.** "The Shifting Industrial Landscape." *Optimize* (April 2005).

**Hammer, Michael.** "Process Management and the Future of Six Sigma." *Sloan Management Review* 43, no. 2 (Winter 2002).

**Hammer, Michael,** and **James Champy.** *Reengineering the Corporation.* New York: HarperCollins (1993).

**Holweg, Matthias,** and **Frits K. Pil.** "Successful Build-to-Order Strategies Start with the Customer." *Sloan Management Review* 43, no. 1 (Fall 2001).

**Iansiti, Marco,** and **Roy Levien.** "Strategy as Ecology." *Harvard Business Review* (March 2004).

**IBM.** "Clarion Malaysia Reduces Design Time by 50 Percent with CATIA V5." http://www.306-ibm.com/software/success, accessed August 31, 2005.

**Kauffman, Robert J.,** and **Yu-Ming Wang.** "The Network Externalities Hypothesis and Competitive Network Growth." *Journal of Organizational Computing and Electronic Commerce* 12, no. 1 (2002).

**Keen, Peter G. W.** *The Process Edge.* Boston: Harvard Business School Press (1997).

**King, William R.,** and **Vikram Sethi.** "An Empirical Analysis of the Organization of Transnational Information Systems." *Journal of Management Information Systems* 15, no. 4 (Spring 1999).

**Konsynski, Benn R.,** and **F. Warren McFarlan.** "Information Partnerships—Shared Data, Shared Scale." *Harvard Business Review* (September–October 1990).

**Koulopoulos, Thomas,** and **James Champy.** "Building Digital Value Chains." *Optimize* (September 2005).

**Levecq, Hugues,** and **Bruce W. Weber.** "Electronic Trading Systems: Strategic Implication of Market Design Choices." *Journal of Organizational Computing and Electronic Commerce* 12, no. 1 (2002).

**McFarlan, F. Warren.** "Information Technology Changes the Way You Compete." *Harvard Business Review* (May–June 1984).

**Piccoli, Gabriele,** and **Blake Ives.** "Review: IT-Dependent Strategic Initiatives and Sustained Competitive Advantage: A Review and Synthesis of the Literature." *MIS Quarterly* 29, no. 4 (December 2005).

**Porter, Michael E.,** and **Scott Stern.** "Location Matters." *Sloan Management Review* 42, no. 4 (Summer 2001).

**Porter, Michael.** *Competitive Advantage.* New York: Free Press (1985).

———. *Competitive Strategy.* New York: Free Press (1980).

———. "Strategy and the Internet." *Harvard Business Review* (March 2001).

**Prahalad, C. K.,** and **Venkatram Ramaswamy.** "The New Frontier of Experience Innovation." *MIS Sloan Management Review* 44, no. 4 (Summer 2003).

**Ray, Gautam, Waleed A. Muhanna,** and **Jay B. Barney.** "Information Technology and the Performance of the Customer Service Process: A Resource-Based Analysis." *MIS Quarterly* 29, no. 4 (December 2005).

**Roche, Edward M.** *Managing Information Technology in Multinational Corporations.* New York: Macmillan (1992).

**Rowsell-Jones, Andrew,** and **Mark McDonald.** "Giving Global Strategies Local Flavor." *Optimize* (April 2005).

**Shapiro, Carl,** and **Hal R. Varian.** *Information Rules.* Boston: Harvard Business School Press (1999).

**Vandenbosch, Mark,** and **Niraj Dawar.** "Beyond Better Products: Capturing Value in Customer Interactions." *Sloan Management Review* 43, no. 4 (Summer 2002).

**Varian, Hal R.** "Technology Levels the Business Playing Field." *The New York Times* (August 25, 2005).

# Chapter 4

**Acharya, Ravi.** "EAI: A Business Perspective," *EAI Journal* (April 2003).

**Barry, Douglas K.** *Web Services and Service-Oriented Architectures: The Savvy Manager's Guide.* New York: Morgan Kaufman (2003).

**Carr, Nicholas G.** "The End of Corporate Computing." *MIT Sloan Management Review* 46, no. 3 (Spring 2005).

**Cegielski, Casey G., Brian J. Reithel,** and **Carl M. Rebman.** "Developing a Timely IT Strategy." *Communications of the ACM* 48, no. 8 (August 2005).

**Champy, James.** "Re-examining the Infrastructure." *Optimize* 23 (September 2003).

**Conry-Murray, Andrew.** "Grid Computing's Promises and Perils." Network Magazine.com, accessed February 5, 2004.

**David, Julie Smith, David Schuff,** and **Robert St. Louis.** "Managing Your IT Total Cost of Ownership." *Communications of the ACM* 45, no. 1 (January 2002).

**DeFelice, Alexandra.** "On Demand Is in Demand." *Customer Relationship Management* (July 2005).

**Dunn, Darrell.** "Power Up with Utility Computing." *Information Week* (August 29, 2005).

**Fox, Armando,** and **David Patterson.** "Self-Repairing Computers." *Scientific American* (May 2003).

**Ganek, A. G.,** and **T. A. Corbi.** "The Dawning of the Autonomic Computing Era." *IBM Systems Journal* 42, no. 1 (2003).

**Gerlach, James, Bruce Neumann, Edwin Moldauer, Martha Argo,** and **Daniel Frisby.** "Determining the Cost of IT Services." *Communications of the ACM* 45, no. 9 (September 2002).

**Hagel, John, III,** and **John Seeley Brown.** "Your Next IT Strategy." *Harvard Business Review* (October 2001).

**IBM.** "Gridlines: The Intersection of Technology and Business." http://www-1.ibm.com/grid/gridlines/January2004/feature/teamwork.shtml, accessed July 2004.

———. "How Customers Are Making On Demand Real." http://www.ibm.com/news/us/2003/11/on_demand_real.html, accessed July 2004.

**Kern, Thomas, Leslie P. Willcocks,** and **Mary C. Lacity.** "Application Service Provision: Risk Assessment and Mitigation." *MIS Quarterly Executive* 1, no. 2 (2002).

**Lee, Jinyoul, Keng Siau,** and **Soongoo Hong.** "Enterprise Integration with ERP and EAI." *Communications of the ACM* 46, no. 2 (February 2003).

**Loo, Alfred W.** "The Future of Peer-to-Peer Computing." *Communications of the ACM* 46, no. 9 (September 2003).

**McAfee, Andrew.** "Will Web Services Really Transform Collaboration?" *MIT Sloan Management Review* 46, no. 2 (Winter 2005).

**McDougall, Paul.** "Dow Hires IBM to Take VoIP Project Over from EDS." *Information Week* (August 3, 2004).

**National Science Foundation.** "Revolutionizing Science and Engineering through Cyberinfrastructure: Report of the National Science Foundation Blue-Ribbon Advisory Panel on Cyberinfrastructure." Washington DC (January 2003).

**Patel, Samir,** and **Suneel Saigal.** "When Computers Learn to Talk: A Web Services Primer." *McKinsey Quarterly* no. 1 (2002).

**Ricadela, Aaron.** "Slow Going on the Global Grid." *Information Week* (February 21, 2005).

**Schuff, David,** and **Robert St. Louis.** "Centralization vs. Decentralization of Application Software." *Communications of the ACM* 44, no. 6 (June 2001).

**Susarla, Anjana, Anitesh Barus,** and **Andrew B. Whinston.** "Understanding the Service Component of Application Service Provision: An Empirical Analysis of Satisfaction with ASP Services." *MIS Quarterly* 27, no. 1 (March 2003).

**Tatemura, Junichi, et al.** "Acceleration of Web Service Workflow Execution through Edge Computing." NEC Laboratories America, Inc. (2003).

**Traudt, Erin,** and **Amy Konary.** "Worldwide and U.S. Software as Service 2005–2009 Forecast and Analysis: Adoption for the Alternative Delivery Model Continues." International Data Center (March 2005).

Walsh, Kenneth R. "Analyzing the Application ASP Concept: Technologies, Economies, and Strategies." *Communications of the ACM* 46, no. 8 (August 2003).

Weill, Peter, and Marianne Broadbent. *Leveraging the New Infrastructure.* Cambridge, MA: Harvard Business School Press (1998).

———. "Management by Maxim: How Business and IT Managers Can Create IT Infrastructures." *Sloan Management Review* (Spring 1997).

Weill, Peter, Mani Subramani, and Marianne Broadbent. "Building IT Infrastructure for Strategic Agility." *Sloan Management Review* 44, no. 1 (Fall 2002).

# Chapter 5

Apte, Chidanand, Bing Liu, Edwin P. D. Pednault, and Padhraic Smith. "Business Applications of Data Mining." *Communications of the ACM* 45, no. 8 (August 2002).

Cappiello, Cinzia, Chiara Francalanci, and Barbara Pernici. "Time-Related Factors of Data Quality in Multichannel Information Systems." *Journal of Management Information Systems* 20, no. 3 (Winter 2004).

Chen, Andrew N. K., Paulo B. Goes, and James R. Marsden. "A Query-Driven Approach to the Design and Management of Flexible Database Systems." *Journal of Management Information Systems* 19, no. 3 (Winter 2002–2003).

Cooper, Brian L., Hugh J. Watson, Barbara H. Wixom, and Dale L. Goodhue. "Data Warehousing Supports Corporate Strategy at First American Corporation." *MIS Quarterly* (December 2000).

DeFelice, Alexander. "What's in a Name?" *Customer Relationship Management* (July 2005).

Eckerson, Wayne W. "Data Quality and the Bottom Line." The Data Warehousing Institute (2002).

Fayyad, Usama, Ramasamy Ramakrishnan, and Ramakrisnan Srikant. "Evolving Data Mining into Solutions for Insights." *Communications of the ACM* 45, no. 8 (August 2002).

Goodhue, Dale L., Laurie J. Kirsch, Judith A. Quillard, and Michael D. Wybo. "Strategic Data Planning: Lessons from the Field." *MIS Quarterly* 16, no. 1 (March 1992).

Goodhue, Dale L., Michael D. Wybo, and Laurie J. Kirsch. "The Impact of Data Integration on the Costs and Benefits of Information Systems." *MIS Quarterly* 16, no. 3 (September 1992).

Hirji, Karim K. "Exploring Data Mining Implementation." *Communications of the ACM* 44, no. 7 (July 2001).

Jukic, Boris, Nenad Jukic, and Manoj Parameswaran. "Data Models for Information Sharing in E Partnerships: Analysis, Improvements, and Relevance." *Journal of Organizational Computing and Electronic Commerce* 12, no. 2 (2002).

Kim, Yong Jin, Rajiv Kishore, and G. Lawrence Sanders. "From DQ to EQ: Understanding Data Quality in the Context of E-Business Systems." *Communications of the ACM* 48, no. 10 (October 2005).

Klau, Rick. "Data Quality and CRM." Line56.com, accessed March 4, 2003.

Kroenke, David. *Database Processing: Fundamentals, Design, and Implementation,* 10th ed. Upper Saddle River, NJ: Prentice Hall (2006).

Lee, Yang W., and Diane M. Strong. "Knowing-Why about Data Processes and Data Quality." *Journal of Management Information Systems* 20, no. 3 (Winter 2004).

Loveman, Gary. "Diamonds in the Datamine." *Harvard Business Review* (May 2003).

McFadden, Fred R., Jeffrey A. Hoffer, and Mary B. Prescott. *Modern Database Management,* 8th ed. Upper Saddle River, NJ: Prentice Hall (2007).

Morrison, Mike, Joline Morrison, and Anthony Keys. "Integrating Web Sites and Databases." *Communications of the ACM* 45, no. 9 (September 2002).

Pierce, Elizabeth M. "Assessing Data Quality with Control Matrices." *Communications of the ACM* 47, no. 2 (February 2004).

Redman, Thomas. "The Impact of Poor Data Quality on the Typical Enterprise." *Communications of the ACM* 41, no. 2 (February 1998).

Strong, Diane M., Yang W. Lee, and Richard Y. Wang. "Data Quality in Context." *Communications of the ACM* 40, no. 5 (May 1997).

Tayi, Giri Kumar, and Donald P. Ballou. "Examining Data Quality." *Communications of the ACM* 41, no. 2 (February 1998).

Wang, Richard Y., Yang W. Lee, Leo L. Pipino, and Diane M. Strong. "Manage Your Information as a Product." *Sloan Management Review* 39, no. 4 (Summer 1998).

# Chapter 6

Banerjee, Snehamay, and Ram L. Kumar. "Managing Electronic Interchange of Business Documents." *Communications of the ACM* 45, no. 7 (July 2002).

Ben Ameur, Walid, and Herve Kerivin. "New Economical Virtual Private Networks." *Communications of the ACM* 46, no. 6 (June 2003).

Bose, Indranil, and Raktim Pal. "Auto-ID: Management Anything Anywhere, Anytime in the Supply Chain." *Communications of the ACM* 48, no. 8 (August 2005).

Brandt, Richard. "Net Assets." *Stanford Magazine* (November–December 2004).

Clancy, Heather. "Flip Open That Cellphone: It's IM on the Move." *The New York Times Circuits* (October 7, 2004).

Damsgaard, Jan, and Kalle Lyytinen. "Building Electronic Trading Infrastructures: A Public or Private Responsibility?" *Journal of Organizational Computing and Electronic Commerce* 11, no. 2 (2001).

Dignan, Larry. "RFID: Hit or Myth?" *Baseline* (February 2004).

Elgin, Ben. "Google at $300? Hold That Cringe." *BusinessWeek Online* (June 10, 2005).

eMarketer, Inc. (Steve Butler). "VoIP: Spending and Trends" (June 2005c).

———. (Noah Elkin). "Wireless Broadband: The Future around the Corner" (May 2005b).

———. (Ben Macklin). "Broadband: Demographics and Usage" (July 2005a).

Farhoomand, Ali, Pauline S. P. Ng, and Justin K. H. Yue. "The Building of a New Business Ecosystem: Sustaining National Competitive Advantage through Electronic Commerce." *Journal of Organizational Computing and Electronic Commerce* 11, no. 4 (2001).

Frauenfelder, Mark. "Sir Tim Berners-Lee." *Technology Review* (October 2004).

Grant, Peter. "Ready for Prime Time." *The Wall Street Journal* (January 12, 2004).

Grover, Varun, and Khawaja Saeed. "The Telecommunication Industry Revisited." *Communications of the ACM* 46, no. 7 (July 2003).

Housel, Tom, and Eric Skopec. *Global Telecommunication Revolution: The Business Perspective.* New York: McGraw-Hill (2001).

Johnson, Keith. "Europe Picks Up 3G, as Phone Hopes Lift." *The Wall Street Journal* (August 25, 2005).

Keen, Peter G. W. *Competing in Time: Using Telecommunications for Competitive Advantage.* Cambridge, MA: Ballinger Publishing Company (1986).

Kocas, Cenk. "Evolution of Prices in Electronic Markets under Diffusion of Price-Comparison Shopping." *Journal of Management Information Systems* 19, no. 3 (Winter 2002–2003).

LaFraniere, Sharon. "Cellphones Catapult Rural Africa to 21st Century." *The New York Times* (August 25, 2005).

Li, Yuan. "Text Messages Sent by Cellphone Finally Catch on in U.S." *The Wall Street Journal* (August 11, 2005).

Madden, Mary, and Lee Rainie. "America's Online Pursuits." Pew Internet and American Life Project (April 25, 2004).

Maes, Patti, Robert H. Guttman, and Alexandros G. Moukas. "Agents That Buy and Sell." *Communications of the ACM* 42, no. 3 (March 1999).

Nasaw, Daniel. "Instant Messages Are Popping Up All Over." *The Wall Street Journal* (June 12, 2003).

National Research Council. *The Internet's Coming of Age.* Washington, DC: National Academy Press (2000).

Netcraft. "Netcraft August 2005 Web Server Survey" (August 2005).

Nicopolitidis, Petros, Georgios Papademitriou, Mohammad S. Obaidat, and Adreas S. Pomportsis. "The Economics of Wireless Networks." *Communications of the ACM* 47, no. 4 (April 2004).

Niemeyer, Alex, Minsok H. Pak, and Sanjay E. Ramaswamy. "Smart Tags for Your Supply Chain." *McKinsey Quarterly* no. 4 (2003).

Overby, Christine Spivey. "RFID at What Cost?" *Forrester Research* (March 1, 2004).

Papazoglou, Mike P. "Agent-Oriented Technology in Support of E-Business." *Communications of the ACM* 44, no. 4 (April 2001).

Pottie, G. J., and W. J. Kaiser. "Wireless Integrated Network Sensors." *Communications of the ACM* 43, no. 5 (May 2000).

Rothfeder, Jeffrey. "What's Wrong with RFID?" *CIO Insight* (August 1, 2004).

Roush, Wade. "The Internet Reborn." *Technology Review* (October 2003).

Spangler, Todd. "Voice on Data Networks: A Sound Move?" *Baseline* (March 2004).

Talbot, David. "The Internet Is Broken." *Technology Review* (December 2005/January 2006).

Varshney, Upkar, Andy Snow, Matt McGivern, and Christi Howard. "Voice Over IP." *Communications of the ACM* 45, no. 1 (January 2002).

Wareham, Jonathan, and Armando Levy. "Who Will Be the Adopters of 3G Mobile Computing Devices? A Profit Estimation of Mobile Telecom Diffusion." *Journal of Organizational Computing and Electronic Commerce* 12, no. 2 (2002).

Weiser, Mark. "What Ever Happened to the Next-Generation Internet?" *Communications of the ACM* 44, no. 9 (September 2001).

Werbach, Kevin. "Using VoIP to Compete." *Harvard Business Review* (September 2005).

Young, Shawn. "Market for Internet Calling, Once Tiny, Gets Crowded Fast." *The Wall Street Journal* (August 26, 2005).

# Chapter 7

Associated Press. "Worm Damage Could Have Been Reduced." (May 5, 2004).

Austin, Robert D., and Christopher A. R. Darby. "The Myth of Secure Computing." *Harvard Business Review* (June 2003).

Backhouse, James, Carol Hsu, and Aidan McDonnell. "Toward Public-Key Infrastructure Interoperability." *Communications of the ACM* 46, no. 6 (June 2003).

Bank, David. "Mydoom Worm Renews Debate on Cybetr-Ethics." *The Wall Street Journal* (November 11, 2004).

———. "Outbreak!" *The Wall Street Journal* (November 15, 2004).

Bank, David, and Riva Richmond. "Where the Dangers Are." *The Wall Street Journal,* Technology Report (July 18, 2005).

———. "What's That Sneaking into Your Computer?" *The Wall Street Journal* (April 26, 2004).

Berghel, Hal. "The Discipline of Internet Forensics." *Communications of the ACM* 46, no. 8 (August 2003).

Biever, Celeste. "Instant Messaging Falls Prey to Worms." (May 14, 2005).

Borzo, Jeannette. "Something's Phishy." *The Wall Street Journal* (November 15, 2004).

Brenner, Susan W. "U.S. Cybercrime Law: Defining Offenses." *Information Systems Frontiers* 6, no. 2 (June 2004).

Byers, Simon, and Dave Kormann. "802.11b Access Point Mapping." *Communications of the ACM* 46, no. 5 (May 2003).

Cam Winget, Nancy, Russ Housley, David Wagner, and Jesse Walker. "Security Flaws in 802.11b Data Link Protocols*." Communications of the ACM* 46, no. 5 (May 2003).

Cavusoglu, Huseyin, Birendra Mishra, and Srinivasan Raghunathan. "A Model for Evaluating IT Security Investments." *Communications of the ACM* 47, no. 7 (July 2004).

Cox, Mark. "Internet Security Threats Increasing in Maliciousness and Criminal Intent: CompTIA." *eChannel Line Daily New* (June 19, 2005).

Darby, Christopher. "The Dollars and Cents of Security." *Optimize* 12 (October 2002).

Datz, Todd. "The Interactive Nightmare." *CSO Magazine* (April 2004).

Delaney, Kevin J. "'Evil Twins' and 'Pharming.'" *The Wall Street Journal* (May 17, 2005).

Di Pietro, Roberto, and Luigi V. Mancini. "Security and Privacy Issues of Handheld and Wearable Wireless Devices." *Communications of the ACM* 46, no. 9 (September 2003).

Duffy, Daintry. "Body of Evidence." *CSO Magazine* (May 2004).

Foley, John. "You Call This Trustworthy Computing?" *Information Week* (February 14, 2005).

Foley, John, and George V. Hulme. "Get Ready to Patch." *Information Week* (August 30, 2004).

Ghosh, Anup K., and Tara M. Swaminatha. "Software Security and Privacy Risks in Mobile E-Commerce." *Communications of the ACM* 44, no. 2 (February 2001).

Giordano, Scott M. "Electronic Evidence and the Law." *Information Systems Frontiers* 6, no. 2 (June 2004).

Gordon, Lawrence A., Martin P. Loeb, and Tashfeen Sohail. "A Framework for Using Insurance for Cyber-Risk Management. "*Communications of the ACM* 46, no. 3 (March 2003).

Gordon, Lawrence A., Martin P. Loeb, William Lucyshyn, and Robert Richardson. "2005 CSI/FBI Computer Crime and Security Survey." Computer Security Institute (2005).

Horowitz, Alan S. "Biting Back." *Computerworld* (January 13, 2003).

Housley, Russ, and William Arbaugh. "Security Problems in 802.11b Networks." *Communications of the ACM* 46, no. 5 (May 2003).

Hulme, George V. "Dial V for Virus." *Information Week* (December 6, 2004).

Hulme, George V., and Thomas Claburn. "Tiny Evil Things." *Information Week* (April 26, 2004).

IBM. "IBM Report: Phishing Attacks in May Jumped More Than 200 Percent; Email Viruses Up 33 Percent." www.businesswire.com, accessed June 30, 2005.

ICSA Labs. "Tenth Annual Computer Virus Prevalence Survey." www.icsalabs.com, www.cybertrust.com, accessed June 17, 2005.

Ives, Blake, Kenneth R. Walsh, and Helmut Schneider. "The Domino Effect of Password Reuse." *Communications of the ACM* 47, no. 4 (April 2004).

Joshi, James B. D., Walid G. Aref, Arif Ghafoor, and Eugene H. Spafford. "Security Models for Web-Based Applications." *Communications of the ACM* 44, no. 2 (February 2001).

Keizer, Gregg. "Trojan Horse Poses as Windows XP Update." *Information Week* (January 9, 2004).

Koch, Christopher. "Don't Maroon Security." *CIO Magazine* (May 15, 2005).

Laudon, Kenneth C. "Data Quality and Due Process in Large Interorganizational Record Systems." *Communications of the ACM* 29 (January 1986a).

Leyden, John. "The Strange Decline in Computer Worms." *The Register,* www.channelregister.co.uk/2005/03/17/f-secure_websec/, accessed March 17, 2005.

Mercuri, Rebeca T. "Analyzing Security Costs." *Communications of the ACM* 46, no. 6 (June 2003).

Mercuri, Rebecca T. "The HIPAA-potamus in Health Care Data Security." *Communications of the ACM* 47, no. 7 (July 2004).

Newman, Robert. *Enterprise Security.* Upper Saddle River, NJ: Prentice Hall (2003).

Panko, Raymond R. *Corporate Computer and Network Security.* Upper Saddle River, NJ: Pearson Prentice Hall (2004).

Reuters. "Sasser Computer Worm Author Confesses in Trial": (July 5, 2005).

Rivlin, Gary. "Purloined Lives." *The New York Times* (March 17, 2005).

Roberts, Paul. "Fake Microsoft Security Trojan on the Loose, Antivirus Firm Says," ID News Service (April 8, 2005).

Roche, Edward M., and George Van Nostrand. *Information Systems, Computer Crime and Criminal Justice.* New York: Barraclough Ltd. (2004).

Schwerha, Joseph J., IV. "Cybercrime: Legal Standards Governing the Collection of Digital Evidence." *Information Systems Frontiers* 6, no. 2 (June 2004).

Shukla, Sudhindra, and Fiona Fui-Hoon Nah. "Web Browsing and Spyware Intrusion." *Communications of the ACM* 48, no. 8 (August 2005).

Straub, Detmar W., and Richard J. Welke. "Coping with Systems Risk: Security Planning Models for Management Decision Making." *MIS Quarterly* 22, no. 4 (December 1998).

Thompson, Roger. "Why Spyware Poses Multiple Threats to Security." *Communications of the ACM* 48, no. 8 (August 2005).

Thomson, Iain. "Akamai Investigates Denial of Service Attack." vunet.com, accessed June 17, 2004.

Vara, Vauhini. "Lurking in the Shadows." *The Wall Street Journal,* Technology Report (July 18, 2005).

Volonino, Linda, and Stephen R. Robinson. *Principles and Practices of Information Security.* Upper Saddle River, NJ: Prentice Hall (2004).

Wang, Huaiqing, and Chen Wang. "Taxonomy of Security Considerations and Software Quality." *Communications of the ACM* 46, no. 6 (June 2003).

Warkentin, Merrill, Xin Luo, and Gary F. Templeton. "A Framework for Spyware Assessement." *Communications of the ACM* 48, no. 8 (August 2005).

Winstein, Keith J. "Bluetooth Gear May Be Open to Snooping." *The Wall Street Journal* (June 16, 2005). http://www.itl.nist.gov/div897/docs/samate.html, accessed August 1, 2005.

Zeller, Tom, Jr. "The Scramble to Protect Personal Data." *The New York Times* (June 9, 2005).

Zhou, Jianying. "Achieving Fair Nonrepudiation in Electronic Transactions." *Journal of Organizational Computing and Electronic Commerce* 11, no. 4 (2001).

## Chapter 8

Anderson, James C., and James A. Narus. "Selectively Pursuing More of Your Customer's Business." *MIT Sloan Management Review* 44, no. 3 (Spring 2003).

D'Avanzo, Robert, Hans von Lewinski, and Luk N. Van Wassenhove. "The Link between Supply Chain and Financial Performance." *Supply Chain Management Review* (November 1, 2003).

Davenport, Thomas H. *Mission Critical: Realizing the Promise of Enterprise Systems.* Boston: Harvard Business School Press (2000).

———. "Putting the Enterprise into Enterprise Systems." *Harvard Business Review* (July–August 1998).

Day, George S. "Creating a Superior Customer-Relating Capability." *MIT Sloan Management Review* 44, no. 3 (Spring 2003).

Dowling, Grahame. "Customer Relationship Management: In B2C Markets, Often Less Is More." *California Management Review* 44, no. 3 (Spring 2002).

Fleisch, Elgar, Hubert Oesterle, and Stephen Powell. "Rapid Implementation of Enterprise Resource Planning Systems." *Journal of Organizational Computing and Electronic Commerce* 14, no. 2 (2004).

Goldenberg, Barton. "Don't Put the Cart before the Horse." *Customer Relationship Management* (September 2004).

Goodhue, Dale L., Barbara H. Wixom, and Hugh J. Watson. "Realizing Business Benefits through CRM: Hitting the Right Target in the Right Way." *MIS Quarterly Executive* 1, no. 2 (June 2002).

Gosain, Sanjay, Arvind Malhotra, and Omar A. El Sawy. "Coordinating for Flexibility in E-Business Supply Chains." *Journal of Management Information Systems* 21, no. 3 (Winter 2004–2005).

Handfield, Robert B., and Ernest L. Nichols, Jr. *Introduction to Supply Chain Management.* Upper Saddle River, NJ: Prentice Hall (1999).

Hitt, Lorin, D. J. Wu, and Xiaoge Zhou. "Investment in Enterprise Resource Planning: Business Impact and Productivity Measures." *Journal of Management Information Systems* 19, no. 1 (Summer 2002).

Jaiswal, M. P. "Implementing ERP Systems." *Dataquest* (June 30, 2003).

Kalakota, Ravi, and Marcia Robinson. *E-Business 2.0.* Boston: Addison-Wesley (2001).

———. *Services Blueprint: Roadmap for Execution.* Boston: Addison-Wesley (2003).

Kanakamedala, Kishore, Glenn Ramsdell, and Vats Srivatsan. "Getting Supply Chain Software Right." *McKinsey Quarterly* no. 1 (2003).

Koch, Christopher. "The ABCs of ERP." CIO Enterprise Resource Planning Research Center. www.cio.com, accessed August 1, 2003.

Kopczak, Laura Rock, and M. Eric Johnson. "The Supply-Chain Management Effect." *MIT Sloan Management Review* 44, no. 3 (Spring 2003).

Lee, Hau. "The Triple-A Supply Chain." *Harvard Business Review* (October 2004).

Lee, Hau, L., V. Padmanabhan, and Seugin Whang. "The Bullwhip Effect in Supply Chains." *Sloan Management Review* (Spring 1997).

LoFrumento, Tony. "How Profitable Are Your Customers?" *Optimize* 18 (April 2003).

Malhotra, Arvind, Sanjay Gosain, and Omar A. El Sawy. "Absorptive Capacity Configurations in Supply Chains: Gearing for Partner-Enabled Market Knowledge Creation." *MIS Quarterly* 29, no. 1 (March 2005).

Palaniswamy, Rajagopal, and Tyler Frank. "Enhancing Manufacturing Performance with ERP Systems." *Information Systems Management* (Summer 2000).

Ranganathan, C., Jasbir S. Dhaliwal, and Thompson S. H. Teo. "Assimilation and Diffusion of Web Technologies in Supply-Chain Management: An Examination of Key Drivers and Performance Impacts." *International Journal of Electronic Commerce* 9, no. 1 (Fall 2004).

Rayport, Jeffrey F. "Who Knows the Customer Best?" *Optimize* (March 2005).

Reinartz, Werner J., and Pankaj Chugh. "Learning from Experience: Making CRM a Success at Last," *Journal of Call Centre Management* (March/April 2002).

Robey, Daniel, Jeanne W. Ross, and Marie-Claude Boudreau. "Learning to Implement Enterprise Systems: An Exploratory Study of the Dialectics of Change." *Journal of Management Information Systems* 19, no. 1 (Summer 2002).

Scott, Judy E., and Iris Vessey. "Managing Risks in Enterprise Systems Implementations." *Communications of the ACM* 45, no. 4 (April 2002).

Slone, Reuben E. "Leading a Supply Chain Turnaround." *Harvard Business Review* (October 2004).

Winer, Russell S. "A Framework for Customer Relationship Management." *California Management Review* 43, no. 4 (Summer 2001).

Yu, Larry. "Successful Customer Relationship Management." *Sloan Management Review* 42, no. 4 (Summer 2001).

## Chapter 9

Adomavicius, Gediminas, and Alexander Tuzhilin. "Personalization Technologies: A Process-Oriented Perspective." *Communications of the ACM* 48, no. 10 (October 2005).

Ba, Sulin, and Paul A. Pavlou. "Evidence of the Effect of Trust Building Technology in Electronic Markets: Price Premiums and Buyer Behavior." *MIS Quarterly* 26, no. 3 (September 2002).

Bakos, Yannis. "The Emerging Role of Electronic Marketplaces and the Internet." *Communications of the ACM* 41, no. 8 (August 1998).

Bhargava, Hemant K., and Vidyanand Chourhary. "Economics of an Information Intermediary with Aggregation Benefits." *Information Systems Research* 15, no. 1 (March 2004).

Bright, Beckey. "Clip Quest." *The Wall Street Journal* (September 12, 2005).

Brynjolfsson, Erik, Yu Hu, and Michael D. Smith. "Consumer Surplus in the Digital Economy: Estimating the Value of Increased Product Variety at Online Booksellers." *Management Science* 49, no. 11 (November 2003).

Chaudhury, Abhijit,, Debasish Mallick, and H. Raghav Rao. "Web Channels in E-Commerce." *Communications of the ACM* 44, no. 1 (January 2001).

Christiaanse, Ellen. "Performance Benefits through Integration Hubs." *Communications of the ACM* 48, no. 5 (April 2005).

Crockett, Roger O., et al. "IPod Killers?" *Business Week Online* (April 21, 2005).

Cuneo, Eileen Colkin. "Web Ads Upend Industry Practices." *Information Week* (June 13, 2005).

Devaraj, Sarv, Ming Fan, and Rajiv Kohli. "Antecedents of B2C Channel Satisfaction and Preference: Validating E-Commerce Metrics." *Information Systems Research* 13, no. 3 (September 2002).

Dewan, Rajiv M., Marshall L. Freimer, and Jie Zhang. "Management and Valuation of Advertisement-Supported Web Sites." *Journal of Management Information Systems* 19, no. 3 (Winter 2002–2003).

eMarketer, Inc. "Comparative Estimates: B2C E-Commerce Revenues in the United States, 1997–2010 (in billions) (August 26, 2005a).

———. (Noah Elkin). "Mobile Marketing and M-Commerce: Global Spending and Trends" (February 2005c).

———. (Jeffrey Grau). "E-commerce in the US: Retail Trends" (May 2005b).

———. "E-Tailing's Next Lift." *Optimize* (July 2005).

Evans, Philip, and Thomas S. Wurster. *Blown to Bits: How the New Economics of Information Transforms Strategy.* Boston: Harvard Business School Press (2000).

Huang, Gregory T. "The Web's New Currency." *Technology Review* (November 2003).

Hui, Kai Lung, and Patrick Y.K. Chau. "Classifying Digital Products." *Communications of the ACM* 45, no. 6 (June 2002).

Iansiti, Marco, F. Warren McFarlan, and George Wessterman. "Leveraging the Incumbent's Advantage." *MIT Sloan Management Review* 44, no. 4 (Summer 2003).

Kaplan, Steven, and Mohanbir Sawhney. "E-Hubs: The New B2B Marketplaces." *Harvard Business Review* (May–June 2000).

Kauffman, Robert J., and Bin Wang. "New Buyers' Arrival under Dynamic Pricing Market Microstructure: The Case of Group-Buying Discounts on the Internet." *Journal of Management Information Systems* 18, no. 2 (Fall 2001).

Kenny, David, and John F. Marshall. "Contextual Marketing." *Harvard Business Review* (November–December 2000).

Kingson, Jennifer A. "Wireless Moves the Cash Register Where You Are." *The New York Times* (November 26, 2005).

Koufaris, Marios. "Applying the Technology Acceptance Model and Flow Theory to Online Consumer Behavior." *Information Systems Research* 13, no. 2 (2002).

Laudon, Kenneth C., and Carol Guercio Traver. *E-Commerce: Business, Technology, Society.* Boston: Addison-Wesley (2006).

Lee, Hau L., and Seungin Whang. "Winning the Last Mile of E-Commerce." *Sloan Management Review* 42, no. 4 (Summer 2001).

Li, Yuan. "Can't Talk Now, I'm Winning," *The Wall Street Journal* (October 11, 2005).

———. "Now, the *Very* Small Screen." *The Wall Street Journal* (September 22, 2005).

———. "TV—Anytime, Anywhere." *The Wall Street Journal* (September 12, 2005).

Lim, Gyoo Gun, and Jae Kyu Lee. "Buyer-Carts for B2B EC: The b-Cart Approach." *Journal of Organizational Computing and Electronic Commerce* 13, nos. 3 & 4 (2003).

Madden, Andrew P. "The Business of Blogging." *Technology Review* (August 2005).

Magretta, Joan. "Why Business Models Matter." *Harvard Business Review* (May 2002).

Markillie, Paul. "A Perfect Market." *The Economist* (May 15–21, 2004).

Markoff, John. "Apple Unveils a New IPod and a Phone Music Player." *The New York Times* (September 8, 2005).

McKnight, D. Harrison, Vivek Choudhury, and Charlea Kacmar. "Developing and Validating Trust Measures for e-Commerce: An Integrative Typology." *Information Systems Research* 13, no. 3 (September 2002).

McWilliam, Gil. "Building Stronger Brands through Online Communities." *Sloan Management Review* 41, no. 3 (Spring 2000).

Mossberg, Walter H. "Sprint Brings Music Direct to Cellphones, But Price Is Too High," *The Wall Street Journal* (November 17, 2005).

Pavlou, Paul A., and David Gefen. "Building Effective Online Marketplaces with Institution-Based Trust." *Information Systems Research* 15, no. 1 (March 2004).

Pinker, Edieal, Abraham Seidmann, and Riginald C. Foster. "Strategies for Transitioning 'Old Economy' Firms to E-Business." *Communications of the ACM* 45, no. 5 (May 2002).

Prahalad, C. K., and Venkatram Ramaswamy. "Coopting Consumer Competence." *Harvard Business Review* (January–February 2000).

Rainie, Lee. "The State of Blogging." Pew Internet & American Life Project (January 2005d).

Riggins, Frederic J. "Market Segmentation and Information Development Costs in a Two-Tiered Fee-Based and Sponsorship-Based Web Site." *Journal of Management Information Systems* 19, no. 3 (Winter 2002–2003).

Roush, Wade. "Social Machines." *Technology Review* (August 2005).

Roy, Cayce. "E-tailing's Next Lift." *Optimize* (July 2005).

Sawhney, Mohanbir, Emanuela Prandelli, and Gianmario Verona. "The Power of Innomediation." *MIT Sloan Management Review* (Winter 2003).

Schultze, Ulrike, and Wanda J. Orlikowski. "A Practice Perspective on Technology-Mediated Network Relations: The Use of Internet-Based Self-Serve Technologies." *Information Systems Research* 15, no. 1 (March 2004).

Smith, Michael D., Joseph Bailey, and Erik Brynjolfsson. "Understanding Digital Markets: Review and Assessment" in Erik Brynjolfsson and Brian Kahin, eds., *Understanding the Digital Economy.* Cambridge, MA: MIT Press (1999).

Sultan, Fareena, and Andrew Rohm. "The Coming Era of 'Brand in Hand' Marketing." *MIT Sloan Management Review* 47, no. 1 (Fall 2005).

Thomke, Stefan, and Eric von Hippel. "Customers as Innovators." *Harvard Business Review* (April 2002).

Urbaczewski, Andrew, Leonard M. Jessup, and Bradley Wheeler. "Electronic Commerce Research: A Taxonomy and Synthesis." *Journal of Organizational Computing and Electronic Commerce* 12, no. 2 (2002).

U.S. Department of Commerce. "E-Stats." Washington, D.C. (May 11, 2005).

Werbach, Kevin. "Syndication: The Emerging Model for Business in the Internet Era." *Harvard Business Review* (May–June 2000).

Westland, J. Christopher. "Preference Ordering Cash, Near-Cash and Electronic Cash." *Journal of Organizational Computing and Electronic Commerce* 12, no. 3 (2002).

Yen, Benjamin P.-C., and Elsie O. S. Ng. "The Impact of Electronic Commerce on Procurement." *Journal of Organizational Computing and Electronic Commerce* 13, nos. 3 & 4 (2003).

Yoo, Byungjoon, Vidyanand Choudhary, and Tridas Mukhopadhyay. "A Model of Neutral B2B Intermediaries." *Journal of Management Information Systems* 19, no. 3 (Winter 2002–2003).

# Chapter 10

Alavi, Maryam, and Dorothy Leidner. "Knowledge Management and Knowledge Management Systems: Conceptual Foundations and Research Issues." *MIS Quarterly* 25, no. 1 (March 2001).

Anandarajan, Murugan. "Profiling Web Usage in the Workplace: A Behavior-Based Artificial Intelligence Approach. " *Journal of Management Information Systems* 19, no. 1 (Summer 2002).

Anson, Rob, and Bjorn Erik Munkvold. "Beyond Face-to-Face: A Field Study of Electronic Meetings in Different Time and Place Modes." *Journal of Organizational Computing and Electronic Commerce* 14, no. 2 (2004).

Babcock, Charles. "Smaller Businesses Try Analytics." *Information Week* (May 9, 2005).

Bargeron, David, Jonathan Grudin, Anoop Gupta, Elizabeth Sanocki, Francis Li, and Scott Le Tiernan. "Asynchronous Collaboration around Multimedia Applied to On-Demand Education." *Journal of Management Information Systems* 18, no. 4 (Spring 2002).

Becerra-Fernandez, Irma, Avelino Gonzalez, and Rajiv Sabherwal. *Knowledge Management.* Upper Saddle River, NJ: Prentice Hall (2004).

Birkinshaw, Julian, and Tony Sheehan. "Managing the Knowledge Life Cycle." *MIT Sloan Management Review* 44, no. 1 (Fall 2002).

Bodendorf, Freimut, and Roland Zimmermann. "Proactive Supply Chain Event Management with Agent Technology." *International Journal of Electronic Commerce* 9, no. 4 (Summer 2005).

Booth, Corey, and Shashi Buluswar. "The Return of Artificial Intelligence." *McKinsey Quarterly* no. 2 (2002).

Burtka, Michael. "Generic Algorithms." *The Stern Information Systems Review* 1, no. 1 (Spring 1993).

**Cavalieri, Sergio, Vittorio Cesarotti,** and **Vito Introna.** "A Multiagent Model for Coordinated Distribution Chain Planning." *Journal of Organizational Computing and Electronic Commerce* 13, nos. 3 & 4 (2003).

**Chittum, Ryan.** "Location, Location Technology." *The Wall Street Journal,* Technology Report (July 18, 2005).

**Cognos Incorporated.** "Integrated CPM Solution from Cognos and SSA Global Drives Performance at Caesars Entertainment." (May 15, 2005).

**Davenport, Thomas H.,** and **Jeanne G. Harris.** "Automated Decision Making Comes of Age." *MIT Sloan Management Review* 46, no. 4 (Summer 2005).

**Davenport, Thomas H.,** and **Lawrence Prusak.** *Working Knowledge: How Organizations Manage What They Know.* Boston: Harvard Business School Press (1997).

**Davenport, Thomas H., David W. DeLong,** and **Michael C. Beers.** "Successful Knowledge Management Projects." *Sloan Management Review* 39, no. 2 (Winter 1998).

**Davenport, Thomas H., Robert J. Thomas,** and **Susan Cantrell.** "The Mysterious Art and Science of Knowledge-Worker Performance." *MIT Sloan Management Review* 44, no. 1 (Fall 2002).

**Dennis, Alan R.,** and **Bryan A. Reinicke.** "Beta versus VHS and the Acceptance of Electronic Brainstorming Technology." *MIS Quarterly* 28, no. 1 (March 2004).

**Dennis, Alan R., Jay E. Aronson, William G. Henriger,** and **Edward D. Walker III.** "Structuring Time and Task in Electronic Brainstorming." *MIS Quarterly* 23, no. 1 (March 1999).

**Dennis, Alan R., Jay F. Nunamaker, Jr.,** and **Douglas R. Vogel.** "A Comparison of Laboratory and Field Research in the Study of Electronic Meeting Systems." *Journal of Management Information Systems* 7, no. 3 (Winter 1990–1991).

**DeSanctis, Geraldine,** and **R. Brent Gallupe.** "A Foundation for the Study of Group Decision Support Systems." *Management Science* 33, no. 5 (May 1987).

**Dhar, Vasant,** and **Roger Stein.** *Intelligent Decision Support Methods: The Science of Knowledge Work.* Upper Saddle River, NJ: Prentice Hall (1997).

**Du, Timon C., Eldon Y. Li,** and **An-pin Chang.** "Mobile Agents in Distributed Network Management." *Communications of the ACM* 46, no. 7 (July 2003).

**Earl, Michael.** "Knowledge Management Strategies: Toward a Taxonomy." *Journal of Management Information Systems* 18, no. 1 (Summer 2001).

**Easley, Robert F., Sarv Devaraj,** and **J. Michael Crant.** "Relating Collaborative Technology Use to Teamwork Quality and Performance: An Empirical Analysis." *Journal of Management Information Systems* 19, no. 4 (Spring 2003).

**El Sawy, Omar.** "Personal Information Systems for Strategic Scanning in Turbulent Environments." *MIS Quarterly* 9, no. 1 (March 1985).

**Fjermestad, Jerry,** and **Starr Roxanne Hiltz.** "An Assessment of Group Support Systems Experimental Research: Methodology, and Results." *Journal of Management Information Systems* 15, no. 3 (Winter, 1998–1999).

**Frangos, Alex.** "New Dimensions in Design." *The Wall Street Journal* (July 7, 2004)

**Gallupe, R. Brent, Geraldine DeSanctis,** and **Gary W. Dickson.** "Computer-Based Support for Group Problem-Finding: An Experimental Investigation." *MIS Quarterly* 12, no. 2 (June 1988).

**Gorry, G. Anthony,** and **Michael S. Scott Morton.** "A Framework for Management Information Systems." *Sloan Management Review* 13, no. 1 (Fall 1971).

**Grover, Varun,** and **Thomas H. Davenport.** "General Perspectives on Knowledge Management: Fostering a Research Agenda." *Journal of Management Information Systems* 18, no. 1 (Summer 2001).

**Holland, John H.** "Genetic Algorithms." *Scientific American* (July 1992).

**Hollis, Emily.** "U.S. Navy: Smooth Sailing for Education." *Chief Learning Officer* (February 2004).

**Housel, Tom,** and **Arthur A. Bell.** *Measuring and Managing Knowledge.* New York: McGraw-Hill (2001).

**Hummingbird Inc.** "Law Firm Discovers Short Cut to Savings on the E-Mail Trail," www.hummigbird.com, accessed August 7, 2005.

**Information Builders Inc.** "Information Builders Underwrites New Enterprise Reporting System for National Life." www.informationbuilders.com, accessed August 7, 2005.

**Jarvenpaa, Sirkka L.,** and **D. Sandy Staples.** "Exploring Perceptions of Organizational Ownership of Information and Expertise." *Journal of Management Information Systems* 18, no. 1 (Summer 2001).

**King, William R., Peter V. Marks, Jr.,** and **Scott McCoy.** "The Most Important Issues in Knowledge Management." *Communications of the ACM* 45, no. 9 (September 2002).

**KPMG.** "Insights from KPMG's European Knowledge Management Survey 2002/2003" (2003a).

———. "Who We Are—Sharing Knowledge." www.kpmgcampus.com September 6 (2003b).

**Kuo, R. J., K. Chang,** and **S. Y. Chien.** "Integration and Self-Organizing Feature Maps and Genetic-Algorithm-Based Clustering Method for Market Segmentation." *Journal of Organizational Computing and Electronic Commerce* 14, no. 1 (2004).

**Latour, Almar.** "After 20 Years, Baby Bells Face Some Grown-Up Competition." *The Wall Street Journal* (May 28, 2004).

**Leidner, Dorothy E.,** and **Joyce Elam.** "Executive Information Systems: Their Impact on Executive Decision Making." *Journal of Management Information Systems* (Winter 1993–1994).

**Leidner, Dorothy E.,** and **Joyce Elam.** "The Impact of Executive Information Systems on Organizational Design, Intelligence, and Decision Making." *Organization Science* 6, no. 6 (November–December 1995).

**Lilien, Gary L., Arvind Rangaswamy, Gerrit H. Van Bruggen,** and **Katrin Starke.** "DSS Effectiveness in Marketing Resource Allocation Decisions: Reality vs. Perception." *Information Systems Research* 15, no. 3 (September 2004).

**Lindorff, Dave.** "How Data Fuels Parkway Corp." *CIO Insight* (February 14, 2003).

**Maglio, Paul P.,** and **Christopher S. Campbell.** "Attentive Agents." *Communications of the ACM* 46, no. 3 (March 2003).

**Maryam, Alavi,** and **Dorothy E. Leidner.** "Knowledge Management and Knowledge Management Systems." *MIS Quarterly* 25, no. 1 (March 2001).

**Microsoft Corporation.** "KPMG Turns Knowledge into Value with Kworld." www.microsoft.com/korea/business/downloads/km/kworld.doc 2003, accessed September 6, 2003.

**Moravec, Hans.** "Robots, After All." *Communications of the ACM* 46, no. 10 (October 2003).

**Murphy, Chris.** "Top-Line Impact." *Information Week* (May 9, 2005).

**O'Keefe, Robert M.,** and **Tim McEachern.** "Web-based Customer Decision Support Systems." *Communications of the ACM* 41, no. 3 (March 1998).

**Perry, Andrew.** "KM in Review: Tracing the Value of Knowledge Assets." *KM World* (October 2002).

**Pinsonneault, Alain, Henri Barki, R. Brent Gallupe,** and **Norberto Hoppen.** "Electronic Brainstorming: The Illusion of Productivity." *Information Systems Research* 10, no. 2 (July 1999).

**ProfitLogic.** "Burlington Coat Factory to Implement ProfitLogic's Markdown Optimization Solution" (April 26, 2005).

**Sadeh, Norman, David W. Hildum,** and **Dag Kjenstad.** "Agent-Based E-Supply Chain Decision Support." *Journal of Organizational Computing and Electronic Commerce* 13, nos. 3 & 4 (2003).

**Saint-Onge, Hubert.** "The Power of Shared Knowledge." *Optimize* (May 2005).

**Schultze, Ulrike,** and **Dorothy Leidner.** "Studying Knowledge Management in Information Systems Research: Discourses and Theoretical Assumptions." *MIS Quarterly* 26, no. 3 (September 2002).

**Schwabe, Gerhard.** "Providing for Organizational Memory in Computer-Supported Meetings." *Journal of Organizational Computing and Electronic Commerce* 9, nos. 2 & 3 (1999).

**Sheng, Yihua Philip, Peter P. Mykytyn, Jr.,** and **Charles R. Litecky.** "Competitor Analysis and Its Defenses in the E-Marketplace." *Communications of the ACM* 48, no. 8 (August 2005).

**Siebel Systems.** "Compass Bank Reduces Loan Write-Offs by 7 Percent Using Siebel Business Analytics." www.siebel.com/business-intelligence/success-stories.shtm, accessed August 14, 2005.

Simon, H. A. *The New Science of Management Decision.* New York: Harper & Row (1960).

Singh, Rahul, A. F. Salam, and Lakshmi Iyer. "Agents in E-Supply Chains." *Communications of the ACM* 48, no. 6 (June 2005).

Suh, Kil-Soo, and Young Eun Lee. "The Effects of Virtual Reality on Consumer Learning: An Empirical Investigation." *MIS Quarterly* 29, no. 4 (December 2005).

Sullivan, Laurie. "Fine-Tuned Pricing." *Information Week* (August 15/22, 2005).

Tanriverdi, Huseyin. "Information Technology Relatedness, Knowledge Management Capability, and Performance of Multibusiness Firms." *MIS Quarterly* 29, no. 2 (June 2005).

Turban, Efraim, and Jay E. Aronson. *Business Intelligence and Decision Support Systems,* 8th ed. Upper Saddle River, NJ: Prentice Hall (2007).

Walczak, Steven. "Gaining Competitive Advantage for Trading in Emerging Capital Markets with Neural Networks. " *Journal of Management Information Systems* 16, no. 2 (Fall 1999).

Wang, Huaiqing, John Mylopoulos, and Stephen Liao. "Intelligent Agents and Financial Risk Monitoring Systems." *Communications of the ACM* 45, no. 3 (March 2002).

Zack, Michael H. "Rethinking the Knowledge-Based Organization." *MIT Sloan Management Review* 44, no. 4 (Summer 2003).

Zadeh, Lotfi A. "Fuzzy Logic, Neural Networks, and Soft Computing." *Communications of the ACM* 37, no. 3 (March 1994).

# Chapter 11

Agarwal, Ritu, and Viswanath Venkatesnh. "Assessing a Firm's Web Presence: A Heuristic Evaluation Procedure for the Measurement of Usability." *Information Systems Research* 13, no. 3 (September 2002).

Andres, Howard P., and Robert W. Zmud. "A Contingency Approach to Software Project Coordination." *Journal of Management Information Systems* 18, no. 3 (Winter 2001–2002).

Aron, Ravi, Eric K. Clemons, and Sashi Reddi. "Just Right Outsourcing: Understanding and Managing Risk." *Journal of Management Information Systems* 22, no. 1 (Summer 2005).

Avison, David E., and Guy Fitzgerald. "Where Now for Development Methodologies?" *Communications of the ACM* 41, no. 1 (January 2003).

Baily, Martin N., and Diana Farrell. "Exploding the Myths of Offshoring." *McKinsey Quarterly* (July 2004).

Barki, Henri, Suzanne Rivard, and Jean Talbot. "An Integrative Contingency Model of Software Project Risk Management." *Journal of Management Information Systems* 17, no. 4 (Spring 2001).

Barthelemy, Jerome. "The Hidden Costs of IT Outsourcing." *Sloan Management Review* (Spring 2001).

Bhattacherjee, Anol, and G. Premkumar. "Understanding Changes in Belief and Attitude toward Information Technology Usage: A Theoretical Model and Longitudinal Test." *MIS Quarterly* 28, no. 2 (June 2004).

Datz, Todd. "Portfolio Management: How to Do It Right," *CIO Magazine* (May 1, 2003).

Davern, Michael J., and Robert J. Kauffman. "Discovering Potential and Realizing Value from Information Technology Investments." *Journal of Management Information Systems* 16, no. 4 (Spring 2000).

Davidson, Elisabeth J. "Technology Frames and Framing: A Socio-Cognitive Investigation of Requirements Determination." *MIS Quarterly* 26, no. 4 (December 2002).

Delone, William H., and Ephraim R. McLean. "The Delone and McLean Model of Information Systems Success: A Ten-Year Update. *Journal of Management Information Systems* 19, no. 4 (Spring 2003).

Feeny, David, Mary Lacity, and Leslie P. Willcocks. "Taking the Measure of Outsourcing Providers." *MIT Sloan Management Review* 46, no. 3 (Spring 2005).

Fingar, Peter. "Component-Based Frameworks for E-Commerce." *Communications of the ACM* 43, no. 10 (October 2000).

Gallivan, Michael J., Valerie K. Spitler, and Marios Koufaris. "Does Information Technology Training Really Matter?" *Journal of Management Information Systems* 22, no. 1 (Summer 2005).

George, Joey, Dinesh Batra, Joseph S. Valacich, and Jeffrey A. Hoffer. *Object Oriented System Analysis and Design,* 2nd ed. Upper Saddle River, NJ: Prentice Hall (2007).

Hickey, Ann M., and Alan M. Davis. "A Unified Model of Requirements Elicitation." *Journal of Management Information Systems* 20, no. 4 (Spring 2004).

Hitt, Lorin, D. J. Wu, and Xiaoge Zhou. "Investment in Enterprise Resource Planning: Business Impact and Productivity Measures." *Journal of Management Information Systems* 19, no. 1 (Summer 2002).

Hoffer, Jeffrey, Joey George, and Joseph Valacich. *Modern Systems Analysis and Design*, 4th ed. Upper Saddle River, NJ: Prentice Hall (2005).

Hoffman, Thomas. "ABN Amro Turns to Global Portfolio Management." *Computerworld* (April 18, 2005).

Hopkins, Jon. "Component Primer." *Communications of the ACM* 43, no. 10 (October 2000).

Housel, Thomas J., Omar El Sawy, Jianfang J. Zhong, and Waymond Rodgers. "Measuring the Return on E-Business Initiatives at the Process Level: The Knowledge Value-Added Approach." *ICIS* (2001).

Irwin, Gretchen. "The Role of Similarity in the Reuse of Object-Oriented Analysis Models." *Journal of Management Information Systems* 19, no. 2 (Fall 2002).

Ivari, Juhani, Rudy Hirscheim, and Heinz K. Klein. "A Dynamic Framework for Classifying Information Systems Development Methodologies and Approaches." *Journal of Management Information Systems* 17, no. 3 (Winter 2000–2001).

Iyer, Bala, Jim Freedman, Mark Gaynor, and George Wyner. "Web Services: Enabling Dynamic Business Networks." *Communications of the Association for Information Systems* 11 (2003).

Jasperson, Jon (Sean), Pamela E. Carter, and Robert W. Zmud. "A Comprehensive Conceptualization of Post-Adoptive Behaviors Associated with Information Technology Enabled Work Systems." *MIS Quarterly* 29, no. 3 (September 2005).

Jeffrey, Mark, and Ingmar Leliveld. "Best Practices in IT Portfolio Management." *MIT Sloan Management Review* 45, no. 3 (Spring 2004).

Johnson, Richard A. "The Ups and Downs of Object-Oriented Systems Development." *Communications of the ACM* 43, no. 10 (October 2000).

Keen, Peter G. W. *Shaping the Future: Business Design through Information Technology.* Cambridge, MA: Harvard Business School Press (1991).

Keen, Peter W. "Information Systems and Organizational Change." *Communications of the ACM* 24 (January 1981).

Keil, Mark, Joan Mann, and Arun Rai. "Why Software Projects Escalate: An Empirical Analysis and Test of Four Theoretical Models." *MIS Quarterly* 24, no. 4 (December 2000).

Kendall, Kenneth E., and Julie E. Kendall. *Systems Analysis and Design,* 6th ed. Upper Saddle River, NJ: Prentice Hall (2005).

Kettinger, William J., and Choong C. Lee. "Understanding the IS-User Divide in IT Innovation." *Communications of the ACM* 45, no. 2 (February 2002).

Kirsch, Laurie J. "Deploying Common Systems Globally: The Dynamic of Control." *Information Systems Research* 15, no. 4 (December 2004).

Klein, Gary, James J. Jiang, and Debbie B. Tesch. "Wanted: Project Teams with a Blend of IS Professional Orientations." *Communications of the ACM* 45, no. 6 (June 2002).

Koh, Christine, Song Ang, and Detmar W. Straub. "IT Outsourcing Success: A Psychological Contract Perspective." *Information Systems Research* 15 no. 4 (December 2004).

Kolb, D. A., and A. L. Frohman. "An Organization Development Approach to Consulting." *Sloan Management Review* 12 (Fall 1970).

Krishna, S., Sundeep Sahay, and Geoff Walsham. "Managing Cross-Cultural Issues in Global Software Outsourcing." *Communications of the ACM* 47, no. 4 (April 2004).

Lapointe, Liette, and Suzanne Rivard. "A Multilevel Model of Resistance to Information Technology Implementation." *MIS Quarterly* 29, no. 3 (September 2005).

Lee, Jae-Nam, Shaila M. Miranda, and Yong-Mi Kim. "IT Outsourcing Strategies: Universalistic, Contingency, and Configurational Explanations of Success." *Information Systems Research* 15, no. 2 (June 2004).

**Lee, Jae-Nam, Minh Q. Huynh, Ron Chi-Wai Kwok,** and **Shih-Ming Pi.** "IT Outsourcing Evolution—Past, Present, and Future." *Communications of the ACM* 46, no. 5 (May 2003).

**Levina, Natalia,** and **Jeanne W. Ross.** "From the Vendor's Perspective: Exploring the Value Proposition in Information Technology Outsourcing." *MIS Quarterly* 27, no. 3 (September 2003).

**Limayem, Moez, Mohamed Khalifa,** and **Wynne W. Chin.** "Case Tools Usage and Impact on System Development Performance." *Journal of Organizational Computing and Electronic Commerce* 14, no. 3 (2004).

**Luftman, Jerry,** and **Hunter Muller.** "Total Value of Ownership: A New Model." *Optimize* (July 2005).

**Majchrzak, Ann, Cynthia M. Beath,** and **Ricardo A. Lim.** "Managing Client Dialogues during Information Systems Design to Facilitate Client Learning." *MIS Quarterly* 29, no. 4 (December 2005).

**Mann, Catherine L.** "What Global Sourcing Means for U.S. I.T. Workers and for the U.S. Economy." *Communications of the ACM* 47, no. 7 (July 2004).

**Markus, M. Lynne,** and **Robert I. Benjamin.** "The Magic Bullet Theory of IT-Enabled Transformation." *Sloan Management Review* (Winter 1997).

**Martin, James.** *Application Development without Programmers.* Englewood Cliffs, NJ: Prentice Hall (1982).

**Martin, James,** and **Carma McClure.** *Structured Techniques: The Basis of CASE.* Englewood Cliffs, NJ: Prentice Hall (1988).

**McFarlan, F. Warren.** "Portfolio Approach to Information Systems." *Harvard Business Review* (September–October 1981).

**Mumford, Enid,** and **Mary Weir.** *Computer Systems in Work Design: The ETHICS Method.* New York: John Wiley (1979).

**Nidumolu, Sarma R.,** and **Mani Subramani.** "The Matrix of Control: Combining Process and Structure Approaches to Managing Software Development." *Journal of Management Information Systems* 20, no. 4 (Winter 2004).

**Overby, Stephanie.** "The Hidden Costs of Offshore Outsourcing," *CIO Magazine* (September 1, 2003).

**Palmer, Jonathan W.** "Web Site Usability, Design and Performance Metrics." *Information Systems Research* 13, no. 3 (September 2002).

**Phillips, James,** and **Dan Foody.** "Building a Foundation for Web Services." *EAI Journal* (March 2002).

**Pitts, Mitzi G.,** and **Glenn J. Browne.** "Stopping Behavior of Systems Analysts during Information Requirements Elicitation." *Journal of Management Information Systems* 21, no. 1 (Summer 2004).

**Prahalad, C. K.,** and **M. S. Krishnan.** "Synchronizing Strategy and Information Technology." *Sloan Management Review* 43, no. 4 (Summer 2002).

**Rai, Arun, Sandra S. Lang,** and **Robert B. Welker.** "Assessing the Validity of IS Success Models: An Empirical Test and Theoretical Analysis." *Information Systems Research* 13, no. 1 (March 2002).

**Ravichandran, T.,** and **Marcus A. Rothenberger.** "Software Reuse Strategies and Component Markets." *Communications of the ACM* 46, no. 8 (August 2003).

**Ribeiro, John.** "Travel Giant TUI Wades Deeper into Indian Outsourcing." *Computerworld* (February 3, 2005).

**Robey, Daniel, Jeanne W. Ross,** and **Marie-Claude Boudreau.** "Learning to Implement Enterprise Systems: An Exploratory Study of the Dialectics of Change." *Journal of Management Information Systems* 19, no. 1 (Summer 2002).

**Ryan, Sherry D., David A. Harrison,** and **Lawrence L Schkade.** "Information Technology Investment Decisions: When Do Cost and Benefits in the Social Subsystem Matter?" *Journal of Management Information Systems* 19, no. 2 (Fall 2002).

**Sircar, Sumit, Sridhar P. Nerur,** and **Radhakanta Mahapatra.** "Revolution or Evolution? A Comparison of Object-Oriented and Structured Systems Development Methods." *MIS Quarterly* 25, no. 4 (December 2001).

**Smith, H. Jeff, Mark Keil,** and **Gordon Depledge.** "Keeping Mum as the Project Goes Under." *Journal of Management Information Systems* 18, no. 2 (Fall 2001).

**Speier, Cheri,** and **Michael. G. Morris.** "The Influence of Query Interface Design on Decision-Making Performance." *MIS Quarterly* 27, no. 3 (September 2003).

**Swanson, E. Burton.** *Information System Implementation.* Homewood, IL: Richard D. Irwin (1988).

**Swanson, E. Burton,** and **Enrique Dans.** "System Life Expectancy and the Maintenance Effort: Exploring Their Equilibration." *MIS Quarterly* 24, no. 2 (June 2000).

**Tam, Kar Yan,** and **Kai Lung Hui.** "A Choice Model for the Selection of Computer Vendors and Its Empirical Estimation." *Journal of Management Information Systems* 17, no. 4 (Spring 2001).

**Thatcher, Matt E.,** and **Jim R. Oliver.** "The Impact of Technology Investments on a Firm's Production Efficiency, Product Quality, and Productivity." *Journal of Management Information Systems* 18, no. 2 (Fall 2001).

**Turetken, Ozgur, David Schuff, Ramesh Sharda,** and **Terence T. Ow.** "Supporting Systems Analysis and Design through Fisheye Views." *Communications of the ACM* 47, no. 9 (September 2004).

**Van Den Heuvel, Willem-Jan,** and **Zakaria Maamar.** "Moving toward a Framework to Compose Intelligent Web Services." *Communications of the ACM* 46, no. 10 (October 2003).

**Venkatesh, Viswanath, Michael G. Morris, Gordon B. Davis,** and **Fred D. Davis.** "User Acceptance of Information Technology: Toward a Unified View." *MIS Quarterly* 27, no. 3 (September 2003).

**Vitharana, Padmal.** "Risks and Challenges of Component-Based Software Development." *Communications of the ACM* 46, no. 8 (August 2003).

**Watad, Mahmoud M.,** and **Frank J. DiSanzo.** "Case Study: The Synergism of Telecommuting and Office Automation." *Sloan Management Review* 41, no. 2 (Winter 2000).

**Wulf, Volker,** and **Matthias Jarke.** "The Economics of End-User Development." *Communications of the ACM* 47, no. 9 (September 2004).

**Xia, Weidong,** and **Gwanhoo Lee.** "Complexity of Information Systems Development Projects." *Journal of Management Information Systems* 22, no. 1 (Summer 2005).

**Zhu, Kevin, Kenneth L. Kraemer, Sean Xu,** and **Jason Dedrick.** "Information Technology Payoff in E-Business Environments: An International Perspective on Value Creation of E-Business in the Financial Services Industry." *Journal of Management Information Systems* 21, no. 1 (Summer 2004).

# Chapter 12

**American Management Association,** and **The ePolicy Institute.** "2005 Electronic Monitoring & Surveillance Survey" (May 18, 2005).

**Association of Computing Machinery.** "ACM's Code of Ethics and Professional Conduct." *Communications of the ACM* 36, no. 12 (December 1993).

**Ball, Kirstie S.** "Situating Workplace Surveillance: Ethics and Computer-Based Performance Monitoring." *Ethics and Information Technology* 3, no. 3 (2001).

**Bank, David.** "Companies Seek to Hold Software Makers Liable for Flaws." *The Wall Street Journal* (February 24, 2005).

**Bellman, Steven, Eric J. Johnson,** and **Gerald L. Lohse.** "To Opt-in or Opt-out? It Depends on the Question." *Communications of the ACM* 44, no. 2 (February 2001).

**Bennett, Colin J.** "Cookies, Web Bugs, Webcams, and Cue Cats: Patterns of Surveillance on the World Wide Web." *Ethics and Information Technology* 3, no. 3 (2001).

**Bowen, Jonathan.** "The Ethics of Safety-Critical Systems." *Communications of the ACM* 43, no. 3 (April 2000).

**Brown Bag Software vs. Symantec Corp.** 960 F2D 1465 (Ninth Circuit, 1992).

**Burk, Dan L.** "Copyrightable Functions and Patentable Speech." *Communications of the ACM* 44, no. 2 (February 2001).

**Carr, David F.,** and **Sean Gallagher.** "BofA's Direct-Deposit Debacle." *Baseline* (May 15, 2002).

**Collins, W. Robert, Keith W. Miller, Bethany J. Spielman,** and **Phillip Wherry.** "How Good Is Good Enough? An Ethical Analysis of

Software Construction and Use." *Communications of the ACM* 37, no. 1 (January 1994).

**Congressional Research Service.** "Internet Privacy: Overview and Pending Legislation" (May 16, 2005).

**Consumer Reports Webwatch.** "Leap of Faith: Using the Internet Despite the Dangers." www.ConsumerWebWatch.org, (2005).

**Earp, Julia B.,** and **David Baumer.** "Innovative Web Use to Learn about Consumer Behavior and Online Privacy." *Communications of the ACM* 46, no. 4 (April 2003).

**eMarketer.** "U.S. Online Sales Lost Due to Privacy/Security Concerns, 2000–2006" (November 23, 2005).

**Farmer, Dan,** and **Charles C. Mann.** "Surveillance Nation." Part I *Technology Review* (April 2003) and Part II *Technology Review* (May 2003).

**Fox, Susannah.** "Digital Divisions." Pew Internet and American Life Project (October 5, 2005).

**Heingartner, Douglas.** "Software Piracy Is in Resurgence, with New Safeguards Eroded by File Sharing." *The New York Times* (January 19, 2004).

**Jackson, Linda A., Alexander von Eye, Gretchen Barbatsis, Frank Biocca, Hiram E. Fitzgerald,** and **Yong Zhao.** "The Impact of Internet Use on the Other Side of the Digital Divide." *Communications of the ACM* 47, no. 7 (July 2004).

**Jackson, Thomas W., Ray Dawson,** and **Darren Wilson.** "Understanding E-mail Interaction Increases Organizational Productivity." *Communications of the ACM* 46, no. 8 (August 2003).

**Kreie, Jennifer,** and **Timothy Paul Cronan.** "Making Ethical Decisions." *Communications of the ACM* 43, no. 12 (December 2000).

**Laudon, Kenneth C.** *Dossier Society: Value Choices in the Design of National Information Systems.* New York: Columbia University Press (1986b).

————. "Ethical Concepts and Information Technology." *Communications of the ACM* 38, no. 12 (December 1995).

**Laudon, Kenneth C.,** and **Carol Guercio Traver.** *E-Commerce: Business, Technology, Society.* Upper Saddle River, NJ: Prentice Hall (2006).

**Lee, Jintae.** "An End-User Perspective on File-Sharing Systems." *Communications of the ACM* 46, no. 2 (February 2003).

**Maltz, Elliott,** and **Vincent Chiappetta.** "Maximizing Value in the Digital World." *Sloan Management Review* 43, no. 3 (Spring 2002).

**Mann, Catherine L.** "What Global Sourcing Means for U.S. I.T. Workers and for the U.S. Economy." *Communications of the ACM* 47. no. 7 (July 2004).

**Martin, David M., Jr., Richard M. Smith, Michael Brittain, Ivan Fetch,** and **Hailin Wu.** "The Privacy Practices of Web Browser Extensions." *Communications of the ACM* 44, no. 2 (February 2001).

**McBride, Sarah.** "For Groskter, It's the Day the Music Died." *The Wall Street Journal* (November 8, 2005).

**Payton, Fay Cobb.** "Rethinking the Digital Divide." *Communications of the ACM* 46, no. 6 (June 2003).

**Petrecca, Laura.** "Memo to Managers: Don't Expect High Workplace Productivity on Monday," *USA Today* (November 27, 2005).

**Pew Internet and American Life Project.** "Demographics of Internet Users." http://www.pewinternet.org/trends/User_Demo_12.05.05. htm, accessed December 9, 2005.

**Reagle, Joseph,** and **Lorrie Faith Cranor.** "The Platform for Privacy Preferences." *Communications of the ACM* 42, no. 2 (February 1999).

**Rifkin, Jeremy.** "Watch Out for Trickle-Down Technology." *The New York Times* (March 16, 1993).

**Rigdon, Joan E.** "Frequent Glitches in New Software Bug Users." *The Wall Street Journal* (January 18, 1995).

**Sewell, Graham,** and **James R. Barker.** "Neither Good, nor Bad, but Dangerous: Surveillance as an Ethical Paradox." *Ethics and Information Technology* 3, no. 3 (2001).

**Smith, H. Jeff.** "The Shareholders vs. Stakeholders Debate." *MIT Sloan Management Review* 44, no. 4 (Summer 2003).

**Smith, Marcia S.** "Spyware: Background and Policy Issues for Congress." Congressional Research Service (May 18, 2005).

"The Real Reasons You're Working So Hard." *Business Week* (October 3, 2005).

**Urbaczewski, Andrew,** and **Leonard M. Jessup.** "Does Electronic Monitoring of Employee Internet Usage Work?" *Communications of the ACM* 45, no. 1 (January 2002).

**U.S. Department of Health, Education, and Welfare.** *Records, Computers, and the Rights of Citizens.* Cambridge: MIT Press (1973).

**Van Kirk, Andrew.** "Platform for Privacy Preferences (P3P): Privacy without Teeth," Working Paper, Duke University (March 10, 2005).

**Wellman, Barry.** "Designing the Internet for a Networked Society." *Communications of the ACM* 45, no. 5 (May 2002).

**Zeller, Tom.** "Critics Press Companies on Internet Rights Issues." *The New York Times* (November 8, 2005).

————. "Study Says Software Makers Supply Tools to Censor Web." *The New York Times* (October 12, 2005).

# INDEX

## International Organizations Index

## Subject Index